Federal Income Taxation
In Focus

Focus Casebook Series

FEDERAL INCOME TAXATION IN FOCUS

Bobby L. Dexter

Wolters Kluwer

Published by Wolters Kluwer in New York.

Wolters Kluwer Legal & Regulatory US serves customers worldwide with CCH, Aspen Publishers, and Kluwer Law International products. (www.WKLegaledu.com)

To contact Customer Service, e-mail customer.service@wolterskluwer.com, call 1-800-234-1660, fax 1-800-901-9075, or mail correspondence to:

    Wolters Kluwer
    Attn: Order Department
    PO Box 990
    Frederick, MD 21705

Printed in the United States of America.

2 3 4 5 6 7 8 9 0

ISBN 978-1-4548-8154-4

Library of Congress Cataloging-in-Publication Data

Names: Dexter, Bobby L., 1967-
Title: Federal income taxation in focus / Bobby L. Dexter.
Description: New York : Wolters Kluwer, [2018] | Series: Focus casebook
  series | Includes bibliographical references and index.
Identifiers: LCCN 2017056962 | ISBN 9781454881544
Subjects: LCSH: Income tax — Law and legislation--United States. | Tax
  deductions — United States. | LCGFT: Casebooks.
Classification: LCC KF6369 .D49 2018 | DDC 343.7305/2 — dc23 LC record available at https://lccn.
loc.gov/2017056962

About Wolters Kluwer Legal & Regulatory U.S.

Wolters Kluwer Legal & Regulatory U.S. delivers expert content and solutions in the areas of law, corporate compliance, health compliance, reimbursement, and legal education. Its practical solutions help customers successfully navigate the demands of a changing environment to drive their daily activities, enhance decision quality and inspire confident outcomes.

Serving customers worldwide, its legal and regulatory solutions portfolio includes products under the Aspen Publishers, CCH Incorporated, Kluwer Law International, ftwilliam.com and MediRegs names. They are regarded as exceptional and trusted resources for general legal and practice-specific knowledge, compliance and risk management, dynamic workflow solutions, and expert commentary.

Hunc Librum Dedico

Universitati Yalensi

Quod Meminit Discipulos

Ex Scholis Publicis

Oppidorum Americae Parvorum

Summary of Contents

Table of Contents

Chapter 20: Tax Avoidance and Tax Shelters   527

Chapter 21: The Alternative Minimum Tax   551

The Focus Casebook Series

Students reach their full potential with the fresh approach of the Focus Casebook Series. Instead of using the "hide the ball" approach, selected cases illustrate key developments in the law and show how courts develop and apply doctrine. The approachable manner of this series provides a comfortable experiential environment that is instrumental to student success.

Students perform best when applying concepts to real-world scenarios. With assessment features, such as Real Life Applications and Applying the Concepts, the Focus Casebook Series offers many opportunities for students to apply their knowledge.

Focus Casebook Features Include:

Ruling or Case Previews and Post-Ruling or Post-Case Follow-Ups — To succeed, law students must know how to deconstruct and analyze cases. Case Previews highlight the legal concepts in a case before the student reads it. Post-Case Follow-Ups summarize the important points.

Case Preview

Blackman v. Commissioner

In approving a given provision of tax law, Congress usually proceeds with a specific intent (or at least some general goal) in mind, and it's fair to say that in most instances, application of the provision is in full accord with the associated legislative intent. From time to time, however, taxpayers will push their luck, hoping to capitalize on the letter of the law while desperately praying that the sovereign's revenue collectors will temporarily overlook its spirit. The ploy rarely succeeds. As you read *Blackman v. Commissioner*, consider the following questions:

1. Did the taxpayer have governing statute?

Post-Case Follow-Up

The Court concluded in *Cottage Savings* that under § 1001, an exchange of properties will constitute a disposition only if the properties are materially different. The Court further concluded that a difference is "material" in this context only if those who hold the properties have legal entitlements that are different in kind or extent. As you might well expect, almost any exchange of properties will give rise to a realization event. What you might not realize, however, is that such an approach to realization might well lead to surprising and unintended consequences. Assume that a given individual is in financial distress and seeks to work out a new arrangement with the bank. If the two parties modify their contract, does the tax law view the transaction as an exchange of one contract (the old one) for another (the new one under which legal rights and obligations differ), thereby triggering a realization event? In the immediate wake of *Cottage Savings*, financial institutions and their obligors had legitimate concerns in this regard. The Treasury Department responded with guidance in the so-called *Cottage Savings* regulations under § 1001. *See generally* Treas. Reg. § 1.1001-3.

The Focus Casebook Series

Real Life Applications — Every case in a chapter is followed by Real Life Applications, which present a series of questions based on a scenario similar to the facts in the case. Real Life Applications challenge students to apply what they have learned in order to prepare them for real-world practice. Use Real Life Applications to spark class discussions or provide them as individual short-answer assignments.

Cesarini v. United States: Real Life Applications

1. After boarding her flight and settling into her seat, Amanda realized that a prior passenger had left an iPad in the seat pocket in front of her. She opened the iPad cover and found an engraving, indicating that the iPad was the property of "Daniel Q. Traveler." She promptly located a flight attendant and handed the property over.

   a. Did Amanda have income as a result of this series of events?
   b. Would Amanda have had income if she had found the iPad but decided to keep it for herself? If so, how much?

2. While walking through the park on a windy day, Casey found what he initially thought was fake money. In actuality, the currency was a real $100 bill. Seeing no one in the immediate vicinity who might have dropped the money, he celebrated his good fortune, pocketed the money, and walked on.

   a. Did Casey have income as a result of finding the money and keeping it?
   b. If Casey had found a gold wedding band (no engraving), would he have had income on finding the wedding band or only upon converting that wedding

Applying the Concepts — These end-of-chapter exercises encourage students to synthesize the chapter material and apply relevant legal doctrine and code to real-world scenarios. Students can use these exercises for self-assessment or the professor can use them to promote class interaction.

Applying the Rules

1. Taxpayer A is contemplating a multi-billion-dollar transaction with Taxpayer B. Taxpayer A hires Fernando, a tax attorney, to assist in obtaining a PLR from the IRS.

   a. How will Fernando find out what steps must be taken to secure a PLR?
   b. If Fernando succeeds in obtaining a favorable ruling from the IRS, which taxpayers, in addition to Taxpayer A, can rely on that PLR?

2. Giovanni, a r[...] the IRS indic[...] taxes.

Federal Income Taxation in Practice

1. Assume that you are a research assistant for one of your tax professors. She plans to write an article on IRC § 108(a)(1)(E) and needs you to conduct some preliminary research. See if you can find out when this provision was added to the Internal Revenue Code. Also check to see if there is a House Report or a Senate Report discussing the new provision.

2. You arrive back to your office one day after lunch to find a litigation partner waiting for you. She informs you that one of her major clients has asked that she litigate a contested liability case in Tax Court. She needs you to find out whether there have been any contested liability cases decided in Tax Court since January 1, 2012. See what you can find and send her a brief e-mail update.

3. You are a partner in a law firm, and one of your clients is The Computer Superstore. The General Counsel of the company contacts you regarding the treatment of employees who receive a computer as part of their compensation. He

Preface

Ensure student success with the Focus Casebook Series.

THE FOCUS APPROACH

In a law office, when a new associate attorney is being asked to assist a supervising attorney with a legal matter in which the associate has no prior experience, it is common for the supervising attorney to provide the associate with a recently closed case file involving the same legal issues so that the associate can see and learn from the closed file to assist more effectively with the new matter. This experiential approach is at the heart of the *Focus Casebook Series*.

Additional hands-on features, such as Real Life Applications, Applying the Concepts, and Federal Income Taxation in Practice provide more opportunities for critical analysis and application of concepts covered in the chapters. Professors can assign problem-solving questions as well as exercises on drafting documents and preparing appropriate filings.

CONTENT SNAPSHOT

This casebook focuses on clear communication of federal income tax fundamentals. On completion of the course, students will have not only the comprehensive substantive knowledge base needed for advanced study in the federal tax arena, but also a healthy degree of familiarity with various tax-related resources. The student will emerge with the ability to perform well in a clinical or practice setting.

- Chapter 1 is introductory and includes basic background with respect to the constitutional authority to tax income and the roles of Congress, the Treasury Department, and the Internal Revenue Service. The chapter also covers standard tax legislation procedure and key sources of tax law and guidance.
- Chapter 2 addresses the concept of realization and the current definition of "income." It also introduces foundational tax terminology (e.g., basis, realization, recognition, etc.) and the fundamentals of the tax computation process.
- Chapter 3 provides coverage of rules regarding gross income inclusions and addresses the diversity of income forms, including windfalls, illegal income, and income from the cancellation of indebtedness. The chapter also explores the contested liability doctrine.

▧ In Chapter 4, the text discusses tax-free basis recovery mechanisms and introduces exclusions from gross income, addressing specific limited exclusions (e.g., gain on the sale of a principal residence).

▧ Chapters 5 and 6 cover specific categorical exclusions, including items received by gift, bequest, devise, or inheritance (and specific basis determination rules). The chapters also cover the exclusion of specific fringe benefits and the treatment of damages received on account of personal physical injury or physical sickness. Chapter 6 addresses cafeteria plans, life insurance contract proceeds, and the treatment of state/local bond interest.

▧ Chapter 7 opens with a discussion of the notion of progressivity before moving on to the standard deduction, itemized deductions (in general terms), tax credits, the meaning of dependent, and the deduction with respect to qualified business income. In Chapter 8, the text transitions decidedly to coverage of specific itemized deductions, starting with the allowance for extraordinary medical expenses (including fertility-related expenses and the characterization and treatment of gender identity disorder).

▧ Chapter 9 continues the coverage of itemized deductions, focusing on the allowance with respect to casualty, theft, and other specific losses by individuals (including the federal disaster limitation with respect to certain losses, the significance of a loss being sustained, and the "suddenness" requirement in the casualty loss context). Public policy considerations are also discussed.

▧ Chapter 10 provides extraordinarily useful background on financing the purchase of a home before devoting focused discussion to the tax treatment of qualified residence interest, including relevant grandfathering rules, the impact of equitable ownership, and application of rules on a per-taxpayer basis. From there, the focus shifts to the treatment of property taxes and state and local income taxes.

▧ With Chapter 11, coverage shifts to a discussion of entities eligible to receive tax-deductible contributions under § 170 and the requirements entities must satisfy to secure tax-exemption under § 501. The chapter addresses the treatment of both standard contributions and quid pro quo transactions in the § 170 context and the role of public policy with respect to tax-exempt entities. Also included is a discussion of private inurement prohibitions.

▧ Chapter 12 focuses on the meaning of "ordinary," "necessary," and "carrying on" a "trade or business" and the general treatment of ordinary and necessary business expenses.

▧ With Chapter 13, the text formally introduces the concept of matching and addresses the treatment of capital expenditures. The chapter also includes coverage of depreciation, the amortization of intangibles, and inventory tax accounting.

▧ Chapter 14 is devoted to discussion of timing and related issues, including the time value of money, annual accounting, the claim of right doctrine, the tax benefit rule, NOL carryovers, and deferred compensation (including the § 83(b) election).

▧ Chapter 15 offers coverage of the cash receipts and disbursement method of accounting, constructive receipt, economic benefit, the accrual method of accounting, and the significance of economic performance. The chapter also includes brief discussion of the installment method of accounting.

▓ In Chapter 16, the text turns to like-kind exchanges of real property and involuntary conversions, providing general discussion of non-recognition and the deferral of gain or loss with respect to a given transaction. Also included is coverage of related basis rules (preserving gain/loss) and the potential impact of boot both on recognition and basis (including the transfer of non-qualifying consideration with built-in gain or loss).

▓ After devoting brief attention to the progressivity of tax rates, Chapter 17 discusses both assignment of income and the transfer of income-producing property as well as the notion of a marriage penalty or marriage bonus.

▓ Chapter 18 focuses on the treatment of various transfers incident to marriage and divorce, including inter-spousal property transfers during marriage, property settlements incident to divorce (or related to the cessation of the marriage), alimony (including fact-specific deduction and inclusion rules), and child support.

▓ In Chapter 19, we take up the treatment of capital gains and losses. In addition to covering the notion of income character, the chapter covers the definition of capital asset, the sale or exchange requirement, and the treatment of long-term and short-term capital gains/losses. There is also discussion of the meaning of "property" under § 1221 as well as the treatment of § 1231 gains and losses and the rules mandating depreciation recapture.

▓ Chapter 20 covers tax avoidance and tax shelters. In addition to discussing the general meaning of passive activity and passive activity losses, the chapter goes on to address material participation, at-risk limitations, and the economic substance doctrine.

▓ Chapter 21 discusses the alternative minimum tax and aims consciously to communicate substantive essentials.

▓ Chapter 22 concludes primary substantive coverage with discussion of federal withholding, estimated taxes, and worker classification. The chapter addresses the meaning of "wages" both in the income tax and in the employment tax contexts as well as the rules regarding FICA, the FICA Wage Base, estimated tax payments, worker classification (including potential § 530 relief), and the imposition of penalties and interest on underpayments.

▓ Appendices 1 and 2 aim largely to impart a substantial dose of practice-readiness by giving students knowledge useful to them in a clinical or early practice setting. Appendix 1 introduces the student to the fundamentals of tax controversy and litigation, including the notion of assessment (including waivers and extensions), offers in compromise, installment agreements, audits (correspondence, office, and field), closing agreements, no-change letters, information document requests, administrative summons, 30-Day Letters, 90-Day Letters, protests, the IRS Office of Appeals, and various tax litigation venues. The chapter also provides a basic introduction to IRS Circular 230. Appendix 2 focuses on tax research fundamentals, including location of current-year and prior versions of the Internal Revenue Code and Treasury Regulations, non-Code tax provisions, legislative history, the "Bluebook," tax cases, IRS pronouncements, and additional research resources (e.g., Bloomberg BNA Tax Management Portfolios and the CCH Standard Federal Tax Reporter). The appendix also references daily tax publications (e.g., CCH Tracker News and the Bloomberg BNA Daily Tax Report) and highlights the importance of monitoring ongoing legal developments.

▪ Materials in Appendix 3 come from a publication of the Congressional Budget Office, Options for Reducing the Deficit: 2017–2026. The materials facilitate discussion of various deficit-reducing tax policy options, including the imposition of a value-added tax and the taxation of greenhouse gas emissions.

RESOURCES

Casebook: The casebook is structured around text, cases, and application exercises. Highlighted cases are introduced with a *Case Preview,* which sets up the issue and identifies key questions. *Post-Case Follow-Ups* expand on the holding in the case. *Real Life Applications* present opportunities to challenge students to apply concepts covered in the case to realistic hypothetical cases. The *Applying the Concepts* feature demands critical analysis and integration of concepts covered in the chapter.

Other resources to enrich your class include: Ask your Wolters Kluwer sales representative or visit the Wolters Kluwer site at *wklegaledu.com* to learn more about building the product package that's right for you.

Acknowledgments

In addition to thanking my friends and family for ongoing encouragement, I'd like to express my sincere appreciation for the mentorship and support provided by Professor Mitch Crusto of the Loyola University (New Orleans) College of Law and the Late Professor M. Katherine B. Darmer of the Chapman University Fowler School of Law. Let me also add to the roster of my personal heroes the Late Dean Brian Bromberger (Loyola) and Dean Emeritus Parham Williams (Chapman), both of whom brought personal warmth, professional integrity, gentlemanly demeanor, and towering leadership to the helm.

Getting this casebook from idea to reality required considerable input and effort from many. Let me extend my sincere thanks to the entire Wolters Kluwer team not only for the work already done but also for the work that lies ahead. Richard Mixter gets my heartfelt thanks for guiding me through the initial project phase and firmly supporting my addition of Federal Income Taxation to the Focus Casebook portfolio. Special recognition is in order for Jane Hosie-Bounar, my editor, for improving the text overall, surviving twenty-two chapters (and several appendices) of federal income taxation, coordinating the review process, and providing regular encouragement with professionalism and grace. My reviewers provided highly valuable input; without question, the casebook emerges stronger as a result of their constructive criticism and guidance. Sarah Hains, my production editor, and the entire production team at The Froebe Group enhanced the quality of the text and ushered it through the critical final production process.

No list of thanks would be complete without the addition of my students. Hundreds of you have trusted me with your legal education, and by doing so you have undoubtedly shaped the content and style of this casebook. I wrote this textbook so that I could tell you the story of tax the way I would like it told, and I remain hopeful that you will do what so many prior students have done; they have taken up the challenge that is federal income taxation and seized the opportunity to thrive. You have allowed me to rediscover tax time and again, all the while reminding me of what the tax labyrinth looks like through student eyes. Your comments, questions, and creative arguments put a decidedly professional polish on my teaching and ultimately made this casebook that much better.

In drafting the text, I called on many resources, including forms and publications of the U.S. Treasury Department (including the Internal Revenue Service), the Congressional Budget Office, and the Joint Committee on Taxation. I further acknowledge reference to sources cited within the text and occasional consultation of various materials for specific information, including The World Book

Encyclopedia, the 2015 Bloomberg BNA Federal Tax Guide, and The Great Courses (The History of the United States, 2nd Edition). In addition to the use of materials within the public domain, I acknowledge the use of specific photographs and document images with the permission of Getty Images (and Stock Montage), Alamy.com (and associated photographers), Shutterstock.com (and associated photographers), the Library of Congress, the Federal Bureau of Investigations, Bloomberg BNA, CCH, and Thomson Reuters. Special thanks are in order for the use of charts with the permission of Statista.com. Finally, I enthusiastically acknowledge the use of comics throughout the text with the permission of the Cartoonist Group and its talented and extraordinarily creative artists.

Federal Income Taxation
In Focus

Introduction

According to recent statistics from the U.S Congressional Budget Office, the taxation of corporate and individual income produces approximately $2 trillion in gross revenue for the United States Treasury during a given **federal budget year** (i.e., October 1 to September 30 of the following year). Individuals pay the lion's share of that total, and much of that, in turn, comes from the regular and systematic withholding of taxes on employee wages as they are earned. Thus, even without actually writing a check to the United States Treasury, most students enrolled in this course have probably paid hundreds (if not thousands) of dollars in federal income taxes over the years. It is equally likely that those of you who suffered what may have felt like the sudden and involuntary withholding of taxes from your paycheck took the further step of filing the appropriate income tax returns, largely in order to comply with federal mandate but also on the off chance that you, like a healthy percentage your fellow taxpayers, might be entitled to a refund. As a law student, I shouldered only modest tax liabilities. I did, however, anticipate landing a job at a big law firm and enrolled in my first tax course as part of a larger strategy to minimize what I felt sure would be substantial future tax liabilities. I soon discovered that Congress had just recently taken away all of the really good stuff, but fortunately, the story had a very good ending. As I made my way through the material, I realized that I had unwittingly stumbled upon an area of law that I found analytically appealing, highly structured, moderately challenging, and yet generally comprehensible; I could navigate the labyrinth and "get it." Also, I occasionally found tax cases to be deeply entertaining, so I was definitely hooked. My hope is that you too will enjoy a similar experience. Allow me, then, to introduce you to the federal income taxation arena.

Key Concepts

- Constitutional authority to lay and collect taxes on income without apportionment
- Roles of Congress, the Department of the Treasury, and the Internal Revenue Service
- Standard tax legislation procedure
- Key sources of tax law and guidance

1

A. THE IMPORTANCE OF STUDYING FEDERAL INCOME TAXATION

The course in federal income taxation typically has a reputation that precedes it, and more often than not, that reputation is a negative one. Many will claim that Federal Income Taxation was the most difficult course they *ever* took in law school. Others will lament that the **Internal Revenue Code** (a collection of the governing statutes) is simply incomprehensible and that the **Treasury Regulations** (which flesh out and further explain the Code provisions) simply complicate matters on a grander scale by using more words, albeit with occasionally helpful examples. And then there is the sin above all sins: Tax apparently involves *math*, a subject reviled by a substantial percentage of law students. The truth, of course, is that the basic tax course has much in common with other law school courses. Some degree of rigor is unavoidable. True to its notorious reputation, tax law does demand rapt attention to precise statutory language. With sufficient focus and diligence, however, a student can readily attain mastery and, over time, some degree of expertise. Indeed, one could say that the course in federal income taxation is largely a "skills" course in that it develops a budding lawyer's ability not only to interpret and apply statutes but also, and perhaps more importantly, to argue and persuade with respect to points of proper statutory construction. Often, the difference between a good or solid lawyer and an outstanding lawyer boils down to the attorney's ability to understand complicated laws quickly and, if need be, to convince a decision maker to resolve statutory ambiguities in a manner consistent with the interests of the lawyer's clients. Even when a statute is clear, applying that statute to a given case may well prove to be an uphill battle for any number of reasons. Consider, for example, the strange case of *Blackman v. Commissioner*. The decision provides an excellent introduction to the course.

Case Preview

Blackman v. Commissioner

In approving a given provision of tax law, Congress usually proceeds with a specific intent (or at least some general goal) in mind, and it's fair to say that in most instances, application of the provision is in full accord with the associated legislative intent. From time to time, however, taxpayers will push their luck, hoping to capitalize on the letter of the law while desperately praying that the sovereign's revenue collectors will temporarily overlook its policy-grounded spirit. The ploy rarely, if ever, succeeds. As you read *Blackman v. Commissioner*, consider the following questions:

1. Did the taxpayer have a rational argument based on the plain language of the governing statute?
2. What standard of conduct did the court conclude would result in a taxpayer losing the ability to take a casualty loss deduction?

3. What specific policy or policies would be frustrated by allowing the taxpayer to take a deduction for the loss under the given circumstances?

Blackman v. Commissioner
88 T.C. 677 (1987)

SIMPSON, Judge

The Commissioner determined a deficiency of $22,737.38 in the petitioner's Federal income tax for 1980 and additions to tax of [approximately $1,800.] * * * After concessions, the issues remaining for decision are: (1) Whether the petitioner is entitled to a deduction for the loss of his residence by fire * * *; (2) whether the petitioner's failure to file a timely Federal income tax return was due to reasonable cause; and (3) whether the petitioner's underpayment of taxes was due to negligence under section 6653(a).

FINDINGS OF FACT

Some of the facts have been stipulated, and those facts are so found.

At the time of the filing of the petition in this case, the petitioner, Biltmore Blackman, resided in Billerica, Massachusetts. He and his wife filed their joint Federal income tax return for 1980 on April 28, 1981, with the Internal Revenue Service Center, Atlanta, Georgia. The petitioner's employer transferred him from Baltimore, Maryland, to South Carolina.

The petitioner relocated his wife and children to South Carolina. Mrs. Blackman was dissatisfied with South Carolina and returned, with the couple's five children, to Baltimore. During the 1980 Labor Day weekend, the petitioner returned to Baltimore, hoping to persuade his wife to give South Carolina another chance. When he arrived at his Baltimore home, he discovered that another man was living there with his wife. The neighbors told the petitioner that such man had been there on other occasions when the petitioner had been out of town on business.

On September 1, 1980, the petitioner returned to his former home to speak to his wife. However, Mrs. Blackman was having a party; her guests refused to leave despite the petitioner's request that they do so. He returned to the house several times, repeating his request, and emphasizing it by breaking windows. Mrs. Blackman's guests did not leave the house until about 3:00 a.m., September 2, 1980.

Later, on September 2, 1980, the petitioner again went to his former home. He wanted to ask his wife whether she wanted a divorce. They quarreled, and Mrs. Blackman left the house. After she left, the petitioner gathered some of Mrs. Blackman's clothes, put them on the stove, and set them on fire. The petitioner claims that he then "took pots of water to dowse the fire, put the fire totally out * * *" and left the house. The fire spread, and the fire department was called. When the firefighters arrived, they found some of the clothing still on the stove. The house and its contents were destroyed.

The petitioner was arrested later that day and charged with one count of Setting Fire while Perpetrating a Crime * * * and one count of Destruction of Property (Malicious

Mischief) * * *. The arson charge was based on the allegation that the petitioner "had set fire to and burned * * * [the house] while perpetrating the crime of Destruction of Property" and the malicious destruction charge was based on the allegation that he "did willfully and maliciously destroy, injure, deface and molest clothing, the property of" Mrs. Blackman. The petitioner pleaded not guilty to both charges. On November 5, 1980, by order of the District Court of Baltimore County, the arson charge was placed on the "stet" docket. The petitioner was ordered to serve 24 months unsupervised probation without verdict on the malicious destruction charge.

Insurance rejects)

The petitioner filed a claim for the fire damage with his insurer, State Farm Fire and Casualty Company of Baltimore, Maryland. The company refused to honor the claim due to the cause of the fire.

The tax return

On his 1980 Federal income tax return, the petitioner deducted as a casualty loss $97,853.00 attributable to the destruction of his residence and its contents. In his notice of deficiency, the Commissioner disallowed the deduction and made other adjustments. He now concedes those other adjustments and does not dispute the amount of the casualty loss, if the loss is allowable. The Commissioner also determined that the petitioner is liable for the additions to tax under section 6651(a) for failure to file a timely return and under section 6653(a) for negligence.

OPINION

The primary issue for our decision is whether the petitioner is allowed to deduct the loss resulting from the fire started by him. Section 165(a) allows a deduction for "any loss sustained during the taxable year and not compensated for by insurance or otherwise." Section 165(c)(3) provides, in pertinent part, that in the case of an individual, the deduction allowed in subsection (a) is to be limited to "losses of property not connected with a trade or business, if such losses arise from fire, storm, shipwreck, or other casualty, or from theft." The Commissioner concedes that the petitioner sustained a loss through fire. However, the Commissioner argues that the petitioner intentionally set the fire which destroyed his home in violation of Maryland's public policy, that allowing the deduction would frustrate that public policy, and that, therefore, under the doctrine of *Commissioner v. Heininger*, 320 U.S. 467 (1943), and subsequent cases, the petitioner is not entitled to a deduction for the damage caused by his fire.

Test: Does it frustrate public Policy?

Courts have traditionally disallowed business expense and casualty loss deductions under section 162 or 165 where national or State public policies would be frustrated by the consequences of allowing the deduction. *Commissioner v. Heininger, supra.* "[T]he test of non-deductibility always is the severity and immediacy of the frustration resulting from allowance of the deduction." *Tank Truck Rentals v. Commissioner*, 356 U.S. 30, 35 (1958). "From the cases, it is clear that the question of illegality to frustrate public policy is, in the last analysis, ONE OF DEGREE, TO BE DETERMINED FROM THE PECULIAR FACTS OF EACH CASE." *Fuller v. Commissioner*, 213 F.2d 102, 106 (10th Cir. 1954) * * *. In examining the facts of each case, courts have examined both the taxpayer's conduct and the policy his conduct is said to frustrate.

How courts decide

Conviction of a crime is not essential to a showing that the allowance of a deduction would frustrate public policy. ***

Moreover, it is well settled that the negligence of the taxpayer is not a bar to the allowance of the casualty loss deduction. On the other hand, gross negligence on the part of the taxpayer will bar a casualty loss deduction. "Needless to say, the taxpayer may not knowingly or willfully sit back and allow himself to be damaged in his property or willfully damage the property himself." *White v. Commissioner*, 48 T.C. 430, 435 (1967). In our judgment, the petitioner's conduct was grossly negligent, or worse. He admitted that he started the fire. He claims that he attempted to extinguish it by putting water on it. Yet, the firemen found clothing still on the stove, and there is no evidence to corroborate the petitioner's claim that he attempted to dowse the flame. The fact is that the fire spread to the entire house, and we have only vague and not very persuasive evidence concerning the petitioner's attempt to extinguish the fire. Once a person starts a fire, he has an obligation to make extraordinary efforts to be sure that the fire is safely extinguished, and this petitioner has failed to demonstrate that he made such extraordinary efforts. The house fire was a foreseeable consequence of the setting of the clothes [on] fire, and a consequence made more likely if the petitioner failed to take adequate precautions to prevent it.

We hold that the petitioner's conduct was grossly negligent and that his grossly negligent conduct bars him from deducting the loss claimed by him under section 165(a) and (c)(3).

In addition, allowing the petitioner a deduction would severely and immediately frustrate the articulated public policy of Maryland against arson and burning. Maryland's policy is clearly expressed. [Applicable Maryland law] makes it a felony to burn a residence while perpetrating a crime. The petitioner admits that he set fire to his wife's clothes, and he has not denied that the residence burned as a result of the fire started by him. The petitioner was charged with violating that section, but that charge was placed on the "stet" docket. As we understand Maryland practice, such action merely postponed any action on the charge. * * * However, the mere fact that the petitioner was never brought to trial for burning the house does not foreclose a finding by this Court that the petitioner acted in violation of that policy. * * *. We are mindful, also, that Maryland has an articulated public policy against domestic violence. We refuse to encourage couples to settle their disputes with fire. We hold that allowing a loss deduction, in this factual setting, would severely and immediately frustrate the articulated public policies of Maryland against arson and burning, and against domestic violence.

Two minor issues remain for our decision. The first is the Commissioner's determination that the petitioner is liable for the addition to tax under section 6651(a). Section 6651(a)(1) imposes a 5-percent addition for a failure "to file any return required * * * on the date prescribed therefor * * *, unless it is shown that such failure is due to reasonable cause and not due to willful neglect * * *." The burden is on the petitioner to show that his failure to timely file returns was due to reasonable cause and not to willful neglect.

The parties stipulated that the petitioner's 1980 return was filed on April 28, 1981. The petitioner claims that he executed a request for an extension of time to file, but he produced no evidence supporting such claim. He also claimed that his delay was due to his difficulty in obtaining Mrs. Blackman's signature, but he produced no details as to why he could not have secured her signature on a timely return. We hold

H: Not on time

that the petitioner has not carried his burden and that he is liable for the addition to tax under section 6651(a)(1).

I: Disregard of rules

The remaining issue concerns the addition, under section 6653(a), for negligence or intentional disregard of rules and regulations. The Commissioner argues that the petitioner is liable for the addition because he claimed a substantial deduction to which he was not entitled and that such a claim justifies imposing the addition. We cannot agree in this case. Under the circumstances of this case, it was not negligent for the petitioner to claim a deduction for his loss by fire. Imposition of the addition is therefore not warranted in this case.

H: No negligence in claiming deduction

Post-Case Follow-Up

Now: mostly restricted to disasters

With the enactment of the Tax Cuts and Jobs Act in 2017, Congress restricted the ability of individuals to deduct personal casualty losses. In general, such losses are now deductible (within numerical limits) only if they are attributable to a federally declared disaster. *See* § 165(h)(5)(A). Accordingly, under current tax law and the stated facts, the Blackmans would have no statutorily grounded basis for pursuing a deduction. Even under prior law, of course, allowing the taxpayers a deduction would have offended various public policies. Two important points do merit emphasis, largely for the limited circumstances (to be discussed in a future chapter) in which a determination must be made as to whether a given individual taxpayer with a non-disaster personal casualty loss may take a deduction. *See generally* § 165(h)(5)(B)(i) (articulating an exception to application of § 165(h)(5)(A)). Even in the absence of a criminal conviction, a taxpayer's gross negligence will prevent the taking of a casualty loss deduction. Further, notwithstanding the fact that a statute appears to apply based on its plain language (i.e., **facial applicability**), public policy concerns and legislative intent may have a decisive impact as to whether a statute will, in fact, apply in a specific situation. We will study personal casualty losses in greater detail in Chapter 9.

According to statistics from the National Fire Protection Association, "[s]moking was the leading cause of civilian home fire deaths" from 2010 to 2014. See http://www.nfpa.org/ news-and-research/fire-statistics-and-reports/fire-statistics/ fires-by-property-type/residential/home-structure-fires. *Credit:* KelvinW/Shutterstock.com.

Blackman v. Commissioner: Real Life Applications

1. Having fallen on hard times, Kenneth and Charles decide to make a living by cooking and selling crystal methamphetamine, an activity which constitutes a felony under federal, state, and local law. The men prepare their product in a large tent located in the forest behind Kenneth's house. Assume that while preparing a batch of methamphetamine, Kenneth accidentally set fire to the tent and the fire spread to the surrounding forest, ravaging nearby homes and structures for several weeks. The fire was ultimately declared a federal disaster. Assume that Kenneth's home was a total loss of $75,000, which was not compensated for by insurance or otherwise. For the moment, disregard any numerical deduction thresholds.

a. Is Kenneth entitled to a casualty loss deduction? Please explain.
b. Does it matter whether Kenneth was being as careful as possible while making the methamphetamine?
c. If Kenneth had merely been preparing a hearty dinner in his kitchen for a group of friends when the fire broke out, would he be entitled to a casualty loss deduction?

2. Late one evening, Taylor fell asleep in bed while smoking a cigarette, and a fire resulted. Given that the home was in close proximity to others and the prevailing winds were exceptionally strong, it was not long before the fire spread to other homes and the surrounding forest. The fire was ultimately declared a federal disaster. Although Taylor managed to escape with minor burns, the house was a total loss of approximately $450,000. Due to nonpayment of premiums, the home was not insured at the time, and the loss has not been compensated for otherwise. For the moment, disregard any numerical deduction thresholds.

a. Is Taylor entitled to a casualty loss deduction? Please explain.
b. Would the presence or absence of operational smoke detectors in the home change your conclusion?
c. Would allowing Taylor a deduction under these circumstances violate any established public policies?

B. THE UNIQUE VALUE OF THE FEDERAL INCOME TAXATION COURSE

The typical law school curriculum includes any number of highly statutory courses, and one might legitimately ask whether studying tax law yields unique skill-development benefits. In my view, the benefits of studying tax law are substantial. Relative to courses focusing almost exclusively on the common law, tax courses more faithfully replicate the actual practice of law by requiring that students focus on and develop an understanding of governing statutes while giving due regard to administrative regulations, official pronouncements, and guiding precedent. Consistent with best teaching practices, the course in federal income taxation also facilitates student success by developing skills in a substantive arena with which the student likely has some baseline familiarity. Most of you, in all likelihood, already understand the notions of **filing status** (e.g., "single," "head of household," or "married filing jointly") and **progressivity** (i.e., tax rates/brackets get progressively higher as one's taxable income rises). Similarly, you understand that tax liability is determined on an annual basis, that taxpayers are subject to audit by the Internal Revenue Service ("IRS"), and that failure to pay taxes can result in the imposition of penalties/fines or even criminal indictment. And even if you have yet to incur extraordinary medical expenses, make substantial charitable contributions, or pay mortgage interest, you probably know that these items may give rise to some form of deduction come tax time. In addition to enhancing critical lawyering skills, the study of tax law has a host of practical benefits, wholly aside from allowing an individual to manage and appreciate his or her own tax affairs. Tax expertise is fully billable in the practice setting, and the more seasoned the expertise, the higher one can charge for it. Legal entities, governments, and individuals with sophisticated financial profiles need the assistance of those with knowledge of the tax law, and given the likely perpetuity of the federal taxing apparatus, one can rest assured that there will always be demand for tax attorney services. Attorneys practicing without sufficient knowledge of tax law are flying the trapeze without a net, and they will often find that their sub-stantive shortcoming places their clients in a financially precarious position. Thus, attorneys demonstrating knowledge of and sensitivity to the tax ramifications of a given course of action can more easily navigate tax-related malpractice threats, even if, as a practical matter, such threats remain remote. At the same time, attorneys should be able to display this hallmark of lawyerly sophistication. Today's clients increasingly come to the table with some degree of tax knowledge, and an attorney who is deficient in that regard may appear to lack full professional competence in a business setting. Tax-savvy attorneys can also spare their clients the headache of finding special tax counsel (and paying multiple retainers). Even if a graduate thinks that he or she can practice law wholly outside the tax arena (e.g., commercial and residential real estate, family law, business law, entertainment law, personal injury law), he or she will quickly find that tax ramifications present at every turn. And this reality should come as no surprise; where money (or property) changes hands (or when financial exigencies present), the IRS will surely take note. Accordingly, attor-neys who don't know the tax ramifications of the transactions they structure tend to draft documents that have to be revised (often substantially) by those who do. Such dereliction enhances both inefficiency and client costs.

C. TAXATION IN WORLD HISTORY

1. Taxation Throughout Ancient and Modern History

Putting modern tax law in the proper context requires that we devote some degree of attention to history. Although today most individuals pay taxes via the periodic withholding of taxes on their wages, those who must make direct tax payment to the government for whatever reason typically do so by sending out a check or money order payable to the United States Treasury or by effecting some form of electronic transfer. In ancient times, people had to pay taxes, but electronic payment options did not exist, nor (for some time at least) did coined money or currency. As a result, people paid taxes by handing over physical goods (e.g., cows, grain, geese, etc.) and by rendering services (e.g., manual labor, military service, etc.).

Eventually, the existence of coined money and currency made it possible to pay taxes in that medium, but what is true today was equally true in ancient times; pay-ing taxes has never been pleasant. Indeed, it has often proven decidedly unpleasant. In centuries past, those suffering under particularly heavy or offensive levies (even in response to specific government needs) were quite capable of and creative in

Scribe in ancient Egypt keeping record of geese.
Credit: World History Archive/Alamy Stock Photo.

communicating their displeasure; history is littered with infamous tax revolts. In early thirteenth century England, barons adamantly resisted King John's effort to impose a heightened **scutage** (i.e., a tax paid in lieu of military service) to fund specific military campaigns. Met finally with armed resistance and faced with a series of demands, the king ultimately signed what we now refer to as the Magna Carta. *See* DAVID F. BURG, A WORLD HISTORY OF TAX REBELLIONS 84–86 (Routledge 2004). Over a century later, a massive peasants' revolt took place in India (circa 1332–1334) when Sultan Muhammad Tughluq substantially increased agrarian taxes. *See id.* at 106–07. After considerable agitation, bloodshed, drought, and famine, the sultan found himself introducing and ultimately implementing programs to support agriculture. *See id.* As tax revolts go, hundreds more can be found in the annals of history, but none was more spectacular than the American Revolution.

2. Taxation of the American Colonies and the American Revolution

In the immediate aftermath of the French and Indian War (fought to some extent in colonial America), Great Britain found itself burdened with considerable war debt. Accordingly, it sought to impose direct taxes on the colonies, starting with the so-called **Stamp Act**, which required that various documents carry a revenue stamp. Colonists had generally grown accustomed to Great Britain's taxation of imperial commerce on the high seas, but they objected vehemently to its attempt to impose taxes with respect to *internal* colonial affairs; that privilege, they reasoned, had always belonged to their colonial legislatures (e.g., the Virginia House of Burgesses). The colonists had no representatives in Parliament and thus, they complained, "Taxation without representation is tyranny!" Faced with active and vocal colonial opposition, Parliament ultimately repealed the Stamp Act, but it later introduced the so-called **Townshend Acts**, which imposed taxes on various mundane items such as glass, tea, and paper. Not surprisingly, colonial unrest mounted, so much so that it was necessary to dispatch British troops to keep order in Boston, Massachusetts. Unfortunately, rather than restoring and maintaining calm, the British troops regularly harassed and taunted the colonists. In one notable incident, a crowd in Boston, which had gathered to watch a fight involving one of the soldiers, grew unruly and refused to disperse, and at least one soldier at the scene was struck by a club. He and others turned, raised their muskets, and fired into the crowd, resulting in the so-called Boston Massacre.

In the aftermath of the event, Parliament ultimately repealed most of the taxes imposed by the Townshend Acts, but to restate and insist on its right to impose taxes on the colonies, it left intact the tax on colonial imports of tea. Rather than rest satisfied with the repeal of most of the Townshend Act taxes and enjoy what was then a relatively cheap cup of tea courtesy of Parliament and the British East India Company, the colonists saw the retention of the tax on tea as an attempt, even if indirect, to secure their acquiescence to and affirmation of Great Britain's asserted right to impose direct taxes on them. They promptly made their opinions known. In a notorious display of outrage and objection, the Sons of Liberty, thinly disguised as Mohawk Indians, boarded ships docked at the port of Boston on the evening of December 16, 1773, and tossed more than 90,000 pounds of tea into the water as Bostonians witnessing the event cheered them on.

Undeterred and enraged, Parliament responded to the event with a series of measures including closing the port of Boston (until the destroyed tea was paid for) and imposing martial law. With a healthy troop presence in Massachusetts and collective colonial resentment rising, it was not long before British redcoats were marching off to Lexington and Concord in search of rebellion leaders and, according to rumor, a stockpile of weapons. The American Revolution was afoot. Years later, of course, in the wake of General Cornwallis's surrender at Yorktown, Virginia, and the signing of the Treaty of Paris of 1783, the American Revolution came to an end, but a host of new problems awaited the fledgling United States of America.

Boston Massacre (March 5, 1770).
Credit: Science History Images/Alamy Stock Photo.

Boston Tea Party (December 16, 1773).
Credit: Pictorial Press Ltd./Alamy Stock Photo.

3. Federal Revenue Needs and the Articles of Confederation

Although the colonies emerged victorious from the American Revolution, it was not without cost. Both the individual states and the federal government found themselves strapped with considerable debt, and although the states could impose taxes on their citizens to begin the process of clearing their debt, the central, federal government found itself in a very real dilemma. In the immediate aftermath of the American Revolution, the United States operated not under the current U.S. Constitution but under the Articles of Confederation, and the Articles did not grant

Constitutional Convention of 1787.
Credit: Everett Historical/Shutterstock.com.

the federal government the power to tax the citizens. To cover its many obligations, the federal government could solicit contributions from the states, but it lacked the power to compel contributions to federal coffers. That reality left the federal government (and, by extension, the collective interests of the states) in a precarious position. To address that and a host of other problems with the Articles of Confederation, the Confederation Congress called a Constitutional Convention in 1787, the end result of which was the adoption and ratification of the U.S. Constitution.

D. TAXATION IN THE UNITED STATES TODAY

1. The Constitutional Authority to Tax Income

The Founding Fathers assembled at Philadelphia in 1787 accomplished a great deal with the U.S. Constitution, laying the foundation of the new government and cloaking the citizens of the United States with a host of important individual rights and liberties. Having just waged a costly war originating, at least in part, over the question of whether Great Britain had the right to impose taxes on the colonies (notwithstanding their consistent, vocal, and active objection), the Founding Fathers were sure to clarify in the new Constitution above and beyond all doubt that the new federal government would, indeed, have the power to tax the citizens of the several states. Thus, Article I, § 8 of the Constitution announces the following with abundant clarity:

> *The Congress shall have power to lay and collect taxes, duties, imposts and excises, to pay the debts and provide for the common defense and general welfare of the United States . . . .*

To ensure that no state would face an unfair burden should taxes be imposed, several other provisions require that any direct taxes be apportioned among the states according to their respective populations. Thus, a state with a small population (e.g., Rhode Island) would not be forced to pay the same amount as a state with an immense population (e.g., Virginia), and a decennial census would ensure an accurate, albeit only periodic, count. To accommodate various interests, it was mandated that only three-fifths of slaves be counted, and the Constitution highlighted such altered counting for direct tax purposes. Article I, §§ 2 and 9 provide, in pertinent part, as follows:

> *Representatives and direct taxes shall be apportioned among the several States which may be included within this Union, according to their respective numbers, which shall be determined by adding to the whole number of free persons, including those bound to service for a term of years, and excluding Indians not taxed, three-fifths of all other persons.*

* * *

> *No capitation or other direct tax shall be laid, unless in proportion to the census or enumeration herein before directed to be taken.*

Although the Constitution authorized the laying and collecting of taxes generally, the *income* tax as we understand it today did not exist at the time of the Constitution's ratification. When the attempt was made to collect taxes on income, some objected that an income tax was a direct tax and that, as such, apportionment was required. Thus, Congress added the Sixteenth Amendment to the Constitution, and the requisite number of states formally ratified the amendment in February of 1913. Although Congress had the power to lay and collect taxes under the Constitution as originally drafted and ratified, the Sixteenth Amendment merely clarified that taxes on income could be laid and collected *without apportionment* and *without regard to the decennial census.* The Sixteenth Amendment provides, in pertinent part, as follows:

> *The Congress shall have power to lay and collect taxes on incomes, from whatever source derived, without apportionment among the several States, and without regard to any census or enumeration.*

2. The Department of the Treasury and the Role of the Internal Revenue Service

Within the larger federal government, the **Department of the Treasury** resides within the executive branch and is responsible for formulating tax policy and administering the tax laws. Its leader, the **Secretary of the Treasury**, delegates administration and enforcement of the tax law to the **Internal Revenue Service** ("**IRS**"), which itself is headed by the **Commissioner of Internal Revenue** ("**Commissioner**"). The IRS has many offices and divisions, each charged with executing a specific function or focusing on a specific group of taxpayers. The IRS's primary divisions include Large Business and International, Small Business/Self-Employed, Tax-Exempt and Government Entities, and Wage and Investment. Its principal offices include the **Office of Chief Counsel** (which provides guidance and advice regarding the tax laws) and the **Office of Appeals** (which aims to settle tax controversies without litigation). As appropriate, we will

Alexander Hamilton (*circa* 1757–1804) served as the first Secretary of the Treasury of the United States.
Credit: FrameAngel/Shutterstock.com.

discuss these divisions and offices in future chapters. For the moment, however, note that as an administrative agency charged with collecting revenue (above and well beyond the corporate and individual income taxes mentioned previously), the IRS managed to bring in gross revenues of approximately $3.3 trillion during the 2016 fiscal year in the form of income, employment, excise, and estate and gift taxes. That impressive revenue total reflects the end result of prevailing tax laws and policies, many of which are in a state of flux and the subject of ongoing debate both in the political arena and in scholarly literature. It bears noting, however, that even with gross revenues measured in the trillions, the United States continues to suffer annual multi-billion-dollar budget deficits, prompting some to argue that the nation's wealthiest taxpayers are asked to pay too little, that loopholes must be closed, and that preferential tax treatment of certain forms of income must be abandoned. Those taxpayers in the top percentiles, in turn, lament not only that they pay the bulk of all federal taxes but also that they are required to pay far too much, and they blame chronic budget deficits largely on profligate federal spending. The debates will rage on, and for better or worse, the tax laws will evolve and change. It can surely be said that by providing for the generation of federal revenue, the Founding Fathers cured one of the more serious defects of the Articles of Confederation, but if recent budget statistics are any indicator, the Constitution's failure to police federal expenditures with sufficient vigilance has emerged as a glaring flaw.

E. NEW TAX STATUTES

1. The Origination Clause and the "Classic" Legislative Process

Students and practitioners of tax law find that although fundamental tax principles and core rules change little over time, tax law constantly shifts and evolves. Tax rates change, new rules appear, old rules suffer repeal, and a stream of temporary provisions make their cameos before riding off into the sunset. The Constitution does not attempt to govern every aspect of the tax legislation process, but it does set forth a few ground rules. In addition to the substantive provisions discussed previously, the Constitution requires, per Article I, § 7, that "[a]ll bills for raising revenue . . . originate in the House of Representatives; but the Senate may propose or concur with amendments as on other bills." Apparently recalling that the English House of Commons had the exclusive power to originate revenue matters, the Founding Fathers decided that the U.S. House of Representatives should have the same power, even if the Senate held the power of amendment. Traditionally, then, a bill for raising revenue will originate in the House of Representatives and then be assigned to the **House Ways and Means Committee,** a standing committee in the House responsible for addressing tax-related measures. The measure may "die" in committee, but if fortune prevails and the committee reports on the measure favorably (i.e., approves), the measure then proceeds to the floor of the House of Representatives for a vote. If the House passes the measure, the bill proceeds to the Senate, where it is assigned to the **Senate Finance Committee,** which handles tax-related measures as a standing committee of the Senate. Assuming that the committee reports on the measure favorably, it goes to the floor of the full Senate for a vote. The version of a measure approved by the House and the version approved by the Senate will likely have discrepancies that must be worked out before the measure can become law. Accordingly, such a measure goes to the **Conference Committee,** a joint committee comprised of members from both chambers who work together to iron out differences in legislation as originally passed by the House and the Senate. The legislation emerging from the Conference Committee proceeds back to the floor of the House and the Senate, and assuming both chambers approve the (now-identical) measure, it goes to the President for signature. With the President's approval, the measure becomes law. If the President vetoes it, Congress, having the power to override a presidential veto, can nonetheless enact the measure.

One should note, at this juncture, that as legislation makes its way through Congress, the various committees generate reports that will ultimately constitute part of the measure's legislative history. Internal Revenue Code provisions may contain ambiguous or perplexing language, making it difficult to ascertain from the face of the statute exactly what Congress intended. Thus, those conducting research in the tax arena can often get a clearer picture of what Congress had in mind when it adopted or amended a given provision of tax law by consulting reports generated during the legislative process. These reports (e.g., the **House Ways and Means Committee Report**, the **Senate Finance Committee Report**, and the **Conference Committee Report**) typically discuss the old law, the reasons for change, and the new law. Consider, for example, the following excerpt from the Senate Report prepared during consideration of what is now § 221 of the Code.

SENATE REPORT NO. 105-33

* * *

3. Deduction for student loan interest (sec. 202 of the bill and new sec. 221 of the Code)

<u>Present Law</u>

The Tax Reform Act of 1986 repealed the deduction for personal interest. Student loan interest generally is treated as personal interest and thus is not allowable as an itemized deduction from income. * * *

<u>Reasons for Change</u>

The [Senate Finance] Committee is aware that many students incur considerable debt in the course of obtaining undergraduate and graduate education. The Committee believes that permitting a deduction for interest on certain student loans will help to ease the financial burden that such obligations represent.

<u>Explanation of Provision</u>

Under the bill, certain individuals who have paid interest on qualified education loans may claim an above-the-line deduction for such interest expenses, up to a maximum . . . .

In addition to the House Report and the Senate Report, the Conference Committee Report can be particularly useful because it will indicate whether the final legislation reflects full or partial adoption of the House provision or the Senate's amendment (if either) and why.

2. The Internal Revenue Code of 1986 (as Amended)

Soon after ratification of the Sixteenth Amendment in 1913, Congress passed the Revenue Act of 1913, and in later years, additional revenue measures were enacted. The various revenue measures were eventually pulled together into a single "Internal Revenue Code," and future changes in tax law simply took the form of amendments to the existing Code. From time to time, the Code would undergo substantial revision/amendment, and the entire Code would be reenacted. Thus, one may see reference to the Internal Revenue Code of 1954. More likely, of course, one will encounter reference to the current version of the Code, the **Internal Revenue Code of 1986 (as amended)** (the "**Code**"). Thus, the statutory supplement in use in your class literally contains select provisions from the Internal Revenue Code as it was reenacted in 1986, albeit reflecting various amendments made thereto since 1986. You may also see reference to the original Internal Revenue Code of 1986 as Public Law 99-514 or P.L. 99-514. Note that although most tax statutes appear in the Code, from time to time, Congress will enact a tax provision and make it part of Statutes-at-Large rather than having the provision codified along with other tax statutes. The practice strikes many as odd, but it persists.

As part of the larger body of federal law, the Code exists as Title 26. That Title is, in turn, subdivided into Subtitles, Chapters, Subchapters, Parts, and Subparts; in this course, we devote our attention to Subtitle A, which addresses income taxes. Individual Code sections generally appear within a Part or a Subpart. And as if that's not enough, it gets better. The individual sections have divisions of their own, and here is where focus is most important. A given Code provision such as § 165(h)(3)(A) has multiple divisions, as exemplified by the following:

165	(h)	(3)	(A)
Section	Subsection	Paragraph	Subparagraph

The good news is that there is method in this madness both at the macro- and micro- levels! If Congress seeks to limit the applicability of a given definition or provision, it can use limiting language; you will often see it. Thus, a special definition for a specific term that should apply only in a given section will be preceded by language akin to "For purposes of this section, ..." Likewise, if a given provision should apply to a range of sections, one might see limiting language akin to "For purposes of this Part, . . ." or "For purposes of this Subpart, ..." If Congress needs restriction within a section, it can use language such as "For purposes of this subparagraph, . . ." or "For purposes of this subsection, ..." Finally, if Congress needs to speak somewhat broadly, it can say "For purposes of this subtitle, . . . " or even "For purposes of this title, ..." Note that even if a particular provision contains language that generally restricts its applicability (e.g., "For purposes of this section"), other provisions may cross-reference that provision to effectively borrow the rules or, perhaps, definitions presented there.

F. OTHER SOURCES OF TAX "LAW"

Although Congress has managed over the years to produce an Internal Revenue Code notorious for its length, Congress has not undertaken to anticipate every situation nor has it attempted to flesh out every revenue provision in baroque detail. Rather, Congress anticipates that the Treasury Department will further interpret and explain the tax law and that, on occasion, courts may be called on for **interstitial law-making** (i.e., filling gaps left by current statutes and regulations). Thus, one should be aware of several important sources of tax "law."

1. Treasury Regulations

Often, Congress will enact a Code provision and explicitly direct, as part of the approved legislation, that the Secretary of the Treasury flesh things out further. The Treasury fulfills this mandate by promulgating Treasury Regulations that generally correspond, numerically, with a specific Code provision. Thus, for further explanation of I.R.C. § 165, discussed by the Tax Court in *Blackman*, one would generally consult Treas. Reg. § 1.165-1 et seq. The Treasury Department may also issue regulations without express congressional directive. Treasury Regulations provide useful information and guidance and are entitled to deference. The Treasury Department will occasionally indicate its intent with respect to a given set of regulations by setting forth a preamble to those regulations, and such preambles can prove useful in a research context. Note also that the Treasury Department normally issues regulations first as **Proposed Treasury Regulations,** which generally serve to provide non-binding but needed taxpayer guidance; only after a public comment period and further administrative procedure are they issued as final Treasury Regulations. The Treasury Department may also issue **Temporary Treasury Regulations** to provide needed rules of immediate applicability, although such regulations are also typically issued in proposed form to elicit feedback and commentary before they are finalized.

2. IRS Pronouncements

Provisions of the Internal Revenue Code and the Treasury Regulations often suffice in terms of clarifying the proper tax treatment of a given transaction or item. The efforts of Congress and the Treasury Department notwithstanding, however, a host of issues may present. If a given provision of the Internal Revenue Code is new, clients may begin pressing their tax advisors for answers before such advisors have the benefit of proposed or temporary Treasury Regulations. Likewise, developments and innovations in any number of arenas (e.g., financial, medical) may have a tax impact, even though in drafting applicable rules as an initial matter Congress did not have those innovations or developments in mind; standard application of the rule might well lead to grossly inappropriate results. Also, in some instances, tax advisors and their clients may have a considerable degree of comfort with respect to the treatment of a given item or transaction, but in light of the significance of the transaction (which might well involve billions of dollars), they seek further assurances from the IRS. Accordingly, from time to time, the IRS will provide guidance by issuing various pronouncements. Some of the more common pronouncements include the following:

Revenue Rulings: This form of pronouncement is the IRS's official position with respect to its treatment of a given transaction or item. One can think of it as the IRS's general indication of its current litigating position, but courts need *not* treat Revenue Rulings as binding, although some may find them persuasive. Note that Revenue Rulings may be amended or superseded by future pronouncements.

Private Letter Rulings ("PLRs"): This form of pronouncement is issued by the IRS to a specific taxpayer with respect to an issue the taxpayer currently faces or an actual transaction the taxpayer contemplates. The ruling confirms how the item or transaction will be treated under the facts as presented by the taxpayer and governing law. Such rulings are binding on the IRS with respect to *that* taxpayer (although the Service does reserve the right to unilaterally revoke a PLR for specific reasons). Other taxpayers may *not* rely on it for their own transactions or cite it as precedent. Note that the IRS is not obligated to rule on every issue, and, in fact, the IRS will often clarify by official announcement that it will not issue PLRs on certain issues.

Revenue Procedures: These pronouncements generally provide guidance with respect to the proper procedure to be followed under varying circumstances. For example, a Revenue Procedure will inform taxpayers about the steps they must take to secure a PLR. Note that Revenue Procedures are subject to amendment and update.

Technical Advice Memoranda: The IRS National Office will issue these pronouncements to fellow IRS personnel as guidance in connection with the examination of a specific taxpayer. The IRS ultimately makes such memoranda available to the public but in a form that would prevent identification of a specific taxpayer.

Action on Decision: These pronouncements are made in response to tax litigation developments, and they are intended to guide IRS personnel working on the same or similar issues. The pronouncements essentially indicate whether the IRS will defer to the holding in certain cases on issues decided against the government that will not be appealed in that case. The IRS issues an "Acquiescence," an "Acquiescence in Result Only," or a "Non-Acquiescence." Note, in particular, that if the IRS issues a Non-Acquiescence, it indicates that for the moment, it's throwing in the towel on the issue in a given jurisdiction (e.g., the Ninth Circuit), but vows to fight the issue elsewhere.

In addition to the preceding items, the IRS issues a wide range of pronouncements. In a practice setting, you will become more familiar with the various pronouncement forms, but for now, the key is to note that in providing advice to clients, one often has several sources of guidance beyond the provisions of the Internal Revenue Code and the Treasury Regulations. These official pronouncements lack the impact of Code provisions and final Treasury Regulations, but one should not take them lightly. A pronouncement on a given issue might well give rise to considerable reverberations throughout the tax-planning community.

3. Tax Cases

As is the case in other areas of law, courts must, from time to time, intervene to resolve differences in the tax arena, and relevant cases can come from any number of courts. Taxpayers facing litigation with the IRS may have to make several important decisions, the first being whether they will pay the asserted tax deficiency before the commencement of litigation or whether they will pay, if at all, only after the commencement or completion of litigation. That initial decision will have an impact on what court they may litigate in. If the taxpayer has the financial wherewithal and decides to pay before commencing litigation, they will ultimately sue the "United States" for a refund either in District Court or the Court of Federal Claims; the rules governing binding and persuasive precedent operate as per usual. Assuming they file in District Court, they may later appeal to the relevant Circuit Court of Appeals and ultimately to the United States Supreme Court. If, instead, they file in the Court of Federal Claims, they may later appeal to the Court of Appeals for the Federal Circuit and ultimately to the United States Supreme Court. Taxpayers who pay before the commencement of litigation may have to part with a considerable amount of money, but their payment stops the tolling of interest on the asserted tax deficiency. Having the ability to pay first also gives them maximum flexibility in terms of shopping for the most favorable forum (based on existing precedent).

Taxpayers lacking the financial wherewithal to pay first or opting to withhold payment until the commencement or completion of litigation, must file suit against the Commissioner of Internal Revenue in **Tax Court**, a court that specializes in tax matters and whose judges have tax expertise. Taxpayers filing in Tax Court may later appeal to the Circuit Court of Appeals for the federal circuit in which they resided at the time the petition was filed and ultimately to the United States Supreme Court. Whether interest continues to accrue on the asserted deficiency depends on whether the taxpayer voluntarily decides to make a preliminary payment after filing a petition (to stop the tolling of interest) or prefers to wait until the litigation phase is complete (allowing interest to accrue in the interim). Note, in particular, that with respect to a given Tax Court case, the court must defer to the decisions of the relevant Circuit Court of Appeals as *binding* precedent. It is also possible for taxpayers litigating in Tax Court to assert a refund claim, essentially arguing not only that they refuse to pay the asserted deficiency but also that they overpaid as an initial matter and will take the opportunity to pursue a refund.

Chapter Summary

- Article I, § 8 of the United States Constitution gives Congress the power to lay and collect taxes for specific purposes.
- Article I, § 2 of the United States Constitution requires that direct taxes be apportioned among the several states.

- Although Article I, § 8 of the Constitution grants Congress the power to lay and collect taxes generally, the Sixteenth Amendment to the U.S. Constitution grants Congress the power to lay and collect taxes on income *without apportionment.*
- Under Article I, § 7 of the U.S. Constitution, all bills for raising revenue must originate in the House of Representatives, although the Senate has the power of amendment.
- The Department of the Treasury resides within the executive branch, and the Secretary of the Treasury delegates administration and enforcement of the tax law to the Internal Revenue Service; the Commissioner of Internal Revenue leads the IRS.
- In the House of Representatives, tax legislation is initially assigned to the House Ways and Means Committee. In the Senate, tax legislation is initially assigned to the Senate Finance Committee. The Conference Committee resolves differences in tax legislation before such legislation is sent for final approval to the House, the Senate, and the President.
- The Internal Revenue Code exists as part of the larger body of federal law as Title 26; some tax statutes are noncodified and generally appear in Statutes-at-Large. Although prior versions exist, the Internal Revenue Code in use today is the Internal Revenue Code of 1986 (as amended). Those providing tax advice with respect to *prior* events must use the version of the Internal Revenue Code as it existed at the time of the relevant events.
- In addition to consulting the Internal Revenue Code, tax advisors may look to various sources for guidance including Treasury Regulations, IRS pronouncements, and tax cases.
- Taxpayers who opt to withhold payment of an asserted deficiency prior to the commencement or close of litigation may proceed only in Tax Court against the Commissioner of Internal Revenue; decisions of both the United States Supreme Court and the Circuit Court of Appeals in which the taxpayer resided at the time of the filing of the petition will be binding precedent while the case is in Tax Court. Taxpayers who pay asserted deficiencies prior to the commencement of litigation (or who otherwise seek refund of taxes paid) may proceed against the United States either in District Court or in the Court of Federal Claims.

Applying the Rules

1. Taxpayer A is contemplating a multi-billion-dollar transaction with Taxpayer B. Taxpayer A hires Fernando, a tax attorney, to assist in obtaining a PLR from the IRS.

   a. How will Fernando find out what steps must be taken to secure a PLR?

   b. If Fernando succeeds in obtaining a favorable ruling from the IRS, which taxpayers, in addition to Taxpayer A, can rely on that PLR?

2. Giovanni, a resident of Los Angeles, California, recently received a notice from the IRS indicating that, with respect to 2017, he owes an additional $2,000 in taxes.

   a. If Giovanni pays the asserted deficiency and then decides to seek a refund, in what trial courts may he proceed?
   b. Who will be the defendant in his refund suit?
   c. What decisions will be binding precedent with respect to his trial court?
   d. If Giovanni refused to pay the asserted deficiency prior to the close of litigation, in what trial court could he proceed? How would you respond to questions (b) and (c) under such altered facts?

Federal Income Taxation in Practice

1. Assume that you have been hired as a summer associate at a large law firm and that your first assignment comes from a tax partner in the firm. The partner already has the relevant version of the Internal Revenue Code and Treasury Regulations but needs legislative history, tax cases, and IRS pronouncements on the issue. Ascertain which electronic legal databases contain the resources/materials you need to locate. Are those databases reliable?

2. Locate Revenue Procedure 2018-1 and find (within it) the start of the general instructions for requesting a letter ruling from the IRS.

3. You have been retained as tax counsel for a specific matter and are unable to obtain access to an electronic database. Fortunately, you do have access to a law library. Go to this library and locate the section containing tax research materials. Find resources that would be helpful if you were conducting research under 26 U.S.C. § 165(c).

4. Use the internet to find and print IRS Form 1040 and Schedule A for the most recent calendar year ("Year Y"). Also locate (but do NOT print) the Instructions for the Form 1040. You will use the "Tax Tables" in the Instructions to complete one of the lines on the second page of the Form 1040. Fill out the Form 1040 using the following information:

   Oliva Wynn (SSN 000-00-0001) and Sergio Wynn (SSN 000-00-0002) reside at 123 Maple Lane in Irvine, CA 92622. At this juncture, they have no children or dependents. They plan to have children in the future, so they steadily save money in the hope that college funds and the like will ultimately be needed. The Bank of Orange paid them $150 in interest in (which they left untouched) in Year Y with respect to their joint savings account.

   Oliva and Sergio both teach high school in Irvine, and each earned an annual salary of $50,000 in Year Y, a real improvement over the $40,000/year they had made back in Baltimore, MD, in Year X. Accepting the positions in Irvine was somewhat of a no-brainer, even though they were not too happy about having to pay their own moving expenses ($5,150). Fortunately, Lady Luck intervened to soften the financial blow. Sergio, the perpetual trivia buff, had managed to win $2,000 as a contestant in a local, popular game show, "Millions!"

In Year Y, Oliva and Sergio had $12,641 withheld from their pay as federal income taxes and $3,000 withheld as California income taxes. They also paid the following:

$1,000 in real property taxes
$5,000 in unreimbursed, uninsured medical expenses related to one of Sergio's wood shop accidents
$5,000 in home mortgage interest
$50 to a local charity

Realization and the Notion of "Income"

Whether we pause to contemplate or acknowledge the fact, we pay a dizzying array of taxes. There are state sales taxes, property taxes, and excises taxes on gasoline, wine, cigarettes, and tanning salon use. We also enjoy F.C.C. taxes for smartphone services, airline ticket taxes, and (for the privilege of summoning the authorities by dialing 9-1-1) the Emergency Tax. We focus squarely in this course on the federal tax on "income," which means that, as an initial matter, we need to define the precise contours of "income"; the task is not always as easy as it might at first appear to be. Assume that a person goes to work, earns money, and gets paid. The money received would certainly appear to constitute income. But what about the gift (in the form of cash) a college graduate receives from her grandparents? Is that income? Even if we correctly assume that she owes no taxes with respect to the gift, does she, nonetheless, have "income"? What if her friend, Khalil, bought Greenacre for $500,000 in the hope that its fair market value would rise? Does Khalil have income each year as the property's value actually rises, even if he continues to own it? In this chapter, you will learn how to answer these questions. Although we will ultimately focus on recent and prevailing notions of income, we must first turn to and spend a fairly healthy amount of time with the concept of "realization." Keep in mind that "income" and "realization" are not synonymous, but they do share an inextricable link.

Key Concepts

- The concept of realization and the multiplicity of realization event forms
- Basis, unrealized gain/loss, amount realized, gain/loss realized, and recognition
- The current standard for ascertaining whether a taxpayer has "income"
- Fundamentals of the tax computation process and the importance of a taxpayer's adjusted gross income ("AGI")

A. THE CONCEPT OF REALIZATION

1. Realization Events Involving Cash; Critical Tax Terminology

Conceptual Fundamentals

Key Statutory Provisions

- IRC § 61(a)
- IRC § 1001(a)–(c)
- IRC § 1012(a)

The Haig-Simons Perspective on "Income"

Although tax law generally views a realization event as a necessary prerequisite to the existence of "income," it is possible to construct notions of income that do not rely on realization event triggers. Economists Robert Haig and Henry Simons essentially defined personal income (for a given period) as the sum of (1) amounts spent by the taxpayer on consumption and (2) the change in the taxpayer's net worth. Under such a formulation, mere increases in the value of a taxpayer's assets would be taken into account in measuring changes in net worth and could ultimately constitute a component of taxable income. Although intriguing to some extent, the Haig-Simons definition of income lacks practical viability and is largely of academic interest.

In the most basic and general terms, the relationship between income and realization is the following: One does not have income for federal tax purposes unless and until **a realization event** occurs.[1] That reality logically leads to the question "What exactly is a realization event?" There is no precise, fixed, or universal definition of the term. Many events alter or influence a taxpayer's economic or financial profile, but one should think of a realization event as an event, the occurrence of which (per Congressional mandate) requires the recognition of income, allows the recognition of loss, or gives rise to some definitive and immediate federal tax consequence. In some instances, the realization event will be the sale, exchange, or other disposition of an asset or the completion of a transaction. In others, it will be the occurrence of an identifiable event or the reduction of property to undisputed personal possession. Statutory rules, Treasury Regulations, IRS pronouncements, and judicial interpretations collectively determine whether a realization event has, in fact, occurred. As you can see, realization events come in many forms, and as you study federal income taxation in greater depth, you will come to appreciate the rich variety. You will also see how sharp differences can arise regarding whether a realization event has occurred, notwithstanding the presence of statutory rules and administrative guidance. For now, let's start with realization events visible to the naked eye, so to speak. Assume that a person buys Greenacre for $500,000 and that the fair market value of Greenacre rises over time to $750,000. At that juncture, the person *could* sell Greenacre at a profit, but for now, as a

---

[1]Later in this chapter, we discuss *Eisner v. Macomber*, which articulates the realization requirement as a common law mandate. The realization requirement has to be understood, however, as both a common law rule and a rule of administrative convenience, not as a constitutional restraint on Congress's taxing power; Congress remains free to tax mere appreciation in value if it so chooses. Although the IRS would face paralyzing difficulty attempting to impose taxes by taking all changes in property value into account, Congress does require that certain increases and decreases in value be recognized before sales, exchanges, or other dispositions occur. *See, e.g.,* § 1256 (discussing mark-to-market rules). For a discussion of the realization requirement's evolution, see Jeffrey L. Kwall, *When Should Asset Appreciation Be Taxed?: The Case for a Disposition Standard of Realization,* 86 IND. L.J. 77 (2011).

matter of established tax doctrine, the $250,000 is mere appreciation in value. Such an increase in value may enhance the individual's net worth, but Greenacre's increase in fair market value by $250,000 is not, itself, an event that results in income cognizable for federal tax purposes. Once the individual sells the land, the potential income represented by the appreciation is no longer hypothetical or "mere paper" gain but *real*, and the Code requires a tax reckoning at that juncture. The sale, then, is the realization event. That's one potential scenario. What if a property's value falls? The concept operates in exactly the same way with respect to a loss. Taxpayers do not suffer a loss for federal income tax purposes unless and until a realization event takes place. Thus, if Redacre is purchased for $100,000 and then falls in value to $80,000, the owner suffers a loss cognizable for tax purposes only upon the occurrence of some realization event. If the owner sells Redacre for $80,000, the sale is the realization event. If, instead, the owner continues to hold Redacre, he does not suffer a tax loss because at that juncture, no realization event has occurred. Keep in mind as you read through this chapter that most realization events are not difficult to see (so don't panic), but given that you are an aspiring attorney (and, possibly, a budding tax specialist at that), you should have a sharpened ability to detect both potential and actual realization events.

The realization events discussed thus far have involved basic sales transactions for cash. Later in this chapter, we examine more subtle or hard-to-detect realization events; but for now, we're going to spend a little more time with simple realization events because doing so allows us to cover some critically important tax terminology. To put it differently, we're going to add a tax vocabulary layer to the straightforward purchase and sale transactions we just discussed. The transaction essentials won't change, but it is imperative that you understand the "tax shorthand" for some of the numbers, because this terminology will appear throughout this and every other tax course you take. As doses of vocabulary go, the following is moderate, but if you master the terminology sooner rather than later, you will thank yourself profusely.

Special Tax Terminology

The tax impact of the following examples makes basic common sense. Take note of the new vocabulary.

Example 1

Assume that Hector buys Greenacre for $200,000 and that it rises in value to $450,000. He sells the property at that point and must include the gain of $250,000 in his gross income. Now, let's reveal the tax vocabulary with respect to this transaction by breaking it down; we'll start at the very beginning.

▨ Hector purchased Greenacre for $200,000. This dollar amount is referred to as his **basis** in Greenacre.[2]

---

[2] Section 1012(a) of the Code generally provides that "the basis of property shall be the cost of such property . . . ."

- The property rose in value to $450,000. At that point (presale), Hector had **unrealized gain** of $250,000 ($450,000 - $200,000). One could use synonymous terminology and say that Hector had **built-in gain** of $250,000.[3]
- Hector sold Greenacre (a realization event), and the purchaser gave him $450,000. We refer to this dollar amount as Hector's **amount realized**.[4]
- Hector made $250,000. We refer to this amount as his **gain realized** because there was a realization event, and $450,000 - $200,000 = $250,000.[5]
- Hector has $250,000 of gross income from this transaction and must include that amount on his federal income tax return. In the tax world, we say that Hector must recognize the gain. Thus, his **gain recognized** is $250,000.[6]

Example 2

Austin buys Blueacre for $400,000 and later sells it for $500,000.

- Basis in Blueacre: $400,000
- Pre-Sale Unrealized/Built-In Gain: $100,000
- Amount Realized: $500,000
- Gain Realized: $100,000
- Gain Recognized: $100,000

Example 3

Kyra purchases Redacre (for use in her business) for $100,000 and later sells it for $80,000.

- Basis in Redacre: $100,000
- Presale Unrealized/Built-In Loss: $20,000
- Amount Realized: $80,000
- Loss Realized: $20,000
- Loss Recognized: $20,000

With basic realization events (and some new tax vocabulary) under your belt, you're now ready to try your hand at more subtle realization events. They're not tough, just different.

---

[3]Both unrealized gain and built-in gain refer to the amount by which the fair market value of a taxpayer's property exceeds its basis or, as we will later learn, its "adjusted basis."

[4]Under § 1001(b), the Code provides that "[t]he amount realized from the sale or other disposition of property shall be the sum of any money received plus the fair market value of the property (other than money) received." In this situation, Hector received money and nothing else. So his amount realized is the amount of money he received.

[5]Section 1001(a) provides, in pertinent part, that the "gain from the sale or other disposition of property shall be the excess of the amount realized therefrom over the . . . basis."

[6]Section 1001(c) provides, in pertinent part, that "[unless a specific exception applies], the entire amount of the gain or loss, determined under this section, on the sale or exchange of property shall be recognized."

> **Note**
> ....
> Based on the preceding examples, it may appear that loss realized will always equal loss recognized and that gain realized will always equal gain recognized. For some transactions, the amounts will be equal, but much later in the course we will encounter transactions in which these amounts may differ because recognition (in whole or in part) will be deferred to a later date.

2. Non-Cash and Non-Transactional Realization Events

Up to this point, all of the realization events portrayed have involved the sale of property for cash, typically at a profit or loss. But, as I mentioned earlier, realization events come in many forms. True enough, some realization events involve the sale of property for cash, but the ambit of "realization event" is, necessarily and by statutory mandate, far broader than that. If a person bought a piece of art for $800,000, and it is now worth $1 million, they cannot escape having a realization event by demanding that the purchaser give them some form of property worth $1 million but not cash. Thus, if a taxpayer sells art in which she has a basis of $800,000 and receives, as consideration, a house worth $1 million, the sale/exchange will constitute a realization event. If a taxpayer hands over a thoroughbred stallion and receives a Clydesdale draft horse (or, more likely, a stable of them), the exchange will constitute a realization event. If they hold Netflix, Inc. stock worth $50,000 and forego the sale of it for cash but, instead, exchange it for Apple, Inc. stock worth $50,000, the exchange will constitute a realization event.

[handwritten margin note: property equal to $1million treated the same as $1 million cash]

By the way, *don't assume that realization events always involve sales, exchanges, or some other transaction.* As we will soon see, the Internal Revenue Code and Treasury Regulations identify a host of non-transactional realization events. A person who walks down the sidewalk, finds $5,000 in cash, and pockets it experiences a realization event just as a person who receives her regular paycheck has a realization event. Likewise, if major disaster strikes and a tornado sweeps up and destroys a taxpayer's SUV (for which no insurance company or other compensation is forthcoming), he has a realization event because he actually sustains a loss, notwithstanding the absence of a negotiated transaction.

B. REALIZATION EVENT V. NONREALIZATION EVENT

If your understanding of realization is still a bit rough around the edges, don't fret. Acquiring the ability to spot realization events requires working knowledge of various statutory and regulatory provisions. It also takes a little practice, and even those with considerable practice can disagree. Various courts have grappled with the issue. In fact, two of the more significant decisions concerning the realization requirement come from the U.S. Supreme Court itself. In one case, the Court found a realization event, and in the other, the Court concluded there was no realization event. Let's start with the latter and see if the Court's finding makes sense to you. In _Eisner v. Macomber_, the alleged realization event concerned the distribution of shares in a corporation to existing shareholders (i.e., a **stock dividend**). Those of you who have yet to take Business Associations should note that those who own shares of stock in a corporation are the corporation's owners. Thus, a person holding 100 percent of the stock of the corporation owns the whole corporation. If, instead, there are two shareholders, the ownership percentages can vary (e.g., 50/50, 25/75, 85/15, 1/99, etc.). Now, assume, for the sake of simplicity, that a corporation has a sole shareholder who holds all 100 shares of the corporation. Assume further that the corporation distributes 900 additional shares to that person and does nothing else. Has there been a realization event? At the beginning of the day, the person held 100 percent of the corporation, and at the end of the day, the person held 100 percent of the corporation. You might initially think there was a realization event because the person actually received something (i.e., stock) from the corporation. To be sure, the corporation did issue an additional 900 shares, but did the person actually get, in substance, something that they did not already have? The only thing that changed was the number of shares. Initially 100 shares represented 100 percent ownership, and at the end of the day, 1,000 shares represented 100 percent ownership. Can we say that the person has derived anything and thus enjoyed a realization event? No. The corporation handed over more shares to its shareholder, but the person did not get _more_ ownership nor, for that matter, did they get money or non-stock property from the corporation. Thus, the shareholder's proportionate interest in the corporation (i.e., 100 percent) was exactly the same before and after the corporation distributed the new stock. The Court held in _Eisner v. Macomber_ that, for income to arise, a realization event is necessary, and under the given facts, a _pro rata_ distribution of shares was not a realization event. The taxpayer owned stock in a corporation along with several others, and they all received additional stock such that they all maintained the same percentage ownership they had held before the distribution. Accordingly, they simply derived nothing, because all of the shareholders held the exact same percentage of stock in the corporation before and after the distribution. No realization event meant no income.

The Supreme Court handed down _Eisner v. Macomber_ in 1920, and its holding regarding the realization requirement remains relevant as a common law rule (although not as a restraint on Congress's taxing power). The realization requirement also serves, for the taxing authorities, as an administrative convenience; rather than tracking and taxing every change in the value of taxpayer property, Congress generally focuses on tax ramifications flowing from realization events. As recently as 1991, there was further development and refinement in the realization event arena; the Court gave us _Cottage Savings Association v. Commissioner_, which dealt with a taxpayer seeking to take a loss deduction. Accordingly, the taxpayer had to establish that a realization event had, indeed, occurred.

Case Preview

Cottage Savings Association v. Commissioner

As we already know, the question of whether a taxpayer has a loss cognizable for tax purposes turns first on whether a realization event has occurred. Answering that question is often fairly easy when one can point to a specific event or even look to a basic sale transaction, but as the transactions become more complex, it can become more difficult to detect the occurrence of a realization event. Consider, for example, a transaction involving financial instruments like basic debt obligations (i.e., IOUs). Banks lend money all the time, so at any given moment, they may have thousands of IOUs (i.e., promissory notes) outstanding. Sometimes, banks require that those promissory notes be backed up by collateral (or "security") in the form of, say, a car or a house; if the debtor defaults on the loan, the bank will repossess the car or commence foreclosure proceedings with respect to the house. When a promissory note is secured by a home, we call the arrangement a mortgage, and for reasons we need not get into, banks and other financial institutions sell and exchange mortgages all the time. If, for good reason, Bank Alpha exchanges some of its mortgages for a group of mortgages held by Bank Beta, can we say that the exchange itself constitutes a realization event for federal income tax purposes? Or is the situation the virtual equivalent of the facts in *Eisner v. Macomber* (i.e., the taxpayer's situation remains essentially unchanged)? The U.S. Supreme Court addressed this tough issue in *Cottage Savings*. As you read the decision, consider the following questions:

The foreclosure crisis of the early 2000s was precipitated, to some extent, by financial institutions making a large number of mortgage loans to borrowers likely to default (i.e., subprime mortgages). *See generally* U.S. Department of Housing and Urban Development, *Report to Congress on the Root Causes of the Foreclosure Crisis* (2010). *Credit:* Andy Dean Photography/Shutterstock.com.

1. When does a given exchange constitute a "disposition" of property for federal income tax purposes under § 1001?
2. The Commissioner argued that the exchanged mortgages were not materially different. What facts supported the Commissioner's argument?
3. What did the Court conclude would constitute a material difference in the context of an exchange?

Cottage Savings Association v. Commissioner
499 U.S. 554 (1991)

Justice Thurgood Marshall

Appointed by President Lyndon B. Johnson, Justice Thurgood Marshall served on the U.S. Supreme Court from 1967 to 1991. Justice Marshall had previously served as Solicitor General of the United States and is well known for the litigation victory he secured in *Brown v. Board of Education*, an enduring landmark of Equal Protection Clause jurisprudence.

Credit: Stock Montage/Getty Images.

Justice MARSHALL delivered the opinion of the Court.

The issue in this case is whether a financial institution realizes tax-deductible losses when it exchanges its interests in one group of residential mortgage loans for another lender's interests in a different group of residential mortgage loans. We hold that such a transaction does give rise to realized losses.

I

Petitioner Cottage Savings Association (Cottage Savings) is a savings and loan association (S & L) formerly regulated by the Federal Home Loan Bank Board (FHLBB). Like many [S & L institutions], Cottage Savings held numerous long-term, low-interest mortgages that declined in value when interest rates surged in the late 1970's. These institutions would have benefited from selling their devalued mortgages in order to realize tax-deductible losses. However, they were deterred from doing so by FHLBB accounting regulations, which required them to record the losses on their books. Reporting these losses consistent with the then-effective FHLBB accounting regulations would have placed many S & L's at risk of closure by the FHLBB.

The FHLBB responded to this situation by relaxing its requirements for the reporting of losses. In a regulatory directive known as "Memorandum R-49," dated June 27, 1980, the FHLBB determined that S & L's need not report losses associated with mortgages that are exchanged for "substantially identical" mortgages held by other lenders. The FHLBB's acknowledged purpose for Memorandum R-49 was to facilitate transactions that would generate tax losses but that would not substantially affect the economic position of the transacting S & L's.

This case involves a typical Memorandum R-49 transaction. On December 31, 1980, Cottage Savings sold "90% participation" in 252 mortgages to four S & L's. It simultaneously purchased "90% participation interests" in 305 mortgages held by these S & L's. All of the loans involved in the transaction were secured by single-family homes, most in the Cincinnati area. The fair market value of the package of participation interests exchanged by each side was approximately $4.5 million. The face value of the participation interests Cottage Savings relinquished in the transaction was approximately $6.9 million.

On its 1980 federal income tax return, Cottage Savings claimed a deduction for $2,447,091, which represented the adjusted difference between the face value of the participation interests that it traded and the fair market value of the participation interests that it received. As permitted by Memorandum R-49, Cottage Savings did not report these losses to the FHLBB. After the Commissioner of Internal Revenue disallowed Cottage Savings' claimed deduction, Cottage Savings sought a redetermination in the Tax Court. The Tax Court held that the deduction was permissible.

On appeal by the Commissioner, the Court of Appeals reversed. The Court of Appeals agreed with the Tax Court's determination that Cottage Savings had realized its losses through the transaction. However, the court held that Cottage Savings was not entitled to a deduction because its losses were not "actually" sustained during the 1980 tax year for purposes of 26 U.S.C. § 165(a).

Because of the importance of this issue to the S & L industry and the conflict among the Circuits over whether Memorandum R-49 exchanges produce deductible tax losses, we granted certiorari. We now reverse.

II

Rather than assessing tax liability on the basis of annual fluctuations in the value of a taxpayer's property, the Internal Revenue Code defers the tax consequences of a gain or loss in property value until the taxpayer "realizes" the gain or loss. * * *

Section 1001(a)'s language provides a straightforward test for realization: to realize a gain or loss in the value of property, the taxpayer must engage in a "sale or other disposition of [the] property." The parties agree that the exchange of participation interests in this case cannot be characterized as a "sale" under § 1001(a); the issue before us is whether the transaction constitutes a "disposition of property." The Commissioner argues that an exchange of property can be treated as a "disposition" under § 1001(a) only if the properties exchanged are materially different. The Commissioner further submits that, because the underlying mortgages were essentially economic substitutes, the participation interests exchanged by Cottage Savings were not materially different from those received from the other S & L's. Cottage Savings, on the other hand, maintains that *any* exchange of property is a "disposition of property" under § 1001(a), regardless of whether the property exchanged is materially different. Alternatively, Cottage Savings contends that the participation interests exchanged were materially different because the underlying loans were secured by different properties.

We must therefore determine whether the realization principle in § 1001(a) incorporates a "material difference" requirement. If it does, we must further decide what that requirement amounts to and how it applies in this case. We consider these questions in turn.

Neither the language nor the history of the Code indicates whether and to what extent property exchanged must differ to count as a "disposition of property" under § 1001(a). Nonetheless, we readily agree with the Commissioner that an exchange of property gives rise to a realization event under § 1001(a) only if the properties exchanged are "materially different." The Commissioner himself has by regulation construed § 1001(a) to embody a material difference requirement:

"Except as otherwise provided . . . the gain or loss realized from the conversion of property into cash, *or from the exchange of property for other property differing materially either in kind or in extent,* is treated as income or as loss sustained." Treas. Reg. § 1.1001-1, 26 CFR § 1.1001-1 (1990) (emphasis added).

* * *

Precisely what constitutes a "material difference" for purposes of § 1001(a) of the Code is a more complicated question. The Commissioner argues that properties are "materially different" only if they differ in economic substance. To determine whether the participation interests exchanged in this case were "materially different" in this sense, the Commissioner argues, we should look to the attitudes of the parties, the evaluation of the interests by the secondary mortgage market, and the views of the FHLBB. We conclude that § 1001(a) embodies a much less demanding and less complex test.

***

Rule: what is materially different?

RC

Under our interpretation of § 1001(a), an exchange of property gives rise to a realization event so long as the exchanged properties are "materially different"-that is, so long as they embody legally distinct entitlements. Cottage Savings' transactions at issue here easily satisfy this test. Because the participation interests exchanged by Cottage Savings and the other S & L's derived from loans that were made to different obligors and secured by different homes, the exchanged interests did embody legally distinct entitlements. Consequently, we conclude that Cottage Savings realized its losses at the point of the exchange.

The Commissioner contends that it is anomalous to treat mortgages deemed to be "substantially identical" by the FHLBB as "materially different." The anomaly, however, is merely semantic; mortgages can be substantially identical for Memorandum R-49 purposes and still exhibit "differences" that are "material" for purposes of the Internal Revenue Code. Because Cottage Savings received entitlements different from those it gave up, the exchange put both Cottage Savings and the Commissioner in a position to [calculate gain or loss]. Thus, there is no reason not to treat the exchange of these interests as a realization event, regardless of the status of the mortgages under the criteria of Memorandum R-49.

III

Although the Court of Appeals found that Cottage Savings' losses were realized, it disallowed them on the ground that they were not sustained under § 165(a) of the Code, 26 U.S.C. § 165(a). Section 165(a) states that a deduction shall be allowed for "any loss sustained during the taxable year and not compensated for by insurance or otherwise." * * *

[W]e conclude that, for purposes of this case, Cottage Savings sustained its losses within the meaning of § 165(a).

IV

For the reasons set forth above, the judgment of the Court of Appeals is reversed, and the case is remanded for further proceedings consistent with this opinion.

So ordered.

Post-Case Follow-Up

The Court concluded in *Cottage Savings* that under § 1001, an exchange of properties will constitute a disposition only if the properties are materially different. The Court further concluded that a difference is "material" in this context only if those who hold the properties have legal entitlements that are different in kind or extent. As you might well expect, almost any exchange of properties will give rise to a realization event. What you might not realize, however, is that such an approach to realization might well lead to surprising and unintended consequences. Assume that a given individual is in financial distress and seeks to work out a new arrangement with the bank. If the two parties modify their contract, does the tax law view the transaction as an exchange of one contract (the old one) for another (the new one under which legal rights and obligations differ), thereby constituting a realization event? In the immediate wake of *Cottage Savings*, financial institutions and their obligors had legitimate concerns in this regard. The Treasury Department responded with guidance in the so-called *Cottage Savings* regulations under § 1001. *See generally* Treas. Reg. § 1.1001-3.

Cottage Savings Association v. Commissioner: Real Life Applications

1. Nancy purchased Brownacre for $50,000, and it now has a fair market value of $200,000. Nancy has an interest in owning Greenacre, which currently has a fair market value of $200,000. Assume that Nancy contacts Greenacre's owner and manages to exchange Brownacre for Greenacre.

   a. Does this exchange constitute a realization event? Please explain.
   b. If Nancy does have a realization event, what is her amount realized? Please explain.
   c. Assuming Nancy has a realization event, what is her gain realized?
   d. Immediately prior to the exchange, what was Nancy's built-in gain?

2. Ming purchased several shares of Banana, Inc. stock for $100,000. The stock now has a fair market value of $125,000. Assume that Ming exchanges his Banana, Inc. stock for $25,000 cash and several shares of Kiwi, Inc. stock worth $100,000.

   a. Will Ming's transaction constitute a realization event? Please explain.
   b. What was Ming's basis in his Banana, Inc. stock?
   c. What was Ming's amount realized in the transaction? Please explain.
   d. What will be Ming's gain realized in connection with this transaction?

> **Friendly Reminder**
>
> As you address these questions, keep a few basic rules in mind. Basis is typically cost, amount realized is the sum of (i) money received and (ii) the fair market value of property (other than money) received, and calculating gain or loss is accomplished by comparing basis and amount realized. *Cf.* §§ 1012, 1001(a) and (b).

3. Solomon purchased several shares of Blueberry, Inc. stock for $250,000. The stock now has a fair market value of $400,000, and Solomon has an interest in acquiring a painting worth $400,000 owned by Hansel. Assume that Solomon hands over the Blueberry, Inc. stock in exchange for Hansel's art.

   a. Will this exchange constitute a realization event for Solomon? Will it constitute a realization event for Hansel?
   b. Immediately before the exchange, what was Solomon's unrealized gain?
   c. On the exchange, what was Solomon's amount realized? What was Hansel's amount realized?
   d. After the exchange, what will be Solomon's gain realized and his gain recognized?

C. THE EVOLVING NOTION OF "INCOME"

At this juncture, we shift our focus to the definition of income. We noted earlier that one does not have income for federal income tax purposes unless and until a realization event occurs, but we also fully understand that "realization" and "income" are not one and the same. Although a taxpayer can experience a realization event and thereby realize gain, the realization event might well result in a loss if, for example, basis exceeds amount realized. Income, then, means something separate and distinct from mere realization, but what exactly? We know that if a person sells land at a profit, they have income. We also know that when people find money in the street or get a direct deposit from their employer they have income. But what about someone who buys a steak on sale at the grocery store for $30 when it would ordinarily cost $50? Does that person have "income" of $20, or was the person simply lucky? What about people who sleep on their friend's couches while in town visiting them? Does the fact that they avoided the cost of a hotel room mean that they have income or just a kind and very understanding friend? The Code, under § 61, generally provides that "gross income means all income from whatever source derived," which essentially means that once a taxpayer identifies various sources of income, "gross income" means all of it (without any offsets like deductions). Great! Section 61 also lists several items constituting income, but the statutory language itself clarifies that the list is not exhaustive. Fortunately, case law gives us something slightly (and only slightly) more definitive to work with.

Case Preview

Commissioner v. Glenshaw Glass Co.

You'll recall that in *Eisner v. Macomber*, the Court confirmed that income arises only upon the occurrence of a realization event; that holding remains good law. Although we did not highlight the fact in prior discussion, the *Eisner v. Macomber* decision also set forth a definition of "income" that controlled for quite some time. The Court noted that income must be understood to mean only gains derived from "capital, labor, or both combined." Thus, under that standard, one's income might be gains from one's investment of money or capital, gains from one's labor (e.g., employment), or some combination of the two. Such a definition reaches far, but as we shall see in *Commissioner v. Glenshaw Glass Co.*, the Court found pressing need to put *Eisner v. Macomber* in proper perspective and to articulate a notion of "income" consistent with and reflective of Congress's broad taxing power. As you read *Commissioner v. Glenshaw Glass Co.*, please focus on the following questions:

1. Why did the taxpayer include only some of its monetary damages in income?
2. What weight did the Court assign to *Eisner v. Macomber*'s definition of income?
3. In this Court's opinion, what is defining characteristic of "income"?

Commissioner v. Glenshaw Glass Co.
348 U.S. 426 (1955)

Mr. Chief Justice WARREN delivered the opinion of the Court.

This litigation involves two cases with independent factual backgrounds yet presenting the identical issue. The two cases were consolidated for argument before the Court of Appeals for the Third Circuit and were heard en banc. The common question is whether money received as exemplary damages for fraud or as the punitive two-thirds portion of a treble-damage antitrust recovery must be reported by a taxpayer as gross income under § 22(a) of the Internal Revenue Code of 1939. In a single opinion, the Court of Appeals affirmed the Tax Court's separate rulings in favor of the taxpayers. Because of the frequent recurrence of the question and differing interpretations by the lower courts of this Court's decisions bearing upon the problem, we granted the Commissioner of Internal Revenue's ensuing petition for certiorari.

The facts of the cases were largely stipulated and are not in dispute. So far as pertinent they are as follows:

Commissioner v. Glenshaw Glass Co. — The Glenshaw Glass Company, a Pennsylvania corporation, manufactures glass bottles and containers. It was engaged in protracted litigation with the Hartford-Empire Company, which manufactures machinery of a character used by Glenshaw. Among the claims advanced by Glenshaw were demands for exemplary damages for fraud and treble damages for injury to its business by reason of Hartford's violation of the federal antitrust laws. In December, 1947, the parties concluded a settlement

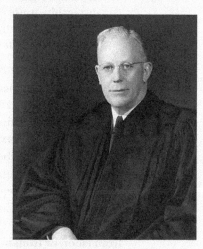

Chief Justice Earl Warren

President Dwight D. Eisenhower appointed Earl Warren to serve as Chief Justice of the United States. In addition to serving as Chief Justice on the U.S. Supreme Court (1953–1969), Warren chaired the commission charged with investigating the assassination of President John F. Kennedy.

Credit: Photo courtesy of the Library of Congress.

[handwritten margin note: Settlement]

of all pending litigation, by which Hartford paid Glenshaw approximately $800,000. Through a method of allocation which was approved by the Tax Court and which is no longer in issue, it was ultimately determined that, of the total settlement, $324,529.94 represented payment of punitive damages for fraud and antitrust violations. Glenshaw did not report this portion of the settlement as income for the tax year involved. The Commissioner determined a deficiency claiming as taxable the entire sum less only deductible legal fees. As previously noted, the Tax Court and the Court of Appeals upheld the taxpayer.

[handwritten margin note: Some not reported]

[Discussion of *Commissioner v. William Goldman Theatres, Inc.* omitted.]

It is conceded by the respondents that there is no constitutional barrier to the imposition of a tax on punitive damages. Our question is one of statutory construction: are these payments comprehended by § 22(a)?

The sweeping scope of the controverted statute is readily apparent:

§ 22. Gross income
(a) General definition. 'Gross income' includes gains, profits, and income derived from salaries, wages, or compensation for personal service * * * of whatever kind and in whatever form paid, or from professions, vocations, trades, businesses, commerce, or sales, or dealings in property, whether real or personal, growing out of the ownership or use of or interest in such property; also from interest, rent, dividends, securities, or the transaction of any business carried on for gain or profit, *or gains or profits and income derived from any source whatever.* * * * (Emphasis added.)

[handwritten margin note: Respondents argument: windfall]

This Court has frequently stated that this language was used by Congress to exert in this field "the full measure of its taxing power." Respondents contend that punitive damages, characterized as "windfalls" flowing from the culpable conduct of third parties, are not within the scope of the section. But Congress applied no limitations as to the source of taxable receipts, nor restrictive labels as to their nature. And the Court has given a liberal construction to this broad phraseology in recognition of the intention of Congress to tax all gains except those specifically exempted.

[handwritten margin note: RE: Court doesn't agree]

Nor can we accept respondents' contention that a narrower reading of § 22(a) is required by the Court's characterization of income in *Eisner v. Macomber,* 252 U.S. 189, 207, 40 S. Ct. 189, 193, 64 L.Ed. 521, as "the gain derived from capital, from labor, or from both combined." The Court was there endeavoring to determine whether the distribution of a corporate stock dividend constituted a realized gain to the shareholder, or changed "only the form, not the essence," of his capital investment. It was held that the taxpayer had "received nothing out of the company's assets for his separate use and benefit." *Id.,* 252 U.S. at page 211. The distribution, therefore, was held not a taxable event. In that context — distinguishing gain from capital — the definition served a useful purpose. But it was not meant to provide a touchstone to all future gross income questions.

Here we have instances of undeniable accessions to wealth, clearly realized, and over which the taxpayers have complete dominion. The mere fact that the payments were extracted from the wrongdoers as punishment for unlawful conduct cannot detract from their character as taxable income to the recipients. Respondents concede, as they must, that the recoveries are taxable to the extent that they compensate for damages actually incurred. It would be an anomaly that could not be justified in the absence of clear congressional intent to say that a recovery for actual damages is taxable but not the additional amount extracted as punishment for the same conduct which caused the injury. And we find no such evidence of intent to exempt these payments. ***

Reversed.

H: Punitive damages are taxable

Post-Case Follow-Up

Commissioner v. Glenshaw Glass Co. established that for federal income tax purposes, income refers to an "undeniable accession to wealth, clearly realized, and over which the taxpayer has complete dominion." Although the Court noted the standard articulated in *Eisner v. Macomber*, the Court reasoned that such a standard was not meant to establish an enduring and governing definition of income for all subsequent cases.

The broad "income" standard set forth in *Glenshaw Glass* better accords with Congress's plenary taxing powers under the Constitution, but note that *Glenshaw Glass* itself does not resolve the "income" determination in every context, nor does it purport to. Wholly aside from the ambiguities inherent in "undeniable accession" and "complete dominion," can taxpayers have "income" even if they do not appear to have enjoyed what some would recognize as an undeniable accession to wealth? Just *I* a few years ago in *Murphy v. IRS*, 493 F.3d 170 (D.C. Cir. 2007), the court noted that in the wake of specific congressional action, an award of damages for nonphysical injury can be included in the taxpayer's gross income "regardless whether the award is an accession to wealth." *Murphy* at 180. The court reasoned that Congress "can *label* a thing income and tax it, so long as it acts within its constitutional authority." *Id.* at 179 (emphasis original). If one recalls that the Sixteenth Amendment allows the taxation of income without apportionment and that under Article I, § 8 of the Constitution Congress has the power to lay and collect taxes, duties, imposts, and excises for specific purposes, it is easier to understand *Glenshaw Glass* as a decision that substantially broadened the common law definition of "income" but did not circumscribe or place a check on Congress's taxing powers with respect to what it deems to be income or with respect to transactions or activities wholly unrelated to a taxpayer's income. Just recently, in fact, the Court noted the following with respect to the penalty previously imposed on certain taxpayers for failing to maintain minimum essential health coverage: "The Affordable Care Act's requirement that certain individuals pay a financial penalty for not obtaining health insurance may reasonably be characterized as a tax. Because the Constitution permits such a tax, it is not our role to forbid it, or to pass upon its wisdom or fairness." *NFIB v. Sebelius*, 567 U.S. 519, 132 S. Ct. 2566, at 2600 (2012). Note that the Tax Cuts and Jobs Act reduced the penalty to zero for months beginning after December 31, 2018.

Commissioner v. Glenshaw Glass Co.: Real Life Applications

1. Responding to an incentive offered by the MusicPatrons Bank of New York, Sandro recently opened a checking account and deposited $1,000. Pursuant to the incentive, Sandro soon received $200, which was deposited directly into his new checking account.

   a. Does Sandro have income upon deposit of the $200 incentive? Why or why not?

   b. Does the MusicPatrons Bank of New York have income as a result of Sandro depositing $1,000 into his new checking account?

2. Bartlett recently relocated to Chicago, IL. Although the electricity in his apartment was connected when he moved in, the leasing office instructed him to have the service switched over to his name by contacting Windy City Edison, Inc. ("WCE"). When he contacted WCE, they told him that his credit history was not as strong as they would like it to be and that he would be required to make a $500 security deposit with them. Illinois law allowed WCE to add security deposits received to its general, unrestricted revenues, but the law also required WCE to return the dollar amount of the deposit on voluntary termination of the service by the customer or after the customer made 12 timely payments for service.

   a. If Bartlett makes the $500 security deposit to commence electricity service in his name, will WCE have income as a result?

   b. Assume that Bartlett fails to pay his electricity bill for three months. If WCE applies all of the security deposit to the outstanding balance, will WCE have income at that point?

3. The First National Bank of Orlando ("FNBO") lent Irma $20,000 (at an annual interest rate of 5 percent for a five-year term) in connection with the purchase of her new car. The vehicle itself served as collateral for repayment of the loan. Irma paid the first three payments on time, was late with the fourth, and missed an additional two payments altogether. At that point, FNBO had the car repossessed and sold. The car sold for $18,858, part of which covered unpaid loan interest (roughly $100) with the remainder covering the unpaid loan balance.

   a. Did Irma have income on receipt of the $20,000 loan?

   b. Did the automobile dealership have income when Irma purchased the car? What information will you need to answer the question?

   c. Did FNBO have income as a result of the repossession and sale of the car? If so, how much?

D. THE TAX COMPUTATION PROCESS

Barring statutory exception, per § 1001(c), gain realized and loss realized must be recognized. Thus, gains realized must ordinarily be included in the taxpayer's gross income (and losses realized may be taken into account as deductions) on the taxpayer's federal income tax return for the year in which the realization events occur. A casual glance at any given tax return will reflect a host of items, line by line, some calling for the inclusion of an income item, others allowing a reduction in income, and yet others calling for numbers or information of relevance in the ongoing calculations. Sprinkled throughout the return one will find special terminology. The ultimate goal of the larger process is to ascertain the taxpayer's tax liability for the year. If he has paid too much, he is entitled to a refund, if he has paid too little, he must make up the difference via payment to the United States Treasury, and if he managed to pay exactly what he owed, all is well (i.e., he still has to file the return, but he neither sends nor receives a check).

Although some of the special vocabulary used below will be explained in further detail later, now is a good time to take a bird's eye view of the entire process.

GROSS INCOME

– Above the Line Deductions (Group A)

ADJUSTED GROSS INCOME

– Below the Line Deductions (Group B)

TAXABLE INCOME

× (Applicable Tax Rates)

Tax

– Prior Payments, Credits, Etc.

FINAL TAX LIABILITY (OR REFUND AMOUNT)

For many individual taxpayers, these calculations occur as they complete IRS Form 1040. We start by adding together all of the sources of taxpayer income for the year to arrive at "gross income." From that number, we subtract certain deductions (if any) available to the taxpayer to arrive at "adjusted gross income" (i.e., "AGI"). Having determined adjusted gross income, we subtract additional items to arrive at "taxable income." You should think of taxable income quite literally. It is not all of the taxpayer's income. Rather, after starting with gross income and deducting various items, we arrive at a figure which represents the part of the taxpayer's income *that can be taxed*. With that figure in hand, we need to ascertain how much actual tax is due, and that requires a little math. Fortunately, most taxpayers don't have to perform actual calculations. Instead, they (or their designated tax return preparers) find the appropriate tax by consulting a chart or by having software calculate the relevant amount. If one had to do the math, one would simply multiply the taxable income figure by the appropriate tax rates. The resulting number is the "tax." We then take into account prior payments (e.g., employer withholding) or other offsets with respect to this tax amount. If the taxpayer has already paid more than the amount due, he is entitled to a refund, and if he has not paid all amounts due, he must make up the deficiency by making payment to the United States Treasury. As Exhibit 2.1 reflects, President Barack Obama and First Lady Michelle Obama were entitled to a refund with respect to their 2015 taxable year.

EXHIBIT 2.1   2015 Form 1040 (Excluding Schedules) of President Barack Obama and First Lady Michelle Obama

Form 1040 U.S. Individual Income Tax Return (09) **2015** OMB No. 1545-0074 | IRS Use Only - Do not write or staple in this space.

For the year Jan. 1-Dec. 31, 2015, or other tax year beginning , 2015, ending , 20 | See separate instructions.

Your first name and initial	Last name	Your social security number
BARACK H.	OBAMA	
If a joint return, spouse's first name and initial	Last name	Spouse's social security number
MICHELLE L.	OBAMA	

Home address (number and street). If you have a P.O. box, see instructions. | Apt. no. | ▲ Make sure the SSN(s) above and on line 6c are correct.

1600 PENNSYLVANIA AVENUE, NW

City, town or post office, state, and ZIP code. If you have a foreign address, also complete spaces below.

WASHINGTON, DC 20500

Foreign country name	Foreign province/state/county	Foreign postal code

Presidential Election Campaign
Check here if you, or your spouse if filing jointly, want $3 to go to this fund. Checking a box below will not change your tax or refund.
[X] You [X] Spouse

Filing Status
Check only one box.

1. [ ] Single
2. [X] Married filing jointly (even if only one had income)
3. [ ] Married filing separately. Enter spouse's SSN above and full name here. ▶
4. [ ] Head of household (with qualifying person). If the qualifying person is a child but not your dependent, enter this child's name here. ▶
5. [ ] Qualifying widow(er) with dependent child

Exemptions

6a [X] Yourself. If someone can claim you as a dependent, do not check box 6a ......
b [X] Spouse ......

c Dependents: (1) First name Last name	(2) Dependent's social security number	(3) Dependent's relationship to you	(4) ✓ if child under age 17 qualifying for child tax credit
MALIA A OBAMA		DAUGHTER	
NATASHA M OBAMA		DAUGHTER	X

If more than four dependents, see instructions and check here ▶ [ ]

d Total number of exemptions claimed ......

Boxes checked on 6a and 6b: **2**
No. of children on 6c who: ● lived with you **2** ● did not live with you due to divorce or separation (see instructions)
Dependents on 6c not entered above
Add numbers on lines above ▶ **4**

Income

Attach Form(s) W-2 here. Also attach Forms W-2G and 1099-R if tax was withheld.

If you did not get a W-2, see instructions.

7	Wages, salaries, tips, etc. Attach Form(s) W-2	7	394,454.
8a	Taxable interest. Attach Schedule B if required	8a	348.
b	Tax-exempt interest. Do not include on line 8a	8b	
9a	Ordinary dividends. Attach Schedule B if required	9a	9.
b	Qualified dividends	9b	
10	Taxable refunds, credits, or offsets of state and local income taxes STMT 1 STMT 3	10	0.
11	Alimony received	11	
12	Business income or (loss). Attach Schedule C or C-EZ	12	56,069.
13	Capital gain or (loss). Attach Schedule D if required. If not required, check here ▶ [ ]	13	-3,000.
14	Other gains or (losses). Attach Form 4797	14	
15a	IRA distributions	15b	
16a	Pensions and annuities	16b	
17	Rental real estate, royalties, partnerships, S corporations, trusts, etc. Attach Schedule E	17	
18	Farm income or (loss). Attach Schedule F	18	
19	Unemployment compensation	19	
20a	Social security benefits 20a	20b	
21	Other income. List type and amount	21	
22	Combine the amounts in the far right column for lines 7 through 21. This is your total income ▶	22	447,880.

(Callout: Gross Income of $447,880)

Adjusted Gross Income

23	Educator expenses	23	
24	Certain business expenses of reservists, performing artists, and fee-basis government officials. Attach Form 2106 or 2106-EZ	24	
25	Health savings account deduction. Attach Form 8889	25	
26	Moving expenses. Attach Form 3903	26	
27	Deductible part of self-employment tax. Attach Schedule SE	27	751.
28	Self-employed SEP, SIMPLE, and qualified plans	28	11,064.
29	Self-employed health insurance deduction	29	
30	Penalty on early withdrawal of savings	30	
31a		31a	
		32	
		33	
		34	
35	Domestic production activities deduction. Attach Form 8903		
36	Add lines 23 through 35	36	11,815.
37	Subtract line 36 from line 22. This is your adjusted gross income ▶	37	436,065.

(Callout: "Above the Line" Deductions")

(Callout: Adjusted Gross Income of $436,065)

510001 12-30-15

LHA For Disclosure, Privacy Act, and Paperwork Reduction Act Notice, see separate instructions.

Form **1040** (2015)

EXHIBIT 2.1   **2015 Form 1040 (Excluding Schedules) of President Barack Obama and First Lady Michelle Obama (*Continued*)**

Taxable Income

Form 1040 (2015)	BARACK H. & MICHELLE L. OBA...			Page 2
Tax and Credits	38	Amount from line 37 (adjusted gross income)	38	436,065.
Standard Deduction for –	39a	Check if: ☐ You were born before January 2, 1951, ☐ Blind. Total boxes ☐ Spouse was born before January 2, 1951, ☐ Blind. checked ▶ 39a		
● People who check any box on line 39a or 39b Of who can be claimed as a dependent, see Instructions.	b	If your spouse itemizes on a separate return or you were a dual-status alien, check here ▶ 39b ☐		
	40	Itemized deductions (from Schedule A) or your standard deduction (see left margin)	40	145,425.
	41	Subtract line 40 from line 38	41	290,640.
	42	Exemptions. If line 38 is $154,950 or less, multiply $4,000 by the number on line 6d. Otherwise, see inst.	42	0.
	43	Taxable income. Subtract line 42 from line 41. If line 42 is more than line 41, enter -0-	43	290,640.
	44	Tax. Check if any from: a ☐ Form(s) 8814 b ☐ Form 4972 c ☐	44	71,440.
● All others: Single or Married filing separately, $6,300.	45	Alternative minimum tax. Attach Form 6251	45	7,743.
	46	Excess advance premium tax credit repayment. Attach Form 8962	46	
	47	Add lines 44, 45, and 46 ▶	47	79,183.
	48	...ign tax credit. Attach Form 1116 if required	48	979.
	49	...enses. Attach Form 2441	49	
	50	...19	50	
	51	...t. Attach Form 8880	51	
	52	...if required	52	
	53	...5695	53	
	54	...900 b ☐ 8801 c ☐	54	
	55	Add lines 48 through 54. These are your total credits	55	979.
	56	Subtract line 55 from line 47. If line 55 is more than line 47, enter -0- ▶	56	78,204.
Other Taxes	57	Self-employment tax. Attach Schedule SE	57	1,502.
	58	Unreported social security and Medicare tax from Form: a ☐ 4137 b ☐ 8919	58	
	59	Additional tax on IRAs, other qualified retirement plans, etc. Attach Form 5329 if required	59	
	60a	Household employment taxes from Schedule H	60a	
	b	First-time homebuyer credit repayment. Attach Form 5405 if required	60b	
	61	Health care: individual responsibility (see instructions) Full-year coverage ☒	61	
	62	Taxes from: a ☒ Form 8959 b ☐ Form 8960 c ☐ Inst.; enter code(s)	62	1,766.
	63	Add lines 56 through 62. This is your total tax ▶	63	81,472.
Payments	64	Federal income tax withheld from Forms W-2 and 1099	64	99,331. STATEMENT 6
	65	2015 estimated tax payments and amount applied from 2014 return	65	5,000.
If you have a qualifying child, attach Schedule EIC.	66a	Earned income credit (EIC)	66a	
	b	Nontaxable combat pay election 66b		
	67	Additional child tax credit. Attach Schedule 8812	67	
	68	American opportunity cred...	68	
	69	Net premium tax cre...	69	
	70	Amount paid with re...	70	
	71	Excess social securi...	71	
	72	Credit for federal tax...	72	
	73	Credits from Form: a ☐ ...	73	
	74	Add lines 64, 65, 66a, and 67 through 73. These are your total payments ▶	74	104,331.
Refund	75	If line 74 is more than line 63, subtract line 63 from line 74. This is the amount you overpaid	75	22,859.
Direct deposit? See instructions.	76a	Amount of line 75 you want refunded to you. If Form 8888 is attached, check here ▶ ☐	76a	22,859.
	b	Routing number ___ ▶ c Type: ☐ Checking ☐ Savings ▶ d Account number ___		
	77	Amount of line 75 you want applied to your 2016 estimated tax ▶ 77		
Amount You Owe	78	Amount you owe. Subtract line 74 from line 63. For details on how to pay, see instructions ▶	78	
	79	Estimated tax penalty (see instructions) 79		
Third Party Designee	Do you want to allow another person to discuss this return with the IRS (see instructions)? ☒ Yes. Complete below. ☐ No	Designee's name ▶ MICHAEL S SOLHEIM	Phone no. ▶	Personal identification number (PIN) ▶

"Below the Line" Deductions (Lines 40 & 42)

"Tax" on Taxable Income

Refund of $22,859

Sign Here
Joint return? See instructions. Keep a copy for your records.

Under penalties of perjury, I declare that I have examined this return and accompanying schedules and statements, and to the best of my knowledge and belief, they are true, correct, and complete. Declaration of preparer (other than taxpayer) is based on all information of which preparer has any knowledge.

Your signature   Date 04/07/16   Your occupation US PRESIDENT   Daytime phone number

Spouse's signature. If a joint return, both must sign   Date 14/09/2016   Spouse's occupation US FIRST LADY   If the IRS sent you an Identity Protection PIN, enter it here

Paid Preparer Use Only

Print/Type preparer's name	Preparer's signature	Date	Check ☐ if self-employed	PTIN
MICHAEL S SOLHEIM		3/31/16		

Firm's name ▶ WINEBERG SOLHEIM HOWELL & SHAIN, PC   Firm's EIN ▶

180 N LASALLE ST, STE 2200   Phone no.

510002 12-30-15   Firm's address ▶ CHICAGO, IL 60601

A special note is in order with respect to adjusted gross income. The AGI figure is an important one because various tax rules may refer to it for specific purposes. For example, assume that Congress would like to make a given deduction available but *only* to low-income individuals. Under those circumstances, Congress could provide that such a deduction is available, but only for those whose AGI is less than $25,000. Congress could be more generous in a different context and allow a deduction, but only for those whose AGI is less than $100,000. Alternatively, rather than making a deduction 100 percent available or 100 percent unavailable, Congress can fine-tune if it so chooses. Thus, Congress could craft a rule making a deduction generally available but requiring gradual reduction of the available deduction amount as a taxpayer's AGI rises. Consider the following table:

TABLE 2.1   **Depiction of Phase-Out of Deduction Based on AGI**

Taxpayer AGI Range	Available Deduction
$0 – $10,000	$5,000
$10,001 – $25,000	$4,000
$25,001 – $75,000	$3,000
$75,001 – $100,000	$1,000
Above $100,000	$0

In the tax world, we call such an approach a "phase-out" because the deduction is reduced in increments or phases. Keep in mind, throughout the course, that AGI can serve as an extremely important benchmark or reference point in some instances.

Given the potential significance of the AGI figure, the point at which a deduction is factored into the calculations matters. Glance for a moment at the "bird's eye view" set forth above. Calculations begin with gross income, and some deductions (Group A) are taken to arrive at AGI. After that figure has been ascertained, one takes additional deductions (Group B) to arrive at taxable income. Assume that taxpayer has gross income of $50,000, Group A deductions of $10,000, and Group B deductions of $8,000. Here's how we would arrive at their taxable income:

Gross Income	$50,000
Group A deductions	**-$10,000**
AGI	$40,000
Group B Deductions	**-$8,000**
Taxable Income	$32,000

The Group A deductions are taken into account in calculating AGI, and for this taxpayer, the AGI of $40,000 is definitively set at that amount; it does not change even though additional calculations are performed. The Group B deductions are taken into account in going from the AGI figure ($40,000) to the Taxable Income figure ($32,000). By convention, tax professionals refer to the Group A deductions as "above-the-line" deductions because they have a direct impact on what will ultimately be the actual AGI figure. Similarly, tax professionals refer to the Group B deductions as "below-the-line" deductions. *Take Home Point:* The fact that a deduction is above-the-line has significance, because the item will impact the calculation of a very important benchmark.

Chapter Summary

- For federal income tax purposes, a taxpayer generally cannot have "income" (or claim a loss) unless and until a realization event has occurred. *See Eisner v. Macomber*. Note that the realization requirement is both a common law mandate and a rule of administrative convenience.
- The "income" definition set forth in *Commissioner v. Glenshaw Glass Co.* displaced the *Eisner v. Macomber* definition. Accordingly, income is an undeniable accession to wealth, clearly realized, over which the taxpayer has complete dominion. Neither decision constrains Congress's ability to define income or to exercise its taxing powers under Article I, § 8 of the U.S. Constitution. *See, e.g., NFIB v. Sebelius*.
- Realization events take many forms. Although they sometimes result from specific transactions, they also occur outside the transactional context (e.g., when a taxpayer derives something or sustains a loss).
- Under § 1012 of the Code, a taxpayer's basis in an asset is its cost to the taxpayer.
- Under § 1001(b) of the Code, a taxpayer's amount realized on the sale or disposition of an asset is the sum of (i) money received and (ii) the fair market value of property (other than money) received. One generally calculates gain realized or loss realized in a transaction by comparing amount realized and basis; the potential use of "adjusted basis" (rather than basis) will be covered in a subsequent chapter. *See* § 1001(a).
- In general, gain or loss realized must be recognized (i.e., included on one's tax return for the year in which the realization event occurs).
- An exchange constitutes a disposition under § 1001 (and thus a realization event) only if the exchanged properties differ materially in kind or extent with respect to legal obligations or entitlements of the property holders. *See Cottage Savings*.

Applying the Rules

1. During her morning walk, Shirley finds a wallet. Inside the wallet is $256, several photos, a driver's license, several credit cards, and a business card. Shirley walks home, calls the number on the business card, and arranges to return the wallet to its rightful owner, Harris. Assuming Shirley meets Harris and returns his wallet to him, did Shirley have a realization event upon finding the wallet?

2. While walking her dog, Nyati witnessed a violent assault that ultimately resulted in the death of the victim. Initially she was unwilling to report anything to the police, but at some point, the police offered a $10,000 reward for any information leading to the arrest and conviction of the perpetrator. Nyati summoned the courage to contact the police, and the perpetrator was eventually arrested and convicted. Two weeks after the conviction, Nyati received her $10,000 reward.

   a. Did Nyati have a realization event upon the announcement of the award?
   b. Did Nyati have a realization event upon receipt of the award?

3. Gary recently purchased 1,000 shares of stock for $1,000. He got very lucky; the stock now has a fair market value of $2,700. Gary considers the stock to be an excellent long-term investment, and he continues to own it.

   a. What is Gary's basis in the stock?
   b. What amount, if any, is Gary's gain realized?
   c. What amount, if any, is Gary's gain recognized?

4. Gloria owns a dining-room table and eight chairs. She purchased the set for $5,000 in 2015. She recently sold it for $4,000 on eBay Inc.'s website.

   a. What was Gloria's amount realized in connection with this transaction?
   b. Immediately before the sale, what was the amount of Gloria's built-in loss?
   c. What was Gloria's loss realized on completion of the transaction?

5. Alex owns Blueacre, which he purchased in 2000 for $325,000. Today, Blueacre has a fair market value of $500,000, but Alex has no interest in selling the land for cash. Rather, he would like to exchange his land for an original painting worth $100,000, and $400,000 of stock, both of which he knows are owned by his friend, Matthew. Assume that Alex contacts Matthew and that the two ultimately execute the transaction.

   a. Will this transaction constitute a disposition of Blueacre within the meaning of § 1001(a)? Please explain.
   b. What is Alex's gain realized in the transaction?
   c. What is Matthew's amount realized in the transaction?
   d. Is Alex required to recognize gain as a result of executing this exchange? If so, how much?

Federal Income Taxation in Practice

1. Locate and read *Grande v. Jennings*, 229 Ariz. 584 (2012). Apply *Commissioner v. Glenshaw Glass Co.* to ascertain whether any construction company workers had income.

2. Over the years, you have accumulated over 100,000 frequent flier miles with Supersonic Air Lines, Inc. You recently redeemed 80,000 miles for a free, round-trip coach ticket to Dubai, UAE. At the time of your redemption, the fair market value of such a ticket was $2,500. Find out whether the IRS has issued any pronouncements governing whether it views such redemptions as realization events giving rise to "income" for federal income tax purposes.

3. The First State Savings & Loan Bank recently opened a local branch in your neighborhood. A week ago, you received an offer from the bank indicating that if you open a new checking or savings account at their local branch, they will give you 50,000 "points" (assuming your account opens with and maintains a specified minimum balance for 90 days). Those receiving the points can redeem them for various forms of merchandise. Ascertain whether any authorities provide guidance with respect to the tax treatment of those who take advantage of these incentives and redeem points for merchandise.

4. Assume that you work as an associate in a large law firm. The partner with whom you work calls you in and tells you that she needs your help on a *Cottage Savings* issue. She understands that Treas. Reg. § 1.1001-3 addresses debt modifications, but she would like to know whether the ABA Tax Section submitted public comments after those regulations were issued as Proposed Treasury Regulations. She asks you to see what you can find and to follow up with her by e-mail.

5. You recently completed your federal income tax return for 2017. A week after you mailed the return in, you woke up in a cold sweat, remembering that during 2017 you received at least $300 cash back from your credit-card issuer as a result of purchases you made. You included none of it in your gross income, and you're concerned that the IRS will audit your return and recommend prosecution for tax evasion. Find out whether any IRS pronouncements or other resources indicate that such amounts should be included in a taxpayer's gross income.

Specific Items Included in Gross Income

In Chapter 2, we discussed both the concept of realization and the *Glenshaw Glass* definition of income. We turn now to § 61 of the Code, which enters the scene and sets forth a broadly worded edict: Barring specific statutory exception, a taxpayer's "gross income" means "all income from whatever source derived." In this chapter, we take a closer look at various forms of income and the rules governing their inclusion in gross income. We will find, as we make our way through the discussion, that in many instances, the propriety of including a given item in gross income presents no real issue. In other contexts, however, we have to proceed with enhanced caution. Even if it appears at first glance that a taxpayer has income under the *Glenshaw Glass* standard, it may be difficult to conclude the fact definitively. And even if one can readily conclude that a taxpayer has income, it may be difficult to ascertain the appropriate time to require inclusion of that amount in gross income. Complicating matters further is the fact that specific events may result in the inclusion of an amount in gross income for some taxpayers but not for others (depending on factors unique to the taxpayers), and inclusion in some contexts turns on whether a taxpayer makes (or foregoes) an available election.

A. SPECIFIC GROSS INCOME ITEMS

1. In General

In addition to providing that gross income includes all income from whatever source derived, section 61 also provides a nonexhaustive list of typical income items, many of which we have already encountered. Thus,

Key Concepts

- The diversity of includible income forms
- Ascertaining whether and when an apparent windfall constitutes includible income
- Illegal income and gross income determinations
- The treatment of income from the discharge of indebtedness, including the impact of taxpayer insolvency
- Understanding the impact of the contested liability doctrine

Key Statutory and Regulatory Provisions

▦ **Internal Revenue Code**
   ▦ **§ 61(a)**
▦ **Treasury Regulations**
   ▦ **§ 1.61-1(a)**
   ▦ **§ 1.61-2(a)(1)**
   ▦ **§ 1.61-2(d)(1)**
   ▦ **§ 1.61-14(a)**

gross income includes gains from dealings in property (e.g., profit from the sale or exchange of assets), interest, rent receipts, royalties, and **dividends** (e.g., a corporate distribution of current or accumulated earnings and profits to its shareholders). Gross income also includes income in the form of compensation for services rendered.

Although it is fair to say that most taxpayers receive compensation in the form of cash, the universe of compensation reflects rich variety. One individual might receive compensation in the form of cash, whereas another might receive both cash and non-cash property. As Exhibit 3.1 reflects, CEOs and other corporate executives may receive a cash salary each year, but the vast and overwhelming majority of their compensation may be in a form other than cash. For example, many executives receive compensation in the form of stock of the company employing them. Some companies, rather providing the stock itself, may simply grant the executive the right or option to purchase the company's stock at a specific price (i.e., a **stock option**). When an individual receives compensation in a form other than cash, we refer to such remuneration as **in-kind compensation**. Because an ownership interest in an entity is generally referred to as **equity interest**, one may see stock-based compensation referred to as equity-based compensation. In any event, keep in mind that gross income includes both cash compensation as well as in-kind compensation.

Non-cash Compensation

EXHIBIT 3.1   **2016 Fiscal Year C.E.O. Compensation (Millions) (www.salary.com/executive-salaries/)**

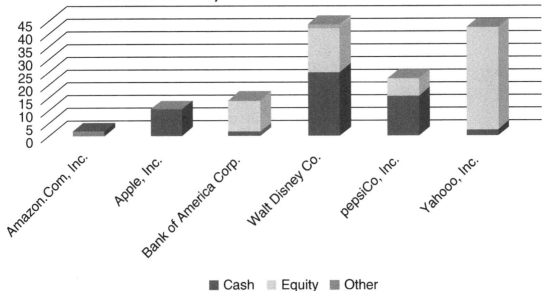

Nonexecutive employees in the same company might be somewhat dissatisfied with the modest salary they themselves receive but take real pleasure in enjoying the company's substantial fringe benefits. Taxpayers outside a traditional employer/employee context may opt to barter. A taxpayer in a **bartering transaction** provides property or services and receives in exchange property or services from someone else (e.g., a barber who provides a haircut to a client with the expectation that "payment" for the haircut will take the form of the client hand washing (and drying) the barber's brand-new car). No money changes hands in that setting, but both the barber and the client have income because they each receive compensation for their services. In future chapters, we will delve into some of the elaborate rules governing various forms of compensation. Some relate to precise timing of the inclusion of the compensation in gross income, others present options to the taxpayer, and yet others clarify the conditions under which items (which many would consider "compensation" as a matter of practical reality) can escape gross income inclusion altogether. For now, the key is to appreciate the fact that many items must be included in gross income; some will take the form of cash, and others will not. Further, within categories like compensation, income can not only take a host of forms but special rules also govern the tax treatment of both the person paying and the person receiving the income. Before we pick our way through that briar patch, however, let's take up cash and the many ways in which it can end up in a taxpayer's gross income.

2. Cash Windfalls, Treasure Trove, and Similar Items

Case Preview

Cesarini v. United States

Most people would agree that an individual receiving cash for services rendered has no real justification for refusing to include the amount in gross income. Indeed, it is safe to say that most people would expect to take a substantial tax hit if they somehow managed to win a $500 million lottery, notwithstanding the fact that the money did not come from an employer. And yet those same individuals will win a $100 bet on a tennis match, basketball game, or hand of blackjack and think nothing of consciously disregarding such winnings when completing their tax returns. They might even chuckle at the thought that some chump would report such a thing. Should some exception exist for de minimis accessions to wealth? Or perhaps situational exceptions? In *Cesarini v. United States*, we grapple with the question of whether a taxpayer who simply finds money should include the amount in gross income. As you read the case, consider the following questions:

1. Is found money listed in § 61 as an income item? If not, what would justify including such amounts in gross income?
2. What rule governs with respect to the proper year in which found money or a treasure trove is to be included in gross income?

Cesarini v. United States
296 F. Supp. 3 (N.D. Ohio 1969), aff'd per curiam, 428 F.2d 812 (6th Cir. 1970)

YOUNG, District Judge.

This is an action by the plaintiffs as taxpayers for the recovery of income tax payments made in the calendar year 1964. Plaintiffs contend that the amount of $836.51 was erroneously overpaid by them in 1964, and that they are entitled to a refund in that amount, together with the statutory interest from October 13, 1965, the date which they made their claim upon the Internal Revenue Service for the refund.

Plaintiffs and the United States have stipulated to the material facts in the case, and the matter is before the Court for final decision. * * * Plaintiffs are husband and wife . . . . In 1957, the plaintiffs purchased a used piano at an auction sale for approximately $15.00, and the piano was used by their daughter for piano lessons. In 1964, while cleaning the piano, plaintiffs discovered the sum of $4,467.00 in old currency, and since have retained the piano instead of discarding it as previously planned. Being unable to ascertain who put the money there, plaintiffs exchanged the old currency for new at a bank, and reported the sum of $4,467.00 on their 1964 joint income tax return as ordinary income from other sources. On October 18, 1965, plaintiffs filed an amended return with the District Director of Internal Revenue in Cleveland, Ohio, this second return eliminating the sum of $4,467.00 from the gross income computation, and requesting a refund in the amount of $836.51, the amount allegedly overpaid as a result of the former inclusion of $4,467.00 in the original return for the calendar year of 1964. On January 18, 1966, the Commissioner of Internal Revenue rejected taxpayers' refund claim in its entirety, and plaintiffs filed the instant action in March of 1967.

***

After a consideration of the pertinent provisions of the Internal Revenue Code, Treasury Regulations, Revenue Rulings, and decisional law in the area, this Court has concluded that the taxpayers are not entitled to a refund of the amount requested, nor are they entitled to capital gains treatment on the income item at issue.

The starting point in determining whether an item is to be included in gross income is, of course, [§ 61 of the Code], and that section provides in part:

> "Except as otherwise provided in this subtitle, *gross income means all income from whatever source derived,* including (but not limited to) the following items: * * *" (Emphasis added.)

Subsections (1) through (15) of Section 61(a) then go on to list fifteen items specifically included in the computation of the taxpayer's gross income, and Part II of Subchapter B of the 1954 Code (Sections 71 *et seq.*) deals with other items expressly included in gross income. While neither of these listings expressly includes the type of income which is at issue in the case at bar, Part III of Subchapter B (Sections 101 *et seq.*) deals with items specifically *excluded* from gross income, and found money is not listed in those sections either. This absence of express mention in any of the code sections necessitates a return to the "all income from whatever source" language of Section 61(a) of the code, and the express statement there that gross income is "not limited to" the following fifteen examples. Section 1.61-1(a) of the Treasury

Regulations, the corresponding section to Section 61(a) in the 1954 Code, reiterates this broad construction of gross income, providing in part:

> "Gross income means all income from whatever source derived, unless excluded by law. *Gross income includes income realized in any form*, whether in money, property, or services. * * *" (Emphasis added.)

The decisions of the United States Supreme Court have frequently stated that this broad all-inclusive language was used by Congress to exert the full measure of its taxing power under the Sixteenth Amendment to the United States Constitution.

In addition, the Government in the instant case cites and relies upon an I.R.S. Revenue Ruling which is undeniably on point:

> "The finder of treasure-trove is in receipt of taxable income, for Federal income tax purposes, to the extent of its value in United States Currency, for the taxable year in which it is reduced to undisputed possession." Rev. Rul. 61, 1953-1[]Cum. Bull. 17.

The plaintiffs argue that the above ruling does not control this case for two reasons. The first is that subsequent to the Ruling's pronouncement in 1953, Congress enacted Sections 74 and 102 of the 1954 Code, § 74 expressly *including* the value of prizes and awards in gross income in most cases, and § 102 specifically *exempting* the value of gifts received from gross income. From this, it is argued that Section 74 was added because prizes might otherwise be construed as non-taxable gifts, and since no such section was passed expressly taxing treasure-trove, it is therefore a gift which is non-taxable under Section 102. This line of reasoning overlooks the statutory scheme previously alluded to, whereby income from all sources is taxed unless the taxpayer can point to an express exemption. Not only have the taxpayers failed to list a specific exclusion in the instant case, but also the Government *has* pointed to express language covering the found money, even though it would not be required to do so under the broad language of Section 61(a) and the foregoing Supreme Court decisions interpreting it.

***

In partial summary, then, the arguments of the taxpayers which attempt to avoid the application of Rev. Rul. 61[] are not well taken. *** While it is generally true that revenue rulings may be disregarded by the courts if in conflict with the code and the regulations, or with other judicial decisions, plaintiffs in the instant case have been unable to point to any inconsistency between the gross income sections of the code, the interpretation of them by the regulations and the Courts, and the revenue ruling which they herein attack as inapplicable. On the other hand, the United States *has* shown a consistency in letter and spirit between the ruling and the code, regulations, and court decisions.

Although not cited by either party, and noticeably absent from the Government's brief, the following Treasury Regulation appears in the 1964 Regulations, the year of the return in dispute:

> "§ 1.61-14 Miscellaneous items of gross income.
>
> "(a) In general. In addition to the items enumerated in section 61(a), there are many other kinds of gross income * * *. *Treasure trove, to the extent of its value in United States currency, constitutes gross income for the taxable year in which it is reduced to undisputed possession.*" (Emphasis added.)

Identical language appears in the 1968 Treasury Regulations, and is found in all previous years back to 1958. This language is the same in all material respects as that found in [Rev. Rul. 61, 1953-1 Cum. Bull. 17], and is undoubtedly an attempt to codify that ruling into the Regulations which apply to the 1954 Code. This Court is of the opinion that Treas.Reg. § 1.61-14(a) is dispositive of the major issue in this case if the $4,467.00 found in the piano was "reduced to undisputed possession" in the year petitioners reported it, for this Regulation was applicable to returns filed in the calendar year of 1964.

This brings the Court to the second contention of the plaintiffs: that if any tax was due, it was in 1957 when the piano was purchased, and by 1964 the Government was blocked from collecting it by reason of the statute of limitations. Without reaching the question of whether the voluntary payment in 1964 constituted a *waiver* on the part of the taxpayers, this Court finds that the $4,467.00 sum was properly included in gross income for the calendar year of 1964. Problems of when title vests, or when possession is complete in the field of federal taxation, in the absence of definitive federal legislation on the subject, are ordinarily determined by reference to the law of the state in which the taxpayer resides, or where the property around which the dispute centers is located. Since both the taxpayers and the property in question are found within the State of Ohio, Ohio law must govern as to when the found money was "reduced to undisputed possession" within the meaning of Treas. Reg. § 1.61-14 and [Rev. Rul. 61, 1953-1 Cum. Bull. 17].

In Ohio, there is no statute specifically dealing with the rights of owners and finders of treasure trove, and in the absence of such a statute the common-law rule of England applies, so that "title belongs to the finder as against all the world except the true owner." *Niederlehner v. Weatherly*, 78 Ohio App. 263, 69 N.E.2d 787 (1946), appeal dismissed, 146 Ohio St. 697, 67 N.E.2d 713 (1946). The *Niederlehner* case held, *inter alia*, that the owner of real estate upon which money is found does not have title as against the finder. Therefore, in the instant case if plaintiffs had resold the piano in 1958, not knowing of the money within it, they later would not be able to succeed in an action against the purchaser who *did* discover it. Under Ohio law, the plaintiffs must have actually *found* the money to have superior title over all but the true owner, and they did not discover the old currency until 1964. Unless there is present a specific state statute to the contrary, the majority of jurisdictions are in accord with the Ohio rule. Therefore, this Court finds that the $4,467.00 in old currency was not "reduced to undisputed possession" until its actual discovery in 1964, and thus the United States was not barred by the statute of limitations from collecting the $836.51 in tax during that year. ***

Post-Case Follow-Up

The court in *Cesarini* confirmed the broad scope of § 61 and the Treasury Regulations promulgated thereunder, specifically Treasury Regulations § 1.61-14(a) concerning the inclusion of treasure trove in income. The court did clarify that at the very earliest, found property or "treasure trove" is not reduced to undisputed possession, under Ohio law at least, until it is actually found, but upon achieving undisputed possession, the finder must include the fair market value of the property in their gross income even if Congress has not separately provided for its inclusion *outside* § 61.

Although *Cesarini* largely reflects straightforward application of governing statutes and regulations, the decision overtly exposes a gap in the broader scheme. The Treasury Regulations § 1.61-14(a) makes reference to and relies critically on "undisputed possession," but the final determination as to whether treasure trove or similar items have been reduced to undisputed possession turns ultimately on state law. Most states, according to the opinion, have the same standard in this regard, but the specter of differential treatment of similarly situated taxpayers cannot be definitively dismissed.

Cesarini v. United States: Real Life Applications

1. After boarding her flight and settling into her seat, Amanda realized that a prior passenger had left an iPad in the seat pocket in front of her. She opened the iPad cover and found an engraving, indicating that the iPad was the property of "Daniel Q. Traveler." She promptly located a flight attendant and handed the property over.

   a. Did Amanda have income as a result of this series of events? No.
   b. Would Amanda have had income if she had found the iPad but decided to keep it for herself? If so, how much?

2. While walking through the park on a windy day, Casey found what he initially thought was fake money. In actuality, the currency was a real $100 bill. Seeing no one in the immediate vicinity who might have dropped the money, he celebrated his good fortune, pocketed the money, and walked on.

   a. Did Casey have income as a result of finding the money and keeping it?
   b. If Casey had found a gold wedding band (no engraving), would he have had income on finding the wedding band or only upon converting that wedding band to cash?

3. While vacationing in the Bahamas, Sean decided to go snorkeling with his friends Leah and Connor. Much to their glee, they discovered (partially buried in underwater sand) a chest full of gold, silver, and precious stones. Bahamian law dictates that any item found in the territorial waters of The Bahamas is officially the property of the Bahamian government. If Sean, Leah, and Connor decide to litigate the matter, must any of them include any amounts in gross income before or during trial? If so, how much?

4. Bill recently purchased a partially furnished home for $100,000. As he was moving in, he noticed a painting hanging in the foyer. He didn't think anything of it at the time. Three years later, one of Bill's dinner guests, an art critic and historian, noticed the painting and eventually confirmed that the picture's artist was

Packed with security features to thwart the efforts of would-be counterfeiters, the current $100 bill includes a security thread, color-shifting ink, a 3D security band, and other features. The federal reserve note also incorporates microprinting. In addition to "USA" appearing along the base of Benjamin Franklin's portrait, one can also find (on his jacket lapel) the words "THE UNITED STATES OF AMERICA."
Credit: Vkilikov/Shutterstock.

The infamous gangster, Al Capone (1899–1947), at the Alcatraz Federal Penitentiary. *Image courtesy of the Federal Bureau of Investigations.*

none other than Learned Hand. Assume that the fair market value of the painting was $120,000. Is Bill required to include the value of the painting in his gross income? If so, when?

3. Illegal Income

Treasury Regulations § 1.61-14(a) plainly states that "[i]llegal gains constitute gross income," and at first glance, the provision would appear to arouse little controversy. After all, if your average individual goes to work, earns an honest living, and pays the appropriate taxes, it would make no sense to excuse embezzlers, drug dealers, prostitutes, inside traders, and the like from paying taxes on their ill-gotten gains. Then again, requiring the inclusion of illegal gains in income opens a rather disturbing door. The illegality of the activity notwithstanding, the federal government has assured itself of getting a piece of the action. Even if the illegal activity involved the theft of money from various victims, tax law dictates that Uncle Sam be allowed to claim his slice from the stash of dough (or, if need be, the perpetrator) first, leaving only whatever remains to those who suffered loss as an initial matter. Can that be right?

The Al Capone Saga

In addition to participating in bootlegging and running both prostitution rings and "protection" rackets, it is believed that during the 1920s Al Capone (a.k.a. "Scarface") ordered the deaths of over 500 men and that over 1,000 more died in Chicago's gang turf wars (also known as the Chicago Beer Wars). In that regard, Capone is perhaps best known for orchestrating the St. Valentine's Day massacre, in which several men from Bugs Moran's North Side gang were gunned down by members of Capone's South Side gang. Ultimately, of course, Capone served time in federal prison not for these crimes but for tax evasion (i.e., failing to pay $215,000 in taxes due with respect to his gambling income). Capone tried to bribe his jury, but the judge changed the jury at the last moment. Capone suffered with syphilitic dementia while serving time at Alcatraz. After being released, he died of a heart attack in 1947 after suffering a stroke. *See generally*, 501 MOST NOTORIOUS CRIMES 328, 330 (Octopus Publishing Group Ltd. 2009).

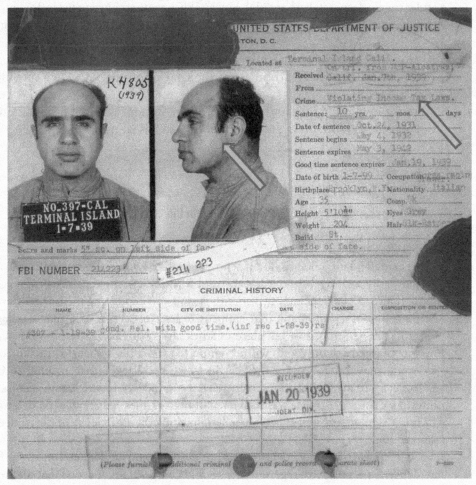

Credit: Photo courtesy of the Federal Bureau of Investigations.

Case Preview

United States v. Ytem

Inasmuch as legal income may take many forms, so can illegal income. Larceny, false pretenses, and embezzlement are all crimes, and each can lead to the obligation to include a given amount in gross income. Embezzlement, however, is particularly offensive in that it involves the conversion of another's property while in lawful possession of it (e.g., an attorney stealing client funds), and this misappropriation remains fully criminal even if the perpetrator feels some degree of guilt and hopes to return the embezzled funds just as soon as he runs into the patch of good luck he thinks is surely just around the corner.

Others do not trouble themselves with the mental irritant of guilt. They steal and struggle desperately to avoid the inevitably negative consequences flowing from their financial derelictions. As you read *Ytem*, consider the following questions:

1. How did the taxpayer effect the embezzlement?
2. On what bases did the court reach the conclusion that Mr. Ytem intended to avoid taxes?
3. In the opinion of the court, what set of circumstances might have caused it to conclude that Mr. Ytem did not *willfully* file a false return?

United States v. Ytem
255 F.3d 394 (7th Cir. 2011)

POSNER, Circuit Judge

The defendant, an accountant who worked in Illinois, embezzled funds of his employer by writing, without authorization, three checks to himself aggregating more than $135,000 during a two-month period and depositing them in his personal account in a Maryland bank that happens to have offices only in that state and in Virginia. The locations of his place of work and of his bank are relevant because he was charged not only with willful failure to report his embezzled income on his federal income tax return for the year in which he received that income, 26 U.S.C. § 7206(1), but also with having transported money obtained by fraud across state lines. 18 U.S.C. § 2314. He was convicted of both crimes, was sentenced to a total of 27 months in prison, and appeals, challenging only the sufficiency of the evidence to convict him.

The appeal bespeaks a deep or perhaps desperate misunderstanding of the law of evidence, especially with regard to the second charge. It is conceded that all the government had to show was that the defendant had caused the checks to be transported across state lines. It is also conceded that the checks indeed ended up in either a Maryland or a Virginia office of the bank in which they were deposited and that one of the checks was accompanied by a note to the bank in the defendant's handwriting

Embezzlement

telling the bank what to do with the check. Presumably the defendant mailed the checks (and the accompanying note) to the bank but there is no direct evidence of this; that is, no one testified to having seen the defendant mail these items and he does not admit having mailed them. He argues that therefore he cannot be proved guilty beyond a reasonable doubt of having caused them to be transported across state lines.

He admits that certainty is not required to establish guilt beyond a reasonable doubt, that a conviction based on fingerprint evidence for example cannot be overturned by pointing out that there is some minute probability of erroneous fingerprint identification. But he insists that a conviction can survive remote doubts about its correctness only when it is based on computed probabilities; common sense probabilities will not do. That is wrong. Common sense as well as science is a source of justified true beliefs, including warranted confidence that certain probabilities though unquantified are so slight that they do not create reasonable doubt. Often this confidence is formed by comparing hypotheses and sensibly adjudging one to be vastly more probable than the others, even taken all together. This case illustrates that routine and unexceptionable reasoning process nicely. While it is conceivable that the defendant did not cause the checks to end up in Maryland or Virginia — maybe after writing them and the accompanying note he changed his mind and threw them in the wastepaper basket in his office and the cleaning people picked them up after hours and mailed them to the defendant's bank — this hypothesis is so unlikely to be true that in the absence of any evidence in support of it (and there is none) a rational trier of fact would be entirely justified in dismissing the probability of its being true as minute in relation to the probability that the defendant himself caused the checks to end up where they did; indeed a trier of fact would be irrational to conclude otherwise.

The situation is a little more doubtful with respect to the defendant's conviction for willfully filing a false return. To be convicted of that offense he had to be proved to have known (at least if he made an issue of his knowledge) that illegal income is taxable and so his income from embezzlement should have been reported, 26 U.S.C. § 7206(1); *Cheek v. United States,* 498 U.S. 192, 201-02, 111 S.Ct. 604, 112 L.Ed.2d 617 (1991), since otherwise the return though false would not be willfully so; and again there is no direct evidence that he knew — evidence that could only have taken the form of an admission by him, for that is the only form that *direct* evidence of a person's state of mind can take. (There are no eyewitnesses to the mental contents of a person's head, as opposed to external phenomena, such as the placing of a letter in a mailbox.) But the circumstantial evidence was convincing, and the absence of direct evidence therefore no bar to conviction. E.g., *United States v. Guidry,* 199 F.3d 1150, 1156-58 (10th Cir. 1999). We are, however, doubtful about the validity of the government's argument, based on the case just cited that the defendant's efforts (which incidentally were rather feeble) to conceal the embezzlement was evidence that he knew that embezzled income is taxable. For he would have had an incentive to conceal the embezzlement in order to save his job and avoid prosecution for embezzlement, even if embezzled income were tax-free. But there is plenty of other circumstantial evidence of the defendant's intent to avoid tax. As in *Guidry,* the defendant was an accountant, moreover an experienced one; he personally prepared the fraudulent tax return; the sums taken were large (they amounted to 75 percent of his total income during the period of the embezzlement), and (the weakest bit of evidence) he used the money for ordinary expenses, the sort of thing people usually defray from taxable income. Furthermore, the fact that illegal income is taxable is widely known, even among lay people. Everyone knows that Al Capone, for example, was nailed for income-tax evasion, not for the bootlegging, loan-sharking, extortion, and prostitution that generated the income. Accountants know better than anyone except tax lawyers that illegal income is taxable.

It is *possible* nevertheless that this experienced accountant who prepared his own tax return thought that illegal income was tax exempt, but it is too remote a possibility to compel an acquittal, at least in the absence of any evidence that might make it plausible, such as that the defendant suffered from some psychiatric disorder that had deranged his knowledge of elementary tax law or his ability to use that knowledge in filling out his income tax return. *Anything* is possible; there are no metaphysical certainties accessible to human reason; but a merely metaphysical doubt (for example, doubt whether the external world is real, rather than being merely a dream) is not a reasonable doubt for purposes of the criminal law. If it were, no one could be convicted. As with the transportation of the checks, so with the charge of willfully filing a false return, the judge had to choose between two hypotheses. One was that the defendant knew that embezzled income is taxable. The other was that he thought embezzled income tax-free — a token of the government's affection for embezzlers and other thieves. The former hypothesis was, in the circumstances, far more likely than the latter. That is enough to compel affirmance.

AFFIRMED.

Post-Case Follow-Up

The fact that taxpayers must include illegal income in their gross income presents no surprise, and the court in *Ytem* basically confirms the standard rule, albeit with a dash of judicial flair. But cases like *Ytem* are easy, at least from a tax perspective. The more challenging cases involve taxpayer conduct that straddles the border between the legitimate and understandable on the one hand and the illegal on the other. In *Gilbert v. Commissioner*, 552 F.2d 478 (2d Cir. 1977), the taxpayer used corporate funds to effect the purchase of another corporation's stock, the thinking being that his corporate employer and the other corporation would ultimately merge and that he was acting in the best interest of his company. The taxpayer was not covert and took steps to ensure repayment of the corporation. Nonetheless, he clearly failed to follow proper fund disbursement procedures. At the trial court level, the Tax Court found him taxable on the funds. On appeal, the Second Circuit concluded that the taxpayer should not suffer taxation under the prevailing facts because he realized no income. He had not acted covertly, he signed promissory notes payable to the corporation, and he backed up those promissory notes with security (i.e., his own personal property) sufficient to ensure that the corporation would ultimately recover the amounts disbursed. But it bears noting that *Gilbert* involved a unique set of facts and is thus of very limited use otherwise. An embezzler cannot escape including embezzled funds in gross income merely by fessing up to the deed and signing a promissory note. It is true that an embezzler who manages to pay back the embezzled funds may not face a gross income inclusion. *See James v. United States*, 366 U.S. 213, 220 (1961). The mere signing of a promissory note, however, will not do the trick. *See Buff v. Commissioner*, 496 F.2d 847 (2d Cir. 1974).

United States v. Ytem: Real Life Applications

1. Paul works as a cashier at a family-owned grocery store. He also has a gambling problem. Recently, one of the store owners, Mr. Baxter, realized that Paul had stolen $5,000 from the business, but rather than report the matter to the police, he forced Paul to sign a promissory note under which the money would be repaid over a five-year period.

   a. Must Paul include the $5,000 in gross income for the year in which he stole the money? *yes, for about rule*

   b. If Paul's promissory note was backed up by $7,000 of collateral, would he have to include any amounts in gross income?

2. Julie works as a cashier at a local racetrack. Although company policies prohibit betting by cashiers, Julie recently placed bets on horses by entering the bet electronically without paying in the requisite dollar amount. At the end of the day, Julie had bet over $10,000 in this manner, but her winnings totaled $35,000. She was able to close out her register without her activity being detected, and she pocketed the $25,000 difference. How much, if any, must Julie include in her gross income in connection with this activity? ~~illegible~~ $25K

Rhymes with Orange

THE STATE PEN

NEXT WINDOW PLEASE

AND HERE ARE THE BANK EMBEZZLERS.

11·22·2014 Dist. by King Features
© HILARY B. PRICE rhymeswithorange.com

4. Income from the Discharge of Indebtedness

In General

Section 61(a) sets forth several forms of income by way of example, including compensation, interest, dividends, and rental receipts. Most taxpayers have working familiarity with these items. In this part of the chapter, we examine the law governing a slightly less familiar form of income referred to in the Code as "income from discharge of indebtedness." A thorough understanding of this form of income, however, requires a brief discussion of loan transactions. From a tax perspective, a traditional loan transaction is largely a non-event. The lender hands over money to the borrower in exchange for the borrower's promise to repay the loan. True, money changes hands, but the borrower has no "undeniable accession to wealth" because the money comes with a clear repayment obligation. Accordingly, the borrower's receipt of the loan funds does not give rise to income to the borrower, and the borrower's repayment of the loan itself does not give rise to a deduction. Now, assume, that for whatever reason (e.g., debtor hardship and/ or begging), the lender decides that the borrower need not repay the loan (i.e., the debt is cancelled or discharged). At that point, the borrower has money but no repayment obligation, so from a tax perspective, the borrower *now* has income from the discharge of indebtedness. If the person owes $1,000 at the time of discharge and must ultimately repay $0, then he has $1,000 of income from the discharge of indebtedness. If, instead, the debtor owes $2,000 at the time of discharge and must repay only $1,500, he would have $500 of income from the discharge of indebtedness. It's as simple as that. The U.S. Supreme Court applied this basic rule in *United States v. Kirby Lumber*, 284 U.S. 1 (1931), a landmark precedent on this issue in the tax arena. In that case, the Kirby Lumber Company sought to acquire additional capital/money. It was able to do so by issuing bonds (i.e., borrowing money from the general public in exchange for corporate IOUs (a.k.a. "bonds")). Thus, a company like Kirby Lumber might receive $10,000 cash and issue a $10,000 IOU/bond. Such a bond would ordinarily obligate Kirby Lumber to pay not only $10,000 but also interest (e.g., 7 percent per year). Bonds are like stock, mortgages, and other financial instruments in that they are bought and sold by investors on a regular basis. In various contexts (including bond transactions) prevailing interest rates are key in terms of valuing or pricing the instrument. Kirby Lumber issued bonds in exchange for $1 million, but was later able to repurchase those bonds in the marketplace for only $862,000 because of an intervening change in prevailing interest rates. The U.S. Supreme Court held that Kirby Lumber had $138,000 in income from the discharge of indebtedness.

[handwritten margin notes:] Loans: No income and no deduction if repaid

Discharge: income

Note (what does not constitute discharge of indebtedness)

The notion of income from the discharge of indebtedness is easy to grasp, but it should not be confused with other events in which a debtor finds himself relieved of a given debt obligation. For example, if a person owed $3,000 to his landlord, and the person's employer paid the landlord, the person has basically received compensation, albeit indirectly, because he enjoyed the economic benefit of having the rent paid. It would be wrong, however, to say that the employee has income from the discharge of indebtedness, because the debt was not cancelled or forgiven by the landlord. The debt was paid. Likewise, if a parent paid a debt for a child, one would likely characterize the payment as a gift from the parent to the child. It would be wrong to say that the child has income from the discharge of indebtedness because the debt itself was not cancelled or discharged. Rather, it was actually paid. As we will soon see, it does in fact matter whether income is technically "income from the discharge of indebtedness."

The Insolvency Exception

Although § 61(a) indicates that gross income includes "income from the discharge of indebtedness" (as well as a host of other items), there's more to the general rule than meets the eye at first glance. If you have focused diligently on the language of the entire section, you have likely noted that it actually begins with "*Except as otherwise provided in this subtitle . . . .*" (Emphasis added.) Thus, there are a number of items that would ordinarily be included in a taxpayer's gross income under the general rule but that are specifically excluded from gross income calculations because Congress has explicitly provided otherwise. An example that readily comes to mind is a gift (excluded by § 102). We will study several exclusions in future chapters, but for the moment, we turn to what one might consider a conditional exclusion.

Under specific circumstances, taxpayers may be able to exclude from gross income some or even *all* of their income from the discharge of indebtedness. The devil, of course, is in the details. Section 108 provides, in pertinent part, as follows:

> Gross income does not include any amount which (but for [this provision]) would be includible in gross income by reason of the discharge (in whole or in part) of indebtedness of the taxpayer **if** . . . the discharge occurs when the taxpayer is insolvent. [Emphasis added.]

If you read through § 108(a)(1), you will see that there are several situations that will allow a taxpayer to exclude income from the discharge of indebtedness, but for the moment, we will focus specifically on the exclusion under § 108(a)(1)(B), the so-called insolvency exception. Let's start with a basic definition of "insolvency." Section 108(d)(3) essentially provides that for purposes of § 108, **insolvent** means the excess of a taxpayer's liabilities over her assets. Accordingly, the following net worth profile of a taxpayer reflects insolvency:

Assets	**Liabilities**
Cash ($1,000)	Bank of Washington Loan ($20,000)
Car ($15,000)	Bank of Vermont Loan ($3,000)
Total Assets = **$16,000**	Total Liabilities = **$23,000**

In fact, we know not only that the taxpayer is insolvent but also that she is insolvent by exactly $7,000 (i.e., her liabilities exceed her assets by $7,000). The fact that the taxpayer is insolvent means that the taxpayer may be able to apply § 108 (to some extent at least) to exclude income from the discharge of indebtedness from her gross income. If the Bank of Vermont alone discharges its entire $3,000 loan under these facts, the taxpayer will *not* be required to include $3,000 in gross income as income from the discharge of indebtedness. What if the Bank of Vermont continued to insist on payment, but the Bank of Washington decided to discharge its entire $20,000 loan? Would the taxpayer be able to plead insolvency and exclude the entire $20,000 under § 108? No. Congress's legislative grace goes only so far. Even though § 108 allows an exclusion of income from the discharge of indebtedness due to taxpayer insolvency, the insolvency exclusion applies *only to the extent of the taxpayer's insolvency. See* IRC § 108(a)(3). Under the facts given, our taxpayer is insolvent by $7,000. Thus, if the Bank of Washington (alone) decided to discharge its entire $20,000 loan, the taxpayer would be able to *exclude* $7,000 of income from the discharge of indebtedness but would be required to *include* the remaining $13,000 in gross income. What if both banks decided to discharge their loans ($23,000 in total) at the same time under these facts? The taxpayer would be able to exclude $7,000 from gross income under § 108(a)(1)(B) but would be required to include $16,000.

You should pay special attention to two key facts regarding the insolvency exception. First, in deciding whether the taxpayer was insolvent and in calculating the extent of insolvency, we started with a list of assets and a list of liabilities. We included the loans (either or both of which might have been discharged) in the list of liabilities. Did we err by doing so? No, because in ascertaining whether a taxpayer is insolvent and in calculating the extent of the insolvency, we have to take a snapshot of her assets and liabilities *immediately before* the discharge. *See* IRC § 108(d)(3). Second, the insolvency exception only applies to income from the *discharge of indebtedness*. Thus, if the employee mentioned had previously enjoyed the economic benefit of having $3,000 rent paid by her employer, she must include the amount in gross income, even if she happens to be insolvent. Section 108(a)'s insolvency exception only operates to exclude amounts that would otherwise constitute gross income "by reason of the discharge . . . of indebtedness," not items that would constitute gross income by reason of economic benefit or something else.

Caveat: Contested Liabilities

Assume that you borrowed $25,000 from a bank and because of an ambiguous clause in the loan contract, a genuine uncertainty existed as to whether the interest rate on the loan went up after your first late payment. You and the bank disagree with respect to the amount currently due. You argue that the amount is $20,000, and the bank argues that the amount is $22,000. If you and the bank finally agree that you have to pay $21,000, and you do so, do you have any income from the discharge of indebtedness? In the end, you paid $1,000 less than the bank initially sought. Did the bank grant you a $1,000 discharge, or did your $21,000 payment constitute payment in full? The contested liability doctrine establishes that to the extent there exists a good faith dispute with respect to the amount a taxpayer owes to a creditor, full payment of the undisputed amount will not result in income from the discharge of indebtedness. If, however, the taxpayer pays *less* than the undisputed amount, the difference will constitute income from the discharge of indebtedness.

Case Preview

McCormick v. Commissioner

McCormick v. Commissioner gives us an opportunity to see the contested liability doctrine in operation. At the same time, we get a more complete sense of what qualifies as a good faith dispute between a debtor and creditor for federal income tax purposes. As you read through the decision, focus on the following questions:

1. Why did the taxpayers have income from the discharge of indebtedness after having paid $7,500 to CitiFinancial?
2. Can debt that is legally unenforceable be "contested" in the federal income taxation sense?

McCormick v. Commissioner
T.C. Memo. 2009-239, 98 T.C.M. (CCH) 357 (2009)

COHEN, Judge.
    Respondent determined a deficiency of $5,067 in petitioners' Federal income tax for 2005 and an accuracy-related penalty of $1,007 pursuant to section 6662(a). * * *

After express concessions and abandoned issues, the issue for decision is whether petitioners must recognize discharge of indebtedness income as a result of settlement of their accounts with CitiFinancial Services and Chase Manhattan Bank.

BACKGROUND

* * * Petitioners resided in Pennsylvania at the time the petition was filed. * * *

From at least 2004 petitioners maintained a loan account with CitiFinancial Services (CitiFinancial). Prior to February 1, 2005, petitioners were advised that the "payoff" amount of the loan was $8,042.10. In a fax sent February 1, 2005, to a branch manager, petitioner challenged the payoff amount, claiming that an insurance refund of $492.44 should have been credited to the account. The following day, the manager offered to settle the dispute for a lump-sum payment of $7,500. Petitioner accepted and paid the $7,500. CitiFinancial sent a Form 109-C, Cancellation of Debt, to the Internal Revenue Service.

Before December 2000, petitioner Mary Lou McCormick, formerly Mary Lou Howard, had a credit card with Chase Manhattan Bank (Chase). The account was placed with collection agencies January 4, 2001, and October 10, 2001. Petitioners disputed the account from at least February 2002. On May 12, 2005, petitioner sent a letter to Chase challenging the alleged account balance of $2,875 and noting that the period of limitations on a suit to collect had expired. Petitioner offered to pay $1,000 as the amount "actually owed." Chase accepted and mailed petitioner Mary Lou McCormick a 2005 Form 1099-C for $1,875, the difference between the balance on the account and the payment.

DISCUSSION

The issue remaining for decision is whether petitioners had cancellation of indebtedness income from CitiFinancial and Chase.

Section 61(a)(12) includes in the general definition of gross income "income from discharge of indebtedness." When the amount of a debt is disputed, "a subsequent settlement of the dispute would be treated as the amount of debt cognizable for tax purposes." *Zarin v. Commissioner,* 916 F.2d 110, 115 (3d Cir.1990) (holding that unenforceable debt is also disputed as to amount, and its settlement does not give rise to cancellation of indebtedness income) revg. 92 T.C. 1084 (1989); *N. Sobel, Inc. v. Commissioner,* 40 B.T.A. 1263, 1265 (1939). There must be evidence of a dispute; a settlement standing alone does not prove that a good-faith dispute existed. See *Rood v. Commissioner,* T.C. Memo.1996–248, affd. without published opinion 122 F.3d 1078 (11th Cir.1997).

In a fax sent to CitiFinancial petitioner argued that the loan payoff amount of $8,042.10 should be reduced by a $492.44 insurance refund. Aside from the insurance refund, petitioners do not argue that the payoff amount was incorrect.

In a letter sent to Chase petitioner argued that the outstanding balance should be $1,000 rather than the $2,875 claimed by the bank. Bank records reflected that the account had been disputed from at least 2002.

The preponderance of the evidence supports a conclusion that a bona fide dispute existed regarding the $492.44 insurance refund on the CitiFinancial debt and the balance of the Chase account over $1,000.

To determine the amount of cancellation of indebtedness income properly attributed to petitioners, we must determine the amount of the CitiFinancial and Chase debt that was definite and liquidated. See *Zarin v. Commissioner, supra* at 116.

In this case, respondent may not rely on the Forms 1099-C submitted by CitiFinancial and Chase as evidence of the amount of debt that was definite and liquidated. Section 6201(d) provides that in any court proceeding, if a taxpayer asserts a reasonable dispute with respect to any item of income reported on an information return and has fully cooperated, the Commissioner shall have the burden of producing reasonable and probative information concerning the deficiency in addition to the information return. Petitioners have asserted reasonable disputes with respect to the amounts reported by CitiFinancial and Chase. Respondent has failed to produce reasonable and probative information independent of the third-party information returns.

Petitioners did not dispute the CitiFinancial claimed payoff amount of $8,042.10, less the disputed insurance refund of $492.44, a total of $7,549.66. That amount is decreased by the settlement payment of $7,500. We conclude that the amount of petitioners' cancellation of indebtedness income from CitiFinancial is $49.66.

Petitioners had an uncontested and liquidated outstanding balance of $1,000 with Chase. Because they paid $1,000 to settle the account, they have no cancellation of indebtedness income from Chase.

In reaching our decision, we have considered all arguments made by the parties. To the extent not mentioned or addressed, they are irrelevant or without merit.

For the reasons explained above,

Decision will be entered under Rule 155.

> *[handwritten note:]* For CF: Loan - refund = 7,549.66 (undisputed). CF discharged $49.66 by their settlement offer of $7,500, so the income is the $49.66 discharged.

Post-Case Follow-Up

The traditional debtor/creditor relationship often proceeds without incident. As the *McCormick* decision well exemplifies, however, misunderstandings occur, and much can go wrong as the parties attempt to sort things out. *McCormick* confirms that no income from the discharge of indebtedness results when there is a good faith dispute with respect to the amount owed and the taxpayer pays the undisputed portion of the debt in full. The court also opines that a debt that is legally unenforceable is disputed as to amount. Do you agree? If the law itself dictates that stale debt is legally unenforceable, shouldn't the amount of the debt legally be set at $0, making any action of the parties (settlement, payment, threatening, badgering, heckling, worrying, pleading) wholly irrelevant from a tax perspective? In *Zarin v. Commissioner*, 916 F.2d 110 (3d Cir. 1990), a compulsive gambler racked up a considerable debt tab, largely by securing multiple extensions of credit from the casino. By extending Zarin credit under the circumstances, the casino violated state law, and the debt was legally unenforceable. Zarin and the casino eventually reached a settlement agreement in which Zarin paid $500,000, prompting the Service to assert that he had approximately $2.9 million of income from the discharge of indebtedness. Although the court appealed to the contested liability doctrine (reasoning

[handwritten margin note:] legally unenforceable debts

that even an unenforceable debt is disputed as to amount and liability), it need not have resorted to such analytical somersaults. The court's strongest rationale for concluding that Zarin had no income from the discharge of indebtedness flows from the simple fact that, under the Code, Zarin had no debt. Per § 108(d)(1), "indebtedness" means indebtedness for which the taxpayer is liable, and by law, Zarin had no liability and thus no debt capable of discharge.

McCormick v. Commissioner: Real Life Applications

1. Breana acquired a smartphone several years ago. She generally managed to pay her bill on time, but at some point, she fell on hard times. Her phone bill climbed to $1,200, and the company, NextCellular, eventually placed her account with its collections department. Hoping to avoid litigation, Breana offered to pay $500 to settle the account. Assume that Breana sent a $500 cashier's check to NextCellular and that the company ultimately wrote off the remainder of the bill as uncollectible. Did Breana have income from the discharge of indebtedness under these facts?

2. Porto, Novo, & Benin LLP ("PNB") recently closed a deal on behalf of Amazonia, Inc. ("Amazonia"), which had retained the firm as lead counsel in Amazonia's acquisition of Whole Nutrition, Inc. Because Amazonia retains PNB for many of its substantial transactional matters, PNB automatically gives the company a 20 percent discount on all attorney hourly rates. Does the PNB discount constitute income from the discharge of indebtedness for Amazonia? What if PNB did not provide a discount but lowered the final bill at Amazonia's request? How, if at all, would your response to the previous question change if PNB refused to lower the final bill but ultimately accepted a partial payment and wrote off the remainder of the bill as uncollectible?

3. Leah had a smartphone account with Vanguard Cellular, and she recently received a bill indicating that she owed $125 for a prior month of service. Arguing that the account representative signed her up for the wrong service plan, she reasoned that she owed no more than $50. She and Vanguard Cellular agreed that the matter would be settled if Leah paid $50, and she did so. Did Leah have income from the discharge of indebtedness in connection with this incident?

4. Salvador recently placed an online order for a couch using his Centurion Express credit card. The couch itself cost $3,000, but charges for tax, shipping, and handling brought the final cost to $3,200. On receiving his bill from Centurion Express Bank ("CEB"), he was quite surprised to see an additional charge of $100 (imposed by CEB) for a "Foreign Transaction." He promptly contacted CEB and demanded that the $100 charge be eliminated because his card featured "No Foreign Transaction Fees." Deeply embarrassed, CEB's representative apologized profusely and emphasized how much the company valued Salvador's business. CEB and Salvador agreed to dispose of the matter if Salvador paid $3,000, and he did so. Did Salvador have any income from the discharge of indebtedness in connection with this transaction?

Chapter Summary

- Barring specific exception, gross income includes all income from whatever source derived. *See* IRC § 61(a). Such income may take the form of cash, property, services, etc. *See* Treas. Reg. § 1.61-1(a).
- Found property (e.g., treasure trove) must be included in gross income to the extent of its value in U.S. currency when such property is reduced to the taxpayer's undisputed possession. *See* Treas. Reg. § 1.61-14(a).
- Gross income includes illegal gains. *See* Treas. Reg. § 1.61-14(a). Those who embezzle during a given tax year but manage to repay the embezzled amount during the same tax year need not include the embezzled amount in gross income.
- Income from the discharge (in whole or in part) of indebtedness constitutes gross income to the taxpayer. An insolvent taxpayer, however, may be able to exclude such income, but only to the extent of her insolvency. *See generally* IRC §§ 61(a)(11), 108(a)(1)(B), and 108(a)(3). Insolvency determinations must occur immediately before the discharge of any indebtedness. *See* IRC § 108(d)(3).
- Taxpayers who, in good faith, dispute a given financial obligation do not realize income from the discharge of indebtedness if they pay 100 percent of the undisputed amount of such obligation.

Applying the Rules

1. Alex is an Executive Vice President at Conglomerate, Inc. Yesterday, his company announced plans to downsize, and Alex now knows that his position has been eliminated. The company did, however, offer him a decent severance package, including a payment of $50,000. Must Alex include this severance payment in his gross income?

2. Garret and Adam recently purchased a home built originally in the late 1920s. They decided that before moving in, they would have extensive renovations done, and they hired Fixer-Uppers, Inc. to do the work. Vikram, one of the employees of the company, found a canister containing $20,000 in the space beneath a floor he was repairing. He promptly gave the canister to his supervisor, Fred, who promised to pass it along to Garret and Adam. Instead, Fred kept the money.

   a. Does Vikram have to include any amount in gross income as a result of his find? No.
   b. Does Fred have to include any amount in gross income as a result of taking and keeping the money in the canister? Yes.

3. Mallory is a registered nurse, and for several years, she has working at Sunset Homes, an assisted living community. With easy access to the elderly, she also has easy access to many of the prescription medications they take. Assume that Mallory steals pain killers from the residents and sells them to a drug dealer. Must Mallory include the money she receives in her gross income? Yes

Insolvency: $5K
Discharged: $7K
Gross income: $2K

4. Assume that Sanjay currently has total assets of $20,000 and total liabilities of $25,000, which includes a $7,000 loan from the First National Bank of Atlantis ("FNBA"). If FNBA discharges the entire loan, how much, if any, must Sanjay include in his gross income as income from the discharge of indebtedness?

5. *Same facts as Question 4*, except that Sanjay has $27,000 in assets. How much, if any, must he include in gross income as a result of FNBA's discharge of the $7,000 loan?

6. Hamilton and Hannah recently divorced, and Hannah is obligated to pay Hamilton $1,000 per month in alimony. Assume that when Hannah is two months behind in payments, her mother, Grace, pays $2,000 to Hamilton as a means of clearing an old obligation (i.e., a loan) that Hannah previously made to her. How much, if any, must Hannah include in gross income as income from the discharge of indebtedness as a result of her mother's payment of the $2,000 obligation on Hannah's behalf?

7. Several weeks ago, Gavin purchased an expensive sculpture for $12,000. His bank initially charged him an additional $200 as a penalty for exceeding his credit limit. Gavin disputed the penalty in good faith, noting that just before the purchase, a representative of the credit card company had authorized a credit line increase from $10,000 to $15,000. Gavin and the company eventually agreed that Gavin could settle the matter by paying $12,000. If Gavin proceeds to pay $12,000, how much, if any, must he include in gross income as income from the discharge of indebtedness?

Federal Income Taxation in Practice

1. Assume that you are a research assistant for one of your tax professors. She plans to write an article on IRC § 108(a)(1)(E) and needs you to conduct some preliminary research. See if you can find out when this provision was added to the Internal Revenue Code. Also check to see if there is a House Report or a Senate Report discussing the new provision.

2. Returning to your office after lunch, you find a litigation partner waiting for you. She informs you that one of her major clients has asked that she litigate a contested liability case in Tax Court. She needs you to find out whether there have been any contested liability cases decided in Tax Court since January 1, 2012. See what you can find and send her a brief e-mail update.

3. You are a partner in a law firm, and one of your clients is The Computer Superstore. The General Counsel of the company contacts you regarding the treatment of employees who receive a computer as part of their compensation. He

notes that the employees take possession of the computer but may not sell it and may forfeit the right to keep it if they do not remain with the company for the next two years. The employees may treat the computers as their own personal property after two years. The General Counsel would like to know whether and when the employees will be required to include the fair market value of the computers in gross income.

Recovery of Basis and Certain Limited Exclusions

In prior chapters, we discussed both the concept of realization and the notion of income. The authorities and provisions covered present a legal landscape in which realization events would appear to occur frequently and a wide range of receipts/events would likely give rise to income. These realities notwithstanding, Congress has never sought to tax all taxpayer receipts. By their nature, some "undeniable accession[s] to wealth, clearly realized and over which the taxpayer has complete dominion," simply fall outside the scope of what Congress intends to tax. In other contexts, exclusion of a given receipt, item, or benefit may facilitate Congress's achievement of a specific policy objective or may simply make sense as a matter of basic fairness or as a rational accommodation of widespread business practice. As you study individual exclusions, bear in mind that an exclusion is not the same thing as a deduction. Deductions are taken into account in arriving at taxable income. Exclusions, on the other hand, simply do not show up on a taxpayer's return because Congress, in its legislative grace and administrative wisdom, has declared that the items shall *not* be included in gross income. Incidentally, you should have noted that we have already stumbled upon the exclusion arena, at least to a limited extent. In discussing income from the discharge of indebtedness, we necessarily addressed the insolvency exception, which one can think of as a conditional exclusion (depending on the taxpayer's balance of assets and liabilities). For many exclusions, Congress offers the relief but requires that taxpayers navigate a statutory labyrinth to access it. It's a worthy pursuit. Foregoing revenue is not Congress's favored pastime, so one must spot and seize exclusion opportunities when they present. Precise understanding of governing rules is key, so let us turn with pointed focus to those items specifically excluded from gross income.

Key Concepts

- Distinguishing exclusions and deductions
- Recovery of basis in different contexts
- Meaning and scope of exclusion of gain from the sale of a principal residence

A.   RECOVERY OF BASIS

As was noted previously, section 1012 of the Code generally provides that a taxpayer's basis in an asset is its cost, and under § 1001(a), on the sale or other disposition of the asset, one calculates gain or loss by reference to the amount realized and taxpayer basis. Thus, a taxpayer with a $4,000 basis in an asset who sells it for $5,000 has gain realized of $1,000. Although the taxpayer clearly received $5,000 on the sale of the asset, taxing him on the full $5,000 makes no sense because he only has profit of $1,000. Put differently, he is entitled to a tax-free recovery of his basis ($4,000). No single Code provision explicitly states that "gross income shall not include the recovery of a taxpayer's basis," but we derive the rule by reading multiple Code provisions together, including § 1001(a) (i.e., "gain . . . shall be the excess of amount realized *over . . . basis*" (emphasis added)) and § 61(a)(3) (i.e., "gross income means all income from whatever source derived . . . including . . . *gains* derived from dealings in property" (emphasis added)).

Taxed on gain only, not recovering the amount paid

In a context involving the sale of a single asset at a gain, ensuring the tax-free recovery of basis is as simple as subtracting a set dollar amount from amount realized in calculating gain. In other contexts, however, getting to the same end result may be a slightly more complicated endeavor, because basis recovery may not occur all at once. Let's consider the treatment of annuities.

B. ANNUITY PAYMENTS

You are probably familiar with the essentials of life insurance. In the typical arrangement, an individual pays monthly premiums to an insurance company, and when the individual dies, the insurance company pays a death benefit to a designated beneficiary. In the typical annuity context, the individual to receive payments (i.e., the **annuitant**) pays premiums to an insurance company, but the expectation is that the annuitant will receive a stream of payments from the insurance company in the future. Think of it as a personal and private means of providing for future income stability and security. The classic retirement annuity involves an annuitant who pays premiums during their working years, and as the years pass, those premiums generate investment returns because the insurance company receiving the money invests it and collects interest and other forms of investment income over time (i.e., the **accumulation phase**). At retirement, the annuitant begins to receive a stream of monthly payments (the **payout phase**) and generally expects to receive, in the aggregate, an amount representing the total premiums paid in plus a substantial portion of the investment earnings those premiums generated over time; if the insurance company is fortunate, it will have generated investment earnings exceeding its obligations under the contract and can pocket the excess. We refer to the total premiums paid in (as of the annuity starting date) as the "investment in the contract." *See* § 72(c)(1). We refer to the *total* amount the annuitant expects to receive as of the annuity starting date (roughly, premiums plus investment earnings) as the "expected return." *See* § 72(c)(3). Let's throw in some numbers to get a working example and to bring out the tax issue. Assume that Samantha is 35 years old on January 1, 2018, and that she decides to make additional provision for her future income security. She pays $1,250 per month to Insurance & Annuity Providers, Inc. ("IAPI"), which receives and invests those premiums and thereby generates investment income over the 30-year period. By January 1, 2048, Samantha has paid a total of $450,000 in premiums. Combined with the investment income that IAPI was able to generate, her total account balance is $1,000,000 (i.e., $450,000 premiums paid in plus $550,000 of investment income). Thus, as of the annuity starting date, her investment in the contract is $450,000, and her expected return is $1,000,000. Assume that at this point, Samantha retires and enters the payout phase of the contract. Her first monthly payment is $5,000.

> ## Annuity Options
>
> Those seeking to enter into an annuity contract often have many arrangements to choose from. As an initial matter, they can pay premiums over time or in a lump sum, and they can elect to defer the payout phase or to have payments start immediately. The annuitant typically has the choice of having payments made for life, for a specific term, or even for life with the guarantee that, in any event, payments must be made to the annuitant or a designated beneficiary for a set minimum term. Annuity payments can be fixed or variable (i.e., dependent on investment returns during the payout phase). For a detailed analysis of the taxation of insurance company financial products, see Pehrson, Bieluch, Christie, and Dexter, Tax Management Portfolio No. 546, *Annuities, Life Insurance, and Long-Term Care Insurance Products* (Bloomberg BNA 2000).

Does she owe any taxes with respect to this amount? One could reason that the payment merely represents a return of her investment in the contract and thus must be treated as a tax-free recovery of her basis. After all, how can we justify taxing someone when they're simply getting their own money back? At the same time, one could argue that the payment effectively amounts to a distribution of some of the accumulated investment income and should be taxed in full; section 61(a) mentions interest, dividends, and annuities, to name just a few income categories. Congress generally resolves the issue by treating annuity payments as including both (1) a tax-free return of taxpayer investment in the contract and (2) a taxable distribution of accumulated investment income. As a result, with respect to each $5,000 payment, Samantha may exclude some portion and must include the remainder in her gross income. We employ a statutory mechanism to break each payment down into its taxable and non-taxable components. If her investment in the contract was $450,000 and her expected return is $1,000,000, then it makes

> ## Life Annuity
>
> If an annuity contract provides that payments are to be made for the life of an annuitant, the expected return must be calculated by taking into account many factors, including the annuitant's life expectancy. *See* IRC § 72(c)(3)(A).

sense to conclude that the *tax-free* portion of each payment should be an amount equivalent to 450,000/1,000,000 or 45/100. To get the amount she may *exclude* from each payment, we multiply the payment amount ($5,000) by this fraction (45/100). Under these facts, we get $5,000 × 0.45 = $2,250. Accordingly, she may exclude $2,250 from each payment but must include $2,750 ($5,000 - $2,250) in income with respect to each $5,000 annuity payment. What if the annuity contract requires IAPI to pay Samantha $5,000 per month for the remainder of her life, no matter how long she lives? At some point, Samantha will have excluded (in the aggregate) $450,000 from her gross income, and from that point on, she must include 100 percent of each annuity payment in her gross income. *See* § 72(b)(2). If she dies before recovering her entire investment in the contract, those filing her final tax return on her behalf may generally deduct the unrecovered amount. *See* § 72(b)(3).

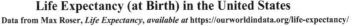

Life Expectancy (at Birth) in the United States
Data from Max Roser, *Life Expectancy*, *available at* https://ourworldindata.org/life-expectancy/

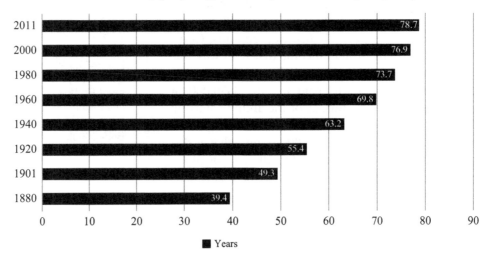

With this understanding in hand, let's see how the Code expresses these concepts.

Section 72(a)(1) generally provides that gross income includes any amount received as an annuity, but the language at the very beginning of the section provides for a potential carve-out. We find our carve-out in § 72(b)(1), which provides, in pertinent part, as follows:

> Gross income does not include that part of any amount received as an annuity . . . which bears the same ratio to such amount as the investment in the contract . . . bears to the expected return under the contract.

That language is not a model of clarity, but at least you have some sense as to what Congress seeks to achieve here. The provision essentially dictates that the left side of the following equation be equal to the right side and that gross income not include the "portion to be excluded."

$$\frac{[\text{Portion to be Excluded}]}{[\text{Payment Amount Received}]} = \frac{[\text{Investment in the Contract}]}{[\text{Expected Return}]}$$

We refer to the right side of this equation (i.e., investment in the contract divided by expected return) as the "exclusion ratio." Under our facts, the equation starts out in the following form:

$$\frac{X}{\$5,000} = \frac{\$450,000}{\$1,000,000}$$

Thus, the excluded portion relative to $5,000 must be the same as $450,000 relative to $1,000,000. As you may recall from math classes, we solve for "X" in this situation by using the following equation:

$$(X)(\$1,000,000) = (\$5,000)(\$450,000).$$

$$(X) = \frac{(\$5,000)(\$450,000)}{(\$1,000,000)}$$

$$X = \$2,250$$

Ultimately, we see that the amount excluded (X) is simply the total amount received multiplied by the exclusion ratio of 45/100. Although we have discussed a relatively simple annuity arrangement, remember that a large number of options exist, so to the extent the parties make various features a part of the contract or engage in certain behavior with respect to the contract, tax ramifications can result. You need not, however, understand the annuity industry in baroque detail to appreciate the key tax points. Focus on the notion that taxpayers get a tax-free return of their investment in the contract but must include investment earnings in gross income when they receive them. A number of the more technical rules regarding the taxation of annuity contracts seek to ensure that the annuitant is not accessing *investment earnings* on a *tax-free* basis. For example, a taxpayer taking out a loan under the terms of the annuity contract (or seeking a loan elsewhere while using the annuity contract as collateral) may find himself facing rather unpleasant tax consequences if the loan terms and conditions do not fit within certain statutory parameters.

C. GAIN ON SALE OF A PRINCIPAL RESIDENCE

Up to this point, we have covered exclusions that essentially involve the tax-free recovery of a taxpayer's basis. We now turn to an exclusion that one might view as a modest display of congressional understanding and accommodation. Current tax law allows a taxpayer to exclude a limited amount of gain realized from the sale or exchange of a principal residence under the appropriate circumstances.

Key Statutory and Regulatory Provisions

■ Internal Revenue Code
- § 121(a)
- § 121(b)(1)–(4)
- § 121(b)(5)(A)–(C)(i)
- § 121(c)
- § 121(d)(3)
- § 121(f)

■ Treasury Regulations
- § 1.121-1(a)
- § 1.121-1(b)(1)–(3)(i)
- § 1.121-1(c)(1)–(2)
- § 1.121-3(a) & (b)

Why would Congress allow such an exclusion? In essence, Congress seeks to encourage and support home ownership, but given that homes tend to appreciate in value over time, taxation of all gain realized on the sale of a home might very well result in the home becoming a trap of sorts. Thus, if Congress seeks to encourage home ownership without unduly burdening alienation of the property or handicapping taxpayer mobility, it should effect measures designed to facilitate tax-effective transfers. For some time, Congress has done exactly that.

1. Prior Law and Reasons for Change

Before 1997, taxpayers had two avenues of relief from the taxation of gain on the sale of a principal residence. The first, under what was then § 1034, allowed taxpayers to avoid immediate taxation of the gain by using the proceeds from the sale of their "old residence" to purchase a "new residence" of equal or greater value. Taking advantage of the provision allowed a taxpayer to "roll over" the gain from the old residence to the new residence. To the extent the taxpayer failed to redeploy the gain to a new residence, inclusion in gross income resulted. If a taxpayer was able to exclude gain, he was required to reduce the basis in his new residence by the amount of excluded gain.

The second approach to escaping the gain from the sale of a principal residence (or at least some of it) took the form of a once-in-a-lifetime exclusion under the old version of § 121. Taxpayers could take advantage of this provision only if, in addition to satisfying various requirements, they had (1) attained age 55 or older on the date of the sale and (2) owned and used the home as their principal residence for three years during the five-year period ending on the date of the sale. The provision generally allowed taxpayers to exclude up to $125,000 of gain, but unlike the provision under § 1034, taxpayers in this particular demographic were not required to purchase a new home to enjoy the benefits of the provision. If you think about it, the logic makes sense. Growing families tend to need more and more space. When two bedrooms will no longer accommodate the family comfortably, the need arises for the four- or five-bedroom home, complete with sufficient bathroom space for peace, order, and thorough hygiene. Twenty years later, all of the children have gone off to live their own lives in their own residences, and the parents (now decades older) have a large principal residence with more bedrooms than they need and (in all likelihood) a substantial amount of built-in gain. A sale of the home for cash (without purchase of a new home of greater or equal value) would generate a hefty tax bill, which middle-aged couples approaching retirement can certainly do without, but at the same time, downsizing to a smaller residence makes sense. This version of § 121 responded to the plight of such taxpayers who might rationally have opted to purchase a smaller, less expensive home or to take up rental living in an apartment community of general availability or in an assisted living environment.

[handwritten margin note: Rollover: Using gain in house sale to buy new house (prior law)]

Whatever the benefits of these alternatives, drawbacks and traps awaited the unwary. Taking advantage of the rollover provision of § 1034 required that taxpayers keep accurate records for extended time periods with respect to the basis in their home, properly adjust basis as they moved from residence to residence, and effectively distinguish between basis-increasing home improvements and mere repairs having no impact on basis. Throughout the larger endeavor, there was ample room for error (and thus potential for the underpayment or overpayment of taxes). Taxpayers seeking to avoid both misfortune and misunderstanding might simply have decided to purchase more expensive homes to ensure that all gain from prior sales was redeployed to the purchase of the next residence. Even though accomplishing such a goal might have been easy when moving from a low-housing-cost area to a high-housing-cost area, a move in the other direction might encourage unnecessary and financially inefficient residential up-sizing. Older taxpayers in a position to take advantage of the once-in-a-lifetime exclusion might have opted to forego sale of the residence altogether if the amount of gain ultimately to be recognized substantially exceeded $125,000 or if they had already taken advantage of the § 121 exclusion. Complicating matters further was the fact that if a taxpayer married an individual who had already taken advantage of the § 121 exclusion, he or she could not take advantage of the exclusion in his or her own right. Current law addresses a number of the difficulties faced by taxpayers under the old statutory framework and thereby facilitates taxpayer mobility and property alienability more broadly. *See generally* Joint Committee on Taxation, General Explanation of Tax Legislation Enacted in 1997 (Part II: Taxpayer Relief Act of 1997 (H.R. 2014)) (1997).

2. Current Law

In General

Under § 121(a) of the Code as it exists today, taxpayers may exclude a limited amount of gain realized from the sale or exchange of their principal residences, assuming they satisfy certain conditions. They must have owned the property *and* used it as their principal residence for at least two years in a specific five-year period; the relevant five-year period *ends* on the date of sale/exchange (e.g., December 31, 2018) and *begins* five years earlier (e.g., December 31, 2013). *See* § 121(a). Also, taxpayers cannot take advantage of this exclusion too frequently. It is available no more than once every two years. *See* § 121(b)(3). Section 121(b) generally provides for an exclusion of up to $250,000 of gain. For married couples filing jointly in the year of the sale or exchange, the exclusion amount rises to $500,000 per § 121(b)(2)(A), assuming the couple satisfies the following requirements:

How much can be excluded

- Either spouse meets the ownership requirement;
- Both spouses meet the use requirement; and

■ Neither spouse is ineligible for the exclusion because such individual took advantage of the § 121 exclusion in the two-year period preceding the date of sale of the current property.

The Treasury Regulations promulgated under § 121 flesh out some of the terminology in the statute. Although most individuals tend to think of "residence" as a house, the term can actually refer to, among other things, a houseboat or a house trailer. *See* Treas. Reg. § 1.121-1(b)(1). And although one might think that identifying one's principal residence presents no difficulty, some taxpayers may have a living situation that makes it necessary to consult a host of factors to nail down the principal residence, including place of employment, tax return addresses, mailing addresses for bills, the taxpayer's bank location, etc. *See* Treas. Reg. § 1.121-1(b)(2). Taxpayers can satisfy the two-year ownership and use requirements by measuring full calendar years, months, weeks, or days, none of which need be rigidly consecutive. *See* Treas. Reg. § 1.121-1(c)(1). Vacations and the like (short temporary absences) do not stop the clock's ticking. *See* Treas. Reg. § 1.121-1(c)(2).

For your standard, plain vanilla situation, these basic rules suffice. Of course, life's flavor is decidedly more neapolitan than plain vanilla, and § 121 contains several special rules for various situations. We will turn to some of these rules later in the chapter. For the moment, let's get our arms around the basics by considering the following examples:

Example 1

Philip purchased a home for $200,000 on January 1, 2007, and since then, he has used it as his principal residence. He sold the home on January 1, 2016 for $525,000, and he has never taken advantage of § 121. How much, if any must Philip include in gross income as a result of this transaction? Under these facts, Philip qualifies for the $250,000 exclusion. The date of sale was January 1, 2016. Further, he owned the home and used it as a principal residence for at least two years in the time period extending from January 1, 2011 to January 1, 2016. His amount realized was $525,000, and his basis in the home was $200,000. Thus, his gain realized was $325,000. He may exclude no more than $250,000 of gain, so he must include $75,000 in gross income (i.e., $325,000 - $250,000).

Example 2

Same facts as Example 1, except that Philip was married to Leah when they purchased the home in 2007, and they have both used it as their principal residence since then. In the year of the sale, they file a joint return. Under the facts given, the couple qualifies for the $500,000 exclusion amount, and accordingly, they will not be required to report any of the $325,000 gain realized on the sale of their old home as income.

Those examples should give you a basic sense as to how § 121 generally operates. As we will soon find out in *Gates v. Commissioner*, what starts out as a straightforward application context can quickly morph into one in which getting exclusionary relief is an uphill battle, and not always one that ends with a taxpayer triumph.

Case Preview

Gates v. Commissioner

The language of § 121 mentions "property," "principal," and "residence" and sets forth a fairly basic rule. A taxpayer who purchases a home and lives in it for the requisite time period should have no difficulty securing the benefits of § 121. But, then again, we all know that homeowners do not always live life with future tax ramifications in mind. They renovate, demolish, remodel, redecorate, etc., for any number of different reasons. Assume that a taxpayer lives in a home for several years and, having concluded that extensive renovations will simply not do, decides to tear it down and have a brand new one built on the same land. If the taxpayer immediately sells the new home without actually living in it, can he appeal to § 121 to exclude any of the gain realized from his gross income? As you read *Gates v. Commissioner*, consider the following questions:

1. Would the taxpayers have been able to take advantage of § 121 if they had sold their old residence?
2. Does the word "property" in § 121 refer to land, a dwelling on the land, or both?
3. Why is legislative history related to § 1034 (which had already been repealed at the time of this case) of any relevance?

Gates v. Commissioner
135 T.C. 1 (2010)

MARVEL, Judge:

Respondent determined a deficiency in petitioners' Federal income tax of $112,553 and an addition to tax under section 6651(a)(1) of $11,211 for 2000. Petitioners filed a timely petition contesting respondent's determination.

After concessions, the issues for decision are: (1) Whether petitioners may exclude from gross income $500,000 of *** gain from the sale in 2000 of property on Summit Road in Santa Barbara, California (Summit Road property), under section 121(a); and (2) whether petitioners are liable for the section 6651(a)(1) addition to tax.

BACKGROUND

*** Petitioners resided in California when the petition was filed.

On December 14, 1984, petitioner David A. Gates (Mr. Gates) purchased the Summit Road property for $150,000. The Summit Road property included an 880–square-foot two-story building with a studio on the second level and living quarters on the first level (original house).

On August 12, 1989, Mr. Gates married petitioner Christine A. Gates. Petitioners resided in the original house for a period of at least 2 years from August 1996 to August 1998.

Change to Property

In 1996 petitioners decided to enlarge and remodel the original house, and they hired an architect. The architect advised petitioners that more stringent building and permit restrictions had been enacted since the original house was built.

Subsequently, petitioners demolished the original house and constructed a new three-bedroom house (new house) on the Summit Road property. The new house complied with the building and permit requirements existing in 1999. During 1999 petitioners had outstanding mortgage loans, but the record does not disclose the identity of the property or properties that secured the mortgage loans or the dates, amounts, or purposes of the loans.

Sale + gain

Petitioners never resided in the new house. On April 7, 2000, petitioners sold the new house for $1,100,000. The sale resulted in a $591,406 gain to petitioners. * * *

On their 2000 return, petitioners did not report as income any of the $591,406 capital gain generated from the sale of the Summit Road property. Petitioners subsequently agreed that $91,406 of the gain should have been included in their gross income for 2000, but they asserted that the remaining gain of $500,000 was excludable from their income under section 121. On September 9, 2005, respondent mailed petitioners a notice of deficiency for 2000 that increased petitioners' income by $500,000 and explained that petitioners had failed to establish that any of the gain on the sale of the Summit Road property was excludable under section 121. Respondent also determined an addition to tax under section 6651(a)(1) for petitioners' failure to timely file their 2000 return.

Because only owns up to $500K

Petitioners timely petitioned this Court seeking a redetermination of the deficiency and addition to tax. Petitioners assert that respondent erred in determining that they were not entitled to exclude $500,000 of the gain under section 121. Petitioners also argue that because they are not liable for a deficiency, respondent erred in determining that they were liable for the section 6651(a)(1) addition to tax.

DISCUSSION

I. Burden of Proof

*** [R]espondent's determination is entitled to the presumption of correctness and that petitioners have the burden of proof. * * *

II.   Sale of the Summit Road Property

Gross income means all income from whatever source derived, unless excluded by law. * * ** Generally, gain realized on the sale of property is included in a taxpayer's income. Section 121(a), however, allows a taxpayer to exclude from income gain on the sale or exchange of property if the taxpayer has owned and used such property as his or her principal residence for at least 2 of the 5 years immediately preceding the sale. Section 121(a) specifically provides:

> SEC. 121(a). Exclusion. — Gross income shall not include gain from the sale or exchange of *property* if, during the 5-year period ending on the date of the sale or exchange, *such property has been owned and used by the taxpayer as the taxpayer's principal residence* for periods aggregating 2 years or more. [Emphasis added.]

The maximum exclusion is $500,000 for a husband and wife who file a joint return for the year of the sale or exchange. A married couple may claim the $500,000 exclusion on the sale or exchange of property they owned and used as their principal residence if either spouse meets the ownership requirement, both spouses meet the use requirement, and neither spouse claimed an exclusion under section 121(a) during the 2-year period before the sale or exchange.

The issue presented arises from the fact that section 121(a) does not define two critical terms — "property" and "principal residence." Section 121(a) simply provides that gross income does not include gain from the sale or exchange of property if "such property" has been owned and used by the taxpayer "as the taxpayer's principal residence" for the required statutory period.

Respondent contends that petitioners did not sell property they had owned and used as their principal residence for the required statutory period because they never occupied the new house as their principal residence before they sold it. Respondent's argument interprets the term "property" to mean, or at least include, a dwelling that was owned and occupied by the taxpayer as his "principal residence" for at least 2 of the 5 years immediately preceding the sale. Respondent urges this Court to conclude that a qualifying sale under section 121(a) is one that includes the sale of a dwelling used by the taxpayer as his principal residence. Because petitioners never resided in the new house before its sale in 2000, respondent maintains that the new house was never petitioners' principal residence.

Predictably, petitioners disagree. Petitioners argue that any analysis of section 121(a) must recognize that the exclusion thereunder applies to the gain on the sale of *property* that was used as the taxpayer's principal residence. Petitioners' argument focuses on two facts — petitioners used the original house as their principal residence for the period required by section 121(a) and they sold the land on which the original house had been situated. Petitioners contend that the term "property" includes not only the dwelling but also the land on which the dwelling is situated. Petitioners seem to argue that the requirements of section 121(a) are satisfied if a taxpayer lived in any dwelling on the property for the required 2-year period even if that dwelling is not the dwelling that is sold. Petitioners contend that because they used the original house and the land on which it was situated as their principal residence for the required term, the Summit Road property qualifies as their principal residence and $500,000 of the gain generated by the sale of the property is excluded under section 121.

Because section 121 does not define the terms "property" and "principal residence," we must apply accepted principles of statutory construction to ascertain Congress' intent. It is a well-established rule of construction that if a statute does not define a term, the term is given its ordinary meaning. It is also well established that a court may look to sources such as dictionaries for assistance in determining the ordinary meaning of a term. We look to the legislative history to ascertain Congress' intent if the statute is ambiguous. Exclusions from income must be construed narrowly, and taxpayers must bring themselves within the clear scope of the exclusion.

[The court proceeds to set forth dictionary definitions of the words "property," "principal," and "residence."]

When the dictionary definitions of "principal" and "residence" are combined, we conclude that "principal residence" may have two possible meanings. It can either mean the chief or primary *place* where a person lives or the chief or primary *dwelling* in which a person resides. Likewise, the term "property" as used in section 121(a) can refer more broadly to a parcel of real estate, or it can refer to the dwelling (and related curtilage) used as a taxpayer's principal residence.

Court says it's ambiguous

Because there is more than one possible meaning for both the term "property" and the term "principal residence," we cannot conclude that the meaning of section 121(a) is clear and unambiguous. Section 121(a) is not explicit as to whether Congress intended section 121 to apply to a sale of property when the property sold does not include the dwelling that the taxpayer used as a principal residence for the period that section 121(a) requires. Because section 121(a) is ambiguous, we may examine the legislative history of section 121 and its predecessor provisions to ascertain Congress' intent regarding the proper tax treatment of principal residence sales.

[The court proceeds to discuss the legislative history of § 121 and former § 1034.]

Section 121 as amended * * * provides that a taxpayer generally may exclude up to $250,000 of gain realized on the sale or exchange of a principal residence occurring after May 6, 1997, each time the taxpayer sells or exchanges a principal residence and meets the eligibility requirements under section 121. Section 121 applies to petitioners' sale of the Summit Road property.

RE on legislative intent

The legislative history of section 121 supports a conclusion that Congress intended the terms "property" and "principal residence" to mean a house or other dwelling unit in which the taxpayer actually resided. In explaining the 1997 amendment to section 121, the House Committee on the Budget used the terms "home" and "house" and their derivations interchangeably with the term "principal residence." * * *

The legislative history demonstrates that Congress intended the term "principal residence" to mean the primary dwelling or house that a taxpayer occupied as his principal residence. Nothing in the legislative history indicates that Congress intended section 121 to exclude gain on the sale of property that does not include a house or other structure used by the taxpayer as his principal place of abode. Although a principal residence may include land surrounding the dwelling, the legislative history supports a conclusion that Congress intended the section 121 exclusion to apply only if the dwelling the taxpayer sells was actually used as his principal residence for the period required by section 121(a).

[The court goes on to discuss the Treasury Regulations promulgated under § 121's predecessor, those under § 1034 (prior to its repeal), and case law interpreting § 1034. The court concludes that those sources support the notion that to reap to benefits of the prior exclusions, a taxpayer selling a dwelling must have actually used it as a principal residence.]

Former section 1034 required that a taxpayer sell "property * * * used by the taxpayer as his principal residence" in order to qualify for deferral. In 1997, when Congress amended section 121 and repealed section 1034, * * * Congress continued to use the wording of former section 1034 to describe the type of property that qualified for exclusion treatment under section 121(a) if sold — "property * * * used by the taxpayer as the taxpayer's principal residence." Congress did not give any indication in the legislative history of section 121 that it intended that wording to have a meaning for the purpose of section 121 different from the meaning it had been accorded under former section 1034; nor did Congress state that it disagreed with the interpretation of that wording in cases that had interpreted former section 1034. We infer from the consistent use of the phrase "property * * * used by the taxpayer as his principal residence" in former section 1034 and in section 121 as amended by Congress in 1997 that Congress intended the comparable wording in the two sections to be interpreted comparably.

Although we recognize that petitioners would have satisfied the requirements under section 121 had they sold or exchanged the original house instead of tearing it down, we must apply the statute as written by Congress. Rules of statutory construction require that we narrowly construe exclusions from income. Under section 121(a) and its legislative history, we cannot conclude on the facts of this case that petitioners sold their principal residence. Accordingly, we hold that petitioners may not exclude from income under section 121(a) the gain realized on the sale of the Summit Road property.

H: It was not their "principal" residence

[The court addressed the penalty issue and concluded that the taxpayer's failure to file a timely return warranted the imposition of the penalties imposed by the Commissioner.]

We have considered all the other arguments made by the parties, and to the extent not discussed above, conclude those arguments are irrelevant, moot, or without merit.

To reflect the foregoing,

Decision will be entered for respondent.

Reviewed by the Court.

COLVIN, COHEN, GALE, THORNTON, WHERRY, GUSTAFSON, PARIS, and MORRISON, JJ., agree with this majority opinion.

COHEN, J., concurring:

I agree with the majority and write to explain my disagreement with the dissent.

The dissent argues that the holding of the majority is inconsistent with the remedial purpose of section 121. This Court's assigned task in the first instance, however, is to apply section 121 as written to the facts of this case. Section 121 requires that we examine the sale or exchange of property and provides that if the property sold was owned and used by the taxpayer as the taxpayer's principal residence for at least 2 of the 5 years preceding the sale or exchange, the taxpayer qualifies for the exclusion under section 121(a).

The focal point of the section 121 analysis is the property sold or exchanged. In this case the property sold consisted of land that petitioners had used for the required period (old land) and a new dwelling in which petitioners had never resided (new house). After concluding that the term "principal residence" means the dwelling (and associated land) in which a taxpayer resided as his or her primary home, the majority examined the facts to see whether what petitioners sold qualified as a principal residence within the meaning of section 121(a).

The fully stipulated facts reveal that the dwelling petitioners sold was not used as their principal residence for the required 2–year period. Petitioners demolished their former principal residence and built a new, much larger house that they never occupied. The facts are decisive and support the holding of the majority.

The dissent maintains that, because petitioners owned and used their former principal residence (old house, now demolished, and old land) for the required 2–year period, the property that they sold (new house and old land) qualifies for the exclusion. The dissent argues that this result is consistent with Congress' intention to liberalize the exclusion rules in 1997 when it amended section 121. However, the dissent ignores the fact that the term " principal residence" has been consistently used by Congress since 1951, and there is no evidence in the legislative history of the Taxpayer Relief Act of 1997 (TRA 1997) * * * to indicate that Congress intended to change the meaning of the term "principal residence" sub silentio when it amended section 121. * * *

The majority's holding is consistent with caselaw that has developed under the predecessor provisions of section 121, most particularly former section 1034. The cases examine the dwelling to decide whether the property sold was used as the tax-payer's principal residence. If a taxpayer sold a dwelling that the taxpayer used as a principal residence, the taxpayer qualified for the deferral provided by former section 1034 if the other requirements of section 1034 (such as the timely purchase of a qual-ifying replacement property) were met. If a taxpayer sold some part of the underlying land but not the dwelling that the taxpayer used as a principal residence, the taxpayer could not defer the recognition of gain on the sale because the taxpayer did not sell his or her principal residence. If a taxpayer sold his or her principal residence with part but not all of the underlying land and then sold the rest of the land close to the time of the sale of the principal residence, at least one court has held that the sales must be integrated in deciding whether the gain on the sale of land could be deferred. * * *

If petitioners had sold their old home instead of demolishing it, they would have qualified for the section 121 exclusion. That is not what they did. They demolished the old home, constructed a new and larger dwelling, and then sold the new dwelling without occupying it for the required 2–year period. The dissent objects to the result and argues that the majority's analysis in this case will distort the result in other cases in which the taxpayer should qualify for the section 121 exclusion. The response to this argument is straightforward — it is not this Court's job to anticipate and decide cases that are not yet before it. As the Supreme Court cautioned in *Dewsnup v. Timm,* 502 U.S. 410, 416–417 [(1992)]:

> Hypothetical applications that come to mind and those advanced at oral argument illustrate the difficulty of interpreting the statute in a single opinion that would apply to all possible fact situations. We therefore focus upon the case before us and allow other facts to await their legal resolution on another day.

We have often stated that we "must decide the case in the light of what was done, not what might have been done." The majority properly limits its analysis to the facts of this case, which were fully stipulated, and to the issues raised by the parties. Petition-ers did not argue for a partial exclusion of gain attributable to the sale of the land, nor did petitioners introduce any evidence that would have permitted the Court to allocate gain between the new house and the land. Petitioners argued only that they were entitled to the full exclusion under section 121. As the majority holds, the prop-erty sold, i.e., the dwelling and related land, must have actually been used as peti-tioners' principal residence for the required 2–year period. Because the new house petitioners sold was never used as their principal residence, the section 121 exclusion does not apply here. We may reach a different conclusion in cases involving different facts if and when the opportunity arises, but we should not distort the result in this case by anticipating those cases.

GALE, THORNTON, MARVEL, WHERRY, GUSTAFSON, and PARIS, JJ., agree with this concurring opinion.

HALPERN, J., dissenting:

There is adequate ground for the majority's conclusion that, to qualify for the section 121 exclusion, the taxpayer must sell not only the land on which her principal residence is located but also the principal residence itself. Nevertheless, I think that there is also adequate ground for concluding that petitioners' sale of the new house qualified for that exclusion.

INTERPRETATION CONTRARY TO THE REMEDIAL INTENT OF SECTION 121(A)

The gain exclusion rule of section 121(a) applies if three conditions are met: (1) There must be a sale or exchange (without distinction, sale); (2) the sale must be of "property* * * owned and used by the taxpayer as the taxpayer's principal residence" (the property use condition), and (3) the property use condition must be satisfied for 2 out of the 5 years ending on the date of sale of the property (the temporal condition). The majority focuses on the second condition (the property use condition) and interprets the condition as being satisfied only if the property sold constitutes, at least in part, "a house or other structure used by the taxpayer as his principal place of abode." * * * The majority does not rely on the text of the statute for that interpretation (which text it concludes is ambiguous) but looks to a report of the Committee on Ways and Means, House of Representatives [and other legislative history of the Taxpayer Relief Act of 1997] explaining the committee's reasons for recommending an amendment to section 121. [The dissent concludes that the legislative history relied on by the majority] provides insufficient grounds to conclude "that Congress intended the section 121 exclusion to apply only if the dwelling the taxpayer sells was *actually used as his principal residence* for the period required by section 121(a)."

While the majority is correct that the Supreme Court has said that exclusions from income are to be narrowly construed, * * * the Supreme Court has also said that, if the meaning of a tax provision liberalizing the law from motives of public policy is doubtful, then it should not be narrowly construed * * * .

With that latter rule of construction in mind, consider a taxpayer whose longtime home is demolished by a natural disaster (a hurricane). The taxpayer lacks insurance. Nevertheless, she rebuilds on the same land (perhaps a bit further from the ocean) and lives in the rebuilt house for 18 months, and then she sells the house and land at a gain. Although the taxpayer satisfies the property use condition, I assume that, nevertheless, under the majority's analysis, she gets no exclusion because she fails the temporal condition; i.e., she has not lived in the rebuilt house for 2 or more of the last 5 years. I assume further that, if her house had been only damaged (and not demolished), and she repaired it, she would get an exclusion. That seems like an untenable distinction to me.[2]

[handwritten margin note: I: At what point does a remodel become a new house?]

DIFFICULT INTERPRETATIVE QUESTIONS

The majority's interpretation of the property use condition naturally suggests that there is some recognizable difference between remodeling a house and demolishing and rebuilding the house. I assume the majority does not mean to suggest that any remodeling of a home (1) terminates the use of that home as the taxpayer's principal residence and (2) resets the temporal clock to zero time elapsed. If not, then is there some level of remodeling that does (1) terminate the use of the home as the taxpayer's principal residence and (2) set the temporal clock to zero? What about a taxpayer who, wanting a bigger house, demolishes the old house (but not the foundation) and constructs a larger (taller) house using the old foundation? Is that remodeling or rebuilding? What about keeping part of the foundation, and expanding horizontally? If that is remodeling, then there may be an easy way for the Court to reach a similar result in the case before us. The parties have stipulated an exhibit, a blueprint, that shows footprints of both the old and the new house. I have examined the exhibit, and the footprints overlap. Might we not conclude that part of the foundation of the old house was incorporated into the new, thus making the case a remodeling case and not a rebuilding case?

The majority's report will undoubtedly raise the kind of remodeling versus rebuilding questions that I have raised. I think that the better course would be to avoid provoking those questions.

DISPOSITION OF HOUSE FOLLOWED BY SALE OF LAND

[Relevant prior cases and interpretive regulations] confirm that, if the principal residence consists of both land and improvements, both a prior sale of the improvements and part of the land and a subsequent sale of the remaining land can qualify under section 121(a). * * *

CONCLUSION

I would treat the demolition and reconstruction of petitioners' house no differently from a renovation. * * *

WELLS, GOEKE, KROUPA, and HOLMES, JJ., agree with this dissent.

Post-Case Follow-Up

Although the court in *Gates* acknowledges that the taxpayers would have been able to take advantage of § 121 had they simply sold their old residence, they ultimately concluded that § 121 was not available under the circumstances because the taxpayers had not used the residence they sold as their principal residence, notwithstanding that the new home was built on the old home site. Calling on relevant legislative history, they surmised that in referring to property and principal residence, Congress meant to refer to a *dwelling* actually used by the taxpayers. The court acknowledged that a disposition of a dwelling might well involve a contemporaneous disposition of related land but refused to accept the notion that Congress meant to allow exclusion of gain from the sale of a residence that the taxpayers never lived in, even if constructed on the very same land upon which the old dwelling had been situated.

Calling on legislative history, regulations, and other sources, the majority in *Gates* hewed a path as close as possible to the letter of § 121, but those in dissent appear to embrace an approach in which the spirit of the provision (or, more literally, Congress's general intent to offer taxpayers relief) should rule the day. To be sure, it seems unduly harsh to strip the taxpayers of the exclusion after they had satisfied the statutory prerequisites, but at the same time, it is unlikely that Congress contemplated granting a $500,000 exclusion with respect to a residence the taxpayers never spent a night in. Should we interpret § 121 as a hard and inflexible rule or as a provision setting forth an overarching standard which, if satisfied, should afford taxpayers relief, notwithstanding failure to fit neatly within the rule's parameters? For scholarly commentary on this perspective, see Abreu, Alice G. and Greenstein, Richard K., *The Rule of Law as Law of Standards: Interpreting the Internal Revenue Code*, 64 Duke L. J. Online 53 (2015). Also, consider the following questions: Even if we view § 121 as a set of standards, can we confidently conclude that the taxpayers satisfied the standard? Did they do something so extraordinary that they ran afoul of even the standards, wholly aside from stepping outside the bounds of the rule? Also, do we swing open the doors of potential abuse if we start interpreting Code provisions as mere standards and not as firm rules of general applicability about which taxpayers have fair warning? Can we rest comfortably with unblinking and strict adherence to the rules as set forth, even though such application would violate the spirit of the provision? Tax law, we shall see, commands that substance take precedence over mere form.

Gates v. Commissioner: Real Life Applications

1. Franklin and Mina purchased a home for $800,000 on March 30, 2010, and they have used it since then as their principal residence. They are particularly fond of the fact that the home sits on 10 acres of land, has an elegant, tree-lined driveway, and boasts several fruit-bearing trees. Assume that they sell the home (and surrounding land) for $1,250,000 on December 31, 2018. How much of the gain, if any, must they include in gross income in connection with this transaction?

2. Ida and Morgan purchased a farm in the countryside for $700,000 on July 1, 2000. The farm included both a house and contiguous land, most of which is used in their farming business. The house alone had a fair market value of $325,000, and they have used it as a principal residence at all times since purchase. If they sell the farm (house plus land) for $900,000 on July 1, 2018, how much, if any, of the gain must they include in gross income, assuming that the house alone had appreciated in value to $500,000?

Special Rules Under § 121: Deemed Ownership and Use

As was mentioned earlier, several special rules apply in the § 121 context, many of them involving spouses and former spouses. You'll recall that for a married couple filing a joint return to enjoy the $500,000 exclusion, they must satisfy the requirements of § 121(b)(2)(A). What happens if they do not satisfy the requirements? Under § 121(b)(2)(B), the couple will qualify for the sum of exclusion amounts they would be entitled to if they were viewed as unmarried individuals, and that approach might well make at least one of them eligible for the $250,000 exclusion. What if, in that context, one spouse could easily satisfy the use requirement but, technically, the home was owned by the other spouse during the entire period? Section 121(b)(2)(B) dictates that for this specific purpose, *each* spouse will be treated as owning the property during any period in which *either* spouse owned the property. Interestingly enough, you will also find similar deemed ownership or deemed use rules under § 121(d)(3) to make the appropriate exclusion available to those receiving property transferred to them from a spouse (or former spouse) and to those whose spouse gets use of the principal residence pursuant to a divorce or separation instrument. Thus, for example, a wife may receive the home she used as a principal residence in the wake of a divorce, and she would benefit from deemed ownership of the house if it was technically owned solely by the husband during the entire marriage. Similarly, if the wife is given sole use of the home (but not ownership) for a limited time after the divorce, the husband will benefit from deemed use during the period in which, technically, only the wife used the residence.

Special Rules Under § 121: Death of a Spouse

If a couple satisfied the requirements of § 121(b)(2)(A) immediately before the death of one spouse, should the surviving spouse automatically lose the ability to take advantage of the $500,000 exclusion amount? Given the harshness of cutting the available exclusion in half, Congress provides for some measure of relief. Under the circumstances contemplated, a surviving spouse (if unmarried) can still take advantage of the $500,000 exclusion amount if the sale or exchange occurs within two years of the death of the deceased spouse. *See* § 121(b)(4).

Special Rules Under § 121: Partial Exclusion Available in Certain Circumstances

The decision to sell a principal residence often comes after serious and careful deliberation, and taxpayers who intend to take advantage of § 121's exclusionary grace can generally plan ahead. In some instances, however, taxpayers find that they must dispose of their current principal residence primarily due to a change in employment, as a result of health-related events, or in the wake of unforeseen circumstances. When these events unfold before the taxpayer has owned and used the relevant dwelling for at least two years prior to the date of sale (or within two years of the taxpayer excluding gain under § 121 in a separate transaction), the Code provides for an exclusion equal to a portion of the amount that would otherwise be available to the taxpayer. To see the relevant provisions in operation, let's start with a simple example.

Example 1

Assume that the taxpayer, Malvolio, purchased and moved into his principal residence on January 1, 2017. Months later, a change in employment made it necessary for him to sell the residence, and he did so on January 1, 2018. Had Malvolio been able to own and use the property as his principal residence for 24 months, he would have been entitled to exclude up to $250,000 of any gain realized. Because he only owned and used the property as his principal residence for 12 months, his maximum exclusion amount is exactly half of $250,000 (i.e., $125,000). We arrive at this figure by multiplying the standard exclusion amount of $250,000 by a fraction which in this instance is 12/24; he was able to own and use the property as his principal residence for 12 of the 24 months necessary to qualify him for a full $250,000 exclusion. In essence, Malvolio qualifies for an exclusion that is directly proportional to the extent to which he satisfied the standard 24-month requirement. *See* § 121(c).

In *Example 1*, the taxpayer multiplied the standard exclusion amount by a fraction, the numerator of which was 12, and the denominator of which was 24. We used 12 as the numerator because the taxpayer owned and used the dwelling as his principal residence for 12 months. It is possible, in some circumstances, that we would do the relevant calculation not by reference solely to the number of months the taxpayer owned and used his dwelling as a principal residence (Option A)[1] but, instead, by using the number of months the taxpayer owned and used the dwelling as a principal residence *after* he took advantage of § 121 with respect to *another* principal residence (Option B). The Code dictates that we choose between Option A or Option B, *whichever period is shorter*. *See* § 121(c)(1)(B)(i). Let's clarify the rule by looking at the next example.

"Unforeseen Circumstances"

In PLR 201628002, the IRS ruled that "unforeseen circumstances" included a wife becoming pregnant and delivering a second child. The couple planned to sell a two-bedroom condominium in which they had lived with their first child. Although the regulations contemplate *multiple* births resulting from the same pregnancy as, per se, an unforeseen circumstance, the taxpayers were wise in seeking a private ruling. The Treasury Regulations give the Commissioner authority to issue rulings sensitive to a taxpayer's unique circumstances. *See* Treas. Reg. § 1.121-3(e)(3).

Credit: Beeboys/Shutterstock.com.

---

[1]Although § 121(c)(1)(B)(i)(I) makes reference to "owned and used," the Treasury Regulations interpreting this provision effectively treat this language as "owned or used." *See* Treas. Reg. § 1.121-3(g)(1) ("The numerator of the fraction is the shortest of the period of time that the taxpayer owned the property during the 5-year period ending on the date of the sale or exchange; the period of time that the taxpayer used the property as the taxpayer's principal residence during the 5-year period ending on the date of the sale or exchange; or the period of time between the date of a prior sale or exchange of property for which the taxpayer excluded gain under section 121 and the date of the current sale or exchange."). Under this interpretation of the statute, the numerator could be one of three numbers. The text adheres to the statutory language of § 121(c)(1)(B)(i)(I) while hereby noting the potential for a given taxpayer to be able to rely solely on use of the property as a principal residence. *See, e.g.,* Treas. Reg. § 1.121-3(g)(2)(Example 2); *see also* § 121(d)(1).

Example 2

Marshall owned Residence #1 for several years. He recently put Residence #1 on the market and proceeded to purchase and move into Residence #2 on November 1, 2016. A few months later, on February 1, 2017, Marshall sold Residence #1 at a profit and took full advantage of the § 121 exclusion. Weeks later, however, a change in employment made it necessary for Marshall to sell Residence #2, and he did so on January 1, 2018. Marshall owned and used Residence #2 as his principal residence for 14 months. But he took advantage of § 121 with respect to Residence #1 a mere 11 months before selling Residence #2. In calculating Marshall's exclusion amount, we will multiply $250,000 by a fraction. Section 121(c)(1)(B) requires that we choose the smaller of 14 or 11 as the numerator for our fraction. Accordingly, we will measure Marshall's exclusion amount by multiplying $250,000 by 11/24. The resulting figure is $114,583.

One might be inclined to think that § 121(c)'s significance is quite limited because homes rarely appreciate so rapidly over a two-year period that they test § 121's limits. But taxpayers occasionally receive homes by gift from living donors. You will learn in the next chapter that, as a donee, the taxpayer must take a basis in the residence equal to their donor's basis. If the donee thereafter finds himself moving for one of the reasons set forth in § 121(c)(2)(B), the ability to exclude substantial amounts of gain becomes quite valuable.

Other Special Rules Under § 121

In the § 121 context, keep the following in mind:

- If a taxpayer has a small amount of built-in gain with respect to one eligible property and a substantial amount of built-in gain with respect to another eligible property, the taxpayer may elect to prevent the application of § 121 with respect to a sale or exchange of the former property and thereby save its benefits for a sale or exchange involving the latter property. *See* § 121(f).
- Congress recently added an anti-abuse provision to § 121. Thus, if a taxpayer owned a given property for several years without using it as a principal residence and hopes to reap the benefits of § 121 by using the property as a principal residence for two years immediately prior to sale, the taxpayer will run into § 121(b)(5). The longer the taxpayer owned the property without using it as a principal residence, the lower the § 121 exclusion amount available to him will be. The provision currently has limited impact because periods of nonqualified use prior to January 1, 2009, are not taken into account. *See* § 121(b)(5)(C)(i). Of course, this anti-abuse provision's impact will grow over time.

Chapter Summary

- A taxpayer may recover basis in an asset tax-free. Amounts received in excess of basis (or, as the case may be, adjusted basis) constitute realized gain.

- Initial annuity payments generally include a tax-free recovery of basis and a taxable disbursement of investment income. The taxpayer calculates the tax-free portion by using an exclusion ratio and must include 100 percent of annuity payments in gross income after full, tax-free recovery of their investment in the contract.

- Assuming taxpayers satisfy certain requirements regarding the ownership and use of a principal residence, they may exclude up to $250,000 of gain on the sale or exchange of the property. Married taxpayers filing jointly in the year of the sale or exchange may exclude up to $500,000 under the appropriate circumstances.

- Special rules under § 121 apply to those who are who are separated or divorced and may result in deemed ownership or deemed use by a spouse. There are also special rules enabling certain surviving spouses to benefit from the $500,000 exclusion.

- Taxpayers may use the exclusion under § 121 no more than once every two years.

- Treasury Regulations promulgated under § 121 clarify that the term "residence" includes houses as well as certain dwellings not affixed to land.

- Treasury Regulations promulgated under § 121 clarify that short, temporary absences do not reduce the number of days of taxpayer use of the property as a principal residence, and the two-year requirement may be satisfied by non-consecutive periods (e.g., years, months, weeks, or days).

- Taxpayers may qualify for a partial § 121 exclusion if they dispose of a residence due to changes of employment, health, or unforeseen circumstances. *See* § 121(c); *see also* Treas. Reg. § 1.121-3.

Applying the Rules

1. Cody recently purchased 1,000 shares of the stock of Oil Company, Inc. for $80,000. Today, he sold those shares for $82,000. How much of his amount realized must he include in gross income?

2. Karen recently took a job as an associate in a large law firm that had recently relocated to posh, new office space. While attending cocktail party hosted by the firm, she struck up a conversation with Stephen, the general counsel of one of the firm's clients. Karen offered to give Stephen a tour of the new offices. Being somewhat inebriated, Stephen managed to spill most of his champagne on a brand new computer that had cost the firm $1,400 and had been in service for no more than a week; the computer was a total loss. If Stephen promptly reimburses the firm $1,400 for destroying the computer, how much, if any, must the firm include in gross income as a result of the incident?

3. James recently retired after teaching at a local university for 50 years. He just received an annuity payment of $2,000. Assume that James's investment in the contract was $800,000 and that his expected return is $1,000,000.

    a. How much, if any, of his $2,000 payment may he exclude from gross income?

    b. How would the answer change if the expected return was $1,600,000?

4. Coltrane purchased his first home on January 1, 2001, and used it as his principal residence until December 31, 2014, at which point he decided to move in with his girlfriend. Although he continued to own his former home immediately thereafter, he rented it out to others until December 31, 2018, at which point he sold it. Coltrane's basis in the home was $300,000, and he sold it for $560,000. How much, if any, of his gain may he exclude from gross income under § 121?

5. Bernie and Bertha purchased their first home on May 1, 1998, for $85,000, and they both used it as their principal residence from then until May 12, 2018. On that date, Bertha passed away quietly in her sleep. Bernie promptly remarried on March 8, 2019, and sold his old home on May 30 of the same year for $525,000. He then moved into the home of his new wife. How much, if any, of the gain from the sale of the old residence must Bernie include in his gross income?

Federal Income Taxation in Practice

1. Jeanne purchased her first home for $100,000 on August 10, 1998, and has used it as her principal residence since then. For medical reasons, she was recently moved to a nursing home, although she continued to own her former residence. Her son would like to have Jeanne sell the home and use the proceeds for her care, but he is concerned about the tax ramifications. If Jeanne has lived at the nursing home for two years, what will be the tax ramifications of a sale of the old home?

2. You are working on an annuity contract matter with a partner in your firm. Although he is familiar with the workings of § 72, he cannot recall how one actually ascertains the expected return for a life annuity. He asks that you conduct some preliminary research and send him an e-mail communicating what you have found.

3. Early this afternoon, you received a phone call from one of the senior attorneys in your personal injury law firm. She has a question concerning § 104 and § 72. She explains her recollection that under § 104 a person receiving damages on account of physical injury may exclude the amount from gross income, even if the amount is received as part of a settlement. One of the firm's clients is due to receive an immediate annuity as compensation for a physical injury, and the investment in the contract will be $1.5 million, with the expected return including that plus interest, etc. She would like to know whether each annuity payment will be received 100 percent tax-free per § 104 or whether any interest or

investment income rolled into the payments must be included in gross income per § 72. She would like to know first if there are any Code provisions, Treasury Regulations, or IRS pronouncements directly addressing this issue, and she will talk with you further regarding future steps, depending on what you find.

Categorical Exclusions: Items Received by Gift, Bequest, Devise, or Inheritance

Although many taxpayers will find themselves able to exclude gain from the sale of a principal residence or to recover their bases tax-free on the sale or disposition of property, almost all taxpayers will find themselves excluding the fair market value of items received by gift, bequest, devise, or inheritance from their gross income. The governing statutory rules appear simple enough on their face, but as we will soon see, the tax dust does not settle immediately on completion of the relevant transfer. Congress may have made an exclusion available, but taxpayers often have to clear hurdles to qualify for its benefits, and as one might well anticipate, collateral tax consequences generally flow from each exclusion event. Given the appeal, significance, and prevalence of these exclusions, you should aim to achieve thorough understanding of the governing law.

A. PROPERTY RECEIVED BY GIFT

1. In General

If a taxpayer receives a gift, the fair market value of the gift is excluded from the taxpayer's gross income under § 102(a), even if the gift is very expensive. Thus, birthday gifts, holiday gifts, engagement rings, wedding presents, gifts for no special

Key Concepts

- Exclusion of fair market value of items received by gift, bequest, devise, or inheritance
- Treatment of income from gifts and gifts of income
- Donee basis in gifts, including gifts with built-in gain or built-in loss in the hands of the donor
- Basis of property received by bequest, devise, or inheritance
- Impact of return of gift to the donor (or the donor's spouse) under certain circumstances

occasion, and the like are simply not included in a taxpayer's gross income. A rule requiring the inclusion of the fair market value of gifts in taxpayer gross income would tend to chill the making of gratuitous transfers, and Congress has no reason to discourage the giving of gifts. Besides, even if Congress sought to tax those receiving gifts, the IRS would encounter considerable administrative difficulty in confirming compliance with governing law. Add to that the fact that many taxpayers would probably resist the IRS's efforts, largely by ignoring the law and hoping that their conscious omissions would escape detection. At the same time, Congress does not want individuals to receive compensation, kickbacks, or other forms of income without paying the appropriate taxes merely because the parties have cast the exchange as a mere "gift" of property from one person to another.

Special Note

Although the recipient of an expensive gift may exclude its fair market value from gross income, the donor may face what we refer to as a "gift" tax. If you take the course in Estate and Gift Taxation, you will learn a great deal more about the gift tax. For now, simply keep in mind that as of 2018, a donor will trigger a gift tax obligation to the extent they transfer more than $15,000 (per donee) by gift during a given tax year; the dollar threshold tends to ease administrative burdens. Note that there are exceptions (e.g., gifts to spouses and gifts to pay certain educational or medical expenses of the donee). Note also that Congress does not seek to discourage gifts (inadvertently) by taxing donors; it's more about making sure taxpayers can't circumvent the estate tax via lifetime gift transfers.

Case Preview

Commissioner v. Duberstein

Section 102 of the Internal Revenue Code refers to "gifts" but does not set forth a statutory definition of the term, nor, for that matter, do the governing Treasury Regulations. How, then, is one to determine whether a given transfer will qualify as a "gift" for federal income tax purposes? A donor may think of the transfer as a gift, while the donee may see it as long overdue compensation, albeit nontraditional in form. What about the impact of prior (or ongoing) business or personal relationships? If a taxpayer claims that property was received as a gift and the IRS disagrees, how is a decision maker to resolve the dispute? In the next case, the U.S. Supreme Court gives us somewhat of a basic standard to be used in determining whether a specific transfer of property constitutes a "gift" for federal income tax purposes. As you read *Commissioner v. Duberstein*, focus on the following questions:

1. What is the articulated standard to be used in future cases?
2. In applying the standard, should a court look to the intent of the donor or the understanding of the donee?
3. Does the standard require an objective assessment or one that is subjective?
4. Does the word "gift" have a special meaning in the tax arena?

Commissioner v. Duberstein
363 U.S. 278 (1960)

Mr. Justice BRENNAN delivered the opinion of the Court.

These two cases concern the provision of the Internal Revenue Code which excludes from the gross income of an income taxpayer "the value of property acquired by gift." They pose the frequently recurrent question whether a specific transfer to a taxpayer in fact amounted to a "gift" to him within the meaning of the statute. * * *

Commissioner v. Duberstein. The taxpayer, Duberstein, was president of the Duberstein Iron & Metal Company, a corporation with headquarters in Dayton, Ohio. For some years the taxpayer's company had done business with Mohawk Metal Corporation, whose headquarters were in New York City. The president of Mohawk was one Berman. The taxpayer and Berman had generally used the telephone to transact their companies' business with each other, which consisted of buying and selling metals. The taxpayer testified, without elaboration, that he knew Berman "personally" and had known him for about seven years. From time to time in their telephone conversations, Berman would ask Duberstein whether the latter knew of potential customers for some of Mohawk's products in which Duberstein's company itself was not interested. Duberstein provided the names of potential customers for

Justice William J. Brennan, Jr.

Justice Brennan served on the U.S. Supreme Court from 1956 to 1990. He was appointed to the Court by President Dwight D. Eisenhower.

Credit: Photo courtesy of the Library of Congress.

these items. One day in 1951 Berman telephoned Duberstein and said that the information Duberstein had given him had proved so helpful that he wanted to give the latter a present. Duberstein stated that Berman owed him nothing. Berman said that he had a Cadillac as a gift for Duberstein, and that the latter should send to New York for it; Berman insisted that Duberstein accept the car, and the latter finally did so, protesting however that he had not intended to be compensated for the information. At the time Duberstein already had a Cadillac and an Oldsmobile, and felt that he did not need another car. Duberstein testified that he did not think Berman would have sent him the Cadillac if he had not furnished him with information about the customers. It appeared that Mohawk later deducted the value of the Cadillac as a business expense on its corporate income tax return. Duberstein did not include the value of the Cadillac in gross income for 1951, deeming it a gift. The Commissioner asserted a deficiency for the car's value against him, and in proceedings to review the deficiency the Tax Court affirmed the Commissioner's determination. It said that "The record is significantly barren of evidence revealing any intention on the part of the payor to make a gift. * * * The only justifiable inference is that the automobile was intended by the payor to be remuneration for services rendered to it by Duberstein." The Court of Appeals for the Sixth Circuit reversed. * * * [B]ecause of the importance of the question in the administration of the income tax laws, we granted certiorari . . . .

[Discussion of *Stanton v. United States* omitted.]

The exclusion of property acquired by gift from gross income under the federal income tax laws was made in the first income tax statute passed under the authority of the Sixteenth Amendment, and has been a feature of the income tax statutes ever since. The meaning of the term "gift" as applied to particular transfers has always been a matter of contention. Specific and illuminating legislative history on the point does not appear to exist. Analogies and inferences drawn from other revenue provisions, such as the estate and gift taxes, are dubious. The meaning of the statutory term has been shaped largely by the decisional law. With this, we turn to the contentions made by the Government in these cases. * * *

First. The Government suggests that we promulgate a new "test" in this area to serve as a standard to be applied by the lower courts and by the Tax Court in dealing with the numerous cases that arise. We reject this invitation. We are of opinion that the governing principles are necessarily general and have already been spelled out in the opinions of this Court, and that the problem is one which, under the present statutory framework, does not lend itself to any more definitive statement that would produce a talisman for the solution of concrete cases. The cases at bar are fair examples of the settings in which the problem usually arises. They present situations in which payments have been made in a context with business overtones — an employer making a payment to a retiring employee; a businessman giving something of value to another businessman who has been of advantage to him in his business. In this context, we review the law as established by the prior cases here.

The course of decision here makes it plain that the statute does not use the term "gift" in the common-law sense, but in a more colloquial sense. This Court has indicated that a voluntarily executed transfer of his property by one to another, without any consideration or compensation therefor, though a common-law gift, is not necessarily a "gift" within the meaning of the statute. For the Court has shown that the mere absence of a legal or moral obligation to make such a payment does not establish that it is a gift. And, importantly, if the payment proceeds primarily from "the constraining force of any moral or legal duty," or from "the incentive of anticipated benefit" of an economic nature, it is not a gift. * * * A gift in the statutory sense, on the other hand, proceeds from a "detached and disinterested generosity," [or] "out of affection, respect, admiration, charity or like impulses." And in this regard, the most critical consideration, as the Court was agreed in the leading case here, is the transferor's "intention." "What controls is the intention with which payment, however voluntary, has been made." The Government says that this "intention" of the transferor cannot mean what the cases on the common law concept of gift call "donative intent." With that we are in agreement, for our decisions fully support this. Moreover, the *Bogardus* case itself makes it plain that the donor's characterization of his action is not determinative — that there must be an objective inquiry as to whether what is called a gift amounts to it in reality. It scarcely needs adding that the parties' expectations or hopes as to the tax treatment of their conduct in themselves have nothing to do with the matter. * * * We take it that the proper criterion, established by decision here, is one that inquires what the basic reason for his conduct was in fact — the dominant reason that explains his action in making the transfer. Further than that we do not think it profitable to go. * * *

The conclusion whether a transfer amounts to a "gift" is one that must be reached on consideration of all the factors. * * * Decision of the issue presented in these cases must be based ultimately on the application of the fact-finding tribunal's experience with the mainsprings of human conduct to the totality of the facts of each case. The nontechnical nature of the statutory standard, the close relationship of it to the data of practical human experience, and the multiplicity of relevant factual elements, with their various combinations, creating the necessity of ascribing the proper force to each, confirm us in our conclusion that primary weight in this area must be given to the conclusions of the trier of fact. This conclusion may not satisfy an academic desire for tidiness, symmetry and precision in this area, any more than a system based on the determinations of various fact-finders ordinarily does. But we see it as implicit in the present statutory treatment of the exclusion for gifts, and in the variety of forums in which federal income tax cases can be tried. If there is fear of undue uncertainty or overmuch litigation, Congress may make more precise its treatment of the matter by singling out certain factors and making them determinative of the matters, as it has done in one field of the "gift" exclusion's former application, that of prizes and awards. * * * A majority of the Court is in accord with the principles just outlined. And, applying them to the *Duberstein* case, we are in agreement, on the evidence we have set forth, that it cannot be said that the conclusion of the Tax Court was "clearly erroneous." It seems to us plain that as trier of the facts it was warranted in concluding that despite the characterization of the transfer of the Cadillac by the parties and the absence of any obligation, even of a moral nature, to make it, it was at bottom a recompense for Duberstein's past services, or an inducement for him to be of further service in the future. We cannot say with the Court of Appeals that such a conclusion was "mere suspicion" on the Tax Court's part. To us it appears based in the sort of informed experience with human affairs that fact-finding tribunals should bring to this task. * * * Accordingly, * * * the judgment of the Court of Appeals is reversed . . . .

It is so ordered.

[Concurring and dissenting opinions omitted.]

Post-Case Follow-Up

Duberstein is landmark precedent in the tax arena. In the decision, the Court held that a given transfer will constitute a "gift" for federal income tax purposes only if it was made out of "detached and disinterested generosity" [or] "out of affection, respect, admiration, charity or like impulses" and not due to moral/legal duty or anticipated economic benefit. The Court also emphasized that the subjective or expressed intent of the donor is not controlling. Rather, a decision maker must call on his or her human experience and undertake an objective assessment of the donor's intent in ascertaining the donor's true motives. The Court readily concedes that the standard articulated will likely frustrate "an academic desire for tidiness, symmetry and precision," but perhaps the Court should not be so hard on itself. Unlike ascertaining whether a taxpayer received property by bequest, devise, or inheritance, ascertaining whether a taxpayer received a "gift" may, of necessity, require that finders of fact be given leeway to explore and develop an appreciation of relevant facts and circumstances and to measure them against their familiarity with the norms of human conduct if they are to reach a sound, well-informed decision.

Commissioner v. Duberstein: Real Life Applications

1. After many trials and tribulations, Eli finally graduated from college. His parents were very proud of him and decided to buy him a new car to celebrate the occasion.

    a. Will Eli be required to include the fair market value of the car in his gross income?

    b. Assume that at the same time his parents also pay off his student loans by writing a check directly to the relevant bank. Is that a "gift"? (And do you remember why Eli will not have income from the discharge of indebtedness?)

2. Mather and Dana have been married for 23 years. Although Mather still loves his wife dearly, he recently started dating Serena, a hot young model partial to the company of very wealthy, married men. As an expression of his ongoing affection and budding love, Mather buys Serena an expensive fur coat. Will Serena be allowed to exclude the value of the coat from her gross income? For an analysis of this issue with additional colorful facts, see *United States v. Harris*, 942 F.2d 1125 (7th Cir. 1991).

3. Michael and his friends have always enjoyed a good steak. In fact, they are regulars at The Executive Grille, a fancy steak house near an upscale mall. Assume that Michael and his friends go to the steak house, enjoy dinner, and leave their waiter a $75 tip. Given the size of their party, the tip was wholly optional.

    a. Should the waiter treat the tip as a mere gift for federal income tax purposes?

    b. Does or should it matter whether state law allows the restaurant to pay waiters less than minimum wage on the assumption that waiters will earn tips?

Case Preview

Goodwin v. United States

Although the decision in *Duberstein* established a governing standard, application of that standard is not always a straightforward matter. How, for example, should one objectively assess the intent of a donor when the donee receives property not from one individual but from a group of individuals? The court in *Goodwin v. United States* tackled this issue.

As you read *Goodwin v. United States*, focus on the following questions:

1. Can one objectively ascertain the intent of a group?
2. Can an employer ever make a "gift" to an employee?
3. Should the fact that a given transfer is optional have an impact on whether a given transfer flows from detached and disinterested generosity?
4. If a given donor truly loves and admires a donee, will transfers from the donor to the donee presumably constitute gifts?

GOODWIN v. UNITED STATES
67 F.3d 149 (8th Cir. 1995)

LOKEN, Circuit Judge.

The Reverend and Mrs. Lloyd L. Goodwin appeal the denial of a refund of income taxes they paid on substantial payments received from members of Reverend Goodwin's congregation. The district court upheld the Commissioner of Internal Revenue's decision that the payments were taxable income, not excludable gifts. We reject the government's proposed standard for resolving this question but nonetheless affirm the district court's decision. * * *

When Reverend Goodwin became pastor of the Gospel Assembly Church in Des Moines, Iowa (the "Church"), in 1963, it had a modest congregation of twenty-five members. Under Goodwin's stewardship, the congregation has grown to nearly four hundred persons. During the three tax years at issue, 1987 through

[handwritten margin notes: Payment at issue; P's: It was income, not gift; H: Wrong standard but agrees it was income]

Extraordinary "Tips"

How should extraordinary tips be treated? Even if one generally thinks of tips as compensation for services rendered (and thus fully includable in income), should one dismiss the possibility that some gifts may be tips in form but largely gifts in substance? Such would certainly appear to have been the case when a Pizza Hut waitress in Angola, Indiana, received a $10,000 "tip" from a very generous customer. *See* http://abcnews.go.com/GMA/OnlyinAmerica/story?id=3374034.

Credit: El Nariz/Shutterstock.com.

1989, Goodwin's annual salary from the Church was $7,800, $14,566, and $16,835; he also received a Church parsonage valued at $6,000 per year. The Goodwins reported these amounts on their joint income tax returns.

[margin note: At issue: Anon. cash payments paid to the tax payers via a procedure]

In 1966, members of the Church congregation began making "gifts" to the Goodwins, initially at Christmas and later on three "special occasion" days each year. At first, the contributors purchased items such as furniture and works of art. But after five years, they began to give cash. By 1987, the congregation had developed a regular procedure for making special occasion gifts. Approximately two weeks before each special occasion day, the associate pastor announced — before Church services, when the Goodwins were not present — that those who wish to contribute to the special occasion gift may do so. Only cash was accepted to preserve anonymity. Contributors placed the cash in envelopes and gave it to the associate pastor or a Church deacon. The associate pastor then gathered the cash and delivered it to the Goodwins.

[margin note: Not reported as income]

The Church did not keep a record of the amount given nor who contributed to each gift. The Goodwins did not report the special occasion gifts as taxable income.

For the tax years 1987–1989, the Commissioner estimated that the Goodwins received $15,000 in "special occasion gifts" each year. The Commissioner assessed deficiencies for the 1987–1989 tax years based upon the estimated unreported special occasion gifts.

[margin note: Eventually paid deficiencies and so this is a refund proceeding]

The Goodwins paid the deficiencies and filed this refund suit in district court, requesting a jury trial. The parties filed cross-motions for summary judgment and a lengthy stipulation that included the following agreed facts:

33. There is no formal written policy or requirement that anyone contribute to the "special occasion gift."

34. No Church member is counseled to give, or encouraged to give specific amounts.

38. All members of the Church deposed or interviewed maintain that the "special occasion gifts" are gifts given to the [Goodwins] out of love, respect, admiration and like impulses and are not given out of any sense of obligation or any sense of fear that [Reverend Goodwin] will leave their parish if he is not compensated beyond his yearly salary.

42. Church members who were deposed or interviewed ... did not deduct the money they gave the [Goodwins] as a charitable contribution to the Church.

47. The Church trustees, who set [Goodwin's] annual compensation, will testify that they do not know the amount of the "special occasion gifts" received and do not consider those "gifts" in setting his annual compensation.

[margin note: Lower court H: It was income]

The district court granted summary judgment in favor of the government, concluding that the special occasion gifts are taxable income to the Goodwins. However, because the parties stipulated and the district court found that the payments totaled $12,750 in 1987, $14,500 in 1988, and $15,000 in 1989, rather than $15,000 each year, as the Commissioner had estimated, the court ordered the government to redetermine the Goodwins' tax liability for 1987 and 1988 and to refund what they had overpaid. The court's order concluded: "Upon payment of the refund of income tax and statutory interest due [the Goodwins], the parties shall execute and file a Satisfaction of Judgment in this matter."

The Goodwins appeal, supported by a brief *amicus curiae* from The Rutherford Institute. They present two related arguments, that the undisputed evidence of the individual Church members' donative intent proves that the special occasion gifts are not taxable income to the Goodwins, and alternatively that summary judgment was improperly granted because donative intent is a question of fact for the jury.

Taxpayer's arg on appeal

* * *

Congress has defined "gross income" broadly in the Internal Revenue Code: "Except as otherwise provided in this subtitle, gross income means all income from whatever source derived." 26 U.S.C. § 61(a). Therefore, unless the Goodwins can prove that the special occasion gifts fall within the statutory exclusion for gifts, these payments are taxable income.

The Code provides that "[g]ross income does not include the value of property acquired by gift, bequest, devise, or inheritance." 26 U.S.C. § 102(a). In the leading case of *Commissioner v. Duberstein,* the Supreme Court rejected the government's proposed "test" to distinguish gifts from taxable income. Instead, the Court adhered to its previous, fact-intensive approach to this recurring issue, explaining that "the problem is one which, under the present statutory framework, does not lend itself to any more definitive statement that would produce a talisman for the solution of concrete cases." The Court clarified, first, that "the statute does not use the term 'gift' in the common-law sense, but in a more colloquial sense"; second, that the transferor's intention is "the most critical consideration"; and third, that "there must be an objective inquiry" into the transferor's intent.

Prior case in book

Despite its lack of doctrinal success in *Duberstein,* the government urges that we adopt the following test to govern whether transfers from church members to their minister are gifts:

> The feelings of love, admiration and respect that professedly motivated the parishoners to participate in the special occasion offerings arose from and were directly attributable to the services that taxpayer performed for them as pastor of the church. Since the transfers were tied to the performance of services by taxpayer, they were, as a matter of law, compensation.

Gov't's arg

We reject that test as far too broad. For example, it would include as taxable income every twenty-dollar gift spontaneously given by a church member after an inspiring sermon, simply because the urge to give was "tied to" the minister's services. It would also include a departing church member's individual, unsolicited five-hundred-dollar gift to a long-tenured, highly respected priest, rabbi, or minister, a result that is totally at odds with the opinions of all nine Justices in *Bogardus v. Commissioner*:

Court rejects

> Has [the payment] been made with the intention that services rendered in the past shall be requited more completely, though full acquittance has been given? If so, it bears a tax. *Has it been made to show good will, esteem, or kindliness toward persons who happen to have served, but who are paid without thought to make requital for the service? If so, it is exempt.*

302 U.S. 34, 45 (1937) (Brandeis, J., dissenting from the Court's decision that unsolicited transfers by shareholders to former employees after a company was sold were

gifts) (emphasis added). We thus turn to the facts of this case, applying *Duberstein* 's objective, no-talisman approach to evaluating transferor intent.

Taxpayer's arg

Court rejects

The Goodwins argue that they must prevail as a matter of law, or at a minimum that the district court erred in granting summary judgment for the government, because it is stipulated that Church members made the special occasion gifts out of love, admiration, and respect, not out of a sense of obligation or fear that Goodwin might otherwise leave. We disagree.

From an objective perspective, the critical fact in this case is that the special occasion gifts were made by the congregation as a whole, rather than by individual Church members. The cash payments were gathered by congregation leaders in a routinized, highly structured program. Individual Church members contributed anonymously, and the regularly-scheduled payments were made to Reverend Goodwin on behalf of the entire congregation.

RE

Viewing the question of transferor intent from this perspective makes it clear that the payments were taxable income to the Goodwins. The congregation funds the Church, including Reverend Goodwin's salary. The special occasion gifts were substantial compared to Goodwin's annual salary. The congregation, collectively, knew that without these substantial, on-going cash payments, the Church likely could not retain the services of a popular and successful minister at the relatively low salary it was paying. In other words, the congregation knew that its special occasion gifts enabled the Church to pay a $15,000 salary for $30,000 worth of work. Regular, sizable payments made by persons to whom the taxpayer provides services are customarily regarded as a form of compensation and may therefore be treated as taxable income.

We also reject the Goodwins' contention that it was error to grant summary judgment on this issue. Although a transferor's objective intent is a fact question under *Duberstein,* summary judgment may nonetheless be appropriate. The stipulated facts of this case demonstrate that the congregation as a whole made special occasion gifts on account of Reverend Goodwin's ongoing services as pastor of the Church. Therefore, no reasonable jury could conclude that these payments were excludable from the Goodwins' taxable income, and summary judgment was appropriate.

The judgment of the district court is affirmed.

Post-Case Follow-Up

Despite the fact that members of the congregation of the Goodwin's church truly loved and admired them and were under no obligation to make special gift contributions, the court concluded that the transfers did not constitute gifts. The opinion underscores the importance of conducting an objective assessment of the prevailing facts and circumstances in ascertaining whether a given transfer constitutes a gift for federal income tax purposes. Under the facts of the case, one can readily understand the court's finding that the group's intent was largely compensatory, but the fact that a group acts in concert to transfer money or property to a specific individual does not always indicate compensatory intent. After all, groups of people often pool their money together to purchase someone a gift, and most of the time, the recipient rightly excludes the fair market value of the gift from their gross income. *Goodwin's* facts reflect more exception than rule.

Goodwin v. United States: Real Life Applications

1. Trajan is a secretary at Pierce, Davenport, & Franklin LLP. To celebrate Trajan's 30th birthday, his colleagues gathered contributions, signed a "Happy Birthday" card, purchased a small cake, and held a brief party for him, passing along the card and a gift purchased with the collected funds. Must Trajan include the fair market value of any of the items he received in his gross income? Please explain.

2. *Same facts as Question #1*, except that Trajan has worked at the firm for 40 years and receives a retirement award of a gold watch worth $5,000 from the law firm rather than a group gift from his colleagues. Will Trajan be able to exclude the value of the watch from his gross income?

3. Filius works for his father, Pater. According to available information, Filius earns a salary that is fully commensurate with his qualifications. If Pater gives Filius $500 during the holiday season, stating that it is a "gift," will Filius be required to include the $500 in his gross income?

One Nation Under God?

According to Pew Research Center data, "[a]mong all U.S. adults, college graduates are considerably less likely that those who have less education to say religion is 'very important' in their lives. . . . ." *See* Pew Research Center, *In America, Does More Education Equal Less Religion?* (April 26, 2017).

Credit: Chris Thompson/ www.shutterstock.com.

Case Preview

Yang v. Commissioner

Family members and intimate familiars ordinarily fall within the ambit of one's natural gift-giving bounty. It is equally true, however, that family members and intimate familiars might rarely, if ever, exchange gifts, even though one regularly pays the other compensation in connection with the collaborative operation of a business venture. Parents operating a business they plan to pass on to their children have special incentive to employ them as a means of grooming them for future responsibilities, but is it necessary (for the sake of tax clarity) that the parent institute a gift-giving ban during the child's employment? That approach hardly seems rational. At the same time, however, we should not allow family members to disguise year-end bonuses and the like as holiday gifts. Nor, for that matter, should we allow what most would consider a gift to morph into "compensation" just because the parties involved have had a falling out and the payor/donor seeks to impose a tax liability on the payee/donee. In *Yang v. Commissioner*, the Tax Court was called on to intervene in a domestic matter and decide whether a given series of transfers between boyfriend and girlfriend constituted compensation (as He said) or gifts (as She said).

As you read *Yang v. Commissioner*, choose a side and consider the following questions:

1. Are transfers of property between intimate familiars presumably gifts?
2. Did the court give any weight to records explicitly indicating that a given transfer constituted "salary" or "wages"?
3. Does the court's experience with the norms of human conduct assist it in conducting the *Duberstein* analysis?

Yang v. Commissioner
T.C. Summ. Op. 2008-156

GERBER, Judge.

* * * Respondent determined a $9,423 deficiency in Federal income tax and a $1,183 accuracy-related penalty under section 6662(a) for petitioner's 2005 tax year. The deficiency determination was based on unreported income adjustments of $40,000 and $10,500. Petitioner conceded that the $40,000 amount was income, but she contends that the $10,500 amount was a gift and not taxable as income. The sole issue for our consideration is whether the $10,500 petitioner received during 2005 was a gift or income.

BACKGROUND

Petitioner, Jue–Ya Yang, resided in California at the time her petition was filed. Petitioner met Howard Shih through a mutual friend and they began dating. Mr. Shih earned his living as an artist and calligrapher. Eventually, petitioner's relationship with Mr. Shih became more intimate. She moved into his home, and they cohabited. Petitioner did some housekeeping and cooking, but she did not work for Mr. Shih under any form of written or oral contract for services. Petitioner did not have any skill or experience in connection with Mr. Shih's artistic endeavors. During 2005 Mr. Shih gave petitioner checks totaling $10,500 to use for herself. Mr. Shih reported to respondent by means of a Form 1099–MISC, Miscellaneous Income, that the $10,500 he paid to petitioner constituted wage income and, ostensibly, he deducted the payments for purposes of computing his income for 2005. Relying on Mr. Shih's filing of Form 1099–MISC, respondent determined that petitioner had received income of $10,500.

DISCUSSION

The conclusion that a transfer amounts to a "gift" is one that must be reached on consideration of all the factors and one that is left to the trier of facts. *Commissioner v. Duberstein,* 363 U.S. 278, 287–289 (1960). In *Duberstein,* the Supreme Court set forth the following principles that underlie the dichotomy between a gift and income:

> This Court has indicated that a voluntarily executed transfer of his property by one to another, without any consideration or compensation therefor, though a common law gift, is not necessarily a "gift" within the meaning of the statute. For the Court has shown that the mere absence of a legal or moral obligation to make such a payment does not establish that it is a gift. And, importantly, if the payment proceeds primarily from "the constraining force of any moral or legal duty," or from "the incentive of anticipated benefit" of an economic nature, it is not a gift. And, conversely, "[w]here the payment is in return for services rendered, it is irrelevant that the donor derives no economic benefit from it." A gift in the statutory sense, on the other hand, proceeds from a "detached and disinterested generosity," "out of affection, respect, admiration, charity or like impulses." And in this regard, the most critical consideration, as the Court was agreed in the leading case here, is the transferor's "intention." * * * *Id.* at 285–286 (citations and fn. refs. omitted).

Mr. Shih was romantically involved with Ms. Yang, and she moved into his home. There were discussions of a formal engagement, and their relationship was intimate. Mr. Shih testified at the trial and his testimony concerning his romantic relationship with Ms. Yang was evasive. Mr. Shih was called by respondent and testified on direct examination that Ms. Yang had performed services in his business in exchange for the payments made to her during 2005. On cross examination, however, after admitting that his relationship with Ms. Yang was more than a professional one, Mr. Shih could not recall taking her out on dates or any intimacy in their relationship, even though their relationship existed only a few years ago. It is obvious that Mr. Shih and Ms. Yang have conflicting interests in the outcome of this controversy and that their positions are diametrically opposed. Mr. Shih structured the payments to Ms. Yang so that they appeared to be wages. He issued a Form W–2, Wage and Tax Statement, and used the notation "salary" or "wages" on some of the checks used for payment. Ms. Yang, however, was forthright in her testimony and answered all questions whether or not they favored her position. On the other hand Mr. Shih professed to remember only those things that supported his position that the payments were income to Ms. Yang. We find his testimony to be evasive and untrue. The facts show that Mr. Shih made payments totaling $10,500 to Ms. Yang with "detached and disinterested generosity" out of his affection for her at the time of payment. We accordingly hold that the $10,500 in payments made during 2005 was a gift and not reportable as income.

Ms. Yang conceded $40,000 in unreported income for 2005, and respondent has carried his burden of production to establish that section 6662(a) applies with respect to that adjustment. Petitioner offered no evidence of reasonable cause with respect to her failure to report the $40,000 in income. Accordingly, we hold that petitioner is liable for an accuracy-related penalty under section 6662(a) with respect to the $40,000 adjustment. Because we have decided that the $10,500 was a gift and not taxable, we need not address the accuracy-related penalty on that adjustment. To reflect the foregoing and petitioner's concession, *Decision will be entered under Rule 155.*

Post-Case Follow-Up

In *Yang*, the court ultimately concludes that Mr. Shih gave Ms. Yang thousands of dollars as a series of gifts, and once again, the *Duberstein* Court's standard (and the directive that finders-of-fact call on their experience with human conduct in applying it) proves its worth. Or does it? One could read *Yang* as a truly disturbing opinion in that it casts a thin cloud over every transfer between intimate familiars who happen to work together and a thick storm cloud over transfers between "EX-intimate" familiars. Ms. Yang may have scored a legitimate victory in this case, but if a given taxpayer hopes to deduct *true* compensation paid to an intimate familiar and is meticulous about keeping accurate records and properly labeling payments, *Yang* may ultimately introduce an unnecessary complication. For additional commentary on the tax ramifications associated with the performance of gratuitous services in contexts involving personal relationships, see Allen D. Madison, *The Taxation of Gratuitous Services Gone Out of "Control,"* 45 U. Mem. L. Rev. 115 (2014) (analyzing the pervasiveness of gratuitous services in intimate relationships and associated tax ramifications).

Yang v. Commissioner: Real Life Applications

1. Mary owns and operates a mid-sized grocery store in a small town. She and Stewart have been dating for three years. As a result of a recent recession, Stewart lost his job, and Mary hired him to work as a secretary in the grocery store's business office. If Mary pays Stewart a salary that is on the high side of average for someone with his qualifications, will he be able to exclude any amounts from his gross income?

2. *Same facts as Question #1.* If Mary decides to take Stewart to Paris, France (nonbusiness travel) and covers all expenses, will Stewart be required to include the fair market value of what he receives (plane ticket, meals, hotel accommodations, etc.) in gross income?

3. Assume that Stewart and Mary decide to live together. Mary's mortgage payment is $3,000 per month, and she does not ask that Stewart pay any of it. Stewart also makes use of utilities and consumes the food that Mary buys for the household. Will Stewart be required to include any amounts in gross income as a result of living with Mary? Would the answer change if Mary allowed Stewart to live rent-free in a home that she would ordinarily rent to others?

2. Specific Rules Regarding Income from Gift Property or Gifts of Income

Up to this point, we have discussed the basic "detached and disinterested" generosity standard set forth in *Duberstein* and the general exclusion rule under § 102(a). We now address two important rules to be kept in mind in the gift context. First, under § 102(b)(1), the general exclusion rule does not apply to income from a gift. Thus, if Donor gives $5,000 to Donee and Donee puts the money in an interest-bearing checking account, Donee may not exclude the interest the bank pays him from gross income under the general exclusion rule of § 102(a). Congress's legislative grace goes only so far. If other taxpayers must generally include interest paid to them in gross income, so must those earning interest on gifts of cash deposited in a financial institution.

The second rule concerns transfers of income by gift, bequest, devise, or inheritance. Assume that Donor has two children (Child #1 and Child #2) and a house the Donor customarily rents out to various tenants. Assume further that Donor decides to transfer the house to Child #1 and the future rents to be collected from renting the house to Child #2. Although Child #1 may exclude the fair market value of the house from gross income under § 102(a), Child #2 cannot appeal to § 102(a). The gift to Child #2 is, itself, a gift of income. Per § 102(b)(2), Congress will not allow Child #2 to exclude the rents from income. The same result follows if the taxpayer receives a bequest or devise of income or if a taxpayer simply inherits an income stream.

[handwritten margin note: Cannot exclude a gift of income]

Before moving on to the next section, let me emphasize a fairly subtle but important point about the relationship between § 102(b) and the general exclusion rule of § 102(a). It's an important lesson in statutory construction. Section 102(b) does not itself require that certain amounts be included in income. Although § 61 may require that a given amount be included in gross income, section 102(b) does not go that far. If you focus rigidly on the language, it simply states that for the items mentioned in § 102(b)(1) and (2), the general exclusion rule of § 102(a) does not apply. If you are lucky enough to find some other provision that would exclude the amount, then you may exclude the amount under that provision, just not § 102(a). For example, if a person receives a house as a wedding gift, uses it as a principal residence for two years, and immediately disposes of it at a gain, the taxpayer may not appeal to § 102(a) to exclude the gain from their gross income (just because the house was a gift), but they *may* appeal to the § 121 exclusion. As you read and analyze various Internal Revenue Code provisions, be sure to avoid analytical leaps not supported by the wording of the statute. In construing tax and other statutes (but especially Code provisions), one must develop and harness the habit of treading very cautiously and very carefully.

3. Donee Basis in Gifts and Transfers by Gift of Unrealized Gain or Loss

We have previously discussed the tax consequences of selling or disposing of various forms of property. Assume that a taxpayer (Donor) purchases a single share of Apple, Inc. stock for $200 and that the fair market value of the stock has risen to $225. At this point, Donor begins to contemplate not the sale of the stock but the transfer of it by gift. We know that Donor holds the stock with a $200 basis. What will be Donee's basis in the stock after the gift transaction? It will be $200. If Donor transfers property with built-in gain, then Donee will take it with a basis equal to Donor's basis. Why so? If Donor had sold the stock for $225, Donor would have been forced to include $25 of gain in gross income. It seems fair and logical that if Donee gets the stock by gift and sells it for $225, then Donee should be required to include $25 of gain in his gross income. To ensure that this happens, Donee is required to "step into the shoes" of Donor with respect to basis in the stock. Section 1015(a) provides that "[i]f property was acquired by gift . . . the basis shall be the same as it would be in the hands of the donor . . . ." So, the rules are pretty straight-forward with respect to a transfer by gift of property with built-in gain. But what about property with built-in loss? The rules governing Donee basis in that context are slightly more complicated.

If the share of stock had fallen in value from $200 to $150 prior to the gift, Donor would have a built-in loss of $50 immediately prior to the gift. That's because Donor's basis was $200, and at the time of the gift, the fair market value of the stock was $150. If the share of stock is transferred by gift at that point, will Donee simply "step into the shoes" of Donor and take a basis in the share of $200? That might make sense, but there is a problem with that approach. Assume that Donor knows that Donee has a lot of income from various sources and wants to transfer built-in loss property to Donee so that Donee can benefit from selling the property at a loss (i.e., use the loss to offset stock transaction gains or perhaps some limited amount of Donee's other income). Allowing Donee to use the built-in loss wouldn't be fair. Donor should not be able to game the system by handing off tax losses to others. Here's how the Code deals with the situation. If Donee ultimately disposes of the stock for a dollar amount *less than* $150, then Donee will calculate loss by using a basis of $150 (i.e., the fair market value of the gift at the time Donee received it). Under § 1015(a), "if [Donor's] basis is greater than the fair market value of the property at the time of the gift, then for the purpose of deter-mining loss [by Donee,] the basis shall be such fair market value." What if there's a built-in loss at the time of the gift, but the stock rises in value and is then sold? The proper treatment will depend on the actual sale price received by Donee relative to Donor's original basis. If Donee ultimately sells the stock for an amount *higher than* $200, then Donee will calculate gain by using a basis of $200. In that situa-tion, Donee has stepped into the shoes of Donor. Thus, for a sale less than $150, we know what basis to use, and for sale higher than $200, we know what basis to use. But what about a sale for a dollar amount at or between $150 and $200? In that situation, there simply is no tax result. The transaction is ignored. Why? Maybe, from a tax policy perspective, such an approach best balances the interests of the taxpayer and the government. If there is a sale at $175, the government might rea-son that Donee's basis was $150 ($25 gain), and Donee might reason that the basis was $200 ($25 loss). Perhaps it just makes sense to ignore the transaction unless there's an undeniable gain in the hands of Donee (an amount realized higher than Donor's basis) or an undeniable loss in the hands of Donee (an amount realized lower than the property's fair market value at the time of the gift).

B. PROPERTY RECEIVED BY BEQUEST, DEVISE, OR INHERITANCE

1. In General

Although we have devoted much attention to transfers by gift, we must give due regard to the fact that section § 102(a) also excludes from gross income property received by bequest, devise, or inheritance. For heirs at

> **Key Statutory Provisions**
>
> ▪ **Internal Revenue Code**
> ▪ **§ 102(a)**
> ▪ **§ 1014(a)(1)**
> ▪ **§ 1014(b)(6)**
> ▪ **§ 1014(e)(1)**

least, death is not all that bad from a tax perspective. Before we take a closer look at rules generally applicable to property received by bequest, devise, or inheritance, we should pause to note that notwithstanding the apparent relevance of § 102 in some circumstances, a taxpayer cannot escape traditional gross income inclusion rules merely by orchestrating a conveyance of the income by will. In *Wolder v. Commissioner*, 493 F.2d 608 (2d Cir. 1974), for example, an attorney agreed to revise a client's will "for free" if she would bequeath various shares of corporate stock to him. Over the years, the lawyer revised the client's will several times, and true to her word, the client bequeathed the shares of stock to the attorney. Having failed to report the fair market value of the stock as income, the lawyer claimed that the stock was an excludable bequest. The court disagreed and held that the stock received constituted compensation for services rendered; as such, the value of the stock did not qualify for exclusion, notwithstanding the fact that the stock was transferred by will as a bequest. With that situational caveat in mind, let's turn to the rules that generally apply in this context.

We know from our study of § 102 that taxpayers may exclude from gross income the fair market value of property received by bequest, devise, or inheritance. Section 1014(a)(1) generally provides that "the basis of property in the hands of a person acquiring the property from a decedent or to whom the property passed from a decedent shall ... be the fair market value of the property at the date of the decedent's death ...." Thus, if the decedent held built-in gain property immediately before death, the recipient of the property will not step into the decedent's shoes with respect to basis. Rather, they will take that property with a basis equal to fair market value. Accordingly, if the decedent held a share of Apple, Inc. stock with a $200 basis and the stock had a fair market value of $225 at the time of the decedent's death, a person who inherits that share of stock will take it with a basis of $225. In tax parlance, the person is said to receive the stock with a "step-up" in basis to fair market value (i.e., a "stepped-up" basis). If the stock was only worth $150 on the date of the death of the decedent (i.e.,

Speed Bump

there was a built-in loss), a person inheriting the stock would take it with a "step-down" in basis to $150. Note that even if one favors such treatment of beneficiaries, the rule tends to provide at least one incentive for those holding appreciated property to maintain it and ultimately pass it along to their heirs with a stepped-up basis (i.e., a **lock-in effect**).

2. Special Issues

Basis in Community Property Received by Bequest, Devise, or Inheritance

One of the good things about the course in Federal Income Taxation is that it is not the course in Community Property. That having been said, we must pay modest attention to the fact that there are community property jurisdictions out there, and there are tax ramifications when a holder of community property "goes on to glory." In that context, the decedent's one-half share of the community property passes to the survivor, and as we learned previously, when a person receives property as a result of the death of a decedent, they take that property with a basis equal to its fair market value on the date of the death of the decedent. We know the survivor holds the decedent's one-half share with a basis equal to fair market value per § 1014(a)(1). But what about the survivor's own half share of the community property in that situation? Does she still hold it with an original cost basis? No. Under the facts given, the survivor will now hold her *own* half share of community property with a basis equal to its fair market value on the date of the death of the decedent. Thus, she will hold the entirety of such property with a basis equal to its fair market value as of the date of the death of the decedent. How do the Code provisions get us there? Under § 1014(a)(1), we know the survivor takes property received from a decedent with a basis equal to fair market. That rule addresses the decedent's one-half share; it literally passes from the decedent to the survivor. We have to turn to § 1014(b)(6) to get the step-up for the *survivor's* one-half share. Under that provision, several different items are *deemed* to have been received from a decedent for purposes of § 1014(a). There is a list, and we know that the items on the list will generally get the step-up in basis. On the list at § 1014(b)(6) is the *surviving* spouse's one-half share of community property (under the appropriate circumstances). That's why the surviving spouse's one-half share of community property generally gets the step-up in basis. Let's consider a simple example. Assume that Husband and Wife purchased a home (community property in the jurisdiction) for $50,000 and that it now has a fair market value of $700,000. Husband and Wife would each have an original cost basis of $25,000 in the home. If Wife passes away, Husband will receive Wife's one-half share of the community property (the house) as a result of her death and take a basis of $350,000 in that half share. Under § 1014(b)(6), he will be deemed to have received his own half share of the house as a result of his Wife's death. Thus, he will take *that* half share with a $350,000 basis. Accordingly, he will hold the entire house with a stepped-up basis of $700,000. And with that, we conclude our thankfully brief discussion of community property, at least for now.

Basis of Property Returned to Initial Donor of Appreciated Property After Death of Donee

Some of you may be thinking that this step-up in basis at death is a good thing. This reality is especially true, you reason, it you have property with a massive built-in gain and know someone who is terminally ill. Just pass it off to them as a "gift" and make sure you are the one who inherits it when they pass away. That way, you get your property back with a fair market value basis and can sell it immediately without realizing any gain. Right? Not exactly. First and foremost, your original transfer would not exactly be flowing from "detached and disinterested generosity." Something more like greed and cunning with more than a trace of callousness. But even if your initial transfer was, under different facts, a true gift, the timing of a return of that gift to you (or your spouse) as a result of the death of the donee matters. If a donor transfers appreciated property by gift to a donee who passes away within one year of the transfer with the result that the gift returns to (e.g., is inherited by) the original donor (or such donor's spouse), the donor (or his spouse) will be required to take a basis in the property equal to the basis of the donee (decedent). Of course, when the donee *originally* received the appreciated property, he took the donor's basis. At the end of the day, the original donor (or his spouse) will get the property back under those circumstances with a basis equal to the donor's basis at the time of the gift.

Chapter Summary

- In general, property received by gift, bequest, devise, or inheritance is excluded from a taxpayer's gross income. An "exclusion" from gross income does not enter a taxpayer's gross income calculations and does not appear on the taxpayer's federal income tax return.
- Per *Commissoner v. Duberstein*, a "gift" in the income tax sense is a transfer flowing from detached and disinterested generosity or out of affection, respect, admiration, charity, or like impulses. The objectively-ascertained intent of the donor is paramount.
- In general, a donee takes gift property with a basis equal to the donor's basis. If the property has a built-in loss at the time of the gift, then for purposes of calculating loss, the donee must use as her basis the fair market value of the gift as of the time of the receipt of the gift.
- Income from gift property is not excluded from gross income by § 102(a). Likewise, a gift *of* income (e.g., a stream of rents) is not excluded from gross income by § 102(a). In either instance, a provision other than § 102(a) may provide an exclusion (or require inclusion).
- The basis of property received by bequest, devise, or inheritance is the fair market value of the property on the date of the death of the decedent. Accordingly, there may be a step-up in basis or a step-down in basis.

▨ If spouses hold community property prior to the death of one of them, the surviving spouse is deemed to receive his own one-half share of the community property from the decedent. As a result, such survivor will hold the entire property with a basis equal to fair market value as of the date of the death of the decedent.

▨ If a donee dies within one year of receiving property (by gift) with built-in gain and the donor (or his spouse) succeeds to the property, then the donor (or his spouse) must take the decedent's basis in the property.

Applying the Rules

1. Darren purchased 100 shares of Blue, Inc. ("Blue") stock at $4 per share in 2000. This week, Darren transferred those shares of Blue stock to Samantha by gift at a time when the shares had a fair market value of $7 per share.

   a. Will Samantha be required to include any amount in income on receipt of the stock from Darren?

   b. What is Samantha's basis in the Blue stock?

   c. If Samantha sells the stock one year after receipt for $8 per share, what will be her amount realized? What about her gain realized? Her gain recognized?

   d. If Samantha sells the stock one year after receipt for $3 per share, what will be her amount realized? What about her loss realized? Her loss recognized?

2. Assume that Morgan purchased Greenacre in 2000 for $600,000. Recently, she transferred that land to Chase by gift at a time when the land had a fair market value of $400,000.

   a. Will Chase be required to include any amount in income on receipt of the land from Morgan?

   b. If Chase sells the land one year after receipt for $300,000, what will be his amount realized? What about his loss realized? His loss recognized?

   c. If Chase sells the land one year after receipt for $750,000, what will be his amount realized? What about his gain realized? His gain recognized?

   d. If Chase sells the land one year after receipt for $500,000, what will be the tax impact on him?

3. Franklin is an old man, but he has a very nice house and would prefer to live out the rest of his years there instead of moving to a nursing home. He promises James that if James will be his caretaker, he will leave the house to him in his will. If James does, in fact, take care of Franklin until Franklin passes away and James receives the home pursuant to Franklin's will, must James include any amount in his gross income as a result of receiving the house after Franklin's death?

4. Assume that Madison purchased Blackacre for $100,000 in 1989. In 2010, she transferred that property by gift to Cooper at a time when the property had a fair market value of $275,000. Cooper recently passed away, and Fenimore inherited the property from Cooper. At the time Fenimore inherited the property, it had a fair market value of $350,000. What was Cooper's basis in the property? What is Fenimore's basis in the property?

5. Assume that Madison and Cooper purchased Mansion (a house) as community property in 2000 for $800,000. Cooper passed away in 2015 at a time when Mansion had a fair market value of $1,000,000. What is Madison's basis in what had been Cooper's half share of Mansion? Why? What is Madison's basis in her half share of Mansion? Why?

6. Percy purchased an original drawing by Leonardo da Vinci for $25,000 in 1990. Assume that Percy transferred the property by gift to Shelly on January 1, 2015, when the property had a fair market value of $95,000. On September 5, 2015, Shelly passed away, and Percy inherited the drawing at a time when its fair market value was $100,000. What will be Percy's basis in the drawing?

Federal Income Taxation in Practice

1. Your law firm has offices in the following states: New York, California, Connecticut, Texas, Oregon, and Illinois. Find out which, if any, of these jurisdictions are community property jurisdictions.

2. One of the partners in your firm asks you to help him with a research question for one of the firm's clients. The partner recalls some of the basic rules under § 1014(a), but he cannot recall what happens when a person inherits the right to receive "income in respect of a decedent." He needs you to refresh his recollection via very brief e-mail. See what you can find.

3. You are a member of Congress, and you serve on the House Ways and Means Committee. The committee will be considering a number of items in the future, including the treatment of capital gains from the sale or exchange of inherited property. Review the material in Exhibit 5.1 from the Congressional Budget Office and prepare a one-page memorandum summarizing your thoughts and arguments.

EXHIBIT 5.1   **Excerpt from Congressional Budget Office, Options for Reducing the Deficit: 2017–2026 (Option 9: Basis of Inherited Assets)**

Revenues—Option 9

Change the Tax Treatment of Capital Gains From Sales of Inherited Assets

Billions of Dollars	2017	2018	2019	2020	2021	2022	2023	2024	2025	2026	Total 2017–2021	Total 2017–2026
Change in Revenues	0.6	4.2	5.2	6.0	6.8	7.5	8.2	8.9	9.8	10.9	22.8	68.0

Source: Staff of the Joint Committee on Taxation.

This option would take effect in January 2017.

When people sell an asset for more than the price at which they obtained it, they realize a net capital gain. That net gain is generally calculated as the sales price minus the asset's adjusted basis. The adjusted basis is generally the price of the asset at the time it was initially acquired plus the cost of any subsequent improvements and minus any deductions for depreciation. Net capital gains are included in taxable income in the year in which the sale occurs.

The tax treatment of capital gains resulting from the sale of inherited assets is different. Taxpayers who inherit assets generally use the asset's fair-market value at the time of the owner's death to determine their basis—often referred to as stepped-up basis—instead of the adjusted basis derived from the time the decedent initially acquired the asset. As a result, when the heir sells the asset, capital gains taxes are assessed only on the change in the asset's value that accrued after the owner's death. Any appreciation in value that occurred while the decedent owned the asset is not included in taxable income and therefore is not subject to capital gains taxation. (However, the estate may be subject to the estate tax.)

Under this option, taxpayers would generally adopt the adjusted basis of the decedent—known as carryover basis—on assets they inherit. As a result, the decedent's unrealized capital gains would be taxed at the heirs' tax rate when they eventually sell the assets. (For bequeathed assets that would be subject to both the estate tax and capital gains tax, this option would adjust the basis of some of those assets to minimize the extent to which both taxes would apply to the appreciation in value.) If implemented, this option would increase revenues by $68 billion from 2017 through 2026, the staff of the Joint Committee on Taxation estimates.

Under the option, most gains accrued between the date a person initially acquired the asset and the date of that person's death would eventually be taxed. As a result, the tax treatment of capital gains realized on the sale of inherited assets would be more similar to the tax treatment of capital gains from the sale of other assets.

One advantage of this approach is that it would encourage people to shift investments to more productive uses during their lifetimes, rather than retaining them so that their heirs could benefit from the tax advantages offered by the stepped-up basis. The option, however, would not completely eliminate the incentive to delay the sale of assets solely for the tax advantages. For an asset that rose in value before the owner's death, replacing stepped-up basis with carryover basis would increase the total amount of taxable capital gains realized when the asset is sold by the heir (unless the asset's value dropped after the owner's death by an amount equal to or greater than the appreciation that occurred while the owner was alive). As a result, heirs might choose to delay sales to defer capital gains taxes (as they might for assets they purchased themselves). An alternative approach would be to treat transfers of assets through bequest as a sale at the time of the transfer, making the capital gains taxable in that year. However, that method might force the owner to sell some portion of the assets at an inopportune time to pay the tax and could be particularly problematic for nonliquid assets.

Another advantage is that using carryover basis to determine capital gains would decrease the incentive for people to devote resources to tax planning rather than to more productive activities. For example, it would lessen the advantages of using certain tax shelters that allow people to borrow against their assets for current consumption and for the loan to be repaid after their death by using the proceeds from the sale of their assets.

Categorical Exclusions: Certain Damage Recoveries, Fringe Benefits, and Other Items

In this chapter, we round out our coverage of the major federal income tax exclusions, directing our focus to the rules governing personal injury recoveries, fringe benefits, death benefits, and tax-exempt interest. Those of you contemplating careers as personal injury attorneys or financial planning/wealth management experts should take special interest in this chapter. Inasmuch as these rules can have an impact after the resolution of a personal injury matter, a smart plaintiff's lawyer will consider tax ramifications of a client victory from the initial pleading stage forward. Likewise, those called on to assist clients with wealth management needs should have working knowledge of investment and quasi-investment options, especially those with particular appeal from a tax planning perspective. This chapter will also prove somewhat useful both to those who plan to develop expertise and advise clients with respect to fringe benefit matters and to those who simply enjoy taking advantage of as many tax-free fringe benefits as the law will allow.

Key Concepts

- Exclusion of non-punitive damages received on account of personal physical injury or physical sickness; special rules governing emotional distress damages
- Exclusion of meals and lodging provided for the convenience of the employer, no-additional-cost services, qualified employee discounts, working condition fringe benefits, and de minimis fringe benefits
- Treatment of cafeteria plan benefits
- Treatment of death benefits and the meaning of life insurance and insurable interest
- Exclusion of interest on state and local bonds and the meaning of arbitrage bond, private activity bond, and qualified bond

A. RECOVERIES FOR SPECIFIC PERSONAL INJURIES

1. Compensation for Physical Injury or Physical Sickness

In the classic cinematic thriller, *Misery*, Annie Wilkes (played by the inimitable Kathy Bates) rescues, rehabilitates, and then forcibly detains her all-time favorite author, Paul Sheldon (played by the acclaimed James Caan). Paul deeply appreciated the fact that Annie rescued him from certain death, but, understandably, he lacked enthusiasm for the notion of living the rest of his life on the Wilkes ranch as Annie's dearly, obsessively, beloved. He attempted escape, Annie found out, and punishment was assured and mercilessly swift. Indeed, Annie inflicted upon Paul many grievous, personal, physical injuries. Her tools? Well, let's just say that Annie's approach to the matter was imaginative yet practical. Bearing those facts in mind, let's consider a few tax-focused hypotheticals.

Assume that Paul somehow managed to escape Annie's clutches and succeeded in collecting damages from her as compensation for his injuries (both physical and mental). How, if at all, would Paul be taxed on those amounts under current federal tax law? If Paul has taken no medical expense deductions in prior years with respect to his injuries, he may exclude from gross income any (non-punitive) damages he receives on account of personal physical injuries or physical sickness. *See* § 104(a)(2). Be careful not to read the rule lightly and with excess sympathy for the victim. Paul recovered for both physical and mental injuries, but as a general matter, § 104(a)(2) only provides for the exclusion of damages received on account of personal *physical* injuries or *physical* sickness. Thus, the physical/mental distinction matters a great deal. Be careful, however, not to etch your mental rule for non-physical damages in stone just yet. Several special rules apply with respect to damages received on account of emotional distress, and we will take up those rules later in the chapter.

Case Preview

Amos v. Commissioner

In the aftermath of an actionable personal injury, the plaintiff may well contemplate damages of every form and flavor: compensatory, exemplary, punitive, etc. It is just as likely, however, that the plaintiff couldn't care less what label the damages are wearing when they are paid, so long as he ends up with a specific dollar amount as compensation for the harm itself and the attendant pain and suffering. Tax law is not so flexible. As *Amos v. Commissioner* makes abundantly clear, damage categorization matters. As you read the case, focus on the following questions:

1. Did the plaintiff receive damages solely "on account of" personal physical injuries?
2. If a settlement agreement does not allocate damage amounts to specific claims, what will determine the proper allocation for federal income tax purposes?
3. If the claim, though settled, is somewhat frivolous, will the tax law require inclusion of the damages received in gross income?

Amos v. Commissioner
86 T.C.M. 663 (2003)

CHIECHI, J.

Respondent determined a deficiency of $61,668 in petitioner's Federal income tax (tax) for 1997.

The only issue remaining for decision is whether the $200,000 settlement amount (settlement amount at issue) that petitioner received in 1997 in settlement of a claim is excludable under section 104(a)(2) from petitioner's gross income for that year. We hold that $120,000 is excludable and that $80,000 is not.

FINDINGS OF FACT

At the time petitioner filed the petition in this case, he resided in Minneapolis, Minnesota. During 1997, petitioner was employed as a television cameraman. In that capacity, on January 15, 1997, petitioner was operating a handheld camera during a basketball game between the Minnesota Timberwolves and the Chicago Bulls. At some point during that game, Dennis Keith Rodman (Mr. Rodman), who was playing for the Chicago Bulls, landed on a group of photographers, including petitioner, and twisted his ankle. Mr. Rodman then kicked petitioner. (We shall refer to the foregoing incident involving Mr. Rodman and petitioner as the incident.)

On January 15, 1997, shortly after the incident, petitioner was taken by ambulance for treatment at Hennepin County Medical Center. Petitioner informed the medical personnel at that medical center (Hennepin County medical personnel) that he had experienced shooting pain to his neck immediately after having been kicked in the groin, but that such pain was subsiding. The Hennepin County medical personnel observed that petitioner was able to walk, but that he was limping and complained of experiencing pain. The Hennepin County medical personnel did not observe any other obvious signs of trauma. Petitioner informed the Hennepin County medical personnel that he was currently taking pain medication for a preexisting back condition. The Hennepin County medical personnel offered additional pain medications to petitioner, but he refused those medications. After a dispute with the Hennepin County medical personnel concerning an unrelated medical issue, petitioner left Hennepin County Medical Center without having been discharged by them.

While petitioner was seeking treatment at Hennepin County Medical Center, he contacted Gale Pearson (Ms. Pearson) about representing him with respect to the incident. Ms. Pearson was an attorney who had experience in representing plaintiffs in personal injury lawsuits. After subsequent conversations and a meeting with petitioner, Ms. Pearson agreed to represent him with respect to the incident.

On January 15, 1997, after the incident and petitioner's visit to the Hennepin County Medical Center, petitioner filed a report (police report) with the Minneapolis Police Department. In the police report, petitioner claimed that Mr. Rodman had assaulted him.

On January 16, 1997, petitioner sought medical treatment at the Veterans Affairs (VA) Medical Center. The medical personnel at that medical center (VA medical personnel) took X-rays of petitioner's back. Petitioner complained to the VA medical personnel about his groin area, but he did not advise them that he was experiencing any symptoms related to that complaint. The VA medical personnel determined that there was no swelling of, but they were unable to ascertain whether there was bruising around, petitioner's groin area. The VA medical personnel gave petitioner some pain medication and told him to continue taking his other prescribed medications. The VA medical personnel prepared a report regarding petitioner's January 16, 1997 visit to the VA Medical Center. That report indicated that, except for certain disk problems that petitioner had since at least as early as February 14, 1995, "the vertebrae are intact and the remaining disk spaces are normal."

Very shortly after the incident on a date not disclosed by the record, Andrew Luger (Mr. Luger), an attorney representing Mr. Rodman with respect to the incident, contacted Ms. Pearson. Several discussions and a few meetings took place between Ms. Pearson and Mr. Luger. Petitioner accompanied Ms. Pearson to one of the meetings between her and Mr. Luger, at which time Mr. Luger noticed that petitioner was limping. Shortly after those discussions and meetings, petitioner and Mr. Rodman reached a settlement.

On January 21, 1997, Mr. Rodman and petitioner executed a document entitled "CONFIDENTIAL SETTLEMENT AGREEMENT AND RELEASE" (settlement agreement). The settlement agreement provided in pertinent part [as follows]:

> For and in consideration of TWO HUNDRED THOUSAND DOLLARS ($200,000), the mutual waiver of costs, attorneys' fees and legal expenses, if any, and other good and valuable consideration, the receipt and sufficiency of which is hereby acknowledged, Eugene Amos [petitioner], on behalf of himself, his agents, representatives, attorneys, assignees, heirs, executors and administrators, hereby releases and forever discharges Dennis Rodman, the Chicago Bulls, the National Basketball Association and all other persons, firms and corporations together with their subsidiaries, divisions and affiliates, past and present officers, directors, employees, insurers, agents, personal representatives and legal counsel, from any and all claims and causes of action of any type, known and unknown, upon and by reason of any damage, loss or injury which heretofore have been or heretoafter may be sustained by Amos arising, or which could have arisen, out of or in connection with an incident occurring between Rodman and Amos at a game between the Chicago Bulls and the Minnesota Timberwolves on January 15, 1997 during which Rodman allegedly kicked Amos ("the Incident"), including but not limited to any statements made after the Incident or subsequent conduct relating to the Incident by Amos, Rodman, the Chicago Bulls, the National Basketball Association, or any other person, firm or corporation, or any of their subsidiaries, divisions, affiliates, officers, directors, employees,

insurers, agents, personal representatives and legal counsel. This Agreement and Release includes, but is not limited to claims, demands, or actions arising under the common law and under any state, federal or local statute, ordinance, regulation or order, including claims known or unknown at this time, concerning any physical, mental or emotional injuries that may arise in the future allegedly resulting from the Incident.

It is further understood and agreed that the payment of the sum described herein is not to be construed as an admission of liability and is a compromise of a disputed claim. It is further understood that part of the consideration for this Agreement and Release includes an agreement that Rodman and Amos shall not at any time from the date of this Agreement and Release forward disparage or defame each other.

It is further understood and agreed that, as part of the consideration for this Agreement and Release, the terms of this Agreement and Release shall forever be kept confidential and not released to any news media personnel or representatives thereof or to any other person, entity, company, government agency, publication or judicial authority for any reason whatsoever except to the extent necessary to report the sum paid to appropriate taxing authorities or in response to any subpoena issued by a state or federal governmental agency or court of competent jurisdiction * * * Any court reviewing a subpoena concerning this Agreement and Release should be aware that part of the consideration for the Agreement and Release is the agreement of Amos and his attorneys not to testify regarding the existence of the Agreement and Release or any of its terms.

It is further understood and agreed that Amos and his representatives, agents, legal counsel or other advisers shall not, from the date of this Agreement and Release, disclose, disseminate, publicize or instigate or solicit any others to disclose, disseminate or publicize, any of the allegations or facts relating to the Incident, including but not limited to any allegations or facts or opinions relating to Amos' potential claims against Rodman or any allegations, facts or opinions relating to Rodman's conduct on the night of January 15, 1997 or thereafter concerning Amos. In this regard, Amos agrees not to make any further public statement relating to Rodman or the Incident or to grant any interviews relating to Rodman or the Incident. * * *

It is further understood and agreed that any material breach by Amos or his attorney, agent or representative of the terms of this Agreement and Release will result in immediate and irreparable damage to Rodman, and that the extent of such damage would be difficult, if not impossible, to ascertain. To discourage any breach of the terms of this Agreement and Release, and to compensate Rodman should any such breach occur, it is understood and agreed that Amos shall be liable for liquidated damages in the amount of TWO HUNDRED THOUSAND and No/100 Dollars ($200,000) in the event such a material breach occurs. Amos agrees that this sum constitutes a reasonable calculation of the damages Rodman would incur due to a material breach.

It is further understood and agreed, that, in the event Rodman or Amos claim a material breach of this Agreement and Release has occurred, either party may schedule a confidential hearing before an arbitrator of the American Arbitration Association for a final, binding determination as to whether a material breach has occurred. If, after the hearing, the arbitrator finds that Amos has committed a material breach, the arbitrator shall order that Amos pay the sum of $200,000 in liquidated damages to Rodman. * * *

Amos further represents, promises and agrees that no administrative charge or claim or legal action of any kind has been asserted by him or on his behalf in any way relating to the Incident with the exception of a statement given by Amos to the Minneapolis Police Department. Amos further represents, promises and agrees that, as part of the consideration for this Agreement and Release, he has communicated to the Minneapolis Police Department that he does not wish to pursue a criminal charge against Rodman, and that he has communicated that he will not cooperate in any criminal investigation concerning the Incident. Amos further represents, promises and agrees that he will not pursue any criminal action against Rodman concerning the Incident, that he will not cooperate should any such action or investigation ensue, and that he will not encourage, incite or solicit others to pursue a criminal investigation or charge against Rodman concerning the Incident.

Petitioner filed a tax return (return) for his taxable year 1997. In that return, petitioner excluded from his gross income the $200,000 that he received from Mr. Rodman under the settlement agreement.

In the notice that respondent issued to petitioner with respect to 1997, respondent determined that petitioner is not entitled to exclude from his gross income the settlement amount at issue.

OPINION

We must determine whether the settlement amount at issue may be excluded from petitioner's gross income for 1997. Petitioner bears the burden of proving that the determination in the notice to include the settlement amount at issue in petitioner's gross income is erroneous.

Section 61(a) provides the following sweeping definition of the term "gross income": "Except as otherwise provided in this subtitle, gross income means all income from whatever source derived". Not only is section 61(a) broad in its scope, * * * exclusions from gross income must be narrowly construed . . . .

Section 104(a)(2) on which petitioner relies provides that gross income does not include [the following]:

["](2) the amount of any damages (other than punitive damages) received (whether by suit or agreement and whether as lump sums or as periodic payments) on account of personal physical injuries or physical sickness;["]

The regulations under section 104(a)(2) restate the statutory language of that section and further provide [as follows]:

["]The term "damages received (whether by suit or agreement)" means an amount received (other than workmen's compensation) through prosecution of a legal suit or action based upon tort or tort type rights, or through a settlement agreement entered into in lieu of such prosecution.["] [Sec. 1.104–1(c), Income Tax Regs.]

[Editor's Note: Under current Treasury Regulations, "[t]he injury need not be defined as a tort under state or common law." Treas. Reg. § 1.104-1(c)(2).]

The Supreme Court summarized the requirements of section 104(a)(2) as follows:

["]In sum, the plain language of § 104(a)(2), the text of the applicable regulation, and our decision in *Burke* establish two independent requirements that a taxpayer must meet before a recovery may be excluded under § 104(a)(2). First, the taxpayer must demonstrate that the underlying cause of action giving rise to the recovery is "based upon tort or tort type rights"; and second, the taxpayer must show that the damages were received "on account of personal injuries or sickness." * * * [*Commissioner v. Schleier, supra* at 336–337.]["]

When the Supreme Court issued its opinion in *Commissioner v. Schleier, supra,* section 104(a)(2), as in effect for the year at issue in *Schleier,* required, inter alia, that, in order to be excluded from gross income, an amount of damages had to be received "on account of personal injuries or sickness." After the Supreme Court issued its opinion in *Schleier,* Congress amended (1996 amendment) section 104(a)(2), effective for amounts received after August 20, 1996, by adding the requirement that, in order to be excluded from gross income, any amounts received must be on account of personal injuries that are physical or sickness that is physical. Small Business Job Protection Act of 1996, Pub.L. 104–188, sec. 1605, 110 Stat. 1755, 1838–1839. The 1996 amendment does not otherwise change the requirements of section 104(a)(2) or the analysis set forth in *Commissioner v. Schleier, supra;* it imposes an additional requirement for an amount to qualify for exclusion from gross income under that section.

Where damages are received pursuant to a settlement agreement, such as is the case here, the nature of the claim that was the actual basis for settlement controls whether such damages are excludable under section 104(a)(2). The determination of the nature of the claim is factual. Where there is a settlement agreement, that determination is usually made by reference to it. If the settlement agreement lacks express language stating what the amount paid pursuant to that agreement was to settle, the intent of the payor is critical to that determination. Although the belief of the payee is relevant to that inquiry, the character of the settlement payment hinges ultimately on the dominant reason of the payor in making the payment. Whether the settlement payment is excludable from gross income under section 104(a)(2) depends on the nature and character of the claim asserted, and not upon the validity of that claim.

The dispute between the parties in the instant case relates to how much of the settlement amount at issue Mr. Rodman paid to petitioner on account of physical injuries. It is petitioner's position that the entire $200,000 settlement amount at issue is excludable from his gross income under section 104(a)(2). In support of that position, petitioner contends that Mr. Rodman paid him the entire amount on account of the physical injuries that he claimed he sustained as a result of the incident.

Respondent counters that, except for a nominal amount (i.e., $1), the settlement amount at issue is includable in petitioner's gross income. In support of that position, respondent contends that petitioner has failed to introduce any evidence regarding, and that Mr. Rodman was skeptical about, the extent of petitioner's physical injuries as a result of the incident. Consequently, according to respondent, the Court should infer that petitioner's physical injuries were minimal. In further support of respondent's position to include all but $1 of the settlement amount at issue in petitioner's gross income, respondent contends that, because the amount of any liquidated damages (i.e., $200,000) payable by petitioner to Mr. Rodman under the settlement agreement was equal to the settlement amount (i.e., $200,000) paid to petitioner under that agreement, Mr. Rodman did not intend to pay the settlement amount at issue in order to compensate petitioner for his physical injuries.

On the instant record, we reject respondent's position. With respect to respondent's contentions that petitioner has failed to introduce evidence regarding, and that Mr. Rodman was skeptical about, the extent of petitioner's physical injuries as a result of the incident, those contentions appear to ignore the well-established principle under section 104(a)(2) that it is the nature and character of the claim settled, and not its validity, that determines whether the settlement payment is excludable from gross income under section 104(a)(2). In any event, we find below that the record establishes that Mr. Rodman's dominant reason in paying the settlement amount at issue was petitioner's claimed physical injuries as a result of the incident.

With respect to respondent's contention that Mr. Rodman did not intend to pay the settlement amount at issue in order to compensate petitioner for his physical injuries because the amount of liquidated damages (i.e., $200,000) payable by petitioner to Mr. Rodman under the settlement agreement was equal to the settlement amount (i.e., $200,000) paid to petitioner under that agreement, we do not find the amount of liquidated damages payable under the settlement agreement to be determinative of the reason for which Mr. Rodman paid petitioner the settlement amount at issue.

On the record before us, we find that Mr. Rodman's dominant reason in paying the settlement amount at issue was to compensate petitioner for his claimed physical injuries relating to the incident. Our finding is supported by the settlement agreement, a declaration by Mr. Rodman (Mr. Rodman's declaration), and Ms. Pearson's testimony.

The settlement agreement expressly provided that Mr. Rodman's payment of the settlement amount at issue ["]releases and forever discharges * * * [Mr.] Rodman * * * from any and all claims and causes of action of any type, known and unknown, upon and by reason of any damage, loss or injury * * * sustained by Amos [petitioner] arising, or which could have arisen, out of or in connection with * * * [the incident].["]

Mr. Rodman stated in Mr. Rodman's declaration that he entered into the settlement agreement "to resolve any potential claims" and that the settlement agreement was intended to resolve petitioner's "claim without having to expend additional defense costs." The only potential claims of petitioner that are disclosed by the record are the potential claims that petitioner had for the physical injuries that he claimed he sustained as a result of the incident. Furthermore, Ms. Pearson testified that Mr. Rodman paid the entire settlement amount at issue to petitioner on account of his physical injuries. As discussed below, Ms. Pearson's testimony that Mr. Rodman paid that *entire* amount on account of petitioner's physical injuries is belied by the terms of the settlement agreement. Nonetheless, her testimony supports our finding that Mr. Rodman's dominant reason in paying petitioner the settlement amount at issue was to compensate him for claimed physical injuries relating to the incident.

We have found that Mr. Rodman's dominant reason in paying petitioner the settlement amount at issue was to compensate him for his claimed physical injuries relating to the incident. However, the settlement agreement expressly provided that Mr. Rodman paid petitioner a portion of the settlement amount at issue in return for petitioner's agreement not to: (1) Defame Mr. Rodman, (2) disclose the existence or the terms of the settlement agreement, (3) publicize facts relating to the incident, or (4) assist in any criminal prosecution against Mr. Rodman with respect to the incident (collectively, the nonphysical injury provisions).

The settlement agreement does not specify the portion of the settlement amount at issue that Mr. Rodman paid petitioner on account of his claimed physical injuries and the portion of such amount that Mr. Rodman paid petitioner on account of the nonphysical injury provisions in the settlement agreement. Nonetheless, based upon our review of the entire record before us, and bearing in mind that petitioner has the burden of proving the amount of the settlement amount at issue that Mr. Rodman paid him on account of physical injuries, we find that Mr. Rodman paid petitioner $120,000 of the settlement amount at issue on account of petitioner's claimed physical injuries and $80,000 of that amount on account of the nonphysical injury provisions in the settlement agreement. On that record, we further find that for the year at issue petitioner is entitled under section 104(a)(2) to exclude from his gross income $120,000 of the settlement amount at issue and is required under section 61(a) to include in his gross income $80,000 of that amount.

We have considered all of the contentions and arguments of respondent and of petitioner that are not discussed herein, and we find them to be without merit, irrelevant, and/or moot.

To reflect the foregoing and the concessions of the parties,

Decision will be entered under Rule 155.

Post-Case Follow-Up

In *Amos v. Commissioner*, the court concludes that whether a given damage amount qualifies for exclusion under § 104(a)(2) ultimately turns on the nature of the underlying claim. Settlement agreements usually indicate the nature of the claim, but in any event, as the court emphasized, ascertaining the fundamental nature of the claim is a factual matter. If the parties fail to allocate the settlement amount, the intent of the payor becomes critical.

Without any real explanation for its allocation, the Tax Court concludes that Amos may exclude $120,000 from his gross income but must include the remaining $80,000. Decisions like this make tax professionals shake their heads in despair. With a little tax-focused strategy, Amos's attorney might very well have gotten his client even more tax-free damages; a $175,000/$25,000 split would have been better to the tune of a few thousand taxpayer dollars. After all, a defendant who has agreed to pay over $200,000, probably doesn't care whether or how the settlement agreement slices it up, so long as the defendant is legally off the hook and the plaintiff agrees not to defame him. The plaintiff has strong incentive to have the damages categorized as compensation for physical injury, pain, suffering, and associated emotional distress. To be sure, the IRS is free to challenge an asserted allocation, and defending it may be difficult in some circumstances, but any good lawyer worth his salt should be able to come up with several reasons why a given dollar amount of damages largely (if not solely) compensates for physical injury. My guess is that if you can establish nerve damage (or bruising), you can probably get away with almost any allocation to "pain and suffering."

Amos v. Commissioner: Real Life Applications

1. While shopping for groceries at Fred's Mini-Mart, Elvia slipped on a thin layer of olive oil and fell; apparently, the person charged with cleaning up a recent spill failed to do a thorough job. Elvia suffered a fractured hip and a sprained wrist. Assume that Elvia and the grocery store settled the incident out of court for $100,000, allocating the entire dollar amount (per the agreement) to "compensatory damages" for personal physical injury.

   a. If the IRS accepts the allocation, will Elvia have to include any of this amount in her gross income?
   b. If the parties had not allocated the dollar amount and the IRS argued that a substantial percentage of the amount should have been included in gross income, how would a court go about ascertaining whether Elvia received any amounts on account of personal physical injury or physical sickness? Who would shoulder the burden of proof in that context?

2. After a fun-filled day shopping at the mall, Gary was driving home. While stopped at a red light, he noticed a small truck approaching from behind. Thanks to the truck driver's last-minute application of the brakes, Gary's vehicle was rear-ended with a very firm tap; there was noticeable damage to the rear bumper but nothing more. Gary immediately grabbed his neck and started complaining of possible whiplash. Subsequent medical examination revealed no definitive evidence of injury, but Gary continued to complain of neck pain. Gary and the driver of the truck eventually settled the matter. In exchange for executing a release for any personal injury claims, Gary received a payment of $10,000 from the truck driver. What additional information will you need to determine whether Gary will have to include any of his recovery in gross income?

---

2. Compensation for Emotional Distress

The basic general rule under § 104(a)(2) allows taxpayers to exclude from gross income non-punitive amounts received on account of personal physical injury or physical sickness. But what about emotional distress associated with the taxpayer's physical injury? For example, a person who purchases a negligently designed product and loses a leg when the product explodes may receive compensation from the manufacturer for the loss of the leg itself, the associated physical pain and suffering, and severe emotional distress resulting from the loss of the leg. Notwithstanding the "mental" character of the emotional distress and depression, Treasury Regulations promulgated under § 104 clarify that taxpayers may exclude from gross income amounts received with respect to emotional distress "attributable to a physical injury or physical sickness." See Treas. Reg. § 1.104-1(c)(1). It also bears noting, at this point, that § 104(a)(2) is also available to those demonstrably harmed in some way as a result of the physical injury or physical sickness of another. When the word "physical" was added to § 104, the legislative history explained that "damages (other than punitive damages) received by an individual on account of a claim for loss of consortium due to the physical injury or physical sickness of such individual's spouse are excluded from gross income. In addition, damages (other than punitive damages) received on account of a claim of wrongful death continue to be excluded from taxable income under present law." Note that in these situations, there is physical injury or physical sickness, but the injury or the sickness was actually suffered by someone other than the plaintiff suing for loss of consortium or wrongful death. Exclusion of such a plaintiff's damages is permitted because, technically, those damages are received "on account of personal physical injuries or physical sickness" — the statutory requirement for excluding damages (other than punitive damages) from gross income.

What about compensation solely for emotional distress unrelated to a physical injury or physical sickness (e.g., for outrageous conduct amounting to the intentional infliction of emotional distress)? Taxpayers receiving such amounts must generally include them in gross income, *but* there is a potential exception. Assuming a taxpayer has incurred medical expenses with respect to emotional distress (and has taken no deduction with respect to such expenses in prior years), damages compensating them for such expenses may be excluded from the taxpayer's gross income. *See* § 104(a) (last two sentences). The carve-out operates as a relief valve of sorts.

> **Tax Policy Perspectives**
>
> In *Devine v. Comm'r*, T.C. Memo. 2017-111, the Tax Court held that under § 104(a)(2), the taxpayer could not exclude from gross income settlement proceeds received on account of sexual harassment and gender discrimination because the funds were not received on account of physical injury or physical sickness. Even if you agree with the court's straightforward application of the statute, do you think Congress's approach is sound as a matter of tax policy? For commentary on whether taxpayers should be able to exclude specific non-physical damages from gross income as reparation for prior conduct, see Bobby L. Dexter, *The Hate Exclusion: Moral Tax Equity for Damages Received on Account of Race, Sex, or Sexual Orientation Discrimination*, 13 PITT. TAX REV. 197 (2016).

[handwritten annotation:] Pure emotional distress stemming from conduct = must include, except med expenses if no prior deductions

> ## Prior Year Medical Expense Deductions
>
> Under § 104, a taxpayer may not exclude a given amount of damages to the extent they took medical expense deductions with respect to the injury in *prior* taxable years. We have yet to study the deduction for medical expenses under § 213, but we will find that the Code provides for such a deduction (within limits) but only if the expense has *not* been compensated for by insurance or otherwise. Thus, a taxpayer might incur medical expenses in 2017 and deduct the relevant amount for that tax year because she received no compensation from her insurance company or otherwise during 2017. Section 104 makes clear that if she recovers for the injury in a subsequent taxable year, it will bar exclusion of the amount received to the extent the taxpayer took medical expense deductions in a prior taxable year. Section 104 thereby forecloses the possibility of "double dipping" (i.e., deducting an expense in one taxable year and excluding a related recovery in a subsequent taxable year). What about medical expenses incurred in the *same* taxable year of the recovery? If there is a medical expense and a compensatory recovery during the same taxable year, the taxpayer cannot deduct the amount under § 213 as an initial matter because the expense would have been compensated for either by insurance or otherwise. Section 104 handles exclusion of the recovery from gross income.

Responding to the Reality of Domestic Terrorism

Prior to its amendment by the Victims of Terrorism Tax Relief Act of 2001, P.L. 107-134, section 104 contemplated exclusionary relief for a limited class of victims with respect to disability income received as a result of injuries incurred in terrorist attacks, but its benefits were limited to attacks occurring outside the United States. Section 104(a)(5) read as follows:

(5) amounts received by an individual as disability income attributable to injuries incurred as a direct result of a violent attack which the Secretary of State determines to be a terrorist attack and which occurred while such individual was an employee of the United States engaged in the performance of his official duties outside the United States.

In the wake of the terrorist attacks occurring in the United States on September 11, 2001, section 104(a)(5) was amended to broaden its exclusionary scope. The statute now reads as follows:

(5) amounts received by an individual as disability income attributable to injuries incurred as a direct result of a terroristic or military action (as defined in section 692(c)(2)) . . .

Section 692(c)(2) generally defines "terroristic or military action" as follows:

(A) any terroristic activity which a preponderance of the evidence indicates was directed against the United States or any of its allies; and

(B) any military action involving the Armed Forces of the United States and resulting from violence or aggression against the United States or any of its allies (or threat thereof).

The Twin Towers of the World Trade Center prior to September 11, 2001.
Credit: Joseph Sohm/Shutterstock.com.

Lower Manhattan with One World Trade Center rising majestically to the historically symbolic height of 1776 feet.
Credit: Allard One/Shutterstock.com.

B. FRINGE BENEFITS AND OTHER ITEMS

Day after day, week after week, and month after month, the drudgery of work continues for those in the labor force. For a fortunate few, however, there is a very nice flip side to the world of work in the form of fringe benefits. The drive-through cashier working the evening shift at the local fast food restaurant gets free dinner and can claim whatever hamburgers, hot dogs, French fries, and the like that are left over at closing time. That person sitting next to you on your flight to Honolulu might have paid $0 for his seat, courtesy of the airline employing him as a baggage handler, and the sales clerk assisting you with garments probably enjoys an enviable discount when shopping in her employer's stores. You or some of your classmates may go to work for a firm that pays bar dues and shoulders the cost of

> **Key Statutory and Regulatory Provisions**
>
> - **Internal Revenue Code**
>   - § 119(a), (b)(1), & (b)(4)
>   - § 125(a) & (d)(1)
>   - § 132(a)–(e), (h), & (i)
> - **Treasury Regulations**
>   - § 1.119-1(a)(2) & (b)
>   - § 1.132-2(a) {except (a)(6)}
>   - § 1.132-4(a) {except (a)(2) & (3)}
>   - § 1.132-6(a) & (e)

continuing education activities for the attorneys who work there. Fringe benefits take many forms, and some of them have considerable dollar value. In fact, some potential employees ask about and consider the menu of fringe benefits that will be available to them if they ultimately get the job. That reality leads us to a fairly salient tax issue. Given that compensation can take many forms (e.g., cash, property, the free use of property, etc.), are fringe benefits merely a disguised form of compensation? If you're inclined to believe that they are, then what about the executive chef who enjoys free breakfast at a restaurant but only because her employer needs her there at 5:00 a.m. so that the restaurant can open promptly at 6:00 a.m.? Should the chef be including the fair market value of her breakfast in gross income, or should the tax law ignore her receipt of a free meal given that her employer's provision of breakfast to her is really just a means of facilitating the timely opening of the employer's business (and accommodation of the fact that the chef, like the rest of us, must eat breakfast at some point)? Maybe we can overlook the free breakfast (and other fringe benefits) as a matter of rational accommodation of common business practices. Chefs, waiters, and waitresses will get free meals from time to time. Flight attendants, ticket agents, and baggage handlers will get free flights, and standard employee discounts tend to boost worker morale. Attempts to tax fringe benefits might also present issues of administrability. Even though the IRS could easily verify the provision and cost of a free flight or the dollar amount of an employee discount, the IRS would encounter considerable administrative difficulty attempting to track every slice of pizza, hot cup of coffee, or doughnut an employee enjoys free of charge at the office over a 12-month period. There are simply bigger fish to fry. At the same time, Congress cannot allow the pendulum to swing too far in the other direction, lest the small fish turn out to be piranha on the public fisc. To some extent, Congress should accommodate common business practices and surrender to administrative practicalities, but at the same time, it must remain vigilant enough to detect compensation in sheep's clothing. The ground rules facilitate discernment in this regard and at the same time establish acceptable fringe benefit boundaries. In this section, we will look at specific rules under § 119 governing the provision of meals and lodging for the convenience of employers before turning to § 132, which addresses employee discounts, de minimis fringes (e.g., free coffee), and no-additional-cost services (e.g., free airline seats). We will then briefly discuss § 125 and "cafeteria plans," which give employees a choice between cash compensation and a specific tax-favored benefit.

1. Meals and Lodging Provided to Employees

In general, § 119(a) of the Code allows employees to exclude the value of meals and lodging provided by their employer to them, their spouses, or their dependents. These items must, however, be provided "for the convenience of the employer," and they must also satisfy additional Code-based and regulatory requirements. Before we explore the various requirement in detail, however, let's look at how courts dealt with the disguised compensation issue before Congress and the Treasury Department intervened.

Case Preview

Benaglia v. Commissioner

Those of you with broad cinematic exposure will likely recall *The Shining*, a horror classic in which Jack Torrance (Jack Nicholson), his wife Wendy (Shelley Duvall), and their son Danny (Danny Lloyd) spent the winter essentially trapped in the remote and isolated Overlook Hotel. As the winter caretaker, Jack (along with his family) enjoyed both free lodging and a huge stockpile of food sufficient to get them safely through the winter with three square meals a day. It's hard to argue that Jack's presence at the resort was not for the convenience of his employer (the resort owner), but what if the Overlook Hotel was not so isolated and Jack frequently took trips away from his winter post? Would it matter if, under the same facts, he openly negotiated the provision of meals and lodging before he would agree to take the position? The Board of Tax Appeals (which we now refer to as the Tax Court) had to grapple with a similar scenario back in the 1930s. As you make your way through *Benaglia v. Commissioner*, consider the following questions:

1. Did the hotel require Benaglia's around-the-clock presence on the property?
2. Did Benaglia negotiate for the meal and lodging benefits? If so, should that fact have an impact on whether the benefits constitute compensation?
3. Must an employer provide fringe benefits solely and exclusively for its benefit with no personal benefit passing to the employee in order for the employee to exclude the fair market value of the benefit from gross income?

Benaglia v. Commissioner
36 B.T.A. 838 (1937)

* * * The Commissioner determined a deficiency in the petitioners' joint income tax for 1933 of $856.68, and for 1934 of $1,001.61, and they contest the inclusion in gross income each year of the alleged fair market value of rooms and meals furnished by the husband's employer.

FINDINGS OF FACT

The petitioners are husband and wife, residing in Honolulu, Hawaii, where they filed joint income tax returns for 1933 and 1934. The petitioner has, since 1926 and including the tax years in question, been employed as the manager in full charge of the several hotels in Honolulu owned and operated by Hawaiian hotels, Ltd., a corporation of Hawaii, consisting of the Royal Hawaiian, the Moana and bungalows, and the Waialae Golf Club. These are large resort hotels, operating on the American plan. Petitioner was constantly on duty, and, for the proper performance of his duties and entirely for the convenience of his employer, he and his wife occupied a suite of *Benefit* rooms in the Royal Hawaiian Hotel and received their meals at and from the hotel.

Petitioner's salary has varied in different years, being in one year $25,000. In 1933 it was $9,625, and in 1934 it was $11,041.67. These amounts were fixed without reference to his meals and lodging, and neither petitioner nor his employer ever regarded the meals and lodging as part of his compensation or accounted for them.

OPINION

STERNHAGEN, J.

The Commissioner has added $7,845 each year to the petitioner's gross income as "compensation received from Hawaiian Hotels, Ltd.," holding that this is "the fair market value of rooms and meals furnished by the employer." * * * The deficiency notice seems to hold that the rooms and meals were not in fact supplied "merely as a convenience to the hotels of the employer."

From the evidence, there remains no room for doubt that the petitioner's residence at the hotel was not by way of compensation for his services, not for his personal convenience, comfort or pleasure, but solely because he could not otherwise perform the services required of him. The evidence of both the employer and employee shows in detail what petitioner's duties were and why his residence in the hotel was necessary. His duty was continuous and required his presence at a moment's call. He had a lifelong experience in hotel management and operation in the United States, Canada, and elsewhere, and testified that the functions of the manager could not have been performed by one living outside the hotel, especially a resort hotel such as this. The demands and requirements of guests are numerous, various, and unpredictable, and affect the meals, the rooms, the entertainment, and everything else about the hotel. The manager must be alert to all these things day and night. He would not consider undertaking the job and the owners of the hotel would not consider employing a manager unless he lived there. This was implicit throughout his employment, and

RE:
Could'nt
perform
duties w/o
the room.
Tx why
a benefit
to employer

when his compensation was changed from time to time no mention was ever made of it. Both took it for granted. The corporation's books carried no accounting for the petitioner's meals, rooms, or service.

Under such circumstances, the value of meals and lodging is not income to the employee, even though it may relieve him of an expense which he would otherwise bear. In *Jones v. United States, supra,* the subject was fully considered in determining that neither the value of quarters nor the amount received as commutation of quarters by an Army officer in included within his taxable income. There is also a full discussion in the English case of *Tennant v. Smith, H. L.* (1892) App.Cas. 150, III British Tax Cases 158. A bank employee was required to live in quarters located in the bank building, and it was held that the value of such lodging was not taxable income. The advantage to him was merely an incident of the performance of his duty, but its character for tax purposes was controlled by the dominant fact that the occupation of the premises was imposed upon him for the convenience of the employer. The Bureau of Internal Revenue has almost consistently applied the same doctrine in its published rulings.

The three cases cited by the respondent . . . are distinguishable entirely upon the ground that what the taxpayer received was not shown to be primarily for the need or convenience of the employer. Of course, . . . it cannot be said as a categorical proposition of law that, where an employee is fed and lodged by his employer, no part of the value of such perquisite is income. If the Commissioner finds that it was received as compensation and holds it to be taxable income, the taxpayer contesting this before the Board must prove by evidence that it is not income. In [a case cited by the respondent,] the Board held that the evidence did not establish that the food and lodging were given for the convenience of the employer. In the present case the evidence clearly establishes that fact, and it has been so found.

The determination of the Commissioner on the point in issue is reversed.

Reviewed by the Board.

Judgment will be entered under Rule 50.

MURDOCK concurs only in the result.

ARNOLD, dissenting:

I disagree with the conclusions of fact that the suite of rooms and meals furnished petitioner and his wife at the Royal Hawaiian Hotel were entirely for the convenience of the employer and that the cash salary was fixed without reference thereto and was never regarded as part of his compensation.

Petitioner was employed by a hotel corporation operating two resort hotels in Honolulu—the Royal Hawaiian, containing 357 guest bed rooms, and the Moana, containing 261 guest bed rooms, and the bungalows and cottages in connection with the Moana containing 127 guest bed rooms, and the Waialae Golf Club. His employment was as general manager of both hotels and the golf club.

His original employment was in 1925, and in accepting the employment he wrote a letter to the party representing the employer, with whom he conducted the negotiations for employment, under date of September 10, 1925, in which he says:

> Confirming our meeting here today, it is understood that I will assume the position of general manager of both the Royal Waikiki Beach Hotel (now under construction) and the Moana Hotel in Honolulu, at a yearly salary of $10,000.00, payable monthly, together with living quarters, meals, etc., for myself and wife. In addition, I am to receive $20.00 per day while traveling, this however, not to include any railroad or steamship fares, and I [am] to submit vouchers monthly covering all such expenses.

While the cash salary was adjusted from time to time by agreement of the parties, depending on the amount of business done, it appears that the question of living quarters, meals, etc., was not given further consideration and was not thereafter changed. Petitioner and his wife have always occupied living quarters in the Royal Hawaiian Hotel and received their meals from the time he first accepted the employment down through the years before us. His wife performed no services for the hotel company.

This letter, in my opinion, constitutes the basic contract of employment and clearly shows that the living quarters, meals, etc., furnished petitioner and his wife were understood and intended to be compensation in addition to the cash salary paid him. Being compensation to petitioner in addition to the cash salary paid him, it follows that the reasonable value thereof to petitioner is taxable income.

Conceding that petitioner was required to live at the hotel and that his living there was solely for the convenience of the employer, it does not follow that he was not benefited thereby to the extent of what such accommodations were reasonably worth to him. His employment was a matter of private contract. He was careful to specify in his letter accepting the employment that he was to be furnished with living quarters, meals, etc., for himself and wife, together with the cash salary, as compensation for his employment. Living quarters and meals are necessities which he would otherwise have had to procure at his own expense. His contract of employment relieved him to that extent. He has been enriched to the extent of what they are reasonably worth.

The majority opinion is based on the finding that petitioner's residence at the hotel was solely for the convenience of the employer and, therefore, not income. While it is no doubt convenient to have the manager reside in the hotel, I do not think the question here is one of convenience or of benefit to the employer. What the tax law is concerned with is whether or not petitioner was financially benefited by having living quarters furnished to himself and wife. He may have preferred to live elsewhere, but we are dealing with the financial aspect of petitioner's relation to his employer, not his preference. He says it would cost him $3,600 per year to live elsewhere.

It would seem that if his occupancy of quarters at the Royal Hawaiian was necessary and solely for the benefit of the employer, occupancy of premises at the Moana would be just as essential so far as the management of the Moana was concerned. He did not have living quarters or meals for himself and wife at the Moana and he was general manager of both and both were in operation during the years before us. Furthermore, it appears that petitioner was absent from Honolulu from March 24 to June 8 and from August 19 to November 2 in 1933, and from April 8 to May 24 and from September 3 to November 1 in 1934 — about 5 months in 1933 and 3 1/2 months in 1934. Whether he was away on official business or not we do not know. During his absence both hotels continued in operation. The $20 per day travel allowance in his letter of acceptance indicates his duties were not confined to managing the hotels in Honolulu, and the entire letter indicates he was to receive maintenance, whether in Honolulu or elsewhere, in addition to his cash salary.

At most the arrangement as to living quarters and meals was of mutual benefit, and to the extent it benefited petitioner it was compensation in addition to his cash salary, and taxable to him as income.

The Court of Claims in the case of *Jones v. United States*, relied on in the majority opinion, was dealing with a governmental organization regulated by military law where the compensation was fixed by law and not subject to private contract. The English case of *Tennant v. Smith*, involved the employment of a watchman or custodian for a bank whose presence at the bank was at all times a matter of necessity demanded by the employer as a condition of the employment.

The facts in both these cases are so at variance with the facts in this case that they are not controlling in my opinion.

SMITH, TURNER, and HARRON agree with this dissent.

Post-Case Follow-Up

Notwithstanding glaring factual peculiarities, the Board of Tax Appeals concluded in *Benaglia* that the provision of meals and lodging to the taxpayer was for the convenience of his employer. Accordingly, Benaglia was not required to include the fair market value of the benefits in his gross income. At the same time, the court did not speak with a single voice. At least one judge concurred only in the result, and four others were in full dissent. Cases like *Benaglia* pushed the envelope, and one can readily imagine a very similar case leading to the opposite result. Congress brought some order to the arena with the enactment of § 119.

Current Law

Section 119(a) generally provides that an employee may exclude from gross income the value of meals and lodging provided to him, his spouse, and his dependents, so long as such items are provided by or on behalf of his employer and for his employer's convenience. Further, additional requirements must be satisfied. Meals, for example, must be provided on the employer's business premises and will be considered as being provided "for the convenience of the employer" only if they are provided for a substantial noncompensatory reason such as the following:

- To have the employee on call and available for emergencies;
- To ensure employee availability when business demands dictate that the employee's own meal periods be very brief (giving them insufficient time to secure nourishment elsewhere);
- To provide proper nourishment when the employee could not secure it elsewhere within a reasonable meal period.

See Treas. Reg. § 1.119-1(a)(2).

The exclusion for lodging applies only (i) if the employee is *required* to accept ~lodging req~ it as a condition of his employment and (ii) such lodging is on the employer's business premises. Treasury Regulations clarify that the requirement that an employee accept lodging as a condition of employment means that the employee must accept such lodging to be able to do the job required (e.g., around-the-clock availability is needed). *See* Treas. Reg. § 1.119-1(b). The reference to business premises generally refers to the place of employment of the employee. *See* Treas. Reg. § 1.119-1(c)(1). Note that with respect to both meals and lodging, the exclusion applies only with respect to provision of the benefit "in kind" (i.e., in a form other than cash). Thus, if an employee can take advantage of the meal or lodging or take additional cash compensation, then § 119 will not apply. *See* Treas. Reg. § 1.119-1(e). Make a quick mental note: When we get to § 125 and cafeteria plans, employees *will* be able to make a choice between a benefit and cash compensation, but do not confuse § 125 cafeteria plans and § 119 meal/lodging benefits in this regard. Finally, recall that in *Benaglia*, the taxpayer specifically negotiated for the provision of meals and lodging. The dissenters harped on this fact, but current law forecloses the argument. Under § 119(b)(1), even if an employment contract or even a state statute deems meals and/or lodging to constitute "compensation," that fact will not prove dispositive on the question of whether such meals or lodging have been provided for the convenience of the employer.

Benaglia v. Commissioner: Real Life Applications (Current Law)

1. Assume that Alliah serves as a waitress at The Veggie GrilleHouse, a fancy restaurant. She works from noon to 9:00 p.m., and to ensure that she remains on the premises and available for work, the restaurant allows her to enjoy both free lunch and dinner on the days she works. She may also enjoy one free meal on the days she does not work.

   a. Must Alliah include in gross income the value of the meals she receives on the days she works?
   b. What about the meals she consumes on days she doesn't work?

2. Phillipe is the night security manager at Dearborn Heights, a luxury apartment building in downtown Chicago, IL. Although he is required to live anywhere within a one-mile radius of the property, he chooses to stay in the security manager's quarters, a one-bedroom suite provided to him free of charge by his employer. Must Phillipe include the fair rental value of the suite in his gross income?

3. Esteban recently accepted the position of Chief Surgical Resident at St. Dominique's Memorial Hospital. As a condition of his employment, he is required to reside in the chief resident's quarters (located in a contiguous wing of the hospital) to be available for emergencies around the clock. The fact that the hospital is located in downtown Boston means that the chief resident's quarters

have considerable market value. Must Esteban include the fair rental value of the chief resident's quarters in his gross income?

2. No-Additional-Cost Services, Employee Discounts, and Other Fringe Benefits

In General

Although § 119 addresses the provision of meals and lodging as excludible fringe benefits, that section covers only one sector of a much broader fringe benefit universe. Section 132 provides for the exclusion of several additional fringe benefits, including employee discounts and what you will come to know as no-additional-cost services and de minimis fringe benefits. We will touch on only a few of the items listed in § 132(a), and even then, we will only scratch the surface long enough to lay out the essentials. Fundamentally, the concepts do not present a challenge, but the language Congress employed in crafting the rules can prove a bit daunting the first time through. Section 132 starts with a fairly straightforward rule of exclusion: "Gross income shall not include any fringe benefit which qualifies as a (1) no-additional-cost service, (2) qualified employee discount, (3) working condition fringe, [or] (4) de minimis fringe . . . ." Further in, the statutory language defines each fringe benefit with some degree of particularity. Focus carefully as you read the statutory language.

No-Additional-Cost Services

In highly generalized terms, a no-additional-cost service is a service an employer is able to provide to an employee without incurring substantial additional cost (including foregoing revenue) in doing so. For example, a company in the hotel industry might make a limited number of rooms available (either free of charge or at a substantially reduced nightly rate) to employees working in that division. In doing so, the company, presumably, can predict what percentage of its rooms at a given property would likely have been left unoccupied based on historical reservation patterns. Another classic no-additional-cost service is the provision of free air transportation by airlines to the employees working in that business division. Given that such employees fly on a standby basis (i.e., he or she takes only those seats left available after paying customers have taken the seats they prefer), the airline foregoes no revenue and incurs scant cost by allowing the employee to occupy the seat for the duration of the flight. Such must be the case in order for the employee to exclude the fair market value of the seat from gross income. Under § 132(b), a fringe benefit will qualify as a *no-additional-cost service* only if it is a service provided by the employer to the employee for the employee's use and (1) the employer offers the service for sale to customers in the ordinary course of the line of business in which the employee works and (2) the employer incurs no substantial additional cost (including foregone revenue) in providing the service to its employees. Assuming the worker enjoying the free seat actually works in the company's *airline* division, the free airplane seat fits the definition comfortably. The airline provides the service to the employee for his use, it offers airplane seats for sale to customers in the ordinary course of the line of business in which the employee works, and by forcing the employee to fly on a standby basis, the airline foregoes no revenue it might have collected from a paying passenger. Note, in particular, the *line of business* requirement. If the company operated a cruise-ship line and an airline, the provision of free flights to employees of the cruise-ship line (or free cruises to the employees of the airline) would not constitute the provision of a no-additional-cost service; accordingly, under those facts, the employees would not be able to exclude from gross income the fair market value of what they received. As for cost to the employer, keep in mind that the employer may incur no substantial additional cost in providing the service to the employee. Such costs include both revenue lost, if any, due to the provision of the service to the employee (vis-à-vis a nonemployee) and the cost of the labor of those employees actually providing the services. *See* § 132(b)(2); Treas. Reg. § 1.132-2(a)(5) (dictating that in this context, one must ignore any amount paid by the employee for the service and, at the same time, factor in labor costs incurred by the employer).

Reciprocal Agreements

Specific employers may enter into reciprocal written agreements such that one employer may provide a no-additional-cost service to another employer's employee (e.g., an employee of Airline A may fly standby on Airline B (and vice versa) under such an agreement). Section 132(i) confirms that the relevant employee may still treat the receipt of this service as an excludible fringe benefit, assuming the arrangement satisfies certain requirements. *See generally* § 132(i); *see also* Treas. Reg. § 1.132-2(b). **WARNING**: The reciprocal agreement rule only applies to no-additional-cost services because § 132(i) applies only "[f]or purposes of [§ 132(a)(1)]." Here we can see the impact of limiting statutory language.

Use by Family of the Employee

Although § 132(b) refers to the provision of a service by an employer to an employee, subsection 132(h)(2)(A) treats any use of the service by a spouse or dependent child as use by the employee. Accordingly, the provision of a free flight (on a standby basis) to an employee's spouse or child (even if the spouse or child is traveling alone) qualifies as a no-additional-cost service provided to the employee. Section 132(b) also refers to the line of business in which the employee provides services, but subsection 132(h)(1) defines *employee* for this purpose to include retirees,

Use by Parents?

Interestingly enough, in the case of air transportation, use by the parent of the employee also qualifies as employee use. *See* § 132(h)(3). These things happen when members of Congress have children employed by airlines.

disabled former employees, and the widows/widowers of those individuals who died while employed in that line of business (or who died while retired/disabled). **WARNING**: These special rules only apply to no-additional-cost services and qualified employee discounts because § 132(h) applies only "[f]or purposes of [§ 132(a)(1) and (2)]." Here again, we see the true impact of limiting statutory language.

Qualified Employee Discounts

Employees typically receive some form of discount when purchasing the products or services of their employer, but given that such discounts allow the employee to retain money they might otherwise have paid, one can easily see how an excessive employee discount can constitute a form of disguised compensation. By rigidly defining and limiting *qualified employee discount* ("QED"), § 132(c) attempts to foreclose this possibility. Section 132(c)(3) defines *employee discount* in straightforward terms as the savings represented by the difference between what the employee pays for property or services and what ordinary customers pay. Section 132(a)(2), however, speaks of a *qualified employee discount*. What's the difference? For an employee discount to constitute a qualified employee discount, the discount must accord with statutory limitations. Section 132(c)(1) provides as follows:

> The term "qualified employee discount" means any employer discount with respect to qualified property or services to the extent such discount does not exceed —
>
> (A) in the case of property, the gross profit percentage of the price at which the property is being offered by the employer to customers, or
>
> (B) in the case of services, 20 percent of the price at which the services are being offered by the employer to customers.

From this language, we see several different things. First, a QED can only be an employee discount with respect to *qualified property or services*; this limitation means that the employee can enjoy an excludible discount only with respect to property or services offered to customers in the ordinary course of business in the line of business in which he or she works. *See* § 132(c)(4). Second, a QED will qualify as such only if it is not excessive. For the purchase of services, an excludible discount cannot exceed 20 percent, and with respect to the purchase of property, the discount cannot exceed the *gross profit percentage* of the price charged to ordinary customers. This term may appear opaque at first glance, but let's see if you can figure out what Congress is doing by capping the excludible employee discount for property purchases at the gross profit percentage. Assume that all of the property offered to customers in a given year by Company cost it $75 million and was sold to customers for $100 million. Looks like a gross profit of $25 million for the period. What is the *gross profit percentage*? Section 132(c)(2) defines the term as follows:

The term "gross profit percentage" means *the percent which —*

    (i) the excess of the aggregate sales price of property sold by the employer to customers over the aggregate cost of such property to the employer, *is of*

    (ii) the aggregate sale price of such property.

Getting a clear understanding of this definition requires that you first step back and view it holistically. If you take a bird's eye view, the term means the percent which (i) is of (ii). Thus, if (i) = 2 and (ii) = 10, the gross profit percentage would be 20 percent (i.e., the percent which 2 is of 10). The only thing we have to do now is ascertain the value of (i) and (ii) under our facts. Item (i) is the *excess* of total sales price over total cost ($100M - $75M), and item (ii) is total sale price ($100M). The gross profit percentage is the percent which $25M is of $100M. We know this to be 25 percent, and accordingly, for the purchase of property under these facts, an excludible employee discount may not exceed 25 percent. Keep in mind that throughout the Code, Congress typically employs the same or a similar statutory approach in setting forth relevant formulas in generic terms. At the end of the day, the impact of the formula at hand is that an employer may give an employee a discount so that, at minimum, the employee pays an amount equal to employer cost (or a rough approximation thereof). Alternatively, one could say that the maximum excludible employee discount is the average mark-up for that employee's line of business expressed as a percentage of customer cost. If the employee is able to get the property from the employer at less than employer cost, then the amount paid less than employer cost constitutes employee compensation. Thus, a discount of 30 percent under the facts given would lead to what result? The amount representing 5 percent of standard cost would constitute compensation, and the amount representing 25 percent of standard cost would be a qualified employee discount. Why not simply declare that the entire discount constitutes income if it exceeds a certain percentage? Because § 132(a) does not state that an employee discount constitutes a QED *if* it does not exceed a certain amount. Rather, it states that an employee discount will constitute a QED *to the extent* it does not exceed a certain amount.

Working Condition Fringe Benefits

To understand the character of a working condition fringe benefit, you must first have basic familiarity with either § 162 or § 167. For our purposes, § 162 will suffice. As you will discover when we study the provision in detail, section § 162(a) generally allows a taxpayer to deduct the ordinary and necessary expenses paid or incurred during a taxable year in carrying on a trade or business. Such expenses include the amount paid as compensation to employees as well as the costs incurred in sending a group of employees out of town for training (e.g., air fare, meals, lodging, etc.). When, for whatever reason, employees pay such costs, the items do not lose their fundamental character as "ordinary" and "necessary" business expenses. Hold that thought for future reference. Fortunately, employers almost always pay such expenses, and when they do, the value of air fare, meals, lodging, etc., paid on behalf of the employee does *not* constitute income to the employee because these items constitute working condition fringe benefits. By definition, a *working condition fringe benefit* is "any property or services provided to an employee of the employer to the extent that, *if the employee* paid for such property or services, such payments would be allowable as a deduction under section 162 or 167." (Emphasis added.) As you might well guess, working condition fringe benefits take many forms (e.g., travel expenses, newspaper/magazine subscriptions, bar dues, etc.), although the author confesses that the coverage of travel expenses associated with attending law professor conferences in exotic locales is particularly enjoyable (even with the generally mandatory presentation of a scholarly paper).

De Minimis Fringe Benefits

Anyone who has enjoyed a free slice of pizza, sandwich, or doughnut courtesy of his employer has enjoyed a *de minimis fringe benefit*. By definition these items are "any property or service the value of which is (after taking into account the frequency with which similar fringes are provided by the employer to the employer's employees) so small as to make accounting for it unreasonable or administratively impracticable." The Treasury Regulations promulgated under § 132 contain more elaborate rules. Common de minimis fringe benefits include coffee, doughnuts, soft drinks, occasional theater or sporting event tickets, traditional birthday or holiday gifts of property with a low fair market value, occasional cocktail parties, and flowers, books, fruit, etc., for special circumstances. *See* Treas. Reg. § 1.132-6(e)(1).

3. Cafeteria Plans

In much the same way that employees may take advantage of qualified employee discounts, no-additional-cost services, and de minimis fringe benefits, taxpayers may also exclude cafeteria plan benefits from their gross income. As the name suggests, a cafeteria plan involves choosing from a menu of options, but instead of deciding whether one will have mashed potatoes, broccoli, or both, employees participating in a cafeteria plan must choose whether they will receive cash compensation on the one hand or a qualified benefit on the other. *See* IRC § 125(d)(1). The menu of qualified benefits includes the following:

■ Accident and health plans (including health care flexible spending arrangements),
■ Dependent care assistance programs,
■ Long-term or short-term disability coverage, and
■ Coverage under an accidental death or dismemberment policy.

See generally Prop. Treas. Reg. § 1.121-1(a)(3). Ordinarily, a taxpayer given the option of receiving cash from his employer or having his employer apply compensation directly to a personal expenditure of the employee would be taxed on the amount applied to the expenditure, but § 125(a) intervenes in this context, providing that "no amount shall be included in the gross income of a participant in a cafeteria plan solely because, under the plan, the participant may choose among the benefits of the plan." In a typical setting, an employee might choose one of the following:

Receive $100,000 in cash compensation

or

Receive $95,000 in cash compensation, $3,000 in dependent care assistance, and $2,000 in health care flexible spending arrangement benefits

or

Receive $95,000 in cash compensation and $5,000 in dependent care assistance

or

Receive $98,000 in cash compensation and $2,000 in health care flexible spending arrangement benefits.

The crucial fact is that the taxpayer will receive the cost of the qualified benefit tax-free. Here's a simple example of how a typical qualified benefit option operates. Assume that an employee is entitled to a salary of $100,000, but under the employer's cafeteria plan, the employee elects to receive $97,600 in salary and to have $2,400 set aside (monthly installments of $200 over 12 months) in a health care flexible spending arrangement ("FSA"). Each month, the employee receives her standard monthly salary amount reduced by $200. The reduced salary amount is part of gross income, but the $200 is not because it is excluded from gross income. The employer holds the $200 in the employee's flexible spending arrangement account and, most likely, engages a third party to administer the account; after the employee pays a medical expense that qualifies for reimbursement from the FSA, the employee submits the appropriate receipts, and the employee ultimately receives reimbursement from the FSA. The employee neither deducts the medical expense nor includes the subsequent reimbursement in gross income. Overall,

Modern Electronic Realities

Today, those with health care FSAs commonly receive a debit card with which to pay for certain medical expenses. If (in the opinion of the administrator) there is no question whether the expense is a qualified medical expense, the matter is resolved. Otherwise, the employee must scan and upload (or mail) an appropriate receipt verifying that the expense was, indeed, a qualifying medical expense.

Carryover or Grace Period for Health Care Flexible Spending Arrangements

Rather than enforcing an absolute "use-it-or-lose-it" rule with respect to their health care FSAs, employers have the option of offering their employees either (i) a 2½ month grace period to "use up" health care FSA funds remaining at the end of the preceding plan year or (ii) a carryover of up to $500 from the health care FSA of one plan year to the next year plan year. *See* IRS Notice 2013-71, 2013-47 I.R.B. 532.

this arrangement results in the employee receiving some portion of compensation tax-free in the form of the qualified benefit. Under the facts given, the employee may receive reimbursement for up to $2,400 in qualifying medical expenses during the taxable year. In fact, the employee could incur and receive reimbursement for up to $2,400 of such expenses in January of a given taxable year, even if his taxable year is the calendar year and he has contributed nothing to his health care FSA at that time.

Participation in a cafeteria plan has its risks and benefits. Taxpayers can forego participation in the cafeteria plan altogether or participate and receive qualified benefits suited to their needs. Those with dependents may favor the dependent care options, those without dependents may opt to have a health care flexible spending arrangement, and some taxpayers will take advantage of several options simultaneously in a given year. Congress limits the qualified benefit election amount for each benefit option, and if an employee fails to "use up" the benefit by the end of the taxable year, he or she will forfeit the balance remaining in the account, unless the plan includes a carryover or grace period provision. Not surprisingly, you will find many taxpayers suddenly realizing that they need prescription sunglasses in December or must tend to a host of medical and dental needs on the eve of the New Year. Bear in mind that cafeteria plans and fringe benefits generally are part of the much broader and substantially more detailed employee benefits arena in federal income taxation. We skim the surface here to lay essential groundwork as part of our ongoing study of exclusions.

> ### Warning
> ....
> Do not confuse health care FSAs with other arrangements such as Medical Savings Accounts (Archer MSAs) or Health Spending Accounts. Those programs operate under distinct, special rules, and coverage of them is beyond the scope of this casebook.

C. LIFE INSURANCE CONTRACT PROCEEDS

1. In General

Under § 101(a)(1), taxpayers may generally exclude from gross income amounts they receive under a life insurance contract if such amounts are paid by reason of the death of an insured individual. Associated rules demonstrate a degree of congressional flexibility in certain contexts. The exclusion provided by the general rule also applies with respect to accelerated death benefits received under a life insurance contract with respect to a terminally or chronically ill individual. *See* IRC § 101(g). In the event that the life insurance contract does not provide for accelerated death benefits, the policyholder may be able to appeal

Key Statutory Provisions

▪ **Internal Revenue Code**
  ▪ **§ 101(a)(1)**
  ▪ **§ 101(g)(1) & (g)(2)(A)**

to *viatical settlement providers* (i.e., persons regularly engaged in the trade/business of purchasing or taking assignment of life insurance contracts on the lives of insured and who satisfy the relevant requirements under § 101(g)(2)(B)). If all or a portion of a death benefit under a life insurance contract is sold or assigned to a viatical settlement provider with respect to a terminally or chronically ill individual, the consideration received for the sale/assignment will be treated as having been paid under a life insurance contract by reason of the insured's death. *See* IRC § 101(g)(2)(A).

2. "Life Insurance" and the Insurable Interest Requirement

The rules under § 101 appear basic and straightforward at first glance, but if you look closely at the language of the statute, you may spot potential issues. Section 101(a) makes specific reference to a *life insurance contract*, but if you search through § 101, you will not find a definition of life insurance contract. For that, you must turn to § 7702(a), which defines the term for purposes of the entirety of Title 26 (i.e., the Internal Revenue Code). Under § 7702, a contract will constitute a *life insurance contract* only if it qualifies as a life insurance contract under applicable (state or foreign) law and satisfies other statutory requirements (far beyond the scope of this text). In addition to clearing statutory and regulatory hurdles, a contract must also satisfy certain common law standards in order to qualify as life insurance. Landmark authority from the U.S. Supreme Court, *Helvering v. Le Gierse*, 312 U.S. 531 (1941), instructs that a life insurance contract must embody risk-shifting and risk-distribution, and ordinarily, these elements exist. A life insurance company receives premiums and takes on the responsibility of paying a death benefit if the insured dies. Thus, the financial risk associated with the death of the insured shifts from the person paying premiums to the life insurance company. Further, by simultaneously collecting premiums from a wide range of individuals of varying levels of mortality risk (e.g., the young, the middle-aged, the old, the healthy, and the sick), the life insurance company distributes this financial risk broadly amongst insureds. Barring catastrophe and assuming favorable mortality experience over time, the life insurance company can use collected premiums (and income generated by investment of such premiums) to meet its regular death benefit obligations. With tax-free death benefits on the line, however, one can be sure that not every transaction structured as life insurance in form will pass muster as life insurance in substance. Assume, for example, that an elderly individual transfers a large amount of money to a life insurance company (enough to cover the entire death benefit) to purchase a "life insurance contract" just a few months before she passes away. Has there been any risk-shifting or risk-distribution? These were the facts in *Le Gierse*, and in that case, the Court held that the contract at issue did not constitute a life insurance contract because the arrangement lacked risk-shifting and risk-distribution. In many, if not most, instances, the contract at hand will readily qualify as life insurance, but because excludible death benefits flow from life insurance contracts, we have to keep fundamental definitional issues on the radar screen as we interpret and apply § 101.

Another intriguing issue that might arise in this context concerns the "insurable interest" requirement. People may enjoy receiving excludible death benefits under the terms of a life insurance contract, but should everyone be able to take out a contract of life insurance on anyone else? Probably not. In fact, insurance law generally provides that an individual taking out a contract of life insurance on the life of another individual for his or her own benefit must have an insurable interest in the continued life of the insured (i.e., they can reasonably expect to reap financial benefit (or to avoid financial loss) as a result of the continuation of the insured's life). *See* 3 Couch on Ins. § 41:20 (3d ed. 2016). Spouses and blood relatives are generally found to have insurable interests in each other's lives, although kinship itself is not required. *See* 3 Couch on Ins. § 41:21 (3d ed. 2016). Interestingly enough, although some jurisdictions only require that this insurable interest be present at the time of the original contract, others will consider the absence of an insurable interest at the time of the insured's death to be fatal to the beneficiary's cause of action. *See* 3 Couch on Ins. § 41:26 (3d ed. 2016). Individuals with contractual capacity, of course, have an insurable interest in their own lives and can designate anyone they deem worthy as beneficiary (even if the beneficiary does not have an insurable interest in the life of the insured), but this rule applies only if the insured acts willfully and is not colluding with others as part of a wagering contract. *See* 3 Couch on Ins. § 41:22 (3d ed. 2016).

Case Preview

Atlantic Oil Co. v. Patterson

Banks and other creditors commonly obtain life insurance policies with respect to their debtors, and on some level, one can argue that this practice does not offend public policy. Those lending large sums of money expect and rely on repayment, and creditors have legitimate reasons to protect themselves against the financial risk of the premature death of the primary obligor. What about employers? Alarming though it may seem to some, employers commonly procure contracts of life insurance with respect to their employees. But should employers have an insurable interest in the lives of their employees? If not all of them, then what about key employees like the chief executive officer or key non-employees like independent members of the Board of Directors of a corporation? As you read *Atlantic Oil Co. v. Patterson*, consider the following questions:

1. Did the company have legitimate financial reason to insure its employees?
2. What conclusion did the court reach, and is its reasoning sound in your opinion?

Atlantic Oil Co. v. Patterson
331 F.2d 516 (5th Cir. 1964)

PER CURIAM.

Proceeds of a life insurance policy are not includable in gross income and therefore not taxable [per § 101]. The question presented by this appeal is whether the accident insurance policy in suit was void as a wagering contract, and its proceeds therefore taxable. The jury so found. We find no basis in the record for disturbing the jury's verdict.

The taxpayer's "company policy" is to have accident insurance on its truck drivers. The life insurance proceeds are to be paid to the employer; certain health benefits are to be paid to the employee. The employer chooses the insurance company and pays the premiums. The employee merely signs his name as the applicant for the policy.

In 1957 when its truck driver, Webster, was killed, the taxpayer applied for and received the $28,750 proceeds on this policy. The Commissioner disallowed the exclusion of the proceeds from gross income. The taxpayer paid the tax and sued for refund. The trial court charged the jury that the taxpayer had no insurable interest in the driver's life that would permit it to take out a valid insurance policy on him. The trial court further charged the jury that if the driver himself voluntarily took out the policy of insurance, it was valid, and he had a "perfect right to name" the taxpayer as beneficiary of the death benefits. The jury was charged, however, that if this action of the driver was the result of "compulsion or some coercion, economic or otherwise," then the jury would find that the taxpayer had really taken out the policy, that the policy was therefore void as a wagering contract, and that therefore the funds were not proceeds excludable from the taxpayer's income. There was no exception to these instructions and appellant does not attack them now.

We have studied the record and find that the jury's verdict has substantial basis therein. Pretermitting the question as to whether or not it is against public policy for an employer to be the death beneficiary on persons who drive its trucks, the evidence at the very least showed that unless the employee, Webster, agreed to take out the policy in behalf of the company, he would not be employed. The jury could well have found that this constituted economic coercion and thus concluded that the death payments were not proceeds of a valid insurance policy excludable from taxpayer's income.

Affirmed.

Post-Case Follow-Up

Although acknowledging Webster's insurable interest in his own life, the court found no reason to disturb the jury's conclusion that the presence of economic coercion resulted in his employer taking out a wagering contract on Webster's life rather than a contract of life insurance paying excludible death benefits. Current law under § 101(j) provides a legal framework in which an employer may secure employer-owned life insurance on the lives of its employees, but even if the employer complies with the notice and consent requirements of § 101(j)(4), one must still ponder the extent to which any consent given is real. Allowing such a contract to continue after the insured terminates employment is particularly disconcerting.

Atlantic Oil Co. v. Patterson: Real Life Applications

1. Calista has been the Chief Executive Officer of International Conglomerate, Inc. ("ICI") for the past 15 years. Longstanding policy requires that ICI have in place an insurance policy on the life of its CEO with ICI as the designated beneficiary. The policy typically insures the life of the CEO for millions of dollars. Assuming Calista knew of this company policy before accepting the position of CEO and gave proper written consent to the procuring of the policy, should any death benefits paid qualify for the exclusion under § 101?

2. Oliver's, Inc. ("Oliver's") is a well-known fast-food restaurant, and it has thousands of locations across the United States, Canada, and Central America. Company policy dictates that Oliver's have in place an insurance contract on the lives of all general managers, and it conditions promotion to that position on the provision of written consent to the issuance of the policy. If an insurance company pays a death benefit with respect to the life of a general manager, should Oliver's be able to exclude the proceeds from its gross income?

D. TAX-EXEMPT INTEREST

1. In General

Under § 103(a), taxpayers may generally exclude the interest on state and local bonds from their gross income, and in this context, the Code defines *state* broadly enough to include the District of Columbia and U.S. possessions. Further, *state and local bond* is defined to include those issued by state political subdivisions such as counties and parishes. *See* § 103(c)(1). Congress, by making this exclusion available, facilitates the funding of state-level activities by eliminating the potential chill of a federal income tax on bond interest, yet Congress has a strong contemporaneous interest in policing this activity so that states do not mislead the investing public or abuse this investor-friendly form of state borrowing. Accordingly, with limited exception, the bond interest exemption will not apply if the bonds are not *registered* (i.e., the state has not disclosed crucial information to the Securities and Exchange Commission and potential investors) or if the bonds constitute *arbitrage bonds* (i.e., those issued by the state in order to enable it to invest the bond proceeds and receive a rate of interest or investment return higher than the rate of interest they must pay on their own bonds). *See* § 103(b)(2) and (3). Further, the exclusion does not apply with respect to *private activity bonds*, unless such bonds are *qualified bonds*. *See* § 103(b)(1).

> **Key Statutory Provisions**
>
> ▪ **Internal Revenue Code**
>   ▪ § 103
>   ▪ § 141(a), (e)(1)(A)
>   ▪ § 142(a)(1)

2. Private Activity Bonds and Qualified Bonds

Unlike investors receiving interest on bonds issued by state and local governments, those investing in bonds issued by private businesses (e.g., corporations) do not receive interest on the bonds tax-free. That reality ultimately means several things: (1) state and local governments can pay a lower rate of interest on their tax-free-interest bonds and (2) investors will demand (and businesses must pay) a higher rate of interest with respect to privately issued bonds. The possibilities are tempting. What if the owner of a major county-level employer (making widgets) manages to convince local county officials to issue "county" bonds, collect the proceeds, and then lend that money to the business, all at the lucrative tax-free-interest bond rate? Should the holders of those "state and local" bonds qualify for the § 103 exclusion? Allowing them to do so would run counter to Congress's intent to facilitate public government operations and projects because the proceeds of the bond issue ended up in the hands of a private actor. Yet, state and local governments often issue bonds for what ultimately turn out to be public purposes (e.g., construction of an airport or public train station), even though the government may have extensive financial interaction with private businesses under contract to do the actual work. Together, sections 103 and 141 of the Code help to sort this out.

Section 103 allows the exclusion of interest on state and local bonds, but the general rule of exclusion does not apply to private activity bonds (unless such private activity bonds happen to be qualified bonds). For our limited purposes, we can forego the technical definition of *private activity bond* under § 141, but one can think of such a bond in simplified terms as one issued by a state or local government with more than some modest amount of the proceeds (5 to 10 percent) going to private business use or to make or finance loans to private businesses. Hit the trigger, and the bond instantly becomes a private activity bond with respect to which holders must include interest received in gross income. If, however, a private activity bond is a *qualified bond* (i.e., a private activity bond with respect to which the proceeds acquired are ultimately used for certain public purposes), the § 103 exclusion will apply. A common example of a qualified bond would be an *exempt facility bond*, which § 142 defines as "any bond issued as part of an issue 95% or more of the net proceeds of which are to be used to provide [airports, docks and wharves, mass commuting facilities, facilities for the furnishing of water, high-speed intercity rail facilities, etc.]." Rather than punishing or deterring public/private interaction in this context, the law paves a broad avenue of opportunity while imposing restrictions sufficient to keep abuses in check.

In addition to the essentials discussed above, the tax-exempt bond arena is rich with special, detailed statutory rules and regulatory provisions. This brief introduction provides basic familiarity with a common yet important exclusion and a firm grip on critical vocabulary.

Exempt Facility Bonds

Municipalities often rely on bonds to finance the construction, expansion, or upgrading or public facilities such as airports. Depicted below is the main hall of the Hartsfield-Jackson Atlanta International Airport, which has been the world's busiest airport (measured by passenger traffic) for several years. The airport's name honors William B. Hartsfield and Maynard H. Jackson, Jr., both of whom played significant roles in making Atlanta an aviation center. Upon his election, Maynard Jackson became the first African-American to serve as mayor of a major city in the southeastern United States.

Credit: ESB Professional/Shutterstock.com.

Chapter Summary

- Taxpayers may exclude from gross income non-punitive damages received on account of personal physical injury or physical sickness. In any event, the Code disallows exclusion to the extent that prior medical expense deductions have been taken with respect to the injury.
- Although damages received solely on account of emotional distress do not qualify for exclusion from gross income, damages compensating for emotional distress associated with physical injury/sickness or compensating for medical care for emotional distress may qualify for exclusion. Again, the Code disallows exclusion to the extent that prior medical expense deductions have been taken with respect to the cost of treating the emotional distress.
- Employees may exclude the value of meals and lodging provided to the employee, his spouse, and his dependents if such items are provided for the convenience of the employer and satisfy specific statutory and regulatory requirements.
- Employees may exclude from gross income the value of specific fringe benefits provided or made available to them. Under the appropriate circumstances, provision of the fringe benefit to the spouse and children of the employee constitutes provision of the benefit to the employee.

▥ Under a cafeteria plan, employees may elect to receive some limited dollar amount of their compensation in the form of qualified benefits in lieu of cash. Congress allows the employee to exclude the value of the qualified benefit from gross income but limits the dollar amount eligible for qualified benefit allocation each taxable year.

▥ Taxpayers may generally exclude death benefits received from their gross income. The contract under which such benefits are paid must constitute insurance (i.e., incorporate the requisite risk-shifting and risk-distribution), and satisfaction of insurable interest requirements may prove critical.

▥ Although taxpayers may generally exclude interest received with respect to state and local bonds from gross income, governing law may disallow such exclusions if the bonds are not registered or constitute arbitrage bonds or private activity bonds that are not qualified bonds.

Applying the Rules

1. Driving home after a movie, Kevin managed to rear-end another vehicle stopped at a red light. The driver-side air bag deployed, and although Kevin did not suffer serious injury as a result of the accident, the air bag deflation caused sharp metal fragments to strike him in the upper torso, resulting in significant loss of blood before paramedics arrived. The air bag turned out to be defective. Kevin ultimately recovered $50,000 as compensation for his physical injuries and $10,000 as compensation for the depression flowing from his personal injury. What amount, if any, must Kevin include in gross income as a result of receiving the aforementioned damages?

2. Incessant cyberbullying by several fellow students sent Thao into deep depression. She began pulling her hair out and ultimately had a nervous breakdown when students persistently spread lies about her. Thao sued several students for libel and slander. The parties ultimately settled out of court for $25,000 and the bullies' promise to leave Thao alone. Must Thao include any amount in gross income in connection with this event?

3. After two years without a vacation, Gabriela finally decided to take a trip to Las Vegas with her family. Because Gabriela is a seasoned pilot with Big Sky Airlines, Inc. ("BSA"), she and her family are able to fly free of charge on regularly scheduled BSA flights. If Gabriela and her husband reserve two coach seats and fly round-trip to Las Vegas free of charge, must Gabriela include any amounts in gross income as a result?

4. *Same facts as Question 3*, except that Gabriela does not go to Las Vegas for vacation. Instead, BSA sends her there (without her husband) to attend a conference on enhanced cockpit security measures. Must Gabriela include the value of air fare, lodging, and meals provided to her in connection with this trip?

5. Estrada is an officer with the Connecticut Highway Patrol. Given that he must remain on patrol and available for emergencies throughout his shift, he must take his meals while he is officially on duty. If the State of Connecticut gives Estrada a meal allowance so that he may purchase his meals while on duty, will he be required to include the dollar amount of the allowance in his gross income?

6. Joanne was recently diagnosed with pancreatic cancer. According to her doctor, she is terminally ill (i.e., she will die within 24 months). If Joanne receives accelerated death benefits in a lump sum under her life insurance contract, will she be required to include any amount in gross income?

7. Marconi Motors, Inc. ("MMI") employs a substantial percentage of the population in Wisteria County in the State of New York, but MMI has recently fallen on hard times, and the local banks have stopped lending it money. If MMI convinces Wisteria County officials to issue bonds, collect the proceeds, and lend the money to MMI, will those holding the bonds be able to exclude any interest received from their gross income?

8. Grand Facility Constructors, Inc. ("GFC") has a strong reputation for building safe, reliable airports. Unfortunately, recent economic stress has made it extremely difficult for GFC to borrow money using traditional channels. Assume that Cook County in the State of Illinois plans to have a new airport (Idlewild International) constructed on vacant land northwest of the city center. If Cook County issues bonds, collects the proceeds, and lends the money to GFC to enable GFC to commence and complete construction of the airport, will the holders of the bonds be able to exclude any interest received from gross income?

Federal Income Taxation in Practice

1. Private University is one of your firm's clients. The partner who serves as the primary contact for that client has asked you to research a question for him. The president of Private University, Dr. Kirkland Capitan, is required, as a condition of his employment, to live in the President's Mansion on the university campus. The university would like to know the tax ramifications for Dr. Capitan in light of the fact that the residence has substantial fair market value and the president pays nothing to the university for living there. The partner needs you to draft a brief memo, but he reminds you that he is not a tax partner and that you should spare him any unnecessary technicalities.

2. One of your friends participates in her employer's cafeteria plan. During the open enrollment period in late 2017, she decided to have $2,000 of her salary put into a health care flexible spending arrangement account for use during

calendar year 2018; the plan does not have a grace period or carryover feature. It is now mid-December in 2018, and she has used only $1,000 of her FSA. She is currently in excellent health and would like to know whether she can just use the FSA in January of next year and, if not, what she can spend it on in order to exhaust the funds. See what you can find and send her an e-mail.

3. Ten years out of law school, you are now financially secure. Notwithstanding the fact that you love your relatives and wish them no harm, you have always found the prospect of receiving tax-free death benefits tantalizing. "Life has its vicissitudes," you reason, and if one of your relatives passes away suddenly, the family (i.e., you) should have sufficient money to cover rudimentary final expenses with perhaps a few thousand dollars left over. Find out whether you have an insurable interest in the lives of any of your blood relatives under California law.

4. The County of Mojave is one of your firm's clients. The tax partner who serves as the client's primary contact has asked whether the county can use a tax-exempt bond issue to finance the construction of wind farms or the installation of vast arrays of solar panels to provide electric energy for county residents. He feels reasonably sure that the county can proceed, but he wanted to check with a tax person before moving forward. Please do the research and follow up with him by brief e-mail message.

5. Orlando Motors, Inc. is one of your firm's clients. The company contacts you with respect to a new matter. They would like to know whether they should be including in employee compensation the fair market value of the holiday ham or holiday turkey they give to each of their employees during the Thanksgiving season. They know that certain holiday bonuses must be included in the employee's gross income, but they are not sure whether the ham/turkey is sufficiently de minimis for them to ignore. They like to think of it as just one of their employees' free fringe benefits. The client does not need a formal memo, but they would like a one-page letter setting forth your conclusions.

The Standard Deduction, Itemized Deductions, Tax Credits, and the Deduction for Qualified Business Income

In calculating taxable income, taxpayers typically can take several deductions. Although some deductions become available to taxpayers only after they have incurred a given expense or suffered a loss, others are generally available to all taxpayers (e.g., the so-called standard deduction). Why is this the case? In a sense, the existence of deductions of general availability seems somewhat odd. If a taxpayer incurs a given expense or suffers a loss, we can easily see the financial impact of the expense or event; allowing the taxpayer to take a deduction appears rational and fair. But allowing deductions unlinked to specific expenses seems, at first glance, to defeat the whole revenue-raising purpose of laying and collecting taxes. In this chapter, we begin our discussion of deductions more generally and devote limited attention to tax credits, but before doing so in earnest, we step back for a more holistic view to develop some appreciation of where various allowances fit in the larger context of rational and equitable tax policy.

A. PROGRESSIVITY, MARGINAL RATES, AND THE PURSUIT OF HORIZONTAL AND VERTICAL EQUITY

In prior chapters, we discussed the concept of realization before turning our focus to specific items included

Key Concepts

- Progressivity, marginal rate, and the notions of horizontal and vertical equity
- The standard deduction and itemized deductions
- The impact of tax credits
- The meaning of *dependent*
- The deduction for qualified business income

in and excluded from a taxpayer's gross income. We now begin our examination of deductions. These items, unlike exclusions, do show up on a taxpayer's federal income tax return as the relevant calculations move from gross income to adjusted gross income and from there to taxable income. Theoretically, Congress could dispense with deductions altogether and impose a tax on gross income or, perhaps, a tax on gross income above a certain exemption amount. Such a regime would give us the **flat tax** many commentators yearn for, but that is not the system we have in place today. In taxing the citizenry, Congress hopes to do so in a manner that is fundamentally fair to everyone. In that vein, Congress seeks to achieve **horizontal equity** by ensuring that those taxpayers who are similarly situated in an economic sense shoulder the same tax burden. Having decided that relying solely on gross income amounts from a given taxable year would be an unacceptably rough means of determining who is similarly situated, Congress achieves greater accuracy by looking to gross income and adjusting that dollar amount by various deductions and allowances to get taxable income. This amount, accordingly, represents an acceptably clear picture of an individual taxpayer's economic profile at the close of a given taxable year relative to the start of that taxable year and thus a proper amount on which to impose tax. Under this approach, per Table 7.1, all unmarried taxpayers with taxable income of $250,000 in 2018 are similarly situated and, accordingly, have the same federal income tax obligation of $45,689.50 plus 35 percent of the amount of taxable income over $200,000. At the same time, as Congress seeks to achieve horizontal equity, it also seeks to achieve **vertical equity**. It does so, as Table 7.1 reflects, by requiring that taxpayers with greater ability to pay (as measured by higher levels of taxable income) pay more taxes *and* at progressively higher rates.

Be sure to keep the following items in mind with respect to vertical equity and tax rate tables:

- Table 7.1 displays tax rates applicable in 2018 for unmarried individuals. Different *dollar* amounts will apply with respect to those with a different filing status (e.g., head of household, married filing separately, etc.).
- Over the years, the dollar amounts for each filing status may change to reflect inflation adjustments. *See generally* § 1(f).

TABLE 7.1   **2018 Rate of Taxation for Those Filing as Unmarried Individuals**

Taxable Income	Tax Due
$0 - $9,525	$0 plus **10%** of the amount over $0
$9,526 - $38,700	$952.50 plus **12%** of the amount over $9,525
$38,701 - $82,500	$4,453.50 plus **22%** of the amount over $38,700
$82,501 - $157,500	$14,089.50 plus **24%** of the amount over $82,500
$157,501 - $200,000	$32,089.50 plus **32%** of the amount over $157,500
$200,001 - $500,000	$45,689.50 plus **35%** of the amount over $200,000
Over $500,000	$150,689.50 plus **37%** of amount over $500,000

■ Congress occasionally alters the tax *rates*. Such changes may reflect a shift in the government's revenue needs (e.g., to finance war or curb budget deficits) or, more likely, a shift in prevailing political sentiment.

■ A taxpayer's **marginal tax rate** refers to the rate of tax applicable to the highest segment of her taxable income under the tax rate tables. Thus, under Table 7.1, an individual with $250,000 of taxable income would have a marginal rate of 35 percent. Just because someone has a marginal rate of 35 percent, however, does *not* mean that all of her taxable income gets taxed at a flat rate of 35 percent. Thus, if an unmarried individual has $250,000 of taxable income and the tax table above applies, some of her income is taxed at 10 percent, some at 12 percent, some at 22 percent, some at 24 percent, and only the last portion at 35 percent. The colloquial fear of being pushed into a "higher tax bracket" should be understood (potentially) as a modest exaggeration; the higher rate may have an impact, but the impact is confined to the uppermost margin of taxable income.

As we move to the deduction arena, we focus first on those that are decidedly personal in nature, reserving those deductions with mixed business and personal elements or only business elements for later. In this chapter, we take up the standard deduction, the itemized deduction election, the impact of tax credits, the meaning of "dependent," and the deduction with respect to qualified business income. We move on to the deduction for extraordinary medical expenses in Chapter 8, before addressing casualty, theft, and other losses in Chapter 9. From there, we discuss the deductions for certain forms of interest and specific taxes in Chapter 10 and the allowance for charitable contributions in Chapter 11.

B. THE STANDARD DEDUCTION AND THE ITEMIZED DEDUCTIONS ALTERNATIVE

As April 15 approaches each year, millions of taxpayers across the United States gather their paperwork and head off to have a paid preparer complete and file their federal income tax return. Others sit down with tax preparation software to complete the task or grab their calculators and set out to tackle IRS Form 1040 or some variant of it. Taxpayers with relatively simple personal and financial profiles, for example, may be able to complete and file IRS Form 1040EZ. Those whose financial profiles or personal situations require a more detailed tax reckoning, however, must complete and file IRS Form 1040. In many instances, completing Form 1040 turns out to be a relatively straightforward task. Many of the line items simply will not apply, and line-by-line instructions are available online at the IRS website (i.e., [Year] Form 1040 Instructions). Our focus is on IRS Form 1040 at the line devoted to taxpayer's standard deduction (or itemized deductions). Taxpayers completing IRS Form 1040 must make a choice at this juncture. They must choose to take *either* (1) a standard deduction *or* (2) a series of itemized deductions. Those who opt for the former deduct a dollar amount corresponding to their filing status. A married taxpayer filing a joint return, for example, would take a standard deduction of $24,000.

> **Key Statutory Provisions**
>
> ■ **Internal Revenue Code**
>   ■ § 63(b), (c)(1)–(4), (e)(1)–(2)
>   ■ § 68(a) and (c)
>   ■ § 262

"Itemized Deductions"

The Code's definition of "itemized deduction" is of critical significance for many reasons. Section 63(d) generally defines itemized deductions as those allowable for income tax purposes, but specific deductions are excluded from the definition, including, among others, (1) those allowable in arriving at adjusted gross income and (2) the deduction under § 199A (concerning qualified business income). Thus a number of available allowances constitute itemized deductions. Within the latter category, there is subdivision into (i) itemized deductions and (ii) miscellaneous itemized deductions. Under prior law, the distinction was significant enough because miscellaneous itemized deductions (as a class) were allowed only to the extent such deductions exceeded two percent of an individual taxpayer's AGI for the taxable year. The distinction is now critical, because currently applicable tax law contains no allowance for the taking of such miscellaneous itemized deductions. Miscellaneous itemized deductions are defined, per § 67(b), as all itemized deductions except designated allowances (e.g., the deduction under § 163 for interest or § 164 for taxes). Viewed holistically, then, deductible items are those that are either non-itemized (e.g., trade or business expenses of employers) or itemized deductions that are not miscellaneous itemized deductions.

Of course, if one's aggregate itemized deductions are higher than one's corresponding standard deduction, it makes more sense to deduct those rather than simply taking the standard deduction. One ascertains the amount of one's itemized deductions by completing IRS Form 1040 Schedule A.

We will examine the law regarding individual itemized and non-itemized deductions in future chapters. For the moment, simply note that those completing IRS Form 1040 must choose between the standard deduction and itemized deductions; those completing IRS Form 1040EZ will automatically take the standard deduction. Congress provides for the standard deduction under IRC § 63. In addition to establishing the statutory amount of the standard deduction for each filing status, the Code also provides for an additional standard deduction for the aged and the blind and requires that the various standard deduction amounts be adjusted for inflation.

The standard deduction can be thought of, in a sense, as a rough approximation of the items one would ordinarily take into account as itemized deductions (e.g., medical expenses, state income taxes, real and personal property taxes, mortgage interest paid, charitable contributions, etc.). For some taxpayers, this rough approximation misses the mark by a wide margin; their mortgage interest deduction, standing alone, might eclipse their standard deduction amount. Completing Schedule A and thereby itemizing one's deductions generally allows the taxpayer to take a larger deduction (relative to the standard deduction), but special rules come into play with respect to each item. As the taxpayer completes Schedule A, he or she may find that a given expense is fully deductible, deductible to a limited extent, or wholly nondeductible.

C. IMPACT OF TAX CREDITS

In completing their returns for a given taxable year, taxpayers generally ascertain their taxable income and proceed to apply the rate schedule that corresponds to their filing status. Thereafter, they will have a figure representing the amount of tax owed. For many taxpayers, calculating their final tax liability (or refund amount) is simply a matter of comparing this amount with amounts previously withheld by their employer or, in the case of the self-employed, amounts previously paid as estimated taxes (to be discussed in Chapter 22). If amounts withheld or paid exceed the tax owed, the taxpayer gets a refund. If, on the other hand, the tax owed exceeds the amounts previously withheld or paid, then the taxpayer must pay the difference. Consider the following examples.

Example 1

Bryce is completing his federal income tax return and has ascertained that his tax owed is $35,000. According to the Form W-2 provided by his employer, Bryce can see that during the taxable year, his employer withheld $36,701 with respect to income taxes. Bryce has overpaid his income taxes and will receive a refund of $1,701.

Example 2

Same facts as Example 1, except that Bryce's employer only withheld $34,000 with respect to income taxes. Bryce will be required to pay $1,000 to the United States Treasury.

In addition to taking withheld amounts and/or estimated tax payments into account in calculating their final tax liability or refund amount, taxpayers may also take into account various tax credits. Tax credits and tax deductions are not the same thing. A **tax credit** is a direct offset to a taxpayer's tax liability. A tax deduction benefits a taxpayer but in a different manner. The following example should highlight the difference between a $1,000 tax deduction and a $1,000 tax credit.

EXHIBIT 7.1   **Sample IRS Form W-2**

22222	a Employee's social security number	OMB No. 1545-0008	
b Employer identification number (EIN)		1 Wages, tips, other compensation	2 Federal income tax withheld
c Employer's name, address, and ZIP code		3 Social security wages	4 Social security tax withheld
		5 Medicare wages and tips	6 Medicare tax withheld
		7 Social security tips	8 Allocated tips
d Control number		9 Verification code	10 Dependent care benefits
e Employee's first name and initial Last name Suff.		11 Nonqualified plans	12a
		13 Statutory employee Retirement plan Third-party sick pay	12b
		14 Other	12c
			12d
f Employee's address and ZIP code			

15 State Employer's state ID number	16 State wages, tips, etc.	17 State income tax	18 Local wages, tips, etc.	19 Local income tax	20 Locality name

Form **W-2**   Wage and Tax Statement   **2017**   Department of the Treasury—Internal Revenue Service

Copy 1—For State, City, or Local Tax Department

Handwritten margin notes:
Deduction: lowers taxing into account tax rate.

Credit: Lowers w/o factoring in that rate

Example 3

Assume that George completed his tax return as soon as he received his Form W-2 from his employer, and it appeared that his total tax liability was $22,000. He realized, however, that he had failed to take into account a $1,000 deduction. If we assume that George's marginal tax rate is 32 percent, then a $1,000 deduction will lower his tax by $320. As a result, his recalculated tax liability will be $21,680 ($22,000 – $320). Based on the foregoing, we can see that a tax deduction benefits a taxpayer, but the level of benefit depends on their marginal tax rate. If we assume that George was entitled to a $1,000 tax *credit* instead of a $1,000 deduction, his tax liability would be reduced from $22,000 to $21,000. Thus, rather than merely reducing tax liability to some extent, a tax credit directly offsets tax liability.

EXHIBIT 7.2 **Sample IRS Form 1040 Excerpt**

62	Taxes from: **a** ☐ Form 8959 **b** ☐ Form 8960 **c** ☐ Instructions; enter code(s)	62	
63	Add lines 56 through 62. This is your **total tax**	63	
Payments 64	Federal income tax withheld from Forms W-2 and 1099	64	
If you have qualifying child, attach Schedule EIC.	65 2016 estimated tax payments and amount applied from 2015 return	65	
66a	**Earned income credit (EIC)**	66a	
b	Nontaxable combat pay election	66b	
67	Additional child tax credit. Attach Schedule 8812	67	
68	American opportunity credit from Form 8863, line 8	68	
69	Net premium tax credit. Attach Form 8962	69	
70	Amount paid with request for extension to file	70	
71	Excess social security and tier 1 RRTA tax withheld	71	
72	Credit for federal tax on fuels. Attach Form 4136	72	
73	Credits from Form: **a** ☐ 2439 **b** ☐ Reserved **c** ☐ 8885 **d** ☐	73	
74	Add lines 64, 65, 66a, and 67 through 73. These are your **total payments** ▶	74	
Refund 75	If line 74 is more than line 63, subtract line 63 from line 74. This is the amount you **overpaid**	75	
76a	Amount of line 75 you want **refunded to you.** If Form 8888 is attached, check ▶ ☐	76a	
Direct deposit? ▶ b	Routing number ▶ **c** Type: ☐ Checking ☐ Savings		
See instructions. ▶ d	Account number		
77	Amount of line 75 you want **applied to your 2017 estimated tax** ▶	77	
Amount You Owe 78	**Amount you owe.** Subtract line 74 from line 63. For details on how to pay, see instructions ▶	78	
79	Estimated tax penalty (see instructions)	79	

Although the Internal Revenue Code sets forth various tax credits, specific taxpayers may or may not be able to take advantage of them. And even those taxpayers eligible for the credit may benefit more or less than others. For example, only those with a qualifying child (or a "dependent" satisfying a statutory standard) may take advantage of the Child Tax Credit provided for by § 24. And although those eligible for the Earned Income Credit (under § 32) need not have a qualifying child, their credit will be enhanced to the extent that they have one or more qualifying children. Keep in mind that a number of tax credits available to individuals are intended to ease the tax burden on those within a specific income range. Thus, as a taxpayer's income rises, she may find that she has been phased out of credit eligibility. Also, keep in mind that not all tax credits are refundable. If a taxpayer has a preliminary tax liability of $10,000 but is eligible for a $12,000 refundable tax credit, the taxpayer will have a final tax liability of $0 *and* get a refund of $2,000. If, on the other hand, the tax credit is nonrefundable, the taxpayer will have a final tax liability of $0 but will get no refund.

EXHIBIT 7.3 **Sample IRS Form 1040 Excerpt**

	62	Taxes from: **a** ☐ Form 8959 **b** ☐ Form 8960 **c** ☐ Instructions; enter code(s) _____	62	
	63	Add lines 56 through 62. This is your **total tax** . . . . ▶	63	
Payments	64	Federal income tax withheld from Forms W-2 and 1099 . .	64	
	65	2016 estimated tax payments and amount applied from 2015 return	65	
If you have a qualifying child, attach Schedule EIC.	66a	**Earned income credit (EIC)**	66a	
	b	Nontaxable combat pay election . . .		
	67	Additional child tax credit. Attach Schedule 8812	67	
	68	American opportunity credit from Form 8863, line 8 . . .	68	
	69	Net premium tax credit. Attach Form 8962	69	
	70	Amount paid with request for extension to file	70	
	71	Excess social security and tier 1 RRTA tax withheld . . .	71	
	72	Credit for federal tax on fuels. Attach Form 4136	72	
	73	Credits from Form: **a** ☐ 2439 **b** ☐ Reserved **c** ☐ 8885 **d** ☐ _____	73	
	74	Add lines 64, 65, 66a, and 67 through 73. These are your **total payments** . . . . . ▶	74	
Refund	75	If line 74 is more than line 63, subtract line 63 from line 74. This is the amount you **overpaid**	75	
	76a	Amount of line 75 you want **refunded to you.** If Form 8888 is attached, check here . ▶ ☐	76a	
Direct deposit? ▶ See instructions.	b	Routing number ⬚⬚⬚⬚⬚⬚⬚⬚⬚ ▶ **c** Type: ☐ Checking ☐ Savings		
	d	Account number ⬚⬚⬚⬚⬚⬚⬚⬚⬚		
	77	Amount of line 75 you want **applied to your 2017 estimated tax** ▶	77	
Amount You Owe	78	**Amount you owe.** Subtract line 74 from line 63. For details on how to pay, see instructions ▶	78	
	79	Estimated tax penalty (see instructions)	79	

D. DEFINING "DEPENDENT"

1. In General

As was noted above, in addition to allowing taxpayers to take the standard deduction or to elect itemization, Congress also generally allows taxpayers a tax credit under § 24 with respect to certain dependents of the taxpayer. Thus, given that lucrative tax credits may be at stake, it matters a great deal not only whether an individual can qualify as a dependent but also which taxpayer may rightfully enjoy the benefits associated with that individual's dependent status.

> **Key Statutory Provisions**
> ▪ **Internal Revenue Code**
>   ▪ 151(d)(5)
>   ▪ § 152(a), (c)(1)–(3), (d)(1)–(2), (e)(1)–(2), (e)(4), and (f)(1)–(4)

Given the potential tax benefits associated with identifying an individual as a dependent, taxpayers might very well conclude that the term *dependent* should be construed broadly and not limited so rigidly to the children they clothed, fed, and housed; random nieces and nephews might suddenly take on a "dependent" aura as tax season dawns, especially if one parent of the purported dependent is incarcerated and the other doesn't really hold what one would call a "job," at least not a stable one. Congress, of course, has a different take on the matter. Although § 152 defines *dependent* with abundant clarity, the rules also reflect a healthy accommodation of a wide range of modern family structures and living arrangements.

Section 152(a) generally defines *dependent* as a *qualifying child* or a *qualifying relative* and subsections 152(c) and (d) provide further definitional clarity with respect to these terms. Under § 152(c), *qualifying child* refers (in highly generalized terms here) to an individual who satisfies the following criteria with respect to the taxpayer:

- Bears a specific type of relationship to the taxpayer (e.g., child, grandchild, brother, stepsister, niece, nephew);[1]
- Shares the taxpayer's principal place of abode for more than one-half of the taxable year;
- Meets an age requirement (i.e., younger than the taxpayer and under 19 (or a student under age 24) as of the close of the taxable year);[2]
- Has not provided more than one-half of their own support for the calendar year; and
- Has not filed a joint return with a spouse for the taxable year.

Section 152(d) defines *qualifying relative*, and as one might expect, the definition sweeps more broadly than the definition of qualifying child but also contains a few restrictions. Stated in highly generalized terms here, qualifying relative refers to an individual who satisfies the following criteria with respect to the taxpayer:

- Bears a specific type of relationship to the taxpayer (*see generally* § 152(d)(2));
- Has gross income for the calendar year below a statutory threshold;
- Received over one-half of their support for the calendar year from the taxpayer; and
- Is not a qualifying child of the taxpayer or any other taxpayer for the relevant taxable year.

Notwithstanding the general clarity and breadth of these rules, the likelihood is strong that your average taxpayer files his tax returns wholly ignorant of the Code's baroque definitional boundaries. Errors will undoubtedly occur. At the same time, there's a big difference between an understandable oversight on the one hand and outright attempts to test the Commissioner's vigilance on the other.

| **Case Preview** | ***Schoen v. Commissioner*** |

Taxpayers called on to assist ailing relatives often do so with no expectation of earthly reward. Others may generally feel the same way, but at some tipping point, they begin to feel that their efforts entitle them to more than mere thanks,

---

1. Section 152(f) contains a host of subdefinitions of specific terms (e.g., "child" includes stepchildren, adopted children, and eligible foster children).
2. An individual who is totally and permanently disabled is deemed to satisfy the age requirement.

appreciative nods, and good feeling. In *Schoen v. Commissioner*, the taxpayer stepped in to help out his father before later helping himself to a deduction on his federal income tax return. That act, and a few more transgressions, got him into hot water with the Commissioner. As you read through *Schoen*, consider the following questions:

1. To what extent did the taxpayer provide for his father's care and support? Was that sufficient to make him the taxpayer's qualifying relative?
2. Do dependents have to be individuals?
3. Given the focus on medical expenses under § 213, why is § 152 even relevant?

Schoen v. Commissioner
T.C. Memo. 1975-167

MEMORANDUM OPINION

RAUM, Judge:

The Commissioner determined a $96.83 deficiency in petitioner's 1971 income tax. At issue is the correctness of the disallowance of two deductions for medical expenses. The deduction for medical expenses is set forth in section 213 of the Code, and it extends to payments made on behalf of the taxpayer's "dependents" as that word is defined in section 152. The issue herein, more particularly, is whether the payments here in question were on behalf of "dependents" of the taxpayer.

The first deduction, in the amount of $400 was claimed by petitioner in respect of his father, who resided in Arizona but who was visiting petitioner at his home in Ipswich, Massachusetts, in June, 1971. At that time the father was arrested and charged with disorderly conduct in Ipswich. It appears that the father was suffering from mental problems and the Massachusetts court ordered on June 11, 1971, that he "be released to son's custody;" the case was then dismissed. Petitioner thereupon promptly arranged to transport his father back to Arizona, where within a very short time the father was committed to a mental institution. Petitioner then returned to Massachusetts. The $400 claimed as a medical deduction related solely to expenses incurred in connection with this trip. Petitioner admits that he did not furnish as much as 50 percent of his father's support during 1971. In the circumstances, the disallowance must be approved.

Section 152(a) of the 1954 Code explicitly requires that in order for petitioner's father to be classified as a "dependent," he must have received over half of his support for the year from petitioner — a condition that was not satisfied here. Accordingly, the claimed medical expense cannot qualify for deduction. The mere fact that for a limited purpose the father was released to petitioner's custody by the Massachusetts court is not sufficient to comply with the requirements of section 152.

Deduction 2:
Dog

The other medical deduction disallowed was an item of $10.30 paid to a veterinarian on behalf of petitioner's dog. In his petition, the taxpayer set forth his position in respect of this item as follows:

> My dog is dependent on me for food & medical care. My family and I are dependent on my dog for protection from harm in the night. A family's dog is part of the family. Again the I.R.S. is simply playing on semantics in disallowing this expense.

4: Dog
doesn't
qualify

While petitioner appears to be entirely sincere, it is quite obvious that the dog cannot qualify as a dependent under section 152. Whatever validity there may be to the ancient maxim that a dog is man's best friend, it is all too clear to us that in no circumstances can a dog qualify as a dependent by reason of being a relative of the taxpayer by blood, marriage or adoption within any of the categories set forth in section 152(a)(1)-(8) and (10), or as an "individual" who is a member of the taxpayer's household within section 152(a) (9).

We hold that there is no sound basis for supporting the claimed medical deductions on any acceptable theory.

Decision will be entered for the respondent.

Case Preview

This short case, included to a healthy extent for its entertainment value, reflects straightforward application of the statutory rules, many of which have not changed fundamentally relative to the version in the Internal Revenue Code of 1954. As you can see, the case technically concerns the deductibility of medical expenses under § 213, but because a taxpayer may deduct only medical expenses of the taxpayer, his spouse, and his dependents, the result in this case ultimately turns on whether the expenses relate to an individual who qualifies, by statutory definition, as the taxpayer's dependent under § 152. We see similar interdependence in § 119 concerning benefits provided for the convenience of the employer ("meals or lodging furnished to [the employee], his spouse, or *any of his dependents*") and § 132(h) concerning certain fringe benefits ("Any use by the spouse *or a dependent child* of the employee shall be treated as use by the employee."). Cross-references appear frequently in the Internal Revenue Code, and you should get comfortable with them. They may require a little legwork, but they need not cause alarm. Attorneys must conduct professional level research and make every effort to achieve thorough understanding.

In *Schoen*, the court confirms that the taxpayer cannot take a medical expense deduction for the cost of assisting his father because the taxpayer's father cannot qualify as a dependent; the taxpayer did not supply over half of the father's support during the calendar year. Taking him into custody, getting him back to Arizona, and checking him into a facility may have been a hassle, but such filial assistance, standing alone, will not give rise to "dependent" status. Likewise, the taxpayer's dog could not qualify as a dependent (and thus no medical expense deduction could follow) because, by definition, dependent (whether a qualifying child or a qualifying relative) must be an "individual." True, unlike the word "person" (which might refer to an individual or a legal person such as a corporation), "individual," refers to flesh and blood, but in the Code that term refers to the flesh and blood *of a human.*

Schoen v. Commissioner: Real Life Applications

1. Four months after celebrating her 85th birthday, Eleanor fell and broke her hip. She moved in with her daughter, Mary Lou, in February of 2017 and has resided there since then. Eleanor has no income, and she relies 100 percent on Mary Lou for her care and support.

   a. What specific Code provision allows Eleanor to satisfy the relationship requirement of § 152(d)(1)(A)?

   b. Is Eleanor Mary Lou's qualifying relative?

   c. Under the same facts, could Mary Lou's uncle (maternal or paternal side of the family) satisfy the relationship requirement of § 152(d)(1)(A)? Please explain.

2. Since an early age, Gary has been legally blind. He now lives independently, but he relies heavily on his seeing-eye dog, Copernicus. Gary generally provides 100 percent of Copernicus's care, although he pays someone to give the dog his daily walks and to take him to the veterinarian for regular checkups.

   a. Does Copernicus qualify as Gary's dependent?

   b. Should Gary be able to deduct the cost of Copernicus's upkeep as a medical expense? *See* PLR 5602244860A (Feb. 24, 1956); *see also* Rev. Rul. 68-295, 1968-1 C.B. 92.

Capuchin Monkeys: Service Animals Extraordinaire

Individuals with impaired mobility often need highly-trained service animals to assist with the activities of daily living. Capuchin monkeys perform extraordinarily well in this capacity for a number of reasons. Their manual dexterity and fine motor skills give them the ability to perform a number of tasks, including turning pages, retrieving objects, activing electronic devices, facilitating drinking, de/activating switches, and repositioning limbs on a wheelchair. *See generally* https://monkeyhelpers.org.

Credit: Little Red on Tour/Shutterstock.com.

2. Children of Divorced, Legally Separated, or Non-Cohabiting Parents

Section 152 contains many special rules, and anyone conducting research on the definition of a dependent should consult an unedited version of the relevant Internal Revenue Code provisions and the associated Treasury Regulations. One should pay special attention to rules governing which parent may enjoy the benefits of a child's dependency status (e.g., tax credits) when the parents are divorced, separated, or not living together.

A child may live with two parents, one parent, or neither parent, and it is not uncommon to find that two individuals seek to designate the same child as a dependent. Assume that two parents support the child but fail to file a joint return. In that context, the parent with whom the child resided for the longest period during the taxable year may designate the child as a dependent. *See* § 152(c)(4)(B)(i). If the same child lived with both parents for the same amount of time during the year, then the parent with the highest AGI gets to designate the child as a dependent. *See* § 152(c)(4)(B)(ii). A child living with one parent and a supporting non-parent who might designate her as a dependent is deemed to be the qualifying child of her parent, and if the child happens to live with two supporting non-parents (e.g., two aunts), then the supporter with the highest AGI gets to designate the child as a dependent.

> **Warning**
>
> Divorce and legal separation may present parents with an opportunity to negotiate which parent will be able to designate the child as a dependent for tax credit and other purposes. Bear in mind that if the IRS requires formalization of this arrangement (e.g., by individual or joint execution of a specific IRS form), the attorneys are ultimately responsible for protecting the interests of their clients by securing the necessary signatures and thereby eliminating any potential issues in this regard.

E. DEDUCTION WITH RESPECT TO QUALIFIED BUSINESS INCOME

Under § 199A, non-corporate taxpayers may generally take a deduction with respect to their qualified business income of the taxable year. By making this allowance available, Congress seeks to offer a measure of tax relief to specific taxpayers operating businesses as sole proprietors or via certain flow-through entities (e.g., partnerships or S corporations). Although we will not undertake exhaustive examination and application of the provision in this introductory setting, we will address certain fundamentals given the impact this provision will have on a number of individuals.

In somewhat oversimplified terms, § 199A generally grants taxpayers a deduction equal to 20 percent of their qualified business income for a given taxable year. Congress, in tailoring the provision to benefit targeted taxpayers within specific taxable income ranges, employed a dense thicket of defined terms. Ultimately, the true extent of a taxpayer's deduction will turn on a number of factors. The general rule set forth in § 199A(a) foreshadows the provision's complexity. Per § 199A(a), a non-corporate taxpayer may take a deduction (the "qualified business deduction") equal to the sum of two amounts, (A) and (B). "(A)" is the lesser of two amounts: (1) the taxpayer's combined qualified business income amount and (2) 20 percent of the taxpayer's taxable income (reduced by any net capital gain and qualified cooperative dividends). "(B)" is the lesser of (1) 20 percent of the taxpayer's qualified cooperative dividends and (2) the taxpayer's taxable income (reduced by any net capital gain). Note that the taxpayer's qualified business deduction can never exceed the taxpayer's taxable income (reduced by any net capital gain). Notwithstanding the relatively straightforward contours of the general rule, it is in exploring the defined terms within it that we truly see how the rule operates, who may take advantage of it, and to what extent. The following terms (as defined for § 199A purposes) are of primary significance:

Taxable Income This is the taxable income of the taxpayer, calculated without taking into account the deduction under § 199A.

Threshold Amount For 2018, this amount is $157,500 for those not filing a joint return and twice this amount ($315,000) for those filing a joint return. Section 199A(e)(2)(B) dictates that the $157,500 amount be adjusted for inflation in taxable years beginning after 2018 (effectively adjusting the joint return amount as well).

Qualified Items of Income, Gain, Deduction, & Loss This term refers to items of income, gain, deduction, and loss to extent they are (1) effectively connected with the conduct of a trade or business within the United States (as defined per § 199A(c)(3)(A)(i)) and (2) included or allowed in determining taxable income for the taxable year. Note that various investment items (e.g., certain interest income and various capital gains or losses) are not taken into account as qualified items of income, gain, deduction, or loss. *See generally* § 199A(c)(3)(B).

Qualified Business Income This term generally refers to the net amount of qualified items of income, gain, deduction, and loss with respect to any qualified trade or business of the taxpayer. It does not include certain defined forms of investment income (e.g., qualified REIT dividends, qualified cooperative dividends, and qualified publicly traded partnership income). Further, qualified business income does not include reasonable compensation paid to a taxpayer by a qualified trade or business for services rendered to the trade or business nor does it include certain payments made to partners for services rendered with respect to the trade or business (e.g., guaranteed payments, among others).

> Note: If, with respect to a given taxable year, the relevant net amount of qualified items of income, gain, deduction, and loss is negative, then this amount will be treated as a loss from a qualified trade or business in the succeeding taxable year.

Qualified Trade or Business Although this term generally refers to any trade or business, the term does not include (i) specified service trades or businesses (as later defined) or (ii) the trade or business of performing services as an employee.

Specified Service Trade or Business This defined term refers to two broad categories. The first is any trade or business described in § 1202(e)(3)(A) (excluding engineering and architecture). The specified trades and businesses described therein include health, law, accounting, performing arts, consulting, athletics, financial services, brokerage services, and those in which the principal business asset is the reputation or skill of one or more employees or owners. The second category includes any trade or business that involves the performance of specific services (i.e., investment, investment management, or trading or dealing in securities, partnership interests, or commodities).

> *Exception for Certain Taxpayers* Although the trade or business of performing services as an employee cannot be a qualified trade or business for § 199A purposes, a given specified service trade or business may be treated as a qualified trade or business if the taxable income of the taxpayer is less than the sum of the threshold amount and $50,000 ($100,000 in the case of a joint return), but in performing calculations under § 199A, the taxpayer will only be allowed to take into account the applicable percentage (defined in § 199A(d)(3)(B)) of specific items.

Combined Qualified Business Income Amount Although one could think of this amount as 20 percent of the taxpayer's total qualified business income with respect to their qualified trades or businesses, the statutory definition is considerably more precise. Technically, a taxpayer's combined qualified business income amount is the sum of (A) and (B), where (A) is the sum of the "Section 199A(b)(2) Amounts" as determined for each of the taxpayer's qualified trades or businesses and (B) is 20 percent of certain investment income of the taxpayer (i.e., qualified REIT dividends plus qualified publicly traded partnership income).

Section 199A(b)(2) Amount In basic technical terms, the § 199A(b)(2) amount is the lesser of the amount determined under § 199A(b)(2)(A) (discussed below) and the amount determined under § 199A(b)(2)(B) (discussed below). On closer examination, however, several possibilities present. Depending on the taxpayer's taxable income, his § 199A(b)(2) amount may be either of the following:

(i) The amount determined under § 199A(b)(2)(A);
(ii) The amount determined under § 199A(b)(2)(A) with a downward adjustment; or
(iii) The lesser of the § 199A(b)(2)(A) amount and the § 199A(b)(2)(B) amount.

If the taxpayer's taxable income does not exceed the threshold amount, the taxpayer ignores the § 199A(b)(2)(B) amount and simply uses the § 199A(b)(2)(A) amount. If the taxpayer's taxable income exceeds the threshold amount but does not exceed it by $50,000 ($100,000 in the case of a joint return) and the § 199A(b)(2)(B) amount would otherwise be less than the § 199A(b)(2)(A) amount, he will use the § 199A(b)(2)(A) amount reduced by a specific amount. If the taxpayer's taxable income exceeds the threshold amount by more than $50,000 ($100,000 in the case of a joint return), then he will use the lesser of the § 199A(b)(2)(A) amount or the § 199A(b)(2)(B) amount.

Section 199A(b)(2)(A) amount refers to 20 percent of the taxpayer's qualified business income with respect to a given qualified trade or business.

Section 199A(b)(2)(B) amount refers to the greater of (i) 50 percent of the W-2 wages (as defined in § 199A(b)(4)) with respect to the qualified trade or business and (ii) the sum of 25 percent of such W-2 wages and 2.5 percent of the unadjusted basis immediately after acquisition of all qualified property (as defined in § 199A(b)(6)).

To the extent the taxpayer is to use a reduced § 199A(b)(2)(A) amount, the reduction is equal to the product of (i) the difference between the § 199A(b)(2)(A) and § 199A(b)(2)(B) amounts and (ii) the quotient obtained by dividing {the taxpayer's taxable income reduced by the relevant threshold amount} by {$50,000 ($100,000 in the case of a joint return)}.

Note that the qualified business income deduction is not an above-the-line item. Further, although it is available to non-itemizers, the deduction, by definition, is not an itemized deduction. *See* § 63(d)(3).

Chapter Summary

- Congress seeks to achieve both vertical and horizontal equity. It does so by ensuring that all taxpayers with the same taxable income shoulder the same tax burden and by requiring that taxpayers pay progressively higher tax rates as their taxable income rises. Rate-specific thresholds vary by taxpayer filing status.
- A taxpayer's marginal tax rate is the rate of tax applicable to the highest segment of their taxable income. Even if a taxpayer has a high marginal tax rate, they still benefit from the lower tax rates imposed on the lower segments of all taxable income.
- In completing IRS Form 1040, taxpayers may take either a standard deduction or a series of itemized deductions. The standard deduction amount varies by taxpayer filing status.
- Tax credits reduce a taxpayer's preliminary tax liability on a dollar for dollar basis. Tax deductions reduce a taxpayer's tax liability in a manner directly proportional to the taxpayer's marginal tax rate.
- The Code defines *dependent* with extensive definitions, subdefinitions, and special rules.
- An IRS determination that an individual does not qualify as a taxpayer's dependent may have wide-ranging impact on the taxpayer.
- Section 199A generally provides for a deduction equal to 20 percent of a non-corporate taxpayer's qualified business income with respect to their qualified trade or business. The deduction is designed to benefit taxpayers with taxable income (as defined in that section) falling within a specific range.

Applying the Rules

1. After wrapping up a rousing senior year of high school, Albert headed off to college on August 20, 2018. He was a single, 17-year-old at the time and had lived with (and been supported 100 percent by) his parents at all times prior to

that date. As his parents complete their joint 2018 Form 1040, will they be able to treat Albert as a dependent (assuming their taxable year is the calendar year)?

2. Emir recently completed high school. He is now 19. He works 40 hours per week as a cashier and lives with and provides 100 percent of the support for his 22-year-old brother, Abdul (who has been unemployed without income for two years). As Emir completes his 2018 Form 1040, may he consider Abdul his dependent as a qualifying child? What about as a qualifying relative?

3. Anna and Claudius are husband and wife. Anna's father passed away three years ago, and Anna's 75-year-old mother, Jessie, has lived in her old home since then. Jessie has gross income of roughly $500 per month from her investments, but she otherwise relies on Anna and Claudius for support (roughly 60 percent). May Anna and Claudius treat Jessie as a dependent for federal income tax purposes?

4. Assume that Heather is an unmarried individual who had $350,000 of taxable income in 2018. Using Table 7.1, ascertain her marginal tax rate and calculate her tax.

5. Tired of regular, heated arguments with her parents over her transgendered status, Jamie Sonoma (who is 15, was born a genetic male (James), prefers to be called Jamie, and identifies as female) asked her long-time neighbors (the Taylors) if she could move into their home. They agreed, and in 2018, Jamie resided with the Taylors. Although the Taylors had no genetic relation to Jamie, they were happy to provide 100 percent of her support. In completing their 2018 Form 1040, may the Taylors treat Jamie as a dependent (assuming Jamie has no income and that the Taylors use the calendar year as their taxable year)? Yes: 152 (d)(2)(H)

Federal Income Taxation in Practice

1. Find Form 1040EZ for 2018 on the IRS website. Also locate Form 1040, Form 1040 Schedule A, and the instructions for Form 1040 and for Form 1040 Schedule A. Also find the form you would file if you needed to amend your 2018 Form 1040.

2. Although Carrie was of the belief that she and her husband, Lance, had an excellent marriage, she recently found out about one of Lance's extramarital affairs. Carrie left Lance and moved in with her parents in April of 2018 (remaining there for the rest of the year). Carrie is 35 years old and had no income during 2018, but she agreed to file a joint return with Lance on the condition that she receive 50 percent of any refund generated. That money, she reasoned, could be used to help pay for a divorce attorney. May Carrie's parents consider her as a dependent with respect to their 2018 Form 1040?

3. Joseph is legally married to Gail. As it turns out, Joseph is also married to Leah and Evelyn because his religion allows plural marriage. State law, however, prohibits bigamy and adultery. Assuming Joseph provides 100 percent of the support of Leah and Evelyn (neither of whom has income) and lives in the same home with them for the entire calendar year, may he and Gail consider them dependents with respect to their joint 2018 Form 1040?

   ↳ violates '52 (f)(3)

4. One of the partners in your law firm is the primary contact of Mr. and Ms. Newton, a couple of generally modest means. They recently suffered the kidnapping of their 10-year-old daughter, Rhea, and continue to be distraught. Your fellow law partner would like to know whether they should be treating Rhea as a dependent on their federal income tax returns during her absence. She lived with them at all times prior to her abduction. Please prepare a brief memorandum summarizing your research findings.

Extraordinary Medical Expenses

Over the course of a given year, most taxpayers spend a modest amount of money on standard health-related items such as band aids, cough syrup, bandages, antiseptics, antihistamines, over-the-counter pain medication, heartburn tablets, and the like. Unfortunately, § 262 generally prohibits any deduction with respect to these items because they are deemed to be mere personal expenses. Congress does realize, however, that at some point expenditures incurred and paid by a taxpayer with respect to the medical care of her family can have a clear and definite impact on her ability to pay her taxes and that, as a matter of fundamental fairness, at least some portion of those expenses should be taken into account in calculating her final tax liability. Accordingly, § 213 presents a potential deduction opportunity, but as you will soon see, the tax relief it provides is decidedly limited. Because the deduction for medical expenses ultimately appears on Form 1040 Schedule A, only those taxpayers who elect to itemize their deductions (and forego the standard deduction amount corresponding to their filing status) can reap its benefits. Even so, the current legal framework essentially guarantees that a deduction will be available only for itemizers with truly extraordinary medical expenses (when measured relative to their adjusted gross income) in a given taxable year.

Key Concepts

- The limited deductibility of medical expenses and the basic meaning of *medical care*
- The treatment of doctor-recommended activities and the specter of differential treatment of taxpayers with respect to identical medical expenses
- The meaning of *cosmetic surgery* and similar procedures
- Evolving conceptions of *disease* and *treatment*

171

A. GENERAL DEDUCTIBILITY RULES

Key Statutory and Regulatory Provisions

■ **Internal Revenue Code**
  ■ § 213(a)–(b)
  ■ § 213(d)(1)–(4)
  ■ § 213(d)(9)
■ **Treasury Regulations**
  ■ § 1.213-1(e)(1)(iv)–(v)
  ■ § 1.213-1(e)(2)

Section 213(a) of the Code generally allows a deduction with respect to expenses paid during the taxable year for medical care of a given taxpayer, his spouse, and his dependents. The rule applies only to expenses that have not been compensated for by insurance (or otherwise), and only a portion of the expenses qualify for deduction; a taxpayer may deduct such expenses but only to the extent they exceed 7.5 percent[1] of his AGI. *See* § 213(a). Exhibit 8.1 depicts the relevant section of IRS Form 1040 Schedule A. The following example demonstrates the operation of the statutory rule:

Example 1

While preparing dinner one evening, Ivan suffered a severe burn to his left hand. He received treatment in the emergency room of a nearby hospital and paid a total of $10,000 for the care he received during the visit. Assuming that Ivan has not been reimbursed by insurance (or otherwise) and that he had AGI of $50,000 during the year he paid the expense, he may deduct a portion of his medical care expense.

Amount paid for medical care:	$10,000
Minus 7.5% of Ivan's AGI ($50,000):	($3,750)
Amount deductible under § 213	**$6,250**

In the above example, Ivan suffered injury to his physical person and sought treatment from medical professionals in a traditional hospital. Most taxpayers, no doubt, incur medical expenses that do not give rise to legal issues, and such individuals are fully content playing by standard deduction rules. But one can easily imagine aggressive taxpayers attempting to deduct the cost of "therapeutic" vacations in lush, tropical resorts or expensive procedures or remedies which (even by modern, alternative-medicine standards) bear disturbing resemblance to outright

EXHIBIT 8.1   **Excerpt from 2016 IRS Form 1040 Schedule A**

Medical and Dental Expenses	Caution: Do not include expenses reimbursed or paid by others.			
	1 Medical and dental expenses (see instructions)	**1**		
	2 Enter amount from Form 1040, line 38 **2**			
	3 Multiply line 2 by 10% (0.10). But if either you or your spouse was born before January 2, 1952, multiply line 2 by 7.5% (0.075) instead	**3**		
	4 Subtract line 3 from line 1. If line 3 is more than line 1, enter -0-		**4**	

---

1. Under the Tax Cuts and Jobs Act, this percentage is 7.5 percent for taxable years beginning after December 31, 2016 and ending before January 1, 2019. If a taxpayer (or the taxpayer's spouse) is 65 or older, this percentage also applies to taxable years beginning after December 31, 2012.

quackery. Taxpayers have been known to make a run at deducting routine personal expenses if there is at least some tangential link to one of their bona fide medical conditions. George and Pearlie Taylor, for example, attempted to deduct the cost of lawn care. In *Taylor v. Commissioner*, T.C. Memo. 1987-399, 54 T.C.M. (CCH) 129, we learned that George suffered with severe allergies, and in accordance with his doctor's recommendations, he avoided mowing his lawn. He did, however, pay someone to complete the task, and he deducted the cost as a medical expense. The Commissioner disallowed the deduction, reasoning that the lawn care expense was merely a nondeductible personal item. The Tax Court concurred, emphasizing that "[d]octor recommended activities have been held in a number of cases not to constitute deductible medical expenses where the expenses did not fall within the parameters of 'medical care.'" Under § 213(d)(1), Congress currently defines the term *medical care* to include only amounts paid for the following:

- The diagnosis, cure, mitigation, treatment, or prevention of disease or for the purpose of affecting any structure or function of the body;
- Transportation primarily for and essential to medical care;
- Qualified long-term care services; and
- Insurance covering medical care or the cost of a qualified long-term care contract (eligible long-term care premiums only).

Even with a fairly comprehensive definition of medical care in place, there remains the need for special rules, targeted carve-outs, exceptions to exceptions, special IRS pronouncements, and the like. We will not take up all of the special rules in their semibaroque detail, but necessity dictates that we address rules of practical significance. Consider, for example, the deductibility of medicine/drug expenses and lodging costs incurred in connection with the receipt of medical care. Medicines and drugs cure, mitigate, treat, and prevent any number of conditions, but their cost is deductible only if the item is a prescribed drug or insulin. *See* § 213(b), (d)(3), and (d)(4). Further, some medicines or drugs may be validly prescribed by a physician under state law but not qualify for deduction under § 213 because knowingly or intentionally possessing them violates federal law. *See* Rev. Rul. 97-9, 1997-1 C.B. 77 (concluding that the cost of medical marijuana was not deductible under § 213); *see also* Treas. Reg. § 1.213-1(e)(2) (defining "medicine and drugs" to include only those legally procured and generally accepted as medicine and drugs).

[handwritten margin note: can't deduct if possession against federal law]

With respect to lodging, the Treasury Regulations provide guidance to address several different scenarios. In general, "[t]he cost of in-patient hospital care (including the cost of meals and lodging therein) is an expenditure for medical care." Treas. Reg. § 1.213-1(e)(1)(v). Indeed, if an individual must be institution-alized principally because he needs medical care (e.g., due to mental illness), the entire cost of his medical care as well as his meals and lodging (furnished as necessary incident to the care) qualify as deductible medical expenses, at least while the individual is in need of constant medical care. *See* Treas. Reg. § 1.213-1(e)(1)(v)(a). On the other hand, if an individual is placed in an institution, albeit not principally because the person is in need of medical care (e.g., because they are very old and cannot safely live alone), then only institutional costs associated with medical care in the facility qualify as deductible medical expenses; meals and lodging do not.

[handwritten margin note: medical why reg]

See Treas. Reg. § 1.213-1(e)(1)(v)(b). Finally, potential lodging expenses may arise from the need to receive medical services far from the patient's home (possibly on an out-patient or minimal-stay basis). A patient in a rural area with access to rudimentary medical care may have to undergo a major procedure that she and her attending physician agree could best be handled by a more sophisticated facility in an urban area hundreds of miles away from her home. Often, the patient arrives a day or so before the procedure and may prefer to stay in the vicinity of the facility a day or so after discharge, given the potential for acute posttreatment complications. Accordingly, if a patient and her caretaker or significant other incur lodging expenses in connection with her receipt of treatment, she may deduct amounts paid (up to $50/person per night) "for lodging (not extravagant or lavish under the circumstances) while away from home primarily for and essential to medical care" under the appropriate circumstances. Such medical care must generally be provided by a physician in a licensed hospital, and the trip may not incorporate "significant element[s] of personal pleasure, recreation, or vacation." *See* § 213(d)(2). The taxpayer's transportation costs would be covered by § 213(d)(1)(B), but the Treasury Regulations promulgated under § 213 warn that "transportation" in this context can stretch only so far and shouldn't be confused with other expenses (some of which may or may not be separately deductible). Technically, *transportation* does not include the cost of meals or lodging while traveling for medical care, nor does it include the cost of traveling merely to improve general health or purely elective travel related to the receipt of medical treatment (e.g., a taxpayer in need of heart surgery decides, of her own volition, to have the surgery done in Paris, France). *See* Treas. Reg. § 1.213-1(e)(1)(iv).

The rules governing the deductibility of medical expenses have evolved over time as Congress has carefully fine-tuned its generosity and scientific advances have complicated the application of existing rules. It used to be the case, for example, that those undergoing procedures to correct balding via hair transplant or to eliminate unwanted hair via electrolysis could deduct the associated costs, given that such procedures did, in fact, affect structures or functions of the body. *See, e.g.*, Rev. Rul. 82-111, 1982-1 C.B. 48 (allowing a medical expense deduction for hair transplant and hair electrolysis

---

Capital Expenditures Related to Medical Care

Although we will study capital expenditures in a subsequent chapter, you should simply understand them at this point as costs that a taxpayer cannot deduct immediately. *See* § 263. In some instances, however, a capital expenditure will also be an item which fits the definition of medical care because, for example, it mitigates the impact of or prevents the worsening of a disease (e.g., a stair lift for a patient with chronic heart disease). In these instances, § 213 will prevail and may allow a partial or full deduction with respect to the item, depending on the extent to which installation of the item increases (if at all) the value of the property to which it is added. *See generally* Treas. Reg. § 1.213-1(e)(1)(iii). For example, if a $2,000 stair lift improves the fair market value of a residence by $1,200, the taxpayer will have a medical expense of $800. If, under the same facts, the addition of the lift has no impact on the value of the residence, the taxpayer will have a $2,000 medical expense. Capital expenditures that relate only to the taxpayer (e.g., wheelchairs, eye glasses, and artificial limbs) also qualify as medical expenses. *See id.*

Credit: Robert Kneschke/Shutterstock.com.

Credit: FXQuadro/Shutterstock.com.

Credit: Ostill/Shutterstock.com.

procedures while denying the deduction for the cost of getting a tattoo or ear piercings). Concluding that only a limited subset of procedures directed at improving appearance should qualify for a medical expense deduction, Congress added § 213(d)(9) to the Code in the Omnibus Budget Reconciliation Act of 1990, P.L. 101-508, 104 Stat. 1388 (1990). In general, § 213(d)(9)(A) provides that medical care does not include *cosmetic surgery* which itself is defined in § 213(d)(9)(B) as "any procedure which is directed at improving the patient's appearance and does not meaningfully promote the proper function of the body or prevent or treat illness or disease." Section 213(d)(9)(A) clarifies, however, that certain forms of cosmetic surgery (and similar procedures) remain within the scope of deductible medical care. Specifically, cosmetic surgery or similar procedures "necessary to ameliorate a deformity arising from, or directly related to, a congenital abnormality, a personal injury resulting from an accident or trauma, or [a] disfiguring disease" constitute medical care and are thus deductible.

Bizarro

I can give you a facelift, but I can't guarantee the villagers won't form a mob and hunt you down.

DR. VICTOR FRANKENSTEIN, COSMETIC SURGEON

Credit: Bizarro used with the permission of Dan Piraro, King Features Syndicate, and the Cartoonist Group. All rights reserved.

Cosmetic Surgery: elective v. non-elective

Ruling Preview

Revenue Ruling 2003–57

Modern advances have made a great deal possible in the world of medicine, and this reality rings especially true in the surgical arena. William T.G. Morton's pioneering work with ether eventually brought about the use of surgical anesthesia, and Joseph Lister (of "Listerine" fame) is largely responsible for the use of antiseptic measures in surgery (substantially reducing postoperative mortality rates). *See* MICHAEL H. HART, THE 100: A RANKING OF THE MOST INFLUENTIAL PERSONS IN HISTORY 195, 295 (Citadel Press 1992). The relative safety of modern-day surgery notwithstanding, surgical interventions may ultimately introduce (for our purposes at least), thorny tax issues. Assume, for example, that a woman undergoes a mastectomy to remove cancerous breast tissue. Even if postoperative examination reveals no cancer, the woman may feel the need for reconstructive breast implant surgery to restore physical symmetry. Would such surgery be purely cosmetic in nature and thus nondeductible? Or can you make an effective argument in favor of deductibility from the language of the statute as written? Give it a try before you read the Revenue Ruling. What argument are you going to make, and are you willing to go to court with it? As you make your way through Rev. Rul. 2003-57 (which, you'll recall, is a pronouncement reflecting the IRS's litigating position on an issue), think over the following questions:

1. Even if breast cancer is potentially fatal, does the current statute necessarily require that the condition itself be a disfiguring disease for reconstructive intervention to escape characterization as cosmetic surgery?
2. Should LASIK surgery qualify as a deductible medical expense if eye glasses or contacts can correct the problem?

Revenue Ruling 2003–57
2003-1 C.B. 959

ISSUE

Are amounts paid by individuals for breast reconstruction surgery, vision correction surgery, and teeth whitening medical care expenses within the meaning of § 213(d) and deductible under § 213 of the Internal Revenue Code?

FACTS

Taxpayer *A* undergoes mastectomy surgery that removes a breast as part of treatment for cancer and pays a surgeon to reconstruct the breast. Taxpayer *B* wears glasses to correct myopia and pays a doctor to perform laser eye surgery to correct the myopia. Taxpayer *C*'s teeth are discolored as a result of age. *C* pays a dentist to perform a teeth-whitening procedure. *A*, *B*, and *C* are not compensated for their expenses by insurance or otherwise.

LAW AND ANALYSIS

Section 213(a) allows a deduction for expenses paid during the taxable year, not compensated for by insurance or otherwise, for medical care of the taxpayer, spouse, or dependent, to the extent the expenses exceed 7.5 percent of adjusted gross income. Under § 213(d)(1)(A), medical care includes amounts paid for the diagnosis, cure, mitigation, treatment, or prevention of disease, or for the purpose of affecting any structure or function of the body.

Medical care does not include cosmetic surgery or other similar procedures, unless the surgery or procedure is necessary to ameliorate a deformity arising from, or directly related to, a congenital abnormality, a personal injury resulting from an accident or trauma, or a disfiguring disease. Section 213(d)(9)(A). Cosmetic surgery means any procedure that is directed at improving the patient's appearance and does not meaningfully promote the proper function of the body or prevent or treat illness or disease. Section 213(d)(9)(B).

A's cancer is a disfiguring disease because the treatment results in the loss of *A*'s breast. Accordingly, the breast reconstruction surgery ameliorates a deformity directly related to a disease and the cost is an expense for medical care within the meaning of § 213(d) that *A* may deduct under § 213 (subject to the limitations of that section).

The cost of *B*'s laser eye surgery is allowed under § 213(d)(9) because the surgery is a procedure that meaningfully promotes the proper function of the body. Vision correction with eyeglasses or contact lenses qualifies as medical care. See Rev. Rul. 74-429, 1974-2 C.B. 83. Eye surgery to correct defective vision, including laser procedures such as LASIK and radial keratotomy, corrects a dysfunction of the body. Accordingly, the cost of the laser eye surgery is an expense for medical care within the meaning of § 213(d) that *B* may deduct under § 213 (subject to the limitations of that section).

In contrast, the teeth-whitening procedure <u>does not treat a physical or mental disease or promote the proper function of the body, but is directed at improving</u> *C*'s appearance. The discoloration is not a deformity and is not caused by a disfiguring disease or treatment. Accordingly, *C* may not deduct the cost of whitening teeth as an expense for medical care.

HOLDING

Amounts paid by individuals for breast reconstruction surgery following a mastectomy for cancer and for vision correction surgery are medical care expenses under § 213(d) and are deductible under § 213 (subject to the limitations of that section). Amounts paid by individuals to whiten teeth discolored as a result of age are not medical care expenses under § 213(d) and are not deductible.

Post-Ruling Follow-Up

The IRS concludes that the cost of reconstructive breast surgery following a mastectomy is a deductible medical expense because the treatment of the original condition is physically disfiguring. LASIK and similar procedures, reasons the IRS, correct a physical dysfunction and thus meet the test of deductibility under § 213. The Service concludes that teeth-whitening merely to correct age-related discoloration, however, serves a largely cosmetic purpose and thus does not qualify for deduction. Is the same true (in whole or in part) with respect to modern-day hormone replacement therapy in the sense that patients are experiencing normal, age-related hormone changes but seek to halt the cosmetic impact and physiological indicia of aging? Commentators note that although hormone supplementation, in the short term, is still useful for the treatment of the intense hot flashes, night sweats, and mood swings that typically arise with the onset of menopause, many women undertake and continue hormone replacement therapy to maintain a "youthful glow" (i.e., for its cosmetic benefits) and may develop an emotional attachment to the hormone replacement regimen. *See, e.g.*, Christine Gorman, et al., *The Truth About Hormones*, TIME (July 22, 2002). Similarly, men may seek the cosmetic benefits associated with testosterone supplementation, although andropause comes with normal hormonal declines and clear physiological manifestations. *See, e.g.*, Datis Kharrazian, *The Role of Andropause for the Practicing Internist*, 17 ORIGINAL INTERNIST, (March 1, 2010) ("Testosterone has impacts on numerous cardiovascular risk factors. For example, the following changes take place as testosterone levels decline: cholesterol and triglycerides increase, arterial plaque increases, coronary artery dilation decreases, lipoproptein A increases, fibrinogen levels increase, insulin levels increase, obesity increases, and estrogen levels increase."). If hormonal intervention is largely, though certainly not exclusively, a cosmetic intervention, shouldn't the Service deny taxpayers the cost of prescribed anti-aging medication such as synthetic estrogen and synthetic testosterone? One could argue that hormonal intervention is hardly "cosmetic," that supplementation affects several functions in a swiftly-changing body, and that the Code requires nothing more. But is hormone therapy (in the absence of clear pathology) just as unnatural as teeth-whitening, and doesn't it come with known risks? *See* Sanjay Gupta, *Should Anyone Take Hormones?*, TIME (Jul. 15, 2002) (pointing out that in one study, hormone replacement therapy for postmenopausal women resulted in increased health risks, i.e., increased risk of developing breast and uterine cancers, while failing to reduce the risk of heart attacks and strokes).

Rev. Rul. 2003–57: Real Life Applications

For each of the following questions, please assume that the taxpayer itemizes deductions, that relevant medical expenses exceed 7.5 percent of the taxpayer's adjusted gross income, and that the taxpayer has not been compensated by insurance or otherwise.

1. A few days after completing a long hike, Victor suffered weakness and atrophy in his left leg. Doctors later confirmed that a tick had attached itself to his calf and infected him with flesh-eating bacteria. After completing a course of very strong antibiotics prescribed by his physician, Victor underwent surgery to have dead calf tissue removed and calf implants inserted to restore anatomical symmetry. May Victor deduct the medical expenses he incurred and paid

with respect to the antibiotics he received and the surgical placement of his calf implants?

2. Since childhood, Mandy has suffered with vitiligo, a condition characterized by the gradual loss of skin pigmentation, often in a patch-like pattern on the hands, arms, face, and feet. If Mandy undergoes treatment to lighten unaffected skin on her face, neck, and hands to match the affected skin, may she deduct the costs paid to secure the treatment?

3. Although he has repeatedly been told that he is attractive, Keith continues to believe that his chin is too narrow. If Keith undergoes surgery to enhance the appearance of his chin, will he be able to deduct any of the associated costs?

B. THE EVOLVING DEFINITION OF "MEDICAL CARE"

The twentieth and twenty-first centuries have witnessed remarkable achievements in the medical arena, and yet, as new medical and technological realities emerge, those who create and administer the law to achieve desirable goals (or to police wayward conduct) find that they must move with dispatch if they are to keep up. Tax experts surely cannot claim exception. Section 213 and many of the Treasury Regulations promulgated thereunder have been around for quite some time, and it should come as no surprise that long-standing rules frequently borrow from and reflect law created in bygone eras. Applying such rules to situations not contemplated at the time of their original drafting often leads to logical, rational, and fair results or, as the case may well be, results that arguably offend established notions of horizontal equity by treating similarly situated taxpayers differently. In this section, we take a closer look at the tax treatment of expenses related to the use of modern reproductive technologies and the surprisingly controversial meaning of key statutory terms such as *disease* and *treatment*.

In Vitro Fertilization

The IVF process involves the fertilization of several eggs by individual sperm by a medical professional in a laboratory setting. After the fertilized eggs have undergone several divisions, a number of embryos are transferred to the woman's uterus in the hope that implantation will occur and that at least one embryo will develop further into a healthy child. In the photo below, the egg is held in place as the sperm is introduced (from the right) by syringe. "In vitro" is Latin for "in glass."

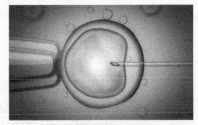

Credit: Vchal/Shutterstock.com.

1. Fertility-Related Expenses

With the birth of Louise Brown (5 pounds and 12 ounces) in Lancashire, England, in the late 1970s, in vitro fertilization left the realm of science fiction and became scientific reality. *See* THE NEW YORK TIMES, THE TIMES OF THE SEVENTIES 144 (Clyde Haberman ed., Black Dog and Leventhal Publishers 2013). In drafting and approving the earliest iterations of § 213, however, Congress surely could not have contemplated more than the traditional and routine costs associated with having a child, which, at the time, did not include the cost of egg-harvesting, microscopic embryo analysis, and multiparty involvement. The next two authorities give us a reasonably clear sense of where Congress has decided to draw the line. See if you agree with the approaches taken.

Case Preview

Magdalin v. Commissioner

Although current medical technology facilitates successful reproduction by those with fertility challenges, that same technology makes it possible for some individuals (demonstrably fertile in every respect) to achieve reproduction via the coordinated effort of donors, surrogates, financial institutions, and legal document specialists. In Private Letter Ruling 200318017, the taxpayer had tried to conceive with assisted reproduction technology (using her own eggs) without success. Rather than assuming that the cost of securing an egg donor (and various related expenses) would be deductible under § 213, she requested a Private Letter Ruling to ascertain definitively how the IRS would treat her if she incurred such expenses, paid them, and took an itemized deduction with respect to them. As a useful comparative backdrop for the main case, review the full ruling set forth below.

Private Letter Ruling 200318017
2003 WL 2009141

Issue: May 2, 2003
January 9, 2003

Section 213 — Medical, Dental, etc., Expenses

Dear *** :

You requested a private letter ruling that egg donor fees and expenses related to obtaining a willing egg donor are allowable as medical care expenses under a flexible spending account. Your ruling request was referred to our office because the answer depends on whether the expenses are deductible under § 213(a) of the Internal Revenue Code.

FACTS:

You have unsuccessfully undergone repeated assisted reproductive technology procedures to enable you to conceive a child using your own eggs. You desire to attempt pregnancy using donated eggs. Your health plan will pay expenses to fertilize and transfer an egg or embryo to you but will not cover expenses to obtain an egg donor. You request a ruling that the following expenses are medical expenses for purposes of § 213:

- The donor's fee for her time and expense in following proper procedures to ensure a successful egg retrieval.
- The agency fee for procuring the donor and coordinating the transaction between the donor and recipient.
- Expenses for medical and psychological testing of the donor prior to the procedure and insurance for any medical or psychological assistance that the donor may require after the procedure.
- Legal fees for preparing a contract between you and the egg donor.

[handwritten margin note: Expenses seeking a definition]

LAW AND ANALYSIS:

A taxpayer may deduct expenses paid during the taxable year, not compensated for by insurance or otherwise, for medical care of the taxpayer, spouse, or dependent, to the extent the expenses exceed 7.5 percent of adjusted gross income, under § 213(a). Section 213(d)(1)(A) provides that medical care includes amounts paid for the diagnosis, cure, mitigation, treatment, or prevention of disease, or for the purpose of affecting any structure or function of the body.

Rev. Rul. 73-201, 1973-1 C.B. 140, and Rev. Rul. 73-603, 1973-2 C.B. 76, hold that vasectomies and operations that render a woman incapable of having children affect a structure or function of the body and thus may qualify as medical care under § 213. A procedure for the purpose of facilitating pregnancy by overcoming infertility similarly affects a structure or function of the body and may be medical care.

[handwritten margin note: Procedure itself is a deduction if needed]

Expenses preparatory to the performance of a procedure that qualifies as medical care that are directly related to the procedure may also constitute medical care for purposes of § 213. For example, Rev. Rul. 68-452, 1968-2 C.B. 111, holds that surgical, hospital, and transportation expenses incurred by a donor in connection with donating a kidney to the taxpayer are deductible medical expenses of the taxpayer-recipient for the years in which the taxpayer pays them, subject to the limits of § 213. Similarly, expenses the taxpayer pays to obtain an egg donor, including the donor's expenses, are directly related and preparatory to the taxpayer's receiving the donated egg or embryo. The expenses are therefore the taxpayer's medical expenses and are deductible by the taxpayer in the year paid.

[handwritten margin note: General rule for related expenses]
[handwritten margin note: examples]
[handwritten margin note: also]

Like other preparatory expenses, legal expenses may be deductible as medical expenses under § 213 if there is a direct or proximate relationship between the legal expenses and the provision of medical care to a taxpayer. *Lenn v. Commissioner,* T.C. Memo 1998-85. For example, legal expenses incurred to create a guardianship in order to involuntarily hospitalize a mentally ill taxpayer were held to be deductible medical expenses because the medical treatment could not otherwise have occurred. *Gerstacker v. Commissioner,* 414 F.2d 448 (6th Cir. 1969). In contrast, the court in *Jacobs v. Commissioner,* 62 T.C. 813 (1974), held that legal expenses related to obtaining a divorce that the taxpayer claimed was necessary for his mental health were not deductible because the divorce would have occurred regardless of the petitioner's depression. Thus, the legal expenses were not directly related to the taxpayer's medical treatment.

[handwritten margin note: Legal expenses deductible if...]
[handwritten margin note: Ex. of non-deductible legal expense]

You have represented that you will pay the fee to the donor, the fee to the agency that procured the donor, the donor's medical and psychological testing expenses, the insurance for post-procedure medical or psychological assistance to the donor, and the cost of the legal contract between you and the donor, in order to enable you to obtain a donated egg for implantation into your body. Because these costs are preparatory to the performance of your own medical procedure, the expenses are medical care for purposes of § 213.

H: All are deductible

HOLDING:

The unreimbursed expenses for the egg donor fee, the agency fee, the donor's medical and psychological testing, the insurance for post-procedure donor assistance, and the legal fees for preparation of the contract, are medical care expenses that are deductible under § 213.

Just a few years after the issuance of this Private Letter Ruling, in *Magdalin v. Commissioner*, we encounter a taxpayer with no physical difficulty reproducing by natural means, but who opted to pursue an egg donor and surrogates to produce two new children. As you read through the case, consider these questions:

I: Deduction if fertile taxpayer chooses surrogate?

1. Are fertile and infertile persons or couples similarly situated with respect to costs incurred in connection with the use of assisted reproduction technology?
2. What, exactly, establishes infertility?
3. What impact, if any, did the previously issued Private Letter Ruling have on the court in *Magdalin v. Commissioner*?

Magdalin v. Commissioner
T.C. Memo. 2008-293, 96 T.C.M. (CCH) 491

WHERRY, Judge:

This case, which involves a petition for redetermination of deficiencies for petitioner's 2004 and 2005 tax years, has been submitted for decision without trial. * * * He challenges only respondent's disallowance of the deductions for medical expenses.

FINDINGS OF FACT

Petitioner is a medical doctor licensed to practice medicine in Massachusetts. At all relevant times, his sperm count and motility were found to be within normal limits. He has twin sons from a marriage to his former spouse, Deborah Magdalin. The twins were born through natural processes and without the use of in vitro fertilization (IVF).

He's capable of having kids

In July 2004 petitioner entered into an Anonymous Egg Donor Agreement under which an anonymous donor was to donate eggs to be fertilized with petitioner's

Sur...

sperm and transferred to a gestational carrier using the IVF process. That same month, petitioner also entered into a Gestational Carrier Agreement in which a woman (the first carrier) agreed to become impregnated through the IVF embryo transfer process with the embryo created from the anonymous donor's egg and petitioner's sperm and to bear a child for petitioner. The first carrier gave birth to a child on September 17, 2005.

[handwritten: Child 1]

On November 18, 2005, petitioner entered into a similar Gestational Carrier Agreement with another woman (the second carrier). The second carrier gave birth to a child on August 12, 2006. The donor was not the spouse or dependent of petitioner. Nor was either of the carriers. Both IVF procedures occurred at the Reproduction Science Center (IVF clinic) in Lexington, Massachusetts.

[handwritten: Child 2]

Petitioner paid the following expenses in 2004 relating to the aforementioned agreements: (1) $3,500 for petitioner's legal fees relating to the first donation cycle under the Anonymous Egg Donor Agreement; (2) $500 for the donor's legal fees relating to the Anonymous Egg Donor Agreement; (3) $10,750 for the donor's fees and expenses; (4) $8,000 for the first carrier's fees and expenses; (5) $25,400 to the IVF clinic; and (6) $2,815 for prescription drugs for the first carrier.

[handwritten: Expenses for child 1]

In 2005 petitioner paid the following relevant expenses: (1) $750 for petitioner's legal fees relating to the second donation cycle under the Anonymous Egg Donor Agreement; (2) $17,000 for the first carrier's fees and expenses; (3) $14,270 for petitioner's legal fees relating to the Gestational Carrier Agreement with the second carrier; (4) $1,000 for the second carrier's legal fees relating to the Gestational Carrier Agreement; (5) $2,615.10 to the IVF clinic; (6) $300 to Lawrence General Hospital for costs relating to the first carrier's stay during delivery of the first child; (7) $1,181.25 for the first carrier's legal fees relating to legal proceedings concerning a dispute over the issuance of the first child's birth certificate; and (8) $838 for prescription drugs for both carriers. There is no evidence that petitioner was compensated for any of those expenses by insurance or otherwise.

[handwritten: Expenses for Child 2]

Petitioner filed his 2004 and 2005 Federal income tax returns on time. On Schedules A, Itemized Deductions, included with those returns he deducted medical expenses of $34,050 for 2004 and $28,230 for 2005. On March 22, 2007, respondent issued petitioner a notice of deficiency for his 2004 and 2005 tax years. Therein, respondent disallowed petitioner's claimed medical expense deductions in their entirety. On April 3, 2007, petitioner, who then resided in Massachusetts, filed a timely petition with this Court.

OPINION

I. Deductions for Medical Expenses

Section 213(a) allows for the deduction of paid expenses "not compensated for by insurance or otherwise, for medical care of the taxpayer, his spouse, or a dependent * * * to the extent that such expenses exceed 7.5 percent of adjusted gross income." While Congress has indicated an intent, once section 213 applies, to broadly define medical care, * * * we have characterized section 213 as carving out "a limited exception" to the general rule in section 262 that prohibits the deduction of personal, living, or family expenses. *Jacobs v. Commissioner*, 62 T.C. 813, 818 (1974). Consequently,

[handwritten: Restriction on personal expenses]

the medical expense deduction has been narrowly construed for many years, as the Court noted more than 40 years ago in *Atkinson v. Commissioner,* 44 T.C. 39, 49 (1965). The deductibility of the expenses at issue hinges on whether they were paid for petitioner's medical care. If so, they are deductible medical expenses under section 213. If not, they are nondeductible personal expenses under section 262.

The term "medical care" includes amounts paid "for the diagnosis, cure, mitigation, treatment, or prevention of disease, or for the purpose of affecting any structure or function of the body". Sec. 213(d)(1)(A). The regulations provide that "Deductions for expenditures for medical care allowable under section 213 will be confined strictly to expenses incurred primarily for the prevention or alleviation of a physical or mental defect or illness." [Treas. Reg. § 1.213-1(e)(1)(ii)].

We have interpreted the statute as requiring a causal relationship in the form of a "but for" test between a medical condition and the expenditures incurred in treating that condition. *See Jacobs v. Commissioner, supra* at 818 (noting that "the payment for which a deduction is claimed must be for goods or services directly or proximately related to the diagnosis, cure, mitigation, treatment, or prevention of the disease or illness"). The "but for" test requires petitioner to prove (1) "that the expenditures were an essential element of the treatment" and (2) "that they would not have otherwise been incurred for nonmedical reasons." *Jacobs v. Commissioner, supra* at 819.

It is also noteworthy that section 213(d)(1)(A), which is not a model of clarity, is phrased disjunctively — it allows for the deduction of any expenses paid "for the diagnosis, cure, mitigation, treatment, or prevention of disease, or for the purpose of affecting any structure or function of the body." Sec. 213(d)(1)(A) (emphasis added); see *Dickie v. Commissioner,* T.C. Memo. 1999–138 ("The deductibility of medical care payments under section 213 is not strictly limited to traditional medical procedures, but it includes payments made for the purpose of affecting any structure or function of the body."). Although the phrase "for the purpose of affecting any structure or function of the body" was historically interpreted by the Internal Revenue Service and the Court to allow taxpayers to deduct the costs of a wide array of cosmetic procedures, Congress felt this was too liberal a tax deduction because it resulted from a personal expense and not a medical one. As a consequence, in 1990 Congress restricted taxpayers' ability to do so.

II. Parties' Contentions

Petitioner argues that it was his civil right to reproduce, that he should have the freedom to choose the method of reproduction, and that it is sex discrimination to allow women but not men to choose how they will reproduce. While he correctly acknowledges that Internal Revenue Service private letter rulings are "not legal precedent[,]" he refers to [PLR 200318017 (Jan. 9, 2003)] to show that "the expenses for egg donor, medical and legal costs are deductible medical expenses."

"Although respondent believes that amounts paid for procedures to mitigate infertility may qualify as deductible medical care[,]" respondent argues that "Petitioner had no physical or mental defect or illness which prohibited him from procreating naturally[,]" as he in fact has, and that "the procedures were not medically indicated." Respondent's position is that the expenses at issue are nondeductible under section 262 because "Petitioner's choice to undertake these procedures was an entirely personal/nonmedical decision."

III. The Expenses at Issue Are Nondeductible Personal Expenses

The expenses at issue were not paid for medical care under the first portion of section 213(d)(1)(A) because the requisite causal relationship is absent. None of the expenses at issue was "incurred primarily for the prevention or alleviation of a physical or mental defect or illness." [Treas. Reg. § 1.213-1(e)(1)(ii)]. In other words, petitioner had no medical condition or defect, such as, for example, infertility, that required treatment or mitigation through IVF procedures. We therefore need not answer lurking questions as to whether (and, if so, to what extent) expenditures for IVF procedures and associated costs (e.g., a taxpayer's legal fees and fees paid to, or on behalf of, a surrogate or gestational carrier) would be deductible in the presence of an underlying medical condition. We leave such questions for another day. Further, petitioner cannot deduct those expenses under the second portion of the statute because they did not affect a structure or function of his body.

[handwritten margin note: RE or no deduction: no medical condition or defect]

[handwritten margin note: H]

Although petitioner at times attempts to frame the deductibility of the relevant expenses as an issue of constitutional dimensions, under the facts and circumstances of his case, it does not rise to that level. Petitioner's gender, marital status, and sexual orientation do not bear on whether he can deduct the expenses at issue. He cannot deduct those expenses because he has no medical condition or defect to which those expenses relate and because they did not affect a structure or function of his body. Expenses incurred in the absence of the requisite underlying medical condition or defect and that do not affect a structure or function of the taxpayer's body are nondeductible personal expenses within the meaning of section 262.

The Court has considered all of petitioner's contentions, arguments, requests, and statements. To the extent not discussed herein, we conclude that they are meritless, moot, or irrelevant.

To reflect the foregoing,
Decision will be entered for respondent.

Post-Case Follow-Up

The IRS concludes in PLR 200318017 that the taxpayer's assisted reproduction expenses are fully deductible because the taxpayer incurred and paid the expenses to overcome infertility. In *Magdalin*, however, the court refused to allow any taxpayer deduction because he demonstrated no physical or mental defect that would have prevented him from reproducing naturally. The court even indulges the luxury of leaving "for another day" questions regarding how the taxpayer's expenses would be treated if he had presented with a medical condition that prevented traditional reproduction. Together, the IRS and the Tax Court have not left the legal landscape in total disarray, but no one would confuse the terrain with academic tidiness. Those who can establish classic medical infertility (whether single or married) will likely enjoy access to assisted reproduction technology and a tax deduction to go along with it.

But where does that leave same-sex couples wholly capable of heterosexual reproduction? What about a fertile heterosexual couple eager to have several children but wary of the unacceptably high risk that their offspring would have sickle cell anemia? These tough questions and others await acceptable resolution. Even if one attempts to insert a uniform standard such as "clear medical necessity," one must still find and articulate a fair, equitable, and administrable definition of that standard. For additional commentary on these issues, see Katherine Pratt, *Deducting the Costs of Fertility Treatment: Implications of* Magdalin v. Commissioner *for Opposite-Sex Couples, Gay and Lesbian Same-Sex Couples, and Single Women and Men*, 2009 Wis. L. Rev. 1283 (2009).

PLR 200318017 and Magdalin v. Commissioner: Real Life Applications

For each of the following questions, please assume that the taxpayer itemizes deductions, that relevant medical expenses exceed 7.5 percent of the taxpayer's adjusted gross income, and that the taxpayer has not been compensated by insurance or otherwise.

1. Rita and Anderson have been trying to have a baby for several years by natural means. They've had no success. A fertility specialist confirmed that Anderson had an abnormally low sperm count, and she recommended in vitro fertilization. If Rita and Anderson complete the in vitro fertilization process, will they be able to deduct the associated costs?

2. Although Jillian and Baker had two children without assisted reproduction technology, Jillian suffered through the latter portion of each pregnancy with preeclampsia, a condition in which the pregnant woman suffers with high blood pressure and other ailments. The condition carries specific risks. If Jillian and Baker decide to use in vitro fertilization and a surrogate to carry their next child to term, will the medical expenses they incur and pay qualify for deduction under § 213?

3. Russell and Annelise have four children, all girls. They understand that current assisted reproduction technology can substantially enhance the likelihood that their next child will be a boy, and they are eager to give it a try. If the couple moves forward with the process (a more sophisticated version of in vitro fertilization that involves using sperm from a select population to effect fertilization), will the associated medical expenses be deductible under § 213?

2. Meaning of Disease and Treatment

Plague, cholera, tuberculosis, dengue, influenza, ebola, malaria, and a host of other diseases and infections have claimed the lives of millions over the centuries, typically announcing their microscopic presence with mild to moderate symptoms before ramping up to full strength and ravaging their victims. Medical professionals confronted with such patients readily confirm the presence of disease and, if possible, proceed with treatment. In other contexts, or, perhaps, with emergent conditions, medical professionals may debate whether a given constellation of symptoms actually coalesce into what would traditionally qualify as a "disease" or "disorder." The outcome, in individual cases, can have real tax consequences in light of the fact that the Code defines medical care to mean amounts paid "for the diagnosis, cure, mitigation, treatment, or prevention, of *disease*, or for the purpose of affecting any structure or function of the body." Section 213(d)(1)(A) (emphasis added). Throw sex, sexuality, or sexual orientation into the mix, and you might end up with a rather perfect, litigation-generating storm.

[handwritten margin note: I: What constitutes "disease"]

Case Preview

O'Donnabhain v. Commissioner

For reasons not fully understood by psychologists or psychiatrists, a number of individuals born genetic males or genetic females identify with the opposite gender, and while some of the affected individuals apparently resolve the mental/physical dissonance without medical or surgical intervention, others find themselves in real, life-threatening distress and seek professional assistance. For years, Robert Donovan struggled with his gender identity. Indeed, even as a child, he dressed secretly in women's clothing. Later in life, having been diagnosed with "gender identity disorder" ("GID"), he sought out and ultimately received sex reassignment surgery becoming Rhiannon O'Donnabhain. She proceeded to deduct various expenses associated with her transition, prompting the Commissioner's disallowance. The Tax Court found itself grappling with the question of whether GID qualified as a *disease* within the meaning of § 213 (and consistent with congressional intent) and, likewise, whether various forms of intervention constituted *treatment* of that disease. As you read *O'Donnabhain v. Commissioner*, consider the following questions:

1. Does the court consider whether Robert Donovan suffered any congenital abnormalities?
2. In the opinion of the court, does a condition qualify as a "disease" only if it can be rooted in some demonstrable physiological abnormality?
3. Why did the court treat Ms. O'Donnabhain's breast augmentation expenses differently than the costs associated with some of her other procedures?

Born a genetic male, Laverne Cox identifies as female and is an award-winning actress. She is well-known for her role in the television series *Orange is the New Black*.

Credit: Kathy Hutchins/Shutterstock. com.

O'Donnabhain v. Commissioner
134 T.C. 34 (2010)

GALE, Judge.

Respondent determined a deficiency of $5,679 in petitioner's Federal income tax for 2001. After concessions, the issue for decision is whether petitioner may deduct as a medical care expense under section 213 amounts paid in 2001 for hormone therapy, sex reassignment surgery, and breast augmentation surgery that petitioner contends were incurred in connection with a condition known as gender identity disorder.

FINDINGS OF FACT

Many of the facts have been stipulated, and the stipulated facts and attached exhibits are incorporated in our findings by this reference. ***

I. Petitioner's Background

Rhiannon G. O'Donnabhain (petitioner) was born a genetic male with unambiguous male genitalia. However, she was uncomfortable in the male gender role from childhood and first wore women's clothing secretly around age 10. Her discomfort regarding her gender intensified in adolescence, and she continued to dress in women's clothing secretly.

As an adult, petitioner earned a degree in civil engineering, served on active duty with the U.S. Coast Guard, found employment at an engineering firm, married, and fathered three children. However, her discomfort with her gender persisted. She felt that she was a female trapped in a male body, and she continued to secretly wear women's clothing.

Petitioner's marriage ended after more than 20 years. After separating from her spouse in 1992, petitioner's feelings that she wanted to be female intensified and grew more persistent.

II. Petitioner's Psychotherapy and Diagnosis

By mid-1996 petitioner's discomfort with her male gender role and desire to be female intensified to the point that she sought out a psychotherapist to address them. After investigating referrals, petitioner contacted Diane Ellaborn (Ms. Ellaborn), a licensed independent clinical social worker (LICSW) and psychotherapist, and commenced psychotherapy sessions in August 1996.

Although not a medical doctor, Ms. Ellaborn had a master's degree in social work and as an LICSW was authorized under Massachusetts law to diagnose and treat psychiatric illnesses. She had specialized training in the diagnosis and treatment of gender-related disorders.

During petitioner's psychotherapy Ms. Ellaborn learned of petitioner's cross-dressing history and of her longstanding belief that she was really female despite her male body. Ms. Ellaborn observed that petitioner was very sad and anxious, had very low self-esteem, had limited social interactions, and was obsessed with issues concerning the incongruence between her perceived gender and her anatomical sex.

In early 1997, after approximately 20 weekly individual therapy sessions, Ms. Ellaborn's diagnosis was that petitioner was a transsexual suffering from severe gender identity disorder (GID), a condition listed in the Diagnostic and Statistical Manual of Mental Disorders (4th ed.2000 text revision) (DSM-IVTR), published by the American Psychiatric Association. The DSMIV-TR states that a diagnosis of GID is indicated where an individual exhibits (1) a strong and persistent desire to be, or belief that he or she is, the other sex; (2) persistent discomfort with his or her anatomical sex, including a preoccupation with getting rid of primary or secondary sex characteristics; (3) an absence of any physical intersex (hermaphroditic) condition; and (4) clinically significant distress or impairment in social, occupational, or other important areas of functioning as a result of the discomfort arising from the perceived incongruence between anatomical sex and perceived gender identity. *See* DSM-IV-TR at 581. Under the classification system of the DSM-IV-TR, a severity modifier — mild, moderate, or severe — may be added to any diagnosis. The term "Transsexualism" is currently used in the DSM-IV-TR to describe GID symptoms that are severe or profound.

Both the DSM-IV-TR and its predecessor the DSM-IV contain the following "Cautionary Statement":

The purpose of DSM-IV is to provide clear descriptions of diagnostic categories in order to enable clinicians and investigators to diagnose, communicate about, study, and treat people with various mental disorders. It is to be understood that inclusion here, for clinical and research purposes, of a diagnostic category * * * does not imply that the condition meets legal or other non-medical criteria for what constitutes mental disease, mental disorder, or mental disability. * * *

III. Treatment of GID

The World Professional Association for Transgender Health (WPATH), formerly known as the Harry Benjamin International Gender Dysphoria Association, Inc., is an association of medical, surgical, and mental health professionals specializing in the understanding and treatment of GID. WPATH publishes "Standards of Care" for the treatment of GID (hereinafter Benjamin standards of care or Benjamin standards). ***

Summarized, the Benjamin standards of care prescribe a "triadic" treatment sequence for individuals diagnosed with GID consisting of (1) hormonal sex reassignment; i.e., the administration of cross-gender hormones to effect changes in physical appearance to more closely resemble the opposite sex; (2) the "real-life" experience (wherein the individual undertakes a trial period of living full time in society as a member of the opposite sex); and (3) sex reassignment surgery, consisting of genital sex reassignment and/or nongenital sex reassignment, more fully described as follows:

Genital surgical sex reassignment refers to surgery of the genitalia and/or breasts performed for the purpose of altering the morphology in order to approximate the physical appearance of the genetically other [sex] in persons diagnosed as gender dysphoric. * * * Non-genital surgical sex reassignment refers to any and all other surgical procedures of non-genital, or non-breast, sites (nose, throat, chin, cheeks, hips, etc.) conducted for the purpose of effecting a more masculine appearance in a genetic female or for the purpose of effecting a more feminine appearance in a genetic male in the absence of identifiable pathology which would warrant such surgery regardless of the patient's genetic sex (facial injuries, hermaphroditism, etc.).

Under the Benjamin standards, an individual must have the recommendation of a licensed psychotherapist to obtain hormonal or surgical sex reassignment. Hormonal sex reassignment requires the recommendation of one psychotherapist and surgical sex reassignment requires the recommendations of two. The recommending psychotherapist should have diagnostic evidence for transsexualism for a period of at least 2 years, independent of the patient's claims.

The Benjamin standards state that hormonal sex reassignment should precede surgical sex reassignment because the patient's degree of satisfaction with hormone therapy "may indicate or contraindicate later surgical sex reassignment." The Benjamin standards further state that "Genital sex reassignment shall be preceded by a period of at least 12 months during which time the patient lives full-time in the social role of the genetically other sex." The standards provide that breast augmentation surgery may be performed as part of sex reassignment surgery for a male-to-female patient "if the physician prescribing hormones and the surgeon have documented that breast enlargement after undergoing hormone treatment for 18 months is not sufficient for comfort in the social gender role."

IV. Ms. Ellaborn's Treatment Plan for Petitioner

After diagnosing severe GID in petitioner in early 1997, Ms. Ellaborn administered a course of treatment that followed the Benjamin standards of care [Petitioner completed the first two phases of treatment, hormonal sex reassignment and the real life experience of living publicly as a female.].

C. Petitioner's Sex Reassignment Surgery

Petitioner's anxiety as a result of having male genitalia persisted, however, and Ms. Ellaborn concluded that her prognosis without genital surgical sex reassignment (sex reassignment surgery) was poor, in that petitioner's anxiety over the lack of congruence between her perceived gender and her anatomical sex would continue in the absence of surgery and would impair her ability to function normally in society.

[Ms. Ellaborn formally recommended petitioner for sex reassignment surgery and secured the additional medical recommendations needed.]

In mid-October 2001 petitioner returned to Portland, and she underwent sex reassignment surgery on October 19, 2001. The procedures that Dr. Meltzer carried out included surgical removal of the penis and testicles and creation of a vaginal space using genital skin and tissue. The procedures were designed to surgically reconfigure petitioner's male genitalia to create female genitalia both in appearance and in function, by reconstructing the penile glans into a neo-clitoris, making sexual arousal and intercourse possible.

[handwritten margin note: Psychotherapist recommends surgery]

Dr. Meltzer also performed breast augmentation surgery designed to make petitioner's breasts, which had experienced some development as a result of feminizing hormones, more closely resemble the breasts of a genetic female.

In May 2002 Dr. Meltzer performed followup surgery on petitioner to refine the appearance of her genitals and remove scar tissue. In February 2005 Dr. Meltzer performed further surgery on petitioner's face, designed to feminize her facial features.[18]

V. Petitioner's Claim for a Medical Expense Deduction

During 2001 petitioner incurred and paid the following expenses (totaling $21,741) in connection with her hormone therapy, sex reassignment surgery, and breast augmentation surgery. ***: These payments were not compensated for by insurance or otherwise.

On her Federal income tax return for 2001, petitioner claimed an itemized deduction for the foregoing expenditures as medical expenses, which respondent subsequently disallowed in a notice of deficiency.

VI. Expert Testimony

A. Petitioner's Expert: Dr. Brown

Petitioner's expert, Dr. George R. Brown (Dr. Brown), is a licensed physician, board certified in adult psychiatry by the American Board of Psychiatry and Neurology. Dr. Brown has been a member of the American Psychiatric Association since 1983 and was elected a Distinguished Fellow of that organization in 2003. At the time of trial Dr. Brown was a professor and associate chairman of the Department of Psychiatry at East Tennessee State University and chief of psychiatry at James H. Quillen Veterans Affairs Medical Center in Johnson City, Tennessee.

Dr. Brown has been an active member of WPATH since 1987, including serving on its board of directors, and he participated in the development of the Benjamin standards of care. He has seen approximately 500 GID patients either in a clinical setting or as an academic researcher. Dr. Brown has published numerous papers in peer-reviewed medical journals and written several book chapters on topics related to GID, including those in the Merck Manuals, one of the most widely used medical reference texts in the world.

Citing its recognition in the DSM-IV–TR, standard medical reference texts, and World Health Organization publications, Dr. Brown contends that there is general agreement in mainstream psychiatry that GID is a legitimate mental disorder. Dr. Brown indicates that there are no biological or laboratory tests that may be used to diagnose GID but notes the same is true of virtually all of the mental disorders listed in the DSM-IV-TR.

In Dr. Brown's view, proper medical treatment of a person diagnosed with GID includes extended psychotherapy and one or more of the triadic therapies in the Benjamin standards. Dr. Brown is not aware of any case in which psychotherapy alone was effective in treating severe GID. For individuals with severe GID, Dr. Brown believes completion of the entire triadic sequence, i.e., through sex reassignment surgery, is usually medically necessary to "cure or mitigate the distress and maladaption caused by GID."

In Dr. Brown's opinion, it is also important to the mental health of a male with severe GID to be able to "pass" convincingly in public as female' — that is, to be perceived as female by members of the public. Failure to pass exacerbates the anxieties associated with GID. Passing includes the use of sex-segregated facilities such as restrooms and locker rooms, where a failure to pass can result in public humiliation, assault, or arrest. Genetic males with GID sometimes have distinctly male facial features that make it difficult to pass, absent surgery to feminize facial features.

According to Dr. Brown, autocastration, autopenectomy, and suicide have been reported in patients who did not receive appropriate treatment for their GID. Dr. Brown rejects the idea that sex reassignment surgery is comparable to cosmetic surgery or is undertaken to improve one's appearance, in view of the social stigma (including rejection by family and employment discrimination) and the pain and complications typically associated with such surgery. Moreover, Dr. Brown observes, normal genetic males generally do not desire to have their penis and testicles removed. Such a desire is regarded in the psychiatric literature as a likely manifestation of psychosis (usually schizophrenia) or GID, followed by a range of other less likely explanations. In Dr. Brown's opinion, people undergo sex reassignment surgery because of the severity of their GID symptoms and the lack of any other known effective treatment.

In Dr. Brown's view, the scientific literature demonstrates positive therapeutic outcomes from sex reassignment surgery. He cites widely used psychiatric reference texts that reach the same conclusion.

On the basis of a review of petitioner's medical records and a telephone interview with petitioner, Dr. Brown opined that petitioner was properly diagnosed with GID and petitioner's treatments, including sex reassignment surgery, were appropriate and medically necessary.

B. *Respondent's Expert: Dr. Schmidt*

Respondent's expert, Dr. Chester W. Schmidt, Jr. (Dr. Schmidt), is a licensed physician, board certified in psychiatry by the American Board of Psychiatry and Neurology, and a member of the American Psychiatric Association. At the time of trial Dr. Schmidt was a professor of psychiatry at the Johns Hopkins University School of Medicine, the chief medical director, Johns Hopkins Health Care, and chair of the medical board, Johns Hopkins Bayview Medical Center.

Dr. Schmidt cofounded the Sexual Behavior Consultation Unit of the Johns Hopkins Hospital, a clinical, teaching, and research program devoted to the evaluation and treatment of sexual disorders, in 1971. Since that time he has been active in the clinical and teaching aspects of transsexualism, having participated in the evaluation of approximately 12 patients per year diagnosed with GID. However, he has not directly treated or managed a patient with GID since the mid-1980s, and his current clinical activity consists of evaluating new cases of GID. Dr. Schmidt's expert report states that he has "participated in the publication" of several peer-reviewed medical journal articles about GID, but none has been identified for which he was a listed author, and he has never written a chapter on the subject in a medical reference text.

In his expert report, Dr. Schmidt asserts that the validity of the GID diagnosis remains the subject of debate within the psychiatric profession and that he currently is undecided about its validity. However, 10 months before submitting his expert report, Dr. Schmidt provided a diagnosis of GID as an expert in a U.S. District Court proceeding and continued to make the diagnosis regularly through the time of trial, as do other practitioners at the Johns Hopkins sexual disorders clinic he cofounded. Further, Dr. Schmidt states that the GID diagnosis is taught to psychiatrists in training at his and other medical schools and is a condition with which they must be familiar.

Dr. Schmidt agreed that GID requires treatment. He has observed that "you can't walk around day after day being ambiguous about your gender identity. It will tear you apart psychologically". Dr. Schmidt likewise agreed that untreated GID in males can sometimes lead to autopenectomy, autocastration, and suicide.

Dr. Schmidt believes that the Benjamin standards of care are merely guidelines rather than true standards of care, in that they do not meet the legal threshold of a "community" standard, the departure from which would constitute malpractice. Dr. Schmidt further believes that the Benjamin standards enjoy only limited acceptance in American medicine generally. He is unaware, however, of any significant disagreement with the Benjamin standards within the psychiatric profession, other than a minority that considers sex reassignment surgery unethical. Dr. Schmidt agrees with the Benjamin standards' treatment protocols, with the exception that he believes psychotherapy should be mandatory rather than merely recommended for candidates for sex reassignment. All GID patients at the sexual disorders clinic where Dr. Schmidt practices are advised to become familiar with the Benjamin standards of care.

Dr. Schmidt believes that cross-gender hormone therapy and sex reassignment surgery have recognized medical and psychiatric benefits for persons suffering from GID, including reinforcement of an internal sense of consistency and balance in their gender identity. Dr. Schmidt has also expressed the view that once a genetic male with GID makes the decision to transition to a female identity, everything that reinforces the identity is helpful for psychological well-being. However, in his opinion a therapist should remain neutral regarding whether a patient should undergo hormone therapy or the surgery because, Dr. Schmidt believes, there is insufficient scientific evidence of the procedures' efficacy in treating GID. A therapist should accordingly only take a position when there are contraindications to the procedures, in his opinion.

Given his view that failure to adhere to the Benjamin standards of care would not constitute malpractice and that a therapist should remain neutral regarding the administration of hormone therapy or sex reassignment surgery, Dr. Schmidt concludes that the procedures are elective and not medically necessary. He acknowledges, however, that the issue of the medical necessity of sex reassignment surgery is "contentious and variable within American medicine."

[handwritten margin note: Arg for not being medically necessary]

Finally, while noting that there is some evidence that GID may have a neurological cause, Dr. Schmidt believes that there is no conclusive scientific proof that GID is the result of a genetic or congenital abnormality.

C. *Respondent's Expert: Dr. Dietz*

[handwritten margin note: Another Dr's testimony supports petitioner]

Respondent's expert, Dr. Park Dietz (Dr. Dietz), is a licensed physician and board certified in psychiatry by the American Board of Psychiatry and Neurology. Like Dr. Brown, he is a Distinguished Fellow of the American Psychiatric Association. At the time of trial Dr. Dietz was a clinical professor of psychiatry and behavioral sciences at the University of California at Los Angeles School of Medicine. Dr. Dietz' specialty is forensic psychiatry, and he has written approximately 100 professional publications, mostly on sexual, criminal, and antisocial behavior from the standpoint of forensic psychiatry, in peer-reviewed journals, reference text chapters, and other media. Dr. Dietz was recognized as an expert in forensic psychiatry. He was retained by respondent for the purpose of addressing the question of whether GID or transsexualism is a disease or illness.

[handwritten margin note: Arg for not being disease or illness]

It is Dr. Dietz' opinion that GID is a mental disorder, susceptible of a correct or incorrect diagnosis, but not a disease or an illness because it has not been shown to arise from a pathological process within the body — a necessary condition for a disease in Dr. Dietz' view. While acknowledging that commentators on the subject have advanced at least three possible "sufficient conditions" for the presence of disease (namely, discomfort, dysfunction, or pathology), Dr. Dietz considers pathology the appropriate sufficient condition. Thus, in Dr. Dietz' opinion, disease is defined as follows:

To be a disease, a condition must arise as a result of a pathological process. It is not necessary that this process be fully known or understood, but it is necessary that the pathology occur within the individual and reflect abnormal structure or function of the body at the gross, microscopic, molecular, biochemical, or neuro-chemical levels. * * *

[handwritten margin note: His definition of "disease"]

Citing the cautionary statement in the DSM-IV-TR (to the effect that inclusion of a condition in a diagnostic category of the DSM does not imply that the condition meets legal criteria for mental disease), Dr. Dietz asserts that the designation of a condition as a mental disorder in the DSM-IV-TR does not indicate that the condition is a disease. To be a disease, a mental disorder must have a demonstrated organic or biological origin in the individual, in his view.

Dr. Dietz testified that since qualification as a disease under his definition depends upon a demonstration of the condition's organic origins, a condition may be a disease but not known as such, pending scientific discoveries concerning its etiology. For example, panic disorder and obsessive-compulsive disorder are now understood to have an organic basis, but their etiology was only discovered as a result of laboratory advances within the last decade or so. Thus, both conditions are diseases under Dr. Dietz' definition, but would not have been recognized as such 20 years ago. Dr. Dietz confirmed that bulimia is psychologically unhealthy but not a disease under his formulation because it has no demonstrated organic etiology. Dr. Dietz was unable to say whether anorexia is a disease under his definition because he was unfamiliar with the current state of scientific knowledge of anorexia's etiology. In Dr. Dietz' view, post-traumatic stress disorder is not a disease as he defines the term, but an injury.

Dr. Dietz agrees that GID is sometimes associated with autopenectomy, autocastration, and suicide.

OPINION

I. Medical Expense Deductions Under Section 213

A. In General

Section 213(a) allows a deduction for expenses paid during the taxable year for medical care that are not compensated for by insurance or otherwise and to the extent that such expenses exceed 7.5 percent of adjusted gross income. In addition, section 213(d)(1)(B) and (2) provides that certain amounts paid for transportation and lodging, respectively, may qualify as amounts paid for medical care under section 213(a) if a taxpayer's travel away from home is primarily for and essential to receiving medical care.

B. Definition of Medical Care

***

The core definition of "medical care" originally set forth in section 23(x) of the 1939 Code has endured over time and is currently found in section 213(d)(1)(A), which provides as follows:

> SEC. 213 (d). Definitions. — For purposes of this section —
> (1) The term "medical care" means amounts paid —
> (A) for the diagnosis, cure, mitigation, treatment, or prevention of disease, or for the purpose of affecting any structure or function of the body * * *

Thus, since the inception of the medical expense deduction, the definition of deductible "medical care" has had two prongs. The first prong covers amounts paid for the "diagnosis, cure, mitigation, treatment, or prevention of disease" and the second prong covers amounts paid "for the purpose of affecting any structure or function of the body."

The regulations interpreting the statutory definition of medical care echo the description of medical care in the Senate Finance Committee report accompanying the original enactment. The regulations state in relevant part:

> (e) Definitions — (1) General. (i) The term "medical care" includes the diagnosis, cure, mitigation, treatment, or prevention of disease. Expenses paid for "medical care" shall include those paid for the purpose of affecting any structure or function of the body or for transportation primarily for and essential to medical care. * * *
> (ii) * * * Deductions for expenditures for medical care allowable under section 213 will be confined strictly to expenses incurred primarily for the prevention or alleviation of *a physical or mental defect or illness.* * * *

[Treas. Reg. § 1.213-1(e)(1) (Emphasis added).]

Notably, the regulations, mirroring the language of the Finance Committee report, treat "disease" as used in the statute as synonymous with "a physical or mental defect or illness." The language equating "mental defect" with "disease" was in the first version of the regulations promulgated in 1943 and has stood unchanged since. In addition, to qualify as "medical care" under the regulations, an expense must be incurred "primarily" for alleviation of a physical or mental defect, and the defect must be specific. "[A]n expenditure which is merely beneficial to the general health of an individual, such as an expenditure for a vacation, is not an expenditure for medical care." [Treas. Reg. § 1.213-1(e)(1)(ii).]

Given the reference to "mental defect" in the legislative history and the regulations, it has also long been settled that "disease" as used in section 213 can extend to mental disorders.

In *Jacobs v. Commissioner*, 62 T.C. 813 (1974), this Court reviewed the legislative history of section 213 and synthesized the caselaw to arrive at a framework for analysis of disputes concerning medical expense deductions. Noting that the medical expense deduction essentially carves a limited exception out of the general rule of section 262 that "personal, living, or family expenses" are not deductible, the Court observed that a taxpayer seeking a deduction under section 213 must show: (1) "the present existence or imminent probability of a disease, defect or illness — mental or physical" and (2) a payment "for goods or services directly or proximately related to the diagnosis, cure, mitigation, treatment, or prevention of the disease or illness." *Id.* at 818. Moreover, where the expenditures are arguably not "wholly medical in nature" and may serve a personal as well as medical purpose, they must also pass a "but for" test: the taxpayer must "prove *both* that the expenditures were an essential element of the treatment *and* that they would not have otherwise been incurred for nonmedical reasons." *Id.* at 819.

C. *Definition of Cosmetic Surgery*

The second prong of the statutory definition of "medical care," concerning amounts paid "for the purpose of affecting any structure or function of the body[,]" was eventually adjudged too liberal by Congress. The Internal Revenue Service, relying on the second prong, had determined in two revenue rulings that deductions were allowed for amounts expended for cosmetic procedures (such as facelifts, hair transplants, and hair removal through electrolysis) because the procedures were found to affect a structure or function of the body within the meaning of section 213(d)(1)(A).

In 1990 Congress responded to these rulings by amending section 213 to include new subsection (d)(9) which, generally speaking, excludes cosmetic surgery from the definition of deductible medical care. *See* Omnibus Budget Reconciliation Act of 1990, Pub.L. 101–508, sec. 11342(a), 104 Stat. 1388–471. A review of the legislative history of section 213(d)(9) shows that Congress deemed the amendment necessary to clarify that deductions for medical care do not include amounts paid for "an elective, purely cosmetic treatment." H. Conf. Rept. 101–964, at 1031

***

In sum, section 213(d)(9)(A) provides the general rule that the term "medical care" does not include "cosmetic surgery" (as defined) unless the surgery is necessary to ameliorate deformities of various origins. Section 213(d)(9)(B) then defines "cosmetic surgery" as any procedure that is directed at improving the patient's appearance but excludes from the definition any procedure that "meaningfully [promotes] the proper function of the body" or "[prevents] or [treats] illness or disease." There appear to be no cases of precedential value interpreting the cosmetic surgery exclusion of section 213(d)(9).

II. The Parties' Positions

Respondent contends that petitioner's hormone therapy, sex reassignment surgery, and breast augmentation surgery are nondeductible "cosmetic surgery or other similar procedures" under section 213(d)(9) because they were directed at improving petitioner's appearance and did not treat an illness or disease, meaningfully promote the proper function of the body, or ameliorate a deformity. Although respondent concedes that GID is a mental disorder, respondent contends, relying on the expert testimony of Dr. Dietz, that GID is not a disease for purposes of section 213 because it does not arise from an organic pathology within the human body that reflects "abnormal structure or function of the body at the gross, microscopic, molecular, biochemical, or neurochemical levels." Respondent further contends that the procedures at issue did not treat disease because there is no scientific proof of their efficacy in treating GID and that the procedures were cosmetic surgery because they were not medically necessary. Finally, respondent contends that petitioner did not have GID, that it was incorrectly diagnosed, and that therefore the procedures at issue did not treat a disease.

Petitioner maintains that she is entitled to deduct the cost of the procedures at issue on the grounds that GID is a well-recognized mental disorder in the psychiatric field that "falls squarely within the meaning of 'disease' because it causes serious, clinically significant distress and impairment of functioning." Since widely accepted standards of care prescribe hormone treatment, sex reassignment surgery, and, in appropriate circumstances, breast augmentation surgery for genetic males suffering from GID, expenditures for the foregoing constitute deductible "medical care" because a direct or proximate relationship exists between the expenditures and the "diagnosis, cure, mitigation, treatment, or prevention of disease," petitioner argues. Moreover, petitioner contends, because the procedures at issue treated a "disease" as used in section 213, they are not "cosmetic surgery" as defined in that section.

III. Analysis

The availability of the medical expense deduction for the costs of hormonal and surgical sex reassignment for a transsexual individual presents an issue of first impression.

A. Statutory Definitions

Determining whether sex reassignment procedures are deductible "medical care" or nondeductible "cosmetic surgery" starts with the meaning of "treatment" and "disease" as used in section 213. Both the statutory definition of "medical care" and the statute's exclusion of "cosmetic surgery" from that definition depend in part upon whether an expenditure or procedure is for "treatment" of "disease." [The court notes that under § 213(d)(1)(A), an expenditure for the treatment of disease is deductible medical care and that under § 213(d)(9)(B), a procedure for the treatment of disease is not cosmetic surgery.]

***

B. *Is GID a "Disease"?*

Petitioner argues that she is entitled to deduct her expenditures for the procedures at issue because they were treatments for GID, a condition that she contends is a "disease" for purposes of section 213. Respondent maintains that petitioner's expenditures did not treat "disease" because GID is not a "disease" within the meaning of section 213. Central to his argument is respondent's contention that "disease" as used in section 213 has the meaning postulated by respondent's expert, Dr. Dietz; namely, "a condition * * * [arising] as a result of a pathological process * * * [occurring] within the individual and [reflecting] abnormal structure or function of the body at the gross, microscopic, molecular, biochemical, or neuro-chemical levels."

On brief respondent cites the foregoing definition from Dr. Dietz' expert report and urges it upon the Court as the meaning of "disease" as used in section 213; namely, that a "disease" for this purpose must have a demonstrated organic or physiological origin in the individual. Consequently, GID is not a "disease" because it has "no known organic pathology," respondent argues.

However, this use of expert testimony to establish the meaning of a statutory term is generally improper. "[E]xpert testimony proffered solely to establish the meaning of a law is presumptively improper." The meaning of a statutory term is a pure question of law that is "exclusively the domain of the judge." * * *

While the Court admitted Dr. Dietz' expert report and allowed him to testify over petitioner's objection, the use to which respondent now seeks to put his testimony is improper, and we disregard it for that purpose. The meaning of "disease" as used in section 213 must be resolved by the Court, using settled principles of statutory construction, including reference to the Commissioner's interpretive regulations, the legislative history, and caselaw precedent.

As a legal argument for the proper interpretation of "disease," respondent's position is meritless. Respondent cites no authority, other than Dr. Dietz' expert testimony, in support of his interpretation, and we have found none. To the contrary, respondent's interpretation is flatly contradicted by nearly a half century of caselaw. Numerous cases have treated mental disorders as "diseases" for purposes of section 213 without regard to any demonstrated organic or physiological origin or cause. *See Fay v. Commissioner*, 76 T.C. 408 (1981). These cases found mental conditions to be "diseases" where there was evidence that mental health professionals regarded the condition as creating a significant impairment to normal functioning and warranting treatment. ***

***

The absence of any consideration of etiology in the caselaw is consistent with the legislative history and the regulations. Both treat "disease" as synonymous with "a physical or mental defect," which suggests a more colloquial sense of the term "disease" was intended than the narrower (and more rigorous) interpretation for which respondent contends.

In addition, in the context of mental disorders, it is virtually inconceivable that Congress could have intended to confine the coverage of section 213 to conditions with demonstrated organic origins when it enacted the provision in 1942, because physiological origins for mental disorders were not widely recognized at the time. As

Dr. Dietz confirmed in his testimony, the physiological origins of various well-recognized mental disorders — for example, panic disorder and obsessive-compulsive disorder — were discovered only about a decade ago. Moreover, Dr. Dietz confirmed that bulimia would not constitute a "disease" under his definition, because bulimia has no demonstrated organic origin, nor would post-traumatic stress disorder. Dr. Dietz was unable to say whether anorexia would meet the definition because he was uncertain regarding the current state of scientific knowledge of its origins. Petitioner's expert, Dr. Brown, testified without challenge that *most* mental disorders listed in the DSM-IV-TR do not have demonstrated organic causes. Thus, under the definition of "disease" respondent advances, many well-recognized mental disorders, perhaps most, would be excluded from coverage under section 213 — a result clearly at odds with the intent of Congress (and the regulations) to provide deductions for the expenses of alleviating "mental defects" generally.

[handwritten margin note: Problems w/ respondent's definition of "disease"]

In sum, we reject respondent's interpretation of "disease" because it is incompatible with the stated intent of the regulations and legislative history to cover "mental defects" generally and is contradicted by a consistent line of cases finding "disease" in the case of mental disorders without regard to any demonstrated etiology.

Having rejected respondent's contention that "disease" as used in section 213 requires a demonstrated organic origin, we are left with the question whether the term should be interpreted to encompass GID. On this score, respondent, while conceding that GID is a mental disorder, argues that GID is "not a significant psychiatric disorder" but instead is a "social construction" — a "social phenomenon" that has been "medicalized." Petitioner argues that GID is a "disease" for purposes of section 213 because it is well recognized in mainstream psychiatric literature, including the DSM-IV-TR, as a legitimate mental disorder that "causes serious, clinically significant distress and impairment of functioning."

***

In view of (1) GID's widely recognized status in diagnostic and psychiatric reference texts as a legitimate diagnosis; (2) the seriousness of the condition as described in learned treatises in evidence and as acknowledged by all three experts in this case; (3) the severity of petitioner's impairment as found by the mental health professionals who examined her; (4) the consensus in the U.S. Courts of Appeal that GID constitutes a serious medical need for purposes of the Eighth Amendment, we conclude and hold that GID is a "disease" for purposes of section 213.

[handwritten margin note: RE]

[handwritten margin note: H: GID is a disease]

C. Did Petitioner Have GID?

[The court concludes that the petitioner's GID diagnosis was amply supported by the record.]

[handwritten margin note: H: Petitioner had GID]

D. Whether Cross-Gender Hormones, Sex Reassignment Surgery and Breast Augmentation Surgery "Treat" GID

1. Cross-Gender Hormones and Sex Reassignment Surgery

Our conclusions that GID is a "disease" for purposes of section 213, and that petitioner suffered from it, leave the question of whether petitioner's hormone therapy, sex reassignment surgery, and breast augmentation surgery "[treated]" GID within the meaning of section 213(d)(1)(A) and (9)(B).

In contrast to their dispute over the meaning of "disease," the parties have not disputed the meaning of "treatment" or "treat" as used in section 213(d)(1)(A) and (9)(B), respectively. We accordingly interpret the words in their ordinary, everyday sense. ***

The regulations provide that medical care is confined to expenses "incurred primarily for the prevention or *alleviation* of a physical or mental defect or illness". Sec. 1.213–1(e)(1)(ii), Income Tax Regs. (emphasis added). A treatment should bear a "direct or proximate therapeutic relation to the * * * condition" sufficient "to justify a reasonable belief the * * * [treatment] would be efficacious." ***

Hormone therapy, sex reassignment surgery and, under certain conditions, breast augmentation surgery are prescribed therapeutic interventions, or treatments, for GID outlined in the Benjamin standards of care. The Benjamin standards are widely accepted in the psychiatric profession, as evidenced by the recognition of the standards' triadic therapy sequence as the appropriate treatment for GID and transsexualism in numerous psychiatric and medical reference texts. Indeed, every psychiatric reference text that has been established as authoritative in this case endorses sex reassignment surgery as a treatment for GID in appropriate circumstances. No psychiatric reference text has been brought to the Court's attention that fails to list, or rejects, the triadic therapy sequence or sex reassignment surgery as the accepted treatment regimen for GID. Several courts have accepted the Benjamin standards as representing the consensus of the medical profession regarding the appropriate treatment for GID or transsexualism.

***

In sum, the evidence establishes that cross-gender hormone therapy and sex reassignment surgery are well-recognized and accepted treatments for severe GID. The evidence demonstrates that hormone therapy and sex reassignment surgery to alter appearance (and, to some degree, function) are undertaken by GID sufferers in an effort to alleviate the distress and suffering occasioned by GID, and that the procedures have positive results in this regard in the opinion of many in the psychiatric profession, including petitioner's *and* respondent's experts. Thus, a "reasonable belief" in the procedures' efficacy is justified. Alleviation of suffering falls within the regulatory and caselaw definitions of treatment, and to "relieve" is to "treat" according to standard dictionary definitions. We therefore conclude and hold that petitioner's hormone therapy and sex reassignment surgery "[treated] * * * disease" within the meaning of section 213(d)(9)(B) and accordingly are not "cosmetic surgery" as defined in that section.

While our holding that cross-gender hormone therapy and sex reassignment surgery are not cosmetic surgery is based upon the specific definition of that term in section 213(d)(9)(B), our conclusion that these procedures treat disease also finds support in the opinions of other courts that have concluded for various nontax purposes that sex reassignment surgery and/or hormone therapy are not cosmetic procedures.

2. Breast Augmentation Surgery

We consider separately the qualification of petitioner's breast augmentation surgery as deductible medical care, because respondent makes the additional argument that this surgery was not necessary to the treatment of GID in petitioner's case because petitioner already had normal breasts before her surgery. Because petitioner had normal breasts before her surgery, respondent argues, her breast augmentation surgery was "directed at improving * * * [her] appearance and [did] not meaningfully promote the proper function of the body or prevent or treat illness or disease," placing the surgery squarely within the section 213(d)(9)(B) definition of "cosmetic surgery."

Reason for treating as separate issue

Petitioner has not argued, or adduced evidence, that the breast augmentation surgery ameliorated a deformity within the meaning of section 213(d)(9)(A). Accordingly, if the breast augmentation surgery meets the definition of "cosmetic surgery" in section 213(d)(9)(B), it is not "medical care" that is deductible pursuant to section 213(a).

For the reasons discussed below, we find that petitioner has failed to show that her breast augmentation surgery "[treated]" GID. The Benjamin standards provide that breast augmentation surgery for a male-to-female patient "may be performed if the physician prescribing hormones and the surgeon have documented that breast enlargement after undergoing hormone treatment for 18 months is not sufficient for comfort in the social gender role." The record contains no documentation from the endocrinologist prescribing petitioner's hormones at the time of her surgery. To the extent Ms. Ellaborn's or Dr. Coleman's recommendation letters to Dr. Meltzer might be considered substitute documentation for that of the hormone-prescribing physician, Ms. Ellaborn's two letters are silent concerning the condition of petitioner's presurgical breasts, while Dr. Coleman's letter states that petitioner "appears to have significant breast development secondary to hormone therapy." The surgeon here, Dr. Meltzer, recorded in his presurgical notes that petitioner had "approximately B cup breasts with a very nice shape." Thus, all of the contemporaneous documentation of the condition of petitioner's breasts before the surgery suggests that they were within a normal range of appearance, and there is no documentation concerning petitioner's comfort level with her breasts "in the social gender role."

H: Surgery was not to treat GID and was cosmetic

RE

Dr. Meltzer testified with respect to his notes that his reference to the "very nice shape" of petitioner's breasts was in comparison to the breasts of other transsexual males on feminizing hormones and that petitioner's breasts exhibited characteristics of gynecomastia, a condition where breast mass is concentrated closer to the nipple as compared to the breasts of a genetic female. Nonetheless, given the contemporaneous documentation of the breasts' apparent normalcy and the failure to adhere to the Benjamin standards' requirement to document breast-engendered anxiety to justify the surgery, we find that petitioner's breast augmentation surgery did not fall within the treatment protocols of the Benjamin standards and therefore did not "treat" GID within the meaning of section 213(d)(9)(B). Instead, the surgery merely improved her appearance.

The breast augmentation surgery is therefore "cosmetic surgery" under the section 213(d)(9)(B) definition unless it "meaningfully [promoted] the proper function of the body". The parties have stipulated that petitioner's breast augmentation "did not promote the proper function of her breasts." Although petitioner expressly declined to stipulate that the breast augmentation "did not meaningfully promote the proper functioning of her body within the meaning of I.R.C. § 213," we conclude that the stipulation to which she did agree precludes a finding on this record, given the failure to adhere to the Benjamin standards, that the breast augmentation surgery "meaningfully [promoted] the proper function of the body" within the meaning of section 213(d)(9)(B). Consequently, the breast augmentation surgery is "cosmetic surgery" that is excluded from deductible "medical care."

E. *Medical Necessity*

***

The mental health professional who treated petitioner concluded that petitioner's GID was severe, that sex reassignment surgery was medically necessary, and that petitioner's prognosis without it was poor. Given Dr. Brown's expert testimony, the judgment of the professional treating petitioner, the agreement of all three experts that untreated GID can result in self-mutilation and suicide, and, as conceded by Dr. Schmidt, the views of a significant segment of knowledgeable professionals that sex reassignment surgery is medically necessary for severe GID, the Court is persuaded that petitioner's sex reassignment surgery was medically necessary.

IV. *Conclusion*

The evidence amply supports the conclusions that petitioner suffered from severe GID, that GID is a well-recognized and serious mental disorder, and that hormone therapy and sex reassignment surgery are considered appropriate and effective treatments for GID by psychiatrists and other mental health professionals who are knowledgeable concerning the condition. Given our holdings that GID is a "disease" and that petitioner's hormone therapy and sex reassignment surgery "[treated]" it, petitioner has shown the "existence * * * of a disease" and a payment for goods or services "directly or proximately related" to its treatment. See *Jacobs v. Commissioner,* 62 T.C. at 818. She likewise satisfies the "but for" test of *Jacobs,* which requires a showing that the procedures were an essential element of the treatment and that they would not have otherwise been undertaken for nonmedical reasons. Petitioner's hormone therapy and sex reassignment surgery were essential elements of a widely accepted treatment protocol for severe GID. The expert testimony also establishes that given (1) the risks, pain, and extensive rehabilitation associated with sex reassignment surgery, (2) the stigma encountered by persons who change their gender role and appearance in society, and (3) the expert-backed but commonsense point that the desire of a genetic male to have his genitals removed requires an explanation beyond mere dissatisfaction with appearance (such as GID or psychosis), petitioner would not have undergone hormone therapy and sex reassignment surgery except in an effort to alleviate the distress and suffering attendant to GID. Respondent's contention that petitioner undertook the surgery and hormone treatments to improve appearance is at best a superficial characterization of the circumstances that is thoroughly rebutted by the medical evidence.

Petitioner has shown that her hormone therapy and sex reassignment surgery treated disease within the meaning of section 213 and were therefore not cosmetic surgery. Thus petitioner's expenditures for these procedures were for "medical care" as defined in section 213(d)(1)(A), for which a deduction is allowed under section 213(a).

To reflect the foregoing and concessions by the parties,

Decision will be entered under Rule 155.

[Concurring and dissenting opinions omitted.]

Post-Case Follow-Up

The court's primary holding in *O'Donnabhain* centers on the conclusion that gender identity disorder is a disease for federal income tax purposes and that sex reassignment surgery is part of treating the severe form of the disorder. One should also view this case as a classic example of the kind of dilemma that practitioners and courts must face from time to time. As an initial matter, Congress may have crafted an effective allowance of widespread general utility, but in light of unanticipated facts and circumstances, there is a real question as to whether disallowing the deduction would effect notable injustice or handily prevent the conferral of unintended legislative grace. In reaching its decision in *O'Donnabhain*, the Tax Court found it necessary to examine industry definitional standards and dissect conflicting expert testimony, all in an effort to determine whether GID constituted a disease and whether the protocol dictated by the Benjamin standards treated the disease. The court's ultimate conclusion that a well-known condition may constitute a disease for purposes of § 213, even if universal medical consensus is lacking, is good news for the deductibility of costs associated with the diagnosis and treatment of emerging conditions. But notable issues do remain on the table. Health-care professionals may render an emerging condition diagnosis prematurely (or excessively), and some apparently emerging conditions ultimately suffer the definitional rejection of the medical community (i.e., deeming the condition not to be a "disease"). Add to that fact the reality that medical experts may play a significant role in influencing a decision maker with respect to whether an emerging condition constitutes a disease, but at the same time, those medical professionals may be heavily influenced by those in the pharmaceutical industry who have a vested interest in the identification and treatment of new diseases and disorders. The difficulty, of course, is that although the pharmaceutical industry has delivered revolutionary advances in the field of medicine, the industry is a business, and the healing benediction of pharmacological intervention does not come free of charge. Far from it.

O'Donnabhain v. Commissioner: Real Life Applications

For each of the following questions, please assume that the taxpayer itemizes deductions, that relevant medical expenses exceed 7.5 percent of the taxpayer's adjusted gross income, and that the taxpayer has not been compensated by insurance or otherwise.

1. Several months ago, Nelson (who now prefers to be called Nefertia) was diagnosed with gender identity disorder. Her psychologist does not consider Nefertia's case to be severe, so she has not recommended surgical intervention. Nonetheless, Nefertia is profoundly uncomfortable with her basic body shape; she would like a more curvaceous figure. If Nefertia undergoes surgery to receive implants in her gluteus maximus muscles to enhance the curvature of her derriere and strategic liposuction to narrow her waistline, will she be able to deduct the expenses under § 213?

2. After surviving a bank robbery, Milton's doctors diagnosed him as having moderately severe post-traumatic stress disorder. If Milton pays for prescription medication and treatment for his PTSD, will he be able to deduct the cost under § 213?

3. For quite some time, Charles has enjoyed working on cars. Unfortunately, he has never been good at taking adequate, precautionary safety measures. As a result, a motor recently crushed one of his legs, and the surgeons were forced to amputate it. Charles made an effective recovery, but from time to time, he suffers excruciating phantom pain in the calf and thigh of the missing leg. Some, but not all, doctors have begun to endorse mirror therapy as a means of reducing or eliminating the phantom pain. If Charles undergoes mirror therapy to alleviate his pain, will the cost of treatment be deductible under § 213?

Bruce Becomes Caitlin Jenner

Although many individuals have transitioned from male to female, perhaps the best known is the Olympic hero, Bruce Jenner (left), who became Caitlin Jenner (right) and was featured on the cover of *Vanity Fair* magazine.

Bruce Jenner *(left): Credit:* Vicki L. Miller/Shutterstock.com.
Caitlin Jenner *(right): Credit:* JStone/Shutterstock.com.

Chapter Summary

- Taxpayers who itemize may deduct expenses incurred and paid with respect to the medical care of the taxpayer, his spouse, and his dependents, but only to the extent that such expenses exceed 7.5 percent of the taxpayer's adjusted gross income (assuming the taxpayer has not received compensation by insurance or otherwise).

- *Medical care* is a defined term and generally includes amounts paid for the diagnosis, cure, mitigation, treatment, or prevention of disease (or to affect a structure or function of the body). Prescription drug costs as well as transportation and lodging costs associated with the receipt of medical care may also be deductible.

- Conduct recommended by a physician may not qualify as *medical care* within the meaning of § 213, notwithstanding the fact that such conduct may prove beneficial to health.

- Amounts paid for cosmetic surgery (or similar procedures) do not qualify as medical care unless the intervention is necessary to ameliorate deformities arising from (or directly related to) congenital abnormalities, certain personal injuries, or disfiguring diseases. By definition, *cosmetic surgery* is directed at improving appearance and does not meaningfully promote the proper function of the body or prevent or treat illness or disease.

- The deductibility of the same medical expense (e.g., the cost of acquiring an egg donor) may ultimately turn on factors unique to the taxpayer.

- Specific capital expenditures may qualify for immediate deduction as medical expenses. If such items take the form of property improvements, the deduction may be unavailable, partial, or full, depending on the impact of the improvement (if any) on the fair market value of the subject property.

- Both physical ailments and mental disorders may qualify as diseases. For federal income tax purposes, verifiable physiological abnormality is not necessary to establish the existence of definitive pathology.

Applying the Rules

Unless otherwise indicated, for each of the following questions, please assume that the taxpayer itemizes deductions, that relevant medical expenses exceed 7.5 percent of the taxpayer's adjusted gross income, and that the taxpayer has not been compensated with respect to the expense by insurance or otherwise.

1. Over the past seven years, Adrienne and Stuart have had seven children. The couple opposes the use of birth control pills, but Adrienne has made it clear that she refuses to have any more children. If Stuart gets a vasectomy, will the expenses incurred be deductible under § 213?

2. *Same facts as Question 1.* Assume that Adrienne, having carried seven children to term, has gained a considerable amount of weight over the years and has been

unable to shed the excess poundage. She is nowhere near morbidly obese, but she tires easily and constantly complains of knee and back pain. If Adrienne undergoes gastric bypass surgery to lose weight, is it likely that she will be able to deduct the associated medical expenses under § 213?

3. *For this question, ignore the assumptions mentioned above.* During 2017, Lee had adjusted gross income of $80,000, and on April 15, 2018, he timely filed his federal income tax return. Lee routinely itemizes, and on his Schedule A, he claimed a medical expense deduction of $9,200 (the amount he paid for emergency room services in connection with a serious injury he sustained while mowing his lawn). He has not been compensated for the expense by insurance or otherwise. What amount, if any, may Lee deduct with respect to this expense?

4. Since her early teenage years, Cherise has suffered with migraine headaches. She's tried everything, including the medication prescribed by her physician. Recently, Cherise discovered that a mild dose of Vicodin does the trick, but given the medication's highly addictive nature, her doctor refuses to prescribe it for her. Undaunted, Cherise has found a steady supplier, a guy who goes by the name of "Dr. V" and typically meets her in dark alleyways. Can Cherise deduct the amount she pays her dealer for her Vicodin?

5. Valerie is a midlevel associate at a large national law firm. She works crazy hours and suffers chronic stress. Her doctor has long advised her to take more vacation time, and this summer, she finally did. Assume that Valerie spent two weeks in Aruba and that her total expense was $7,000 ($2,000 air fare and $5,000 hotel accommodations). May Valerie deduct any portion of her costs under § 213?

Federal Income Taxation in Practice

Unless otherwise indicated, for each of the following questions, please assume that the taxpayer itemizes deductions, that relevant medical expenses exceed 7.5 percent of the taxpayer's adjusted gross income, and that the taxpayer has not been compensated with respect to the expense by insurance or otherwise.

1. While playing outside an abandoned house with other neighborhood children, Virginia stepped on a piece of broken glass. The resulting cut ultimately required that she receive several stitches in the emergency room at the local hospital. Although Virginia ordinarily lives with her mother during the year, she spends the summer months (June through August) with her father, who divorced her mother several years ago. The incident occurred during one of Virginia's summer visits with her father, and it was he who covered the cost of the emergency room visit. Will he be able to deduct the relevant medical expenses?

2. By all accounts, Cleo was a promising gymnastics student. She recently suffered an accident that left her paralyzed from the waist down; she now uses a motorized wheelchair. Her parents have asked you whether the cost of the wheelchair (and ongoing maintenance on it) is deductible under § 213. They would also like to know whether they can deduct the cost of constructing a ramp outside their home for Cleo's benefit.

3. You recently prepared a memo for one of the senior tax partners in your law firm. In the memo, you note that medical care expenses are deductible to the extent they exceed 7.5 percent of AGI. The tax partner can see that language in the current statute, but she would like to know how and when the number changed in recent years. See what you can find, and draft a brief memo for her.

4. Due to chronic low back pain, one of your friends has expressed an interest in acupuncture, but he is concerned about the cost. He plans to give acupuncture serious consideration, but only if he can deduct the cost. Are there any IRS pronouncements on this issue?

Casualty, Theft, and Other Losses

In much the same way that taxpayers may have income from various sources, they may also suffer economic losses in various contexts. A sole proprietor or a major corporate taxpayer may be forced to endure considerable economic strife if the local or national economy veers into recession or if a substantial line of business falls out of consumer favor. Equally likely to occur are losses flowing from natural disasters or other casualties that have nothing to do with the regular ebb and flow of the business cycle. For example, the Great Fire that raged through Chicago in the 1870s, the spectacular eruption of Mt. St. Helens in the 1980s, and the flooding surge following Hurricane Katrina left death and economic devastation in their wake. Fortunately for all affected, the tax law does not turn a blind eye to the financial impact of these unfortunate events in taxpayers' lives. In this chapter, we will briefly address the basic treatment of business and nonbusiness losses before turning our attention to the tax treatment of casualty and theft losses suffered by individuals.

A. GENERAL RULES

Section 165(a) of the Code generally allows taxpayers a deduction for losses sustained during the taxable year. A corporate taxpayer in the parcel delivery business, for example, might suffer the loss of one of its airplanes or trucks in severe weather, and an individual taxpayer might suffer the loss of his home and all of its contents due to a tornado. In each instance, the deduction is available only to the extent that such losses have not been compensated for by

Key Concepts

- The meaning of "casualty" and the role of "suddenness" in the federal income taxation context
- The meaning and ramification of a loss being "sustained"
- Limitations on the losses of individuals
- Loss amount and the significance of taxpayer substantiation
- The impact of public policy on loss deductibility

insurance or otherwise, and under the appropriate circumstances, taxpayers must adjust loss amounts (typically measured by adjusted basis in the case of property) for any salvage value remaining in the asset after the fact. Section 165(a) is best understood as a default, foundational rule, because several special rules may come into play and thereby alter its impact. Later in this chapter, we will discuss several special rules applicable to the losses of individuals. As you will see, individuals, per § 165(c), may deduct only those losses falling within discrete categories and, in certain instances, only in limited amounts. Gamblers suffering losses at the casino (or placing bets elsewhere) may offset wagering losses only with wagering gains, and whether one is a gambler or not, those suffering capital losses (e.g., by selling stock) must take such losses into account in compliance with special rules designed for the tax treatment of capital gains and capital losses. *See generally* § 165(d) and (f).

B. TIMING THE DEDUCTION OF LOSSES

1. Requirement That Losses Be "Sustained" During the Taxable Year

Although taxpayer losses arising from isolated events (e.g., fires, tornados, thefts, etc.) generally present no timing issues, the possibility for temporal ambiguity exists. Insurance companies may promptly acknowledge the existence of a potential claim but feel the need to conduct an investigation before confirming coverage and tendering forth payment or denying coverage altogether. How should an affected taxpayer treat these unresolved situations when faced with the unavoidable obligation to file a timely federal income tax return? And what happens if a taxpayer takes a loss deduction in one taxable year and accepts some form of (unexpected) compensation from an insurance company (or other actor) in a subsequent taxable year? Section 165 sets forth the relevant rules, and the associated Treasury Regulations provide useful guidance.

Let's start by taking a close look at the language of § 165(a). The statute provides that "[t]here shall be allowed as a deduction any loss *sustained* during the taxable year and not compensated for by insurance or otherwise." (Emphasis added.) The Treasury Regulations promulgated under § 165 clarify what it means for a loss to be sustained, and by doing so, they control the timing of a loss deduction. In general, the regulations provide that "a loss shall be treated as sustained during the taxable year in which the loss occurs as evidenced by closed and completed transactions and as fixed by identifiable events occurring in such taxable year."

Treas. Reg. § 1.165-1(d)(1). A sale of stock at a loss would be a closed and completed transaction, and the destruction of a personal residence by fire or hurricane would be an identifiable event. In the case of certain casualties or other loss events, insurance may cover the loss or some alternative form of reimbursement may be forthcoming, and a loss deduction might ultimately prove premature. The Treasury Regulations clarify that so long as a reasonable prospect of recovery exists, the loss (technically) has not been "sustained" for federal income tax purposes:

> If a casualty or other event occurs which may result in a loss and, in the year of such casualty or event, there exists a claim for reimbursement with respect to which there is a reasonable prospect of recovery, no portion of the loss with respect to which reimbursement may be received is sustained, for purposes of section 165, until it can be ascertained with reasonable certainty whether or not such reimbursement will be received.

Treas. Reg. § 1.165-1(d)(2)(i).

As a matter of logic, several possibilities are on the table after an incident. There may be no claim for reimbursement (e.g., because of the taxpayer's failure to secure insurance). There may be a claim for reimbursement, albeit with no reasonable prospect of recovery (e.g., the insurance company is bankrupt). And there may be a claim for reimbursement with respect to which there is a reasonable prospect of recovery; in that event, the regulations bar deduction *until* it can be ascertained with reasonable certainty whether such reimbursement is forthcoming. Settlement, adjudication, or objective abandonment of the claim effectively establish reasonable certainty (for good or ill). *See* Treas. Reg. § 1.165-1(d)(2)(i). Note also that even if some form of reimbursement may be forthcoming, taxpayers may be able to proceed with a limited loss deduction if it can be established that any recovery will be partial (e.g., an item was not fully insured) or that an anticipated recovery has, in fact, fallen short of original expectation. *See* Treas. Reg. § 1.165-1(d)(2)(ii).

2. Special Timing Situations: Theft and Disaster Losses

Special timing rules apply with respect to theft and disaster losses. Losses arising from theft are deemed to have been sustained in the taxable year in which the taxpayer discovers the theft, but even in that context, the existence of a claim for reimbursement with respect to which there is a reasonable prospect of recovery may delay the deduction of the loss until it has (technically) been sustained. *See* Treas. Reg. § 1.165-1(d)(3). The timing rules for certain disasters reflect Congress's attempt to offer taxpayers more immediate relief than they might otherwise enjoy. If a loss occurs in a disaster area and is attributable to a federally declared disaster, the affected taxpayer may deduct the loss on his return for *either* the taxable year in which the disaster actually occurs *or* for the taxable year immediately preceding the year of the disaster. *See* § 165(i). Thus, in the latter context, in the wake of a qualifying event occurring on March 1, 2017, the taxpayer may elect to deduct the loss on the 2016 federal income tax return he files on April 15, 2017 (i.e., as though the event had occurred and the loss sustained in 2016). If the taxpayer has already filed his 2016 return (e.g., on February 7, 2017), he may file an amended return for that taxable year and take the deduction.

3. Subsequent Recoveries

Taxpayers validly deducting a loss under § 165 in one taxable year and receiving some form of reimbursement in a subsequent taxable year will not likely have the luxury of simply enjoying receipt of the money and doing nothing else. They may be called on to reconcile the inconsistency; but to the extent they must take corrective action, they will not do so by amending the prior year's return. Instead, as a general matter, they must include the amount received in gross income in the year of the recovery, but note the potential for an alternative outcome. If taking the deduction in the prior year did not result in a reduction of the taxpayer's liability (e.g., taxable income had already been reduced to $0 by other deductions), then the loss deduction taken gave rise to no tax benefit; in that situation, a subsequent recovery will be a non-event for tax purposes. That's putting it very succinctly. We will return to this situation (i.e., deduction followed by recovery) and consider more detailed recovery exclusion prerequisites when we study § 111 in a future chapter.

Excess Business Losses of Non-Corporate Taxpayers

Although § 165(c)(1) generally provides for the deduction of trade or business losses by an individual, section 461(*l*) bars the deduction of excess business losses in a given taxable year by a non-corporate taxpayer. Rather than mandating permanent disallowance, Congress essentially requires that such losses be saved for another day. In technical terms, losses disallowed by § 461(*l*) must be treated as net operating loss carryovers [a concept we will cover in a subsequent chapter] to the next taxable year. "Excess business loss" refers to the excess of (1) total trade or business deductions over (2) the sum of (i) income/gain from the business and (ii) $250,000 ($500,000 for married taxpayers filing jointly).

C. LOSSES OF INDIVIDUALS

1. General Rules

Although § 165(a) generally allows taxpayers a deduction for losses sustained during the taxable year, individuals face specific hurdles and limitations. Section 165(c) provides that an individual may deduct losses under § 165(a) only if (1) such losses were incurred in a trade or business; (2) such losses were incurred in a transaction entered into for profit (even if not a trade or business); or (3) within numerical limits, such losses fail to fall into the preceding categories and were property losses arising from fire, storm, shipwreck, or other casualty or from theft. The losses referred to in the last category (i.e., personal casualty losses) are set forth in § 165(c)(3). In addition to taking numerical limitations of general applicability into account, individual taxpayers must ascertain whether a given personal casualty loss remains available in light of other Code-based restrictions discussed below. *See generally*

§ 165(h). Note also that to the extent an individual suffered losses described in § 165(c)(3) that were covered by insurance, such losses will be taken into account (assuming the insurance company's ultimate refusal/failure to cover the loss) under § 165 only if the taxpayer files a timely insurance claim. *See* § 165(h)(4)(E). A claim denial establishes that the loss was not compensated for by insurance, but the taxpayer may not simply ignore what would appear to be a viable insurance claim and expect to be able to take advantage of the loss deduction provided for in § 165.

Tornados

Although tornados strike in various parts of the world, most occur in the United States. Winds in the storm can spin at hundreds of miles per hour and turn both small and large items into lethal projectiles. One of the deadliest tornados in U.S. history struck on March 18, 1925. Touching down near Ellington, Missouri, it left death and destruction in its wake as it tore across Illinois and Indiana. The so-called Tri-State Tornado killed 652 people and left more than 2,000 injured. Although tornados typically last approximately 15 minutes, this storm raged for over three hours. See 501 Most Devastating Disasters 29 (Bounty Books 2010).

Tornado: *Credit:* Justin Hobson/ Shutterstock.com.

Aftermath: *Credit:* Martin Haas/ Shutterstock.com.

Limitations Generally Applicable to Personal Casualty Losses of Individuals

Barring limited situational exception, for taxable years beginning after December 31, 2017 and before January 1, 2026, individuals may deduct personal casualty losses only if such losses are attributable to a federally declared disaster. *See* § 165(h)(5)(A) and (i)(5). Moreover, as was noted previously, the extent to which taxpayers may deduct such losses is limited numerically. Bear in mind that the federal disaster requirement generally applies to § 165(c)(3) losses; it does not apply to losses of an individual under § 165(c)(1) or (c)(2).

Stated in grossly oversimplified terms, § 165(h) provides that individuals with personal casualty losses may deduct them but only to the extent such losses exceed 10 percent of the taxpayer's adjusted gross income. The unabridged version of the rule is more accurate but decidedly more complicated. Let's consider the rule in

§ 165(h)(1) before tackling the rule in § 165(h)(2). Section 165(h)(1) is simple in its application. It clarifies that a personal casualty loss is allowed (with respect to each casualty) only to the extent the loss exceeds $100. In practical terms, then, the provision requires an immediate $100 reduction or "haircut" with respect to the amount of any personal casualty loss; this mandatory reduction is simply an across-the-board rule and is intended to render irrelevant minor losses such as broken plates, damaged trinkets, and the like. Thus, if a tornado causes a taxpayer to lose 10 place settings of bone china dinnerware in which the taxpayer had an aggregate basis of $900, the taxpayer must first reduce the loss amount to $800. Because the tornado was a single casualty, only one "haircut" is required, *not* one "haircut" for each place setting; the Code requires the reduction for *each* casualty or *each* theft. But if the taxpayer suffered a casualty loss in January of a given year and a second casualty loss in July of the same year, a separate haircut would apply with respect to each casualty event.

Section 165(h)(2) resists easy digestion, but you can attain a better understanding of its provisions if you first get two technical definitions under your belt, the first for personal casualty gain and the second for personal casualty loss. A *personal casualty loss* is any loss described in § 165(c)(3), although for § 165(h)(2) calculation purposes, this amount is reduced by the $100 haircut. A *personal casualty gain* is any recognized gain flowing from the involuntary conversion of property as a result of a § 165(c)(3) event. Involuntary conversion results, for example, if a taxpayer loses property due to a fire and receives payment from an insurance company as a result; the fire involuntarily converts the property to cash. Personal casualty gains may arise, for example, if a taxpayer insures an item for an amount (e.g., $10,000) exceeding the item's adjusted basis (e.g., $8,000); if a casualty or theft occurs and the taxpayer receives the full coverage amount, the taxpayer will have a personal casualty gain (e.g., $2,000).

With those definitions in mind, let's take a closer look at the inner workings of § 165(h)(2). The provision contemplates two scenarios. In one, personal casualty gains for a given year exceed personal casualty losses, and in the other, the situation is reversed. If gains exceed losses, then both the gains and losses are treated as capital in nature. For our purposes, this treatment simply means that the capital losses can be used to offset the capital gains. What about the much more likely scenario in which the personal casualty losses exceed the personal casualty gains? In that scenario, the personal casualty losses are first allowed to the extent necessary to offset all personal casualty gains. The taxpayer may then deduct any personal casualty losses remaining after the offset but only to the extent such losses exceed 10 percent of the taxpayer's adjusted gross income. Bear in mind throughout the entire analysis

Potential Use of Non-Disaster Personal Casualty Losses

Under § 165(h)(5)(A), for certain taxable years beginning after December 31, 2017, taxpayers may generally deduct only those personal casualty losses attributable to a federally declared disaster. Note, however, that if a taxpayer has personal casualty gains in those taxable years, then non-disaster personal casualty losses can be used to offset such gains. See § 165(h)(5)(B)(i). If such an offset occurs, then the amount of personal casualty gains taken into account for purposes of § 165(h)(2)(A) must be reduced by the amount of the gains offset under § 165(h)(5)(B)(i). See § 165(h)(5)(B)(ii).

that before any loss is allowed, the loss must first be sustained (during the taxable year) within the meaning of § 165 and the regulations promulgated thereunder. The following example demonstrates application of the rules under § 165(c) and (h).

Example

In 2019, Sirius had adjusted gross income of $70,000. During that year, he sustained a personal casualty loss of $17,000 when an earthquake struck in the vicinity of his home. The event was later declared to be a federal disaster. Given the application of § 165(h)(1), Sirius's personal casualty loss was reduced to $16,900 ($17,000 - $100) for purposes of 165(h)(2) calculations. In connection with the same earthquake, Sirius also had a personal casualty gain of $2,000 because he received an insurance company payout of $5,000 for an item with an adjusted basis of $3,000. His personal casualty losses are first allowed to the extent of his personal casualty gains ($2,000). Thereafter, he may deduct remaining personal casualty losses ($14,900), but only to the extent they exceed 10 percent of his AGI. Because 10 percent of his AGI is $7,000, he may deduct an additional $7,900. Sirius's total loss deduction as a result of the earthquake will be $2,000 + $7,900 = $9,900.

2. Special Issues

Given that current law generally bars deductions with respect to personal casualty losses unless such losses were attributable to a federally declared disaster, taxpayers will rarely face the issue of whether a specific event qualifies as a "casualty" within the meaning of § 165(c)(3), at least with respect to taxable years affected by § 165(h)(5). That having been said, taxpayers seeking to appeal to the exception in § 165(h)(5)(B)(i) may take advantage of its allowance only with respect to eligible items. The relevant portion of the personal casualty loss need not be attributable to a federally declared disaster, but in that context, qualification of an item as a personal casualty loss (i.e., a § 165(c)(3) loss) becomes critical. Further, taxpayers may find it necessary to address the qualification issue for taxable years unaffected by § 165(h)(5). Let's turn, then, to the oft-subsidiary issue of whether a given event qualifies as a casualty within the meaning of § 165(c)(3), bearing in mind the limited circumstances requiring resolution of this issue.

Defining "Casualty"

Under appropriate circumstances and within specified limits, individuals may take a loss deduction when they suffer a theft loss or a loss caused by fire, storm, shipwreck, or other casualty. Courts and commentators generally agree that for an event to qualify as an "other casualty," it must be akin to a fire, storm, or shipwreck. But what exactly does that mean? According to one authority, "[a] casualty is the damage, destruction, or loss of property that results from an identifiable event that is sudden (i.e., swift, not gradual or progressive), unexpected (i.e., ordinarily unanticipated and unintended), or unusual (i.e., not a day-to-day occurrence and not typical of the activity engaged

Defining "Sudden"

Although many events that constitute casualties under § 165(c) often last no more than a few seconds or minutes, an event may qualify as "sudden," even if it occurs over a multiday period. In Revenue Ruling 79-174, 1979-1 C.B. 99, the taxpayer owned 40 ornamental pine trees, all of which were attacked by a massive swarm of southern pine beetles. The onslaught occurred over a 5- to 10-day period, and it left all of the trees dead. The Service pointed out that progressive deterioration (including that caused by insects) does not qualify as "sudden," but under the given circumstances, the fact that the insects attacked in epidemic proportions and decimated the trees within a matter of days made the event sufficiently swift and precipitous to qualify as sudden.

Credit: KC_Film/Shutterstock.com.

in)." BLOOMBERG BNA, 2015 FEDERAL TAX GUIDE 420 (Tax Management Inc. 2014). Under that standard, the destruction of a home over the course of several years by termites would not constitute a casualty, but destruction of the same home by a falling tree (e.g., one struck by lightning or uprooted and tossed by strong winds) would. The toughest cases likely to end up in Tax Court reside uncomfortably between these extremes.

Case Preview

Popa v. Commissioner

Where, along the continuum of casualty to non-casualty events, does loss occasioned by political upheaval fall? In *Popa v. Commissioner*, the taxpayer suffered the loss of household goods when the City of Saigon in the Republic of Vietnam fell to the North Vietnamese in the mid-1970s. Can we say that he simply abandoned his property in the same way that someone might abandon a couch on the sidewalk (suffering no cognizable loss), or is his situation decidedly akin to one suffering a loss due to fire, storm, or shipwreck? A notably divided Tax Court struggled with this issue in *Popa*. As you read through the opinion, consider the following questions:

1.   What is *ejusdem generis* and why does it matter in this and similar cases?
2.   Must a taxpayer establish, in every instance, by weight of relevant evidence, that he suffered a loss in a manner akin to fire, storm, or shipwreck, or can he rely solely on strong likelihood and ask the decision maker to embrace assumptions?
3. How does the court reconcile this opinion with other decisions in which no casualty loss was found, notwithstanding factual similarity?

Popa v. Commissioner
73 T.C. 130 (1979)

STERRETT, Judge

By letter dated October 27, 1977, respondent determined a deficiency in petitioner's income taxes paid for his taxable year ended December 31, 1975, in the amount of $3,206.23. After concessions, the only issue for our decision is whether or not petitioner sustained a casualty loss within the meaning of section 165(c)(3), I.R.C. 1954, when various of his personal possessions, located in the Republic of Vietnam, were lost when the government of that nation fell to the North Vietnamese.

FINDINGS OF FACT

Some of the facts have been stipulated and are so found. * * *

Petitioner Justin Popa timely filed his cash basis individual Federal income tax return for his taxable year ended December 31, 1975, with the Internal Revenue Service Center at Philadelphia, Pa. Mr. Popa's petition was timely filed with this Court on March 23, 1978. At the time he filed his petition herein, Mr. Popa resided in Seoul, Korea.

During the calendar year 1975, petitioner resided in the Republic of Vietnam, serving as the vice president and general manager of the Transworld Services Corp.***. On April 26, 1975, petitioner left Vietnam on one of his frequent business trips to Bangkok, Thailand. He took with him only a suitcase and a briefcase. Everything else petitioner owned, such as furniture, clothing, appliances, books, and stored food stuffs, was left at his rented home in an affluent part of Saigon. Within a matter of days after Mr. Popa's departure from the Republic of Vietnam, that country's government collapsed. United States nationals were ordered evacuated by the President. Petitioner was never able to return to that country and has no reasonable hope of ever recovering his property or its value. None of the goods lost were insured.

In his return, petitioner attached a list of the items which he claims he had to abandon in Vietnam. Petitioner assigned a total fair market value of $12,691 to these items and deducted this amount, less the $100 section 165(c)(3) floor, as a casualty loss on his calendar year 1975 return.

Items left in Vietnam once govt collapsed

OPINION

[T]he only issue left for our decision is whether petitioner is entitled to a casualty loss deduction under

The Vietnam War and the Fall of Saigon

Seeking to halt the "domino effect" spread of Communism throughout Southeast Asia, the United States sent troops to South Vietnam to support the local government against the aggression of the North Vietnamese and the Viet Cong (militant South Vietnamese opposed to the local government). The conflict was bloody and included the United States' use of napalm (an incendiary liquid) and Agent Orange (to defoliate jungle and thereby expose opposition supply lines). Although the United States left South Vietnam in 1973 in the wake of the Paris Peace Accords, a subsequent communist attack resulted in the capture of Saigon in 1975, and the country was unified as the Socialist Republic of Vietnam. Over one million refugees escaped the new communist regime and ultimately settled in the United States of America. *See* HISTORY: THE DEFINITIVE VISUAL GUIDE 430–31 (Covent Garden Books 2010).

Saigon is now officially called Ho Chi Minh City.
Credit: Pavalena/Shutterstock.com.

section 165(c)(3) with respect to the loss of his household goods following the fall of Saigon to the North Vietnamese.

By contending that petitioner abandoned his property in Saigon, respondent concedes the fact that petitioner has suffered an economic loss. Further, we take it as implicit in respondent's memorandum brief that he also concedes that the loss took place when Saigon fell to enemy troops a day or two after petitioner left on a business trip to Bangkok. Nevertheless, respondent argues that petitioner's loss is nondeductible because it "does not constitute a casualty loss as is contemplated by I.R.C. section 165(c)(3)." Petitioner, on the other hand, argues that his loss in Vietnam was due to an "identifiable event of a sudden, unexpected and unusual nature" which event is ejusdem generis to the events specifically described in section 165(c)(3).

We believe that petitioner's loss of his goods is an "other casualty" within the meaning of section 165(c)(3). We think that petitioner's loss in the fall of Saigon is ejusdem generis to losses due to "fire, storm (and), shipwreck." It was a sudden, cataclysmic, and devastating loss — just the sort of loss section 165(c)(3) was designed to address. We have previously noted that the application of the principle of ejusdem generis — has been consistently broadened so that wherever unexpected, accidental force is exerted on property and the taxpayer is powerless to prevent application of the force because of the suddenness thereof or some disability, the resulting direct and proximate damage causes a loss which is like or similar to losses arising from the causes specifically enumerated in section 165(c)(3).

As "the events giving rise to the undisputed loss here were sudden, unexpected, violent and not due to deliberate or willful actions by petitioner," we conclude that these losses are deductible. See *White v. Commissioner*, [48 T.C. 430, 433-434 (1967)].

Our review of the cases convinces us that the only circumstance which could possibly have existed that would require us to deny petitioner his casualty loss would be that the property was confiscated under color of some hastily enacted local law. All the other possibilities (fire, theft, looting, etc.) are such that entitle him to a section 165(c)(3) casualty loss.

Respondent notes in his memorandum brief that "It is extremely doubtful that petitioner knows or will ever know what became of his property, since he was precluded from returning to Vietnam after the U.S. military evacuation." We are, of course, well aware of the legion of cases that hold that the taxpayer must be put to his proof. However, in unusual circumstances such as this, we do not think it fair or reasonable to require that the taxpayer eliminate all possible noncasualty causes of his loss. We do not believe that we unduly stretch the bounds of judicial notice when we take into account the abruptness with which the United States abandoned Saigon and the stories with respect to the heavy damage to the city. A few days before the city fell, the United States Government was actively evacuating its citizens from the city. We can hardly fault petitioner for not remaining to determine whether his property was destroyed by gun fire, by looting, by fire, or some form of seizure by the remaining Saigon residents, the Vietcong, or the North Vietnamese. Certainly, petitioner's failure to return to the city was not a matter of personal choice. Nor can his inexactitude in this matter be held against him.

We note here that the difficulties in South Vietnam did not arise from a revolution from within such as occurred recently in Iran and Nicaragua, thus making less likely the possibility that even a despotic law authorized the taking at issue.

Accordingly, we believe that the most reasonable conclusion, on the particular facts of this case, is that the property at issue was either destroyed or pilfered with criminal intent. Hence, we find the decision in *Farcasanu v. Commissioner*, 436 F.2d 146 (D.C. Cir. 1970), *affg.* 50 T.C. 881 (1968), relied on by respondent, to be inapposite.

We find more apposite our holding in *Solt v. Commissioner*, 19 T.C. 183 (1952), wherein we allowed a section 23(e) deduction (the 1939 Code predecessor to sec. 165) for the loss in 1954 of a farm, including a residence, attributable to confiscation by the Government of Hungary.

We, therefore, conclude that petitioner suffered a section 165(c)(3) loss when he lost his goods in Vietnam.

However, while we hold that petitioner sustained a casualty loss within the ~~BUT~~ meaning of section 165(c)(3), we are not satisfied that petitioner has adequately documented the deductible amount of this loss. For example, petitioner claimed a $1,000 loss with respect to two air conditioners. The $1,000 claim represents petitioner's estimate of the fair market value of these items as of their loss date. Petitioner testified that he had purchased the air conditioners for $800. Of course, only $800 would, therefore, be allowed as a casualty deduction with respect thereto. Sec. 1.165-7(b)(1), Income Tax Regs. In the face of this, and other similar failures in petitioner's proof, we allow petitioner 75 percent of his claimed loss ***.

Decision will be entered under Rule 155.

Reviewed by the Court.

CHABOT, J., concurring:

Respondent does not dispute the fact of petitioner's loss of the property left behind when petitioner departed Vietnam on April 26, 1975.

The parties dispute the amount of the loss; that dispute is resolved in the majority opinion ***.

The parties also dispute the deductibility of the loss.

In the usual case, only one cause of loss is alleged and the issue either is whether that was the cause or whether that cause qualifies the loss for deduction. This case is unusual only in that any of several forces might have caused the loss. In such a situation, I see no warrant for requiring petitioner to show which of several forces, each of which would qualify the loss for deduction, was the cause of the loss.

Petitioner has the burden of proving that it is more likely than not that the loss resulted from "fire, storm, shipwreck, or other casualty, or from theft," within the meaning of section 165(c)(3). The judge who presided at the trial has concluded that petitioner has borne that burden of proof * * *, and nothing in the record herein appears to justify disagreement with that conclusion.

Since the trier of fact has drawn his conclusion "on the particular facts of this case" (*Purvis v. Commissioner*, 65 T.C. 1165, 1169 (1976)), and that conclusion seems to be consistent with the record before us, I see no reason to speculate as to what the record might show if the loss occurred in Iran or Nicaragua. Also, it does not seem to me to be relevant to weigh the difficulty or cost for petitioner, or the Department of State, or someone else, to return to the scene to gather additional evidence, unless it is thought that some variant of the doctrine of *Wichita Terminal Elevator Co. v. Commissioner*, 6 T.C. 1158, 1165 (1946), *affd.* 162 F.2d 513 (10th Cir. 1947), applies to the case. Since respondent does not raise that question, I would not attempt to analyze the difficulties that petitioner might have faced.

The question before us is whether petitioner has borne his burden of proof. I cannot join in any suggestion that some might read into the majority opinion that the practical hazards of an unsettled world somehow justify a lesser burden of proof. However, I concur in the result because of the majority's conclusion that petitioner has borne his burden of proof, however narrowly, as to deductibility.

GOFFE, J., agrees with this concurring opinion.

FAY, J., dissenting:

While I sympathize with petitioner, I must nevertheless respectfully dissent from the majority's conclusion that he sustained a deductible loss.

At the outset, I think it important to bear in mind that not all uninsured economic losses suffered by an individual are deductible. Were that the case, there would be no question that petitioner would be entitled to some deduction for the unfortunate loss of his property. However, section 165(c), I.R.C. 1954, expressly provides otherwise:

(c) LIMITATIONS ON LOSSES OF INDIVIDUALS. — In the case of an individual, the deduction under subsection (a) shall be limited to —
(1) losses incurred in a trade or business;
(2) losses incurred in any transaction entered into for profit, though not connected with a trade or business; and
(3) losses of property not connected with a trade or business, if such losses arise from fire, storm, shipwreck, or other casualty, or from theft. * * *

Thus, if an individual's loss is not connected with a trade or business or incurred in a profit-seeking transaction, it is deductible only if it arises from casualty, as defined, or theft.

For example, if petitioner abandoned his property as respondent contends, petitioner is not entitled to any deduction, since there is no evidence his personal property was used in a trade or business. *Shea v. Commissioner*, 24 B.T.A. 798, 803 (1931). Indeed, the findings of fact state petitioner himself claimed "he had to abandon (his property) in Vietnam," ***. Yet, the majority opinion does not address this possibility despite its statements that "Saigon fell to enemy troops a day or two after petitioner left," ***; "the United States abandoned Saigon"; and "A few days before the city fell, the United States Government was actively evacuating its citizens from the city."

Similarly, it is clear petitioner would not be entitled to a loss deduction in the event his property was seized by the North Vietnamese Government after entering Saigon because that would not constitute a "theft." *Farcasanu v. Commissioner*, 50 T.C. 881 (1968), affd. 436 F.2d 146 (D.C. Cir. 1970).

In the instant case, petitioner and the majority rely upon that part of section 165(c)(3) which permits an individual to deduct the loss of property arising from a "fire, storm, shipwreck, or other casualty." The relevant inquiry therefore is whether petitioner has produced sufficient evidence to "show that he comes within (the statute's) terms." *New Colonial Ice Co. v. Helvering*, 292 U.S. 435, 440 (1934). I submit that he has not.

In *Powers v. Commissioner*, 36 T.C. 1191 (1961), the taxpayer purchased an automobile in West Berlin, Germany. Three days later, while enroute from Berlin to Hamburg, the taxpayer's automobile was seized by the East German police and never returned to him. In holding that the taxpayer was not entitled to a deduction for the clear loss he sustained, we stated:

> Petitioner offers some suggestion that his loss was a "casualty" in any event. Assuming that that change of position is now open to him, it is of no assistance. What happened was not like a "fire, storm or shipwreck." Sec. 23(e)(3), I.R.C. 1939. It did not embody the requisite element of "chance, accident or contingency." *Alice P. Bachofen von Echt*, 21 B.T.A. 702, 709 (1930). The deduction was not permissible either as a theft or as a casualty. Petitioner's loss, though unfortunate, "was no more than a personal expense to petitioner, for the deduction of which the statute makes no provision." *Thomas F. Gurry*, 27 B.T.A. 1237, 1238 (1933). (36 T.C. at 1193.)

In light of *Powers*, and cases which have followed it, it is clear that if petitioner's property was confiscated by the Communist government after the fall of Saigon, he would not be entitled to a casualty loss deduction under section 165(c)(3). However, based upon petitioner's complete lack of knowledge, the wartime circumstances, and judicially noticed "stories with respect to the heavy damage to the city," *** the majority infers that the property was most likely destroyed or criminally pilfered.

Admittedly, if petitioner's property were destroyed by ordnance or destroyed or pilfered before order was restored, he would be entitled to a casualty loss deduction. See *Davis v. Commissioner*, 34 T.C. 586 (1960) (vandalism). Unfortunately, under the circumstances, petitioner cannot prove the cause of his loss and for that reason, in my opinion, has failed to meet his burden of proof.

In *Allen v. Commissioner*, 16 T.C. 163 (1951), the taxpayer, Mary Allen, entered the Metropolitan Museum of Art in New York wearing a diamond brooch on the left side of her dress. Before leaving the museum less than 2 hours later, Mary discovered that her brooch was missing. After carefully retracing her steps, she was unable to find the brooch. Although she testified that she didn't know whether the brooch was lost or stolen, she nevertheless argued that since the record showed that she was present only in well-lighted rooms that were so constructed that no article could have been lost, someone must have stolen her brooch and she was therefore entitled to a theft loss deduction. The trial judge felt this evidence was sufficient to substantiate her claim of a theft loss. *Allen v. Commissioner*, 16 T.C. at 167 (Judge Opper dissenting). However, in rejecting her claim, we stated:

> She does not, and cannot, prove that the pin was stolen. All we know is that the brooch disappeared and was never found by, or returned to, petitioner.
>
> Petitioner has the burden of proof. This includes presentation of proof which, absent positive proof, reasonably leads us to conclude that the article was stolen. If the reasonable inferences from the evidence point to theft, the proponent is entitled to prevail. If the contrary be true and reasonable inferences point to another conclusion, the proponent must fail. If the evidence is in equipoise preponderating neither to the one nor the other conclusion, petitioner has not carried her burden. (16 T.C. at 166; emphasis added.)

In the present case, the record does not show whether petitioner's property was abandoned by him, confiscated by the North Vietnamese Government, pilfered, or destroyed. In my opinion, any of the above are reasonable inferences. That being so, based on *Allen*, I would hold that petitioner has not met his burden of proof by a preponderance of the evidence.

The majority would, however, relieve petitioner of his burden because his inability to determine what happened to his property was not his fault. This problem was addressed in *Burnet v. Houston*, 283 U.S. 223 (1931), wherein the taxpayer claimed it was impossible for him to prove his 1913 basis for stock which became worthless in 1920. The Supreme Court held:

> We cannot agree that the impossibility of establishing a specific fact, made essential by the statute as a prerequisite to the allowance of a loss, justifies a decision for the taxpayer based upon a consideration only of the remaining factors which the statute contemplates. * * * The impossibility of proving a material fact upon which the right to relief depends, simply leaves the claimant upon whom the burden rests with an unenforcible [sic] claim, a misfortune to be borne by him, as it must be borne in other cases, as the result of a failure of proof. (283 U.S. at 228.)

Finally, I think it important to note that in the past, Congress has enacted special legislation to deal with cases similar to that of petitioner. For example, section 165(i) (repealed 1976) allowed a deduction for losses sustained when a Communist regime came to power in Cuba. In the absence of such legislation, on these facts, I think respondent should prevail. *See Farcasanu v. Commissioner*, 50 T.C. at 890.

TANNENWALD, SIMPSON, and NIMS, JJ., agree with this dissenting opinion.

Post-Case Follow-Up

In *Popa*, the Tax Court concluded that the taxpayer's loss of property due to the fall of Saigon was sufficiently sudden and cataclysmic to characterize it as an "other casualty" comparable to a loss by fire, storm, or shipwreck. Moreover, as the dissent promptly brings to our attention, it reached that result notwithstanding the existence of several cases in which taxpayers in similar situations were met with disallowance. *Popa* itself is like many other cases in the distinct sense that the court was called on to apply a statute to a situation not likely contemplated by the drafters of the legislation or even those drafting associated Treasury Regulations. Faced with the patent reality of taxpayer loss, the majority chose to adopt an accommodating stance with respect to proof of the loss. The dissent argued the need to await congressional action, noting Congress's response to the Communist regime coming to power in Cuba. Years later, in fact, when the reality of domestic terrorism surfaced in the United States, we saw Congress respond with the Victims of Terrorism Tax Relief Act of 2001, P.L. 107-134, § 101(a). Even if the court is jumping the gun or bending the rules a bit, one can certainly understand its effort to ensure that the taxpayers before it at the time get the same treatment Congress will likely extend to similarly situated taxpayers in the future.

Popa v. Commissioner: Real Life Applications

For the following questions, please (1) assume that there has been no compensation by insurance or otherwise, (2) ignore § 165(h) deductibility thresholds, and (3) assume that § 165(h)(5) does not apply.

1. Françoise d'Alsace is a United States citizen who owns a residence in the country of Sparta. He has lived there for several years and has noted growing unrest in the population. In fact, protests are a daily occurrence, and in light of the government's increasingly hostile responses, Françoise fears that a revolution is at hand. In the immediate aftermath of a massive protest (and an aggressive and deadly response from the government), Françoise packs a few articles of clothing and flies to the United States, leaving his home and its contents. Days later, a full-fledged revolution erupts, and the power struggle continues. Is Françoise's loss attributable to a casualty?

2. Determined to get the most out of her vehicle, Lorin was driving her old Chevy truck when the transmission finally gave out. Reasoning that she had gotten over 350,000 miles out of the truck, she collected her possessions, called a tow truck, and had the Chevy delivered to a junkyard for automobiles. She left it there and had the tow truck driver take her home. Will this series of events give rise to a deductible loss for Lorin?

3. *Same facts as Question #2*, except that Lorin is driving the truck and it continues to operate. She hears of a tornado warning on the radio and soon sees the tornado approaching rapidly from the west. She jumps out of her truck, seeks shelter under an overpass, and sees her beloved Chevy swept up and ripped apart by the tornado. Is Lorin's loss attributable to a casualty?

Basis Determinations

Although § 165(a) generally allows taxpayers to take a deduction with respect to losses sustained during the taxable year, other provisions bear on the basic amount of the loss to be taken into account as an initial matter. Section 165(b) dictates that taxpayers measure the amount of loss by reference to the adjusted basis of the relevant property, but in some instances, the approach to be taken differs. In the event of a casualty or theft, the Treasury Regulations generally limit the amount to be taken into account for § 165(a) purposes to the *lesser* of (1) the fair market value of the property immediately before the event (less its fair market value afterwards) or (2) the adjusted basis of the property. *See* Treas. Reg. §§ 1.165-7(b)(1); 1.165-8(c). Today, with computerized records and in-the-cloud storage of data, establishing the original/adjusted basis of an asset (and its fair market value over time) may be much easier than it was in the past, but the course of human events can quickly complicate matters.

Case Preview

Adel v. Commissioner

In *Adel v. Commissioner*, the taxpayers managed to flee a country in turmoil with some of their property in hand. Years later, unfortunately, they suffered the loss of that property by theft. Even with asset appraisals in hand, however, they found themselves at odds with the Commissioner. As you read through the case, consider the following questions:

1. What is the Commissioner's primary argument against the allowance of a theft loss deduction?
2. What evidence did the taxpayers produce to support their deduction? Was that evidence deemed credible and sufficient?
3. If taxpayers have difficulty establishing the basis or fair market value of property lost to theft, will replacement value suffice as a measure of their loss?

War in Afghanistan

With Marxists in control of the government in Afghanistan in the late 1970s, the United States authorized the covert training, support, and funding of volunteer opposition forces, the Mujahideen (the Arabic word for "warriors"). The Soviet invasion of Afghanistan in 1979 was met with the armed resistance of the Mujahideen, and years later, bowing to international pressure, the Soviet Union withdrew its troops. Statistics indicate that approximately one million Afghans died in the war, and approximately five million became refugees in surrounding countries. *See* HISTORY: THE DEFINITIVE VISUAL GUIDE 444–45 (Covent Garden Books 2010).

Adel v. Commissioner
T.C. Summ. Op. 2008-65

GOLDBERG, Special Trial Judge.
Respondent determined a $3,034 deficiency in petitioners' Federal income tax for 2002. The sole issue for decision is whether petitioners are entitled to a theft loss deduction for the taxable year at issue.

BACKGROUND

Some of the facts have been stipulated and are so found. *** Petitioners resided in Virginia when they filed their petition.

Petitioners were born and raised in Afghanistan, where they met and were married. In 1980 in the midst of the Soviet-Afghan War, petitioners fled Afghanistan for Pakistan. Needing cash for their journey but unable to sell their greatest assets (a house and a Mercedes-Benz automobile) because of government-imposed restrictions on the sale of such assets, petitioners arranged to sell their car to an uncle for $25,000. The uncle had some cash on hand to complete the transaction but not to pay the full price of the car, $25,000. Petitioners and the uncle agreed that the difference would be satisfied by the transfer of a gold and emerald jewelry set that the uncle had in his possession as a result of a bequest from his grandmother.

Before embarking upon their journey to Pakistan, petitioners took the jewelry set (comprising a necklace, ring, earrings, and a bracelet) to an Afghani jewelry appraiser. The appraiser, who was both appraising the pieces and setting a price in case petitioners wished to sell him the set, valued the jewelry at "11,300 U.S. dollars." Because of the unstable political environment causing many similarly situated families to attempt to sell such jewelry sets, petitioners decided to retain the set in the hope of attaining a higher price for it in either Pakistan or another country.

After one year in Pakistan, petitioners emigrated to Canada, where they lived from 1981 through 1998. While they lived in Canada, petitioners kept the jewelry in a safe deposit box at their bank. They did not have any further appraisal done on the set while living in Canada.

In 1998 petitioner husband (Mr. Shah) was offered a position with the "U.S. Trade Office" and later as a military consultant and translator. Petitioners moved to Virginia sometime in 1998 and have lived there since in a three-story, single-family home. Petitioners have family in Canada and Afghanistan and occasionally travel to both places to visit their relatives.

In late February 2002 petitioner wife traveled to visit her ailing mother in Canada. At or about this same time, Mr. Shah had oral surgery. While Mr. Shah was recuperating, he stayed in a bedroom on the top floor of their three-story home. Sometime between February 24 and February 26, 2002, petitioners' home was burglarized. The burglary occurred in the basement of the home while Mr. Shah was on the top floor convalescing.

On February 26, 2002, petitioners filed a police report with the Prince William County Police Department in Manassas, Virginia, wherein they detailed the items stolen as follows: (1) A Sony Playstation 2 video game console, game controllers, and a memory card ($850 value); (2) a stereo ($110 value); (3) a camcorder ($500 value); and (4) an emerald and gold jewelry set. The values reported for the articles in the set were as follows: (1) Necklace — $12,000; (2) earrings — $7,000; (3) ring — $5,000; and (4) bracelet — $8,000. The total value on the police report for all items reported stolen was $33,460. None of the items stolen were ever recovered, and petitioners' homeowners' insurance covered only the value of the non-jewelry items taken in the burglary and the damage done to petitioners' home.

During the year in issue, petitioners filed a joint Form 1040, U.S. Individual Income Tax Return . . . . Petitioners reported adjusted gross income of $47,870. * * * Petitioners' Form 4684 listed their cost basis in the items stolen as $33,767 less an insurance reimbursement of $3,985. After subtracting the $100 limitation imposed on theft losses under section 165(h)(1), and the adjusted gross income limitation under section 165(h)(2), petitioners computed the amount of their total theft loss on Form 4684 to be $24,895 and claimed a casualty and theft loss deduction for the same amount on Schedule A, Itemized Deductions.

On October 13, 2005, respondent sent petitioners a statutory notice of deficiency wherein respondent determined a deficiency of $3,034 resulting from the disallowance of petitioners' claimed deduction for theft loss for lack of substantiation.

DISCUSSION

In general, the Commissioner's determination in a notice of deficiency is presumed correct, and the burden of proof is on the taxpayer to prove otherwise. Tax deductions are a matter of legislative grace, and the taxpayer bears the burden of proving entitlement to deductions claimed on a return. * * *

Respondent's position is that petitioners have failed to substantiate either their bases in or the fair market values immediately before the theft of the items stolen for which they claimed a theft loss deduction on their 2002 return. Petitioners have presented evidence only with respect to the jewelry set, and it is petitioners' contention that the car sale price, the Afghani jeweler's appraisal of the set, and their own estimate of the appreciated value of the set over the course of 22 years adequately substantiate their basis in, and the fair market value of, the set.

Section 165(a) allows a deduction for any loss sustained during the taxable year and not compensated for by insurance or otherwise. For individuals, section 165(c) (3) allows a taxpayer to deduct a loss from theft. The deduction is only allowed to the extent that the loss exceeds $100 and to the extent that the net loss exceeds 10 percent of adjusted gross income. Sec. 165(h)(1) and (2). The amount allowed as a deduction is the lesser of: (1) The difference between the fair market value of the property immediately before and after the theft, and (2) the adjusted basis in the property. In applying section 1.165–7(b), Income Tax Regs., the fair market value of the property immediately after the theft is zero. Sec. 1.165–8(c), Income Tax Regs.

Inherent in section 165 are several requirements. First, the taxpayer must have been the owner of the property at the time of the loss. The parties agree that petitioners owned the jewelry set at the time of the theft. In addition to the ownership requirement, either the taxpayer's basis in the stolen property or the fair market value of the property immediately before the theft must be ascertained. Secs. 1.165–7(b), 1.165–8(c), Income Tax Regs. Where a taxpayer fails to credibly establish either the basis or the fair market value of the property immediately preceding the theft, we are unable to determine the amount of loss deductible.

On the basis of petitioners' account of the sale of their car in 1980, we are unclear as to how much of the $25,000 purchase price was satisfied by petitioners' uncle through the transfer of his grandmother's jewelry set. While we believe that petitioners did sell the car to their uncle for $25,000, we also believe that their uncle gave them cash for at least one-half of the stated value of the car, $25,000. Therefore, on the basis of this analysis, we find that petitioners' basis in the jewelry set could be no more than $12,500, although petitioners themselves provided no documentation or credible testimony to establish the amount of cash their uncle gave them for the car. Accordingly, we find that petitioners have failed to adequately substantiate their basis in the jewelry set for purposes of determining the deductible amount of theft loss.

Petitioners next argue that the Afghani jeweler's 1980 appraisal, coupled with their estimate of the appreciation of the jewelry set over the course of 22 years, should suffice as credible substantiation of the fair market value of the jewelry set for purposes of their claiming a $24,895 theft loss deduction. For the following reasons, we disagree.

First, petitioners claimed a $24,895 deduction for the loss of four pieces of gold and emerald jewelry. This amount reflects petitioners' estimate of the replacement cost of those items and therefore is not the appropriate standard. With respect to the $24,895 figure claimed on their return, petitioners presented no evidence to establish the fair market value of the jewelry immediately before the theft. The only credible evidence presented was a translated copy of the Afghani jeweler's

1980 appraisal. While we find the appraisal to be credible, we have serious doubts as to petitioners' estimate of the fair market value of the jewelry before the theft. We acknowledge, generally, that the prices of gold and gemstones have risen markedly over the past 22 years, and we are confident that that amount would be greater than even the highest basis we have already presumed that petitioners could have had in the jewelry ($12,500). However, because the amount allowed as a deduction is limited to the lesser of either the fair market value of the property immediately preceding the theft or the taxpayer's basis, the amount of the allowable deduction would be limited to petitioners' basis in the jewelry set. See sec. 1.165–8(c), Income Tax Regs.

As previously discussed, we lack credible evidence to specifically determine petitioners' basis in the jewelry set. In the absence of such evidence, we will apply our best judgment to approximate this amount. *See Cohan v. Commissioner,* 39 F.2d 540 (2d Cir.1930). Bearing heavily against the taxpayer "whose inexactitude is of his own making," *id.* at 544, we find that petitioners' basis in the jewelry set before the theft was $5,000.

Because petitioners did not receive any insurance reimbursement for the jewelry, no amount for such reimbursement must be deducted. The amount of theft loss deduction to which petitioners are entitled is, however, limited: petitioners must first deduct $100 from the total amount of allowable loss under section 165(h)(1). Second, under section 165(h)(2), petitioners are allowed a deduction only to the extent that the amount allowable exceeds 10 percent of the petitioners' adjusted gross income. The allowable amount is $4,900. After applying section 165(h)(2), the total theft loss amount allowable is $113.

Decision will be entered under Rule 155.

Post-Case Follow-Up

In *Adel v. Commissioner*, the court acknowledged that the taxpayers suffered a loss but resorted largely to its own judgment to measure that loss rather than relying on any objective measures. Substantiation requirements serve the useful purpose of keeping taxpayers honest, but the likelihood is strong that only a handful of taxpayers feel the need to keep track of the basis and the fair market value of their assets beyond, perhaps, an initial appraisal. Does that mean that they should be vulnerable to judicial whim? Or does is simply mean that the benefit of the casualty/theft loss deduction will be reserved largely for those suffering cataclysmic losses while others, if challenged, must clear substantiation hurdles or risk not a mere haircut, but a brutal scalping?

Adel v. Commissioner: Real Life Applications

For the following questions, please (1) assume that there has been no compensation by insurance or otherwise, (2) ignore § 165(h) deductibility thresholds, and (3) assume that § 165(h)(5) does not apply.

Bizarro

Alcohol-Impaired Drivers

During 2014, approximately 10,000 individuals were killed in crashes involving an alcohol-impaired driver. Typically, a blood alcohol concentration of 0.08 percent results in impaired judgment/reasoning, and poor muscle coordination (e.g., altered balance, speech, reaction time, and vision). Drivers can expect impairment in speed control and information processing (e.g., signal detection). For more information on impaired driving consult the CDC's website.

1. In celebration of her 40th birthday, Kyra purchased a brand new truck for $42,000. Immediately after purchase and upon her taking possession, the value of the truck fell to $40,000. She drove it around showing it off to her relatives, friends, and neighbors. As it turns out, the truck caught the attention of neighborhood thieves, and one week later, the truck was stolen. Because of Kyra's failure to deliver a check, the vehicle was technically uninsured at the time of the theft, so she has not been compensated by insurance or otherwise. What is the amount of Kyra's loss (ignoring § 165(h) thresholds)?

2. Allen was a rising senior at Palm Beach High School. His parents purchased him a 10kt yellow gold ring for $700. Two years later, the ring was stolen from his dorm room by a burglar. Because the price of gold had risen recently, the ring's fair market value at the time of the theft was $1,000. He was not compensated for the theft by insurance or otherwise. What is the amount of Allen's loss (ignoring § 165(h) thresholds)?

3. Mia recently inherited a Cartier diamond cuff from her grandmother, Anjung. At the time of her grandmother's death, the cuff had a fair market value of $370,000, and that value has remained constant. Returning home from the opera one evening, Mia was confronted by a gun-wielding thug who forced her to hand over the cuff. Assuming she was not compensated by insurance or otherwise for the theft, what is the amount of Mia's loss (ignoring § 165(h) thresholds)?

Gross Negligence and Public Policy Limitations

In Chapter 1, we discussed *Blackman v. Commissioner,* and you'll likely recall that even though the taxpayer suffered a loss by fire (which he set), he was not allowed to take a casualty loss deduction because allowing such a deduction would have rewarded gross negligence *and* offended public policy. Given the broader factual context, few would object to the court's ruling. But where exactly should the line be drawn between negligence and gross negligence, and who should have the final word as to what does or does not violate public policy? Are we to look to Congress, should the Treasury Department weigh in via pronouncement or regulations, or are these questions best left to the courts based on their assessment of the prevailing public mindset and a careful analysis of the relevant facts and circumstances?

Case Preview

Rohrs v. Commissioner

In *Rohrs v. Commissioner*, we find a taxpayer seeking a casualty loss deduction after crashing his truck. But this was no mere crash. According to evidence obtained after the incident, Mr. Rohrs was operating his vehicle with a blood alcohol level just above the legal limit. Accordingly, he was cited for driving under the influence of alcohol. But does that mean that a casualty loss deduction should be off the table as a matter of course? As you read *Rohrs*, consider the following questions:

1. What constitutes "gross negligence" under California law?
2. Does the court view driving under the influence of alcohol as per se gross negligence?
3. If state law prohibits driving under the influence of alcohol (at a specified blood alcohol level), what degree of intoxication should result in the barring of a casualty loss deduction? Why?

Rohrs v. Commissioner
T.C. Summ. Op. 2009 - 190

GERBER, Judge.

* * * For petitioner's 2005 tax year respondent determined a $6,230 income tax deficiency and a $1,246 accuracy-related penalty under section 6662(a). The issues for our consideration are: (1) Whether petitioner is entitled to a casualty loss deduction for 2005; and (2) whether petitioner is liable for the section 6662(a) accuracy-related penalty. *Issues*

BACKGROUND

Some of the facts have been stipulated and are so found. The stipulation of facts and the attached exhibits are incorporated herein by this reference. Petitioner resided in California when his petition was filed.

On August 12, 2005, petitioner purchased a 2006 Ford F-350 pickup truck for $40,210.65. On October 28, 2005, petitioner attended a gathering at a friend's house. Anticipating that he would be drinking alcohol, he arranged for transportation to and from his home. After returning home petitioner decided to drive to his parents'

Crash of
truck/DUI

house. On the way there he failed to successfully negotiate a turn, and his truck slid off an embankment. The truck rolled over and was severely damaged. Because his blood-alcohol level was 0.09 percent, he was cited and arrested for driving under the influence of alcohol (DUI). The legal threshold for blood-alcohol level in the State of California is 0.08 percent. He was then taken to the hospital.

Petitioner's loss claim filed with his automobile insurance carrier was denied in accordance with the terms of his policy because of his DUI citation and arrest.

On April 13, 2006, petitioner filed his 2005 Form 1040, U.S. Individual Income Tax Return. On that return he claimed a $33,629 casualty loss deduction for the damage to his truck. On March 25, 2008, respondent issued a notice of deficiency disallowing petitioner's casualty loss deduction and determining a $6,230 income tax deficiency and a $1,246 section 6662(a) accuracy-related penalty for petitioner's 2005 tax year. On June 9, 2008, petitioner filed a timely petition with this Court.

DISCUSSION

Section 165(a) allows a deduction for losses not compensated for by insurance or otherwise. If a loss is not incurred in connection with a trade or business or in a transaction entered into for profit, it may be deducted by an individual if it arises from a fire, storm, shipwreck, or other casualty, or from theft, except as provided in section 165(h). Sec. 165(c)(3). There is no question about whether petitioner's loss generally qualified as a casualty loss under section 165.

Although negligence may not be a bar to a casualty loss deduction, courts have held that gross negligence may be. In addition, [Treas Reg. § 1.165-7(a)(3)] provides that an automobile may be the subject of a casualty loss when the damage is not due to the willful act or willful negligence of a taxpayer.

Conflict: was
DUI grossly
negligent?

Petitioner concedes that his act of driving while intoxicated constitutes negligence. Petitioner, however, disagrees with respondent's contention that his behavior rose to the level of gross or willful negligence, thereby barring a casualty loss deduction.

Neither the Internal Revenue Code nor the underlying regulations define "willful negligence" for purposes of [Treas Reg. § 1.165-7(a)(3)]. Respondent argues that the definitions of "willful negligence" and "gross negligence" are supplied by caselaw. Respondent relies upon *People v. Bennett*, 819 P.2d 849 (Cal.1991), in support of his position.

In *People v. Bennett, supra,* a driver was convicted of vehicular manslaughter and gross negligence while driving under the influence of alcohol. Before driving, Mr. Bennett and three friends shared the entire contents of a keg of beer. He was then involved in a single-car accident in which one of his friends died. Mr. Bennett's blood-alcohol level was measured at 0.20 percent 2 hours after the accident. In affirming his conviction, the California Supreme Court defined gross negligence as "the exercise of so slight a degree of care as to raise a presumption of conscious indifference to the consequences." *Id.* at 852. The court further explained that "The state of mind of a person who acts with conscious indifferences to the consequences is simply, 'I don't care what happens.'" *Id.* (quoting *People v. Olivas*, 218 Cal. Rptr. 567, 569 (Ct. App. 1985)). The court held that conscious indifference could be inferred from the severity of defendant's intoxication:

gross
negligence
issue on

"one who drives with a very high level of intoxication is indeed more negligent, more dangerous, and thus more culpable than one who drives near the legal limit of intoxication, just as one who exceeds the speed limit by 50 miles per hour exhibits greater negligence than one who exceeds the speed limit by 5 miles per hour."

Id. at 853 (quoting *People v. Von Staden,* 241 Cal. Rptr. 523, 527 (Ct. App. 1987)).

We agree with petitioner that his actions did not amount to willful or gross negligence. While petitioner's decision to drive after drinking was negligent, that alone does not automatically rise to the level of gross negligence. "'[G]ross negligence cannot be shown by the *mere fact* of driving under the influence and violating the traffic laws.'" *Id.* at 852 (emphasis added) (quoting *People v. Von Staden, supra* at 527). The overall circumstances of the defendant's actions, including the level of intoxication and/or the manner in which he drove must be considered. *Id.* at 853.

The circumstances do not support a holding that petitioner was willfully or grossly negligent. Petitioner's level of intoxication and the manner in which he drove do not suggest that he was consciously indifferent to the hazards of drunk driving. Unlike the defendant in *People v. Bennett, supra,* petitioner was less impaired and not severely intoxicated when he chose to drive. At the time of the accident petitioner's blood-alcohol level was 0.09 percent, which is slightly over California's legal limit of 0.08 percent. See Cal. Veh. Code sec. 23152 (West 2000). Further and significantly distinguishing petitioner's situation from that in *People v. Bennett, supra,* petitioner made arrangements not to drive immediately after consuming alcohol. He arranged for transportation home and thus allowed some time for his body to process the alcohol before driving. If petitioner truly did not care what happened, he would not have gone to the trouble to arrange for transportation.

Likewise, there is no evidence in the record that petitioner was aware his actions would result in injury. In addition, there was no evidence that excess speed or alcohol directly caused petitioner's accident. On brief, petitioner claimed he lost control of his vehicle because of the windy conditions on the road, and no evidence was presented at trial as to what the precise cause of petitioner's accident was.

In the alternative, respondent contends that petitioner's casualty loss deduction should not be allowed because to do so would frustrate public policy.

Courts have disallowed deductions where national or State public policy would be frustrated by the allowance of a deduction. However, this rule is not applied indiscriminately. *Tank Truck Rentals, Inc. v. Commissioner,* 356 U.S. 30, 35 (1958). "[T]he test of nondeductibility always is the severity and immediacy of the frustration resulting from allowance of the deduction." *Id.*

California, like most other States, has "a strong public policy against * * * drunk driving." *Carrey v. Dept. of Motor Vehicles,* 228 Cal. Rptr. 705, 708 (Ct. App. 1986). But the fact that petitioner's loss may have resulted from his drunk driving does not ipso facto mean a casualty loss deduction would severely and immediately frustrate public policy. "It has never been thought * * * that the mere fact that an expenditure bears a remote relation to an illegal act makes it non-deductible." *Commissioner v. Heininger,* [320 U.S. 467, 474 (1943)].

In cases where a deduction has been denied, the taxpayers typically knew their actions encouraged an illegal activity or were illegal. In contrast, petitioner believed that he was no longer impaired or intoxicated at the time he chose to drive. Moreover, he had taken precautions to avoid driving immediately after drinking. There was no evidence that intoxication, high speed, or reckless driving was the ultimate cause of petitioner's accident. Where the taxpayer is reasonably unaware that he is doing something wrong, it is less likely that allowance of a casualty loss deduction would so severely frustrate public policy as to require disallowance.

In *Tank Truck Rentals, Inc. v. Commissioner, supra,* the taxpayer attempted to deduct as business expenses fines imposed for violations of State maximum weight laws. The Court disallowed the deduction because the "Deduction of fines and penalties uniformly has been held to frustrate state policy in severe and direct fashion by reducing the 'sting' of the penalty prescribed by the state legislature." *Id.* at 35–36.

By contrast, allowing petitioner's casualty loss deduction would not in any way alleviate the "sting" of any punishment imposed by the State of California. In California, a first-time DUI offense is punishable by imprisonment of at least 96 hours and a fine of at least $390. See Cal. Veh.Code sec. 23536 (West Supp. 2009). Petitioner's casualty loss deduction would have no impact on either the sentence or the fine.

This Court is not empowered to judge petitioner's actions from a criminal perspective or to punish him for his actions. In reaching our decision, we do not reflect upon or in any way condone the act of driving under the influence of alcohol. It is our obligation to decide whether petitioner's actions amounted to gross or willful negligence and/or whether the allowance of a casualty loss deduction in the setting of this Federal income tax case would frustrate public policy.

We hold that petitioner is entitled to the claimed casualty loss deduction and, accordingly, is not liable for the section 6662(a) accuracy-related penalty.

To reflect the foregoing,

Decision will be entered for petitioner.

Post-Case Follow-Up

Consistent with *Blackman v. Commissioner* and other cases, the court here finds that simple negligence on the part of a taxpayer does not serve to bar a casualty loss deduction. The difficulty, of course, arises because what the court considers mere negligence is, at the same time, conduct deemed criminal by the State of California. The court openly notes that it lacks the ability to judge or punish the taxpayer's criminal conduct, and there's no harm in stating the obvious. But the court is charged with deciding whether allowing a deduction is consistent with public policy, and the state legislature has made it abundantly clear that the conduct targeted threatens the safety and well-being of its citizens and thus merits *criminal* sanction; current statistics in Exhibit 9.1 confirm the risk drunk drivers pose to the public. How can a court rationally and logically conclude that allowing a federal income tax deduction in connection with the conduct doesn't offend public policy? In an effort to distinguish *Tank Truck Rentals, Inc.*, the court reasons that although allowing a deduction for fines or penalties imposed by a state would "frustrate state policy in severe and direct fashion," allowing the taxpayer a casualty loss deduction would have no impact on whatever sanctions or fines followed from violating the California Vehicle Code. But allowing a given deduction can severely and immediately

EXHIBIT 9.1   **Select Drunk-Driving Fatality Statistics**

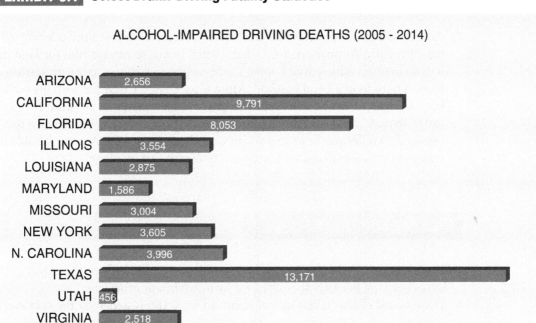

ALCOHOL-IMPAIRED DRIVING DEATHS (2005 - 2014)

ARIZONA	2,656
CALIFORNIA	9,791
FLORIDA	8,053
ILLINOIS	3,554
LOUISIANA	2,875
MARYLAND	1,586
MISSOURI	3,004
NEW YORK	3,605
N. CAROLINA	3,996
TEXAS	13,171
UTAH	456
VIRGINIA	2,518

See https://data.cdc.gov/Motor-Vehicle/Occupant-and-Alcohol-Impaired-Driving-Deaths-in-St/haed-k2ka (visited September 19, 2016).

offend public policy even if the taxpayer's attempt is not to deduct a fine or avert some penalty imposed by the state. In *Blackman*, wholly aside from its gross negligence finding, the court separately denied the taxpayer's casualty loss deduction with respect to his former residence because allowing it would have offended Maryland's public policies against arson and domestic violence. The court reached this conclusion notwithstanding the fact that allowing a casualty loss deduction would have had no impact on the sanctions imposed by the State of Maryland with respect to the taxpayer's conduct. Perhaps there is room on the landscape beyond the line of deduction demarcation for both gross negligence and mere negligence punishable by criminal sanction. Even if we willingly acknowledge that people make mistakes, surely we can do so without extending to them the legislative grace of a tax deduction.

Rohrs v. Commissioner: Real Life Applications

For the following questions, please (1) assume that there has been no compensation by insurance or otherwise, (2) ignore § 165(h) deductibility thresholds, and (3) assume that § 165(h)(5) does not apply.

1. While driving to make an appointment, Olabisi attempted to send a text message to her administrative assistant. Such conduct constitutes a misdemeanor under state law and can subject the perpetrator to a fine of $500. If Olabisi wrecks her

car because she was distracted by her texting activity, is it likely that her loss would qualify for deduction under § 165?

2. Ammar is a junior partner in a law firm with several very wealthy celebrity clients. Recently, Ammar received a substantial bonus to reward him for landing a new client, an athlete well known for his ability to perform at the professional level in both football and baseball. Ammar purchased a new car with his bonus but managed to wreck the vehicle only a few weeks later as he raced through traffic to make a dinner date. According to the police report, Ammar was driving over 90 miles per hour in a 55 mile per hour zone. Will Ammar be able to take a casualty loss deduction in connection with this incident?

Chapter Summary

- Taxpayers may deduct sustained losses under § 165 but only to the extent such losses have not been compensated for by insurance or otherwise.
- The amount of loss taken into account under § 165 is generally the taxpayer's adjusted basis in the property. The loss amount with respect to a casualty or a theft will be the lower of the taxpayer's adjusted basis in the property or the property's fair market value immediately before the loss (reduced by any value remaining after the loss).
- Special rules apply with respect to certain losses (e.g., capital losses and those arising from wagering transactions).
- Losses of individuals are limited to those occurring in a trade or business, an activity undertaken for profit, and (within numerical limits) those arising from fire, storm, shipwreck, other casualty or from theft. Special rules apply for losses sustained in taxable years beginning after December 31, 2017, both with respect to the excess trade or business losses of non-corporate taxpayers and with respect to personal casualty losses of individuals.
- In order to qualify for deduction, a loss must have been sustained during the taxable year. Whether a loss has been sustained has ramifications on basic deductibility and timing.
- A loss is not sustained for federal income tax purposes to the extent a claim for reimbursement exists with respect to which the taxpayer has a reasonable prospect of recovery. Settlement, adjudication, abandonment of a claim may establish the extent to which the taxpayer has a reasonable prospect of recovery.
- Taxpayers may suffer a loss but be unable to take a deduction with respect to the loss because such an allowance would offend public policy. Although mere negligence is not a bar to deductibility, gross negligence is.
- A taxpayer taking a loss deduction in one taxable year and recovering with respect to that loss in a future taxable year may be required to include all or part of the recovery in gross income in the year of the recovery; the taxpayer will not amend the prior year's return in any event.

Applying the Rules

1. In the latter portion of 2017, Lily and Pierce Wilson purchased a brand new home for $450,000. Due to an electrical problem caused by the home builders, a fire started, and the fire alarms failed to sound. The entire home burned to the ground, and to worsen matters, the Wilsons found out that their insurance company was bankrupt and would not be obligated to cover any portion of the loss. They have not been compensated otherwise. At this juncture, may the Wilsons take a casualty loss deduction in connection with this event?

2. In July 2017, Yasser sustained a casualty loss of $28,600. During 2017, Yasser had adjusted gross income of $120,000 and no personal casualty gains. To what extent, if any, may Yasser take a casualty loss deduction with respect to this event?

3. Tyson owns an expensive bicycle. He left it secured just outside his apartment on the evening of December 28, 2017. He visited family and friends for a two-week period, returning home in January 2018, and it was at that time that he discovered that his bicycle had been stolen. How would Tyson have been treated under § 165 prior to the enactment of § 165(h)(5)? How will Tyson be treated under current law, assuming he has no personal casualty gains?

4. *Same facts as Question #3*, except that Tyson lost his bike due to a hurricane (later declared a federal disaster) sweeping through the area in his absence on January 3, 2018.

5. In an effort to improve his cash flow, Brad decided to make and sell crystal methamphetamine ("meth"). Such conduct constitutes a felony under both state and federal law. If Brad's home burns down because of an accident occurring during his manufacturing of meth, will he be able to take a casualty loss deduction?

6. *Same facts as Question #5*, except that thieves break in and steal Brad's newly manufactured supply of meth. Will Brad be allowed a theft loss deduction?

Federal Income Taxation in Practice

1. One of your neighbors knows that you are a tax expert. She tells you that in November of 2017, prior to preparing Thanksgiving dinner, she removed her diamond ring and placed it on the counter. Somehow, she managed to knock the ring into the sink, and it found its way into the garbage disposal. She was distraught but still wanted to know whether she might be able to get a tax deduction out of the incident. You vaguely recollect reading casualty loss cases involving

diamond rings, and you tell her that you think that she may be able to take the deduction. What cases, if any, might support your position?

2. You are preparing your federal income tax return for 2017. Although it is abundantly clear that you sustained a loss during 2017 and that you must take the $100 "haircut," you wonder whether the haircut must be doubled if you are filing a joint return with your spouse. Does the Code require a $200 haircut for taxpayers filing jointly?

3. One of the senior tax partners has a wealthy client whose home was recently rendered uninhabitable by a storm passing through Louisiana. She believes that § 165(k) applies, but she would like to get a better sense of exactly what Congress had in mind when it enacted the provision in the Deficit Reduction Act of 1984 (P.L. 98-369). She would like you to research the legislative history of the provision and prepare a brief memo summarizing your findings.

4. The partner was impressed with your work on Question #3, and she is back with another assignment. She tells you that one of her clients living in Beverly Hills, California, happens to live two houses away from the scene of a horrific double murder which occurred in January of 2017. Appraisers confirmed that the client's home promptly decreased in value, and the partner would like to know whether this diminution in value constitutes a loss deductible under § 165. She vaguely recollects taxpayers attempting to make similar arguments in the wake of the murders of Nicole Brown Simpson and Ronald Goldman back in 1994. She would like you to research the question and communicate your findings in a brief memo to her.

Interest and Taxes

Individual taxpayers borrowing money to purchase a home find that they must pay both mortgage interest with respect to the debt incurred and real property taxes. Neither experience is particularly pleasant. Congress, realizing that home ownership tends to benefit the larger community in many ways, offers a home ownership subsidy of sorts by allowing taxpayers to deduct specific forms of interest, so long as the underlying debt satisfies certain statutory requirements and is within prescribed limits. Likewise, Congress makes provision for the deduction of a limited amount of real property taxes by individuals. In this chapter, we look at the governing rules and, by examining specific issues, solidify our understanding of the applicable limits and how they operate in various situations, some of which have been addressed by Treasury Regulations and others of which have attained clarity only because the courts intervened to fill in statutory gaps. Before diving into the relevant provisions, however, we first take a tour of a fairly standard home purchase process. Code-based rules do not operate in a vacuum, so having some sense of the role they play and the influence they have in the real world will broaden your knowledge base in general and deepen your understanding of the rules and associated authorities.

A. PURCHASING A HOME

Most of you have not purchased a home or taken out a mortgage at this stage in your life, but the likelihood remains strong that such an event lies in your future. Although one can certainly master the law regarding the deductibility of mortgage interest and certain taxes by studying the governing statutory and regulatory

Key Concepts

- General deductibility of interest paid and the prohibition on deducting *personal interest* by non-corporate taxpayers
- The meaning of *acquisition indebtedness* and *qualified residence*
- Deductibility of *qualified residence interest* by legal or equitable owner of qualified residence
- Application of statutory caps in § 163(h) on a per-taxpayer and not a per-qualified-residence basis

provisions in the abstract, having a basic understanding of the home purchase process will yield practical benefits in your personal lives, may assist you in advising clients, and should deepen your understanding of this specific area of tax law. The operating assumption, for our purposes, is that we are dealing with an unmarried taxpayer who seeks to purchase a home by making a down payment and borrowing the bulk of the purchase price from a financial institution. Such a taxpayer is said to "finance" the purchase of the home (rather than to purchase it for cash). Bear in mind that no home purchase process is typical. Indeed, wide variation is the norm. There are, however, several common elements.

1. Preliminary Matters

Ideally, an individual seeking to purchase a home has taken the time over the preceding years to put himself or herself in a position to move through the home mortgage process with ease. As you might imagine, the process typically involves very large dollar amounts, and emotions often run high as lifelong hopes and dreams materialize or threaten to evaporate at critical moments. In gearing up for the process, consider the following nuggets of advice:

- *Save money.* Although banks are willing to facilitate home purchases by lending money to qualified borrowers, one will rarely, if ever, find a bank willing to lend 100 percent of the home's purchase price. Accordingly, the aspiring homeowner must make a down payment towards the purchase, and the more one can pay down the better. Several factors are at play. The bank seeks to enhance the likelihood that it can recover the unpaid loan balance if sale of the home becomes necessary (even after a modest decline in home value), and at the same time, it expects the borrower to have "skin in the game." Borrowers putting down less than 20 percent of the home's purchase price must pay monthly premiums for "mortgage insurance" in addition to making the standard monthly mortgage payments.

- *Keep good financial records.* Individuals seeking a home mortgage must often produce several relevant documents, including recent bank statements and tax returns. It's always a good idea, in any event, to keep *signed* copies of both federal and state income tax returns on hand (including the relevant schedules and forms (e.g., W-2) submitted along with those returns). Lenders will also require recent pay stubs, so a borrower should have ready access to these documents whether electronically or physically.

- *Maintain excellent credit.* Banks preparing to make mortgage loans must assess the risk of nonpayment, and loan officers will invariably consult an applicant's credit report. Good news should await them. Borrowers should pay credit cards, rent, utilities, student loans, and any other obligations on time. As the mortgage application process nears (e.g., 12 to 14 months preapplication), future borrowers should attempt to reduce outstanding debt balances to $0 and avoid applying for or seeking any form of new credit (from any source). Both strong payment histories and delinquencies remain on a credit report for several years, and each will significantly influence a borrower's **FICO score** (i.e., a number generated by the Fair Isaac Corporation using information in an individual's credit report and based on a host of factors, including an individual's history of managing personal debt). *See* Exhibit 10.1. Some credit card companies facilitate credit report monitoring by providing free FICO scores to their cardholders, so borrowers should take advantage of those resources to the extent they are available. As the mortgage process nears (and perhaps on a regular basis), borrowers should obtain free copies of their credit reports (via the Annual Credit Report web page resource) from each of the major reporting agencies (i.e., Experian, Equifax, and TransUnion). Potential borrowers should also be sure to clear up any errors or outdated information. Prospective homeowners must also be wary of cosigning credit obligations and offering "additional" credit cards to others.

2. Starting the Mortgage Application Process

Once a potential homeowner is ready to enter the home search marketplace, she should consider contacting a financial institution and undergoing the prequalification process. The bank will take a very brief look at the potential applicant's financial profile by reviewing pay stubs and checking FICO scores. Based on that fairly cursory review, the bank (though far from being obligated to lend money at that juncture) will likely give the borrower a sense of whether moving forward makes sense and, if so, the home price range that would likely suit the borrower comfortably. From there, it's time to search for a home, choose one, and submit an offer. If

EXHIBIT 10.1   **FICO Score Components**

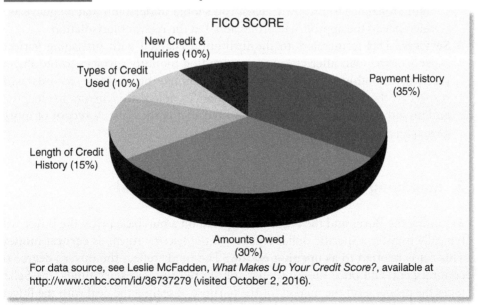

FICO SCORE

New Credit & Inquiries (10%)

Types of Credit Used (10%)

Payment History (35%)

Length of Credit History (15%)

Amounts Owed (30%)

For data source, see Leslie McFadden, *What Makes Up Your Credit Score?*, available at http://www.cnbc.com/id/36737279 (visited October 2, 2016).

the home seller decides to accept the buyer's offer, the process will move forward. The following cast of characters will likely be involved:

- **Seller:** This term refers to the current owner of the home, who is offering it for sale.
- **Buyer:** This term refers to the purchaser of the home. As the person borrowing money from the Lender and using the home as collateral (i.e., security) for repayment of the loan, the Buyer is referred to as the **mortgagor**.
- **Lender:** This term generally refers to the financial institution lending money to the Buyer to facilitate purchase of the home from the Seller. As the Lender extending credit to the Buyer and the holder of a lien on the home (collateral/security for repayment), the Lender is referred to as the **mortgagee**. A **lien** links a specific obligation to a specific item serving as collateral/security (e.g., a car loan and a specific car). Failure to pay the obligation results in the creditor, in this case the mortgagee, proceeding against the collateral and selling it to obtain loan repayment.
- **Underwriters:** These individuals (generally associated with the Lender) ultimately decide, based on all relevant facts and circumstances, whether the mortgage loan application is to be approved or denied. Underwriters will issue approvals conditioned on the mortgagor's provision of satisfactory responses to questions or the submission of certain documents.
- **Escrow Agent:** The escrow agent is a trusted third party who facilitates execution of the transaction. Among other things, the escrow agent receives and holds money from the Buyer and the Lender, disburses funds to the Seller on the closing date, ensures an effective transfer of title to the property from the Seller to the Buyer, and confirms that the Lender's lien on the home is properly and effectively recorded in the appropriate public records (typically at the local county level).
  - *Note*: In some jurisdictions, escrow agents are not used. Instead, brokers or attorneys may fulfill the duties of an escrow agent. To the extent the text makes future reference to Escrow Agents, you should understand that language as a reference to the appropriate professional in the relevant jurisdiction.
- **Servicer:** This term refers to the institution charged with managing various aspects of the loan after closing (e.g., sending monthly invoices to the Buyer, receiving monthly mortgage payments, maintaining accurate records with respect to the loan (e.g., outstanding balances, interest payments made, etc.), and providing relevant documents to interested parties (e.g., a record of mortgage interest paid during a calendar year)).

3. Managing the Process and Closing the Deal

Assuming the Buyer and the Seller have agreed on a purchase price, the Buyer will typically transfer a specific dollar amount to the Escrow Agent as **earnest money.** This act is referred to as **opening escrow**. The funds reflect the Buyer's degree of commitment, and once the Buyer has transferred the necessary funds, the Seller takes the property off the market for the purpose of sealing the deal with the Buyer. If the deal falls apart through no fault of the Seller, the Buyer may stand to lose her earnest money. After the opening of escrow, many things happen, and the order or events is not set in stone. Transactions will differ. The parties ultimately seek to complete all tasks necessary to effect the legal transfer of the home from the Seller to the Buyer, and the process completes when the parties **close escrow** on the closing date.

At some point after the Seller accepts the Buyer's offer and the parties open escrow, the Buyer will submit a complete mortgage loan application to the Lender; if prevailing interest rates are to the Buyer's liking, she should "lock" those rates at the time of application; otherwise, the interest rate on the loan will "float" and be set at a later date (prior to closing). In addition to supplying basic identifying information, the Buyer must typically submit up-to-date pay stubs, recent bank statements, income tax returns, and other documents. The Underwriters then proceed to scrutinize the application, and they commonly present questions, require additional documents/letters, solicit further explanation, and present demands or conditions before they indicate willingness to approve the loan. Loan applicants should respond promptly and abandon any and all hope of maintaining financial privacy. Assuming the Buyer survives the underwriting process, she will receive a Loan Estimate that will provide basic details about the proposed loan, including the interest rate (the basic rate of interest to be paid over time on outstanding loan principal) and the annual percentage rate (an interest rate that factors in all costs and fees associated with the loan transaction). For federal income tax purposes, it is the interest rate that will prove significant. If a Buyer considers the prevailing interest rate too steep, she may be able to lower the rate by prepaying interest to the Lender. Such prepaid interest amounts are called **points.**

Although the Buyer must survive underwriting, the Lender's Underwriters must assure themselves that the Seller's property is actually worth the loan amount; after all, the property itself may be the ultimate source of repayment. Accordingly, it will be necessary that the Seller's property be inspected and appraised. With these hurdles cleared, the Lender can prepare loan documents for the Buyer's signature, and the transaction can move forward. Once the relevant documents have been prepared, the Buyer typically sits down with a notary public and proceeds to sign various documents, including the promissory note for the loan. The Buyer receives a **Closing Disclosure,** which is a document setting forth the final loan details and associated transaction facts. Execution of the relevant documents to the Lender's satisfaction sets the stage for a straightforward transfer of property ownership on the appointed date.

Potential Significance of Points

In the mortgage lending context, the term points (i.e., "discount points") refers to prepaid interest, and a borrower can lower the interest rate to be paid over time on borrowed funds by paying points to the Lender. Mathematically, a point is 1 percent of the amount borrowed, and it reduces the interest rate by a specific amount. Thus, for a $500,000 loan at 4.125 percent, one point is $5,000, and the payment of this amount at closing might lower the interest rate to 4.000 percent. Remember that the loan amount is still $500,000 because payment of a point prepays *interest*, not loan principal. If you hope to purchase a home early in your career while you still have student loan debt and credit card obligations, a mortgage loan application may result initially in an interest rate that is too high for you to service with limited income. Paying points (i.e., "buying down the interest rate") could be the difference between qualifying and failing to qualify for the mortgage loan. By the way, keep in mind that points must be distinguished from closing costs, which include the fees for title insurance, inspection, appraisal, etc.

Speed Bump

WHEN THE HUFFING AND PUFFING DIDN'T WORK, I TALKED HIM INTO A LOW INTEREST SUBPRIME MORTGAGE.

The closing of escrow can be a moment of very high drama if last-minute issues arise, but things often proceed smoothly and quickly. As the date scheduled for the close of escrow approaches, the Buyer must transfer the full down payment amount to the Escrow Agent (less the earnest money deposit amount already on hand). The Lender will then proceed, on the eve of the closing date, to fund the loan (i.e., provide the remainder of the purchase price) by transferring the funds to the Escrow Agent. On the closing date, the Escrow Agent transfers the Buyer's down payment and the loan funds to the Seller, records the transfer of title from the Seller to the Buyer, and records the Lender's security interest in the property (making it clear to the public that the Buyer's recently-purchased home is encumbered by the Lender's lien). At that juncture, escrow closes, and the Buyer can pick up the keys to the house and move in. Thereafter, the Buyer proceeds to make monthly payments of principal and interest to the loan's Servicer, which may be the Lender itself.

Mortgage terms vary considerably, although most borrowers opt to pay down the debt over 30, 20, 15, or even 10 years. Some will opt for a fixed rate of interest during the entire term, and others may opt for a rate of interest that is fixed for a limited time (often enticingly low relative to other rates at the time) but may adjust or vary within limits thereafter. A 10-year adjustable rate mortgage ("**ARM**"), for example, would have a fixed rate of interest for the first 10 years of a 30-year term, but after the first ten years, the interest rate could vary (within limits), which means that monthly mortgage payments can vary considerably after the first 10 years. As you might suspect, ARMs pose a significant threat for some borrowers. Those who have difficulty qualifying for a traditional or "conventional" mortgage may be offered a **subprime mortgage,** which you should generally think of as a mortgage loan generally made available to those with poor credit histories. Such loans typically have a higher interest rate, but if the subprime loan has an adjustable rate, then the rate applicable in the first few years may be quite manageable. Considerable financial strife may loom, however, when the interest rate inevitably spikes upward. If the residence has appreciated in value over time and the mortgagor can no longer afford the home, he can promptly sell it and use the proceeds to pay off the old debt. If such a mortgagor finds that the value of his home has fallen *below* the amount of the outstanding mortgage debt (i.e., he is **underwater**), a sale of the home will not yield funds sufficient to retire the debt in full. If the mortgagor faces liability for the shortfall, financial hardship (or worse) awaits.

Preferring to avoid the risks associated with ARMs, many borrowers opt for a fixed-rate mortgage. Regardless of the loan chosen by the borrower, each monthly mortgage payment includes both a payment of interest and a payment reducing the outstanding loan principal balance. The percentage of each payment allocated to interest and to principal changes over time. Initial payments are largely interest. *See* Table 10.1.

If we change the mortgage term to 15 years (and thereby obtain a slightly lower interest rate), the amortization schedule, as partially depicted in Table 10.2, adjusts accordingly. Principal payment dominates, notwithstanding the existence of a healthy interest component.

The borrower with the 30-year fixed mortgage will pay $271,076 in loan interest over the term of the loan, and the borrower with the 15-year fixed mortgage will pay $116,127 in loan interest, reaping the benefits of both a lower interest rate and, more importantly, a reduced loan term. Note that only payments of *principal* reduce the outstanding loan balance. Although many find new home ownership exhilarating, few welcome the payment of mortgage interest, and that's not the whole of it. In addition to paying a hefty monthly mortgage, homeowners must also

What Is Foreclosure?

Homeowners failing to satisfy their mortgage obligations go into "default." The Lender then has the right to accelerate the debt (i.e., the entire outstanding loan balance becomes due). Rather than being forced to surrender the home in any event, the debtor has the right to pay off the mortgage if, that is, he can pay the full amount due (i.e., he has an "equitable right of redemption"). That right is not everlasting. At some point, the Lender will ask a court to intervene and cut off or "foreclose" that equitable right. The foreclosure sale generally terminates the equitable right of redemption, although some jurisdictions may provide for a post-sale right of redemption.

TABLE 10.1 **Amortization Schedule for 30-Year Fixed Mortgage of $500,000 at an Interest Rate of 3.125 Percent**

Date	Payment	Interest	Principal	Balance
Sept. 2016	$2,142	$1,302	$840	$499,160
Oct. 2016	$2,142	$1,300	$842	$498,318
Nov. 2016	$2,142	$1,298	$844	$497,474
Dec. 2016	$2,142	$1,296	$846	$496,628
Jan. 2017	$2,142	$1,293	$849	$495,779
Feb. 2017	$2,142	$1,291	$851	$494,928
March 2017	$2,142	$1,289	$853	$494,075
~~	~~~~~	~~~~	~~~~	~~~~~~
Feb. 2046	$2,142	$39	$2,103	$12,735
March 2046	$2,142	$33	$2,109	$10,626
April 2046	$2,142	$28	$2,114	$8.512
May 2046	$2,142	$22	$2,120	$6,392
June 2046	$2,142	$17	$2,125	$4,267
July 2046	$2,142	$11	$2,131	$2,136
Aug. 2046	$2,142	$6	$2,136	$0

See http://www.amortization-calc.com (visited Sept. 25, 2016).

| TABLE 10.2 | Amortization Schedule for 15-Year Fixed Mortgage of $500,000 at an Interest Rate of 2.875 Percent | | | |

Date	Payment	Interest	Principal	Balance
Sept. 2016	$3,423	$1,198	$2,225	$497,775
Oct. 2016	$3,423	$1,193	$2,230	$495,545
Nov. 2016	$3,423	$1,187	$2,236	$493,309
~~	~~~~~~	~~~~~~	~~~~~~	~~~~~~~
June 2031	$3,423	$24	$3,398	$6,821
July 2031	$3,423	$16	$3,407	$3,415
Aug. 2031	$3,423	$8	$3,415	$0

See http://www.amortization-calc.com (visited Sept. 25, 2016).

pay property taxes, which frequently serve as a source of revenue for local schools and other public functions. In fact, commentators have long noted that home ownership supports a community's economic vitality because in addition to providing property tax revenues, homeowners tend to demand a wide range of goods and services (e.g., furniture, lawn mowers, paint, wallpaper, refrigerators, computers, televisions, carpets, and decorative accessories). Congress, by way of the tax law, supports the venture by easing the financial burden of home ownership.

B. THE DEDUCTION FOR THE PAYMENT OF CERTAIN MORTGAGE INTEREST

Section 163(a) of the Code generally allows taxpayers to take a deduction with respect to interest paid during the taxable year on indebtedness. Non-corporate taxpayers, however, face the limitations set forth in § 163(h), which contains several defined terms. In fact, we will find multiple layers of definition, so focus carefully. Section 163(h)(1) counters the general rule of § 163(a) by providing that non-corporate taxpayers, such as individuals, may not deduct so-called "personal interest." Section 163(h)(2) goes on to define *personal interest* very broadly such that the term includes pretty much all interest (e.g., interest paid on car loans, credit cards, etc.). But several items listed in § 163(h)(2) are simply deemed (by statutory fiat) *not* to constitute personal interest, including student loan interest (to be discussed later) and "qualified residence interest."

> **Key Statutory and Regulatory Provisions**
>
> ■ Internal Revenue Code
>   ■ § 163(a)
>   ■ § 163(h)(1)–(2)
>   ■ § 163(h)(3)(A)(i) and (B)
>   ■ § 163(h)(3)(F)(i)
>   ■ § 163(h)(4)(A)
> ■ Treasury Regulations
>   ■ § 1.163-1(b)(first sentence)

Under current law, the term *qualified residence interest* includes interest paid during the taxable year on acquisition indebtedness with respect to a qualified residence of the taxpayer.

Consider the visual representation set forth in Exhibit 10.2.

EXHIBIT 10.2 Visual Representation of Specific Individual Interest Categories

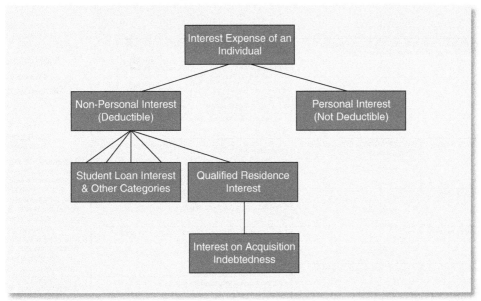

You will have noted that in defining qualified residence interest, the Code refers to acquisition indebtedness with respect to a qualified residence of the taxpayer. What exactly does qualified residence mean? As generally defined in § 163(h)(4)(A), *qualified residence* refers to (1) the taxpayer's principal residence, and (2) one other taxpayer-designated residence used by the taxpayer as a residence. Thus, the term can refer to two of the taxpayer's properties (e.g., a principal residence and a vacation home). With this basic definition in hand, we can now develop a more technical appreciation of the meaning of acquisition indebtedness.

1. Acquisition Indebtedness

As we previously discussed, qualified residence interest includes interest paid on acquisition indebtedness with respect to a qualified residence of the taxpayer. An amount qualifies as *acquisition indebtedness* only if it is (1) debt used to acquire, construct, or substantially improve a qualified residence of the taxpayer and (2) secured by that residence (i.e., the home serves as collateral for repayment of the debt). Further, for taxable years beginning after December 31, 2017, and before

Home Equity Indebtedness

Although § 163(h)(3)(A)(ii) makes reference to interest on home equity indebtedness with respect to any qualified residence of the taxpayer, § 163(h)(3)(F)(i)(I) provides that for taxable years beginning after December 31, 2017, and before January 1, 2026, § 163(h)(3)(A)(ii) shall not apply. Accordingly, for the relevant taxable years, qualified residence interest does not include any interest on home equity indebtedness. Note that this rule applies *regardless of the year in which the taxpayer originally incurred the home equity indebtedness.*

Warning: Even if a financial institution refers to a give debt as a "home equity loan" or a "home equity line of credit," the actual use of the funds may qualify the amount, technically, as acquisition indebtedness (e.g., if (i) the loan is secured by the qualified residence, (ii) the funds are used to acquire, construct, or substantially improve it, and (iii) the total amount of outstanding acquisition indebtedness (including the new funds) does not exceed the relevant statutory cap in a given taxable year).

EXHIBIT 10.3 Sample 2016 IRS Form 1098

RECIPIENT'S/LENDER'S name, street address, city or town, state or province, country, ZIP or foreign postal code, and telephone no.	*Caution: The amount shown may not be fully deductible by you. Limits based on the loan amount and the cost and value of the secured property may apply. Also, you may only deduct interest to the extent it was incurred by you, actually paid by you, and not reimbursed by another person.	OMB No. 1545-0901 2016 (Rev. July 2016) Form **1098**	Mortgage Interest Statement
	1 Mortgage interest received from payer(s)/borrower(s)* $		Copy B For Payer/ Borrower
RECIPIENT'S/LENDER'S federal identification number	PAYER'S/BORROWER'S taxpayer identification no.	2 Outstanding mortgage principal as of 1/1/2016 $	3 Mortgage origination date	The information in boxes 1 through 9 is important tax information and is being furnished to the Internal Revenue Service. If you are required to file a return, a negligence penalty or other sanction may be imposed on you if the IRS determines that an underpayment of tax results because you overstated a deduction for this mortgage interest or for these points, reported in boxes 1 and 6; or because you didn't report the refund of interest (box 4); or because you claimed a non-deductible item.
		4 Refund of overpaid interest $	5 Mortgage insurance premiums $	
PAYER'S/BORROWER'S name		6 Points paid on purchase of principal residence $		
Street address (including apt. no.)		7 Is address of property securing mortgage same as PAYER'S/BORROWER'S address? If Yes, box is checked . . . . ☐ If No, see box 8 or 9, below		
City or town, state or province, country, and ZIP or foreign postal code		8 Address of property securing mortgage		
10 Other		9 If property securing mortgage has no address, below is the description of the property		
Account number (see instructions)				

Form **1098**   (Keep for your records)   www.irs.gov/form1098   Department of the Treasury - Internal Revenue Service

January 1, 2026, the Code places a $750,000 cap on the dollar amount of debt that can qualify as acquisition indebtedness. Thus, if a taxpayer purchases a home for $1,400,000 by making a down payment of $200,000 and borrowing $1.2 million, only the first $750,000 of the $1.2 million loan will constitute acquisition indebtedness. That means that even though the taxpayer must pay interest on the full $1.2 million loan, only the interest on the first $750,000 will be deductible as interest on acquisition indebtedness. Interestingly enough, even if only part of the interest paid by a taxpayer on a loan is deductible (due to statutory limits), the loan Servicer does not automatically provide a break-down. Servicers simply report the interest paid to the IRS and send the borrower a form (see Exhibit 10.3) providing the same basic information. At best, the borrower gets a warning.

Borrowers paying mortgage interest during a given taxable year will receive this form at some point during the following January, but note that even if an individual is paying mortgage interest, they may not end up deducting it on their federal income tax returns. The deduction for mortgage interest is an itemized deduction appearing on Schedule A. Accordingly, if a taxpayer opts for the standard deduction amount, he will not take a mortgage interest deduction. The amount of mortgage interest paid (along with the amount of other itemized deductions) will prove determinative. Those with substantial mortgage debt are, of course, more likely to itemize because they will pay a considerable amount of interest. The fact that homeowners stand to pay extraordinary amounts of interest with respect to mortgage debt affords an excellent segue to the subject of refinancing.

Assume that an individual has a 30-year, fixed-rate mortgage of $500,000 on which they pay interest at a rate of 4.125 percent per year. Three years in, the individual has paid the principal balance down to $472,000, and prevailing mortgage rates have come down considerably (around 2.5 percent for the most creditworthy borrowers). The individual could pay less interest overall by getting a New Loan of $472,000 at 2.5 percent, using that money to pay off the Old Loan of $472,000 at 4.125 percent, and resuming monthly mortgage payments on the New Loan. When individuals do this, they are said to "refinance" their mortgage. If we assume that the Old Loan constituted acquisition indebtedness, then we know that interest paid on that debt was deductible as qualified residence interest. Will the interest on the New Loan get the same treatment if the home serves as security for the New Loan? Yes, up to the amount of the acquisition indebtedness outstanding at the time of the refinancing. Section 163(h)(3)(B)(i) defines acquisition indebtedness and then provides the following:

> [Acquisition indebtedness] also includes any indebtedness secured by such residence resulting from the refinancing of [acquisition indebtedness]; but only to the extent the amount of indebtedness resulting from such refinancing does not exceed the amount of the refinanced indebtedness.

Put more directly, if the individual refinancing his mortgage in our example had been able to get a New Loan of $480,000, only $472,000 would technically constitute acquisition indebtedness resulting from the refinancing. What about the other $8,000? Under the stated facts, the treatment of interest on this remaining indebtedness will turn on the use to which those funds are put. If the taxpayer uses the funds, for example, to substantially improve the qualified residence and the full loan amount is secured by the residence, the remaining $8,000 will constitute acquisition indebtedness, and the interest paid with respect to it will constitute deductible qualified residence interest.

2. Grandfather Rules for Certain Acquisition Indebtedness

Taxpayers who incurred acquisition indebtedness on or before December 15, 2017, are not affected by the $750,000 cap set forth in § 163(h)(3)(F)(i)(II) with respect to such indebtedness. If, however, a taxpayer incurs debt satisfying the requirements of § 163(h)(3)(B)(i) after December 15, 2017, the $750,000 cap will have an impact. The

---

Timing the Deduction of Points

Discount points paid in the mortgage lending context represent prepaid interest. Ordinarily, taxpayers may not immediately deduct prepaid interest that relates to (and, technically, would have been due in) future years. *See* § 461(g)(1). This general prohibition does not apply, however, with respect to points paid in connection with the acquisition or improvement of a principal residence. *See* § 461(g)(2). Thus, points paid in connection with those events are currently deductible. Taxpayers who pay points in connection with refinancing mortgage debt may be able to deduct currently some portion of the points paid if (and to the extent) they used a portion of the proceeds to substantially improve their principal residence.

Caveat: Do not equate principal residence and qualified residence in this context. These rules apply with respect to principal residences.

$750,000 cap generally applicable to new acquisition indebtedness will be reduced (but not below zero) by the amount of any indebtedness incurred on or before December 15, 2017, which was treated as acquisition indebtedness for purposes of § 163(h) for the taxable year. Thus, for example, assume that a taxpayer incurred acquisition indebtedness of $500,000 on December 14, 1999, and has $200,000 of such indebtedness outstanding on January 2, 2019. If they incur additional debt satisfying the requirements of § 163(h)(3)(B)(i) on January 2, 2019, only $550,000 of such additional debt ($750,000-$200,000) may qualify as acquisition indebtedness; at that point, then, the taxpayer would have aggregate acquisition indebtedness of $750,000. Likewise, assume that a taxpayer incurred acquisition indebtedness of $1,000,000 on December 14, 2015, and has $900,000 of such indebtedness outstanding on January 2, 2019. The taxpayer may deduct the interest on this indebtedness, because the limitation in § 163(h)(F)(i)(II) does not apply; the debt is grandfathered. But, if such a taxpayer incurs additional debt satisfying the requirements of § 163(h)(3)(B)(i) on January 2, 2019, none of it will qualify as acquisition indebtedness; the taxpayer's acquisition indebtedness cap is $0. Given that $750,000-$900,000 would yield a negative number, § 163(h)(3)(F)(i)(III) effectively reduces the cap for new acquisition indebtedness to $0 for this taxpayer.

> **Note**
> ....
> *The rules set forth under § 163(h)(3)(F)(iii)(I) generally allow refinanced indebtedness resulting from grandfathered acquisition indebtedness to be treated as acquisition indebtedness, so long as the debt resulting from the refinancing does not exceed the amount of the refinanced indebtedness. Congress achieves this result by treating the refinanced indebtedness as having been incurred on the date that the original indebtedness was incurred, but this treatment is time-restricted under § 163(h)(3)(F)(iii)(II).*

> **Caveat**
> ....
> Do not leave the chapter thinking that a taxpayer may deduct $750,000 *of interest* under the appropriate circumstances. The taxpayer may only deduct the interest on up to $750,000 of *loan principal*.

3. Special Issue: Deducting Mortgage Interest as the Legal or Equitable Owner of Property

Case Preview

Jackson v. Commissioner

Under normal circumstances, taxpayers encounter little difficulty in applying the rules of § 163. They borrow the money, grant the lien on their new home, pay the loan principal and interest, and use the form sent to them by the bank to fill in the appropriate amount on their Form 1040 (Schedule A). But taxpayers have a way of complicating matters, and the Treasury Regulations have managed to adjust and accommodate to some extent. Under Treasury Regulations § 1.163-1(b), a taxpayer may be able to deduct mortgage interest paid even if he happens not to be legally obligated to pay the promissory note secured by the residence. The taxpayer must, however, be the legal or equitable owner of the subject property. Legal ownership is straightforward enough as concepts go, but just how far does equitable ownership reach, and how far are courts willing to bend and strain to acknowledge its existence? The Tax Court offered up some guidance on the question in *Jackson v. Commissioner*. Contemplate the following as you read through the case:

1. Who was the legal owner of the property?
2. What factors point to the existence of equitable ownership?
3. What did the taxpayer offer as proof of equitable ownership, and did the court find it sufficient?

Jackson v. Commissioner
T.C. Summ. Op. 2016-33

SUMMARY OPINION

GUY, Special Trial Judge:

Respondent determined deficiencies of $3,104 and $2,119 in petitioner's Federal income tax for 2011 and 2012, respectively (years in issue). Petitioner filed timely petitions for redetermination with the Court pursuant to section 6213(a). At the time the petitions were filed, petitioner resided in Nevada.

The issue for decision is whether petitioner is entitled to deductions for qualified residence interest that he claimed on Schedules A, Itemized Deductions, for the years in issue.

Background

Some of the facts have been stipulated and are so found. The stipulation of facts and the accompanying exhibits are incorporated herein by this reference.

I. The Mortgaged Property

During the years in issue petitioner lived with his girlfriend, Julie Furney, in a residence in Nevada that she had purchased in 2005. Ms. Furney had financed the purchase of the residence with a mortgage provided by Countrywide Financial (a mortgage lender subsequently acquired by Bank of America). She is listed as the sole owner on the deed to the property and as the only person responsible on the mortgage. Petitioner was not able to join Ms. Furney in obtaining a mortgage on the residence in 2005 because of personal debt problems. Nevertheless, he maintains that he and Ms. Furney are "domestic partners" and, as such, share equal ownership of the residence.

[handwritten margin note: F: Cash Phymts made by taxpayer to gf for mortgage Phymts. No evidence though.]

Petitioner further testified that during the years in issue he transferred $1,000 in cash to Ms. Furney each month to make "interest-only" mortgage payments on the residence. Although he explained that he always paid Ms. Furney in cash to avoid bank fees, he did not produce any objective evidence, such as records or receipts, to show that he transferred any amounts to Ms. Furney.

[handwritten margin note: Letter from gf confirming]

Petitioner did not call Ms. Furney as a witness. He testified that Ms. Furney pays all homeowners insurance premiums and property taxes assessed on the residence and that he shares all maintenance costs with her. The record includes a copy of a letter from Ms. Furney to respondent's counsel, dated April 7, 2015, stating in pertinent part that petitioner "has paid the amount of $1,000 per month on the Mortgage payment * * * for the past 10 years." Although the parties agree that Bank of America issued Forms 1098, Mortgage Interest Statement, to Ms. Furney for the years in issue, showing that she paid interest of $13,794 in both years, those forms were not made part of the record.

II. Petitioner's Tax Returns

[handwritten margin note: Deduction at Issue]

Petitioner filed Forms 1040, U.S. Individual Income Tax Return, for 2011 and 2012, reporting wages of $39,392 and $33,022, respectively. On Schedules A attached to his tax returns he claimed matching mortgage interest deductions of $15,720.

III. Notices of Deficiency

Respondent issued notices of deficiency to petitioner for the years in issue disallowing for lack of substantiation the mortgage interest deductions that he had claimed. Respondent determined that the deductions claimed did not match amounts reported on Forms 1098.

Discussion

As a general rule, the Commissioner's determination of a taxpayer's liability in a notice of deficiency is presumed correct, and the taxpayer bears the burden of proving that the determination is incorrect. Tax deductions are a matter of legislative grace, and the taxpayer bears the burden of proving entitlement to any deduction claimed. A taxpayer must substantiate deductions claimed by keeping and producing adequate records that enable the Commissioner to determine the taxpayer's correct tax liability.

* * *

In general, section 163(h)(3) and (4) allows a deduction for interest paid or accrued on certain indebtedness, including acquisition indebtedness on a qualified residence. The acquisition indebtedness generally must be an obligation of the taxpayer and not an obligation of another. Section 1.163-1(b), Income Tax Regs., provides in relevant part, however, that "[i]nterest paid by the taxpayer on a mortgage upon real estate of which he is the legal or equitable owner, even though the taxpayer is not directly liable upon the bond or note secured by such mortgage, may be deducted as interest on his indebtedness."

Thus, if the taxpayer can establish legal, equitable, or beneficial ownership of mortgaged property, the taxpayer may be entitled to a deduction for qualified residence interest. In *Uslu v. Commissioner*, T.C. Memo. 1997-551, for example, the taxpayers could not qualify for a mortgage loan because of a recent bankruptcy. Consequently, the taxpayer husband and his brother agreed that the brother would obtain the loan for the property and the taxpayers would pay the mortgage and all other expenses for maintenance and improvements. The Court held that although the taxpayers did not hold legal title to the property, they were the equitable owners and were entitled to deduct mortgage interest they paid with respect to the property. ***

[margin note: General Rule]

In contrast, where the taxpayer is unable to establish legal, equitable, or beneficial ownership of mortgaged property, this Court has disallowed the taxpayer a mortgage interest deduction. See *Daya v. Commissioner*, T.C. Memo. 2000-360.

Petitioner had no legal obligation to make mortgage payments on the residence, nor did he hold legal title to the property in 2011 or 2012. To prevail, he was obliged to establish that he paid the mortgage interest and that he held beneficial or equitable ownership of the residence during the years in issue. As explained below, he failed to show either.

[margin note: H: Taxpayer failed to show beneficial or equitable ownership]

State law determines the nature of property rights, and Federal law determines the tax consequences of those rights. The Supreme Court of Nevada recognizes that unmarried cohabiting adults may expressly or impliedly agree to hold property as though it were community property. In *Hay v. Hay*, 678 P.2d 672, 674 (Nev. 1984), the court cited with approval the holding in *Marvin v. Marvin*, 557 P.2d 106 (Cal. 1976), that courts should enforce express or implied contracts between nonmarital partners.

This Court has long recognized that a taxpayer may become the equitable owner of property when he or she assumes the benefits and burdens of ownership. In determining whether a taxpayer possesses any of the benefits and burdens of ownership of property, the Court considers whether the taxpayer: (1) has the right to possess the property and to enjoy its use, rents, or profits; (2) has a duty to maintain the property; (3) is responsible for insuring the property; (4) bears the property's risk of loss; (5) is obligated to pay the property's taxes, assessments, or charges; (6) has the right to improve the property without the owner's consent; and (7) has the right to obtain legal title at any time by paying the balance of the purchase price. See *Blanche v. Commissioner*, T.C. Memo. 2001-63; *Uslu v. Commissioner*, T.C. Memo. 1997-551.

[margin note: Rule and Factors for determining equitable ownership]

Petitioner did not provide any objective evidence that he paid the mortgage interest in issue or that he was the equitable or beneficial owner of the property in question. He did not produce any bank statements, receipts, or similar records to show that he transferred any amounts to Ms. Furney to pay the mortgage or other expenses related to the residence. Petitioner testified that Ms. Furney paid all of the homeowners insurance premiums and property taxes on the residence. There was no showing that petitioner could make improvements to the property without Ms. Furney's consent or that he could obtain legal title to the property by paying the balance due on the mortgage.

[margin note: RE: Lack of statements, receipts, etc.]

Considering the shared ownership arrangement that petitioner described, one would reasonably expect that petitioner and Ms. Furney would have committed the terms of their agreement regarding ownership of the residence to writing. Yet the record is bare of any written statement of their respective rights to possess the property or to share in the benefits and burdens of ownership. Because she held legal title to the residence and was the sole [mortgagor], Ms. Furney's testimony would have been highly relevant to the question whether she and petitioner had agreed (expressly or impliedly) that he would hold an interest in the property (akin to that of a community property interest). Despite ample advance notice of the trial date and the Court's considerable flexibility in scheduling the trial in these cases, Ms. Furney did not appear as a witness. Under the circumstances, we give no weight to Ms. Furney's April 2015 letter to respondent's counsel related to petitioner's history of transferring funds to her.

The only evidence remaining in support of petitioner's position was his own testimony, which is unsubstantiated and unconvincing. We are not required to accept such testimony, and we decline to do so.

In sum, we conclude that petitioner failed to show that he paid any mortgage interest in the years in issue or that he held any ownership interest in the residence. Consequently, we sustain respondent's determination disallowing the mortgage interest deductions that petitioner claimed for the years in issue.

To reflect the foregoing,

Decisions will be entered for respondent.

Post-Case Follow-Up

The court in *Jackson* readily acknowledges that a taxpayer may be entitled to a deduction for mortgage interest paid if he or she can establish equitable or legal ownership of the subject property. The court found, however, that Mr. Jackson simply failed to submit sufficient evidence to establish legal or equitable ownership. One could criticize the court for expecting all taxpayers to formalize their relationships and have the ability produce bank records and the like; not everyone feels the need to interact with intimate familiars at arm's length. Even so, taxpayers asserting entitlement to a five-figure deduction must be able to produce something, even if it is simply the testimony of a knowledgeable person. Perhaps the good news is that even if Mr. Jackson paid the interest yet was unable to take a mortgage interest deduction, at least he had the benefit of the standard deduction.

Jackson v. Commissioner: Real Life Applications

1. Theresa recently inherited a four-bedroom home from her grandmother. The home was built in the late 1920s, and Theresa would like to improve the residence substantially before moving in. The problem, unfortunately, is that Theresa has been quite irresponsible in managing her personal finances, and no bank is willing to lend her money. Assume that Theresa's brother, Phil, borrows $200,000 from Renaissance Bank (secured, with Theresa's permission, by the residence) and uses the funds to substantially improve the home. If Theresa

provides 100 percent of the funds for each monthly payment and is responsible for the payment of property taxes and ongoing maintenance, will she be able to deduct the mortgage interest paid on the note?

2. *Same facts as Question #1*, except that Theresa did not inherit a home. Instead, she grew tired of paying rent and convinced her brother, Elliot, to borrow money and acquire a home on her behalf. Assuming that Theresa lives in the home, provides 100 percent of the funds for each monthly payment, and is responsible for the payment of property taxes and ongoing maintenance, will she be able to deduct the interest paid on the mortgage?

4. Special Issue: Applying Statutory Limits on a Per Taxpayer or Per Residence Basis

Case Preview

Voss v. Commissioner

Under prior law, § 163(h) generally established a $1 million cap with respect to acquisition indebtedness and a $100,000 cap with respect to home equity indebtedness. If an individual borrowed money to acquire both a principal residence and a vacation home, the interest on up to $1.1 million of indebtedness constituted deductible qualified residence interest (assuming statutory requirements had been satisfied). We know that a married couple is treated as one taxpayer for this purpose, but what about two unmarried individuals jointly owning a principal residence and a vacation home (or other qualified residence)? Under currently applicable law, is the cap $750,000 for the couple, or does the absence of marriage result in what is effectively a $1.5 million cap? In other words, do the statutory caps apply in a per-qualified-residence basis or per-taxpayer basis? Although states generally allow joint ownership of property, it wasn't too long ago that a number of states prohibited and refused to recognize same-sex marriage. Even today, both same-sex and opposite-sex couples may opt to live together as registered domestic partners while owning several properties as joint tenants with the right of survivorship. The Tax Court and the U.S Court of the Appeals for the Ninth Circuit came to different conclusions as to how § 163's limits operate in this context. As you read the decision, consider the following questions:

1. What conclusion did the Tax Court come to, and why?
2. Has Congress ever clarified that a given tax benefit is to be limited when unmarried individuals might be in a position to obtain multiple benefits?
3. What statutory language serves as the key focal point of the court's analysis?

Voss v. Commissioner
796 F.3d 1051 (9th Cir. 2015)

BYBEE, Circuit Judge:

This is a tax dispute brought by two unmarried co-owners of real property, Bruce Voss and Charles Sophy. For the 2006 and 2007 tax years, Voss and Sophy each claimed a home mortgage interest deduction under § 163(h)(3) of the Internal Revenue Code, which allows taxpayers to deduct interest on up to $1 million of home acquisition debt and $100,000 of home equity debt. After an audit, the IRS determined that Voss and Sophy were jointly subject to § 163(h)(3)'s $1 million and $100,000 debt limits and thus disallowed a substantial portion of their claimed deductions. Voss and Sophy challenged the IRS's assessment in Tax Court, arguing that the statute's debt limits apply per taxpayer such that they were entitled to deduct interest on up to $1.1 million of home debt each. The Tax Court agreed with the IRS.

We are now called upon to decide how § 163(h)(3)'s debt limit provisions apply when two or more unmarried co-owners of a residence claim the home mortgage interest deduction. Although the statute is silent as to unmarried co-owners, we infer from the statute's treatment of married individuals filing separate returns that § 163(h)(3)'s debt limits apply to unmarried co-owners on a per-taxpayer basis. We accordingly reverse the decision of the Tax Court and remand for a recalculation of petitioners' tax liability.

Section 163 of the Internal Revenue Code governs the deductibility of interest on a taxpayer's indebtedness. This section of the Tax Code, like much of the Code, is complex — it requires attention to definitions within definitions and exceptions upon exceptions. To assist the reader, we begin with a brief overview of the section's relevant provisions.

[At this point, the court discusses the Code provisions governing the deduction of qualified residence interest.]

Significantly, the statute does not allow taxpayers to deduct interest payments on an unlimited amount of acquisition and home equity indebtedness. Instead, the statute limits "[t]he aggregate amount treated as acquisition indebtedness for any period" to $1,000,000 and "[t]he aggregate amount treated as home equity indebtedness for any period" to $100,000. *Id.* § 163(h)(3)(B)(ii), (C)(ii). "[I]n the case of a married individual filing a separate return," however, the statute reduces the debt limits to $500,000 and $50,000 [respectively]. *Id.* We shall refer to these provisions as the debt limit provisions

* * *

Although the statute is specific with respect to a married taxpayer filing a separate return, the Code does not specify whether, in the case of residence co-owners who are not married, the debt limits apply per residence or per taxpayer. That is, is the $1.1 million debt limit the limit on the qualified residence, irrespective of the number of owners, or is it the limit on the debt that can be claimed by any individual taxpayer? That gap in the Code is the source of the present controversy. * * *

Bruce Voss and Charles Sophy are domestic partners registered with the State of California. They co-own two homes as joint tenants — one in Rancho Mirage, California and the other, their primary residence, in Beverly Hills, California.

When Voss and Sophy purchased the Rancho Mirage home in 2000, they took out a $486,300 mortgage, secured by the property. Two years later, they refinanced that mortgage and obtained a new mortgage, also secured by the property, in the amount of $500,000. Voss and Sophy are jointly and severally liable for the refinanced Rancho Mirage mortgage.

Voss and Sophy purchased the Beverly Hills home in 2002. They financed the purchase of the Beverly Hills home with a $2,240,000 mortgage, secured by the Beverly Hills property. About a year later, they refinanced the mortgage by obtaining a new loan in the amount of $2,000,000. Voss and Sophy are jointly and severally liable for the refinanced Beverly Hills mortgage, which, like the original mortgage, is secured by the Beverly Hills property. At the same time as they refinanced the Beverly Hills mortgage, Voss and Sophy also obtained a home equity line of credit of $300,000 for the Beverly Hills home. Voss and Sophy are jointly and severally liable for the home equity line of credit as well.

The total average balance of the two mortgages and the line of credit in 2006 and 2007 (the two taxable years at issue) was about $2.7 million — $2,703,568.05 in 2006 and $2,669,135.57 in 2007. Thus, whether § 163(h)(3)'s debt limit provisions are interpreted as applying per taxpayer (such that Voss and Sophy can deduct interest on up to $2.2 million of debt) or per residence (such that Voss and Sophy can deduct interest on up to $1.1 million of debt), it is in either event clear that Voss and Sophy's debt exceeds the statutory debt limits.

* * *

[Voss and Sophy claimed mortgage interest deductions by applying the statutory caps on a per-taxpayer basis rather than on a per-residence basis. The IRS issued a Notice of Deficiency, treating Voss and Sophy as one taxpayer and limiting their mortgage interest deduction to the interest paid with respect to $1.1 million of indebtedness, as opposed to the interest paid on $2.2 million of indebtedness.]

* * *

Voss and Sophy each filed a petition with the Tax Court, and the two cases were consolidated for joint consideration. The Tax Court granted the parties' joint motion to submit the cases for decision without trial and on the basis of stipulated facts and exhibits, and directed the parties to submit proposed computations for entry of decision.

Based on the stipulated facts, exhibits, and proposed computations submitted by the parties, the Tax Court reached a decision and issued an opinion in the IRS's favor. The Tax Court framed the question presented as "whether the statutory limitations on the amount of acquisition and home equity indebtedness with respect to which interest is deductible under section 163(h)(3) are properly applied on a per-residence or per-taxpayer basis when residence co-owners are not married to each other." *Sophy v. Comm'r*, 138 T.C. 204, 209 (2012).

The Tax Court began its analysis by looking to the definitions of acquisition indebtedness and home equity indebtedness in § 163(h)(3)(B)(i) and (C)(i). *Id.* at 210. The Tax Court noted that the term "any indebtedness" in both definitions is not qualified by language relating to an individual taxpayer (as in "any indebtedness *of the taxpayer*"). *Id.* The Tax Court also pointed out that the phrase "of the taxpayer" in the definition of acquisition indebtedness "is used only in relation to the qualified residence [as in "qualified residence *of the taxpayer*"], not the indebtedness." *Id.*

The Tax Court then examined the definition of qualified residence interest. *Id.* The Tax Court noted that the phrase "with respect to any qualified residence" in that definition appeared to be superfluous, as acquisition indebtedness and home equity indebtedness were already defined in relation to a qualified residence. *Id.* at 211. The Tax Court nevertheless found that the phrase was not superfluous because, in its view, "Congress used these repeated references to emphasize the point that qualified residence interest and the related indebtedness limitations are residence focused rather than taxpayer focused." *Id.* at 212.

The Tax Court further reasoned that the married-person parentheticals were consistent with its per-residence interpretation, as the parentheticals made clear that married couples — whether filing separately or jointly — are, as a couple, limited to deducting interest on $1 million of acquisition indebtedness and $100,000 of home equity indebtedness. *Id.* The purpose of the parentheticals, the Tax Court explained, was simply

> to set out a specific allocation of the limitation amounts that must be used by married couples filing separate tax returns, thus implying that co-owners who are not married to one another may choose to allocate limitation amounts among themselves in some other manner, such as according to percentage of ownership.

Id. at 213.

Noting that nothing in the legislative history of § 163(h)(3) suggested any contrary intention, the Tax Court concluded that "the limitations in section 163(h)(3)(B)(ii) and (C)(ii) on the amounts that may be treated as acquisition and home equity indebtedness with respect to a qualified residence are properly applied on a per-residence basis." *Id.*

We have jurisdiction to review the decisions of the Tax Court "in the same manner and to the same extent as decisions of the district courts in civil actions tried without a jury." 26 U.S.C. § 7482(a)(1). Accordingly, we review the Tax Court's factual findings for clear error, and we review the Tax Court's conclusions of law — including its interpretation of the Internal Revenue Code — de novo. *Suzy's Zoo v. Comm'r*, 273 F.3d 875, 878 (9th Cir.2001).

* * *

We are asked to decide an issue of first impression: When multiple unmarried taxpayers co-own a qualifying residence, do the debt limit provisions found in 26 U.S.C. § 163(h)(3)(B)(ii) and (C)(ii) apply per taxpayer or per residence? We conclude that § 163(h)'s debt limits apply per taxpayer.

* * *

We begin with the text of the key provisions at issue — § 163(h)(3)'s debt limit provisions. They provide:

(B) Acquisition indebtedness. —

. . .

(ii) $1,000,000 Limitation. — The aggregate amount treated as acquisition indebtedness for any period shall not exceed $1,000,000 ($500,000 in the case of a married individual filing a separate return).

(C) Home equity indebtedness. —

. . .

(ii) Limitation. — The aggregate amount treated as home equity indebtedness for any period shall not exceed $100,000 ($50,000 in the case of a separate return by a married individual).

Id. § 163(h)(3)(B)(ii), (C)(ii).

The parties dispute whether the $1 million and $100,000 debt limits in these provisions apply per taxpayer or per residence. If they apply per taxpayer, then Voss and Sophy are each entitled to a $1.1 million debt limit, such that together they can deduct interest payments on up to $2.2 million of acquisition and home equity debt. If the debt limit provisions apply per residence, as the Tax Court held, then the $1 million and $100,000 debt limits must be divided up in some way between Voss and Sophy.

Discerning an answer from § 163(h) requires considerable effort on our part because the statute is silent as to how the debt limits should apply in co-owner situations. Both provisions limit "[t]he aggregate amount treated" as acquisition or home equity debt, but neither says to whom or what the limits apply. Had Congress wanted to make clear that the debt limits apply per taxpayer, it could have drafted the provisions to limit "the aggregate amount *each taxpayer* may treat as" acquisition or home equity debt. But it did not. Or, had Congress wanted to make clear that the debt limits apply per residence, it could have provided that the debt limits must be divided or allocated in the event that two or more unmarried individuals co-own a qualified residence. *Cf.* 26 U.S.C. § 36(a)(1)(C) ("If two or more individuals who are not married purchase a principal residence, the amount of the [first-time home-buyer] credit allowed . . . shall be allocated among such individuals in such manner as the Secretary may prescribe, except that the total amount of the credits allowed to all such individuals shall not exceed $8,000"). But, again, it did not.

Although Congress did neither of these things, we are not altogether without textual guidance. The statute is *mostly* silent about how to deal with co-ownership situations, but it is not *entirely* silent. Both debt limit provisions contain a parenthetical that speaks to one common situation of co-ownership: married individuals filing separate returns. *See id.* § 163(h)(3)(B)(ii), (C)(ii). The parentheticals provide half-sized debt limits "in the case of a married individual filing a separate return." *Id.* Congress's use of the phrase "in the case of" is important. It suggests, first, that the parentheticals contain an exception to the general debt limit set out in the main clause, not an illustration of how that general debt limit should be applied. At the same time, the phrase "in the case of" also suggests a certain parallelism between the parenthetical and the main clause of each provision: other than the debt limit amount, which differs, we can expect that in all respects the case of a married individual filing a separate return should be treated like any other case. It is thus appropriate to look to the parentheticals when interpreting the main clauses' general debt limit provisions. These parentheticals offer us at least three useful insights.

First, the parentheticals clearly speak in per-taxpayer terms: the limit on acquisition indebtedness is "$500,000 in the case of *a married individual* filing a separate return," *id.* § 163(h)(3)(B)(ii) (emphasis added), and the limit on home equity indebtedness is "$50,000 in the case of a separate return by *a married individual*," *id.* § 163(h)(3)(C)(ii) (emphasis added). And they speak in such terms even though married individuals commonly (and perhaps usually) co-own their homes and are jointly and severally liable on any mortgage debt. Had Congress wanted to draft the parentheticals in per-residence terms, doing so would not have been particularly difficult. Congress could have written, "in the case of any qualified residence of a married individual filing a separate return." Yet, once again, Congress did not draft the statute in that way. The per-taxpayer wording of the parentheticals, considered in light of the parentheticals' use of the phrase "in the case of," thus suggests that the wording of the main clause — in particular, the phrase "aggregate amount treated" — should likewise be understood in a per-taxpayer manner.

Second, the parentheticals don't just speak in per-taxpayer terms; they operate in a per-taxpayer manner. The parentheticals give each separately filing spouse a separate debt limit of $550,000 so that, together, the two spouses are effectively entitled to a $1.1 million debt limit (the normal limit for single taxpayers). They do not subject both spouses jointly to the $550,000 debt limit specified in the statute. Were the parentheticals to work in that way, the result would be quite anomalous. Rather than ensuring that a married couple filing separate returns is treated the same as a couple filing a joint return, the parentheticals, under a per-residence reading, would result in disparate treatment of married couples filing separate returns. The separately filing couple would have a $550,000 debt limit, whereas the jointly filing couple, and even the single individual, would have a $1.1 million debt limit.

This is surely not what the statute intended, and we don't understand the Tax Court or the IRS to say otherwise. Quite to the contrary, both acknowledge that the parentheticals' lower limits apply per spouse — which is just another way of saying per taxpayer. And if the debt limits for spouses filing separately apply per spouse, we see no reason in the statute why the debt limits for unmarried individuals should not apply per unmarried individual. The per-taxpayer operation of the debt limits for married individuals filing separately thus suggests that the general debt limits also operate per taxpayer.

Third, and finally, the very inclusion of the parentheticals suggests that the debt limits apply per taxpayer. "It is a well-established rule of statutory construction that courts should not interpret statutes in a way that renders a provision superfluous." *Chubb Custom Ins. Co. v. Space Sys./Loral, Inc.*, 710 F.3d 946, 966 (9th Cir. 2013), *cert. denied*, ___ U.S. ___, 134 S. Ct. 906, 187 L. Ed. 2d 833 (2014). If the $1.1 million debt limit truly applied per residence, as the Tax Court held it does, the parentheticals would be superfluous, as there would be no need to provide that two spouses filing separately get $550,000 each. If the $1.1 million debt limit applies per taxpayer, by contrast, the parentheticals actually do something: they give each separately filing spouse half the debt limit so that the separately filing couple is, as a unit, subject to the same debt limit as a jointly filing couple.

The Tax Court interpreted the married-person parentheticals differently. The purpose of the parentheticals, according to the Tax Court, is not to lower the debt limits for spouses filing separate returns — the spouses are already jointly subject to the $1.1 million debt limit. Rather, the Tax Court explained,

> this language simply appears to set out a *specific allocation* of the limitation amounts that must be used by married couples filing separate tax returns, thus implying that co-owners who are not married to one another may choose to allocate the limitation amounts among themselves in some other manner, such as according to percentage of ownership.

Sophy, 138 T.C. at 213 (emphasis added).

We find this interpretation unpersuasive. In particular, we think it unlikely that Congress would go out of its way to prevent spouses (and only spouses) from allocating § 163(h)(3)'s debt limit amounts, especially when in most cases spouses presumably own their home as equal partners. The much more likely intent of the parentheticals, we think, is to ensure that married couples filing a separate return are treated the same, for purposes of § 163(h)(3), as married couples filing a joint return — in other words, to ensure that *all* married couples, not just joint filers, are treated as though they were a single taxpayer.

[margin note: Intent of Parentheticals]

Section 163(h)(3) is not the only provision in the Tax Code that does this. Congress has on a number of occasions provided half-sized deductions, credits, or limits for separately filing spouses. * * *

The purpose of these provisions is obvious. In each provision, each taxpayer gets some tax benefit — a credit, an exclusion up to some limit, allowable losses up to some limit, or, here, a deduction on interest on home debt up to some limit. Congress, knowing that joint filers are treated as a single taxpayer and that separate filers are treated as two separate taxpayers, wants to ensure that the separately filing spouses don't get double the benefit that jointly filing couples get. And so, in each of these provisions, Congress provides that separately filing spouses each get half the benefit. The intent of these provisions is not to prevent separately filing spouses from allocating the benefit; it is to ensure that the separately filing spouses don't get double the credit, the exclusion, the losses, or the debt limit that the jointly filing couple gets.

If Congress wants to go further and ensure that two or more *unmarried* taxpayers are treated as a single taxpayer for purposes of a particular deduction or credit, it can do that too. And it has. Take § 36 of the Tax Code, for example. That section sets an $8,000 limit on the first-time homebuyer credit but adds two caveats. *See id.* § 36(b)(1). The first caveat is very similar to (and, indeed, has much of the same language as) the limitation provisions here. The statute states, "In the case of a married individual filing a separate return, subparagraph (A) [the provision containing the $8,000 cap] shall be applied by substituting '$4,000' for '$8,000.'" *Id.* § 36(b)(1)(B). But, unlike the limitation provisions here, § 36 does not stop there. It has an additional provision — the second caveat — which states:

> If two or more individuals *who are not married* purchase a principal residence, the amount of the credit allowed . . . shall be allocated among such individuals in such

manner as the Secretary may prescribe, except that the total amount of the credits allowed to all such individuals shall not exceed $8,000.

Id. § 36(b)(1)(C) (emphasis added).

As § 36 makes clear, Congress knows how to treat a group of unmarried taxpayers as a single taxpayer for purposes of a particular tax benefit or burden. Congress could have done so here, but tellingly it did not. Instead, Congress did what it has done many times before, using the same language it has used before: It eliminated what would otherwise be a significant discrepancy between separately filing and jointly filing married couples by expressly reducing the debt limits for spouses filing separately.

In sum, the married-person parentheticals' language, purpose, and operation all strongly suggest that § 163(h)(3)'s debt limit provisions apply per taxpayer, not per residence. Absent some contrary indication in the statute, then, we shall read the debt limit provisions as applying on a per-taxpayer basis. * * *

***

The IRS argues that applying § 163(h)(3)'s debt limit provisions on a per-taxpayer basis creates a marriage penalty. We agree that it does, but we do not believe the marriage penalty is as significant a concern as the IRS urges.

Congress may have had perfectly legitimate reasons for distinguishing between married and unmarried taxpayers. Married individuals, unlike unmarried individuals, have the option under the Tax Code of filing a joint return. This option offers significant benefits — in particular, lower tax rates at various levels of income. But it's not all honeymoon; filing jointly also comes with certain drawbacks. A couple filing a joint return might, for example, receive one $1,000 tax credit where the same couple filing separate tax returns might receive two $1,000 credits. It would appear that, in Congress's view, the home mortgage interest deduction is one such drawback. If two individuals who are engaged to be married each own their own house and each have their own $1 million mortgage, both get to deduct all of their interest. But if they get married and file a joint return, they are treated as one taxpayer and can then only deduct half of their interest. *See Pau,* 73 T.C.M. (CCH) at 1819, 1826. This is a marriage penalty, but Congress presumably allows the marriage penalty because the couple also receives offsetting benefits available only to married couples filing a joint return.

Of course, a married couple filing separate returns does not receive the benefits of filing a joint return. Is it unfair, then, that they are treated as a single taxpayer while the unmarried couple is not? Perhaps not, for the married couple, unlike the unmarried couple, can usually elect to file a joint return. And perhaps Congress did not want separately filing married couples to have a significant advantage over jointly filing married couples. * * *

We thus agree that the debt limit provisions of § 163(h)(3) result in a marriage penalty; but we are not particularly troubled. Congress may very well have good reasons for allowing that result, and, in any event, Congress clearly singled out married couples for specific treatment when it explicitly provided lower debt limits for married couples yet, for whatever reason, did not similarly provide lower debt limits for unmarried co-owners.

* * *

We hold that 26 U.S.C. § 163(h)(3)'s debt limit provisions apply on a per-tax-payer basis to unmarried co-owners of a qualified residence. We infer this conclusion from the text of the statute: By expressly providing that married individuals filing separate returns are entitled to deduct interest on up to $550,000 of home debt each, Congress implied that unmarried co-owners filing separate returns are entitled to deduct interest on up to $1.1 million of home debt each. We accordingly reverse the Tax Court's decision and remand for the limited purpose of allowing the parties to determine, in a manner consistent with this opinion, the proper amount of quali-fied residence interest that petitioners are entitled to deduct, as well as the proper amount of any remaining deficiency.

REVERSED and REMANDED.

[Dissenting opinion omitted.]

Post-Case Follow-Up

In *Voss*, the court concludes that the $1.1 million statutory cap with respect to acquisition and home equity indebted-ness applies on a per-taxpayer basis as opposed to a per-qual-ified-residence basis. The court reached this result by noting that married taxpayers are treated as one taxpayer and by focusing on language in § 163(h)(3) mandating that mar-ried taxpayers filing separately apply standard statutory caps reduced by one-half. This approach, reasoned the court, ensures that "one" tax-payer (whether that be an individual or a married couple filing jointly) is limited to the standard statutory caps on a per-taxpayer basis. The court acknowledges that its reading of the statute imposes a marriage penalty, but it also points out that Congress has clearly demonstrated its ability to limit the availability of a tax benefit in the housing context when unmarried individuals might be in a position to reap undue largesse. In the majority's view, Congress's decision not to alter the language set forth in § 163(h) suggests that Congress was unperturbed by the status quo. The court might also have pointed out that the Code's references to "any indebtedness" and not "any indebtedness of the taxpayer" is fully consistent with the notion that a legal or equitable owner of real estate may take a deduction for paying qualified residence interest even if that person is not legally obligated to pay the mortgage. *See* Treas. Reg. § 1.163-1(b).

Even if one agrees with the holding in *Voss*, one must acknowledge that it involved two taxpayers and two residences. As one individual buying one home, each of them would have no difficulty deducting interest on $1.1 million of indebt-edness with respect to a qualified residence. But what about two unmarried tax-payers co-owning three homes (e.g., the summer residence, the winter residence, and the beach residence) or two unmarried individuals occupying one qualified residence encumbered by at least $2.2 million of indebtedness? Because *Voss* con-cludes that the $1.1 million caps apply on a per-taxpayer basis, the factual variations should yield the same result, and the IRS is in express agreement. The following pronouncement is an Action on Decision concerning *Voss v. Commissioner*.

ACTION ON DECISION

Subject: *Voss v. Commissioner*, 796 F.3d 1051 (9th Cir. 2015), *rev'g Sophy v. Commissioner*, 138 T.C. 204 (2012)

Issue: Whether the § 163(h)(3) debt limitations on deductions for qualified residence interest apply on a per-taxpayer basis, rather than on a per-residence basis.

Discussion: Section 163(h)(2)(D) of the Internal Revenue Code allows taxpayers to deduct a limited amount of personal interest paid on residential mortgages. The mortgage must be secured by a "qualified residence," defined by § 163(h)(4)(A) to include the taxpayer's principal residence plus one other residence. Section 163(h)(3) limits the amount of deductible interest to interest paid on $1 million of acquisition indebtedness (or refinanced acquisition indebtedness, up to the amount of the original loan's balance), plus interest paid on $100,000 of home equity indebtedness.

Mr. Voss and Mr. Sophy, unmarried co-owners of two residences, each filed an individual tax return claiming a deduction for qualified residence interest paid on acquisition indebtedness and home equity indebtedness in excess of $1.1 million (for a combined amount in excess of $2.2 million). The IRS disallowed portions of each taxpayer's deduction for qualified residence interest on the grounds that § 163(h)(2) and (3) limit the aggregate amount of indebtedness to $1 million and $100,000, respectively, on any qualified residence, allocated among all taxpayers entitled to an interest expense deduction for that qualified residence.

Mr. Voss and Mr. Sophy petitioned the Tax Court, challenging the Service's determinations. The Tax Court agreed with the IRS, finding that the language of the statute limits the total amount of indebtedness with respect to acquisition indebtedness and home equity indebtedness that may be claimed in relation to the qualified residence, rather than in relation to an individual taxpayer. The taxpayers appealed to the United States Court of Appeals for the Ninth Circuit.

The Ninth Circuit reversed the Tax Court decision, agreeing with the taxpayers that the statutory limitations apply to unmarried co-owners of a qualified residence on a per- taxpayer basis. The court based its conclusion largely on its interpretation of the language of the statute that expressly provides that married individuals filing separate returns are entitled to deduct interest on up to $500,000 of acquisition indebtedness and $50,000 of home equity indebtedness. By providing lower debt limits for married couples, and not for unmarried co-owners, Congress singled out married couples for specific treatment, implying that an unmarried co-owner filing a separate return is entitled to deduct interest on up to $1,000,000 of acquisition indebtedness and $100,000 of home equity indebtedness.

The Internal Revenue Service will follow the *Voss* opinion and will apply the § 163(h)(2) and (3) limitations on a per-taxpayer basis, allowing each taxpayer to deduct mortgage interest on indebtedness of up to $1 million and $100,000, respectively, on a qualified residence.

Recommendation: Acquiescence

2016-31 Internal Revenue Bulletin 193.

Voss v. Commissioner: Real Life Applications

1. While vacationing in Martha's Vineyard, Sterling and his wife, Anne, noted that a beautiful beachside home was being "Offered" at $1.2 million by the owners (i.e., the residence was for sale). Although the couple already had $900,000 of acquisition indebtedness outstanding on their principal residence, they decided that they could not pass up the home on "The Vineyard," especially in light of the fact that they could borrow at historically low interest rates. If they purchase the new residence by making a down payment of $240,000 and borrowing $960,000, how much acquisition indebtedness will they have with respect to their qualified residences?

2. *Same facts at Question #1*, except that Sterling and Anna are unmarried domestic partners who co-own their principal residence and their home on Martha's Vineyard as joint tenants with the right of survivorship. How much acquisition indebtedness will they have with respect to their qualified residences?

C. THE DEDUCTION FOR INTEREST PAID ON EDUCATION LOANS

In addition to clarifying that qualified residence interest does not constitute personal interest, section 163 also indicates that personal interest does not include interest paid under § 221 with respect to qualified education loans. The Code, in turn, defines *qualified education loans* (which may relate to the taxpayer, his spouse, or a dependent) as those incurred to cover qualified education expenses (i.e., the cost of attending an eligible educational institution, reduced by certain exclusions, scholarships, and allowances). *See generally* § 221(a) and (d). Notwithstanding the initial excitement generated by the apparent availability of this deduction, many taxpayers with substantial educational debt (and the well-paying jobs that tend to go along with it), will find that the gentle breeze of modest financial success has slammed shut the § 221 door. Section 221(b) caps any available deduction at $2,500, but a taxpayer soon finds that the Code gradually phases out this allowance as modified adjusted gross income rises. *See* § 221(b)(2). Note also that taxpayers may not take the student loan interest deduction if they are dependents of another taxpayer. *See* § 221(c).

Key Statutory Provisions

- **Internal Revenue Code**
  - **§ 221(a)**
  - **§ 221(b)–(d) (skim)**

Student Debt Relief

In recent years, a number of universities offering need-based financial aid have made it possible for certain students to attend without incurring debt. Qualifying families must present a specific gross income/financial asset profile.

Credit: Littlenystock / Shutterstock.com.

D. THE DEDUCTION FOR THE PAYMENT OF CERTAIN TAXES

Key Statutory Provisions

■ **Internal Revenue Code**
  - ■ § 164(a)(1)–(3)
  - ■ § 164(b)(2) and (b)(5)(A)
  - ■ § 164(b)(6)

Impact of Sale of Real Property During a Real Property Tax Year

If real property is sold during a real property tax year, the taxes imposed with respect to that property must be apportioned between the seller and the purchaser. In general, the apportionment tracks the period before the sale date and the period on and after the sale date. *See* § 164(d)(1). For this purpose, real property tax year refers to the "period which, under the law imposing the tax, is regarded as the period to which the tax relates." Treas. Reg. § 1.164-6(c).

In addition to allowing individuals to take an itemized deduction with respect to certain interest paid during the taxable year, Congress also allows such taxpayers to take an itemized deduction under § 164 for certain taxes paid or accrued during the taxable year (up to $10,000 in the aggregate for the period). Such taxes include the following:

- ■ State and local real property taxes that were not paid or accrued in carrying on a trade or business (or profit-seeking activity) (e.g., taxes on land ownership);
- ■ State and local personal property taxes that were not paid or accrued in carrying on a trade or business (or profit-seeking activity) (e.g., taxes on car ownership); and
- ■ State and local income taxes.

The Code provides that a reference to a state or local tax includes taxes imposed by U.S. possessions and political subdivisions (counties, parishes, etc.) as well as those imposed by the District of Columbia. *See* § 164(b)(2).

In light of the fact that some U.S. jurisdictions do not impose income taxes, the Code allows taxpayers to elect the deduction of either state income taxes or state and local general sales taxes. *See* § 164(b)(5). Bear in mind that, in any instance, only those who itemize their deductions will benefit from the provisions of § 164 in these respects.

NOTE: Separate rules govern the deductibility of state, local, and foreign taxes paid by individuals in connection with a trade or business.

Chapter Summary

- ■ Section 163(a) generally allows taxpayers a deduction with respect to interest paid during the taxable year on indebtedness.
- ■ Individuals and other noncorporate taxpayers may not deduct personal interest paid on indebtedness. The Code defines personal interest as all interest otherwise deductible except interest falling into designated defined categories (including qualified residence interest).
- ■ *Qualified Residence Interest* refers, under current law, only to interest on acquisition indebtedness with respect to any qualified residence of the taxpayer.

- *Qualified Residence* refers to both the taxpayer's principal residence and one other residence chosen by the taxpayer and used as a residence.
- A taxpayer may take a deduction with respect to qualified residence interest paid during a taxable year so long as such taxpayer is the legal or equitable owner of the qualified residence.
- The statutory dollar cap established with respect to acquisition indebtedness applies on a per-taxpayer basis as opposed to a per-qualified-residence-basis. For this purpose, a married couple filing jointly constitutes one taxpayer.
- Taxpayers may be able to take a deduction with respect to interest paid on certain qualified education loans. The Code phases this deduction out as the taxpayer's modified adjusted gross income rises.
- Per § 164, individual taxpayers itemizing their deductions may take a limited deduction with respect to specific real property taxes, personal property taxes, and income taxes paid during the taxable year. Taxpayers may elect to take an itemized deduction for general sales taxes paid instead of income taxes paid.

Applying the Rules

1. Having been a renter for 10 years, Bram decided to purchase a home and to use it as his principal residence. On September 1, 2018, he found a beautiful place in an upscale neighborhood and offered the existing owners $1.5 million. They accepted. Assume that in acquiring the home, Bram made a $300,000 down payment and borrowed $1.2 million from Citizens Financial Bank (using the home as security for repayment of the loan). How much acquisition indebtedness does Bram have? *750k because of limitation*

2. Assume that you are reading a document concerning § 163. Which of the following, if any, accurately reflect the law and why?

   a. Interest on acquisition indebtedness is a form of qualified residence interest.
   b. Qualified residence interest is a form of deductible personal interest.

3. Timothy and Shelley Brown purchased a home in 2012 for $1.1 million by making a down payment of $200,000 and borrowing $900,000. The home serves as security for repayment of the 30-year, fixed rate loan, and the outstanding principal balance is $800,000. Assume that prevailing interest rates have fallen since the Browns made their purchase, and they have decided to refinance. If the Browns refinance by borrowing $1 million (again using the home as their principal residence and as security for repayment of the new loan), on what portion of this amount may they take deductions for payments of qualified residence interest? *$800k because grandfathered in, and they don't lose the benefit by refinancing.*

4. During calendar year 2018, Alejandro paid $8,000 in real property taxes, $1,000 in personal property taxes, $12,000 in interest on acquisition indebtedness, and

$200 in interest on his credit card obligations. No amounts were paid in connection with Alejandro's conduct of a trade or business or profit-seeking activity. Which of these items may Alejandro deduct on Form 1040 Schedule A as itemized deductions?

Federal Income Taxation in Practice

1. One of your clients is under audit for his 2016 taxable year. During that year, he paid mortgage insurance premiums with respect to a mortgage he took out in calendar year 2014. He would like to know whether mortgage insurance premiums constituted qualified residence interest if those amounts were paid during calendar year 2016 with respect to a qualified residence. See what you can find, and prepare a brief letter for him.

2. You are a partner with a large law firm, and one of your clients is a major manufacturer of mobile homes. His sales force routinely tells customers that their mobile home can serve as a qualified residence for mortgage interest deduction purposes so long as the mobile home serves as security for repayment of the relevant loan. The General Counsel of the company understands that if a bank seeks to hold a lien on a mobile home, it must make a public filing at a centralized location in the state, but with the mobility of mobile homes, he wonders whether moving a mobile home to another jurisdiction (without a new filing being made in that jurisdiction) will result in the mobile home not being secured for purposes of § 163. He expects to be in long meetings this week but would appreciate a short e-mail letting him know what you have found.

3. One of your relatives recently started paying a considerable amount of attention to his pay stub. He recalls you telling him that certain real and personal property taxes are deductible. He would like to know whether amounts paid as FICA, which he has special hatred for, is something he can deduct. What do you tell him?

Charitable Contributions and Tax-Exempt Entities

Recent statistics from the Office of Management and Budget estimate that for fiscal year 2018, the United States will forego approximately $63 billion in revenue as a result of allowing corporate and individual taxpayers a deduction with respect to their charitable contributions. *See* Office of Management and Budget, Analytical Perspectives, Budget of the United States Government, Fiscal Year 2018, at 132–33. It is money well spent. Charitable organizations undertake a vast array of beneficial activities. Although many of them exist primarily to assist those in need or to alleviate suffering, others aim to enrich the everyday lives of the citizenry, to support meaningful advances in the sciences, or to spark creativity in the fine arts. Taxpayers have ample reason to support these worthy causes, and by making the charitable contribution deduction available, Congress encourages donations and provides a degree of indirect financial support to the organizations. Notwithstanding the opportunity to do good works by way of a charitable organization, however, unsavory organizers and administrators may attempt to reap illicit personal benefits by capitalizing on the availability of the charitable contribution deduction. Accordingly, governing statutory provisions carefully and restrictively define both the types of organizations eligible to receive tax-deductible contributions and those that qualify for tax-exempt status. In each instance, the rules also limit or prohibit certain forms of conduct.

Key Concepts

- The determination (1) whether an entity may receive tax-deductible contributions and (2) whether an entity is, itself, tax-exempt
- The meaning and impact of engaging in a quid pro quo transaction with an organization eligible to receive tax-deductible contributions
- The impact of public policy violations on the tax-exempt status of an organization
- The meaning and impact of private inurement in specific contexts

A. DEDUCTION FOR CHARITABLE CONTRIBUTIONS

1. General Rules

Most people tend to think of charitable organizations as falling into one broad category. In some contexts, such thinking may well be appropriate, but in the tax world, we have to draw an extraordinarily important distinction by recognizing two organization types. Category 1 includes all entities eligible to receive tax-deductible contributions, and Category 2 includes all tax-exempt entities. Congress defines Category 1 organizations under § 170, and it generally defines Category 2 organizations under § 501.[1] In *many* instances, a tax-exempt entity is also, at the same time, an entity eligible to receive tax-deductible contributions. *See* Exhibit 11.1. Even if the entity type overlap is notable, it is critical that you understand that the entity types are distinct and that the overlap is not 100 percent. Although entities eligible to receive tax-deductible contributions are generally tax-exempt, some tax-exempt entities may well be able to receive contributions, but the donor will *not* be entitled to a tax deduction as a result.

> **Key Statutory Provisions**
>
> ▨ **Internal Revenue Code**
>   ▨ § 115
>   ▨ § 170(a)(1)
>   ▨ § 170(b)(1)(A)(i)–(iii) and language after (ix)
>   ▨ § 170(b)(1)(G)
>   ▨ § 170(c) and skim (d)(1)(A)
>   ▨ § 170(f)(8) and (f)(11)(A)–(D)
>   ▨ § 501(a)
>   ▨ § 501(c)(3)
>   ▨ § 6115

Later in this chapter, we will turn to the tax laws governing tax-exemption. At this juncture, we focus on the rules governing the deduction for certain charitable contributions and the organizations receiving them.

Section 170(a) of the Code generally allows taxpayers to take a deduction for charitable contributions made during a taxable year. For individual taxpayers,

EXHIBIT 11.1 **Charitable Organization Bifurcation**

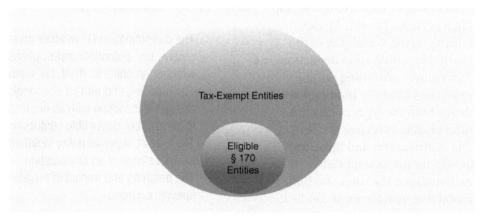

---

[1] Although not deemed tax-exempt under § 501, certain government entities (listed at § 170(c)(1)) enjoy income exclusion under § 115.

the deduction appears on Form 1040 Schedule A, so it is available only to those itemizing their deductions, and even in that context, the taxpayer may run into an annual statutory limit with respect to the charitable contribution line item. Individual taxpayers may deduct charitable contributions made during a taxable year to churches, educational organizations, medical facilities, and other entities described in § 170(b)(1)(A), but as a general matter, the deduction for a given period may not exceed 50 percent of the taxpayer's contribution base (i.e., their adjusted gross income). Note that for taxable years beginning after December 31, 2017, deductions with respect to contributions of *cash* are limited to 60% of the taxpayer's contribution base. *See* § 170(b)(1)(G)(i). Amounts taken into account under this rule will reduce (but not below zero) the amount that would otherwise have been allowable under § 170(b)(1)(A). The deduction cap for contributions to entities not described in § 170(b)(1)(A) may be lower. *See, e.g.,* § 170(b)(1)(B). If an individual's contribution for a given year exceeds the statutory cap, the excess amount may be deductible in future years. Under § 170(d)(1)(A), a taxpayer may carry forward excess contribution amounts to each of the five succeeding taxable years, but again, the amount the taxpayer may deduct will be subject to statutory restriction. Thus, a taxpayer unable to offset excessive amounts of income by making charitable contributions in one year will not be able to do so in a succeeding taxable year.

Although it is possible to think of charitable contribution in the colloquial sense, the Code employs the phrase as a defined term. For purposes of § 170, a *charitable contribution* is a contribution/gift for the use of specific organizations listed in § 170(c), including states (and their political subdivisions), veterans' organizations/posts, cemetery corporations/companies, and a host of organizations satisfying the requirements of § 170(c)(2) (i.e., entities one would traditionally think of as a charity). By definition, an organization described in § 170(c)(2) is a corporation, trust, community chest, fund, or foundation that satisfies the following criteria:

- It is "created or organized in the United States or in any possession thereof, or under the law of the United States, any State, the District of Columbia, or any possession of the United States";
- It is "organized and operated exclusively for religious, charitable, scientific, literary, or educational purposes, or to foster national or international amateur sports competition . . . or for the prevention of cruelty to children or animals";
- "No part of [its] net earnings . . . inures to the benefit of any private shareholder or individual"; and
- It is "not disqualified for tax exemption under section 501(c)(3) by reason of attempting to influence legislation, and [it] does not participate in, or intervene in (including the publishing or distributing of statements), any political campaign on behalf of (or in opposition to) any candidate for public office."

26 U.S.C. § 170(c)(2).

As charitable organization requirements go, the preceding items have basic, common-sense appeal, and conceptually, most are fairly straightforward. The private inurement prohibition might be unfamiliar. A charity can and should benefit the general public, and that reality will result in specific individuals enjoying the organization's goods and services over time as the charitable organization fulfills its mission (e.g., providing education, feeding the poor, offering musical entertainment, facilitating spiritual awareness, or providing shelter to the homeless). But, no charity can operate so as to allow any specific individual to "cash in" or "line his pockets" with the charity's money/property. Prohibiting "private inurement" concisely captures this notion, and we will discuss it at greater depth later in this chapter. For the moment, let's turn to the subject of deduction amounts and mandatory substantiation requirements.

If a donee organization satisfies the statutory requirements, donors may take the charitable contribution deduction provided by § 170(a). Bearing in mind the limitations imposed by § 170(b), donations of cash yield a deduction in the amount of cash contributed, and donations of property typically yield a deduction equal to the fair market value of the property. *See* Treas. Reg. § 1.170A-1(c). In the latter instance, however, the amount ultimately available as a deduction may reflect the intervention of specific rules applicable to donation of specific forms of property. *See, e.g.,* § 170(e) (rules governing contributions of ordinary income and capital gain property), § 170(f)(12) (rules governing contributions of qualified vehicles), and § 170(f)(16) (rules governing the contribution of clothing and household items). In addition to complying with deduction limitation rules, taxpayers contributing $250 or more in a given taxable year will also face substantiation requirements (i.e., they will have to submit some form of proof that they made the donation). At minimum, the taxpayer will have to submit a written acknowledgement from the donee organization. *See* § 170(f)(8)(A). At higher levels (e.g., a deduction above $500 is claimed), special rules generally dictate that donors submit a property description or (for claimed deductions exceeding $5,000) a qualified appraisal with respect to the subject property in order to avail themselves of the charitable contribution deduction. *See* § 170(f)(11).

2. Quid Pro Quo Contributions

As charitable organizations go about their fundraising activities, they often offer donors some small token of appreciation for the donation made. When this happens, donors must adjust the basic amount of the deduction they plan to take to account for the fact that some portion of their contribution actually constituted consideration for the token provided. Thus, a donor who hands over a $500 check payable to a charity may only count $470 as a charitable contribution if the organization provides the donor with a teddy bear valued at $30. Section 6115 generally requires that a charity described in § 170(c) receiving a quid pro quo contribution in excess of $75 provide both a written statement, which essentially informs the donor that only a portion of their contribution is deductible (i.e., the amount exceeding the value of goods/services provided by the charity), and a good faith estimate of the value of such goods or services. We see similar deduction policing on the donor side. As was noted above, donors contributing $250 or more to a charity (regardless of whether it occurs in a quid pro quo context) must substantiate the contribution by providing a written acknowledgment (containing specific information) from the organization. *See* § 170(f)(8)(B). The acknowledgement must include information concerning the amount of money received (along with a description of any non-cash items received), indicate whether the organization provided goods or services in consideration (in whole or in part) for the donation, and provide a description and good faith estimate of the value of any goods or services the charity provided to the donor in exchange for the donation. *See* § 170(f)(8)(B). An acknowledgement must also clarify whether an individual received solely intangible religious benefits in connection with their contribution. *See id.* Interestingly enough, the Code defines *intangible religious benefit* in a rather circular fashion as "any intangible religious benefit which is provided by an organization organized exclusively for religious purposes and which generally is not sold in a commercial transaction outside the donative context." Congress added § 170(f)(8), including this language, to the Code in the Omnibus Budget Reconciliation Act of 1993 (P.L. 103-66), just a few years after the decision in our next case was handed down. As you make your way through this authority, consider whether this statutory language can, at the least, inform an analysis of the issue presented in *Hernandez*.

Case Preview

Hernandez v. Commissioner

Parishioners attending church commonly pay tithes (or make some voluntary financial contribution) at some point during the services. Assuming the contribution recipient qualifies as a religious organization described in § 170(c), the parishioners may take a deduction (to the extent allowed) under § 170(a) with respect to the donations made. Rarely, if ever, does a parishioner think they are in any sense paying for the good reverend's sermon. Members of the Church of Scientology, however, pay for "training" and "auditing" sessions both to enhance spiritual growth and to prevent spiritual decline. In *Hernandez v. Commissioner*, the U.S. Supreme Court had to determine whether the payments made by Scientologists for these sessions constituted charitable contributions to a religious organization or, instead, payments for services rendered in a quid pro quo exchange. Consider the following questions as you read through the opinion:

1. Why do Scientologists require payment for training and auditing?
2. Does the IRS consider the subjective motivations or beliefs of those making the payments in determining whether the donations constitute charitable contributions?
3. How does the IRS treat those adhering to faiths other than Scientology with respect to mandatory or quasi-mandatory payments made for specific religious benefits?

Famous Scientologists

Tom Cruise and Elisabeth Moss are well-known actors who have been associated with the Church of Scientology.

Tom Cruise *(left)*
Credit: Bakounine/Shutterstock.com.
Elizabeth Moss *(right)*
Credit: Featureflash Photo. Agency/Shutterstock.com.

Hernandez v. Commissioner
490 U.S. 680 (1989)

Justice Thurgood Marshall

Appointed by President Lyndon B. Johnson, Justice Thurgood Marshall served on the U.S. Supreme Court from 1967 to 1991. Justice Marshall had previously served as Solicitor General of the United States and is well-known for the litigation victory he secured in *Brown v. Board of Education,* an enduring landmark of Equal Protection Clause jurisprudence.

Credit: Stock Montage/Getty Images.

Justice MARSHALL delivered the opinion of the Court.

Section 170 of the Internal Revenue Code of 1954 (Code) permits a taxpayer to deduct from gross income the amount of a "charitable contribution." The Code defines that term as a "contribution or gift" to certain eligible donees, including entities organized and operated exclusively for religious purposes. We granted certiorari to determine whether taxpayers may deduct as charitable contributions payments made to branch churches of the Church of Scientology (Church) in order to receive services known as "auditing" and "training." We hold that such payments are not deductible.

Scientology was founded in the 1950's by L. Ron Hubbard. It is propagated today by a "mother church" in California and by numerous branch churches around the world. The mother Church instructs laity, trains and ordains ministers, and creates new congregations. Branch churches, known as "franchises" or "missions," provide Scientology services at the local level, under the supervision of the mother Church.

Scientologists believe that an immortal spiritual being exists in every person. A person becomes aware of this spiritual dimension through a process known as "auditing." Auditing involves a one-to-one encounter between a participant (known as a "preclear") and a Church official (known as an "auditor"). An electronic device, the E-meter, helps the auditor identify the preclear's areas of spiritual difficulty by measuring skin responses during a question and answer session. Although auditing sessions are conducted one on one, the content of each session is not individually tailored. The preclear gains spiritual awareness by progressing through sequential levels of auditing, provided in short blocks of time known as "intensives."

The Church also offers members doctrinal courses known as "training." Participants in these sessions study the tenets of Scientology and seek to attain the qualifications necessary to serve as auditors. Training courses, like auditing sessions, are provided in sequential levels. Scientologists are taught that spiritual gains result from participation in such courses.

The Church charges a "fixed donation," also known as a "price" or a "fixed contribution," for participants to gain access to auditing and training sessions. These charges are set forth in schedules, and prices vary with a session's length and level of sophistication. *** This system of mandatory fixed charges is based on a central tenet of Scientology known as the "doctrine of exchange," according to which any time a person receives something he must pay something back. In so doing, a Scientologist maintains "inflow" and "outflow" and avoids spiritual decline.

The proceeds generated from auditing and training sessions are the Church's primary source of income. The Church promotes these sessions not only through newspaper, magazine, and radio advertisements, but also through free lectures, free personality tests, and leaflets. The Church also encourages, and indeed rewards with a 5% discount, advance payment for these sessions. The Church often refunds unused portions of prepaid auditing or training fees, less an administrative charge.

Petitioners in these consolidated cases each made payments to a branch church for auditing or training sessions. They sought to deduct these payments on their federal income tax returns as charitable contributions under § 170. [The] Commissioner * * * disallowed these deductions, finding that the payments were not charitable contributions within the meaning of § 170.

Petitioners sought review of these determinations in the Tax Court. * * * Before trial, the Commissioner stipulated that the branch churches of Scientology are religious organizations entitled to receive tax-deductible charitable contributions under the relevant sections of the Code. This stipulation isolated as the sole statutory issue whether payments for auditing or training sessions constitute "contribution[s] or gift[s]" under § 170.

The Tax Court held a 3-day bench trial during which the taxpayers and others testified and submitted documentary exhibits describing the terms under which the Church promotes and provides auditing and training sessions. Based on this record, the court upheld the Commissioner's decision. It observed first that the term "charitable contribution" in § 170 is synonymous with the word "gift," which case law had defined "as a *voluntary transfer* of property by the owner to another *without consideration* therefor." It then determined that petitioners had received consideration for their payments, namely, "the benefit of various religious services provided by the Church of Scientology." The Tax Court also rejected the taxpayers' constitutional challenges based on the Establishment and Free Exercise Clauses of the First Amendment.

[Circuit Courts of Appeal affirmed the Tax Court.]

We granted certiorari to resolve a Circuit conflict concerning the validity of charitable deductions for auditing and training payments. We now affirm.

For over 70 years, federal taxpayers have been allowed to deduct the amount of contributions or gifts to charitable, religious, and other eleemosynary institutions. Section 170, the present provision, was enacted in 1954; it requires a taxpayer claiming the deduction to satisfy a number of conditions. The Commissioner's stipulation in this case, however, has narrowed the statutory inquiry to one such condition: whether petitioners' payments for auditing and training sessions are "contribution[s] or gift[s]" within the meaning of § 170.

The legislative history of the "contribution or gift" limitation, though sparse, reveals that Congress intended to differentiate between unrequited payments to qualified recipients and payments made to such recipients in return for goods or services. Only the former were deemed deductible. The House and Senate Reports on the 1954 tax bill, for example, both define "gifts" as payments "made with no expectation of a financial return commensurate with the amount of the gift." Using payments to hospitals as an example, both Reports state that the gift characterization should not apply to "a payment by an individual to a hospital *in consideration of* a binding obligation to provide medical treatment for the individual's employees. It would apply only if there were no expectation of any quid pro quo from the hospital."

In ascertaining whether a given payment was made with "the expectation of any quid pro quo," the IRS has customarily examined the external features of the transaction in question. This practice has the advantage of obviating the need for the IRS to conduct imprecise inquiries into the motivations of individual taxpayers. The lower courts have generally embraced this structural analysis. We likewise focused on external features in *United States v. American Bar Endowment* to resolve the taxpayers' claims that they were entitled to partial deductions for premiums paid to a charitable organization for insurance coverage; the taxpayers contended that they had paid unusually high premiums in an effort to make a contribution along with their purchase of insurance. We upheld the Commissioner's disallowance of the partial deductions because the taxpayers had failed to demonstrate, at a minimum, the existence of comparable insurance policies with prices lower than those of the policy they had each purchased. In so doing, we stressed that "[t]he *sine qua non* of a charitable contribution is a transfer of money or property *without adequate consideration*."

In light of this understanding of § 170, it is readily apparent that petitioners' payments to the Church do not qualify as "contribution[s] or gift [s]." As the Tax Court found, these payments were part of a quintessential *quid pro quo* exchange: in return for their money, petitioners received an identifiable benefit, namely, auditing and training sessions. The Church established fixed price schedules for auditing and training sessions in each branch church; it calibrated particular prices to auditing or training sessions of particular lengths and levels of sophistication; it returned a refund if auditing and training services went unperformed; it distributed "account cards" on which persons who had paid money to the Church could monitor what prepaid services they had not yet claimed; and it categorically barred provision of auditing or training sessions for free. Each of these practices reveals the inherently reciprocal nature of the exchange.

Petitioners do not argue that such a structural analysis is inappropriate under § 170, or that the external features of the auditing and training transactions do not strongly suggest a *quid pro quo* exchange. Indeed, the petitioners in the consolidated *Graham* case conceded at trial that they expected to receive specific amounts of auditing and training in return for their payments. Petitioners argue instead that they are entitled to deductions because a *quid pro quo* analysis is inappropriate under § 170 when the benefit a taxpayer receives is purely religious in nature. Along the same lines, petitioners claim that payments made for the right to participate in a religious service should be automatically deductible under § 170.

We cannot accept this statutory argument for several reasons. First, it finds no support in the language of § 170. Whether or not Congress could, consistent with the Establishment Clause, provide for the automatic deductibility of a payment made to a church that either generates religious benefits or guarantees access to a religious service, that is a choice Congress has thus far declined to make. Instead, Congress has specified that a payment to an organization operated exclusively for religious (or other eleemosynary) purposes is deductible *only* if such a payment is a "contribution or gift." The Code makes no special preference for payments made in the expectation of gaining religious benefits or access to a religious service. The House and Senate Reports on § 170, and the other legislative history of that provision, offer no indication that Congress' failure to enact such a preference was an oversight.

Second, petitioners' deductibility proposal would expand the charitable contribution deduction far beyond what Congress has provided. Numerous forms of payments to eligible donees plausibly could be categorized as providing a religious benefit or as securing access to a religious service. For example, some taxpayers might regard their tuition payments to parochial schools as generating a religious benefit or as securing access to a religious service; such payments, however, have long been held not to be charitable contributions under § 170. Taxpayers might make similar claims about payments for church-sponsored counseling sessions or for medical care at church-affiliated hospitals that otherwise might not be deductible. Given that, under the First Amendment, the IRS can reject otherwise valid claims of religious benefit only on the ground that a taxpayers' alleged beliefs are not sincerely held, but not on the ground that such beliefs are inherently irreligious, the resulting tax deductions would likely expand the charitable contribution provision far beyond its present size. We are loath to effect this result in the absence of supportive congressional intent.

Finally, the deduction petitioners seek might raise problems of entanglement between church and state. If framed as a deduction for those payments generating benefits of a religious nature for the payor, petitioners' proposal would inexorably force the IRS and reviewing courts to differentiate "religious" benefits from "secular" ones. If framed as a deduction for those payments made in connection with a religious service, petitioners' proposal would force the IRS and the judiciary into differentiating "religious" services from "secular" ones. We need pass no judgment now on the constitutionality of such hypothetical inquiries, but we do note that "pervasive monitoring" for "the subtle or overt presence of religious matter" is a central danger against which we have held the Establishment Clause guards.

Accordingly, we conclude that petitioners' payments to the Church for auditing and training sessions are not "contribution[s] or gift[s]" within the meaning of that statutory expression.

[Discussion of Establishment Clause and Free Exercise Clause claims omitted.]

We turn, finally, to petitioners' assertion that disallowing their claimed deduction is at odds with the IRS' longstanding practice of permitting taxpayers to deduct payments made to other religious institutions in connection with certain religious practices. Through the appellate stages of this litigation, this claim was framed essentially as one of selective prosecution. The Courts of Appeals for the First and Ninth Circuits summarily rejected this claim, finding no evidence of the intentional governmental discrimination necessary to support such a claim.

In their arguments to this Court, petitioners have shifted emphasis. They now make two closely related claims. First, the IRS has accorded payments for auditing and training disparately harsh treatment compared to payments to other churches and synagogues for their religious services: Recognition of a comparable deduction for auditing and training payments is necessary to cure this administrative inconsistency. Second, Congress, in modifying § 170 over the years, has impliedly acquiesced in the deductibility of payments to these other faiths; because payments for auditing and training are indistinguishable from these other payments, they fall within the principle acquiesced in by Congress that payments for religious services are deductible under § 170.

Although the Commission[er] demurred at oral argument as to whether the IRS, in fact, permits taxpayers to deduct payments made to purchase services from other churches and synagogues, the Commissioner's periodic revenue rulings have stated the IRS' position rather clearly. A 1971 ruling, still in effect, states: "Pew rents, building fund assessments, and periodic dues paid to a church . . . are all methods of making contributions to the church, and such payments are deductible as charitable contributions within the limitations set out in section 170 of the Code." Rev.Rul. 70-47, 1970-1 Cum.Bull. 49 (superseding A.R.M. 2, Cum.Bull. 150 (1919)). We also assume for purposes of argument that the IRS also allows taxpayers to deduct "specified payments for attendance at High Holy Day services, for tithes, for torah readings and for memorial plaques." *Foley v. Commissioner,* 844 F.2d, at 94, 96.

The development of the present litigation, however, makes it impossible for us to resolve petitioners' claim that they have received unjustifiably harsh treatment compared to adherents of other religions. The relevant inquiry in determining whether a payment is a "contribution or gift" under § 170 is, as we have noted, not whether the payment secures religious benefits or access to religious services, but whether the transaction in which the payment is involved is structured as a *quid pro quo* exchange. To make such a determination in this case, the Tax Court heard testimony and received documentary proof as to the terms and structure of the auditing and training transactions; from this evidence it made factual findings upon which it based its conclusion of nondeductibility, a conclusion we have held consonant with § 170 and with the First Amendment.

Perhaps because the theory of administrative inconsistency emerged only on appeal, petitioners did not endeavor at trial to adduce from the IRS or other sources any specific evidence about other religious faiths' transactions. The IRS' revenue rulings, which merely state the agency's conclusions as to deductibility and which have apparently never been reviewed by the Tax Court or any other judicial body, also provide no specific facts about the nature of these other faiths' transactions. In the absence of such facts, we simply have no way (other than the wholly illegitimate one of relying on our personal experiences and observations) to appraise accurately whether the IRS' revenue rulings have correctly applied a *quid pro quo* analysis with respect to any or all of the religious practices in question. We do not know, for example, whether payments for other faiths' services are truly obligatory or whether any or all of these services are generally provided whether or not the encouraged "mandatory" payment is made.

The IRS' application of the "contribution or gift" standard may be right or wrong with respect to these other faiths, or it may be right with respect to some religious practices and wrong with respect to others. It may also be that some of these payments are appropriately classified as partially deductible "dual payments." With respect to those religions where the structure of transactions involving religious services is established not centrally but by individual congregations, the proper point of reference for a *quid pro quo* analysis might be the individual congregation, not the religion as a whole. Only upon a proper factual record could we make these determinations. Absent such a record, we must reject petitioners' administrative consistency argument.

[handwritten margin note: Court's R[?] for rejecting for unfair treatment arg.]

Petitioners' congressional acquiescence claim fails for similar reasons. Even if one assumes that Congress has acquiesced in the IRS' ruling with respect to "[p]ew rents, building fund assessments, and periodic dues," Rev.Rul. 70-47, 1970-1 Cum.Bull. 49, the fact is that the IRS' 1971 ruling articulates no broad principle of deductibility, but instead merely identifies as deductible three discrete types of payments. Having before us no information about the nature or structure of these three payments, we have no way of discerning any possible unifying principle, let alone whether such a principle would embrace payments for auditing and training sessions.

For the reasons stated herein, the judgments of the Courts of Appeals are hereby *Affirmed.*

Justice BRENNAN and Justice KENNEDY took no part in the consideration or decision of these cases.

Justice O'CONNOR, with whom Justice SCALIA joins, dissenting.

The Court today acquiesces in the decision of the Internal Revenue Service (IRS) to manufacture a singular exception to its 70-year practice of allowing fixed payments indistinguishable from those made by petitioners to be deducted as charitable contributions. Because the IRS cannot constitutionally be allowed to select which religions will receive the benefit of its past rulings, I respectfully dissent.

* * *

Post-Case Follow-Up

Concluding that payments made for training and auditing sessions did not constitute deductible charitable contributions, the Court in *Hernandez* emphasized that the larger transaction was a "quintessential quid pro quo" exchange. In full dissent, Justices O'Connor and Scalia opined that disallowing a charitable contribution deduction in this context was tantamount to allowing the IRS to decide which religions it would favor and which religions it would frown upon. They had a point, to be sure, but there remains the basic question whether those facing mandatory fees in order to realize a specific benefit in the religious context should, as a group, enjoy a charitable contribution deduction or be barred from taking such a deduction. Maybe the best and brightest line to draw would be one at which only wholly voluntary contributions are deductible, but even this line is problematic. Some church members pay tithes (which appear wholly voluntary in a sense) because they consider it religious obligation. Do you think Congress would seek to eliminate the deductibility of tithes?

Can § 170(f)(8)(B) inform the analysis? That provision addresses substantiation requirements and dictates that if an individual receives solely an intangible religious benefit as a result of making a donation at or above a specific dollar threshold, the receiving entity's contribution acknowledgement must state this fact.

Even if this provision established a clear and bright line, little justifies the conclusion that a substantiation rule supports or bars a charitable contribution deduction. In the end, it appears that the dissenters in *Hernandez* won the war, at least as far as Scientologists are concerned. A few years after the Court's decision, the IRS and the Church of Scientology entered into a closing agreement under which those paying for "training" or "auditing" sessions could take a charitable contribution deduction under § 170. *See* Allan J. Samansky, *Deductibility of Contributions to Religious Institutions*, 24 VA. TAX REV. 65 (2004). Indeed, the IRS went so far as to withdraw a prior Revenue Ruling that was fully consistent with the Court's holding in *Hernandez*. *See* Rev. Rul. 93-73, 1993-2 C.B. 75 (stating in its entirety: "Revenue Ruling 78-189, 1978-1 C.B. 68, is obsoleted."). These developments work rather well for Scientologists with respect to auditing and training, but where does that leave those that the IRS has not sanctified? Apparently, they now stand on fairly firm though not altogether holy ground. Revenue Ruling 70-47 and decisions like *Foley* leave considerable room for optimism, but not every transaction is in the clear. In *Sklar v. Commissioner*, the taxpayers attempted to take a charitable contribution deduction with respect to part of the cost of sending their children to a Jewish day school. They reasoned that the deduction was warranted because their children spent part of the day receiving religious instruction. The courts have not been sympathetic, typically reasoning that the Sklars simply paid for the education of their children and cannot be viewed as having made a charitable contribution to a religious organization. *See Sklar v. Comm'r*, 125 T.C. 28 (2005), *aff'd*, 549 F.3d 1252 (9th Cir. 2008), *cert. den.*, 558 U.S. 829 (2009).

Hernandez v. Commissioner: Real Life Applications

For the following questions, please assume that the taxpayer itemizes deductions and is not at risk of exceeding deduction caps.

1. In celebration of their son's 30th birthday, Maggie and Bert Hamilton purchased him a motorcycle. Sadly enough, their son, Glenn, died a few months later in an accident that occurred as he raced on his motorcycle against one of his friends. Although Maggie and Bert pleaded with the Board of Deacons at their local church to allow Glenn's funeral services to be held there, the Board refused, noting that their son was not a member of the church and, worse yet, was known to be a long-time troublemaker (i.e., incorrigible sinner) in the community. Maggie and Bert promised that if the Board allowed the services to be held at the church, they would contribute $1,000. The Board agreed. Assuming the church is described in § 170(c), may the Hamiltons take a charitable contribution deduction in connection with this donation?

2. Angelina and her husband, Mark, are members of the Greater Greenfield Baptist Church. In fact, they were married at the facility 10 years ago in a thrilling and majestic double-ring ceremony. Unfortunately, they have not found domestic bliss or anything remotely resembling it, and they now feel the need for

counseling to stave off divorce. The church offers faith-based marital counseling to couples but requires that they make a fixed, regular donation to the church (prior to each session and in accord with a fixed fee schedule) during the course of therapy. Assume that the church is described in § 170(c). May Angelina and Mark take a deduction with respect to any fee-schedule-based donations made to the church in exchange for marital counseling?

3. Esther has been religious all her life, and she credits her financial success to her enduring faith and God's benevolence. She has fond memories of attending Sunday school, and she recently decided to donate $10,000 to the church she attended as a child to fund the purchase of both Sunday school books and inscribed, leather-bound bibles for graduating high school seniors on their way to college. Assume that Esther's church is described in § 170(c). May Esther take a charitable contribution deduction with respect to her donation?

TABLE 11.1   Funding-Raising by the Church: The Decidedly Mixed Results

Sagrada Família	Christ the Redeemer	The Protestant Reformation
Funded by private donations and consecrated as a minor basilica in 2010, the magnificent Sagrada Família is Antoni Gaudí's crowning architectural achievement. Work on the structure began in 1882, but it remains unfinished (with a 2026 projected completion date). The structure has the following three façades: Nativity (scenes from Christ's birth), Passion (scenes from Christ's betrayal and crucifixion), and Glory (ascent of sinners from death to judgment and then to glory (or hell)). *See* B. Jollands and P. Fisher, 100 Landmarks of the World 136–39 (Parragon 2011).	An inspiring and visually commanding presence, the statue Christ the Redeemer stands atop Corcovado Mountain in Rio de Janeiro, Brazil. Construction of a religious monument on "hunchback" mountain was the brainchild of Father Pedro Maria Boss. The Catholic Circle of Rio began fundraising for the effort in 1921. The statue's inauguration ceremony took place on October 12, 1931. The work remains one of the largest Art Deco structures ever built and ranks as one of the New Seven Wonders of the World. *See* B. Jollands and P. Fisher, 100 Landmarks of the World 42–43 (Parragon 2011).	During the sixteenth century, the Roman Catholic Church undertook the sale of indulgences. A purchase would remit sin, thereby reducing a given soul's time in purgatory prior to its entry into the glory of paradise. Incensed by this practice, Martin Luther nailed his infamous 95 theses to the church door at Wittenburg and thereby sparked the Protestant Reformation. *See* Michael H. Hart, The 100: A Ranking of the Most Influential Persons in History 123–24 (Citadel Press 1992).

Sagrada Família.
Credit: Genova/Shutterstock.com.

Christ the Redeemer.
Credit: Dmitry Petrenko/
Shutterstock.com.

Martin Luther.
Credit: Everett Historical/
Shutterstock.com.

B. TAX-EXEMPT ENTITIES

1. General Rules

As was noted earlier in this chapter, § 170 governs the deductibility of charitable contributions and generally defines the types of organizations eligible to receive such tax-deductible contributions. We now turn to § 501 which does *not* address the deductibility of charitable contributions. Instead, that section clarifies which organizations or entities will qualify as tax-exempt. In general, organizations eligible to receive tax-deductible contributions are, at the same time, tax-exempt entities, but the key is to appreciate that an organization may fall into one category but not the other.

Section 501(a) generally provides that an organization described in § 501(c) or (d) "shall be exempt from taxation under this subtitle." Section 501(c), in turn, sets for a list of organizations with individual paragraphs describing each organization. Most of you have, no doubt, heard of § 501(c)(3) organizations. What you may not have done is examine the language of the statute carefully. Packed with requirements you should take note of, section 501(c)(3) defines (in fairly generic terms) a specific type of tax-exempt organization:

> Corporations, and any community chest, fund, or foundation, organized and operated *exclusively* for religious, charitable, scientific, testing for public safety, literary, or educational purposes, or to foster national or international amateur sports competition (but only if no part of its activities involve the provision of athletic facilities or equipment), or for the prevention of cruelty to children or animals, *no part of the net earnings of which inures to the benefit of any private shareholder or individual,* no *substantial* part of the activities of which is carrying on propaganda, or otherwise attempting, to influence legislation (except as otherwise provided in subsection (h)), and which *does not participate in, or intervene in* (including the publishing or distributing of statements), *any political campaign* on behalf of (or in opposition to) any candidate for public office.

26 U.S.C. § 501(c)(3) (Emphasis added).

As you can see from the statutory language, in order for an entity to qualify as a § 501(c)(3) organization it must be organized and operated for an enumerated purpose; it cannot allow private inurement; it cannot allow a substantial part of its activities to take the form of carrying on propaganda or attempting to influence legislation; and it cannot participate in or intervene in the political campaigns of those seeking public office. Organizations willing to play by the rules should encounter little difficulty getting and maintaining their tax-exempt status. As we will soon see, however, there's more to maintaining tax-exempt status than meets the eye.

2. Public Policy Restrictions

In addition to satisfying and adhering to statutory prerequisites, an organization's activities must also harmonize with prevailing notions of sound public policy if it is to maintain its tax-exempt status. But who gets to decide what does or does not constitute established public policy at a given point in time? Who *should* make that decision? Turn the clock back a few decades and one would find society completely comfortable with segregating the races, preventing women from practicing law, and refusing to allow gays and lesbians to serve openly in the military. Without question, public policy evolves. Does that mean that those seeking to maintain tax-exemption must evolve as well? Maybe so. After all, with tax-exemption, we see Congress's legislative grace at its very height. No organization can claim entitlement to it as matter of right.

Case Preview

Bob Jones University v. United States

For years, Bob Jones University enjoyed tax-exemption even though its policies openly discriminated on the basis of race. Faced with the specter of losing its tax-exemption, it altered its policies but maintained prohibitions regarding interracial dating and marriage. Ultimately, the IRS revoked the university's tax-exempt status. The central issue, of course, is whether the revocation was warranted and whether the IRS or Congress should be the final arbiter as to what does or does not accord with prevailing notions of public policy. As you read *Bob Jones University*, consider the following questions:

1. On what basis did Bob Jones University prohibit interracial dating and marriage?
2. Does the Internal Revenue Code expressly or implicitly condition tax-exemption on adherence to prevailing notions of public policy?
3. If Congress was well aware that the IRS routinely made decisions regarding public policy in this context and failed to intervene, can one conclude, in essence, that Congress ratified or endorsed the IRS's conduct?

Bob Jones University v. United States
461 U.S. 574 (1983)

Chief Justice BURGER delivered the opinion of the Court.

We granted certiorari to decide whether petitioners, nonprofit private schools that prescribe and enforce racially discriminatory admissions standards on the basis of religious doctrine, qualify as tax-exempt organizations under § 501(c)(3) of the Internal Revenue Code of 1954.

Until 1970, the Internal Revenue Service granted tax-exempt status to private schools, without regard to their racial admissions policies, under [§501(c)(3) of the Internal Revenue Code] and granted charitable deductions for contributions to such schools under § 170 of the Code.

Chief Justice Warren E. Burger

Appointed to the U.S. Supreme Court by President Richard M. Nixon, Warren Burger served as Chief Justice of the United States from 1969 to1986.

Credit: Photo courtesy of the Library of Congress.

→ New policy

On January 12, 1970, a three-judge District Court for the District of Columbia issued a preliminary injunction prohibiting the IRS from according tax-exempt status to private schools in Mississippi that discriminated as to admissions on the basis of race. Thereafter, in July 1970, the IRS concluded that it could "no longer legally justify allowing tax-exempt status [under § 501(c)(3)] to private schools which practice racial discrimination." At the same time, the IRS announced that it could not "treat gifts to such schools as charitable deductions for income tax purposes [under § 170]." By letter dated November 30, 1970, the IRS formally notified private schools, including those involved in this case, of this change in policy, "applicable to all private schools in the United States at all levels of education."

On June 30, 1971, the three-judge District Court issued its opinion on the merits of the Mississippi challenge. That court approved the IRS' amended construction of the Tax Code. *** The revised policy on discrimination was formalized in Revenue Ruling 71–447, 1971–2 Cum. Bull. 230:***

Approved

Based on the "national policy to discourage racial discrimination in education," the IRS ruled that "a private school not having a racially nondiscriminatory policy as to students is not 'charitable' within the common law concepts reflected in sections 170 and 501(c)(3) of the Code." *Id.,* at 231.

The application of the IRS construction of these provisions to petitioners, two private schools with racially discriminatory admissions policies, is now before us.

No. 81–3, Bob Jones University v. United States

Bob Jones University is a nonprofit corporation located in Greenville, South Carolina. Its purpose is "to conduct an institution of learning . . ., giving special emphasis to the Christian religion and the ethics revealed in the Holy Scriptures." The corporation operates a school with an enrollment of approximately 5,000 students, from kindergarten through college and graduate school. Bob Jones University is not affiliated with any religious denomination, but is dedicated to the teaching and propagation of its fundamentalist Christian religious beliefs. It is both a religious and educational institution. Its teachers are required to be devout Christians, and all courses at the University are taught according to the Bible. Entering students are screened as to their religious beliefs, and their public and private conduct is strictly regulated by standards promulgated by University authorities.

Religious University

The sponsors of the University genuinely believe that the Bible forbids interracial dating and marriage. To effectuate these views, Negroes were completely excluded until 1971. From 1971 to May 1975, the University accepted no applications from unmarried Negroes, but did accept applications from Negroes married within their race.

discrimination by university

Following the decision of the United States Court of Appeals for the Fourth Circuit in *McCrary v. Runyon,* 515 F.2d 1082 (4th Cir. 1975), prohibiting racial exclusion from private schools, the University revised its policy. Since May 29, 1975, the University has permitted unmarried Negroes to enroll; but a disciplinary rule prohibits interracial dating and marriage. That rule reads:

There is to be no interracial dating

1. Students who are partners in an interracial marriage will be expelled.
2. Students who are members of or affiliated with any group or organization which holds as one of its goals or advocates interracial marriage will be expelled.
3. Students who date outside their own race will be expelled.
4. Students who espouse, promote, or encourage others to violate the University's dating rules and regulations will be expelled.

The University continues to deny admission to applicants engaged in an interracial marriage or known to advocate interracial marriage or dating.

Until 1970, the IRS extended tax-exempt status to Bob Jones University under § 501(c)(3). By the letter of November 30, 1970, *** the IRS formally notified the University of the change in IRS policy, and announced its intention to challenge the tax-exempt status of private schools practicing racial discrimination in their admissions policies.

***

On January 19, 1976, the IRS officially revoked the University's tax-exempt status, effective as of December 1, 1970, the day after the University was formally notified of the change in IRS policy. ***

The United States District Court for the District of South Carolina held that revocation of the University's tax-exempt status exceeded the delegated powers of the IRS, was improper under the IRS rulings and procedures, and violated the University's rights under the Religion Clauses of the First Amendment. ***

The Court of Appeals for the Fourth Circuit, in a divided opinion, reversed. ***[T]he Court of Appeals concluded that § 501(c)(3) must be read against the background of charitable trust law. To be eligible for an exemption under that section, an institution must be "charitable" in the common law sense, and therefore must not be contrary to public policy. In the court's view, Bob Jones University did not meet this requirement, since its "racial policies violated the clearly defined public policy, rooted in our Constitution, condemning racial discrimination and, more specifically, the government policy against subsidizing racial discrimination in education, public or private." The court held that the IRS acted within its statutory authority in revoking the University's tax-exempt status. Finally, the Court of Appeals rejected petitioner's arguments that the revocation of the tax exemption violated the Free Exercise and Establishment Clauses of the First Amendment. The case was remanded to the District Court with instructions to dismiss the University's claim . . . . ***

[Discussion of *Goldsboro Christian Schools, Inc. v. United States* omitted.]

We granted certiorari in both cases, and we affirm in each.

In Revenue Ruling 71–447, the IRS formalized the policy first announced in 1970, that § 170 and § 501(c)(3) embrace the common law "charity" concept. Under that view, to qualify for a tax exemption pursuant to § 501(c)(3), an institution must show, first, that it falls within one of the eight categories expressly set forth in that section, and second, that its activity is not contrary to settled public policy.

Rule {

Section 501(c)(3) provides that "[c]orporations . . . organized and operated exclusively for religious, charitable . . . or educational purposes" are entitled to tax exemption. Petitioners argue that the plain language of the statute guarantees them tax-exempt status. They emphasize the absence of any language in the statute expressly requiring all exempt organizations to be "charitable" in the common law sense, and they contend that the disjunctive "or" separating the categories in § 501(c)(3) precludes such a reading. Instead, they argue that if an institution falls within one or more of the specified categories it is automatically entitled to exemption, without regard to whether it also qualifies as "charitable." The Court of Appeals rejected that contention and concluded that petitioners' interpretation of the statute "tears section 501(c)(3) from its roots."

It is a well-established canon of statutory construction that a court should go beyond the literal language of a statute if reliance on that language would defeat the plain purpose of the statute:

> "The general words used in the clause . . ., taken by themselves, and literally construed, without regard to the object in view, would seem to sanction the claim of the plaintiff. But this mode of expounding a statute has never been adopted by any enlightened tribunal — because it is evident that in many cases it would defeat the object which the Legislature intended to accomplish. And it is well settled that, in interpreting a statute, the court will not look merely to a particular clause in which general words may be used, *but will take in connection with it the whole statute . . . and the objects and policy of the law. . . ."* Brown v. Duchesne,* 19 How. 183, 194, 15 L.Ed. 595 (1857) (emphasis added).

Section 501(c)(3) therefore must be analyzed and construed within the framework of the Internal Revenue Code and against the background of the Congressional purposes. Such an examination reveals unmistakable evidence that, underlying all relevant parts of the Code, is the intent that entitlement to tax exemption depends on meeting certain common law standards of charity — namely, that an institution seeking tax-exempt status must serve a public purpose and not be contrary to established public policy.

Congressional intent {

This "charitable" concept appears explicitly in § 170 of the Code. That section contains a list of organizations virtually identical to that contained in § 501(c)(3). It is apparent that Congress intended that list to have the same meaning in both sections. In § 170, Congress used the list of organizations in defining the term "charitable contributions." On its face, therefore, § 170 reveals that Congress' intention was to provide tax benefits to organizations serving charitable purposes. The form of § 170 simply makes plain what common sense and history tell us: in enacting both § 170 and § 501(c)(3), Congress sought to provide tax benefits to charitable organizations, to encourage the development of private institutions that serve a useful public purpose or supplement or take the place of public institutions of the same kind.

Tax exemptions for certain institutions thought beneficial to the social order of the country as a whole, or to a particular community, are deeply rooted in our history, as in that of England. The origins of such exemptions lie in the special privileges that have long been extended to charitable trusts.

***

A corollary to the public benefit principle is the requirement, long recognized in the law of trusts, that the purpose of a charitable trust may not be illegal or violate established public policy. ***

When the Government grants exemptions or allows deductions all taxpayers are affected; the very fact of the exemption or deduction for the donor means that other taxpayers can be said to be indirect and vicarious "donors." Charitable exemptions are justified on the basis that the exempt entity confers a public benefit — a benefit which the society or the community may not itself choose or be able to provide, or which supplements and advances the work of public institutions already supported by tax revenues. History buttresses logic to make clear that, to warrant exemption under § 501(c)(3), an institution must fall within a category specified in that section and must demonstrably serve and be in harmony with the public interest. The institution's purpose must not be so at odds with the common community conscience as to undermine any public benefit that might otherwise be conferred.

We are bound to approach these questions with full awareness that determinations of public benefit and public policy are sensitive matters with serious implications for the institutions affected; a declaration that a given institution is not "charitable" should be made only where there can be no doubt that the activity involved is contrary to a fundamental public policy. But there can no longer be any doubt that racial discrimination in education violates deeply and widely accepted views of elementary justice. Prior to 1954, public education in many places still was conducted under the pall of *Plessy v. Ferguson,* 163 U.S. 537, 16 S. Ct. 1138, 41 L. Ed. 256 (1896); racial segregation in primary and secondary education prevailed in many parts of the country. This Court's decision in *Brown v. Board of Education,* 347 U.S. 483, 74 S. Ct. 686, 98 L. Ed. 873 (1954), signalled an end to that era. Over the past quarter of a century, every pronouncement of this Court and myriad Acts of Congress and Executive Orders attest a firm national policy to prohibit racial segregation and discrimination in public education.

An unbroken line of cases following *Brown v. Board of Education* establishes beyond doubt this Court's view that racial discrimination in education violates a most fundamental national public policy, as well as rights of individuals. ***

Few social or political issues in our history have been more vigorously debated and more extensively ventilated than the issue of racial discrimination, particularly in education. Given the stress and anguish of the history of efforts to escape from the shackles of the "separate but equal" doctrine of *Plessy v. Ferguson, supra,* it cannot be said that educational institutions that, for whatever reasons, practice racial discrimination, are institutions exercising "beneficial and stabilizing influences in community life," *Walz v. Tax Comm'n,* 397 U.S. 664, 673, 90 S. Ct. 1409, 1413, 25 L. Ed. 2d 697 (1970), or should be encouraged by having all taxpayers share in their support by way of special tax status.

***

Whatever may be the rationale for such private schools' policies, and however sincere the rationale may be, racial discrimination in education is contrary to public policy. Racially discriminatory educational institutions cannot be viewed as conferring a public benefit within the "charitable" concept discussed earlier, or within the Congressional intent underlying § 170 and § 501(c)(3).

Petitioners contend that, regardless of whether the IRS properly concluded that racially discriminatory private schools violate public policy, only Congress can alter the scope of § 170 and § 501(c)(3). Petitioners accordingly argue that the IRS overstepped its lawful bounds in issuing its 1970 and 1971 rulings.

Yet ever since the inception of the tax code, Congress has seen fit to vest in those administering the tax laws very broad authority to interpret those laws. ***

Congress, the source of IRS authority, can modify IRS rulings it considers improper; and courts exercise review over IRS actions. In the first instance, however, the responsibility for construing the Code falls to the IRS. Since Congress cannot be expected to anticipate every conceivable problem that can arise or to carry out day-to-day oversight, it relies on the administrators and on the courts to implement the legislative will. Administrators, like judges, are under oath to do so.

In § 170 and § 501(c)(3), Congress has identified categories of traditionally exempt institutions and has specified certain additional requirements for tax exemption. Yet the need for continuing interpretation of those statutes is unavoidable. For more than 60 years, the IRS and its predecessors have constantly been called upon to interpret these and comparable provisions, and in doing so have referred consistently to principles of charitable trust law. ***

Guided, of course, by the Code, the IRS has the responsibility, in the first instance, to determine whether a particular entity is "charitable" for purposes of § 170 and § 501(c)(3). This in turn may necessitate later determinations of whether given activities so violate public policy that the entities involved cannot be deemed to provide a public benefit worthy of "charitable" status. We emphasize, however, that these sensitive determinations should be made only where there is no doubt that the organization's activities violate fundamental public policy.

On the record before us, there can be no doubt as to the national policy. *** Clearly an educational institution engaging in practices affirmatively at odds with this declared position of the whole government cannot be seen as exercising a "beneficial and stabilizing influenc[e] in community life," *Walz v. Tax Comm'n, supra,* 397 U.S., at 673, 90 S. Ct., at 1413, and is not "charitable," within the meaning of § 170 and § 501(c)(3). We therefore hold that the IRS did not exceed its authority when it announced its interpretation of § 170 and § 501(c)(3) in 1970 and 1971.

The actions of Congress since 1970 leave no doubt that the IRS reached the correct conclusion in exercising its authority. It is, of course, not unknown for independent agencies or the Executive Branch to misconstrue the intent of a statute; Congress can and often does correct such misconceptions, if the courts have not done so. Yet for a dozen years Congress has been made aware — acutely aware — of the IRS rulings of 1970 and 1971. As we noted earlier, few issues have been the subject of more vigorous and widespread debate and discussion in and out of Congress than those related to racial segregation in education. Sincere adherents advocating contrary views have ventilated the subject for well over three decades. Failure of Congress to modify the IRS rulings of 1970 and 1971, of which Congress was, by its own studies and by public discourse, constantly reminded; and Congress' awareness of the denial of tax-exempt status for racially discriminatory schools when enacting other and related legislation make out an unusually strong case of legislative acquiescence in and ratification by implication of the 1970 and 1971 rulings.

***

Petitioners contend that, even if the Commissioner's policy is valid as to nonreligious private schools, that policy cannot constitutionally be applied to schools that engage in racial discrimination on the basis of sincerely held religious beliefs. As to such schools, it is argued that the IRS construction of § 170 and § 501(c)(3) violates their free exercise rights under the Religion Clauses of the First Amendment. This contention presents claims not heretofore considered by this Court in precisely this context. ***

The governmental interest at stake here is compelling. [T]he Government has a fundamental, overriding interest in eradicating racial discrimination in education — discrimination that prevailed, with official approval, for the first 165 years of this Nation's history. That governmental interest substantially outweighs whatever burden denial of tax benefits places on petitioners' exercise of their religious beliefs. The interests asserted by petitioners cannot be accommodated with that compelling governmental interest, and no "less restrictive means," are available to achieve the governmental interest.

***

The judgments of the Court of Appeals are, accordingly,
Affirmed.
Justice POWELL, concurring in part and concurring in the judgment.
I join the Court's judgment, along with [its holding] that the denial of tax exemptions to petitioners does not violate the First Amendment. I write separately because I am troubled by the broader implications of the Court's opinion with respect to the authority of the Internal Revenue Service (IRS) and its construction of §§ 170(c) and 501(c)(3) of the Internal Revenue Code.

Federal taxes are not imposed on organizations "operated exclusively for religious, charitable, scientific, testing for public safety, literary, or educational purposes . . . ." 26 U.S.C. § 501(c)(3). The Code also permits a tax deduction for contributions made to these organizations. § 170(c). It is clear that petitioners, organizations incorporated for educational purposes, fall within the language of the statute. It also is clear that the language itself does not mandate refusal of tax-exempt status to any private school that maintains a racially discriminatory admissions policy. Accordingly, there is force in Justice REHNQUIST's argument that §§ 170(c) and 501(c)(3) should be construed as setting forth the only criteria Congress has established for qualification as a tax-exempt organization. Indeed, were we writing prior to the history detailed in the Court's opinion, this could well be the construction I would adopt. But there has been a decade of acceptance that is persuasive in the circumstances of this case, and

I conclude that there are now sufficient reasons for accepting the IRS's construction of the Code as proscribing tax exemptions for schools that discriminate on the basis of race as a matter of policy.

I cannot say that this construction of the Code, adopted by the IRS in 1970 and upheld by the Court of Appeals below, is without logical support. The statutory terms are not self-defining, and it is plausible that in some instances an organization seeking a tax exemption might act in a manner so clearly contrary to the purposes of our laws that it could not be deemed to serve the enumerated statutory purposes. And, as the Court notes, if any national policy is sufficiently fundamental to constitute such an overriding limitation on the availability of tax-exempt status under § 501(c)(3), it is the policy against racial discrimination in education. Finally, and of critical importance for me, the subsequent actions of Congress present "an unusually strong case of legislative acquiescence in and ratification by implication of the [IRS'] 1970 and 1971 rulings" with respect to racially discriminatory schools. ***

I therefore concur in the Court's judgment that tax-exempt status under §§ 170(c) and 501(c)(3) is not available to private schools that concededly are racially discriminatory. I do not agree, however, with the Court's more general explanation of the justifications for the tax exemptions provided to charitable organizations. ***

With all respect, I am unconvinced that the critical question in determining tax-exempt status is whether an individual organization provides a clear "public benefit" as defined by the Court. Over 106,000 organizations filed § 501(c)(3) returns in 1981. I find it impossible to believe that all or even most of those organizations could prove that they "demonstrably serve and [are] in harmony with the public interest" or that they are "beneficial and stabilizing influences in community life." Nor I am prepared to say that petitioners, because of their racially discriminatory policies, necessarily contribute nothing of benefit to the community. It is clear from the substantially secular character of the curricula and degrees offered that petitioners provide educational benefits.

Even more troubling to me is the element of conformity that appears to inform the Court's analysis. The Court asserts that an exempt organization must "demonstrably serve and be in harmony with the public interest," must have a purpose that comports with "the common community conscience," and must not act in a manner "affirmatively at odds with [the] declared position of the whole government." Taken together, these passages suggest that the primary function of a tax-exempt organization is to act on behalf of the Government in carrying out governmentally approved policies. In my opinion, such a view of § 501(c)(3) ignores the important role played by tax exemptions in encouraging diverse, indeed often sharply conflicting, activities and viewpoints. ***

I am unwilling to join any suggestion that the Internal Revenue Service is invested with authority to decide which public policies are sufficiently "fundamental" to require denial of tax exemptions. Its business is to administer laws designed to produce revenue for the Government, not to promote "public policy." ***

The Court's decision upholds IRS Revenue Ruling 71–447, and thus resolves the question whether tax-exempt status is available to private schools that openly maintain racially discriminatory admissions policies. There no longer is any justification for *Congress* to hesitate — as it apparently has — in articulating and codifying its desired policy as to tax exemptions for discriminatory organizations. Many questions remain, such as whether organizations that violate other policies should receive tax-exempt status under § 501(c)(3). These should be legislative policy choices. *** The contours of public policy should be determined by Congress, not by judges or the IRS.

Justice REHNQUIST, dissenting.

The Court points out that there is a strong national policy in this country against racial discrimination. To the extent that the Court states that Congress in furtherance of this policy could deny tax-exempt status to educational institutions that promote racial discrimination, I readily agree. But, unlike the Court, I am convinced that Congress simply has failed to take this action and, as this Court has said over and over again, regardless of our view on the propriety of Congress' failure to legislate we are not constitutionally empowered to act for them.

can't take power away from congress

***

Therefore, it is my view that unless and until Congress affirmatively amends § 501(c)(3) to require more, the IRS is without authority to deny petitioners § 501(c)(3) status. For this reason, I would reverse the Court of Appeals.

Post-Case Follow-Up   Bob Jones University proved willing to admit African-Americans but remained aggressively hostile to interracial dating. Notwithstanding the fact that the university's policies were rooted in religious belief, the Court concluded that such policies were offensive to prevailing notions of public policy and, accordingly, that the university's conduct was not charitable in the common law sense. The Court went on to hold that the IRS had not exceeded its authority in revoking the university's tax-exempt status. Any burden on the university's free exercise of religion, noted the Court, was necessary to achieve a compelling governmental interest. Although the Court reasoned that Congress had effectively ratified the IRS's determinations in this regard, Justice Powell (in his concurring opinion) emphasized that Congress had no reason to delay definitive action. Waxing passive, Justice Rehnquist (in dissent) argued that even in the face of clear public policy, the Court simply lacked the authority to effect change.

The U.S. Constitution clearly provides for a division of labor within the federal government, and in theory at least, we have an effective system of checks and balances. But practical realities matter. Congress may hold the legislative power, but that branch of government continues to prove itself most vulnerable to the shifting whims of the voting public and increasingly prone to spectacular displays of gridlock. Modern history confirms that if American society needs to make a giant leap forward, appeal to the highly political branches may leave us standing in place for decades. Only from the U.S. Supreme Court did we get earth-shifting, landmark decisions like *Brown v. Board of Education*, 347 U.S. 483 (1954), *Roe v. Wade*, 410 U.S. 113 (1973), and *Obergefell v. Hodges*, 135 S. Ct. 2584 (2015). The Court may not always get it right, even when acting in accord with prevailing public senti-ment — *see e.g.*, *Plessy v. Ferguson*, 163 U.S. 537 (1896) — but in the wake of healthy evolution of the public mindset, it has the power to move the nation forward with dispatch.

Bob Jones University answered the pressing question of the day. In recent years, however, that decision has given rise to new issues. For example, a faith-based edu-cational institution might have any number of policies prohibiting premarital sex (applicable to students, faculty, administrators, and staff). But what if that univer-sity (1) refuses to hire gays or lesbians and (2) suspends those guilty of heterosexual premarital sex (including adultery) but terminates or expels those it discovers to be gay, bisexual, or lesbian? If such an institution is tax-exempt and eligible to receive tax-deductible charitable contributions, does *Bob Jones University* mandate (or at least provide clear justification for) revocation of the university's tax-exempt status under § 501 and its ability to receive tax-deductible charitable contributions under § 170?

Bob Jones University v. United States: Real Life Applications

1. The School is an accredited institution providing religious and secular educa-tion for students between the ages of 6 and 18. Its stated policies allow admis-sion only of boys who are adherents of Gregarianism, a well-known religion. Students must comply with various rules concerning diet, dress, holy day obser-vances, and daily prayers. Assuming it otherwise complies with § 501(c)(3), should The School qualify as tax-exempt?

2. *Same facts as Question #1*, except that the school admits all qualified students, regardless of faith or gender but prohibits any interfaith dating or marriage.

3. The Institution is a nationally accredited, faith-based university. Its founders and administrators, devout Puritans, believe that any form of same-sex conduct is sinful. Accordingly, it refuses to admit or hire anyone who identifies as gay, lesbian, or bisexual. Employees or students found to have engaged in any form of same-sex conduct are expelled or terminated. Assuming The Institution is described in § 501(c)(3), should it qualify as tax-exempt?

3. The Private Inurement Prohibition

Pride, sloth, gluttony, envy, lust, and wrath are six of the seven deadly sins, and although each of the foregoing claims many victims, it is only the seventh that promises swift and potentially unpleasant federal income tax consequences. Ava-rice. Ideally, an organization fulfilling its charitable mission will enjoy tax-exempt status under § 501 and the ability to receive tax-deductible contributions under § 170. But those interested more in executing their personal, financial missions than in advancing the commonweal may perceive an opportunity to line their pockets with the donations of others, all under the monkish hooded cloak of good intent. Accordingly, Congress explicitly forbids private inurement both in defining tax-exempt entities in § 501 and in defining entities eligible to receive tax-deductible contributions under § 170. Without doubt, entities may lose their tax-exemption or fall outside the bounds of § 170 for any number of reasons, but in many instances, private inurement is the culprit.

Case Preview

Freedom Church of Revelation v. United States

The taxpayers in *Freedom Church of Revelation* founded the organization and soon secured tax-exempt status from the IRS. Thereafter, the church actively sought out new "adherents," but as it turns out an individual interested in the organization could get "minister" credentials merely by paying a fee, and if he arranged his personal and church affairs in accord with church directives, he could substantially lower his federal income tax obligations. These realities prompted the IRS to take a closer look at the organization to ascertain whether it operated exclusively for appropriate charitable purposes, whether it managed to steer clear of private inurement, and whether its tax-exempt status merited retroactive revocation. The Service's findings should not come as a surprise. Nonetheless, consider the following questions as you read the case:

1. Why was the Freedom Church of Revelation founded, and what are its core and central tenets?
2. What is the operational test, and did this organization satisfy it?
3. Do you believe that the IRS should have the power to revoke tax-exempt status retroactively?

Freedom Church of Revelation v. United States
588 F. Supp. 693 (D. D.C. 1984)

JUNE L. GREEN, District Judge.

In this action, plaintiff seeks a declaratory judgment *** that it continues to qualify as an exempt organization under [§ 501(c)(3) of the Internal Revenue Code of 1954]. *** For the reasons stated below, the Court revokes retroactively the exempt status of plaintiff, effective for all tax years beginning with 1978.

H: Tax exempt status revoked

FINDINGS OF FACT

On March 8, 1979, plaintiff Freedom Church of Revelation ("Freedom Church") applied for recognition as a tax-exempt organization pursuant to section 501(c)(3) of the Code. On June 8, 1979, the Commissioner of IRS determined that plaintiff was exempt under section 501(c)(3), based upon information supplied by plaintiff in its application for recognition of exemption, as well as the assumption that plaintiff would operate in the manner it had represented in its application.

On October 14, 1979, following an examination of plaintiff's operations, the IRS informed plaintiff that it was proposing to revoke plaintiff's exemption under section 501(c)(3). Plaintiff appealed this proposed revocation to the IRS. On September 30, 1982, plaintiff received a final determination that its recognition as a tax-exempt organization under section 501(c)(3) had been revoked, effective for the tax year 1978 and all subsequent years.

IRS then revokes because →

In revoking the tax-exempt status of plaintiff, the IRS gave the following reasons:

1. You are not organized and operated exclusively for religious, charitable, educational or any other § 501(c)(3) purpose.
2. You are not organized and operated exclusively for public purposes.
3. You are operated for the benefit of private individuals.

As a result of this decision, on December 28, 1982, plaintiff filed the instant action under the declaratory judgment provisions of 26 U.S.C. § 7428. ***

In lieu of trial in this matter, the parties agreed to submit their respective cases on the papers. ***

CONCLUSIONS OF LAW

Section 501(a) of the Code exempts certain organizations from taxation, including those organizations described in Section 501(c)(3) as follows:

> Corporations . . . organized and operated exclusively for religious, charitable, scientific . . . or educational purposes . . . no part of the net earnings of which inures to the benefit of any private shareholder or individual, no substantial part of the activities of which is carrying on propaganda, or otherwise attempting, to influence legislation . . . and which does not participate in, or intervene in (including the publishing or distributing of statements), any political campaign on behalf of any candidate for public office.

26 U.S.C. § 501(c)(3).

Section 7428(a) of the Code states in relevant part:

> (a) *Creation of remedy.* — In the case of actual controversy involving —
> (1) a determination by the Secretary —
> (A) with respect to the initial qualification or continuing qualification of an organization as an organization described in section 501(c)(3) which is exempt from tax under section 501(a) or as an organization described in section 170(c)(2),
>
> upon the filing of an appropriate pleading, the United States Tax Court, the United States Claims Court, or the district court of the United States for the District of Columbia may make a declaration with respect to such initial qualification or continuing qualification . . . . Any such declaration shall have the force and effect of a decision of the Tax Court or a final judgment or decree of the district court or the Claims Court, as the case may be, and shall be reviewable as such. For purposes of this section, a determination with respect to a continuing qualification or continuing classification includes any revocation of or other change in a qualification or classification.

26 U.S.C. § 7428(a).

At the outset, the Court notes that an action brought by an organization under section 7428(a), challenging revocation of its existing section 501(c)(3) recognition, is a *de novo* proceeding in which neither the parties nor the Court is limited to the administrative record. The burden of proof is on the organization to overcome the grounds set forth in the IRS' revocation letter.

To qualify as an exempt organization under section 501(c)(3), plaintiff must prove (1) that it is "operated exclusively" for tax-exempt purposes and (2) that no part of its net earnings inured to the benefit of any private individual.

With regard to the first requirement of section 501(c)(3), *i.e.,* that an organization must be operated exclusively for an exempt purpose, the applicable regulations state as follows:

> (c) *Operational test* — (1) *Primary activities.* An organization will be regarded as "operated exclusively" for one or more exempt purposes only if it engages primarily in activities which accomplish one or more of such exempt purposes specified in section 501(c)(3). *An organization will not be so regarded if more than an insubstantial part of its activities is not in furtherance of an exempt purpose.*

26 C.F.R. § 1.501(c)(3)–1(c)(1) (emphasis added).

Therefore, if the nonexempt activities of plaintiff are more than incidental or insubstantial, it is not entitled to continuing qualification as an exempt organization.

The Court has examined the entire record in this action, including all of the material submitted by plaintiff. The documents, affidavits and letters submitted by plaintiff's leaders and members do not establish that plaintiff operated exclusively for religious, charitable or educational purposes. Plaintiff has failed to provide any financial records to buttress its claims that it is organized primarily for exempt purposes under section 501(c)(3). Moreover, the United States has presented evidence, which has not been refuted, that a substantial activity engaged in by plaintiff was the promotion of tax-avoidance schemes.

The Declarations of Prince L. Davis, a former high official of Freedom Church, and Charles L. Henry, a former "minister" of Freedom Church, submitted as two of defendant's supplemental exhibits, indicate that they became aware of Freedom Church by attending a seminar conducted by Dorothy Turner, a Director of Freedom Church, and Ruben Jiggetts, the avowed Bishop of Freedom Church for the Washington metropolitan area. These seminars were advertised as a way for people to reduce their tax liability legally by approximately seventy to 100 percent. Individuals who attended these seminars were told that they could obtain ministers' credentials by donating $4,100 to Freedom Church. A donation of $3,600 was acceptable if individuals joined within ten days of the seminar. It was strongly suggested that this donation be made in cash. They also were told that once an individual became a minister he could reduce his tax liability legally by:

> open[ing] a bank account in the name of Freedom Church of Revelation using a charter number that would be contained in the "letter of direction," and could "donate" 50% of his income to this account, deducting this 50% of his income on his Federal income tax return as a charitable contribution. Ms. Turner outlined how the "minister" could then use the funds in this account as a "parsonage allowance" for personal expenses, such as mortgage, rent, interest, taxes, utilities, and [other items.

They could] also use the funds in this account for such items as investments, automobiles, insurance, and [other specific items]. The "Freedom or Control?" flyer *** was one of the slides presented at the seminar. Among the other slides was a slide of the original letter of determination from the Internal Revenue Service stating that Freedom Church of Revelation was tax-exempt, and a slide containing a portion of the text of Section 170 of the Internal Revenue Code.

Ms. Turner stated at the seminar that all "ministers" were required to send 1% of all funds passing through their "church" bank accounts to the Freedom Church of Revelation office in Boca Raton, Florida.

The documentary evidence submitted by plaintiff verifies the existence of a substantial nonexempt purpose, *i.e.*, tax avoidance. The "Congregational Management Guidebook," submitted to the Government by plaintiff on July 19, 1983, includes a sample filled-in IRS form, a reprinted IRS publication on valuing donated property, and advice on avoiding social security taxes, state sales taxes, and Federal income taxes. Moreover, Mr. Henry and Mr. Davis bought a booklet and chart at the seminar they attended which corroborate their declarations as to the principal nature of plaintiff's activities. The Court also notes that:

At no time during [the] seminar[s] [attended by Mr. Davis and Mr. Henry] did Ms. Turner or Mr. Jiggetts ever mention anything relating to a specific religion, or church worship services, or any actual charitable acts that the "church" or its "ministers" could perform. Ms. Turner stated that Freedom Church of Revelation was a non-denominational church, and that all "ministers" were free to believe whatever they wanted, and to continue to belong to any other churches or religious organizations.

Davis Declaration at ¶ 9; Henry Declaration at ¶ 9.

The fact that plaintiff has shown independently that it did engage in some charitable work, such as distributing food to the needy, donating $1,000 to Providence House/Willingboro Shelter, a refuge for battered wives and abused children, and donating clothing and money to the Staten Island Development Center, is not enough to entitle plaintiff to continued recognition as an exempt organization. Section 501(c)(3) clearly states that an organization must be operating *exclusively* for religious, charitable, educational or other exempt purposes. Tax avoidance schemes do not qualify as "other exempt purposes." Because more than an insubstantial part of its activities is not in furtherance of an exempt purpose, plaintiff has not met the "operational test" set forth at 26 C.F.R. § 1.501(c)(3)–1(c)(1).

Therefore, the Court finds that plaintiff has failed to meet the first requirement of section 501(c)(3) that it be "operated exclusively" for one or more exempt purposes.

Even assuming *arguendo* that plaintiff did meet its burden of proving that it is "operated exclusively" for an exempt purpose, plaintiff fails to meet the second requirement of section 501(c)(3), *i.e.*, that its assets do not inure to the private benefit of private shareholders or individuals. *See* 26 C.F.R. § 1.501(c)(3)–1(c)(2). A "'private shareholder or individual' refer [s] to persons having a personal and private interest in the activities of the organization[,]" and includes the creator of the organization and his family. 26 C.F.R. §§ 1.501(a)–1(c); 1–501(c)(3)–1(d)(1)(ii). The requirement that there be no private inurement overlaps the requirement that an organization must operate exclusively for exempt purposes. Clearly, if part of an organization's earnings inure to the benefit of private individuals, the organization cannot be operating exclusively for exempt purposes.

The Court must determine whether any individuals benefit financially in a private capacity from the operation of Freedom Church. The amount or extent of the inurement or benefit is not relevant. If any portion of the organization's net earnings inures to the benefit of a private individual, the organization cannot meet the second requirement of section 501(c)(3).

In the instant case, plaintiff has failed to carry its burden of establishing that its earnings did not inure to private individuals. Freedom Church has failed to provide any information on its operation and finances. It has failed to respond to the Davis and Henry Declarations; to explain what happened to the initial "donations" of $3,600 to $4,100 collected from each individual who decided to become a minister; to explain what happened to the one percent (now two percent) of all church accounts collected from each minister; or to explain what happened to the $250 fees collected from each "missionary." Freedom Church has failed to state specifically how it uses this money or even that this money is used by the organization rather than by individual members of Freedom Church. Instead, the record is replete with very general statements by plaintiff's leaders and members extolling its religious, charitable, and educational activities.

In a similar case, *Basic Unit Ministry of Alma Karl Schurig v. United States,* the court stated in pertinent part:

In factual situations such as [these], where there is evident potential for abuse of the exemption provisions and avoidance of taxes, plaintiff must openly and candidly disclose all facts bearing upon the operation and the finances of the organization. *Bubbling Well Church v. Commissioner,* 74 T.C. 531, 535 (1980). That has not been done. Plaintiff did not proffer sufficiently detailed evidence as to the nature of the charitable disbursements, or as to the extent of the maintenance and support of the members. The services which plaintiff claims its members performed for it are characterized more by generalizations than specifics.

Although the Court recognizes that some of the members and officials of Freedom Church have submitted letters, affidavits, and documents describing some of the religious, charitable, and educational activities engaged in by plaintiff, as in *Basic Unit Ministry,* plaintiff has failed to provide sufficiently detailed evidence as to the nature of the charitable disbursements and more importantly, the extent of the maintenance and support of its members. *See id.* The information submitted by plaintiff is not enough to demonstrate positively that a portion of its earnings did not inure to private individuals.

The record also indicates that in July 1980, a Special Agent of the IRS issued administrative summonses to several banks and other institutions in New Jersey, seeking records of accounts in the names of several organizations, including Freedom Church of Revelation, over which Francis John Conti, the founder and overall leader of Freedom Church, or his wife, Marie Conti, had signatory authority. *** On December 11, 1980, the court ordered that the summonses were to be enforced.

Pursuant to these summonses, the IRS obtained, *inter alia,* records of Account No. 031980–3 at Midland Bank and Trust Company, and records of Account No. 129–583–7 at National Community Bank. Both of the accounts were in the name of

Re: Account activity

Freedom Church of Revelation, and both Frank J. Conti and his wife had signatory authority over the accounts.

Summaries of these accounts for the periods specified in the respective summonses (*i.e.,* through the end of 1979) were prepared by the IRS as official agency documents. These accounts contain checks made out to such entities as American Express, New Jersey Bell Telephone, Diners Club, Blue Cross-Blue Shield, and various doctors, dentists, schools, utilities, insurance companies, newspapers, and stores.

A total of $335,592.23 was disbursed by check from these two accounts between July 28, 1979, and December 31, 1979, including $5,489.64 to American Express, and $66,325.09 to International Precious Metals. In the absence of any evidence submitted by plaintiff to explain how the funds in these church accounts were used for legitimate church purposes, the Court must conclude that the funds in these accounts inured to Mr. Conti's personal benefit.

Under any standard of proof, plaintiff has not established that its earnings did not inure to private individuals as required under section 501(c)(3) of the Code. Because plaintiff has failed to meet the requirements of section 501(c)(3), the Court finds that it is not entitled to continuing qualification as an exempt organization.

[The court went on to conclude that retroactive revocation of the taxpayer's tax-exempt status was appropriate.]

CONCLUSION

In accordance with the above, the Court affirms the final determination of the IRS, dated September 30, 1982; declares pursuant to section 7428 of the Code that plaintiff is not entitled to continuing qualification as an exempt organization under sections 501(a) and 501(c)(3) of the Code, and revokes retroactively the exempt status of Freedom Church, effective for all tax years beginning with 1978. An appropriate order is attached.

Post-Case Follow-Up

In this case, the court readily concludes that the Freedom Church of Revelation failed to qualify for tax-exemption under § 501(c)(3) because it failed the operational test and existed largely for the sake of prohibited private inurement. Moreover, the court validated the IRS's retroactive revocation of that tax-exemption. Of course, dressing up a tax-avoidance scheme as a church makes the task of revoking tax-exempt status that much easier. One can rationally assume, however, that private inurement rarely presents itself in such a highly visible manner. Effective lawyering skill will prove key in close cases.

Freedom Church of Revelation v. United States: Real Life Applications

1. For years, Walter has been a diehard football fan. He recently donated $500,000 to his college alma mater (an educational organization described in § 170(c) and § 501(c)(3)), but he restricted the use of the funds to the school's football program. During the past academic year, the school's star quarterback, Michael Firenzi, received a $50,000 athletic scholarship. From a tax perspective, will the award of the scholarship prove problematic for Walter's alma mater?

2. Rev. George Whytfield has been a gifted orator all his life. His is currently the senior pastor at his church and earns a salary far higher than his peers around town. If Rev. Whytfield's church is tax-exempt under § 501(c)(3), will the payment of his extraordinary salary constitute private inurement?

3. The Freedom Church of Genesis enjoys tax-exemption under § 501(c)(3) and is described in § 170(c). Unfortunately, the church's Treasurer takes seriously only a small handful of the Ten Commandments, excluding "Thou shalt not steal." If the Treasurer regularly embezzles $100 from the church, will her activities constitute private inurement and call into question the church's tax-exemption or its ability to receive tax-deductible contributions?

Chapter Summary

- Section 170 provides for the charitable contribution deduction. It also describes which organizations qualify to receive tax-deductible contributions.
- Individuals may not deduct as charitable contributions under § 170 amounts exceeding 50 percent of their contribution base in a given taxable year; for cash contributions made after December 31, 2017, the limit is 60%. A taxpayer may, however, carry forward any excess amounts for five consecutive years. Use of the excess contribution amount in future years will be subject to specific limitations during those taxable years.
- Donations and claimed deductions at certain threshold levels may require donor substantiation (e.g., description, written organization acknowledgement, or a qualified appraisal).
- Section 501(c) describes tax-exempt organizations. It does *not* determine which entities may receive tax-deductible contributions.
- Entities eligible to receive tax-deductible contributions under § 170 are also generally tax-exempt entities under § 501, but do not assume that the two organization types are synonymous.
- Taxpayers making quid pro quo contributions must reduce their contribution amount by the fair market value of the goods and/or services received from the donee organization.
- Even if an organization is described in § 501(c), it may not qualify for tax-exemption if its activities are counter to prevailing notions of public policy.

◼ Entities do not qualify as tax-exempt (or as organizations eligible to receive tax
-deductible contributions) if their operations result in private inurement.

Applying the Rules

1. Javier and Celina Cruz are the founders of Church of the Holy Scriptures, and
   each serves as one of its ministers. Although the Church of the Holy Scriptures
   was originally granted tax-exempt status under § 501(c)(3) of the Code, an audit
   reveals that 90 percent of its funds derive from contributions made by Javier
   and Celina and 90 percent of its expenditures take the form of a housing allowance paid to the couple. Does the church currently qualify as tax-exempt under
   § 501(c)(3)?

2. During 2018, Dahlia had adjusted gross income of $60,000. No longer willing
   to pay for the storage of property she inherited several years ago, Dahlia sold
   the items and contributed $40,000 to The Charity, an organization described
   in § 170(c). How much may Dahlia take as a charitable contribution deduction
   with respect to her 2018 taxable year?

3. Donahue recently attended a fundraising dinner to support an organization
   described in § 170(c). The event cost $550 per plate, and the meal provided to
   each donor had a fair market value of $150. How much may Donohue take as a
   charitable contribution deduction, assuming he does not have to contend with
   numerical caps set forth in § 170 and provides any required substantiation?

4. For several decades, The Hawk Scouts of America ("HSA") has been a tax-
   exempt organization described in § 501(c) and an entity eligible to receive
   tax-deductible contributions (per § 170). Recently, the governing body of HSA
   passed a resolution stating that no individual openly identifying as gay or bisexual could serve as the leader of a troop. Does HSA continue to qualify as a tax-
   exempt organization under § 501(c)?

5. Mark and his wife, Esther, actively participate in the religious life of their community. They recently donated $1,000 to their local temple which is a religious
   organization described in § 170(c). May the couple take a charitable contribution deduction as a result of making this donation?

6. After surviving a mild heart attack, Jamal decided to have as much fun as he
   possibly could in his life. He started a local club, and its central and core mission
   is "the pursuit of happiness and pleasure." Substantially all of the club's activities
   are for those specific purposes, the club's activities are not contrary to public
   policy, and no part of the net earnings of the club inures to the benefit of any private shareholder or individual. Does this club qualify for tax-exemption under
   § 501(c)? Is the club eligible to receive tax-deductible contributions per § 170?

Federal Income Taxation in Practice

1. One of your clients is in the process of purchasing a new home and a new car. Although the new home has enough garage space to accommodate two cars, the client has decided to donate her old used car (worth approximately $2,000) to a charity described in § 170(c). That way, she will not have to have the old car towed to her new home. Please prepare a brief memo summarizing how this donation with be treated for federal income tax purposes and what the donor will be required to provide as substantiation.

2. Assume that you are a junior associate in a large law firm. One of the partners in the tax department would like you to do some research on charitable contributions by individuals and charitable contributions by corporations. He left you a terse voicemail message indicating that "You should find out ASAP whether there are any BNA Portfolios on this." You have never heard of BNA Portfolios, but you plan to be as responsive and helpful as possible. Find out if such a portfolio exists, and update the partner by e-mail.

3. One of the firm's clients (an organization described in § 170(c)) is preparing to host a fund-raising dinner. Although each plate will cost $1,000, each plate purchaser will receive a "swag bag" packed with goodies from the organization. The partner on the matter would like a brief memo outlining any federal income tax consequences flowing from this event (for both the organization and the individual donors).

4. It's the late 1960s, and one of the tax partners in your group has heard other attorneys making reference to Revenue Ruling 69-545. He'd like you to take a quick look at the pronouncement and dictate a short client update for your secretary to type. Go to the tax section of your law library, find the authority, copy it, and prepare the client update (you may avoid the dictaphone and prepare the update on your own).

Ordinary and Necessary Business Expenses

In this chapter, we turn our focus to the treatment of so-called "ordinary" and "necessary" business expenses. After focusing on the concepts of ordinary and necessary in general, we will devote some attention to a few rules that may intervene to alter the treatment of (or even disallow) what would otherwise qualify as a deductible expense.

Key Concepts

- Meaning of "ordinary" and "necessary" business expenses
- Meaning of "carrying on" and "trade or business"
- Limited and situational deductibility of specific items
- Categorical deduction prohibitions

A. "ORDINARY" AND "NECESSARY" IN THE TAX ARENA

During the course of a given tax year, businesses often look to generate revenue by performing fee-based services on behalf of customers, selling goods to consumers at a profit, or undertaking other revenue-generating activities. But rather than taxing businesses on total revenue (i.e., gross receipts), Congress allows businesses to deduct various expenses incurred in connection with their revenue-generating efforts. In

Key Statutory Provisions

- **Internal Revenue Code**
  - § 162(a)(1)–(3)(excluding terminal right-justified language)
  - § 162(c)(1)
  - § 162(e)(1), (3), and (4)
  - § 162(e)(5)(A)–(B)
  - § 162(f)(1)–(4)

Current "Expenses" Versus Capital "Expenditures"

In this chapter, we discuss the various rules and doctrines governing current expenses. These items qualify for immediate deduction. You should mentally distinguish these items from capital expenditures. In general, capital expenditures yield long-term, multiyear benefits, and to the extent that any deduction or offset is available with respect to such expenditures, the allowance is not full and immediate in the current taxable year. We will explore capital expenditures in a later chapter.

that way, Congress more accurately measures business "income." A restaurant, for example, must pay chefs, waiters, and managers, in addition to bearing the costs associated with obtaining electricity and prompt waste disposal. An airline must buy jet fuel in addition to paying pilots, flight attendants, baggage handlers, and customer service personnel. Notwithstanding Congress's generally accommodating legislative grace, businesses (and those active in the business arena) do not have a blank check enabling them to write off any expense with some tangential or remote connection to business activity. Necessarily, boundaries and limits exist. Section 162(a) speaks with a degree of exactitude in allowing a deduction for "all the *ordinary* and *necessary* expenses paid or incurred during the taxable year in carrying on any trade or business ..." (emphasis added). In the next case, we explore the precise meaning of ordinary and necessary in the tax context.

Case Preview

Welch v. Helvering

Welch v. Helvering is landmark precedent. The case involves a taxpayer who, in a stroke of reputation-restoring "brilliance," decided to pay off certain debts of his former (bankrupt) employer. One can certainly understand the taxpayer's desire to restore his reputation. After all, he was working in the same industry and encountering some of the same customers who had recently suffered losses in the wake of the bankruptcy. But should Welch's payment of the debts of his former employer (even if to enhance and restore his own professional reputation) qualify as an ordinary and necessary business expense? Answering that questions requires, as a preliminary matter, agreement on the meaning of "ordinary" and "necessary." As you read the case, consider the following questions:

1. Why did Welch decide to pay the debts of his former employer?
2. How did the Commissioner characterize the payments?
3. Must an expense be regular and habitual to qualify as ordinary in the tax sense?
4. Can discretionary expenditures qualify as necessary in the tax sense?

Welch v. Helvering
290 U.S. 111 (1933)

Mr. Justice CARDOZO delivered the opinion of the Court.

The question to be determined is whether payments by a taxpayer, who is in business as a commission agent, are allowable deductions in the computation of his income if made to the creditors of a bankrupt corporation in an endeavor to strengthen his own standing and credit.

In 1922 petitioner was the secretary of the E. L. Welch Company, a Minnesota corporation, engaged in the grain business. The company was adjudged an involuntary bankrupt, and had a discharge from its debts. Thereafter the petitioner made a contract with the Kellogg Company to purchase grain for it on a commission. In order to re-establish his relations with customers whom he had known when acting for the Welch Company and to solidify his credit and standing, he decided to pay the debts of the Welch business so far as he was able. In fulfillment of that resolve, he made payments of substantial amounts during five successive years. * * * The Commissioner ruled that these payments were not deductible from income as ordinary and necessary expenses, but were rather . . . for the development of reputation and good will. The Board of Tax Appeals sustained the action of the Commissioner, and the Court of Appeals for the Eighth Circuit affirmed. The case is here on certiorari.

"In computing net income there shall be allowed as deductions * * * all the ordinary and necessary expenses paid or incurred during the taxable year in carrying on any trade or business."

We may assume that the payments to creditors of the Welch Company were necessary for the development of the petitioner's business, at least in the sense that they were appropriate and helpful. He certainly thought they were, and we should be slow to override his judgment. But the problem is not solved when the payments are characterized as necessary. * * * There is need to determine whether they are both necessary and ordinary. Now, what is ordinary . . . is none the less a variable affected by time and place and circumstance. Ordinary in this context does not mean that the payments must be habitual or normal in the sense that the same taxpayer will have to make them often. A lawsuit affecting the safety of a business may happen once in a lifetime. The counsel fees may be so heavy that repetition is unlikely. None the less, the expense is an ordinary one because we know from experience that payments for such a purpose, whether the amount is large or small, are the common and accepted means of defense against attack. The situation is unique in the life of the individual affected, but not in the life of the group, the community,

Justice Benjamin N. Cardozo

Associate Justice Benjamin N. Cardozo joined the U.S. Supreme Court in 1932. He was appointed by President Herbert Hoover.

Credit: Photo courtesy of the Library of Congress.

of which he is a part. At such times there are norms of conduct that help to stabilize our judgment, and make it certain and objective. * * * *

We try to classify this act as ordinary or the opposite, and the norms of conduct fail us. No longer can we have recourse to any fund of business experience, to any known business practice. **Men do at times pay the debts of others without legal obligation or the lighter obligation imposed by the usages of trade or by neighborly amenities, but they do not do so ordinarily,** not even though the result might be to heighten their reputation for generosity and opulence. Indeed, if language is to be read in its natural and common meaning, we should have to say that payment in such circumstances, instead of being ordinary is in a high degree extraordinary. There is nothing ordinary in the stimulus evoking it, and none in the response. Here, indeed, as so often in other branches of the law, the decisive distinctions are those of degree and not of kind. One struggles in vain for any verbal formula that will supply a ready touchstone. The standard set up by the statute is not a rule of law; it is rather a way of life. Life in all its fullness must supply the answer to the riddle.

The Commissioner of Internal Revenue resorted to that standard in assessing the petitioner's income, and found that the payments in controversy came closer to [expenditures yielding long-term benefits] than to ordinary and necessary expenses in the operation of a business. His ruling has the support of a presumption of correctness, and the petitioner has the burden of proving it to be wrong. Unless we can say from facts within our knowledge that these are ordinary and necessary expenses according to the ways of conduct and the forms of speech prevailing in the business world, the tax must be confirmed. * * *

The decree should be

Affirmed.

Post-Case Follow-Up

Unwilling to indulge Mr. Welch's attempts to shore up his good will in his business community, the Court concluded that although his expenses were "necessary," they were far from "ordinary." That reality doomed any taxpayer attempt at deduction. The Court notes in passing that "[o]ne struggles in vain for any verbal formula that will supply a ready touchstone. The standard set up by the statute is not a rule of law; it is rather a way of life. Life in all its fullness must supply the answer to the riddle." Even so, the Court left us with language generally embraced as a governing standard. "Ordinary" in the tax sense does not mean "habitual." Rather, an expense will be considered ordinary if incurring and paying it is the common and accepted means of addressing a given business situation in the taxpayer's community. And notwithstanding its everyday, conversational meaning, the word "necessary" does not translate to "required" in the tax world. Instead, so long as incurring and paying a given expense is appropriate and helpful, it will qualify as necessary in the tax sense. One might criticize these standards as hopelessly vague and amorphous, especially in light of the fact that they divorce familiar words from their generally understood meaning. Nonetheless, these standards have served well over the years. To their credit, they are general enough to accommodate various taxpayers, flexible enough to evolve alongside business developments, and yet restrictive enough to keep taxpayers from taking undue advantage (even inadvertently).

Welch v. Helvering: Real Life Applications

For the following questions, please assume that neither statutory nor regulatory rules require that the purchase of the relevant item be treated as a capital expenditure or included in inventory costs.

1. HealerSupply.com, Inc. ("HS") is a corporation operating an online medical supply business. Employees of HS work in a large warehouse. They fill orders by locating inventory via handheld devices (i.e., iPads) and pulling together order items into packages prior to shipment. At this juncture, HS is unique in the sense that no other business filling orders from warehouse inventory provides or even uses iPads in this manner, given that the devices are quite new. If HS buys iPads for all of its warehouse personnel for use in order fulfillment, will such an expense qualify as an ordinary and necessary business expense of HS?

2. Abacus, Inc. ("Abacus") manufactures and sells personal computers. In some of its research facilities, employees must wear "clean room" uniforms, which Abacus provides and maintains at no cost to the employee. Others in the industry follow the same practice. May Abacus deduct the cost of purchasing and maintaining the clean room uniforms as ordinary and necessary business expenses?

3. Disturbed by a recent wave of mass shootings (some of which occurred in the workplace), Annelise Oakley (a sole proprietor) purchased handguns for each of her eighty employees, noting that the gun was for use in keeping the workplace environment safe and for responding to any outbreaks of sudden violence. No other business in the area follows this practice. May Annelise deduct the cost of the firearms as ordinary and necessary business expenses?

4. Grant Kennedy is an American movie star. Recently, he decided to vacation. As per usual, he brought along security personnel to protect him and his family from fans and the ever-present and perpetually aggressive paparazzi. Some movie stars and celebrities maintain a constant private security detail, but others have been known to employ "camouflage" as a means of protecting themselves and their privacy. May Grant deduct the cost of bringing his security personnel with him on vacation as an ordinary and necessary business expense?

5. ***Same facts as Question #4***, except that Grant pays a major amusement park to dismiss all other park guests one hour before standard closing time so that he may enjoy the park without being mobbed by adoring fans, paparazzi, and others. The amusement park accommodated Grant but has never done this for anyone in the past. May Grant deduct the amount paid to the park as an ordinary and necessary business expense?

6. Assume that Grant is a pop star making a cameo appearance in one of the many shows featured at the amusement park. If Grant bears the cost of providing his

own security personnel in connection with the performance (to control fans and paparazzi), may he deduct the cost as an ordinary and necessary business expense, or is this merely a personal expense?

B. PERSONAL EXPENSES REMOTELY CONNECTED TO BUSINESS ACTIVITY

Although taxpayers regularly incur and pay ordinary and necessary expenses in the course of ongoing business operations, personal expenses arise regularly throughout the work day. The cost of a snack purchased during one's break is a nondeductible personal expense, and the cost of lunch shared with colleagues (in a purely social context) surely does not constitute an ordinary and necessary business expense simply because the lunch hour occurs in the middle of the business day. Under some circumstances, however, it's much harder to draw the line between wholly personal and wholly business-related expenses, especially when the personal expense arises while one is "on the clock" or while one is clearly in the process of going about the conduct of one's trade or business. As the next case well demonstrates, the line-drawing exercise can get exceedingly tricky. What passes muster under one set of facts will not clear the hurdle in what some might consider highly analogous circumstances.

Case Preview

Gilliam v. Commissioner

From time to time and in various contexts, businesses incur legal expenses. Attorneys may act as part of a larger team planning and executing a transaction, or they may be retained to defend against or pursue business litigation. No real question arises with respect to whether there is a link between the legal expense and the carrying on of the taxpayer's trade or business. But as the link between the attorney's efforts and the business activity gets progressively weaker, the following question arises: Just how robust must the linkage be to justify a deduction of the legal expense? In *Gilliam*, the Tax Court faced this intriguing issue. An individual on a business trip engaged in activities that gave rise to potential legal liability, but was the fact that he was on a business trip sufficient to characterize the resulting legal expenses as deductible ordinary and necessary business expenses? As you might guess, proper characterization ultimately turns on the nature of the individual's activities in the larger factual context. As you read *Gilliam*, ask yourself the following questions:

1. Does the court consider Gilliam's legal expenses ordinary or necessary?
2. Can an expense qualify as ordinary even if a given taxpayer has never encountered the expense before and may never encounter it again?
3. In your opinion, does the court convincingly distinguish *Dancer* and *Clark*?

Gilliam v. Commissioner
T.C. Memo. 1986-81

CHABOT, JUDGE:

Respondent determined deficiencies in Federal individual income taxes against petitioners for 1975 and 1976 in the amounts of $4,529 and $3,159, respectively. After concessions by petitioners, the issue for decision is whether petitioners are entitled to deduct under section 162 the amounts paid in defense of a criminal prosecution and in settlement of a related civil claim.

FINDINGS OF FACT

*** When the petition was filed in the instant case, petitioners Sam Gilliam, Jr. ["Gilliam"], and Dorothy B. Gilliam, husband and wife, resided in Washington, D.C.

Gilliam was born in Tupelo, Mississippi, in 1933, and raised in Louisville, Kentucky. In 1961, he received a master of arts degree in painting from the University of Louisville.

Gilliam is, and was at all material periods, a noted artist. His works have been exhibited in numerous art galleries throughout the United States and Europe, including the Corcoran Gallery of Art, Washington, D.C.; the Philadelphia Museum of Art, Philadelphia, Pennsylvania; the Karl Solway Gallery, Cincinnati, Ohio; the Phoenix Gallery, San Francisco, California; and the University of California, Irvine, California. His works have also been exhibited and sold at the Fendrick Gallery, Washington, D.C. In addition, Gilliam is, and was at all material periods, a teacher of art. On occasion, Gilliam lectured and taught art at various institutions.

Gilliam accepted an invitation to lecture and teach for a week at the Memphis Academy of Arts in Memphis, Tennessee. On Sunday, February 23, 1975, he flew to Memphis to fulfill this business obligation.

Gilliam had a history of hospitalizations for mental and emotional disturbances and continued to be under psychiatric care until the time of his trip to Memphis. ***

Before his Memphis trip, Gilliam created a 225-foot painting for the Thirty-fourth Biennial Exhibition of American Painting at the Corcoran Gallery of Art ["the Exhibition"]. The Exhibition opened on Friday evening, February 21, 1975. In addition, Gilliam was in the process of preparing a giant mural for an outside wall of the Philadelphia Museum of Art for the 1975 Spring Festival in Philadelphia. The budget plans for this mural were due on Monday, February 24, 1975.

On the night before his Memphis trip, Gilliam felt anxious and unable to rest. On Sunday morning, Gilliam contacted Ranville Clark ["Clark"], a doctor Gilliam had been consulting intermittently over the years, and asked Clark to prescribe some medication to relieve his anxiety. Clark arranged for Gilliam to pick up a prescription of the drug Dalmane on the way to the airport. Gilliam had taken medication frequently during the preceding 10 years. Clark had never before prescribed Dalmane for Gilliam.

On Sunday, February 23, 1975, Gilliam got the prescription and at about 3:25 p.m., he boarded American Airlines flight 395 at Washington National Airport,

Washington, D.C., bound for Memphis. Gilliam occupied a window seat. He took the Dalmane for the first time shortly after boarding the airplane.

About one and one-half hours after the airplane departed Washington National Airport, Gilliam began to act in an irrational manner. He talked of bizarre events and had difficulty in speaking. According to some witnesses, he appeared to be airsick and held his head. Gilliam began to feel trapped, anxious, disoriented, and very agitated. Gilliam said that the plane was going to crash and that he wanted a life raft. Gilliam entered the aisle and, while going from one end of the airplane to the other, he tried to exit from three different doors. Then Gilliam struck Seiji Nakamura ["Nakamura"], another passenger, several times with a telephone receiver. Nakamura was seated toward the rear of the airplane, near one of the exits. Gilliam also threatened the navigator and a stewardess, called for help, and cried. As a result of the attack, Nakamura sustained a one-inch laceration above his left eyebrow which required four sutures. Nakamura also suffered ecchymosis of the left arm and pains in his left wrist. Nakamura was treated for these injuries at Methodist Hospital in Memphis.

On arriving in Memphis, Gilliam was arrested by Federal officials. On March 10, 1975, Gilliam was indicted. He was brought to trial in the United States District Court for the Western District of Tennessee, Western Division, on one count of violation of 49 U.S.C. section 1472(k) (relating to certain crimes aboard an aircraft in flight) and two counts of violation 49 U.S.C. section 1472(j) (relating to interference with flight crew members or flight attendants). Gilliam entered a plea of not guilty to the criminal charges. The trial began on September 8, 1975, and ended on September 10, 1975. After Gilliam presented all of his evidence, the district court granted Gilliam's motion for a judgment of acquittal by reason of temporary insanity.

Petitioners paid $8,250 and $8,600 for legal fees in 1975 and 1976, respectively, in connection with both the criminal trial and Nakamura's civil claim. In 1975, petitioners also paid $3,800 to Nakamura in settlement of the civil claim.

Petitioners claimed deductions for the amounts paid in 1975 and 1976 on the appropriate individual income tax returns. Respondent disallowed the amounts claimed in both years attributable to the incident on the airplane.

* * *

Gilliam's trip to Memphis was a trip in furtherance of his trades or businesses.

Petitioners' expenses for the legal fees and claim settlement described, supra, are not ordinary expenses of Gilliam's trades or businesses.

OPINION

Petitioners contend that they are entitled to deduct the amounts paid in defense of the criminal prosecution and in settlement of the related civil claim under section 162. Petitioners maintain that the instant case is directly controlled by our decision in *Dancer v. Commissioner*, 73 T.C. 1103 (1980). According to petitioners, "(t)he clear holding of *Dancer* is * * * that expenses for litigation arising out of an accident which occurs during a business trip are deductible as ordinary and necessary business expenses." Petitioners also contend that *Clark v. Commissioner*, 30 T.C. 1330 (1958), is to the same effect as *Dancer*.

Respondent maintains that *Dancer* and *Clark* are distinguishable. Respondent contends that the legal fees paid are not deductible under either section 162 or section

212 because the criminal charges against Gilliam were neither directly connected with nor proximately resulted from his trade or business and the legal fees were not paid for the production of income. Respondent maintains that "the criminal charges which arose as a result of * * * (the incident on the airplane), could hardly be deemed 'ordinary', given the nature of (Gilliam's) profession." Respondent contends "that the provisions of section 262 control this situation." As to the settlement of the related civil claim, respondent asserts that since Gilliam committed an intentional tort, the settlement of the civil claim constitutes a nondeductible personal expense.

We agree with respondent that the expenses are not ordinary expenses of Gilliam's trade or business.

Section 162(a) allows a deduction for all the ordinary and necessary expenses of carrying on a trade or business. In order for the expense to be deductible by a taxpayer, it must be an ordinary expense, it must be a necessary expense, and it must be an expense of carrying on the taxpayer's trade or business. If any one of these requirements is not met, the expense is not deductible under section 162(a). *Deputy v. du Pont*, 308 U.S. 488 (1940); *Welch v. Helvering*, 290 U.S. 111 (1933); *Kornhauser v. United States*, 276 U.S. 145 (1928). In *Deputy v. du Pont*, the Supreme Court set forth a guide for application of the statutory requirement that the expense be "ordinary," as follows (308 U.S. at 494-497):

> In the second place, these payments were not "ordinary" ones for the conduct of the kind of business in which, we assume arguendo, respondent was engaged. The District Court held that they were "beyond the norm of general and accepted business practice" and were in fact "so extraordinary as to occur in the lives of ordinary business men not at all" and in the life of the respondent "but once." Certainly there are no norms of conduct to which we have been referred or of which we are cognizant which would bring these payments within the meaning of ordinary expenses for conserving and enhancing an estate. We do not doubt the correctness of the District Court's finding that respondent embarked on this program to the end that his beneficial stock ownership in the du Pont Company might be conserved and enhanced. But that does not make the cost to him an "ordinary" expense within the meaning of the Act. Ordinary has the connotation of normal, usual, or customary. To be sure, an expense may be ordinary though it happen but once in the taxpayer's lifetime. *Cf. Kornhauser v. United States, supra.* Yet the transaction which gives rise to it must be of common or frequent occurrence in the type of business involved. *Welch v. Helvering, supra,* 114. Hence, the fact that a particular expense would be an ordinary or common one in the course of one business and so deductible under section 23(a) [currently 162(a)] does not necessarily make it such in connection with another business. * * * As stated in *Welch v. Helvering, supra,* pp. 113-114: ". . . What is ordinary, though there must always be a strain of constancy within it, is none the less a variable affected by time and place and circumstance."
>
> One of the extremely relevant circumstances is the nature and scope of the particular business out of which the expense in question accrued. The fact that an obligation to pay has arisen is not sufficient. It is the kind of transaction out of which the obligation arose and its normalcy in the particular business which are crucial and controlling.

****

Petitioners bear the burden of proving entitlement to a deduction under section 162. Gilliam is a noted artist and teacher of art. It undoubtedly is ordinary for people in Gilliam's trades or businesses to travel (and to travel by air) in the course of such trades or businesses; however, we do not believe it is ordinary for people in such trades or businesses to be involved in altercations of the sort here involved in the course of any such travel. The travel was not itself the conduct of Gilliam's trades or businesses. Also, the expenses here involved are not strictly a cost of Gilliam's transportation. Finally, it is obvious that neither the altercation nor the expenses were undertaken to further Gilliam's trades or businesses.

We conclude that Gilliam's expenses are not ordinary expenses of his trades or businesses.

It is instructive to compare the instant case with *Dancer v. Commissioner, supra,* upon which petitioners rely. In both cases, the taxpayer was travelling on business. In both cases, the expenses in dispute were not the cost of the travelling, but rather were the cost of an untoward incident that occurred in the course of the trip. In both cases, the incident did not facilitate the trip or otherwise assist the taxpayer's trade or business. In both cases, the taxpayer was responsible for the incident; in neither case was the taxpayer willful. In *Dancer,* the taxpayer was driving an automobile; he caused an accident which resulted in injuries to a child. The relevant expenses were the taxpayer's payments to settle the civil claims arising from the accident. In the instant case, Gilliam was a passenger in an airplane; he apparently committed acts which would have been criminal but for his temporary insanity, and he injured a fellow passenger. Gilliam's expenses were the costs of his successful legal defense, and his payments to settle Nakamura's civil claim.

In *Dancer,* we stated as follows (73 T.C. at 1108-1109):

> It is true that the expenditure in the instant case did not further petitioner's business in any economic sense; nor is it, we hope, the type of expenditure that many businesses are called upon to pay. Nevertheless, neither factor lessens the direct relationship between the expenditure and the business. Automobile travel by petitioner was an integral part of this business. As rising insurance rates suggest, the cost of fuel and routine servicing are not the only costs one can expect in operating a car. As unfortunate as it may be, lapses by drivers seem to be an inseparable incident of driving a car. *Anderson v. Commissioner* (81 F.2d 457 (CA10 1936)). Costs incurred as a result of such an incident are just as much a part of overall business expenses as the cost of fuel. (Emphasis supplied.)

Dancer is distinguishable.

In *Clark v. Commissioner, supra,* also relied on by petitioners, the expenses consisted of payments of (a) legal fees in defense of a criminal prosecution [for allegations of assault with intent to rape that were dismissed] and (b) amounts to settle a related civil claim. In this regard, the instant case is similar to *Clark.* In *Clark,* however, the taxpayer's activities that gave rise to the prosecution and civil claim were activities directly in the conduct of [the taxpayer's] trade or business. [The taxpayer had a practice of interviewing husbands and getting their permission before he hired women as outside salespeople. The victim alleged assault with intent to rape when the taxpayer came to her home at time when, according to the taxpayer, he expected her husband to be home.] In the instant case, Gilliam's activities were not directly in the conduct of his trades or businesses. Rather, the activities merely occurred in the course of transportation connected with Gilliam's trades or businesses. And, as we noted in *Dancer v. Commissioner*, 73 T.C. at 1106, "in cases like this, where the cost is an adjunct of and not a direct cost of transporting an individual, we have not felt obliged to routinely allow the expenditure as a transportation cost deduction."

Petitioners also rely on *Commissioner v. Tellier*, 383 U.S. 687 (1966), in which the taxpayer was allowed to deduct the cost of an unsuccessful criminal defense to securities fraud charges. The activities that gave rise to the criminal prosecution in *Tellier* were activities directly in the conduct of Tellier's trade or business. Our analysis of the effect of *Clark v. Commissioner*, applies equally to the effect of *Commissioner v. Tellier*.

In sum, Gilliam's expenses were of a kind similar to those of the taxpayers in *Tellier* and *Clark*; however the activities giving rise to Gilliam's expenses were not activities directly in the conduct of his trades or businesses, while Tellier's and Clark's activities were directly in the conduct of their respective trades or businesses. Gilliam's expenses were related to his trades or businesses in a manner similar to those of the taxpayer in *Dancer*; however Gilliam's actions giving rise to the expenses were not shown to be ordinary, while Dancer's were shown to be ordinary. *Tellier*, *Clark*, and *Dancer* all have similarities to the instant case; however, *Tellier*, *Clark*, and *Dancer* are distinguishable in important respects. The expenses are not deductible under section 162(a).

We hold for respondent.

Decision will be entered for respondent.

Post-Case Follow-Up

Emphasizing that a deductible expense must be ordinary, necessary, and one incurred in carrying on the taxpayer's trade or business, the Tax Court in *Gilliam* promptly concluded that the taxpayer's legal expenses were neither ordinarily and customarily incurred by noted teachers and artists (at least not for the conduct complained of) nor actually incurred in carrying on the taxpayer's trade or business. Drawing on factual particulars, the court distinguished *Dancer* and *Clark*, noting that in each instance, the legal expenses incurred related directly to employee conduct undertaken to carry on the employer's business, notwithstanding the fact that the actual or alleged conduct did not advance that business in an economic sense and deviated substantially from standard business operations (e.g., child injury and allegations of intent to rape). On a purely emotional level, one can certainly sympathize with Mr. Gilliam, but at

Legal Expenses

Under prior law, employees incurring legal expenses (or other unreimbursed ordinary and necessary business expenses) were entitled to a limited deduction because the items constituted miscellaneous itemized deductions. Current law generally bars the taking of miscellaneous itemized deductions. Employers (including sole proprietors) continue to be able to deduct legal expenses, so long as such expenses are ordinary and necessary business expenses paid or incurred in connection with carrying on the relevant trade or business.

the same time, it is not difficult to understand why legal expenses to defend against criminal and civil charges for assault during business travel fail to qualify as ordinary and necessary business expenses of artists and teachers. If, instead, Mr. Gilliam operated a night club and employed several bouncers, his assault-related legal expenses would likely fall comfortably in the realm of the ordinary and necessary for those in that business.

Gilliam v. Commissioner: Real Life Applications

1. Parcel Service of America, Inc. ("PSA") specializes in the delivery of large orders of boxed goods. Miles, one of PSA's new employees, drove his vehicle over the speed limit on one of the local interstate highways and received a ticket from a state patrol officer. If PSA employs an attorney to fight payment of the ticket, will the legal expenses incurred qualify as ordinary and necessary business expenses?

2. *Same facts as Question #1*, except that Miles strikes a pedestrian with his vehicle while making deliveries. Will the legal expenses incurred in litigating or settling the matter be deductible?

3. Under normal circumstances, Kiev is a mild-mannered software engineer. Recently, however, while traveling for business, he assaulted and battered someone as they appeared to be stealing his work computer. His employer, Cerebral Solutions, Inc. ("CSI"), retained a law firm to defend against the suit instituted by the victim (who claimed that he had simply mistaken Kiev's computer for his own). CSI deducted the legal expenses on its tax return, and the IRS has issued a Notice of Deficiency, disputing the deductibility of the legal expenses. Who is likely to prevail?

4. Byron works for Behemoth Pharmaceuticals, Inc. ("BPI"), and he spends a lot of time on the road visiting with and assisting medical professionals. Most do not know it, but Byron has a short temper when it comes to what he views as careless driving. Recently, while traveling from one hospital to another, Byron encountered a badly distracted driver who almost caused a serious accident. In a fit of rage, Byron threw several objects from his car, most of which struck the offending vehicle, damaging its paint job and shattering at least one driver-side window. BPI incurred several thousand dollars in attorney's fees defending against the claims asserted by the distracted driver. Can BPI deduct these legal expenses?

C. "CARRYING ON" A "TRADE OR BUSINESS"

1. The "Carrying On" Requirement

The court in *Gilliam* ultimately concluded that the taxpayer could not deduct any of the legal expenses he incurred as a result of his midflight mishap. Although one can expect artists and teachers to incur legal expenses for any number of business-related reasons, paying an attorney to handle charges of assault and battery is not what most, if any, artists or teachers would consider a regular, commonplace occurrence in their day-to-day business activities. Thus, Gilliam's legal expenses were not ordinary in the tax sense. Further, the court concluded that the expenses failed to qualify as items paid in "carrying on" Gilliam's trade or business, noting that "neither the altercation nor the expenses were undertaken to further Gilliam's trades or businesses." To be sure, Gilliam was on a business trip, but the payment of attorney's fees in this instance was not for the purpose of advancing, operating, or protecting his trade or business. The question of whether a given taxpayer's business expenses were incurred or paid in "carrying on" that trade or business can arise in many contexts because (1) not every expense with a business link serves to "carry on" that business and (2) the statutory language refers to an existing trade or business. A taxpayer fully engaged in a specific commercial endeavor has little to worry about in this regard so long as the expenses clearly relate to the advancement of the business of the enterprise, but what about a taxpayer incurring expenses in connection with transitioning to a new trade or business? They aren't carrying on their old trade or business, and they haven't yet started their new trade or business. Are the expenses deductible as ordinary and necessary expenses as long as they are "carrying on" or plan to carry on *any* trade or business? And what about those who were gainfully employed in a trade or business before they were terminated? When they go back on the market to find a new job in that same line of business, can we view them as "carrying on" their old trade or business? The answers to these questions may prove dispiriting. Individuals entering the job market for the first time or transitioning to a new trade or business may not deduct job-seeking expenses as ordinary and necessary expenses. Although individuals promptly seeking re-employment in

Start-Up Expenditures

Section 162 allows taxpayers to deduct the ordinary and necessary expenses of carrying on a trade or business. Given the reference to an existing trade or business in § 162 and the standard treatment of capital expenditures (to be discussed in a future chapter), certain items related to starting a business must qualify for deduction elsewhere to the extent they will be deductible at all. Section 195 addresses the treatment of start-up expenditures. In general, under the terms of the provision, taxpayers may elect to deduct a limited amount of start-up expenditures in the year an active trade or business begins. The taxpayer may deduct any remaining start-up expenditures ratably over a 15-year period. In order to qualify as *start-up expenditures* for § 195 purposes, an item must clear two hurdles. First, the item must be one paid or incurred in one of the following contexts:

- Investigating the creation or acquisition of an active trade or business;
- Creating an active trade or business; or
- Engaging in an activity for profit and the production of income (before an active trade or business emerges) with ultimate intent that the activity become an active trade or business.

Second, the item must be one which would have been allowable as a deduction if paid or incurred in connection with the operation of an existing active trade or business in the same field.

   The Code excludes from the definition of start-up expenditures those items deductible under §§ 163, 164, or 167. Note that if a taxpayer fails to make the election provided by § 195(b), the general rule of § 195(a) bars any deduction with respect to start-up expenditures.

the same line of business used to be entitled to a limited deduction with respect to job-seeking expenses (i.e., as miscellaneous itemized deductions), current tax law does not include such an allowance.

2. Defining "Trade or Business"

Notwithstanding the relative ubiquity of the "trade or business" language throughout the Internal Revenue Code, neither the Code nor the Treasury Regulations define the precise meaning of the phrase. Courts have made valuable contributions in terms of attempting to bring the notion into sharper focus, but even they lament the difficulty (if not the impossibility) of eradicating the prevailing blurriness. Back in the 1940s, U.S. Supreme Court Justice Felix Frankfurter reasoned that "'carrying on any trade or business' . . . involves holding one's self out to others as engaged in the selling of goods or services." *Deputy v. Du Pont*, 308 U.S. 488, at 499 (Frankfurter, J., concurring). More recent precedent frowns on Justice Frankfurter's attempt to craft a manageable standard, but surely meaningful doctrinal advancement requires a great deal more than expressing formal discontent.

Case Preview

Commissioner v. Groetzinger

In *Groetzinger*, the Court ultimately had to determine whether an individual who made his living from gambling was engaged in a trade or business. You may recall from our study of § 165 that a taxpayer may use gambling losses only to offset gambling winnings. *See* § 165(d). But does that provision relegate all gambling to an arena of special and focused treatment outside the realm of legitimate trade or business activity, or was the provision simply meant to prevent individuals from using sporadic gambling losses to offset income from other sources (e.g., salary, dividends, etc.)? Major casinos make their money, at least in part, by offering patrons the opportunity to gamble, but does that mean they are not engaged in a trade or business? Can it be that their losses at the blackjack and craps tables (however rare) cannot offset income from hotel room sales, restaurant space rent, and other sources? Consider the following questions as you read *Groetzinger*:

1. What standard did Justice Frankfurter articulate in *Deputy v. Du Pont* for determining whether specific taxpayer activity constituted a trade or business?
2. What was this Court's view of Justice Frankfurter's standard?
3. Is this case about a retiree with a gambling habit or one with a legitimate business?
4. What standard, if any, does this Court articulate for distinguishing a trade or business from a mere profit-seeking venture?

Commissioner v. Groetzinger
480 U.S. 23 (1987)

[handwritten: I: Is gambling a trade or business?]

Justice BLACKMUN delivered the opinion of the Court.

The issue in this case is whether a full-time gambler who makes wagers solely for his own account is engaged in a "trade or business," within the meaning of §§ 162(a) and 62(1) of the Internal Revenue Code of 1954, as amended. The tax year with which we here are concerned is the calendar year 1978; technically, then, we look to the Code as it read at that time.

I

There is no dispute as to the facts. *** Respondent Robert P. Groetzinger had worked for 20 years in sales and market research for an Illinois manufacturer when his position was terminated in February 1978. During the remainder of that year, respondent busied himself with parimutuel wagering, primarily on greyhound races. He gambled at tracks in Florida and Colorado. He went to the track 6 days a week for 48 weeks in 1978. He spent a substantial amount of time studying racing forms, programs, and other materials. He devoted from 60 to 80 hours each week to these gambling-related endeavors. He never placed bets on behalf of any other person, or sold tips, or collected commissions for placing bets, or functioned as a bookmaker. He gambled solely for his own account. He had no other profession or type of employment.

Respondent kept a detailed accounting of his wagers and every day noted his winnings and losses in a record book. In 1978, he had gross winnings of $70,000, but he bet $72,032; he thus realized a net gambling loss for the year of $2,032.

Justice Harry A. Blackmun

Appointed by President Nixon, Associate Justice Harry A. Blackmun joined the U.S. Supreme Court in 1970.

Credit: Photo courtesy of the U.S. Library of Congress.

Respondent received $6,498 in income from other sources in 1978. This came from interest, dividends, capital gains, and salary earned before his job was terminated.

On the federal income tax return he filed for the calendar year 1978 respondent reported as income only the $6,498 realized from nongambling sources. He did not report any gambling winnings or deduct any gambling losses. He did not itemize deductions. Instead, he computed his tax liability from the tax tables. *[handwritten: Tax Return]*

Upon audit, the Commissioner of Internal Revenue determined that respondent's $70,000 in gambling winnings were to be included in his gross income and that, pursuant to § 165(d) of the Code, a deduction was to be allowed for his gambling losses to the extent of these gambling gains. But the Commissioner further determined that, under the law as it was in 1978, a portion of respondent's $70,000 gambling-loss deduction [would not be allowed because gambling was not the taxpayer's trade or business. Accordingly, the taxpayer faced an asserted tax deficiency of $2,522 for 1978.] *[handwritten: Findings by Commissioner]*

Respondent sought redetermination of the deficiency in the United States Tax Court. That court, in a reviewed decision, with only two judges dissenting, held that *[handwritten: P/S: He was involved in trade or business]* respondent was in the trade or business of gambling, and that, as a consequence, no part of his gambling losses [would be disallowed].

The United States Court of Appeals for the Seventh Circuit affirmed. Because of a conflict on the issue among Courts of Appeals, we granted certiorari.

II

The phrase "trade or business" has been in § 162(a) and in that section's predecessors for many years. Indeed, the phrase is common in the Code, for it appears in over 50 sections and 800 subsections and in hundreds of places in proposed and final income tax regulations. The slightly longer phrases, "carrying on a trade or business" and "engaging in a trade or business," themselves are used no less than 60 times in the Code. The concept thus has a well-known and almost constant presence on our tax-law terrain. Despite this, the Code has never contained a definition of the words "trade or business" for general application, and no regulation has been issued expounding its meaning for all purposes. Neither has a broadly applicable authoritative judicial definition emerged. Our task in this case is to ascertain the meaning of the phrase as it appears in the sections of the Code with which we are here concerned.

In one of its early tax cases, *Flint v. Stone Tracy Co.,* 220 U.S. 107 (1911), the Court . . . said: " 'Business' is a very comprehensive term and embraces everything about which a person can be employed." [*Id.* at 171]. It embraced the Bouvier Dictionary definition: "That which occupies the time, attention and labor of men for the purpose of a livelihood or profit." *Ibid.* ***

With these general comments as significant background, we turn to pertinent cases decided here. *Snyder v. Commissioner,* 295 U.S. 134 (1935), . . . held, in that context, that an investor, seeking merely to increase his holdings, was not engaged in a trade or business. ***

In *Deputy v. Du Pont,* 308 U.S. 488, 60 S.Ct. 363, 84 L.Ed. 416 (1940), the Court was concerned with what were "ordinary and necessary" expenses of a taxpayer's trade or business ***[T]he Court *assumed* that the activities of the taxpayer in conserving and enhancing his estate constituted a trade or business, but nevertheless disallowed the claimed deductions because they were not "ordinary" or "necessary." Justice Frankfurter, in a concurring opinion joined by Justice Reed, did not join the majority. He took the position that whether the taxpayer's activities constituted a trade or business was "open for determination," [Id. at 499], and observed:

> " '. . . carrying on any trade or business,' within the contemplation of § 23(a), involves holding one's self out to others as engaged in the selling of goods or services. This the taxpayer did not do. . . . Without elaborating the reasons for this construction and not unmindful of opposing considerations, including appropriate regard for administrative practice, I prefer to make the conclusion explicit instead of making the hypothetical litigation-breeding assumption that this taxpayer's activities, for which expenses were sought to be deducted, did constitute a 'trade or business.' "

Ibid.

Next came *Higgins v. Commissioner,* 312 U.S. 212 (1941). There the Court, in a bare and brief unanimous opinion, ruled that salaries and other expenses incident to looking after one's own investments in bonds and stocks were not deductible . . . as expenses paid or incurred in carrying on a trade or business. * * *

[handwritten margin note: Deputy's dissent addressed "trade or business"]

Less than three months later, the Court considered the issue of the deductibility, as business expenses, of estate and trust fees. In unanimous opinions issued the same day and written by Justice Black, the Court ruled that the efforts of an estate or trust in asset conservation and maintenance did not constitute a trade or business. The *Higgins* case was deemed to be relevant and controlling. * * *

From these observations and decisions, we conclude [that] . . . [t]he Court's cases, thus, give us results, but little general guidance.

III

Federal and state legislation and court decisions, perhaps understandably, until recently have not been noticeably favorable to gambling endeavors and even have been reluctant to treat gambling on a parity with more "legitimate" means of making a living. And the confinement of gambling-loss deductions to the amount of gambling gains, . . . closed the door on suspected abuses, . . . but served partially to differentiate genuine gambling losses from many other types of adverse financial consequences sustained during the tax year. Gambling winnings, however, have not been isolated from gambling losses. The Congress has been realistic enough to recognize that such losses do exist and do have some effect on income

The issue this case presents has "been around" for a long time and, as indicated above, has not met with consistent treatment in the Tax Court itself or in the Federal Courts of Appeals. The Seventh Circuit, in the present case, said the issue "has proven to be most difficult and troublesome over the years." 771 F.2d, at 271. The difficulty has not been ameliorated by the persistent absence of an all-purpose definition, by statute or regulation, of the phrase "trade or business" which so frequently appears in the Code. Of course, this very frequency well may be the explanation for legislative and administrative reluctance to take a position as to one use that might affect, with confusion, so many others.

Be that as it may, this taxpayer's case must be decided and, from what we have outlined above, must be decided in the face of a decisional history that is not positive or even fairly indicative, as we read the cases, of what the result should be. There are, however, some helpful indicators.

If a taxpayer, as Groetzinger is stipulated to have done in 1978, devotes his full-time activity to gambling, and it is his intended livelihood source, it would seem that basic concepts of fairness (if there be much of that in the income tax law) demand that his activity be regarded as a trade or business just as any other readily accepted activity, such as being a retail store proprietor or, to come closer categorically, as being a casino operator or as being an active trader on the exchanges.

It is argued, however, that a full-time gambler is not offering goods or his services, within the line of demarcation that Justice Frankfurter would have drawn in *Du Pont*. Respondent replies that he indeed is supplying goods and services, not only to himself but, as well, to the gambling market; thus, he says, he comes within the Frankfurter test even if that were to be imposed as the proper measure. "It takes two to gamble." Surely, one who clearly satisfies the Frankfurter adumbration usually is in a trade or business. But does it necessarily follow that one who does not satisfy the Frankfurter adumbration is not in a trade or business? One might well feel that a full-time gambler ought to qualify as much as a full-time trader, as Justice Brandeis in *Snyder* implied and as courts have held. The Commissioner, indeed, accepts the trader result. In any event, while the offering of goods and services usually would qualify the activity as a trade or business, this factor, it seems to us, is not an absolute prerequisite.

We are not satisfied that the Frankfurter gloss would add any helpful dimension to the resolution of cases such as this one, or that it provides a "sensible test," as the Commissioner urges. It might assist now and then, when the answer is obvious and positive, but it surely is capable of breeding litigation over the meaning of "goods," the meaning of "services," or the meaning of "holding one's self out." And we suspect that-apart from gambling-almost every activity would satisfy the gloss. A test that everyone passes is not a test at all. We therefore now formally reject the Frankfurter gloss which the Court has never adopted anyway.

Of course, not every income-producing and profit-making endeavor constitutes a trade or business. The income tax law, almost from the beginning, has distinguished between a business or trade, on the one hand, and "transactions entered into for profit but not connected with . . . business or trade," on the other. Congress "distinguished the broad range of income or profit producing activities from those satisfying the narrow category of trade or business." We accept the fact that to be engaged in a trade or business, the taxpayer must be involved in the activity with continuity and regularity and that the taxpayer's primary purpose for engaging in the activity must be for income or profit. A sporadic activity, a hobby, or an amusement diversion does not qualify.

It is suggested that we should defer to the position taken by the Commissioner and by the Solicitor General, but, in the absence of guidance, for over several decades now, through the medium of definitive statutes or regulations, we see little reason to do so. We would defer, instead, to the Code's normal focus on what we regard as a common-sense concept of what is a trade or business. Otherwise, as here, *** it is not too extreme to say that the taxpayer is being taxed on his gambling losses, a result distinctly out of line with the Code's focus on income.

We do not overrule or cut back on the Court's holding in *Higgins* when we conclude that if one's gambling activity is pursued full time, in good faith, and with regularity, to the production of income for a livelihood, and is not a mere hobby, it is a trade or business within the meaning of the statutes with which we are here concerned. Respondent Groetzinger satisfied that test in 1978. Constant and large-scale effort on his part was made. Skill was required and was applied. He did what he did for a livelihood, though with a less-than-successful result. This was not a hobby or a passing fancy or an occasional bet for amusement.

We therefore adhere to the general position of the *Higgins* Court, taken 46 years ago, that resolution of this issue "requires an examination of the facts in each case." This may be thought by some to be a less-than-satisfactory solution, for facts vary. But the difficulty rests in the Code's wide utilization in various contexts of the term "trade or business," in the absence of an all-purpose definition by statute or regulation, and in our concern that an attempt judicially to formulate and impose a test for all situations would be counterproductive, unhelpful, and even somewhat precarious for the overall integrity of the Code. We leave repair or revision, if any be needed, which we doubt, to the Congress where we feel, at this late date, the ultimate responsibility rests.

The judgment of the Court of Appeals is affirmed.

It is so ordered.

[Dissenting opinion omitted.]

A: He was engaged in trade or business

Post-Case Follow-Up

The Court in *Groetzinger* ultimately concluded that the taxpayer was, in fact, in the trade or business of gambling, a result that would allow him full deductibility of his gambling losses. Though critical of prior cases for offering little general guidance, the Court itself adopts a decidedly unworkable approach to addressing the core definitional issue at hand. Early on, the Court appears to embrace the notion that a full-time gambler who gambles for a living merits the same treatment as one who plays the stock market or operates a casino as a trade or business. Further, in speaking more generally, the Court appears to offer a litmus test to be applied across the board, emphasizing that "to be engaged in a trade or business, the taxpayer must be involved in the activity with continuity and regularity and . . . the taxpayer's primary purpose for engaging in the activity must be for income or profit." *Groetzinger*, at 35. But the Court dealt a blow to its own test by throwing up its hands near the opinion's end. Noted the Court, "an attempt judicially to formulate and impose a test for all situations would be counterproductive, unhelpful, and even somewhat precarious for the overall integrity of the Code." *Id*. at 36. *Groetzinger* thus leaves us with a crutch of sorts (in the form of apparently relevant verbiage) but, per its own terms, nothing truly bulletproof to rely on. Even so, *Groetzinger*'s articulation of the trade or business standard has demonstrated considerable staying power.

The difficulty of properly categorizing an activity as a trade or business can only grow more pressing over time. Arguably, many online businesses do (or should) qualify as trades or businesses even if the proprietor need not tend to it full time or even with continuity and regularity. Congress drafted many of the governing statutes before the internet existed, but much has changed. Although some standards update easily and automatically, others need a more hands-on approach, whether the intervention takes the form of conscious judicial gap-filling or, perhaps more appropriately, clarification from Congress and the Treasury Department.

Commissioner v. Groetzinger: Real Life Applications

1. Since his sophomore year in college, Coleman Heath has always enjoyed weightlifting. For years, he was to content to work out several times a week, but he is now going to the gym six days per week. In fact, Coleman reduced his regular work hours as an accountant from full-time to part-time and decided to do competitive bodybuilding. He has already won several regional titles. In addition to planning each of his seven daily meals carefully, he also keeps meticulous records with

respect to his lifting progress and is sure to sleep on a fixed and regular schedule. He plans to earn money by winning competitions and securing endorsements for athletic apparel, protein powders, meal supplements, and related items. Does Coleman's bodybuilding activity qualify as a trade or business?

2. Rhea recently lost her job as a registered nurse. Although she spends part of each day looking for new work, she spends a healthy amount of time (20 hours/ week) posting entries to a blog on various medical issues from a nurse's perspective. Interestingly enough, the blog has far exceeded her modest expectations. It now gets thousands of hits per day, and she has several corporate advertisers who pay her to post their banners on her blog page. Does Rhea's blogging qualify as a trade or business?

3. Herman and Nam are both custodians at the local middle school, but for several years, each worked as a house painter. As a result, they are both somewhat comfortable on ladders. During the months of November and December, they install Christmas lights for friends, neighbors, and others; the fee they charge varies according to the complexity of the home owner's "vision." Naturally, some projects consume more time than others, but on average, they spend approximately 20 to 30 hours per week doing the work. The job itself requires only modest planning, and most of the expenditures they incur relate to safety equipment, basic supplies, and vehicle operation. During the remainder of the year, their only occupation is their custodial work. Can Herman and Nam treat the seasonal Christmas light installation activity as a trade or business?

D. SPECIFIC DEDUCTION PROHIBITIONS AND RELEVANT EXCEPTIONS

1. Illegal Bribes/Kickbacks, Fines, Etc.

Although one might generally think of § 162 as a provision making various deductions available, the provision also sets forth specific deduction prohibitions. Section 162(c), for example, prohibits the deduction of illegal bribes or kickbacks under § 162(a) when paid to specific government personnel, agencies, or instrumentalities or when such payments violate the Foreign Corrupt Practices Act of 1977. Likewise, § 162(f)(1) generally prohibits the deduction of any fines or penalties paid to, or at the direction of, a government or governmental entity in connection with violations of the law (or investigations regarding potential violations). *See, e.g., Tank Truck Rentals, Inc. v. Commissioner*, 356 U.S. 30 (1958) (barring any deduction for fines imposed for even inadvertent violation of a state's maximum truck weight laws). Note, however, that §§ 162(f)(2)–(4) set forth exceptions to this general rule for certain payments (e.g., amounts constituting restitution or paid to effect compliance with the law, certain court-ordered payments, and amounts paid or incurred as taxes due).

2. Client Entertainment

In the business world, those offering goods and services to consumers regularly entertain their best clients. Indeed, many consider such entertainment to be a matter of effective competitiveness, if not basic survival. Good clients generally expect some degree of wooing, and a business that fails to entertain as much (or as well) as the competition might well find the flow of new business slowing to a trickle or, worse yet, drying up altogether. Notwithstanding those realities, it's hard to ignore the fact that in some instances, a taxpayer doing business can look an awful lot like a taxpayer doing pleasure. After all, how onerous is it to go to dinner with clients at the city's finest restaurants, take them to professional basketball games (with courtside seats), or schmooze with them over cocktails? Congress would be among the first to acknowledge that client entertainment is common and accepted in the business community and certainly qualifies as appropriate and helpful. Notwithstanding historic accommodation of these practical business realities, Congress has firmly closed the door to actual and potential taxpayer abuses. Section 274 provides that no deduction (otherwise allowable) is permitted "[w]ith respect to an activity which is of a type generally considered to constitute entertainment, amusement, or recreation" or with respect to a facility used for such activities. To accommodate specific taxpayer categories and special circumstances, the Treasury Regulations promulgated under § 274 provide additional clarity. Thus, although all interested parties must employ an objective test in determining whether a given activity constitutes "entertainment," the taxpayer's trade or business must be taken into account such that those whose trades or businesses are intimately associated with entertainment (e.g., theater critics, etc.) are not inadvertently penalized. *See* Treas. Reg. § 1.274–2(b)(1)(ii). Similar protective rules apply to the extent (i) taxpayers incur expenses for entertainment (including facilities) made available to the general public and (ii) taxpayers incur expenses for entertainment (including facilities) sold to customers (e.g., the costs of operating a night club). *See* Treas. Reg. § 1.274–2(f)(2)(viii)–(ix).

Is Posting Videos on YouTube a "Trade or Business"?

In 2009, Bethany Mota started posting videos on YouTube, and by 2014, she was making $40,000 per month (according to Business Insider estimates). *See* http://www.businessinsider.com/haul-teenage-youtube-shopping-star-bethany-mota-2014-1. Would this activity satisfy Justice Frankfurter's trade or business standard (i.e., holding oneself out to others as providing goods and services)? If so, when? And, notwithstanding substantial profits, how would this activity fare under the "continuity and regularity" standard articulated in *Groetzinger*?

Credit: FashionStock.com/Shutterstock.com.

3. Lobbying

Congress (being of the belief that certain taxpayer activities should rarely, if ever, enjoy even a partial or indirect government subsidy) generally disallows any deduction under § 162(a) for lobbying or political expenditures. Such expenditures include amounts paid or incurred in connection with the following:

- Influencing legislation;
- Participating or intervening in candidate campaigns for public office;
- Attempting to influence the public regarding elections, referenda, or legislation; and
- Direct communications with certain covered executive branch officials in an attempt to influence their official actions or positions.

See IRC § 162(e)(1).

Note that this general rule does not apply to those in the trade or business of providing lobbying services for others or to certain de minimis in-house expenditures. *See generally* § 162(e)(4).

The *Citizens United* Decision

In *Citizens United v. Federal Election Commission*, 558 U.S. 310 (2010), the U.S. Supreme Court held that regulation of free speech based on the speaker's corporate identity was inconsistent with the First Amendment of the U.S. Constitution. Students of tax law should not, however, confuse a corporate taxpayer's ability to make electioneering communications as a matter of fundamental constitutional right with the ability to deduct the cost of making such communications. Keep § 162's limitations in mind.

Golden Parachute Payments

High-level corporate executives forced to relinquish their positions after certain transactional events (e.g., a change in corporate control or ownership) often get large sums of money as terminal compensation (i.e., golden parachutes). In addition to limiting deductions for applicable employee remuneration under § 162(m), Congress also bars deductions for *excess parachute payments*. *See* § 280G(a).

4. Sale of Certain Controlled Substances

Those of you familiar with the AMC series *Breaking Bad* will promptly recall that the two principal characters were carrying on a trade or business. The business was flagrantly illegal, but it was a trade or business nonetheless. Assume that the authorities apprehended them and charged them with, among other things, tax evasion. How would the federal prosecutor measure the amount of tax actually evaded? At the outset, she would have to calculate the venture's taxable income, and if the manufacture of methamphetamine were treated like any other trade or business, one would start with gross receipts and then reduce this amount by various ordinary and necessary business expenses incurred and paid in carrying on the venture (e.g., the cost of bags for storage, marketing, distribution, electricity, internet service, accounting, vehicle repair, phone service, body disposal expenses, weaponry, ammunitions, security, and, of course, occasional mortuary expenses). As it turns out, Congress has greatly simplified the prosecutor's job in this regard. The Tax Equity and Fiscal Responsibility Act of 1982 added § 280E to the Code. *See generally* P.L. 97-248, § 351(a) (1982). That provision dictates that "[n]o deduction or credit shall be allowed for any amount paid or incurred . . . in carrying on any trade or business if such trade or business (or the activities which comprise such trade or business) consists of trafficking in controlled substances . . . which is prohibited by Federal law or the law of any State in which such trade or business is conducted." IRC § 280E. The rule is simple enough on its face, but should it apply in *every* instance? One would think so, but what about situations not contemplated by Congress at the time of the provision's drafting? After all, today, many states allow the medicinal and recreational use of certain drugs (e.g., marijuana), notwithstanding the fact that the items are controlled substances under federal law. Let's see how the Court of Appeals for the Ninth Circuit has dealt with this issue.

Case Preview

Olive v. Commissioner

The taxpayer in *Olive* operated the Vapor Room Herbal Center ("Vapor Room") in San Francisco, California. In addition to providing medical marijuana to those with valid prescriptions, the Vapor Room also offered other goods and services to its patrons. The taxpayer's returns for the years at issue reported net income, but the taxpayer derived the net income figure by taking into account various expenses associated with operation of the business. Notwithstanding the fact that operation of a medical marijuana dispensary violated no California law, the Commissioner appealed to § 280E to deny the taxpayer any deductions or credits associated with carrying on the enterprise. At the time that Congress enacted § 280E, however, medical marijuana dispensaries did not exist. Accordingly, from the taxpayer's perspective, there was a genuine issue as to whether Congress could have intended § 280E's prohibitions to apply beyond the illicit drug trade context. As you read the case, consider the following questions:

1. What factors did the court consider in deciding whether The Vapor Room was the taxpayer's trade or business?
2. Why is the taxpayer arguing that the business does not "consist of" the selling of controlled substances?
3. Should laws enacted primarily to address problems in one context apply to similar yet distinct activities? What is the court's perspective on this question?

Olive v. Commissioner
792 F.3d 1146 (9th Cir. 2015)

GRABER, Circuit Judge:

Petitioner Martin Olive appeals the Tax Court's decision assessing deficiencies and penalties for tax years 2004 and 2005, which arise from Petitioner's operation of the Vapor Room Herbal Center ("Vapor Room"), a medical marijuana dispensary in San Francisco. The Tax Court held, among other things, that 26 U.S.C. (I.R.C.) § 280E precluded Petitioner from deducting any amount of ordinary or necessary business expenses associated with operation of the Vapor Room because the Vapor Room is a "trade or business . . . consist [ing] of trafficking in controlled substances . . . prohibited by Federal law." I.R.C. § 280E. Reviewing that legal conclusion de novo, . . . we agree and, therefore, affirm the Tax Court's decision.

marijuana

Established in 2004, the Vapor Room provides its patrons a place where they can socialize, purchase medical marijuana, and consume it using the Vapor Room's vaporizers. The Vapor Room sells medical marijuana in three forms: dried marijuana leaves, edibles, and a concentrated version of THC. Customers who purchase marijuana at the Vapor Room pay varying costs, depending on the quantity and quality of the product and on the individual customer's ability to pay.

The Vapor Room is set up much like a community center, with couches, chairs, and tables located throughout the establishment. Games, books, and art supplies are available for patrons' general use. The Vapor Room also offers services such as yoga, movies, and massage therapy. Customers can drink complimentary tea or water during their visits, or they can eat complimentary snacks, including pizza and sandwiches. The Vapor Room offers these activities and amenities for free.

Business Expenses

Each of the Vapor Room's staff members is permitted under California law to receive and consume medical marijuana. Petitioner purchases, for cash, the Vapor Room's inventory from licensed medical marijuana suppliers. Patrons who visit the Vapor Room can buy marijuana and use the vaporizers at no charge, or they can use the vaporizers (again, at no charge) with marijuana that they bought elsewhere. Sometimes, staff members or patrons sample Vapor Room inventory for free. When staff members interact with customers, occasionally one-on-one, they discuss illnesses; provide counseling on various personal, legal, or political matters related to medical marijuana; and educate patrons on how to use the vaporizers and consume medical marijuana responsibly. All these services are provided to patrons at no charge.

The tax return

Petitioner filed business income tax returns for tax years 2004 and 2005, which reported the Vapor Room's net income during those years as $64,670 and $33,778, respectively. Although Petitioner reported $236,502 and $417,569 in Vapor Room business expenses for 2004 and 2005, the Tax Court concluded that § 280E of the Internal Revenue Code precluded Petitioner from deducting any of those expenses. Petitioner timely appeals.

The Internal Revenue Code provides that, for the purpose of computing taxable income, an individual's or a business's "gross income" includes "all income from whatever source derived," including "income derived from business." I.R.C. § 61(a)(2). The Code further allows a business to deduct from its gross income "all the ordinary and necessary expenses paid or incurred during the taxable year in carrying on [the] trade or business." *Id.* § 162(a). But there are exceptions to § 162(a). *See, e.g., id.* §§ 261–280H (listing "Items Not Deductible"). One such exception applies when the "amount paid or incurred during the taxable year" is for the purpose of "carrying on any trade or business . . . consist[ing] of trafficking in controlled substances." *Id.* § 280E. Although the use and sale of medical marijuana are legal under California state law, *see* Cal. Health & Safety Code § 11362.5, the use and sale of marijuana remain prohibited under federal law, *see* 21 U.S.C. § 812(c).

Controlled Substances exception

We turn first to the text of I.R.C. § 280E. To determine whether Petitioner may deduct the expenses associated with the Vapor Room, then, we must decide whether the Vapor Room is a "trade or business [that] consists of trafficking in controlled substances . . . prohibited by Federal law." We start with the phrase "trade or business."

First: Is it a trade or business?

The test for determining whether an activity constitutes a "trade or business" is "whether the activity 'was entered into with the dominant hope and intent of realizing a profit.' " *United States v. Am. Bar Endowment*, 477 U.S. 105, 110 n. 1, 106 S. Ct. 2426, 91 L. Ed. 2d 89 (1986) (quoting *Brannen v. Comm'r*, 722 F.2d 695, 704 (11th Cir. 1984)); *see also Vorsheck v. Comm'r*, 933 F.2d 757, 758 (9th Cir. 1991) (per curiam) (applying the same standard to § 162(a) deductions). The parties agree, and the Tax Court found, that the *only* income-generating activity in which the Vapor Room engaged was its sale of medical marijuana. The other services that the Vapor Room offered — including, among other things, the provision of vaporizers, food and drink, yoga, games, movies, and counseling — were offered to its patrons at no cost to them. The only activity, then, that the Vapor Room "entered into with the dominant hope and intent of realizing a profit," *Am. Bar Endowment*, 477 U.S. at 110 n. 1, 106 S. Ct. 2426, was the sale of medical marijuana. Accordingly, Petitioner's "trade or business," for § 162(a) purposes, was limited to medical marijuana sales.

Given the limited scope of Petitioner's "trade or business," we conclude that the business "consist[ed] of trafficking in controlled substances . . . prohibited by Federal law." The income-generating activities in which the Vapor Room engaged consisted *solely* of trafficking in medical marijuana which, as noted, is prohibited under federal law. Under § 280E, then, the expenses that Petitioner incurred in the course of operating the Vapor Room cannot be deducted for federal tax purposes.

Petitioner's argument relies primarily on the phrase "consists of," rather than on the phrase "trade or business." According to Petitioner, the use of the words "consists of" is most appropriate "when a listing is meant to be exhaustive"; the word "consisting," he argues, is not synonymous with the word "including." Relying on that proposition, Petitioner contends that, for § 280E purposes, a business "consists of" a service only when that service is the *sole* service that the business provides. Because the Vapor Room provides caregiving services *and* sells medical marijuana, Petitioner concludes that his business does not "consist of" either one alone and therefore does not fall within the ambit of § 280E.

To support that line of reasoning, Petitioner cites the Tax Court's decision in *Californians Helping to Alleviate Medical Problems, Inc. v. Commissioner* (*CHAMP*), 128 T.C. 173 (2007). His reliance on *CHAMP* is misplaced. In *CHAMP*, the petitioner's income-generating business included the provision not only of medical marijuana, but also of "extensive" counseling and caregiving services. *Id.* at 175. The Tax Court noted that the business's "primary purpose was to provide caregiving services to its members" and that its "secondary purpose was to provide its members with medical marijuana." *Id.* at 174. The court found, after considering the "degree of economic interrelationship between the two undertakings," that the petitioner was involved in "more than one trade or business." *Id.* at 183. That is not the case here. Petitioner does not provide counseling, caregiving, snacks, and so forth for a separate fee; the only "business" in which he engages is selling medical marijuana.

An analogy may help to illustrate the difference between the Vapor Room and the business at issue in *CHAMP*. Bookstore A sells books. It also provides some complimentary amenities: Patrons can sit in comfortable seating areas while considering whether to buy a book; they can drink coffee or tea and eat cookies, all of which the bookstore offers at no charge; they can obtain advice from the staff about new authors, book clubs, community events, and the like; they can bring their children to a weekend story time or an after-school reading circle. The "trade or business" of Bookstore A "consists of" selling books. Its many amenities do not alter that conclusion; presumably, the owner hopes to attract buyers of books by creating an alluring atmosphere. By contrast, Bookstore B sells books but also sells coffee and pastries, which customers can consume in a cafe-like seating area. Bookstore B has two "trade[s] or business[es]," one of which "consists of" selling books and the other of which "consists of" selling food and beverages.

Petitioner's arguments related to congressional intent and public policy are similarly unavailing. He contends that I.R.C. § 280E should not be construed to apply to medical marijuana dispensaries because those dispensaries did not exist when Congress enacted § 280E. Congress added that provision, he maintains, to prevent street dealers from taking a deduction. According to Petitioner, Congress could not have intended for medical marijuana dispensaries, now legal in many states, to fall within the ambit of "items not deductible" under the Internal Revenue Code. We are not persuaded.

That Congress might not have imagined what some states would do in future years has no bearing on our analysis. It is common for statutes to apply to new situations. And here, application of the statute is clear. Application of the statute does not depend on the illegality of marijuana sales under state law; the only question Congress allows us to ask is whether marijuana is a controlled substance "prohibited by Federal law." I.R.C. § 280E. If Congress now thinks that the policy embodied in § 280E is unwise as applied to medical marijuana sold in conformance with state law, it can change the statute. We may not.

***

In summary, the Tax Court properly concluded that I.R.C. § 280E precludes Petitioner from deducting, pursuant to I.R.C. § 162(a), the ordinary and necessary business expenses associated with his operation of the Vapor Room. We therefore affirm the Tax Court's decision.

AFFIRMED.

Post-Case Follow-Up

With little fanfare, the Ninth Circuit confirms that § 280E bars the deduction of all ordinary and necessary expenses associated with the operation of the taxpayer's "trade or business," reasoning that it need look no further than ascertaining whether the business consists of the trafficking in a controlled substance in contravention of state or federal law. The court reached this conclusion notwithstanding the fact that the activity was legal under California law and that Congress could not have contemplated the existence of medical marijuana dispensaries when crafting and enacting § 280E. The Ninth Circuit's decision makes logical sense, but the likelihood remains strong that the specific issue presented in *Olive* (and a host of others) will resurface as more states embrace the medicinal and recreational use of marijuana. As Exhibit 12.1 reflects, more than half of all states allow some form of legal marijuana use, and even if further legalization expands in halting steps, the tide of public opinion regarding marijuana appears to have made a definitive shift. In fact, citizens themselves often transition jurisdictions to legal recreational use by statewide referendum. What is more, even though marijuana remains a controlled substance under federal law, the government apparently sees no need to halt the purchase and sale of it so long as state law allows it; alcohol sales during the Prohibition Era fared far worse.

Special Note: The Cost of Goods Sold

Although the court in *Olive* addresses the impact of § 280E on certain ordinary and necessary expenses, note that the rule does not alter the calculation of profit from the sale of marijuana. Thus, if the Vapor Room paid $5,000 for marijuana it sold for $7,500, its profit of $2,500 takes into account the cost of the goods it sold. *See CHAMPS v. Commissioner*, 128 T.C. 173, 177 n.4 (2007) (noting the IRS's concession that § 280E does not apply to C.O.G.S. and that the IRS's concession is consistent with the underlying statute and legislative history).

EXHIBIT 12.1 **Marijuana Legalization by State as of November 2016**

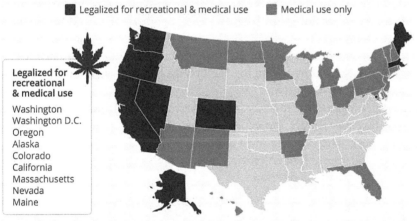

The States Where It's Legal To Smoke Marijuana
Laws on recreational and medical marijuana use in the US*

■ Legalized for recreational & medical use   ■ Medical use only

Legalized for recreational & medical use

Washington
Washington D.C.
Oregon
Alaska
Colorado
California
Massachusetts
Nevada
Maine

* As of Nov 10, 2016 - laws in some states have not yet taken effect.
Some states not highlighted allow limited medical marijuana access
@StatistaCharts Source: NY Times

statista

Original image located at https://www.statista.com/chart/6681/the-states-where-its-legal-to-smoke-marijuana/ (last visited January 11, 2017).

Olive v. Commissioner: Real Life Applications

1. In early 2016, Harrold was involved in a serious traffic accident. After his discharge from the hospital, he complained of occasional pain, and his doctor prescribed

reasonably strong painkillers. Harrold's complaints were largely a hoax. Harrold suffered pain, but he could alleviate it with over-the-counter medication. He told his doctor that such medication did not work because he hoped his doctor would give him the "good stuff." Harrold now collects disability and spends most days of the week scoring painkillers from the sick, filling his many prescriptions, and selling all of his "inventory" to customers in violation of state and federal law. Do Harrold's activities constitute a trade or business, and if so, will his associated expenses (e.g., storage containers, phone service, gasoline, automobile maintenance, etc.) qualify as deductible ordinary and necessary business expenses?

2. Several years ago, Glenn finally realized his dream of opening a sports supplement store. He soon realized that the industry was quite competitive. To augment his business income, he started selling anabolic steroids to amateur bodybuilders in violation of state and federal law. In any given year, at least 40 percent of Glenn's revenue from the store comes from the sale of anabolic steroids. To what extent, if any, may Glenn deduct the ordinary and necessary expenses of operating his store?

Chapter Summary

- For federal income tax purposes, an expense qualifies as "ordinary" if the expense is common and accepted in the business community of which the taxpayer is a part. "Ordinary" does not mean "regular" and "habitual" (i.e., one-time expenditures may qualify).
- For federal income tax purposes, an expense qualifies as "necessary" if it is appropriate and helpful in advancing the taxpayer's business interests. "Necessary" does not mean "required."
- Fundamentally, personal expenses remain personal (and thus nondeductible) even if the taxpayer incurs the expense during business hours or while conducting business. The expense must actually relate to and advance conduct of the taxpayer's business. Tangential connection of an expense to the conduct of business will not justify deduction.
- Expenses an individual incurs in connection with seeking new employment in the same line of business do not qualify as deductible ordinary and necessary expenses incurred in "carrying on" a trade or business. Likewise, when such expenses are associated with entering the job market or transitioning to a new trade or business, they will not qualify as deductible expenses.
- An activity will generally qualify as a "trade or business" if the taxpayer engages in it with continuity and regularity for the purpose of generating income or profit. Prevailing facts and circumstances will play an important role in proper categorization.
- Specific fines, penalties, illegal kickbacks, and bribes are not deductible.
- Notwithstanding the fact that an expense qualifies as "ordinary" and "necessary," special rules may alter or eliminate the deductibility of the item.

Applying the Rules

1. For the past eight years, Federico has worked for National Parcel Service, Inc. ("NPS") driving their delivery trucks and dropping off packages to customers. Recently, he was involved in an accident while working, and according to police reports, the other driver (Steven) was at fault. Steven had no insurance, and because NPS's insurance company covered only a portion of the total cost of vehicle repair, NPS had to pay the remainder. To recover this amount, NPS retained an attorney for the purpose of obtaining a judgment against Steven and proceeding against his assets. May NPS deduct the attorney's fees paid in connection with the lawsuit against Steven?

2. *Same facts as Question #1*, except that Federico apparently caused the accident. Steven claims that Federico was reading text messages on his smartphone at the time of the accident. Federico denies the accusation, and NPS paid a notoriously aggressive law firm to defend it in the litigation.

3. International Conglomerate, Inc. ("ICI") hopes to expand its business operations to Cuba. In an effort to expedite matters, ICI authorized its agents to pay illegal bribes to several high-ranking government officials because according to the agents, "this is just the way things work in this part of the world. All the businesses do it." May ICI deduct the bribes as "ordinary and necessary" business expenses?

4. Although Amanda has worked at Dante, Ballantine, and Forth, LLP for five years as an aspiring corporate litigation attorney, she has tired of the grueling hours regularly demanded of her. She has started looking around for a new position, and she has made it abundantly clear to all potential employers that she will only do transactional corporate work. Do any of Amanda's job-hunting expenses qualify as having been incurred in "carrying on" her trade or business of being an attorney?

5. Brandon does construction work for The Pyramid Group, LP ("TPG"). While working on a new building in a highly trafficked area downtown in his city, he overheard a passerby making disparaging remarks about construction workers. Brandon and the pedestrian exchanged words, and a fight ensued. If the pedestrian retains legal counsel to pursue damages from TPG, may TPG deduct any of the legal expenses it incurs in its defense?

Federal Income Taxation in Practice

1. One of your longtime clients, Darryl "Blackjack" Thames, recently received a Notice of Deficiency from the IRS challenging Darryl's deduction of gambling losses in his capacity as a professional gambler. You need to get more facts, but

in the interim, you'd like to find out whether any Ninth Circuit opinions have applied *Commissioner v. Groetzinger* to gamblers. See what you can find, and prepare a memo for your files.

2. One of your professors is thinking about writing a scholarly article in which she will devote some discussion to *Olive v. Commissioner*. She understands that someone recently published a comment on the decision in a law review. She has asked that you track it down and send her a copy. See if you can find it and send it to her via e-mail.

Capital Expenditures, Depreciation, and Amortization

In Chapter 12, we discussed § 162's provision for the deduction of all the ordinary and necessary expenses paid or incurred during the taxable year in carrying on a trade or business. Although we have devoted considerable attention to various prohibitions and limitations with respect to § 162(a)'s default operation, it remains true that the general rule properly allows the immediate deduction of a wide range of standard business expenses. An airline, for example, must purchase fuel to operate its jets, and even if best airline industry practices dictate the maintenance of emergency fuel reserves, we rationally think of airlines as consuming or "using up" most of the fuel purchased during a given year in transporting passengers to their final destinations. A full deduction for the cost of fuel in the year of purchase makes sense. Airlines, however, must also purchase airplanes, luggage transport vehicles, and mainframe computers. Logically enough, we do not think of these items as being used up, consumed, or rendered obsolete during the same taxable year in which the airline purchases them. In fact, we think of them as lasting for several years if not for decades. Should the tax law allow a full and immediate deduction for the purchase of an airplane or luggage transport vehicle in the same way that it allows such a deduction for the purchase of jet fuel? The purchase of jet fuel yields an ephemeral benefit, whereas the purchase of a multi-million-dollar, wide-body jet yields enduring, long-term benefits. In light of these realities, the tax law generally demands that these items and those yielding similarly short-term and long-term benefits be treated differently. In this chapter, we take a closer look at the treatment of expenditures incurred to acquire business assets likely to yield benefits to the taxpayer beyond a single tax year.

Key Concepts

- Capital expenditures and the significance of matching income and expense
- Depreciation of tangible, wasting assets and the amortization of intangibles
- Inventory tax accounting

A. OVERVIEW

Assume that Carnival Air Lines, Inc. ("Carnival") purchases a jumbo jet for $432 million in January of 2019 and immediately places it in service on the route between Boston's Logan International Airport and Rio de Janeiro's Galeão International Airport. The plane will likely serve Carnival for decades, and there's no doubt that for an international airline, the purchase of a jet with high mileage range qualifies as both "ordinary" and "necessary". Jet purchases are common and accepted in the airline industry, and such purchases are certainly appropriate and helpful in transporting passengers. And yet, allowing Carnival to deduct the full cost of the jet in 2019 might cause any number of problems and misperceptions. For example, if the company would have had net income of $100 million (disregarding the jet purchase), then allowing an immediate deduction of $432 million might lead to the erroneous belief that the company operated at a *loss* in 2019. But we can't ignore the asset purchase altogether; doing so would be equally misleading. The airline's books and records must reflect the purchase of a significant asset, and the company should be able to adjust its gross income to reflect that it has incurred a substantial business expense, albeit one that will help to generate revenue over time. Congress's solution deftly threads the needle. When Carnival purchases a jet, it cannot take a full and immediate deduction with respect to the jet's cost. Instead, Carnival records the jet as an asset in its financial books and records. When that approach is taken, we say that the cost has been **capitalized**, and we refer to the item as a **capital expenditure**. But that's not the end of the story. The jet will help the airline generate income over time, but even with adherence to rigid maintenance and safety protocols, the jet will also suffer the effects of continued use and gradually show its age. Thus, for a tangible, wasting business asset like a jet, the cost of the item may face initial capitalization, but Congress allows deductions over time for exhaustion and wear and tear with respect to the asset in the form of annual **depreciation** deductions. *See* § 167 (discussed below). The deductions do not go on in perpetuity. Taxpayers generally take depreciation deductions with respect to their business assets until they have deducted an amount equal to the asset's cost (i.e., basis). One may encounter references to depreciation deductions as **cost recovery**. When the cost recovery process is complete, the asset is **fully depreciated**. The multiyear period during which cost recovery deduction will occur varies according to the asset, per rules set forth in the Code. *See* § 168 (discussed below). In general, those rules allow cost recovery deductions for a period that roughly approximates the period during which the asset will be of use to the business (i.e., its **useful life**). With this system in place, the company's records reflect

Key Statutory and Regulatory Provisions

- Internal Revenue Code
  - § 162(a)(1)–(3)(excluding terminal right-justified language)
  - § 167(a) and (c)
  - § 168(a)
  - § 179(a)–(b)(3)
  - § 197(a), (c)(1) and (2)
  - § 197(d)(1)(A)–(C)
  - § 263(a)(1) (first sentence)
  - § 263(a)(2)
  - § 263A(a)(1)(A) and (B)
  - § 263A(b)
  - § 1016(a)(2)
- Treasury Regulations
  - § 1.162-4
  - § 1.167(a)-2
  - § 1.197-2(d)(2)(ii)
  - § 1.263(a)-1(b) and (d)(1)
  - § 1.263(a)-2(d)(1)
  - § 1.263(a)-3(d)
  - § 1.263(a)-5(a)

the existence of the asset, but the company takes the cost of the asset into account over its useful life as it helps the company generate income. As a practical matter, annual depreciation deductions with respect to the asset will generally appear on the same return as the income flowing from use of the asset. In that way, we achieve the mathematical **matching** of gross income from use of the asset with the cost of the asset and thereby achieve the clearest reflection of the company's net income during that time period. We avoid potential distortions and misperceptions with respect to the success of the company's operations during a given taxable year while truthfully and accurately accounting for the asset purchase.

There's one more wrinkle. When taxpayers take a deduction with respect to an ordinary and necessary business expense, they may do so only once. Similarly, for a capital expenditure subject to depreciation, taxpayers may take the appropriate deductions but only up to the amount of the item's basis, and they may do so only once. But what if a taxpayer purchases a $1 million asset, capitalizes the cost, recovers the cost via depreciation until the asset is fully depreciated, and then sells the asset? Over time, the taxpayer will have taken $1 million in depreciation deductions. It would be inappropriate to allow the taxpayer to sell the asset for $1 million and then (on sale or other disposition) offset that amount realized by a basis of $1 million. If we take that approach, no gain would be realized, and we would have allowed both $1 million in deductions and $1 million in basis offset on sale of the asset. That approach cannot be right. Governing rules aggressively ensure that such a series of events, in any event, will never come to pass. Under § 1016(a)(2), we see provision for the periodic mandatory adjustment of the basis measured by the amount allowed or (at minimum) allowable as a deduction for wear, tear, exhaustion, depletion, obsolescence, etc. Although adjustment may be made by reference to deductions actually taken (i.e., allowed), the basis adjustment is not contingent on deductions actually taken; minimal adjustment occurs to the extent such a deduction is "allowable." *See generally* Treas. Reg. § 1.1016–3. We refer to this changing number as the asset's **adjusted basis**. If the cost recovery occurs in equal annual installments, we refer to the schedule of deductions as **straight line depreciation**. *See* Table 13.1. If, for some reason, the governing rules or available elections allow higher initial deductions, we refer to the schedule as **accelerated depreciation** or **accelerated cost recovery**. *See* Table 13.2.

TABLE 13.1 Straight Line Depreciation: Original Cost Basis of $1,000,000

Years Since Asset Placed in Service	Depreciation Amount	Adjusted Basis
1	$100,000	$900,000
2	$100,000	$800,000
3	$100,000	$700,000
4	$100,000	$600,000
5	$100,000	$500,000
6	$100,000	$400,000
7	$100,000	$300,000
8	$100,000	$200,000
9	$100,000	$100,000
10	$100,000	$0

TABLE 13.2 **Accelerated Cost Recovery: Original Cost Basis of $1,000,000**

Years After Asset Placed in Service	Depreciation Amount	Adjusted Basis
1	$300,000	$700,000
2	$200,000	$500,000
3	$100,000	$400,000
4	$100,000	$300,000
5	$100,000	$200,000
6	$100,000	$100,000
7	$100,000	$0

If a sale or other disposition of the asset occurs, the adjusted basis is used to calculate any gain or loss realized. *See* § 1001(a).

Our brief discussion of the tax impact of a jet purchase by Carnival communicates certain fundamentals but belies the complexity of the governing rules. Because different assets have different cost recovery periods, the treatment of capital expenditures varies, depending on the asset. An airplane might have a recovery period of twenty years, a building one of thirty years, a computer one of five years, and a printer one of three to four years. Further, even though one might think that annual amounts taken into account with respect to a capital expenditure should be equal, actual adjustments may vary over time (or they might, in fact, be equal annual adjustments). We also have to keep in mind that for some capital expenditures, the Code prohibits annual cost recovery adjustments; the item is purchased, the expense is capitalized, and only on sale or other disposition does one take its cost into account in calculating any gain or loss realized. If, for example, a taxpayer acquires a tangible, nonwasting asset (e.g., land), they will not be able to take cost recovery adjustments over time. On the flip side, some taxpayers may have the limited ability to deduct currently (as opposed to charging to a capital account) the full cost of certain tangible, depreciable assets (among other things) under § 179(a). For property placed in service in taxable years starting after December 31, 2017, taxpayers may generally expense the cost of up to $1,000,000 of § 179 property, although this limit is subject to reduction to the extent the aggregate cost of § 179 property placed in service in a particular tax year exceeds $2,500,000. The amount of the § 179(a) deduction cannot, in any event, exceed the taxpayer's taxable income derived from the active conduct of any trade or business during that taxable year; Code-based rules provide for the carryover of disallowed amounts. We will not cover the rules in this arena in elaborate detail. What's key is that you grasp the essentials.

At least one critical question confronts us at the outset. In light of the significance of the existence (or absence) of a future benefit to accurate categorization of an item as current expense or capital expenditure, what subsidiary standards, if any, inform a future benefit analysis? Does the sword of "future benefit" hang above the taxpayer's head by a thread or by a good, beefy rope? Taxpayers typically (though certainly not always) prefer to characterize a given item as noncapital (and thus currently deductible in full as yielding no real future benefit), and the IRS often takes the stance that a taxpayer must capitalize the cost of the item as an initial matter (given the existence of notable future benefit). If sizeable deductions are on the table, the stage is set for an epic battle. Fortunately, over time, Congress, the Treasury Department, and the courts have given us useful standards to apply, and in the next section, we develop a greater appreciation of them. From there, we will take a closer look at specific rules governing the tax treatment of capital expenditures before turning to the rules governing the tax treatment of inventory.

B. CURRENT EXPENSE V. CAPITAL EXPENDITURE

Although both current expenses and capital expenditures benefit a business, it is critically important that you develop an understanding of what these categories have in common and what distinguishes them. We think of items currently deductible under § 162 expenses as ordinary and necessary expenses incurred in carrying on a trade or business. A capital expenditure may well satisfy the common law definitions of ordinary and necessary, but as was noted previously, such an expenditure differs from a current expense in that it yields benefits to the taxpayer *beyond* the current taxable year. *United States v. Akin*, 248 F.2d 742, at 744 (10th Cir. 1957) ("It may be said in general terms that an expenditure should be treated as one in the nature of a capital outlay if it brings about the acquisition of an asset having a period of useful life in excess of one year or if it secures a like advantage to the taxpayer which has a life of more than one year.") (Citation omitted.) In light of the long-term benefit the taxpayer will enjoy as a result of acquiring the asset, § 263 intervenes to prevent the taking of a full and immediate deduction with respect to its cost. *See* Treas. Reg. § 1.263(a)-1(b) ("Nothing in this section changes the treatment of any amount that is specifically provided for under any provision of the Internal Revenue Code or the Treasury Regulations *other than* section 162(a) or section 212 and the regulations under those sections.") (Emphasis added.) The purchase of a jumbo jet by an airline is a good example of a capital expenditure, as is the purchase of a cement truck by a construction company. *See* Treas. Reg. § 1.263(a)-2(d)(1); *see also* Treas. Reg. § 1.263(a)-1(d)(1) (referring, in highly generalized terms, to "[a]n amount paid to acquire or produce a unit of real or personal property").

Although the purchase of a distinct, tangible asset may constitute a capital expenditure, it would be erroneous to assume that such expenditures only appear in that form. The durable, tangible asset is often the easy case, but whatever the expense, it will qualify as a capital expenditure if it yields benefits to the taxpayer beyond the immediate taxable year. As you might well guess, a number of items resist easy categorization. An expense may not appear rigidly related to a specific asset, but it may promise to yield some form of benefit to the taxpayer beyond a single taxable year (e.g., the salary of a hard-working and faithful employee). Other expenses may relate to a specific long-lived asset but, at the same time, have nothing to do with the initial asset purchase (e.g., a vehicle repair). We have to search for workable categorization standards in the governing statutes, Treasury Regulations, and judicial pronouncements. Even then, we may encounter frustration. Treasury Regulations § 1.162-4, for example, provides that a taxpayer "may deduct amounts paid for repairs and maintenance to tangible property," but this generous rule applies only "if the amounts paid are not otherwise required to be capitalized." Ascertaining the proper treatment of an item, then, may well require resort to judicial interpretations.

Case Preview

Midland Empire Packing Co. v. Commissioner

In *Midland Empire*, the taxpayer incurred various expenses to prevent the seepage of oil and water into its business premises. Given that the work involved shoring up concrete walls and floors, the question arose as to whether the associated expenses were currently deductible repairs or so substantial and enduring that they should be categorized as capital expenditures. As you read the case, consider the following questions:

1. Did the work undertaken by the taxpayer result in enhancement of the value of its business premises?
2. Did the work done on the taxpayer's basement extend the useful life of the facility?
3. Is the *American Bemberg Corporation* decision mentioned by the court factually analogous to the taxpayer's case, or is it distinguishable?

Midland Empire Packing Co. v. Commissioner
14 T.C. 635 (1950)

FINDINGS OF FACT

The petitioner, herein sometimes referred to as Midland, is a Montana corporation and the owner of a meat-packing plant which is located adjacent to the city of Billings, Yellowstone County, State of Montana. ***

The basement rooms of petitioner's plant were used by it in its business for the curing of hams and bacon and for the storage of meat and hides. These rooms have been used for such purposes since the plant was constructed in about 1917. The original walls and floors, which were of concrete, were not sealed against water. There had been seepage for many years and this condition became worse around 1943. At certain seasons of the year, when the water in the Yellowstone River was high, the underground water caused increased seepage in the plant. Such water did not interfere with petitioner's use of the basement rooms. They were satisfactory for their purpose until 1943.

The Yale Oil Corporation, sometimes referred to herein as Yale, was the owner of an oil-refining plant and storage area located some 300 yards upgrade from petitioner's meat-packing plant. The oil plant was constructed some years after petitioner had been in business in its present location. Yale expanded its plant and storage from year to year and oil escaping from the plant and storage facilities was carried to the ground surround[ing] the [] plant of petitioner. In 1943 petitioner found that oil was seeping into its water wells and into water which came through the concrete walls of the basement of its packing plant. The water would soon drain out through the sump, leaving a thick scum of oil on the basement floor. Such oil gave off a strong

[Handwritten margin notes: "Petitioner's argument", "2nd condition", "made worse by oil co."]

odor, which permeated the air of the entire plant. The oil in the basement and fumes therefrom created a fire hazard. The Federal meat inspectors advised petitioner to oilproof the basement and discontinue the use of the water wells or shut down the plant. ***

Midland decided to proceed with the work in the basement.... The Yale officials refused to do the repair work themselves. ***

The original walls and floor of petitioner's plant were of concrete construction. For the purpose of preventing oil from entering its basement, petitioner added concrete lining to the walls from the floor to a height of about four feet, and also added concrete to the floor of the basement. Since the walls and floor had been thickened, petitioner now had less space in which to operate. Petitioner had this work done by independent contractors . . . at a cost of $4,868.81. Petitioner paid for this work during [1943].

oilproofing

The oilproofing work was effective in sealing out the oil. While it has served the purposes for which it was intended down to the present time, it did not increase the useful life of the building or make the building more valuable for any purpose than it had been before the oil had come into the basement. The primary object of the oilproofing operation was to prevent the seepage of oil into the basement so that the petitioner could use the basement as before in preparing and packing meat for commercial consumption.

***

Midland charted the $4,868.81 to repair expense on its regular books and deducted that amount on its tax returns as an ordinary and necessary business expense for the fiscal year 1943. The Commissioner, in his notice of deficiency, determined that the cost of oilproofing was not deductible, either as an ordinary and necessary expense or as a loss in 1943.

Tax Return

OPINION

ARUNDELL, Judge:

The issue in this case is whether an expenditure for a concrete lining in petitioner's basement to oilproof it against an oil nuisance created by a neighboring refinery is deductible as an ordinary and necessary expense *** on the theory it was an expenditure for a repair, or, in the alternative, whether the expenditure may be treated as the measure of the loss sustained during the taxable year and not compensated for by insurance or otherwise . . . .

I

The respondent has contended, in part, that the expenditure is for a capital improvement and should be recovered through depreciation charges and is, therefore, not deductible as an ordinary and necessary business expense or as a loss.

Respondent's way

It is none too easy to determine on which side of the line certain expenditures fall so that they may be accorded their proper treatment for tax purposes. Treasury Regulations 111, from which we quote in the margin, is helpful in distinguishing between an expenditure to be classed as a repair and one to be treated as a capital outlay. In *Illinois Merchants Trust Co., Executor*, 4 B.T.A. 103, at page 106, we discussed this subject in some detail and in our opinion said:

It will be noted that the first sentence of the article (now Regulations 111, sec. 29.23(a)-4) relates to repairs, while the second sentence deals in effect with replacements. In determining whether an expenditure is a capital one or is chargeable against operating income, it is necessary to bear in mind that purpose for which the expenditure was made. To repair is to restore to a sound state or to mend, while a replacement connotes a substitution. A repair is an expenditure for the purpose of keeping the property in an ordinarily efficient operating condition. It does not add to the value of the property nor does it appreciably prolong its life. It merely keeps the property in an operating condition over its probable useful life for the uses for which it was acquired. Expenditures for that purpose are distinguishable from those for replacements, alterations, improvements, or additions which prolong the life of the property, increase its value, or make it adaptable to a different use. The one is a maintenance charge, while the others are additions to capital investment which should not be applied against current earnings.

It will be seen from our findings of fact that for some 25 years prior to the taxable year petitioner had used the basement rooms of its plant as a place for the curing of hams and bacon and for the storage of meat and hides. The basement had been entirely satisfactory for this purpose over the entire period in spite of the fact that there was some seepage of water into the rooms from time to time. In the taxable year it was found that not only water, but oil, was seeping through the concrete walls of the basement of the packing plant and, while the water would soon drain out, the oil would not, and there was left on the basement floor a thick scum of oil which gave off a strong odor that permeated the air of the entire plant, and the fumes from the oil created a fire hazard. It appears that the oil which came from a nearby refinery had also gotten into the water wells which served to furnish water for petitioner's plant, and as a result of this whole condition the Federal meat inspectors advised petitioner that it must discontinue the use of the water from the wells and oilproof the basement, or else shut down its plant.

To meet this situation, petitioner during the taxable year undertook steps to oil-proof the basement by adding a concrete lining to the walls from the floor to a height of about four feet and also added concrete to the floor of the basement. It is the cost of this work which it seeks to deduct as a repair. The basement was not enlarged by this work, nor did the oilproofing serve to make it more desirable for the purpose for which it had been used through the years prior to the time that the oil nuisance had occurred. The evidence is that the expenditure did not add to the value or prolong the expected life of the property over what they were before the event occurred which made the repairs necessary. It is true that after the work was done the seepage of water, as well as oil, was stopped, but, as already stated, the presence of the water had never been found objectionable. The repairs merely served to keep the property in an operating condition over its probable useful life for the purpose for which it was used.

While it is conceded on brief that the expenditure was "necessary," respondent contends that the encroachment of the oil nuisance on petitioner's property was not an "ordinary" expense in petitioner's particular business. But the fact that petitioner had not theretofore been called upon to make a similar expenditure to prevent damage and disaster to its property does not remove that expense from the classification of "ordinary" for, as stated in *Welch v. Helvering*, 290 U.S. 111, "ordinary in this context does not mean that the payments must be habitual or normal in the sense that the same taxpayer will have to make them often. * * * [T]he expense is an ordinary one because we know from experience that payments for such a purpose, whether the amount is large or small, are the common and accepted means of defense against attack. *Cf. Kornhauser v. United States*, 276 U.S. 145. The situation is unique in the life of the individual affected, but not in the life of the group, the community, of which he is a part." Steps to protect a business building from the seepage of oil from a nearby refinery, which had been erected long subsequent to the time petitioner started to operate its plant, would seem to us to be a normal thing to do, and in certain sections of the country it must be a common experience to protect one's property from the seepage of oil. Expenditures to accomplish this result are likewise normal.

In *American Bemberg Corporation*, 10 T.C. 361, we allowed as deductions, on the ground that they were ordinary and necessary expenses, extensive expenditures made to prevent disaster, although the repairs were of a type which had never been needed before and were unlikely to recur. In that case the taxpayer, to stop cave-ins of soil which were threatening destruction of its manufacturing plant, hired an engineering firm which drilled to the bedrock and injected grout to fill the cavities were practicable, and made incidental replacements and repairs, including tightening of the fluid carriers. In two successive years the taxpayer expended $734,316.76 and $199,154.33, respectively, for such drilling and grouting and $153,474.20 and $79,687.29, respectively, for capital replacements. We found that the cost (other than replacement) of this program did not make good the depreciation previously allowed, and stated in our opinion:

> In connection with the purpose of the work, the Proctor program was intended to avert a plant-wide disaster and avoid forced abandonment of the plant. The purpose was not to improve, better, extend, or increase the original plant, nor to prolong its original useful life. Its continued operation was endangered; the purpose of the expenditures was to enable petitioner to continue the plant in operation not on any new or better scale, but on the same scale and, so far as possible, as efficiently as it had operated before. The purpose was not to rebuild or replace the plant in whole or in part, but to keep the same plant as it was and where it was.

The petitioner here made the repairs in question in order that it might continue to operate its plant. Not only was there danger of fire from the oil and fumes, but the presence of the oil led the Federal meat inspectors to declare the basement an unsuitable place for the purpose for which it had been used for a quarter of a century. After the expenditures were made, the plant did not operate on a changed or larger scale, nor was it thereafter suitable for new or additional uses. The expenditure served only to permit petitioner to continue the use of the plant, and particularly the basement for its normal operations.

In our opinion, the expenditure of $4,868.81 for lining the basement walls and floor was essentially a repair and, as such, it is deductible as an ordinary and necessary business expense. This holding makes unnecessary a consideration of petitioner's alternative contention that the expenditure is deductible as a business loss, nor need we heed the respondent's argument that any loss suffered was compensated for by "insurance or otherwise."

Decision will be entered under Rule 50.

Post-Case Follow-Up

Midland Empire is a long-standing, landmark precedent in the tax arena. In the decision, the Tax Court concluded that lining the taxpayer's basement with concrete did not increase the property's value, prolong its longevity, or make it suitable for new uses. Rather, the concrete lining allowed the continued use of the property for its stated purpose for the remainder of its useful life. Accordingly, the court concluded that the cost of the concrete lining was a repair that was deductible as an ordinary and necessary business expense. Despite *Midland Empire's* soaring status as governing precedent, it's hard to see how adding something so durable and effective as a concrete lining to basement walls and floors fails to prolong at least part of the structure's useful life. Moreover, a basement free of oil and water leaks would certainly appear to be more valuable than one with that notable, business-threatening flaw left intact. Even so, the Tax Court equated the concrete lining with minor patchwork that might be done on other parts of the property, and the decision continues to provide support for the deductibility of repairs. In light of subsequent decisions of the Tax Court (set forth or referenced in later cases), one has to wonder whether it would reach the same conclusion today under similar facts.

Midland Empire Packing Co. v. Commissioner: Real Life Applications

1. Delivery Demon, Inc. ("DDI") owns a fleet of delivery trucks. A recent thunderstorm produced golf-ball-sized hail, some of which damaged several of DDI's trucks (e.g., causing chipped paint and minor windshield damage). If DDI pays independent contractors to restore the vehicles, will the cost constitute a current expense or a capital expenditure?

2. Carnival Air Lines, Inc. ("Carnival") offers regular passenger service between various cities in the United States and Rio de Janeiro, Brazil. Due to a recent air traffic control mishap, one of Carnival's airplanes was delayed on the runway for over three hours. Irate, the passengers demanded that the plane return to the terminal. When the pilot refused to do so, several passengers expressed their displeasure by damaging several of the small screens on the back of the passenger seat in front of them. If Carnival incurs various costs to fix the screens, will the aggregate cost constitute a current expense or a capital expenditure?

3. Airport Luxury Transport, Inc. specializes in transporting high net worth individuals from their residences to private air terminals. Recently, the company discovered that the transmissions in several vehicles were failing and replaced them. May the company deduct the associated cost as a current expense?

Case Preview

Norwest Corp. v. Commissioner

Midland Empire addressed the tax treatment of hazard-reducing repairs made with respect to part of a taxpayer's business premises. Would more extensive repairs warrant the same treatment? In *Norwest Corp. v. Commissioner*, the taxpayer decided to remodel its business premises. For a host of reasons, the taxpayer also decided (as part of the larger remodeling plan) to have asbestos-containing materials removed from the relevant facility. At the time of the building's construction, the dangers of volatile asbestos fibers were not known, but at the time of the remodeling, no one would have questioned the soundness of a business decision to have the material removed. Given that the company's action terminated an employee health hazard and facilitated a broader remodeling effort, should the cost of removal be treated as a currently deductible ordinary and necessary business expense or as a capital expenditure? Let's see how the Tax Court handled this issue. Consider the following questions as you make your way through the case:

Asbestos and Mesothelioma

Exposure to asbestos particles can cause malignant mesothelioma, a rare and dangerous form of cancer. The photo below depicts asbestos fibers.

Credit: Farbled/Shutterstock.com.

1. On what theory or theories does the Commissioner argue for capitalization of the relevant items?
2. What is the basic difference between a "repair" and a "capital improvement"?
3. What is the so-called *Plainfield-Union* test, and how does it factor into the analysis?

Norwest Corp. v. Commissioner
108 T.C. 265 (1997)

JACOBS, Judge:

[The Commissioner] determined deficiencies in petitioner's 1987 and 1988 Federal income taxes in the respective amounts of $93,413 and $3,999,398, as well as additional interest under section 6621(c) for 1988. Pursuant to an amended answer filed on September 23, 1994, respondent increased the amount of the 1988 deficiency to $4,644,201. ***

The issue[] for decisions [is]: (1) Whether petitioner is entitled to deduct the costs of removing asbestos-containing materials from its Douglas Street bank building. * * *

GENERAL FINDINGS

Norwest Corporation (hereinafter petitioner or Norwest), a Delaware corporation, had its principal place of business in Minneapolis, Minnesota, at the time the petitions were filed. ***

The first issue is whether petitioner is entitled to deduct the costs of removing asbestos-containing materials from its Douglas Street bank building. Petitioner argues that the expenditures constitute section 162(a) ordinary and necessary expenses. Respondent, on the other hand, contends that the expenditures must be capitalized pursuant to section 263(a)(1). Alternatively, respondent contends that the expenditures must be capitalized pursuant to the "general plan of rehabilitation" doctrine. ***

One of petitioner's subsidiaries, Norwest Bank Nebraska, N.A. (Norwest Nebraska), owns a building at 1919 Douglas Street in Omaha, Nebraska (the Douglas Street building or building). The Douglas Street building is a three-story commercial office building that occupies half a square block and has a lower level parking garage. Norwest Nebraska constructed the building in 1969 at a $4,883,232 cost. During all relevant periods, Norwest Nebraska used the Douglas Street building as an operations center as well as a branch for serving customers. ***

In 1985 and 1986, Norwest Nebraska consolidated its "back room" operations at the Douglas Street building. Pursuant to that process, Norwest Nebraska undertook to determine the most efficient means for providing more space to accommodate the additional operations personnel within the building. The planning process indicated that the building needed a major remodeling. (The building had not been remodeled since its construction; Norwest Nebraska usually remodels its banks every 10 to 15 years.) Thus, by the end of 1986, petitioner and Norwest Nebraska had decided to completely remodel the Douglas Street building. In December 1986, both petitioner and Norwest Nebraska approved a preliminary budget of $2,738,000 for carpet, furniture, and improvements. ***

The Douglas Street building was constructed with asbestos-containing materials as its main fire-retardant material. (The local fire code required that buildings contain fireproofing material.) Asbestos-containing materials were sprayed on all columns, steel I-beams, and decking between floors. The health dangers of asbestos were not widely known when the Douglas Street building was constructed in 1969, and asbestos-containing materials were generally used in building construction in Omaha, Nebraska.

A commercial office building's ventilation system removes existing air from a room through a return air plenum as new air is introduced. The returned air is subsequently recycled through the building. The area between the decking and the suspended ceiling in the Douglas Street building functioned as the return air plenum. The top part of the return air plenum, the decking, was one of the components of the building where asbestos-containing materials had been sprayed during construction.

Over time, the decking, suspended ceiling tiles, and light fixtures throughout the building became contaminated. This contamination occurred because the asbestos-containing fireproofing had begun to delaminate, and pieces of this material reached the top of the suspended ceiling. ***

In the 1970s and 1980s, research confirmed that asbestos-containing materials can release fibers that cause serious diseases when inhaled or swallowed. Diseases resulting from exposure to asbestos can reach the incurable stage before detection and can cause severe disability or death. Asbestosis is a progressive and disabling lung disease caused by inhaling asbestos fibers that become lodged in the lungs. Persons exposed to asbestos may develop lung cancer or mesothelioma, an extremely rare form of cancer.

On March 29, 1971, the Environmental Protection Agency (EPA) designated asbestos a hazardous substance. The parties have stipulated that Federal, State, and local laws and regulations at all relevant times did not require asbestos-containing materials to be removed from commercial office buildings if they could be controlled in place. Nevertheless, building owners had to take precautions against the release of asbestos fibers.

The presence of asbestos in a building does not necessarily endanger the health of building occupants. The danger arises when asbestos-containing materials are damaged or disturbed, thereby releasing asbestos fibers into the air (when they can be inhaled). ***

Asbestos removal must be performed by specially trained professionals wearing protective clothing and respirators. The work area must be properly contained to prevent release of fibers into other areas. Containment typically requires barriers of polyethylene plastic sheets with folded seams, complete with air locks and negative air pressure systems. Asbestos-containing materials that are removed must be wetted to reduce fiber release. Once removed, the materials must be disposed of in leak-tight containers in special landfills. ***

In October 1985, petitioner's general liability and property damage insurer, the St. Paul Property and Liability Insurance Co. (St. Paul), tested a bulk sample of fire-retardant material from the Douglas Street building's steel I-beams to determine whether the building contained asbestos. The results indicated that the material contained 8 to 10 percent chrysotile asbestos, the most common type of asbestos. ***

The highest level of airborne fiber concentration at the Douglas Street building (0.006 fiber per cubic centimeter of air) did not exceed either the EPA or OSHA guidelines. There was, however, the expectation that the airborne asbestos-fiber concentrations would continue to increase. Moreover, the asbestos-containing fireproofing at the Douglas Street Building had characteristics that the EPA had identified as warranting removal of the material, such as evidence of delamination, presence of debris, proximity to an air plenum, and necessity of access for maintenance.

After considering the circumstances, petitioner decided to remove the asbestos-containing materials from the Douglas Street building (other than the parking garage) in coordination with the overall remodeling project. Indeed, the remodeling could not have been undertaken without disturbing the asbestos-containing fireproofing. Thus, because petitioner and Norwest Nebraska chose to remodel, it became a matter of necessity to remove the asbestos-containing materials. Petitioner essentially decided that "managing the asbestos in place" was not a viable option, given the extent of remodeling that would disturb the asbestos.

Removing the asbestos-containing materials from the Douglas Street building at the same time as, and in connection with, the remodeling was more cost efficient than conducting the removal and renovations as two separate projects at different times. It also minimized the amount of inconvenience to building employees and customers. ***

The asbestos removal and remodeling were basically performed in 13 phases; each phase involved a defined area of the Douglas Street building. ***

Removing all the asbestos-containing materials from the Douglas Street building was a large project, entailing an enormous amount of work. Nearly every suspended ceiling and light fixture on all four levels of the building had to be taken down. Asbestos-containing materials were removed from the entire building.

The asbestos fireproofing in the Douglas Street building was replaced with Cafco, a mineral wool material. The ceiling tiles on the Farnam parking level, as well as the floor tiles in the customer lobbies, were replaced with new, asbestos-free materials. ***

The removal of the asbestos-containing materials from the Douglas Street building was substantially completed by the end of May 1989. ***

The removal of the asbestos-containing materials from the Douglas Street building did not extend the building's useful life. ***

The total cost of renovating the Douglas Street building was close to $7 million, comprising nearly $4,998,749 in remodeling costs and approximately $1.9 million in asbestos removal costs. ***

On its 1987 and 1988 returns, petitioner claimed neither depreciation nor ordinary deductions with respect to the costs of removing the asbestos-containing materials from the Douglas Street building. On its 1989 return, however, petitioner claimed a $7,696 depreciation deduction and a $902,206 ordinary and necessary business deduction with respect to such expenditures.

Petitioner asserts in its petitions that it properly deducted the $902,206 on its 1989 return. In addition, petitioner claims that it is also entitled to ordinary and necessary business deductions for the costs of removing the asbestos-containing materials from the Douglas Street building for tax years 1987 and 1988 in the respective amounts of $175,095 and $863,764 (which amounts, petitioner claims, were inadvertently omitted from its 1987 and 1988 returns). ***

In the notice of deficiency, respondent disallowed petitioner's $902,206 ordinary and necessary deduction for asbestos-removal expenditures.

DISCUSSION

At issue is whether petitioner's costs of removing the asbestos-containing materials are currently deductible pursuant to section 162 or must be capitalized pursuant to section 263 or as part of a general plan of rehabilitation.***

Section 263 requires taxpayers to capitalize costs incurred for permanent improvements, betterments, or restorations to property. In general, these costs include expenditures that add to the value or substantially prolong the life of the property or adapt such property to a new or different use. Sec. 1.263(a)-1(b), Income Tax Regs. In contrast, section 162 permits taxpayers to currently deduct the costs of ordinary and necessary expenses (including incidental repairs) that neither materially add to the value of property nor appreciably prolong its life but keep the property in an ordinarily efficient operating condition.

Deductions are exceptions to the norm of capitalization. *INDOPCO, Inc. v. Commissioner,* 503 U.S. 79, 84, 112 S. Ct. 1039, 117 L. Ed. 2d 226 (1992). An income tax deduction is a matter of legislative grace; the taxpayer bears the burden of proving its right to a claimed deduction. Rule 142(a); *Welch v. Helvering,* 290 U.S. 111, 115, 54 S. Ct. 8, 78 L. Ed. 212 (1933). ***

The distinction between repairs and capital improvements has also been characterized as follows:

> "The test which normally is to be applied is that if the improvements were made to 'put' the particular capital asset in efficient operating condition, then they are capital in nature. If, however, they were made merely to 'keep' the asset in efficient operating condition, then they are repairs and are deductible." *[Test]*

Moss v. Commissioner, 831 F.2d 833, 835 (9th Cir. 1987)***.

The Court in *Plainfield-Union Water Co. v. Commissioner,* 39 T.C. 333, 338, 1962 WL 1262 (1962), articulated a test for determining whether an expenditure is capital by comparing the value, use, life expectancy, strength, or capacity of the property after the expenditure with the status of the property before the condition necessitating the expenditure arose (the *Plainfield-Union* test). Moreover, the Internal Revenue Code's capitalization provision envisions an inquiry into the duration and extent of the benefits realized by the taxpayer. See *INDOPCO, Inc. v. Commissioner, supra* at 88.

Whether an expense is deductible or must be capitalized is a factual determination. *Plainfield-Union Water Co. v. Commissioner, supra* at 337–338. Courts have adopted a practical case-by-case approach in applying the principles of capitalization and deductibility. *Wolfsen Land & Cattle Co. v. Commissioner,* 72 T.C. 1, 14, 1979 WL 3856 (1979). The decisive distinctions between current expenses and capital expenditures "are those of degree and not of kind." *Welch v. Helvering, supra* at 114.***

General Plan of Rehabilitation Doctrine

Expenses incurred as part of a plan of rehabilitation or improvement must be capitalized even though the same expenses if incurred separately would be deductible as ordinary and necessary. Unanticipated expenses that would be deductible as business expenses if incurred in isolation must be capitalized when incurred pursuant to a plan of rehabilitation. Whether a plan of capital improvement exists is a factual question "based upon a realistic appraisal of all the surrounding facts and circumstances, including, but not limited to, the purpose, nature, extent, and value of the work done." *[Statement of rule]*

An asset need not be completely out of service or in total disrepair for the general plan of rehabilitation doctrine to apply. For example, in *Bank of Houston v. Commissioner,* T.C. Memo.1960–110, the taxpayer's 50-year-old building was in "a general state of disrepair" but still serviceable for the purposes used (before, during, and after the work) and was in good structural condition. The taxpayer hired a contractor to perform the renovation (which included nonstructural repairs to flooring, electrical wiring, plaster, window frames, patched brick, and paint, as well as plumbing repairs, demolition, and cleanup). Temporary barriers and closures were erected during work in progress. The Court recognized that each phase of the remodeling project, removed in time and context, might be considered a repair item, but stated that "The Code, however, does not envision the fragmentation of an over-all project for deduction or capitalization purposes." The Court held that the expenditures were not made for incidental repairs but were part of an overall plan of rehabilitation, restoration, and improvement of the building. ***

Petitioner contends that the costs of removing the asbestos-containing materials are deductible as ordinary and necessary business expenses because: (1) The asbestos removal constitutes "repairs" within the meaning of section 1.162-4, Income Tax Regs.; (2) the asbestos removal did not increase the value of the Douglas Street building when compared to its value before it was known to contain a hazardous substance — a hazard was essentially removed and the building's value was restored to the value existing prior to the discovery of the concealed hazard; (3) although performed concurrently, the asbestos removal and remodeling were not part of a general plan of rehabilitation because they were separate and distinct projects, conceived of independently, undertaken for different purposes, and performed by separate contractors; and (4) using the principles of section 213 (which allows individuals to deduct certain personal medical expenses that are capital in nature) and section 1.162-10, Income Tax Regs. (which allows a trade or business to deduct medical expenses paid to employees on account of sickness), the cost of removing a health hazard is deductible under section 162.

Respondent, on the other hand, contends that the costs of removing the asbestos-containing materials must be capitalized because: (1) The removal was neither incidental nor a repair; (2) petitioner made permanent improvements that increased the value of the property by removing a major building component and replacing it with a new and safer component, thereby improving the original condition of the building; (3) petitioner permanently eliminated the asbestos hazard that was present when it built the building, creating safer and more efficient operating conditions and reducing the risk of future asbestos-related damage claims and potentially higher insurance premiums; (4) the asbestos removal and the remodeling were part of a single project to rehabilitate and improve the building; (5) the purpose of the expenditure was not to keep the property in ordinarily efficient operating condition, but to effect a general restoration of the property as part of the remodeling; and (6) section 213 and section 1.162-10, Income Tax Regs., are not analogous to the present case.

The parties also disagree as to whether the *Plainfield-Union* test is appropriate for determining whether petitioner's asbestos removal expenditures are capital. Petitioner contends that it is the appropriate test because the condition necessitating the asbestos removal was the discovery that asbestos is hazardous to human health. Accordingly, until the danger was discovered, petitioner argues that the physical presence of the asbestos had no effect on the building's value. Only after the danger was perceived could the contamination affect the building's operations and reduce its value.

Petitioner points to Rev. Rul. 94-38, 1994-1 C.B. 35, which cites *Plainfield-Union* in addressing the proper treatment of costs to remediate soil and treat groundwater that a taxpayer had contaminated with hazardous waste from its business. The ruling treats such costs (other than those attributable to the construction of groundwater treatment facilities) as currently deductible.

Respondent, on the other hand, argues that the discovery that asbestos is hazardous and that the Douglas Street building contained that substance is not a relevant or satisfactory reference point. Respondent contends that the *Plainfield-Union* test does not apply herein because a comparison cannot be made between the status of the building before it contained asbestos and after the asbestos was removed; since construction, the building has *always* contained asbestos. In cases where the *Plainfield-Union* test has been applied . . ., respondent continues, the condition necessitating the repair resulted from a physical change in the property's condition. In this case, no change occurred to the building's physical condition that necessitated the removal expenditures. The only change was in petitioner's awareness of the dangers of asbestos. Accordingly, respondent argues that the *Plainfield-Union* test is inapplicable, and the Court must examine other factors to determine whether an increase in the building's value occurred.

Respondent also disagrees with petitioner's reliance on Rev. Rul. 94-38, *supra,* arguing that the present facts are distinguishable. The remediated property addressed in the ruling was not contaminated by hazardous waste when the taxpayer acquired it. The ruling permits a deduction only for the costs of remediating soil and water whose physical condition has changed during the taxpayer's ownership of the property. Under this analysis, the taxpayer is viewed as restoring the property to the condition existing before its contamination. Thus, respondent contends, unlike Rev. Rul. 94-38, petitioner's expenditures did not return the property to the same state that existed when the property was constructed because there was never a time when the building was asbestos free. Rather, the asbestos-abatement costs improved the property beyond its original, unsafe condition.

Analysis

We believe that petitioner decided to remove the asbestos-containing materials from the Douglas Street building beginning in 1987 primarily because their removal was essential before the remodeling work could begin. The extent of the asbestos-containing materials in the building or the concentration of airborne asbestos fibers was not discovered until after petitioner decided to remodel the building and a budget for the remodeling had been approved. Because petitioner's extensive remodeling work would, of necessity, disturb the asbestos fireproofing, petitioner had no practical alternative but to remove the fireproofing. Performing the asbestos removal in connection with the remodeling was more cost effective than performing the same work as two separate projects at different times. (Had petitioner remodeled without removing the asbestos first, the remodeling would have been damaged by subsequent asbestos removal, thereby creating additional costs to petitioner.) We believe that petitioner's separation of the removal and remodeling work is artificial and does not properly reflect the record before us. The parties have stipulated that the asbestos removal did not increase the useful life of the Douglas Street building. We recognize (as did petitioner) that removal of the asbestos did increase the value of the building compared to its value when it was known to contain a hazard. However, we do not find, as respondent advocates, that the expenditures for asbestos removal materially increased the value of the building so as to require them to be capitalized. We find, however, that had there been no remodeling, the asbestos would have remained in place and would not have been removed until a later date. In other words, *but for* the remodeling, the asbestos removal would not have occurred.

The asbestos removal and remodeling were part of one intertwined project, entailing a full-blown general plan of rehabilitation, linked by logistical and economic concerns. "A remodeling project, taken as a whole, is but the result of various steps and stages." *Bank of Houston v. Commissioner,* T.C. Memo. 1960-110. In fact, removal of the asbestos fireproofing in the Douglas Street building was "part of the preparations for the remodeling project." See *id.* Before remodeling could begin, nearly every ceiling light fixture in the building was ripped down and crews removed all the asbestos-containing materials that had been sprayed on the columns, I-beams, and decking between floors, as well as the floor tiles in the customer lobbies. Only then could the remodeling contractor perform its work. As described above, the entire project required close coordination of the asbestos removal and remodeling work.

Clearly, the purpose of removing the asbestos-containing materials was first and foremost to effectuate the remodeling and renovation of the building. Secondarily, petitioner intended to eliminate health risks posed by the presence of asbestos and to minimize the potential liability for damages arising from injuries to employees and customers.

In sum, based on our analysis of all the facts and circumstances, we hold that the costs of removing the asbestos-containing materials must be capitalized because they were part of a general plan of rehabilitation and renovation that improved the Douglas Street building.

4. Costs must be capitalized

Post-Case Follow-Up

Although acknowledging that specific repairs (in isolation) might justify an immediate deduction, the Tax Court emphasizes in *Norwest Corporation* that the extensive repairs and remodeling effected by the taxpayer pursuant to a coordinated plan merited capitalization under the general rehabilitation doctrine. As doctrinal evolution goes, the opinion adds useful balance to *Midland Empire* by clarifying that at some point extensive repairs go beyond mere patchwork and begin to yield notable, long-term benefits. Capitalization is the only appropriate treatment. The persistent difficulty, however, is drawing the line between extensive repairs on the one hand and general rehabilitation on the other. The court notes the following:

> Expenses incurred as part of a plan of rehabilitation or improvement must be capitalized even though the same expenses if incurred separately would be deductible as ordinary and necessary. Unanticipated expenses that would be deductible as business expenses if incurred in isolation must be capitalized when incurred pursuant to a plan of rehabilitation. Whether a plan of capital improvement exists is a factual question "based upon a realistic appraisal of all the surrounding facts and circumstances, including, but not limited to, the purpose, nature, extent, and value of the work done."

Perhaps it is impossible to state in generic terms when individual repairs coalesce into a general plan of rehabilitation. Taxpayer situations differ, and one can certainly argue that giving courts flexibility to weigh unique factors and decide accordingly has its merits.

Norwest Corp. v. Commissioner: Real Life Applications

1. Bibbs Enterprises, Inc. ("BEI") has extensive warehouse storage facilities. Although most of its facilities have held up over the years, a number of warehouses have developed extensive roof problems. If BEI replaces all of its warehouse roofs, will the cost constitute a capital expenditure? *Yes*

2. ***Same facts as Question #1***, except that the roofs have generally held up well. On occasion, lightning will strike one of the warehouses and cause minor damage; modest leaks may or may not result. If BEI has contractors fix all minor lightning damage, may it deduct the cost currently?

3. Assume that Carnival Air Lines, Inc. ("Carnival") decides to upgrade several of the more geriatric planes in its long-range fleet by replacing the seats in coach and upgrading the seats in the First Class cabin so that each has direct aisle access and reclines to "flat" for passengers desiring to sleep on overnight flights. Will the associated costs be capital expenditures for Carnival?

4. Somerset, Inc. ("Somerset") owns several apartment buildings. After a tenant moves out, Somerset generally has its employees repaint the unit and steamclean the carpets. During 2019, Somerset decided to do more with recently vacated units on the top five floors. Regarding a vacancy in those units, Somerset instructed its employees to renovate the kitchens and bathrooms and repaint the entire unit. Will Somerset be able to deduct the cost of repainting in these units?

Case Preview

INDOPCO, Inc. v. Commissioner

Although neither *Midland Empire* nor *Norwest Corp.* dealt with the acquisition of a distinct, tangible asset, they both involved expenses incurred with respect to such assets, and in *Norwest Corp.*, at least, the court found that the expenses constituted capital expenditures. But, as we already know, one cannot assert that capital expenditures arise only from the acquisition or modification of a distinct, tangible asset. A business may incur expenses that effect meaningful and lasting change but cannot be associated with a distinct asset. In *INDOPCO, Inc. v. Commissioner*, 503 U.S. 79 (1992), for example, the taxpayer paid various professional service providers in connection with a significant corporate transaction. The transaction promised to prove beneficial to the corporation for years to come, but there was a distinct issue as to whether the costs paid with respect to the professional service providers (who helped to facilitate and seal the deal) warranted capitalization or qualified for full and immediate deduction as ordinary and necessary business expenses. As you make your way through the facts and discussion in the opinion, consider the following questions:

1. Why is the U.S. Supreme Court's decision in *Commissioner v. Lincoln Savings & Loan Association* of relevance here?
2. What future benefits did INDOPCO secure as a result of the transaction?
3. In the opinion of the Court, does the existence of any future benefit warrant capitalization?

INDOPCO, Inc. v. Commissioner
503 U.S. 79 (1992)

Justice BLACKMUN delivered the opinion of the Court.

In this case we must decide whether certain professional expenses incurred by a target corporation in the course of a friendly takeover are deductible by that corporation as "ordinary and necessary" business expenses under § 162(a) of the Internal Revenue Code.

I

Justice Harry A. Blackmun

Appointed by President Nixon, Associate Justice Harry A. Blackmun joined the U.S. Supreme Court in 1970.

Credit: Photo courtesy of the U.S. Library of Congress.

Most of the relevant facts are stipulated. Petitioner INDOPCO, Inc., formerly named National Starch and Chemical Corporation and hereinafter referred to as National Starch, is a Delaware corporation that manufactures and sells adhesives, starches, and specialty chemical products. In October 1977, representatives of Unilever United States, Inc., also a Delaware corporation (Unilever), expressed interest in acquiring National Starch, which was one of its suppliers, through a friendly transaction. National Starch at the time had outstanding over 6,563,000 common shares held by approximately 3,700 shareholders. The stock was listed on the New York Stock Exchange. Frank and Anna Greenwall were the corporation's largest shareholders and owned approximately 14.5% of the common. The Greenwalls, getting along in years and concerned about their estate plans, indicated that they would transfer their shares to Unilever only if a transaction tax free for them could be arranged.

[National Starch and Unilever completed the transaction with the assistance of investment bankers and attorneys. The court proceeds to address the tax treatment of various costs (including fees for professional services) associated with the transaction.]

Morgan Stanley charged National Starch a fee of $2,200,000, along with $7,586 for out-of-pocket expenses and $18,000 for legal fees. The Debevoise firm charged National Starch $490,000, along with $15,069 for out-of-pocket expenses. National Starch also incurred expenses aggregating $150,962 for miscellaneous items — such as accounting, printing, proxy solicitation, and Securities and Exchange Commission fees — in connection with the transaction. No issue is raised as to the propriety or reasonableness of these charges.

On its federal income tax return for its short taxable year ended August 15, 1978, National Starch claimed a deduction for the $2,225,586 paid to Morgan Stanley, but did not deduct the $505,069 paid to Debevoise or the other expenses. Upon audit, the Commissioner of Internal Revenue disallowed the claimed deduction and issued a notice of deficiency. Petitioner sought redetermination in the United States Tax Court, asserting, however, not only the right to deduct the investment banking fees and expenses but, as well, the legal and miscellaneous expenses incurred.

The Tax Court, in an unreviewed decision, ruled that the expenditures were capital in nature and therefore not deductible under § 162(a) in the 1978 return as "ordinary and necessary expenses." The court based its holding primarily on the long-term benefits that accrued to National Starch from the Unilever acquisition. The United States Court of Appeals for the Third Circuit affirmed, upholding the Tax Court's findings that "both Unilever's enormous resources and the possibility of synergy arising from the transaction served the long-term betterment of National Starch." In so doing, the Court of Appeals rejected National Starch's contention that, because the disputed expenses did not "create or enhance . . . a separate and distinct additional asset," see *Commissioner v. Lincoln Savings & Loan Assn.,* 403 U.S. 345, 354, 91 S. Ct. 1893, 1899, 29 L. Ed. 2d 519 (1971), they could not be capitalized and therefore were deductible under § 162(a). We granted certiorari to resolve a perceived conflict on the issue among the Courts of Appeals.

II

Section 162(a) of the Internal Revenue Code allows the deduction of "all the ordinary and necessary expenses paid or incurred during the taxable year in carrying on any trade or business." In contrast, § 263 of the Code allows no deduction for a capital expenditure — an "amount paid out for new buildings or for permanent improvements or betterments made to increase the value of any property or estate." The primary effect of characterizing a payment as either a business expense or a capital expenditure concerns the timing of the taxpayer's cost recovery: While business expenses are currently deductible, a capital expenditure usually is amortized and depreciated over the life of the relevant asset, or, where no specific asset or useful life can be ascertained, is deducted upon dissolution of the enterprise. Through provisions such as these, the Code endeavors to match expenses with the revenues of the taxable period to which they are properly attributable, thereby resulting in a more accurate calculation of net income for tax purposes.

In exploring the relationship between deductions and capital expenditures, this Court has noted the "familiar rule" that "an income tax deduction is a matter of legislative grace and that the burden of clearly showing the right to the claimed deduction is on the taxpayer." The notion that deductions are exceptions to the norm of capitalization finds support in various aspects of the Code. Deductions are specifically enumerated and thus are subject to disallowance in favor of capitalization. Nondeductible capital expenditures, by contrast, are not exhaustively enumerated in the Code; rather than providing a "complete list of nondeductible expenditures," § 263 serves as a general means of distinguishing capital expenditures from current expenses. For these reasons, deductions are strictly construed and allowed only "as there is a clear provision therefor."

The Court also has examined the interrelationship between the Code's business expense and capital expenditure provisions. In so doing, it has had occasion to parse § 162(a) and explore certain of its requirements. For example, in *Lincoln Savings*, we determined that, to qualify for deduction under § 162(a), "an item must (1) be 'paid or incurred during the taxable year,' (2) be for 'carrying on any trade or business,' (3) be an 'expense,' (4) be a 'necessary' expense, and (5) be an 'ordinary' expense." 403 U.S., at 352, 91 S. Ct., at 1898. The Court has recognized, however, that the "decisive distinctions" between current expenses and capital expenditures "are those of degree and not of kind," *Welch v. Helvering,* 290 U.S., at 114, 54 S. Ct., at 9, and that because each case "turns on its special facts," the cases sometimes appear difficult to harmonize.

National Starch contends that the decision in *Lincoln Savings* changed these familiar backdrops and announced an exclusive test for identifying capital expenditures, a test in which "creation or enhancement of an asset" is a prerequisite to capitalization, and deductibility under § 162(a) is the rule rather than the exception. We do not agree, for we conclude that National Starch has overread *Lincoln Savings.*

In *Lincoln Savings,* we were asked to decide whether certain premiums, required by federal statute to be paid by a savings and loan association to the Federal Savings and Loan Insurance Corporation (FSLIC), were ordinary and necessary expenses under § 162(a), as Lincoln Savings argued and the Court of Appeals had held, or capital expenditures under § 263, as the Commissioner contended. We found that the "additional" premiums, the purpose of which was to provide FSLIC with a secondary reserve fund in which each insured institution retained a pro rata interest recoverable in certain situations, "serv[e] to create or enhance for Lincoln what is essentially a separate and distinct additional asset." 403 U.S., at 354, 91 S. Ct., at 1899. "[A]s an inevitable consequence," we concluded, "the payment is capital in nature and not an expense, let alone an ordinary expense, deductible under § 162(a)." *Ibid.*

Lincoln Savings stands for the simple proposition that a taxpayer's expenditure that "serves to create or enhance . . . a separate and distinct" asset should be capitalized under § 263. It by no means follows, however, that *only* expenditures that create or enhance separate and distinct assets are to be capitalized under § 263. We had no occasion in *Lincoln Savings* to consider the tax treatment of expenditures that, unlike the additional premiums at issue there, did not create or enhance a specific asset, and thus the case cannot be read to preclude capitalization in other circumstances. In short, *Lincoln Savings* holds that the creation of a separate and distinct asset well may be a sufficient, but not a necessary, condition to classification as a capital expenditure.

Nor does our statement in *Lincoln Savings,* that "the presence of an ensuing benefit that may have some future aspect is not controlling" prohibit reliance on future benefit as a means of distinguishing an ordinary business expense from a capital expenditure. Although the mere presence of an incidental future benefit — "*some future aspect*" — may not warrant capitalization, a taxpayer's realization of benefits beyond the year in which the expenditure is incurred is undeniably important in determining whether the appropriate tax treatment is immediate deduction or capitalization. Indeed, the text of the Code's capitalization provision, § 263(a)(1), which refers to "permanent improvements or betterments," itself envisions an inquiry into the duration and extent of the benefits realized by the taxpayer.

III

In applying the foregoing principles to the specific expenditures at issue in this case, we conclude that National Starch has not demonstrated that the investment banking, legal, and other costs it incurred in connection with Unilever's acquisition of its shares are deductible as ordinary and necessary business expenses under § 162(a).

Although petitioner attempts to dismiss the benefits that accrued to National Starch from the Unilever acquisition as "entirely speculative" or "merely incidental," the Tax Court's and the Court of Appeals' findings that the transaction produced significant benefits to National Starch that extended beyond the tax year in question are amply supported by the record. For example, in commenting on the merger with Unilever, National Starch's 1978 "Progress Report" observed that the company would "benefit greatly from the availability of Unilever's enormous resources, especially in the area of basic technology." Morgan Stanley's report to the National Starch board concerning the fairness to shareholders of a possible business combination with Unilever noted that National Starch management "feels that some synergy may exist with the Unilever organization given a) the nature of the Unilever chemical, paper, plastics and packaging operations . . . and b) the strong consumer products orientation of Unilever United States, Inc."

In addition to these anticipated resource-related benefits, National Starch obtained benefits through its transformation from a publicly held, freestanding corporation into a wholly owned subsidiary of Unilever. ***

Courts long have recognized that expenses such as these, " 'incurred for the purpose of changing the corporate structure for the benefit of future operations are not ordinary and necessary business expenses.' " Deductions for professional expenses thus have been disallowed in a wide variety of cases concerning changes in corporate structure. Although support for these decisions can be found in the specific terms of § 162(a), which require that deductible expenses be "ordinary and necessary" and incurred "in carrying on any trade or business," courts more frequently have characterized an expenditure as capital in nature because "the purpose for which the expenditure is made has to do with the corporation's operations and betterment, sometimes with a continuing capital asset, for the duration of its existence or for the indefinite future or for a time somewhat longer than the current taxable year." The rationale behind these decisions applies equally to the professional charges at issue in this case.

IV

The expenses that National Starch incurred in Unilever's friendly takeover do not qualify for deduction as "ordinary and necessary" business expenses under § 162(a). The fact that the expenditures do not create or enhance a separate and distinct additional asset is not controlling; the acquisition-related expenses bear the indicia of capital expenditures and are to be treated as such.

The judgment of the Court of Appeals is affirmed.

It is so ordered.

Post-Case Follow-Up

Rejecting the notion that a capital expenditure arises only upon the creation of a separate and distinct asset, the *INDOPCO* court held that expenditures giving rise to future taxpayer benefit (beyond the merely incidental) warrant capitalization. The decision's initial impact was jarring given that one could read its holding to require the capitalization of almost any expense. Given the far-reaching and potentially calamitous impact of such a pronouncement, prompt guidance from the Treasury Department was needed. Treasury Regulations § 1.263(a)-5 now clarifies the extent to which amounts paid or incurred to facilitate acquisitions of trades or businesses or to effect changes in the capital structure of a business must be capitalized. The rules devote special attention to the meaning and extent of "facilitate" and thereby offer taxpayers a more accurate sense as to whether a given expense falls within or without the mandatory capitalization regime. As a response, the guidance from the Treasury accomplishes a great deal in terms of diluting *INDOPCO* and rescuing taxpayers from the decision's full and potentially caustic strength.

INDOPCO, Inc. v. Commissioner: Real Life Applications

Note: Answering the following questions will require not only application of the case but also consultation of the relevant Treasury Regulations.

1. The Board of Directors of Acquiring Corporation ("Acquiring") has reached agreement with the Board of Directors of Target Corporation ("Target") to effect a friendly merger of Target with and into Acquiring. Acquiring instructs its General Counsel to have regular outside counsel, Global Law Firm, LLP ("GLF") draft the merger agreement. If Acquiring pays $25,000 to GLF for a completed merger agreement, must Acquiring capitalize the cost?

2. *Same facts as Question #1*, except that Acquiring must pay a fee to a federal regulatory agency to complete an antitrust review of the transaction. Must Acquiring capitalize the fee payment?

3. *Same facts as Question #1*, except the cost at issue is the salary earned by Pat, the Executive Secretary of Acquiring's CEO. Pat worked full-time for the CEO during all phases of the transaction and performed a wide range of tasks related directly to the acquisition of Target by Acquiring. Must Acquiring capitalize amounts paid to Pat in connection with work on this transaction?

C. DEPRECIATION AND AMORTIZATION

1. In General

Earlier in this chapter we devoted brief attention to depreciation or "cost recovery." At this juncture, we explore the statutory provisions regarding depreciation and focus briefly on the rules governing a subject we have yet to address: amortization. In each instance, our coverage is intentionally limited, given that a substantial percentage of these rules serve largely, as a practical matter, to guide accountants and others charged with tax compliance.

2. Depreciation

Section 167 of the Code provides, in pertinent part, that "[t]here shall be allowed as a depreciation deduction a reasonable allowance for the exhaustion, wear and tear (including a reasonable allowance for obsolescence) of property used in the trade or business or of property held for the production of income." Section § 167(a). The provision goes on to indicate, in essence, that the amount one may take into account with respect to exhaustion, wear, and tear is determined by the asset's basis (as adjusted from time to time). Although § 167 provides for a depreciation allowance, it is § 168 which fleshes out the practical details. In general, for tangible property, depreciation must be in accordance with the following:

- The applicable depreciation method;
- The applicable depreciation recovery period; and
- The applicable convention.

See § 168(a).

The *applicable depreciation method* refers to the rate at which the taxpayer may depreciate the total asset cost. We have discussed the concepts previously. For some assets, the applicable method will be the straight line method, and for others depreciation will occur at an accelerated rate (e.g., the 200 percent declining balance method or the 150 percent declining balance method). *See generally* § 168(b). The *applicable recovery period* refers to the number of years over which the depreciation deduction will take place, which, in turn, is determined by the property's classification (e.g., 3-year property, 10-year property, 20-year property, "residential rental property," etc.). *See generally* § 168(c) and (e)(1). Finally, the *applicable convention* refers to the default assumption to be made with respect to when items were placed in service and thus made eligible for depreciation (or when they were disposed of and thus made no longer eligible for depreciation by the disposing taxpayer). The relevant conventions include the half-year convention, the mid-month convention, and the mid-quarter convention. *See generally* § 168(d).

By the way, note that from time to time, Congress will allow taxpayers to take additional or even extraordinary up-front depreciation deductions (i.e., bonus depreciation) as a means of stimulating investment in specific assets. If first-year bonus depreciation is 100% of the asset's basis, then the bonus depreciation is, in effect, an immediate expensing allowance.

Keep in Mind

Under the Treasury Regulations, the depreciation deduction only applies to tangible property subject to wear and tear, decay, or decline from natural causes, exhaustion, and obsolescence. *See* Treas. Reg. § 1.167(a)-2. The deduction does not apply to land (apart from improvements or physical developments added to it), items in taxpayer inventory, personal automobiles, buildings used solely as personal residences (including furnishings), personal effects, or clothing. *See id.*

---

3. Amortization

Having addressed the depreciation of tangible, wasting assets, we can now turn to the rules governing cost recovery with respect to certain intangible assets. In a manner similar to the depreciation of tangible assets, the Code allows a taxpayer to recover the cost of certain intangible assets by providing for "amortization" deductions. But what, you might ask, is an intangible asset, and which intangible assets qualify for the amortization deduction? Let's answer the basic definitional question first. An **intangible asset** is a business asset that lacks a tangible or physical manifestation. Consider, for example, a business's good name or reputation (i.e., **goodwill**). A small neighborhood grocery store may have a host of tangible assets with readily ascertainable fair market values (e.g., $50,000), but a significant component of the store's true fair market value (e.g., $85,000) may come from its 30-year presence in the same prime location and its owners' excellent, long-standing relationships with almost everyone in the surrounding community. A different taxpayer, such as a large manufacturer, may employ thousands of reliable workers hired over years of ongoing operations. Anyone attempting to create such a business from scratch would need to go through the onerous process of recruiting, screening, and hiring thousands of individuals. Accordingly, it is possible to assign some value to the fact that a well-established business has the intangible asset of "workforce in place." One might even assign "going concern value" to an enterprise merely because it exists as a functioning business unit and is not merely a motley collection of tangible assets.

Even if a given business has intangible assets, § 197 may permit amortization of such assets only in specific situations. Section 197(a) provides that the allowance is available only with respect to an *amortizable* § 197 intangible, and the statute goes on to define both "section 197 intangible" and "amortizable section 197 intangible." Under § 197(d), we see that § 197 intangibles include many of the items previously discussed (e.g., goodwill, going concern value, workforce in place) in addition to a great many more. What's key, from a definitional perspective, is that the item be an amortizable § 197 intangible.

From the outset, note that § 197(c) has a rule, an exception, and an exception to the exception. Section 197(c)(1) generally provides that a § 197 intangible qualifies as amortizable if (1) it was acquired by the taxpayer after the statute's enactment and (2) it is held in connection with the conduct of the taxpayer's trade or business (or § 212 activity). But, what § 197(c)(1) giveth, § 197(c)(2) taketh away (at least on occasion). It does so by excluding from the ambit of amortizable § 197 intangible *certain* intangibles created by the taxpayer (e.g, those described in § 197(d)(1)(A)–(C)). Per the Treasury Regulations, "created by the taxpayer" means that the taxpayer "makes payments or otherwise incurs costs for [the asset's] creation, production, development, or improvement." Treas. Reg. § 1.197-2(d)(2)(ii).

Example 1

Calvin recently opened a new restaurant. Over the years, he spent a healthy amount of money building up the restaurant's reputation, and as a result, the business soon had considerable goodwill. Notwithstanding the fact that the restaurant's goodwill appears to qualify as an amortizable § 197 intangible, the exception under § 197(c)(2) excludes it. Thus, Calvin may not amortize the goodwill because it is self-created.

This example shows the operation of § 197(c)(2), but there is the exception to the exception. As § 197(c)(2) clarifies, it does not apply to intangibles created in connection with transactions involving the acquisition of "assets constituting a trade or business or substantial portion thereof." Thus, if Calvin decides to sell his restaurant (which will include the goodwill) to Restaurant Conglomerate, Inc. ("RCI"), RCI will be able to amortize the goodwill.

Treatment of Cost of Acquired Leasehold Interests (Lessor and Lessee)

Because a leasehold interest is literally a contractual right to use property, one cannot classify it as tangible real or personal property. Nonetheless, a leasehold interest can have considerable value. For example, a taxpayer purchasing an office building (in which floors have been leased to tenants on terms very favorable to the landlord) might simultaneously purchase the right to assume the leases from the current owner/landlord. Under different circumstances, a taxpayer purchasing a business might, simultaneously, be purchasing the right to continue (as lessee) an existing lease entered into on terms highly favorable to the former owner/lessee. Whether the purchaser will ultimately be a lessor or lessee, the leasehold when purchased does not constitute a separate and distinct intangible asset subject to amortization under § 197. See § 197(e)(5)(A). The taxpayer who purchases a building (including favorable leases) and becomes the lessor must include the cost of purchasing the leases in the basis of the building and recover that cost as the taxpayer depreciates the building. Likewise, the taxpayer who purchases a business (including favorable leases) and becomes the lessee generally recovers the cost of purchasing the lease-hold over the remaining term of the lease. Consider the following example:

Lessee holds the lease on a warehouse. The remaining term of the lease is five years. On October 1, 2018, Taxpayer pays $6,000 to Lessee to purchase Lessee's leasehold interest in the property. After Taxpayer acquires Lessee's leasehold, Taxpayer will have to pay the landlord $2,000 per month as rent for the remaining five-year term. Rather than being forced to capitalize the cost of the lease, Taxpayer will amortize the $6,000 paid over the remaining five-year term (i.e., $100 per month over a 60-month period). If we assume that Taxpayer uses the calendar year as its taxable year, $300 will be deductible with respect to 2018 (i.e., October to December). For 2019 to 2022, Taxpayer may deduct $1,200 each year, and for taxable year 2023, the taxpayer may deduct $900 (January to September). The monthly rent of $2,000 is an ordinary and necessary business expense deductible under § 162.

Special Note

A lessee amortizing the cost of acquiring the lease may employ the approach discussed above, so long as at least 75 percent of the cost of acquiring the lease is attributable to the remaining lease term on the acquisition date. Otherwise, the amortization term would have to include renewal periods, etc. *See* § 178.

Years ago, taxpayers did *not* enjoy an amortization allowance with respect to specific intangible assets covered by § 197 (e.g., goodwill and going concern value). They simply recorded those intangible assets on their books and records and proceeded to depreciate their tangible, wasting assets alongside those intangible assets for which a specific value and a determinable useful life could be established (e.g., a five-year covenant not to compete). As you can well imagine, taxpayers were generally fond of the treatment accorded depreciable assets, and if one business acquired another, the acquiring business made every effort to allocate the bulk of the cost of the acquired business (i.e., the "purchase price") to depreciable assets. To the extent that it was necessary to allocate purchase price to intangible assets, every effort was made to establish that a given intangible asset had an ascertainable value and a limited useful life, thereby justifying amortization of the value over the useful life. The Commissioner took the contrary approach, maximizing purchase price allocations to nondepreciable intangible assets while minimizing allocations to both depreciable assets and amortizable intangible assets. High-stakes litigation in the arena was not uncommon. *See, e.g., Newark Morning Ledger v. United States*, 507 U.S. 546 (1993). To the extent the taxpayer and the Commissioner proceeded to litigate the matter, both parties could be counted on to summon experts favorable to their position. With the Omnibus Budget Reconciliation Act of 1993, P.L. 103-66, Congress officially intervened, effectively mandating a cease-fire and compromise with the enactment of § 197. Under current law, § 197 provides for the ratable (i.e., straight line) amortization of specific intangible assets over a 15-year period, beginning with the month the intangible was acquired. *See* § 197(a).

Example 2

Acquiring Corporation ("Acquiring") purchased Target Corporation for $167 million (of which $18 million is properly allocable to amortizable § 197 intangibles) on October 1, 2020. Over a 15-year period, Acquiring may amortize $1.2 million every 12 months (i.e., $100,000 per month). If we assume that Acquiring uses the calendar year as its taxable year, Acquiring may take an amortization deduction of $300,000 for its taxable year ending December 31, 2020. Thereafter, it may take amortization deductions of $1.2 million for each full calendar year, and $100,000 per month to the extent that it completes amortization prior to the end of a given calendar year.

D. INVENTORY

Capitalizing an asset's cost and depreciating or amortizing that amount over time achieves the matching of income and expense and thereby prevents short-term distortions or misperceptions with respect to the taxpayer's net income. Up to this point, we have focused on the costs associated with acquiring or modifying a business's tangible and intangible assets, but in each instance, such assets were not intended for sale to others. From there, we shift our focus to those businesses that generate some measure of income from the sale of inventory. Although many businesses operate largely to offer services to the public, many manufacture or produce items for sale to customers or purchase items for ultimate resale to others. In each instance, a potential matching problem looms. A producer, for example, might incur any number of expenses in connection with manufacturing merchandise (e.g., the cost of raw materials, delivery expenses, employee compensation, warehouse heating and cooling, etc.), but (in the absence of § 263A) the business might incur and deduct these ordinary and necessary business expenses in one taxable year and sell the merchandise (collecting revenue) in a subsequent taxable year. The basic approach taken is to require that taxpayers roll all inventory production costs into the inventory's cost basis (vis-à-vis deducting the costs currently) and deduct that basis from the amount realized *only* on sale of the inventory (assuming a profitable sale). By preventing a current deduction of relevant costs as the inventory is produced, the rules effectively match revenue from inventory sale with the cost of producing that inventory.

Let's focus, for the sake of example, on a company in the business of manufacturing and selling automobiles, Voiture Motors, Inc. ("VMI"). In manufacturing automobiles, VMI must incur many costs. In addition to paying suppliers for tires, glass, leather, engine parts, fiberglass, windshield wipers, carpeting, and electrical components, it must also pay assembly-line workers, cool and heat the manufacturing facilities, offer employee benefits, pay accountants, and arrange for the safe disposal of hazardous materials. Rather than taking current deductions with respect to these items, VMI must include these costs in the bases of the fleet of vehicles it produces. When VMI sells a vehicle at a profit, it calculates gain realized by deducting its cost basis from the amount realized on the sale. By this mechanism it matches revenue from sales with the expenses of production and thereby avoids distortions with respect to its net income during a given taxable period. Let's see how Congress provides for this system in Internal Revenue Code terms.

As for governing statutory rules, § 263A is command central, providing for what are termed "uniform capitalization" rules. In general, the provision applies to (i) real or tangible personal property produced by taxpayers and (ii) real or personal property that is stock in trade, inventory, or held primarily for sale to customers and acquired by the taxpayer for resale (assuming the taxpayer (or predecessor) had average annual gross receipts of more than $10 million for the three-taxable-year period immediately preceding the relevant taxable year). *See* § 263A(b). If § 263A applies to a taxpayer, certain costs must be given certain treatment. In the case of items that will constitute taxpayer inventory, the costs must be included in inventory costs, and in the case of other property, the costs must be capitalized. *See* § 263A(a)(1)(A) and (B). The costs referred to include so-called direct manufacturing costs and certain indirect manufacturing costs. Applying these rules to VMI, we see that VMI produces tangible personal property that will be inventory in its hands. Accordingly, VMI must include certain direct and indirect production costs in the inventory's basis.

If VMI is fortunate, its production costs will be low, and its volume of profitable car sales will be high. Chances are slim, however, that VMI will manage to steer clear of the ebb and flow of the business cycle. Both production costs and sales volume will likely change over time, and as it turns out, additional rules are necessary to ensure some degree of consistency with respect to VMI's calculation of its income from inventory sales. Let's see why. Assume the following facts in Tables 13.3 and 13.4.

The facts indicate that during 2019, VMI sold 800 vehicles, and for the sake of simplicity, let's assume that it sold each vehicle for $25,000, because they are essentially the same. Thus, VMI's gross revenue from vehicle sales was $20,000,000. In order to calculate VMI's gain, we need to know its basis in the vehicles sold (also referred to as its "cost of goods sold" or "COGS"). Of the 1,200 vehicles available for sale, which 800 did it sell? The first 800 produced during the year (for a basis of

TABLE 13.3 **Vehicle Inventory Data**

Data Category	Totals
2019 Opening vehicle inventory (01/01/2019)	0
2019 Vehicle production	1,200
2019 Inventory available for sale	1,200
2019 Closing vehicle inventory (12/31/2019)	400
2019 Inventory sold (total available – closing)	800

| TABLE 13.4 | **Vehicle Production Totals and Costs by Month (2019)** | | |

Month	Cost	No. of Vehicles Produced	Monthly Production Cost
January	$10,000	100	$1,000,000
February	$10,000	100	$1,000,000
March	$10,000	100	$1,000,000
April	$10,000	100	$1,000,000
May	$12,000	100	$1,200,000
June	$12,000	100	$1,200,000
July	$12,000	100	$1,200,000
August	$12,000	100	$1,200,000
September	$ 8,000	100	$ 800,000
October	$ 8,000	100	$ 800,000
November	$ 8,000	100	$ 800,000
December	$ 8,000	100	$ 800,000

$8,800,000), the last 800 (for a basis of $8,000,000), or 800 produced in the middle of the year (March through October) (for a basis of $8,400,000)? If VMI is consistent from year to year and adopts various conventions and methods that accurately reflect its income according to generally accepted accounting principles, it may make an assumption regarding how it sold vehicles. It can assume (i) that it sells the first 800 vehicles manufactured first, or (ii) that it sells the last 800 vehicles manufactured first. We refer to the initial approach as "first in first out" or "FIFO" and the latter approach as "last in first out" or "LIFO."

The rules governing the treatment of taxpayer inventory are complex. As with depreciation and amortization, detailed study of precise mechanisms and calculations are best left to accounting professionals specializing in tax compliance.

Chapter Summary

- To minimize potential misperceptions and distortions with respect to a taxpayer's net income for a specific period, the tax law generally aims to match income earned in a given tax period with the various expenses incurred or paid in connection with the generation of that income.
- Although taxpayers may generally take a current deduction with respect to ordinary and necessary expenses incurred or paid in connection with their trade or business, certain items must be capitalized. To the extent that a given expenditure will give rise to benefits to the taxpayer extending beyond the taxable year, the item must be capitalized. In many instances, the capitalized cost will be recovered via depreciation or amortization deductions.
- Repairs constitute currently deductible ordinary and necessary expenses.

- Although taxpayers might ordinarily deduct various repairs if made in isolation, they must capitalize repair costs incurred as part of a general plan of rehabilitation.
- Taxpayers must capitalize costs incurred to facilitate certain corporate transactions. Such treatment follows notwithstanding the fact that the transaction gives rise to intangible assets and does not create or enhance a separate and distinct asset.
- Certain taxpayers producing real or tangible personal property for sale to customers or purchasing certain items for resale must include direct and indirect costs associated with the production or acquisition of such items in the inventory's basis. Such costs are recovered on sale or other disposition of the inventory.

Applying the Rules

1. Just a few years ago, American Hotel Group, Inc. ("AHG") was on the verge of bankruptcy. In no small part due to federal intervention, AHG now thrives, so much so that it now plans to purchase a new building to serve as its corporate headquarters. If AHG pays $7 million to purchase a new building, must it capitalize the cost, or may it take a current deduction with respect to the acquisition?

2. Spiffy, Inc. ("Spiffy") operates a laundromat in a strip mall. The attendants have informed the general manager that two of the dryers need minor repairs. If the company has an independent contractor repair the dryers, may Spiffy take a current deduction with respect to the cost of the repairs?

3. Barry has long enjoyed inventing safe toys for children. Recently, he formed a corporation, Yay!, Inc. ("Yay!"), and the company now makes toys for sale to a wide network of wholesalers and retailers. How should Yay! treat the various costs incurred in producing the toys?

4. For several years Hamza has served as the general manager of The Royal Oasis. Hotel reviews by guests state that they return to The Royal Oasis and never frequent its competitors because of the extraordinary service they receive from Hamza and the staff he supervises. May the owner of The Royal Hotel deduct the salary it pays to Hamza, or should Hamza's salary be capitalized because his services have increased the goodwill of The Royal Oasis?

5. Quick Mart, Inc. ("QMI") operates a chain of supermarkets throughout the southeastern United States. QMI recently decided to renovate its store to enhance its overall ambience. In addition to installing hard-wood flooring in all of its locations, it also plans to enhance lighting fixtures and upgrade each store's air filtration system. Will QMI be able to deduct the costs associated with these changes as ordinary and necessary business expenses?

Federal Income Taxation in Practice

1. You are a partner in a law firm, and one of your clients, Atlas Construction, Inc. ("Atlas"), is a major construction company. As it turns out, Atlas recently constructed its own headquarters building, and its general counsel has an interesting question she'd like you to look into. She generally believes that Atlas can depreciate the cost of its construction equipment, but she wonders whether the company can take depreciation with respect to equipment used during the taxable year in constructing the new headquarters building. She understands that the costs associated with the construction of the new building constitute capital expenditures, but she is unsure just how broadly she should construe construction cost in this instance. See what you can find, and follow up with her by letter.

2. One of the partners you work for is aware of *INDOPCO* and is still unsure just how far it reaches. He understands that *INDOPCO* dealt with an acquisition, but he knows that some Treasury Regulations tend to restrict *INDOPCO*'s reach. One of the firm's clients is thinking about transitioning from a sole proprietorship to a corporation. Section 351 of the Code would be relevant if the incorporation proceeds. The partner would like to know whether the taxpayer would have to capitalize amounts paid to facilitate the "351." "It's just a basic corporate organization," he reasons. See what you can find, and follow up with him by e-mail.

3. Your good friend, Sarah, has owned and operated a fine dining establishment for ten highly profitable years. She opened the restaurant herself in a prime location, and her customer reviews are quite favorable. A potential purchaser recently approached Sarah concerning the restaurant. Sarah expressed no interest in selling her restaurant, but she was intrigued enough to have the establishment appraised. According to the appraisal report, her restaurant now has a fair market value of $750,000 of which at least $100,000 represents the goodwill Sarah has created over the years. May Sarah now amortize this goodwill? Consult § 197, and send Sarah a brief letter communicating your research findings.

Timing and Related Issues

In several of the preceding chapters, we discussed the technical aspects of many of the governing rules and closely examined facts to ascertain, for example, whether a given amount constituted income or whether the taxpayer's expense itself even qualified for deduction. Only on occasion did we focus squarely on proper timing of the item. We noted briefly, in covering the inclusion of treasure trove, that it constitutes gross income "for the taxable year in which it is reduced to undisputed possession." Treas. Reg. § 1.61-14. And as we turned to the deduction for losses under § 165, we paid close attention to the meaning of "sustained" and noted how the Treasury Regulations controlled timing by clarifying precisely when a taxpayer actually sustains a loss (and, conversely, when the taking of a loss deduction would be premature). Chapter 13, of course, brought a host of timing concerns to the fore, and we saw firsthand the mechanisms Congress forces taxpayers to employ to achieve the proper temporal matching of income and associated income-generation expenses. In this chapter, we bring timing itself to center stage and with good reason: It has considerable dramatic potential. On occasion, neither the taxpayer nor the Commissioner disputes whether an item constitutes income or qualifies for deduction. Rather, in light of potential tax liability ramifications, the parties are at odds over whether the item belongs in an earlier tax period, the current tax period, or possibly a later one. Then again, an interested party can attempt to wield timing as a weapon; if paralyzed by apparent or likely defeat on the substantive merits, a taxpayer (or the Commissioner) might very well raise timing as an issue in a last ditch and desperate effort to score a victory.

A. THE TIME VALUE OF MONEY

On a fairly basic level, one can understand why a taxpayer would generally prefer to delay including

Key Concepts

- Time value of money
- Annual accounting
- Claim of right doctrine and the tax benefit rule
- Net operating loss, carryover, and carryback
- Deferral of compensation and the § 83(b) election

an item in gross income or, on the flip side, to promptly take advantage of an available deduction. The operation of the tax system, however, can create timing incentives that might, at first glance, appear contrary to Average Joe logic. A pending increase in tax rates might result in a taxpayer seeking to accelerate income recognition such that it falls in a current taxable period as opposed to a later one. If a rate decrease appears likely, incentives shift, and the taxpayer would likely seek to delay income recognition to the future period. At root, the taxpayer seeks to minimize taxable income and thereby maximize the amount of revenue he can retain. Even if the taxpayer must face the reality of including the item in gross income, delaying inclusion often makes a great deal of sense because money on hand can be set aside to generate interest over time. As tax professionals put it, money has time value.

> **Key Statutory Provisions**
>
> ▦ **Internal Revenue Code**
>   - ▦ § 83(a) and (b)
>   - ▦ § 83(c)(1) and (2)
>   - ▦ § 83(e)(1)
>   - ▦ § 111(a)
>   - ▦ § 172(a)
>   - ▦ § 172(b)(1)(A)
>   - ▦ § 172(b)(2)(first 2 sentences)
>   - ▦ § 172(c)
>   - ▦ § 1273(a)(1)
>   - ▦ § 1341(a)

Assume that a taxpayer must eventually pay a tax of $50,000. If the obligation must be paid on April 15, 2019, he will have to pay exactly $50,000. But what if he can somehow manage to alter the due date to April 15, 2020 by making a successful timing argument? Better yet, what if he can argue his way to a due date of April 15, 2021 or possibly later? With victory in hand, he can actually make the time value of money work in his favor by setting aside money on April 15, 2019, letting that money generate interest, and using the final total to satisfy the future obligation. The key fact is that he would be able to set aside *less than* $50,000 up front because the accumulated interest will ultimately make up the rest. Under the given facts (and assuming an interest rate of 5 percent per year), if the taxpayer opts to set aside money on April 15, *2019* to pay a total of $50,000 on April 15, *2020*, he will only have to set aside approximately $47,619. Move the final payment date to April 15, 2021, and he would have to set aside approximately $45,351. As Table 14.1 reflects, the amount to be set aside on April 15, 2019, gets lower as the final payment date gets delayed further. The following formula can be used to perform the necessary calculations:

$$PV = FV \div (1 + r)^n$$

PV = Present Value (e.g., $47,619)
FV = Future Value (e.g., $50,000)
r = Interest Rate expressed as a decimal (e.g., 0.05)
n = Number of years (e.g., 1)

TABLE 14.1   **Present and Future Value Data Using Baseline Assumptions**

Approximate Amount Set Aside on April 15, 2019	Interest Rate	Number of Years	Future Value
$47,619	5%	1	$50,000
$45,351	5%	2	$50,000
$43,192	5%	3	$50,000
$41,135	5%	4	$50,000
$39,176	5%	5	$50,000
$37,311	5%	6	$50,000
$35,534	5%	7	$50,000

In discussing the numbers, one could state, for example, that the future value of $47,619 set aside for one year at 5 percent is $50,000. Alternatively, one could state that "reduced to present value," $50,000 as of April 15, 2020, is $47,619 on April 15, 2019 (assuming an interest rate of 5 percent).

Although the time value of money clearly helps the taxpayer under discussion minimize the up-front amount he must set aside to satisfy a future obligation, the time value of money appeals more broadly because money can generate interest over time (provided that it remains in the taxpayer's bank account or is properly invested in an interest-producing obligation). The larger the dollar amounts involved (and they are often quite substantial in tax practice), the more important timing becomes.

B. ANNUAL ACCOUNTING AND ITS IMPACT

We previously noted in Chapter 13 that capitalization, depreciation, amortization, and inventory cost recovery rules aim, to some extent, to match income and associated income-generation expenses. Although a taxpayer able to deduct an expense currently may, from time to time, elect to capitalize the item, only on occasion do they have the ability to deduct currently an expense that would otherwise constitute a capital expenditure. *See, e.g.,* Treas. Reg. 1.162-3(h) (Example 7). Thus, the taxpayer is at the mercy of the governing rules. Should the matching mandate apply with equal force to the Commissioner as well? Let's see how the tax law effects a rational compromise between fairness and administrative efficiency.

Case Preview

Burnet v. Sanford & Brooks

Taxpayers operating in the business world incur and pay income-generation expenses throughout the taxable year. In a perfectly-timed world, the expenses encountered and the income from the activity would automatically show up on the same tax return. Unfortunately, it is often the case that expenses must be incurred and paid long before the associated income arrives, and once it does, taxpayers may be of the opinion that the income received simply balanced out the expenses (or net losses) previously incurred, with the result that no reportable income arose from the transaction. The taxpayer in *Burnet v. Sanford & Brooks* took this approach over the Commissioner's objection. As you read the opinion, consider the following questions:

1. On what basis does the taxpayer argue for exclusion of the amounts ultimately recovered?
2. Why does the Court insist that even an approach requiring a focus solely on gain or profit would not resolve the key issue at hand?
3. Does the Court acknowledge mismatching potential?

Burnet v. Sanford & Brooks
282 U.S. 359 (1931)

Mr. Justice STONE delivered the opinion of the Court.

In this case certiorari was granted to review a judgment of the Court of Appeals for the Fourth Circuit reversing an order of the Board of Tax Appeals which had sustained the action of the Commissioner of Internal Revenue in making a deficiency assessment against respondent for income and profits taxes for the year 1920.

From 1913 to 1915, inclusive, respondent, a Delaware corporation engaged in business for profit, was acting for the Atlantic Dredging Company in carrying out a contract for dredging the Delaware River, entered into by that company with the United States. In making its income tax returns for the years 1913 to 1916, respondent added to gross income for each year the payments made under the contract that year, and deducted its expenses paid that year in performing the contract. The total expenses exceeded the payments received by $176,271.88. The tax returns for 1913, 1915, and 1916 showed net losses. That for 1914 showed net income.

In 1915 work under the contract was abandoned, and in 1916 suit was brought in the Court of Claims to recover for a breach of warranty of the character of the material to be dredged. Judgment for the claimant was affirmed by this Court in 1920. It held that the recovery was upon the contract and was "compensatory of the cost of the work, of which the government got the benefit." From the total recovery, petitioner received in that year the sum of $192,577.59, which included the $176,271.88 by which its expenses under the contract had exceeded receipts from it, and accrued interest amounting to $16,305.71. Respondent having failed to

Justice Harlan F. Stone

Having joined the U.S. Supreme Court as an Associate Justice in 1925, Harlan Fiske Stone became Chief Justice of the United States in 1941 on the nomination of President Franklin D. Roosevelt.

Credit: Photo courtesy of the U.S. Library of Congress.

include these amounts as gross income in its tax returns for 1920, the Commissioner made the deficiency assessment here involved, based on the addition of both items to gross income for that year.

The Court of Appeals ruled that only the item of interest was properly included, holding, erroneously as the government contends, that the item of $176,271.88 was a return of losses suffered by respondent in earlier years and hence was wrongly assessed as income. Notwithstanding this conclusion, its judgment of reversal and the consequent elimination of this item from gross income for 1920 were made contingent upon the filing by respondent of amended returns for the years 1913 to 1916, from which were to be omitted the deductions of the related items of expenses paid in those years. Respondent insists that as the Sixteenth Amendment and the Revenue Act of 1918, which was in force in 1920, plainly contemplate a tax only on net income or profits, any application of the statute which operates to impose a tax with respect to the present transaction, from which respondent received no profit, cannot be upheld.

If respondent's contention that only gain or profit may be taxed under the Sixteenth Amendment be accepted without qualification, the question remains whether the gain or profit which is the subject of the tax may be ascertained, as here, on the basis of fixed accounting periods, or whether, as is pressed upon us, it can only be net profit ascertained on the basis of particular transactions of the taxpayer when they are brought to a conclusion.

All the revenue acts which have been enacted since the adoption of the Sixteenth Amendment have uniformly assessed the tax on the basis of annual returns showing the net result of all the taxpayer's transactions during a fixed accounting period, either the calendar year, or, at the option of the taxpayer, the particular fiscal year which he may adopt. Under [the governing revenue act], respondent was subject to tax upon its annual net income, arrived at by deducting from gross income for each taxable year all the ordinary and necessary expenses paid during that year in carrying on any trade or business, interest and taxes paid, and losses sustained, during the year. [Per governing law,] gross income "includes * * * income derived from * * * business * * * or the transaction of any business carried on for gain or profit, or gains or profits and income derived from any source whatever." The amount of all such items is required to be included in the gross income for the taxable year in which received by the taxpayer. ***

That the recovery made by respondent in 1920 was gross income for that year within the meaning of these sections cannot, we think, be doubted. The money received was derived from a contract entered into in the course of respondent's business operations for profit. While it equalled, and in a loose sense was a return of, expenditures made in performing the contract, still, as the Board of Tax Appeals found, the expenditures were made in defraying the expenses incurred in the prosecution of the work under the contract, for the purpose of earning profits. ***

That such receipts from the conduct of a business enterprise are to be included in the taxpayer's return as a part of gross income, regardless of whether the particular transaction results in net profit, sufficiently appears from [the governing statute] and from the character of the deductions allowed. Only by including these items of gross income in the 1920 return would it have been possible to ascertain respondent's net income for the period covered by the return, which is what the statute taxes. The excess of gross income over deductions did not any the less constitute net income for the taxable period because respondent, in an earlier period, suffered net losses in the conduct of its business which were in some measure attributable to expenditures made to produce the net income of the later period. ***

But respondent insists that if the sum which it recovered is the income defined by the statute, still it is not income, taxation of which without apportionment is permitted by the Sixteenth Amendment, since the particular transaction from which it was derived did not result in any net gain or profit. But we do not think the amendment is to be so narrowly construed. A taxpayer may be in receipt of net income in one year and not in another. The net result of the two years, if combined in a single taxable period, might still be a loss; but it has never been supposed that that fact would relieve him from a tax on the first, or that it affords any reason for postponing the assessment of the tax until the end of a lifetime, or for some other indefinite period, to ascertain more precisely whether the final outcome of the period, or of a given transaction, will be a gain or a loss.

The Sixteenth Amendment was adopted to enable the government to raise revenue by taxation. It is the essence of any system of taxation that it should produce revenue ascertainable, and payable to the government, at regular intervals. Only by such a system is it practicable to produce a regular flow of income and apply methods of accounting, assessment, and collection capable of practical operation. It is not suggested that there has ever been any general scheme for taxing income on any other basis. The computation of income annually as the net result of all transactions within the year was a familiar practice, and taxes upon income so arrived at were not unknown, before the Sixteenth Amendment. It is not to be supposed that the amendment did not contemplate that Congress might make income so ascertained the basis of a scheme of taxation such as had been in actual operation within the United States before its adoption. While, conceivably, a different system might be devised by which the tax could be assessed, wholly or in part, on the basis of the finally ascertained results of particular transactions, Congress is not required by the amendment to adopt such a system in preference to the more familiar method, even if it were practicable. It would not necessarily obviate the kind of inequalities of which respondent complains. If losses from particular transactions were to be set off against gains in others, there would still be the practical necessity of computing the tax on the basis of annual or other fixed taxable periods, which might result in the taxpayer being required to pay a tax on income in one period exceeded by net losses in another. ***

The assessment was properly made under the statutes. Relief from their alleged burdensome operation which may not be secured under these provisions, can be afforded only by legislation, not by the courts.

Reversed.

Post-Case Follow-Up

Notwithstanding the potential mismatching of expenses and income, the *Sanford & Brooks* Court confirms that the income tax system requires annual reporting. The result is, of course, harsh. When the taxpayer received the litigation damages (plus interest), it was obligated to report the amount as income. Yet in prior years, when the taxpayer's expenses exceeded income, the taxpayer may have had no tax liability, but the taxpayer could expect nothing from the government as a result of having *negative* taxable income. With strictly annual accounting, those loss-generating expense items were confined to a single tax year and of no use in other years in which income (even from a related transaction) might have been available for offset. The taxpayer found itself trapped in an inescapable mismatch nightmare, courtesy of Justice Stone and his brethren. Fortunately, current law provides relief under § 172 (discussed below), but note that *Sanford & Brooks* retains its vitality as an annual accounting mandate.

Burnet v. Sanford & Brooks: Real Life Applications

For these questions, please ignore any potential impact of § 172. Further, assume that all taxpayers use the cash disbursements and receipts method of accounting and that they use the calendar year as their taxable year.

1. Produce Transport, Inc. ("PTI") makes its services available to farmers throughout the southeastern United States. PTI understands that, in some instances, produce must be brought to market soon after it is harvested to outpace spoilage. At the same time, the selling farmer needs the revenue from sales in order to pay PTI. Assume that during its taxable year ending December 31, 2017, PTI had a net loss of $50,000, due solely to performing services and deducting related costs prior to receiving the revenue from payment of its invoices. When PTI receives the payments in 2018, must it include all amounts in gross income or only amounts received in excess of $50,000?

2. Tangerine Express, Inc. ("TEI") has a long-standing business relationship with Fruit Farms, Inc, ("FFI"), a company specializing in growing genetically modified tangerines. TEI's pricing is very competitive, but its financial success is highly susceptible to fluctuations in gasoline prices. During 2019, TEI's profit from the FFI contract was $350,000, but due to soaring gasoline prices, TEI suffered a $200,000 loss on the FFI

Taxpayer Method of Accounting

Although individuals and small businesses tend to report income when received and deduct items upon actual payment (e.g., using the **cash disbursements and receipts method of accounting**), larger businesses likely use a method of accounting that is not always tied to actual cash payments and actual cash receipts (i.e., the so-called **accrual method of accounting**). The accrual method of accounting results in more accurate matching and would likely have prevented the mismatch and resulting tax headaches in *Sanford & Brooks*. We will discuss the basic methods of accounting in Chapter 15.

Speaking of Timing: The Gregorian Calendar

For centuries, the so-called Julian calendar, named after the Roman General Julius Caesar, enjoyed widespread use. The calendar featured a standard year of 365 days, leap years of 366 days, a start date of January 1, and the month of July (named after Julius Caesar).

Julius Caesar.
Credit: Andrei Nekrassov/Shutterstock.com.

Today, the dominant calendar is the Gregorian calendar, named after Pope Gregory XIII who called for a revision of the Julian calendar to better align Easter and the vernal equinox.

Pope Gregory XIII.
Credit: Eddy Galeotti/ Shutterstock.com.

The modern calendar, of course, retains many features of the Julian calendar. *See* R. Ferguson, The Handy History Answer Book 2d 497 (Visible Ink Press 2006).

contract in 2020. May TEI amend its 2019 return and use the $200,000 FFI contract loss from 2020 to offset some of its prior $350,000 profit from the FFI contract?

---

1. Section 172 and Net Operating Losses

Burnet v. Sanford & Brooks vividly demonstrates the harshness that might well flow from the strict and inflexible enforcement of annual tax accounting. Current law provides relief via § 172, which you should think of as generally applying to taxpayers operating businesses. As several of the problems and cases have made clear, a taxpayer might end a tax year with more total deductions than total income. By definition, the excess of deductions over gross income constitutes a net operating loss. *See* § 172(c). Thus, a taxpayer with total deductions of $2 million and total income of $1.75 million has a net operating loss (i.e., "NOL") of $250,000 for that taxable year (i.e., the "loss year"). Under § 172, taxpayers have the ability to use NOLs from one taxable period (the "loss year") to offset a portion of their taxable income from separate taxable periods. Although the rules in § 172 do not operate in the same manner with respect to each taxpayer, the terminology used in this area is common. When an NOL is used to offset income from a tax year preceding the NOL loss year, it is referred to as a carryback to that year, and when the NOL is used to offset income in a tax year following the NOL loss year, it is referred to as a carryover to that year; the use of carrybacks tends to trigger refunds with respect to prior tax years. Some taxpayers (e.g., those with farming losses) may be able to use NOL carrybacks, but as a general matter, taxpayers are barred by statute from doing so. Thus, § 172(b)(1)(A) provides, in pertinent part, as follows:

[A] net operating loss for any taxable year –

(i) except as otherwise provided in this paragraph, shall not be a net operating loss carryback to any taxable year preceding the taxable year of such loss, and

(ii) shall be a net operating loss carryover to each taxable year following the taxable year of the loss.

With that general limitation in mind, let's consider some additional statutory technicalities and deduction mechanics. Given that only a limited number of taxpayers may use NOL carrybacks, we will focus exclusively on the use of carryovers from the loss year to future tax years. When a taxpayer has a net operating loss in a particular tax year, they may carry over that loss to a future tax year and use it to lower the taxable income derived in that future tax year (as calculated before use of the NOL carryover). For example, if a taxpayer has taxable income of $100,000 for 2019 (before use of a $10,000 NOL from 2018), the taxpayer may employ the 2018 NOL carryover to reduce 2019 taxable income to $90,000. What if the 2018 NOL was $40,000? In that case, the 2019 taxable income would be reduced from $100,000 to $60,000. It would appear, at first glance, that the taxpayer can use the 2018 NOL in full to offset future taxable income, and in the examples given, the taxpayer could use the entire 2018 NOL carryover. In other situations, however, the taxpayer will hit a hard ceiling. Congress's legislative grace goes only so far. A taxpayer may use an NOL carryover to offset taxable income of a given year, but they may offset no more than 80% of the taxable income of that year (as calculated before use of the NOL carryover). Thus, under the stated facts in which 2019 taxable income started out at $100,000, use of an NOL from a prior period would be capped at $80,000. The rule that emerges is one with which an NOL carryover can be used to offset taxable income in a given year, but the actual amount used will be the lower of (i) the full NOL carryover or (ii) 80% of the taxable income of the current period. Any NOL carryover not used to offset taxable income in a particular year simply becomes an NOL carryover to the next tax year (and so on) until the NOL carryover from the loss year is fully consumed. Consider the visual depiction set forth in Exhibit. 14.1.

The $700,000 NOL from 2018 was used to offset taxable income in the years 2019–2022. Notwithstanding the $700,000 NOL from 2018, it could be used to offset no more than 80% of the taxable income in 2019 (as calculated before application of the NOL). The portion of the 2018 NOL not used in 2019 was carried over as an NOL to future periods and gradually consumed. In 2022, we know that 80% of the original $100,000 taxable income is $80,000, but the amount of the 2018 NOL remaining is only $60,000, and accordingly, no more than that amount can be used to offset the original $100,000 of taxable income in 2022.

Using NOL Rules to Effect Economic Stimulus

Under prior law, § 172 generally provided for a 2-year carryback period and a 20-year carryover period. Congress occasionally alters the operative NOL rules as a means of offering specific taxpayers a form of economic stimulus. For example, in the Job Creation and Worker Assistance Act of 2002, Congress extended the carryback period to five years, reasoning as follows: "The current uncertain economic conditions have resulted in many taxpayers incurring unexpected financial losses. A temporary extension of the NOL carryback period will provide taxpayers in all sectors of the economy who experience such losses the ability to increase their cash flow through the refund of income taxes paid in prior years. The provision will free up funds that can be used for capital investment or other expenses that will provide stimulus to the economy." H.R. Rep. 107-251, at 29. Note that Congress also liberalized the carryback rules in the American Recovery and Reinvestment Tax Act of 2009 (Pub. L. No. 111-5) and the Worker, Homeownership, and Business Assistance Act of 2009 (Pub. L. No. 111-92). The most recent changes to NOL rules in the Tax Cuts and Jobs Act (Pub. L. No. 115-97) eliminated the use of NOL carrybacks for most taxpayers but made it possible to use NOL carryovers indefinitely.

As we prepare to move away from further discussion of NOLs, two matters merit acknowledgment. First, the rules governing NOLs are considerably more complex than warrants discussion in this text, but you should be warned of the larger technical mass lurking beneath the tip of the iceberg we have sighted here. Second, because NOLs from one tax year can offset income from other periods indefinitely, fake or aggressively inflated NOLs have considerable appeal to those seeking to evade taxes. Indefinitely. Thus, if an individual client claims that he suffered a billion-dollar NOL in a single tax year and hopes to use that loss to offset the

EXHIBIT 14.1   **Carryover of NOL Arising in 2018**

2018	2019	2020	2021	2022	2023
($700,000)	$100,000	$200,000	$500,000	$100,000	$100,000
	−$80,000	−$160,000	−$400,000	−$60,000	
	$20,000	$40,000	$100,000	$40,000	

bulk of his future taxable income, you should probably exercise extreme caution and view the claim with considerable skepticism.

2. Claim of Right Doctrine

Although § 172 helps taxpayers offset the business income from profitable years with losses from other years, taxpayers face potential timing and mismatch challenges in numerous contexts. For example, in *United States v. Lewis*, 340 U.S. 590 (1951), the taxpayer received a $22,000 bonus in one year only to find out a few years later that he had to return half of it. Prior to the partial repayment, of course, he held the money and used it as his own under the mistaken belief that he was entitled to keep all of it. The disputed question was whether the taxpayer should (i) amend his prior year return and reduce the amount of gross income reported because he was ultimately unable to keep all amounts he received or (ii) simply compute his tax for the current year, adhering to the annual reporting mandate while taking a deduction for the amount of the repayment into account. In resolving the matter, the Court called on established precedent:

> In the *North American Oil* case we said: "If a taxpayer receives earnings under a claim of right and without restriction as to its disposition, he has received income which he is required to [report on his tax] return, even though it may still be claimed that he is not entitled to retain the money, and even though he may still be adjudged liable to restore its equivalent." Nothing in this language permits an exception merely because a taxpayer is "mistaken" as to the validity of his claim. ***

United States v. Lewis, 340 U.S. 590, at 591 (1951). Thus, the Court ultimately concluded that the taxpayer was obligated to include the full amount of the bonus on his tax return for the year it was paid to him because he held it under claim of right. Deducting the amount repaid on his tax return for the year of repayment corrected the situation while preserving the sanctity of individual tax years.

The approach taken in *United States v. Lewis* was corrective in a sense but left the taxpayer exposed. If an individual included $10,000 in taxable income and paid taxes on it at a rate of 28 percent, he would have handed over $2,800. He might have been forced, however, to repay that amount later and take a latter-year deduction when rates were lower. Thus, he could have taken a $10,000 deduction, but at a time when the applicable rate on taxable income was 20 percent. That deduction would reduce his taxes by only $2,000. Congress opted to protect taxpayers from this adverse shift in rates with § 1341. A taxpayer may invoke that provision if the following is true (stated generally):

- The taxpayer included an item in gross income in a prior taxable year while under the belief that the right to the item was unrestricted; ~~1341~~
- A deduction is allowable in the current taxable year because it was later established that the taxpayer did not have an unrestricted right to the item (or some portion thereof); and
- The amount of the available deduction exceeds $3,000.

Assuming the conditions are satisfied, the taxpayer's tax liability for the current year will be the lower of the following:

- A tax computed by taking a current-year deduction of the amount repaid; or
- A tax computed by foregoing the deduction but taking a tax credit in the current year equal to the amount by which the taxes would have been reduced had the amount repaid been excluded from taxable income as an initial matter in the prior year.

See generally § 1341(a).

Case Preview

McKinney v. United States

Innocently enough, *United States v. Lewis* dealt with a taxpayer forced to repay a portion of a bonus. Today, a similarly situated taxpayer could handily escape negative tax consequence by invoking § 1341. Can the same be said of someone forced to repay money they embezzle? We know as a matter of elementary tax law that illegal income is includible in gross income, but what ramifications flow from that reality? If the taxpayer must include embezzled funds in income, can she legitimately claim that she apparently had an unrestricted (albeit potentially temporary) right to the money? An affirmative answer would appear to make the protections of § 1341 available to her at the time she is forced to repay the funds. The Fifth Circuit Court of Appeals took up this issue in *McKinney v. United States*. Consider the following questions as you read the opinion:

1. What theories of deduction did the taxpayer advance?
2. How does the taxpayer attempt to circumvent the court's interpretation of the statute?
3. Were embezzlers required to include their ill-gotten gains in income when Congress enacted § 1341?

McKinney v. United States
574 F.2d 1240 (5th Cir. 1978)

TUTTLE, Circuit Judge:

The taxpayer, Herman E. McKinney, having embezzled the sum of $91,702.06 from his employer, reported and paid taxes on the fund in 1966. He refunded the entire amount in 1969 and now seeks to be made whole tax-wise under the terms of a special statutory relief provision of the Internal Revenue Code, [section 1341].

The facts are not in dispute. Over a period of years McKinney, who was employed by the Texas Employment Commission, arranged matters in such a manner that in 1966 he was able to siphon off $91,702.06 of the state's money. Because of the requirements of the federal taxing statutes following the Supreme Court's decision in *James v. United States*, 366 U.S. 213 (1961), McKinney reported the embezzled funds as "miscellaneous income" on his 1966 federal income tax return. Subsequently, the embezzlement was discovered, and McKinney was convicted in the state courts of embezzlement. He repaid the embezzled funds in 1969. On his tax return for that year, taxpayer claimed a deduction for this repayment as a trade or business loss, resulting in a reported "net operating loss" for that year. He then claimed a net operating loss carryback deduction for 1966. Alternatively, taxpayer filed a claim for refund for 1969, claiming the benefit of the provisions of § 1341.

The Government does not dispute the taxpayer's entitlement to a deduction for the year 1969, but this does not give him the full benefits that would be enjoyed if he could treat the loss as if it had occurred in 1966, the year of payment. The taxpayer has abandoned his original claim that he is entitled to a carryback of the loss as a "net operating loss." *** He therefore relies solely on his contention that by the enactment of § 1341, Congress intended that a taxpayer, who reported as income funds acquired by theft or embezzlement, be able to obtain, if required subsequently to refund the amounts, the full benefit of a deduction in the year of repayment that would effectively wipe out the economic loss suffered from the prior payment of taxes on the illegally acquired funds.

In 1954, Congress enacted § 1341 to alleviate perceived inequities created by operation of the so-called "claim-of-right doctrine." The classic formulation of the doctrine is that:

> If a taxpayer receives earnings *under a claim of right and without restriction as to its disposition*, he has received income which he is required to [report on his tax] return, even though it may still be claimed that he is not entitled to retain the money, and even though he may still be adjudged liable to restore its equivalent.

North American Oil Consolidated v. Burnet, 286 U.S. 417, 424 (1952) (emphasis added). The statute merely allows, as an alternative to a deduction in the year of repayment, taxes for the current year to be reduced by the amount taxes were increased in the year of receipt because the funds in question were included in gross income.

The Court first applied the doctrine in the context of embezzled funds in *Commissioner of Internal Revenue v. Wilcox*, 327 U.S. 404 (1946). In *Wilcox* the IRS argued that embezzled funds should be treated as taxable income to the wrongdoer under

§ 22(a) of the Code. The Court disagreed. After noting that the essence of taxable income is "the accrual of some gain, profit or benefit to the taxpayer," the Court held:

> For present purposes . . . it is enough to note that a taxable gain is conditioned upon (1) the presence of a claim of right to the alleged gain and (2) the absence of a definite, unconditional obligation to repay or return that which would otherwise constitute a gain. Without some bona fide legal or equitable claim, . . . the taxpayer cannot be said to have received any gain or profit within the reach of § 22(a).
>
> It is obvious that the taxpayer in this instance, in embezzling the $12,748.60, received the money without any semblance of a bona fide claim of right. And he was at all times under an unqualified duty and obligation to repay the money . . . .

Id. at 408, 66 S. Ct. at 549 (emphasis added) (citation omitted). On this basis the Court concluded that embezzled money did not constitute taxable income to the embezzler.

Fifteen years later, the Court expressly overruled *Wilcox* in *James v. United States*, 366 U.S. 213 (1961). The Court reasoned:

> A gain "constitutes taxable income when its recipient has such control over it that, as a practical matter, he derives readily realizable economic value from it." Under these broad principles, we believe that petitioner's contention, that all unlawful gains are taxable except those resulting from embezzlement, should fail.
>
> When a taxpayer acquires earnings, lawfully or unlawfully, without the consensual recognition, express or implied, of an obligation to repay and without restriction as to their disposition, "he has received income which he is required to [report on his tax] return, even though it may still be claimed that he is not entitled to retain the money, and even though he may still be adjudged liable to restore its equivalent." This standard brings wrongful appropriations within the broad sweep of "gross income" . . . .

Id. at 219 [internal citations omitted].

Because the benefit conferred by the statute depends upon whether it "appear(s) that the taxpayer had an unrestricted right to such [item,"] it is necessary for us to determine whether in its *James* decision, the Supreme Court modified its conclusion in *Wilcox* that in embezzling funds a taxpayer "received the money without any semblance of a bona fide claim of [right,"] or whether the Court merely said that embezzled funds are to be returned [i.e., reported on his tax return] for tax purposes as part of gross income regardless of whether they were held under a "claim of right."

We agree with the reasoning of the trial court here:

> The decision . . . in *James* cannot properly be read to say that the Supreme Court concluded that embezzled funds are held under a claim of right. On the contrary, *James* does not in any way contradict or weaken the Court's statement in *Wilcox* that embezzled funds are not held under a claim of right; it only says that this is immaterial in determining whether embezzled funds must be included in gross income.

The *James* Court merely held that the term "gross income" in the tax statute was broad enough to include money received "when its recipient has such control over it that, as a practical matter, he derives readily realizable economic value from it," without regard to whether its recipient had a "claim of right" to the funds.

Since the language of § 1341 makes its benefits available to a taxpayer only if he "had an unrestricted right to such item," we agree with the trial court that the plain language of the statute prevents its application in favor of appellant. The language of § 1341(a)(1), i.e. "because it appeared that the taxpayer had an unrestricted right to such item," must necessarily mean "because it appeared (to the taxpayer) that (he) had an unrestricted right to such item." When the item was embezzled funds it is clear that it could not appear to the taxpayer that he had any right to the funds, much less "an unrestricted right" to them. ***

The taxpayer contends that, notwithstanding the plain meaning of the words, the statute should be interpreted to read that whenever gains are enjoyed by a taxpayer which, under applicable laws, he is required to report as income, this requirement of itself converts such gains into income held under a "claim of right." The chronology of the two Supreme Court cases and the enactment of this statute precludes such a determination. ***At the time this statute was enacted, *Wilcox* was the law. Embezzled funds were not reportable as income. It could not have been the intent of Congress to give the benefits of this new relief section to holders of embezzled funds.

Our conclusion comports with the prior affirmance by us of the judgment of the district court in *Hankins v. United States*, 403 F. Supp. 257 (N.D. Miss. 1975). In that case, on facts identical to those in the present case, the district court held:

> (A)s an embezzler, plaintiff never received his employer's funds under a claim of right and the benefits of Section 1341 of the Code (26 U.S.C. § 1341) are not available to him.

***

The judgment is AFFIRMED.

Post-Case Follow-Up

In this case, the Fifth Circuit Court of Appeals rejected the notion that embezzled funds includible in gross income are held by the embezzler under a claim of right. Given that § 1341 applies only to those holding original funds under the belief that they have an unrestricted right to them, the court rationally concluded that § 1341 does not apply to embezzlers forced to repay stolen funds. Under the facts of this case, the embezzler apparently found himself in a tax environment in which application of § 1341 would have offered measurable benefits. Even though the court deprived him of § 1341's protections, the facts of the case do bring to light an oddity (assuming § 1341 applies in a specific situation). Having been required to include income in gross income in a prior period, a given taxpayer might find himself able to take a deduction (on repayment of the funds) in a later period in which tax rates have *increased* substantially (i.e., they get the benefit of a current deduction even if a tax credit would yield a lesser benefit). Add to that the fact that the taxpayer is also spared fines, penalties, and prison time.

Real Life Applications: McKinney v. United States

1. For eight years, Dr. Allan Connolly has consciously overbilled insurance companies for the care he has provided to patients. In total, he collected more than $900,000 in excess fees. An investigation revealed the overbilling, and Dr. Connolly was required to reimburse the relevant companies the amounts overbilled. For federal income tax purposes, will Dr. Connolly be able to apply § 1341 after he repays the insurance companies?

2. *Same facts as Question #1*, except that the overbilling was a result of a clerical error by one of Dr. Connolly's administrative assistants.

3. Jeremiah recently received a $5,000 check from the state lottery commission. Reasoning that he had gotten lucky in a "second chance" drawing, he deposited the funds and declared them on his 2019 federal income tax return. As it turns out, the check was sent to Jeremiah in error; the proper winner had the same first and last name as Jeremiah, and a clerk had sent the check to the wrong Jeremiah. Assume that Jeremiah ultimately had to repay the $5,000 to the state lottery commission. Will § 1341 apply to Jeremiah in this situation?

As the prior discussion indicates, the claim of right doctrine resolves a potential issue concerning the timing of a gross income inclusion, and to the extent that subsequent events call for corrective tax computations, § 1341 protects taxpayers from the potentially negative impact of adverse rate changes. What happens when the problem is not prior inclusion but *prior deduction* followed by events necessitating a correction? For that issue, we call on and apply the tax benefit rule.

3. Tax Benefit Rule

Section 111 generally provides that if a taxpayer deducted an amount in a prior period and subsequent events prove inconsistent with the prior deduction (e.g., a loss is unexpectedly reimbursed), the current treatment of the taxpayer will turn on whether the prior deduction did (or could) prove beneficial from a tax perspective. If the prior deduction did not (and cannot) give rise to a tax benefit to the taxpayer, she may exclude a related recovery. *See* § 111(a) and (c). Consider the following examples:

Example 1

In 2018, Veronica contributed several pieces of art to an organization eligible to receive tax-deductible contributions under § 170. As a result, Veronica deducted $10,000 on her federal income tax returns for the taxable year. In 2020, however, the organization returned the art to Veronica. To the extent that the taking of the charitable contribution deduction in 2018 lowered her tax liability, she must include the value of the art in her gross income in 2020.

Example 2

In 2019, Miles itemized his deductions. On Schedule A, he was able to take a medical expense deduction of $500, although in truth, his tax liability would have been the same without the medical expense deduction because of other items on his return. If Miles's insurance company pays him $500 with respect to his medical expense, he will not be required to include the amount in gross income because the prior deduction did not reduce his original tax liability.

Example 3

Bunsen Chemical Enterprises, Inc. ("BCEI") recently found it necessary to pay various independent contractors to decontaminate soil near one of its facilities. The cost contributed to BCEI's net operating loss of $850,000 for that taxable year. Three years later, after conducting an extensive investigation, BCEI's insurance company reimbursed BCEI for the expense, but as of the beginning of the taxable year of the reimbursement, a portion of the NOL previously generated remained available to the company for use as a carryforward. Accordingly, BCEI may not exclude the amount of the recovery from its gross income.

C. DEFERRED COMPENSATION

1. In General

Among the benefits employers often offer employees, various forms of deferred compensation often play a key role. In general, **deferred compensation** refers to compensation provided for during a specific period of employee service but made available to (or accessed by) the employee at a later date. An employer, for example, might make contributions to a § 401(k) plan or annuity over the years such that an employee can enjoy its benefits in retirement. Similarly, a company might have a plan by which employees eventually earn the right to purchase their employer's stock after years of continued service. Entire courses are devoted to the tax rules governing specific employee benefits, and an exhaustive treatment of those rules is left to those courses. We pause briefly to appreciate the potential timing issues and to take a glimpse at one rule of key significance in certain contexts.

Both employers and employees value the ability to take advantage of deferred compensation arrangements. The employer gets to offer a rich, tax-friendly compensation package while, at the same time giving the employee the opportunity to plan for income in the retirement years or, as the case may be, allowing them to benefit from the increasing value of the company's stock. Considerable difficulty arises, however, if either party offends established timing rules. Deferred compensation is not tax-free compensation. Rather, taxation is merely deferred to a later date (e.g., when the taxpayer actually receives the funds), and such deferral cannot be in perpetuity. If employees somehow end up with ready access to funds supposedly unavailable to them until retirement, immediate taxation is the appropriate, accurate, and fair result (e.g., early access to § 401(k) funds outside a stated exception). On the flip side, those entitled to deferred compensation must, at some point, commence the receipt of minimum required distributions. Many of the rules governing deferred compensation arrangements focus ultimately on the proper timing of income inclusion.

2. Section 83 and the § 83(b) Election

Section 83 plays a key role in certain segments of the deferred compensation arena. In plain English, the statute generally requires that a service provider (e.g., employee) include in gross income the value of property transferred to them as compensation, but such inclusion must only occur when the property can truly be thought of as "theirs" (i.e., it "vests"). Assume, for example, that Healthy Nutrition, Inc. ("HNI") transfers 1,000 shares of common stock to one of its employees, Rama, in connection with her performance of services. All parties understand that the shares will vest in 250 share increments per year over the next four years, so long as Rama continues to work for HNI. Prior to share vesting, Rama cannot transfer the stock, and if she does not continue working for HNI, her right to receive shares she has yet to earn will be forfeited. Under those limited facts, Rama will have income over the next four years as measured by the fair market value of the 250 shares that vest each year. If we assume that the stock has a fair market value of $1/share at all times and that Rama pays nothing to receive it, she will include $250 in gross income each year over the four-year period; if the stock changes in value before it vests, then Rama must include in gross income an amount equal to 250 times the fair market value of 1 share of stock then vesting.

Stated in highly generalized statutory terms, section 83 provides that if property is transferred to a person in connection with the performance of services, he or she must include in gross income the difference between the fair market value of the property and the amount paid for it "in the first taxable year in which the rights of the person having the beneficial interest in such property are transferable or are not subject to a substantial risk of forfeiture, whichever is applicable." Under the facts previously given, Rama will include $250 in gross income each year because it is only after the completion of each year of work that she no longer stands to lose or forfeit 250 shares, and once the shares vest, she is free to transfer or do with them as she pleases. If the fair market value of the stock about to vest for a given year has risen to $3/share, then Rama will include $750 in gross income (i.e., the fair market value of the 250 shares then vesting).

Rama will be receiving stock in lieu of cash compensation. As a result, she will pay taxes with respect to that stock at so-called "ordinary" income tax rates, which, under current law, can be as high as 37 percent. Often, individuals buying and selling stock qualify for lower tax rates (i.e., "capital gains" rates, which vary considerably but often fall in the 10 to 15 percent range); in this instance, however, Rama will pay taxes at ordinary income rates on receipt of the stock; she's not buying or selling the stock at that point but receiving it as compensation. *Thereafter*, if she disposes of the stock for cash, *then* the more favorable capital gains rates may apply; the applicable rate will ultimately depend on the amount of time she continues to hold the stock after it vests. Now, if Rama is willing to suffer the payment of ordinary income tax rates sooner rather than later (and endure a little risk), she could potentially lower her tax bill considerably. Enter the § 83(b) election.

If Rama is willing to pay tax at ordinary income rates on the fair market value of the 1,000 shares of stock when they are initially transferred to her *and have yet to vest*, then (1) she will not have to include any amounts in income when the stock eventually vests, and (2) on disposition of the stock, she will be able to apply capital gains rates. Of course, if Rama pays something to acquire the stock (e.g., $0.25/share), then she will pay taxes at ordinary income rates at initial transfer only on the difference between what she paid (e.g., $250) and the fair market value of the stock ($1,000). *See* § 83(b). Under the given facts, that difference is $750 (i.e., $1,000 - $250). Assuming the stock ultimately rises substantially in value, Rama will have taken a tax hit up front, but on final disposition of the stock, she will enjoy capital gains treatment. That's huge — but there's a catch. If Rama makes the election, and the property is subsequently forfeited (e.g., she leaves after one year to work for another company), Rama can take no deduction with respect to the forfeiture. *See* § 83(b) (last sentence). If she paid money to acquire the stock, she will, however, be able to treat the forfeiture as a capital loss (i.e., amount paid initially minus the amount received, if any, at forfeiture). Also, if Rama seeks to make a § 83(b) election, she must do so within 30 days of the transfer of the property to her. *See* § 83(b)(2).

> **Note**
> ·········
> Section 83 does not apply in every context involving stock or stock option transfers from employers to employees. It does not, for example, apply with respect to incentive stock options or employee stock purchase plans. *See generally* § 83(e).

D. ORIGINAL ISSUE DISCOUNT

No general discussion of timing would be complete without some attention to the notion of original issue discount ("OID"). The rules governing original issue discount make up their own statutory and regulatory edifice, and we will not be exploring them in detail. Even so, you should have some rudimentary appreciation of what OID is and how Congress has resolved the timing issue it presents. Let's start with a loan transaction that does not involve OID and then contrast that with a transaction in which OID is present.

Assume that a given company would like to secure needed capital (i.e., money) by borrowing it, and let's also assume that the company has chosen to borrow money from the public at large. The company could offer to hand out IOUs entitling the holder to payment of $1 million on a given date in the future in exchange for a $1 million loan today, with interest to be paid at the market rate of interest in the interim. Such an IOU would not have original issue discount. The persons lending the money and acquiring the IOU would part with $1 million because that would be the price at which the company offered its IOUs to the public. That amount would be the "issue price." In turn, the company would be obligated to pay $1 million in the future (along with a market rate of interest in the interim) to the holder presenting the IOU to the company at the maturity date. In that case, the stated redemption price at maturity ("SRPM") would be $1 million. We know from prior study that borrowing and repaying loan principal does not give rise to tax consequences. The interest, however, will constitute income to the recipient and may be deductible by the payor. Under the stated facts, the holder of the IOU would literally have interest income as it is paid by the company, and the company would deduct the payment of interest under § 163(a).

Original issue discount arises in many contexts, but let's keep it simple. Assume that the company decides to issue an IOU with an SRPM of $1 million but an issue price of $800,000 with no actual payments of interest in the interim. In essence, the lender parts with $800,000 today and understands that it will receive $1 million from the company in a lump sum in the future, some of which will represent a deferred payment of interest with the remainder constituting repayment of the $800,000 loan principal. Because the stated redemption price at maturity exceeds the issue price, the IOU has original issue discount; numerically, the OID is the difference between the two figures. *See* § 1273(a). Rather than simply treating the interest as having been paid by the payor and received by the lender when the $1 million actually changes hands at the maturity date, the tax law will treat the parties *as if* they had exchanged the appropriate interest payments throughout the term of the transaction. Accordingly, the lender will be *deemed* to have received periodic interest payments throughout the term of the IOU and must include that interest in income as it is deemed received. Likewise, the company will be *deemed* to have made periodic interest payments at the same time and will be allowed to deduct the interest as though it had actually paid it. By this mechanism, Congress interferes with the transaction long enough to impose its vision of sensible financial reality rather than tolerating the timing distortions the parties arranged.

Chapter Summary

- The time value of money is a notion reflecting the fact that money can generate interest income over time.
- Taxpayers must calculate taxable income on an annual as opposed to a transactional basis. Unless the Code dictates otherwise, a taxpayer may use the calendar year or a fiscal year (i.e., a 12-month period other than the calendar year) as their taxable year.
- Taxpayers must include an item in income when they hold it under claim of right (i.e., it appeared to that taxpayer that they had an unrestricted right to the item).

▨ If a given taxpayer includes an item in income under claim of right and they must later restore part of all of the income in a subsequent taxable year, their current tax liability (assuming § 1341 applies) will be the lower of their taxes calculated with (1) a deduction measured by the amount restored or (2) a tax credit determined by reference to the enhanced tax liability resulting from the prior inclusion. The taxpayer will not amend the prior year return to effect the correction.

▨ Taxpayers may use NOLs from the loss year to offset income in other taxable years. Although some taxpayers may enjoy the use of NOL carrybacks, most taxpayers may only use NOL carryovers. NOL carryovers may be used until the NOL is fully utilized, but the amount used with respect to any taxable year will be the lower of (i) the amount of the NOL carryover remaining from the loss year and (ii) 80 percent of the taxable income of the current taxable year (as calculated before application of the NOL carryover).

▨ Deferred compensation arrangements consciously alter the timing rules, but if taxpayers offend established timing rules, negative tax consequences will follow.

▨ A taxpayer receiving property in connection with the performance of services must include in gross income the fair market value of the property (minus any amounts paid for the property) when their right to the property is transferable and no longer subject to a substantial risk of forfeiture. Under appropriate circumstances, taxpayers may make an election under § 83(b) in an effort to maximize the benefits achieved by the application of favorable capital gains rates.

▨ A financial obligation with an issue price less than its stated redemption price at maturity has original issue discount, and the transaction parties will be deemed to have paid and received interest during the term of the obligation, notwithstanding the deferral of actual interest payments.

Applying the Rules

1. Package Delivery Express, Inc. ("PDE") is a taxpayer using the cash disbursements and receipts method of accounting, and it uses the calendar year as its taxable year. In late December of 2018, PDE incurred considerable operating expenses in delivering packages during the holiday season. In light of the fact that most of the accounting personnel at its corporate clients were on vacation during the holiday season, PDE received approximate $75,000 in January 2019 with respect to delivery services actually performed in 2018. In what taxable year should PDE include the $75,000 in gross income?

2. Assuming an interest rate of 5 percent, reduce $100,000 paid on December 31, 2020 to its present value on December 31, 2018.

3. PDE (from Problem #1) had an NOL of $400,000 in 2021. Assume that the company had taxable income of $100,000 in 2022 and $50,000 in 2023. How much was the NOL deduction in 2023?

4. In the aftermath of litigation, Annie Pearl received damages of $5 million in October 2019, none of which was excludible from her gross income. Subsequent litigation favored her opponent, and Annie Pearl had to repay $2 million in 2022. Should Annie Pearl have included the full $5 million in her gross income in 2019? What should Annie Pearl do now in light of the fact that she had to repay $2 million?

5. In April 2019, Timothy lost his home in a massive fire (later declared a federal disaster). Because the insurance company considered the circumstances suspicious (i.e., Timothy appeared to have started the conflagration while engaging in illegal activity), it refused to cover the claim. Timothy took a casualty loss deduction of $80,000 for the taxable year, resulting in a substantial tax savings. One year later, and after thorough investigation, the insurance company decided to cover the loss. What should Timothy do now to account for the fact that the insurance company covered the loss?

Federal Income Taxation in Practice

1. The partner with whom you work has a § 83 question she would like you to look into. She is well aware of how § 83(a) operates, but she has some concerns regarding one of her clients. She believes that the client intends to transfer property with an apparent risk of forfeiture, but she doubts that there will be enforcement of the forfeiture provisions. She would like to know whether the Treasury Regulations promulgated under § 83 flesh out the meaning of *substantial risk of forfeiture* and if they speak to the issue at hand. Conduct the research and follow up with her by e-mail.

2. During lunch with two partners, you overheard one of the partners mention an "incentive stock option." The other partner (with whom you work a great deal) has asked that you hunt down a basic definition of an "ISO" and prepare a one-pager that will familiarize him with the essentials. See what you can find and prepare the summary.

Methods of Accounting

In Chapter 14, we started our focused discussion of timing by devoting attention to the annual accounting mandate and the general goal of matching income and income-generation expenses. Allowing the current deduction of specific expenses and requiring that others be capitalized (with or without the gradual recovery of cost via depreciation or amortization allowances) gets the tax system closer to a "matching" ideal, as does requiring the adoption of specific cost recovery conventions with respect to inventory. But all of these rules operate and have specific impact within broad, overarching timing schemes: the taxpayer methods of accounting rules. Under § 446 of the Code, taxpayers must compute their taxable income under the method of accounting they regularly use in keeping their financial books and records. Taxpayers may generally employ either the *cash receipts and disbursements* method of accounting or an *accrual* method of accounting, but if the chosen method does not clearly reflect income, the Commissioner may impose a more accurate methodology. *See generally* § 446(b) and (c). Further, if a taxpayer seeks to change its method of accounting, it must apply to do so and secure consent from the Secretary of the Treasury (i.e., the IRS). *See generally* § 446(e). In this chapter, we take a closer look at the standards regarding income inclusion and deduction under the various methods of accounting while, at the same time, giving due regard to significant doctrines operating in this context.

Key Concepts

- *Cash receipts and disbursements method of accounting*
- Constructive receipt and economic benefit
- *Accrual method of accounting*
- Economic performance
- Installment method of accounting

A. CASH METHOD OF ACCOUNTING

1. Taxable Year of Income Inclusion

In General

Most individual taxpayers employ and are familiar with the cash receipts and disbursements method of accounting. We include items like salary in income upon actual receipt and deduct items like mortgage interest upon actual payment. Although, as you recall, § 61 and common law standards tell us what does or does not constitute "income," it is § 451(a) that tells us when these items must show up on a tax return. The statute provides that items of gross income must be included on the return "for the taxable year in which [such items are] received by the taxpayer, [unless the taxpayer's method of accounting requires otherwise.]" Section 451(a). For most individual taxpayers, the taxable year is the calendar year, and for the most part, we have little difficulty determining whether we received income during a given taxable year. Issues arise, however, when there are real and legitimate questions as to whether a taxpayer truly has received an item of income or when the taxpayer has taken steps to manipulate receipt in an effort to manage the timing of income inclusion to his preferences. If the taxpayer properly plans and executes a given transaction, he can achieve his timing goals, but as the next case demonstrates, there is room for error.

Key Statutory and Regulatory Provisions

■ Internal Revenue Code
   ▪ § 446
   ▪ § 448(a)-(c)(1)
   ▪ § 451(a)
   ▪ § 451(b)(1)
   ▪ § 451(b)(3)(A) (skim)
   ▪ § 451(c)(1) and (4)
   ▪ § 453(a)–(d)(1)
   ▪ § 461(a), (h)(1), (2), and (4)
■ Treasury Regulations
   ▪ § 1.446-1(c)(2)(i)
   ▪ § 1.451-1(a) (1st 2 sentences)
   ▪ § 1.451-2(a) (1st 2 sentences)
   ▪ § 1.461-1(a)(1) (1st 2 sentences)
   ▪ § 1.461-1(a)(2) (1st sentence)

Case Preview

Warren v. United States

The vast majority of buying and selling of standard consumer goods involves immediate payment for merchandise on hand or, perhaps, for merchandise the purchaser will receive by delivery in short order. A typical commodities transaction (e.g., for the purchase or sale of corn, pork bellies, oranges, etc.) is more complicated. Almost invariably, such deals involve several parties and normally occur in stages over time. Corn growing in the field may be sold (i.e., put under contract) months before it is ripe for harvesting, and the parties involved understand not only that delivery and payment will occur in the future but also that the goods (and payment for them) may necessarily pass through several hands. Although farmers place a premium on selling their carefully raised crop at a good price, the structure of a commodities deal presents opportunities for timing manipulation that they might seek to use to their advantage. The

Commissioner, of course, is hardly a novice at timing games. As you read through *Warren v. United States*, consider the following questions:

1. Did the Warrens actually have the right to receive immediate payment for their cotton upon its sale?
2. Were the cotton gin companies mere independent contractors expected to accomplish a task with respect to cotton processing, or did they play a larger role?
3. Were the Warrens consistent, year to year, with respect to the transactions at hand?

Warren v. United States
613 F.2d 591 (5th Cir. 1980)

SAM D. JOHNSON, Circuit Judge.

This is a refund action brought by the Warrens for the recovery of federal income taxes for the years 1969 and 1970. The question before us is whether sale proceeds received by cotton gins for the taxpayers are properly included in the taxpayer's gross income for the years in which the sales were made.

Bobby and Modelle Warren are Texas cotton growers using the cash receipts and disbursements method of accounting for tax purposes. In 1969 and 1970 they took their cotton to the Cotton King Gin and the Sand Gin Company.

These gins, in addition to ginning and baling, also arranged sales of the cotton for producers interested in selling. The gin obtained prices from a number of prospective buyers and relayed the information to the producer. When a producer was satisfied with a price, he could authorize the gin to sell the cotton and obtain the proceeds of the transaction. As an additional option, the producer could instruct the gin to "defer" the cotton. When cotton was "deferred" the purchase price was paid directly to the gin and not to the producer; the proceeds of the sale were retained by the gin and were not transferred to the producer until the following year. In return for the gin[']s services, the buyer of the cotton paid the gin a set fee based solely upon the bales obtained. The producer paid the gin only for the actual ginning of the cotton.

The Warrens followed this procedure with both the Cotton King Gin and the Sand Gin Company in the years 1969 and 1970. Their cotton was sold in November and December of both years. King Gin deposited the sale proceeds for the Warrens' cotton in its own account and issued a check to the Warrens on January 2nd of the following year. Sand Gin Company deposited the funds in an escrow account at Lamesa National Bank. On January 2, 1970, the bank issued a check to the Warrens for their sale proceeds.

In reporting their income from 1969 and 1970, the Warrens did not include these sales proceeds. The sale proceeds for each year were included in the following year's tax return. After an audit, the IRS determined the proceeds should have been included in the Warrens' income for the year in which the sale occurred. The

Warrens paid the tax deficit and sought a refund. The IRS disallowed their claim and in May, 1976, suit was filed by the Warrens in the Northern District of Texas.

The case was tried to a jury in August, 1977. The United States moved for a directed verdict during trial, and the motion was denied. The jury retired with four special interrogatories, and returned a verdict for the Warrens. After final judgment for the Warrens was entered, the United States filed a motion for judgment notwithstanding the verdict or for a new trial. This motion was denied and this appeal was instituted.

Section 451 of the Internal Revenue Code provides that income is to be included in gross income for the taxable year in which received by the taxpayer. Even so, courts are often called upon to determine exactly when a taxpayer is deemed to have "received" income. One doctrine that has been adopted for the resolution of these disputes is the proposition that receipt by an agent is receipt by the principal. *Maryland Casualty Co. v. United States*, 251 U.S. 342, 346, 40 S. Ct. 155, 156, 64 L. Ed. 297 (1920). The government's contention throughout this dispute has been that the gins were the Warrens' agents.

The government raises two points of error on appeal. It argues initially that the district court erred in not granting either the motion for a directed verdict or the motion for judgment n.o.v. Alternatively, the appellants contend that the trial court erred in instructing the jury. We agree with the government's first contention and reverse.

The standard to be applied by a district court when passing on a motion for directed verdict or judgment n.o.v. is well settled. "If the facts and inferences point so strongly and overwhelmingly in favor of one party that the Court believes that reasonable men could not arrive at a contrary verdict, granting of the motions is proper." *Boeing Co. v. Shipman*, 411 F.2d 365, 374 (5th Cir. 1969) (en banc). Our review of the record supports the United States' argument that there is no conflict in substantial evidence the gins were the Warrens' agents for the sale of cotton.

The primary function of the Cotton King Gin and the Sand Gin was to gin, bale and prepare the cotton for sale. Secondarily, as a service for its customers, the gins would also help find buyers. The evidence shows that in performing this secondary function for the Warrens, the cotton gins were serving as their agents. The Warrens decided that the gins should help sell the cotton. The gins then solicited bids from various buyers. This information was relayed to the Warrens. At that point the appellees decided whether to instruct the gins to accept the highest bid offered or to wait for a better price. When they decided to sell, the Warrens also had the option of receiving their monies immediately or instructing the gins to hold the proceeds until the following year. It was the Warrens' decision to defer payments.

The relationship between the Warrens and the gins for the purpose of selling the cotton was indisputably that of principal and agent. The Warrens instructed the gins to solicit bids, the Warrens decided whether to accept the highest price offered, and the Warrens determined whether or not to instruct the gins to hold the proceeds from the sale until the following year. The gins' role in the sale of the cotton was to adhere to the appellees' instructions. The Warrens were the owners of the cotton held for sale; the Warrens were in complete control of its disposition.

This case is distinguishable from *Kasper v. Banek*, 214 F.2d 125 (8th Cir. 1954) and *Amend v. Commissioner*, 13 T.C. 178 (1949). In those cases, it was recognized that proceeds from the sale of a crop by a farmer, pursuant to a bona fide arms-length contract between the buyer and seller calling for payment in the taxable year following delivery, are includable in gross income for the taxable year in which payment is received. In the case at bar the bona fide arms-length agreement was not between the buyer and seller but rather between the seller and his agent. The Warrens' decision to have the gins hold the sales proceeds until the following year was a self-imposed limitation, not a part of the sales transaction between the buyer and seller. Such a self-imposed limitation does not serve to change the general rule that receipt by an agent is receipt by the principal. See *Williams v. United States*, 219 F.2d 523 (5th Cir. 1955). The income was received by the Warrens' agents in the year of the sale. The fact that the Warrens restricted their access to the sales proceeds does not change the tax status of the money received.

How this case differs

Since we conclude that the district court erred in not granting the government's motions for a directed verdict or for judgment n. o. v., we do not address the alleged error in the jury instructions. For the reasons stated above, the judgment entered by the district court is

REVERSED.

Post-Case Follow-Up

Concluding that the cotton gins acted as agents of the taxpayers in arranging for the sale of cotton, the Fifth Circuit held that receipt of the proceeds by the gins constituted actual receipt of such proceeds by the Warrens. Accordingly, as cash basis taxpayers, they had no choice but to include the proceeds in gross income in the year such proceeds were paid over by the purchasers to the gins. Standing alone, the holding comes as no surprise, but placed next to cases reaching the opposite result, the factual distinctions are decidedly modest. In *Amend v. Commissioner*, the taxpayer contracted directly with a purchaser for the sale of his wheat crop. The wheat was delivered in August 1944, and per contract, the purchaser paid for the wheat in January 1945. Reasoning that the cash basis taxpayer held nothing more than a promise of future payment in 1944, the Tax Court held that the taxpayer had income only in 1945. Although the court in *Warren* distinguished *Amend*, it did so by highlighting the fact that the Warrens had contracted with their agent to defer payment rather than contracting directly with the purchaser of their freshly ginned cotton. The distinction, while real enough, is not particularly compelling. Getting from *Warren* to *Amend* would appear to be as simple as directing the agent to contract only with purchasers willing to defer payment to the gin. Then again, maybe the gin could expect compensation for its work only from the proceeds of sale, but that factor would merely require the purchaser to make two payments rather than one; retaining money surely would not appear to be an onerous yoke for a purchaser to bear. In the end, it hardly seems appropriate for the final result to turn on whether the taxpayer does the rain dance clockwise rather than counterclockwise.

Warren v. United States: Real Life Applications

For the following applications, please assume that the relevant taxpayer uses the cash receipts and disbursements method of accounting and has adopted the calendar year as its taxable year.

1. Barret Semper (a sole proprietor) owns and operates Semper Farms, and the business's primary crop is cotton. Semper Farms has a long-standing relationship with the King Cotton Gin, which gins and sells Semper Farms's cotton (disbursing the proceeds to Semper Farms on receipt). Recently, a customer attempting to pay King Cotton Gin with respect to cotton produced by Semper Farms sent a certified check to the Cotton King Gin, a business having no relationship with Semper Farms. Although the error was later corrected, is Semper Farms (i.e., Barret Semper) obligated to include in income the funds erroneously sent to Cotton King Gin on the date received by Cotton King Gin?

2. Western Steer Co. ("WSC") operates a cattle ranch. Recently, in connection with the sale of a steer, the purchaser paid a WSC employee cash on December 30, 2018. Due to the pending holidays and his vacation schedule, the employee did not surrender the funds to the company until January of 2019. When must WSC include the sale proceeds in income?

3. **Same facts as Question #2**, except that when the employee attempts to surrender the funds to the company, he is told to take the money directly to a feed supplier to settle an outstanding company obligation. When must Western Steer Co. include the sale proceeds in income, if at all?

Commodities Trading

Although electronic trading platforms exist, commodities transactions also occur live on the floor of exchanges such as the Chicago Board of Trade. Those at the exchanges seeking to purchase or sell commodities gather in the "pit" and use a combination of hand gestures and open outcry to communicate their intentions and to strike deals. The action in the pit can be frantic; it is *not* a place for the meek.

Credit: Joseph Sohm/ Shutterstock.com.

Constructive Receipt

In *Warren v. United States*, the court concluded that the taxpayer *actually* received the consideration paid for his cotton because the appropriate funds were paid over to his duly-authorized agent. Although taxpayers with actual receipt present the easiest and most understandable case for immediate income inclusion, taxpayers must also include in income amounts they receive constructively during the taxable year. A taxpayer is in constructive receipt of income if she has received the income in effect, even if she has not reduced the income to actual possession. A classic example would be a taxpayer who has retrieved her physical weekly check from payroll but has yet to deposit it or present it to a financial institution for payment. Because she can do so at any time, she is in *constructive receipt* of the income. Under Treas. Reg. § 1.451-2(a), "[i]ncome although not actually reduced to a taxpayer's possession is constructively received by him in the taxable year during which it is credited to his account, set apart for him, or otherwise made available so that he may draw upon it at any time, or that he could have drawn upon it during the taxable year if notice of intention to withdraw had been given." The Treasury Regulations go on to emphasize, however, that income is not constructively received "if the taxpayer's control of its receipt is subject to substantial limitations or restrictions." Treas. Reg. § 1.451-2(a). It follows, then, that if a financial institution credits interest to a depositor's account and makes the funds available for withdrawal, the taxpayer is in constructive receipt of it. If, however, the institution credits the interest to the account but does not allow immediate withdrawal, then the depositor is not in constructive receipt of the interest until it is available for withdrawal. *See id.*

Treas Reg

Economic Benefit

Up to this point, we have dealt with taxpayers deemed to be in actual or constructive receipt of income either because amounts were paid to them (or their agents) or amounts were readily available to them. But what if a taxpayer manages to get funds that would constitute income if reduced to his actual possession (or constructive receipt) paid directly to a third party (e.g., a landlord or credit card company)? The taxpayer could argue that he was never in actual receipt of the income and that direct payment to a third party makes it impossible for him to gain access to it. These arguments, though rational, will fail to prevent inclusion of the relevant amounts in income. Under the **economic benefit theory**, taxpayers must include amounts in gross income to the extent that such amounts have been (1) paid over to a third party on the taxpayer's behalf or (2) set aside for the taxpayer irrevocably and in such a manner that the amounts are no longer within the reach of the payor's creditors.

Case Preview	*Old Colony Trust Co. v. United States*

Today, when most workers receive their paychecks, they note that their employer has withheld any number of different items (e.g., federal income taxes, state income taxes, FICA, Medicare, etc.). The employee understands that "gross pay" reflects his baseline earnings, but he accepts the reality employers must withhold some percentage of their pay and send it to the relevant taxing authorities. But what if the employee received his gross pay in full and his employer miraculously decided to use its own funds to pay the employee's various tax liabilities? Should the employee include in income only those amounts paid to him, or must he also include the amounts paid on his behalf by his employer? In *Old Colony Trust Co. v. United States*, the U. S. Supreme Court addressed this issue. Consider the following questions as you make your way through the opinion:

1. Were the tax payments compensation, even if paid to a third party?
2. Could the payment of the taxes have constituted a gift under *Duberstein*?

Old Colony Trust Co. v. United States
279 U.S. 716 (1929)

Mr. Chief Justice TAFT delivered the opinion of the Court.

We have before us for consideration two questions certified from the same Circuit Court of Appeals, No. 130 and No. 129. ***

No. 130 comes here by certificate from the Circuit Court of Appeals for the First Circuit. ***

The facts certified to us are substantially as follows:

William M. Wood was president of the American Woolen Company during the years 1918, 1919, and 1920. In 1918 he received as salary and commissions from the company $978,725, which he included in his federal income tax return for 1918. In 1919 he received as salary and commissions from the company $548,132.87, which he included in his return for 1919.

August 3, 1916, the American Woolen Company had adopted the following resolution, which was in effect in 1919 and 1920:

"Voted: That this company pay any and all income taxes, State and Federal, that may hereafter become due and payable upon the salaries of all the officers of the company, including the president, William M. Wood; the comptroller, Parry C. Wiggin; the auditor, George R. Lawton; and the following members of the staff, to wit: Frank H. Carpenter, Edwin L. Heath, Samuel R. Haines, and William M. Lasbury, to the end that said persons and officers shall receive their salaries or other compensation in full without deduction on account of income taxes, State or Federal, which taxes are to be paid out of the treasury of this corporation."

***

[T]he American Woolen Company paid to the collector of internal revenue Mr. Wood's federal income and surtaxes due to salary and commissions paid him by the company . . . . ***

The decision of the Board of Tax Appeals here sought to be reviewed was that the income taxes of $681,169.88 and $351,179.27 paid by the American Woolen Company for Mr. Wood were additional income to him for the years 1919 and 1920. [Author Note: Old

Chief Justice William H. Taft

Appointed by President Warren G. Harding, William Howard Taft joined the U.S. Supreme Court as Chief Justice in 1921. Taft had previously served as President of the United States from 1909 to 1913. The sinking of the *Titanic* and the ratification of the Sixteenth Amendment occurred during Taft's administration. He died in 1930 and was the first president interred at Arlington National Cemetery. *See* David H. Burton, *William Howard Taft*, 19 WORLD BOOK ENCYCLOPEDIA 8 (World Book 2013).

Credit: Photo courtesy of the Library of Congress.

Colony Trust Co. and others were the executors of Mr. Wood's estate. The executors petitioned for review of the decision of the Board of Tax Appeals.]

The question certified by the Circuit Court of Appeals for answer by this Court is:

"Did the payment by the employer of the income taxes assessable against the employee constitute additional taxable income to such employee?"

***

Coming now to the merits of this case, we think the question presented is whether a taxpayer, having induced a third person to pay his income tax or having acquiesced in such payment as made in discharge of an obligation to him, may avoid the making of a return thereof and the payment of a corresponding tax. We think he may not do so. The payment of the tax by the employers was in consideration of the services rendered by the employee, and was again derived by the employee from his labor. The form of the payment is expressly declared to make no difference. It is therefore immaterial that the taxes were directly paid over to the government. The discharge by a third person of an obligation to him is equivalent to receipt by the person taxed. The certificate shows that the taxes were imposed upon the employee, that the taxes were actually paid by the employer, and that the employee entered upon his duties in the years in question under the express agreement that his income taxes would be paid by his employer. This is evidenced by the terms of the resolution passed August 3, 1916, more than one year prior to the year in which the taxes were imposed. The taxes were paid upon a valuable consideration, namely, the services rendered by the employee and as part of the compensation therefor. We think, therefore, that the payment constituted income to the employee. ***

This result is sustained by many decisions.

Nor can it be argued that the payment of the tax in No. 130 was a gift. The payment for services, even though entirely voluntary, was nevertheless compensation within the statute. ***

The question in this case is, "Did the payment by the employer of the income taxes assessable against the employee constitute additional taxable income to such employee?" The answer must be "Yes."

[Separate opinion of Mr. Justice McReynolds omitted]

Post-Case Follow-Up

In *Old Colony Trust Co.*, the Court had little difficulty concluding that the taxes paid by the company on Mr. Wood's behalf constituted additional compensation to him and, though reflecting the company's voluntary largesse, was not a gift. Had the Court decided otherwise, taxpayers could easily eliminate a substantial portion of their tax liabilities by arranging to have some of their compensation paid directly to mortgage lenders, credit card companies, automobile finance companies, grocery stores, dry cleaners, appliance sellers, and the like. Necessarily, then, the economic benefit theory is alive and well. In fact, but for the existence of specific Code provisions authorizing deferral, taxpayers who receive matching § 401(k) contributions from their employers would face immediate taxation on the matching amounts under the economic benefit theory because often the relevant funds are paid over to a third party on the employee's behalf and remain beyond the reach of the employer's creditors. Once employees begin receiving distributions from their § 401(k) plans, they must pay taxes on the amounts received, and if those distributions are premature, the taxpayer must also pay a penalty. By the way, do you see why the economic benefit theory would apply to § 401(k) matching contributions but constructive receipt would not?

Rameses II (a.k.a. Rameses the Great) of Egypt ruled as pharaoh for almost 70 years. During his lifetime, he sired well over 100 children. He also had several monuments and temples built during his reign, including those at Abu Simbel. *See* HISTORY: THE DEFINITIVE VISUAL GUIDE 66–67 (D.K. Publishing 2010).

Credit: Anton_Ivanov/Shutterstock.com.

Old Colony Trust Co. v. United States: Real Life Applications

1. For 24 years, Elijah has worked as a truck driver for Lumber Transport Enterprises, a sole proprietorship owned by his longtime friend, Rusty. Recently, a local police officer arrested Elijah for driving while intoxicated. At the jail, Elijah called Rusty who eventually paid $500 to bail him out. Profusely thankful, Elijah promised that he would pay Rusty back. Rusty replied that the money was something Elijah would not have to worry about. Must Elijah include the $500 in income as compensation from his employer?

2. Ramses is a bachelor who has managed to sire several children. Paying child support, however, is not his strong suit. Recently, the sheriff delivered a writ of garnishment to Ramses's employer, and in compliance with the writ, his employer subsequently withheld $400 per paycheck from his gross earnings and paid it over to the authorities. Must Ramses include the amounts withheld pursuant to the writ in his gross income?

3. For several years, Ariel made timely payments on her new car. Unfortunately, she recently encountered a series of financial difficulties, and the bank repossessed her vehicle. Without her car, Ariel had considerable difficulty getting to work, so she appealed to her employer for assistance. Her employer paid off the balance due on her car but made it clear that the amount paid over would be deducted from Ariel's pay in small installments over time. Must Ariel include in income the amount paid by her employer to recover her car? As she receives future pay, must she include the full amount of the pay or only the amount remaining after reduction by the installment amount?

2. Taxable Year of Deduction

Section 461(a) governs the timing of taxpayer deductions. In simple terms, it states that taxpayers may take deductions (or credits) into account "for the taxable year which is the proper taxable year under the method of accounting used in computing taxable income." The Treasury Regulations provide necessary clarity. Taxpayers using the cash receipts and disbursements method of accounting may generally take deductions "into account for the taxable year in which paid." Treas. Reg. § 1.461-1(a)(1). Likewise, such taxpayers may also take appropriate deductions (in accordance with statutory requirements) for amounts not flowing directly from a cash disbursement (e.g., depreciation, amortization, losses, and other items). *See id.*

3. Limitation on Use of Cash Receipts and Disbursement Method of Accounting

Section § 446(b) generally provides that taxpayers may employ either (i) the cash receipts and disbursements method of accounting, (ii) an accrual method of accounting, or (iii) a designated permissible method. Section 448, however, prohibits the use of the cash receipts and disbursement method of accounting by tax shelters. Additionally, as a general rule, section 448 prohibits use of the cash method by C corporations (and partnerships with a C corporation as a partner) if the entity has gross receipts exceeding $5,000,000 during a statutory testing period. Such businesses have reached a scale of operations such that use of the cash method of accounting could lead to stark timing-related distortions. The Code thus demands that such ventures use a method of accounting that achieves proper matching regardless of actual cash receipts or disbursements. Accordingly, most large businesses use the accrual method of accounting. Finally, most businesses with inventories are required to use the accrual method. *See* Treas. Reg. § 1.446-1(c)(2)(i).

B. ACCRUAL METHOD OF ACCOUNTING

1. Taxable Year of Income Inclusion

In General

Although § 451(a) generally requires that taxpayers include an amount in income in their year of receipt, it clarifies that such rule applies unless, under the taxpayer's method of accounting, "such amount is to be properly accounted for as of a different period." Thus, under the standards governing the accrual method, the taxable year of actual receipt and the taxable year of income accrual can be different. Traditionally, an accrual method taxpayer includes an item in gross income upon satisfaction of the so-called all events test. Section 451(b)(1)(C) indicates that for § 451 purposes, the all events test is met "with respect to any item of gross income if all the events have occurred which fix the right to receive such income and the amount of such income can be determined with reasonable accuracy." Section § 451(b)(1)(A) goes on to clarify that the all events test is deemed to have been met no later than when a given item (or portion thereof) is taken into account as revenue in an applicable financial statement or other Treasury-prescribed financial statement. Accrual method taxpayers lacking financial statements are not subject to this rule and thus continue to include amounts in income upon satisfaction of the all events test (barring application of a provision allowing deferral of inclusion or exclusion altogether). Although various documents may satisfy the definition of "applicable financial statement" set forth in § 451(b)(3), a standard example would be a 10-K (or annual statement to shareholders) certified as having been prepared in accordance with generally accepted accounting principles ("GAAP"). *See generally* § 451(b)(3)(A)–(C).

Example 1

Spiffy Windows, Inc. ("Spiffy") operates a major window-cleaning service in Las Vegas, Nevada. It uses the accrual method of accounting, and its taxable year runs from January 1 to December 31. From December 26 to 30, 2018, Spiffy employees cleaned the exterior windows of several major hotels. Although Spiffy immediately billed the hotels for services rendered, the hotels did not pay Spiffy until January 2019. By December 31, 2018, Spiffy's employees had completed the work. Thus, by that date, all events that fixed Spiffy's right to receive the income had occurred, and the amount of income earned could be determined with reasonable accuracy. Accordingly, Spiffy must accrue the income for its 2018 taxable year, notwithstanding the fact that it receives actual cash payment in 2019.

Advance Payments

Accrual method taxpayers receiving advance payments are subject to the rules set forth in § 451(c) which generally require inclusion of the amount in gross income unless the taxpayer elects application of § 451(c)(1)(B). In that event, the taxpayer must (i) include relevant advance payments in income in the year of receipt if and to the extent § 451(b) requires inclusion and (ii) include the remainder in income in the taxable year following the year of receipt. Section 451(c)(4)(C) clarifies that receipt (for § 451(c) purposes) occurs when an item is actually or constructively received or is due and payable to the taxpayer. Advance payment generally refers to a payment for goods or services, but note that additional definitional requirements exist. *See generally* § 451(c)(4)(A) & (B).

Example 2

Dougie's Laundry Service and Repair, Inc. ("Dougie's") operates a thriving business. It uses the accrual method of accounting, and its taxable year is a fiscal year running from July 1 to June 30. On June 28, 2019, Dougie's arranged to repair eight well-used washing machines at a local laundromat, and per Dougie's established policy, the customer paid in advance on the same date. The parties scheduled the repair work for the early afternoon of July 6, 2019. Dougie's employees completed the repairs as scheduled. Assume that Dougie's properly elects the application of

§ 451(c)(1)(B) and takes none of the advance payment into account as revenue in any of its financial statements for its taxable year ended June 30, 2019. Dougie's would not be required to accrue any of the advance payment as income for the taxable year beginning July 1, 2018 and ending June 30, 2019. Section 451(c)(1)(B)(ii) would, however, require accrual of the income in Dougie's taxable year starting July 1, 2019 and ending June 30, 2020. Even if (under alternative facts) Dougie's had not managed literally to satisfy the all events test during that time period, the election would not permit failure to accrue the income in the 2019–2020 taxable year.

2. Taxable Year of Deduction

Section 461(a) generally provides that taxpayers deduct amounts (or take credits) for the taxable year dictated by their method of accounting. The rule for deducting items under the accrual method shares similarities with the rule for accruing income, but with one key difference, the so-called *economic performance requirement*. Treasury Regulations § 1.461-1(a)(2) provides that "under an accrual method of accounting, a liability . . . is incurred, and generally is taken into account for Federal income tax purposes, in the taxable year in which all the events have occurred that establish the fact of the liability, the amount of the liability can be determined with reasonable accuracy, and economic performance has occurred with respect to the liability." The notion of economic performance often relates to the provision of services whether this means services provided to the taxpayer or services the taxpayer must provide to others. The taxpayer may not accrue the cost of providing services or compensating others for services rendered until (in either event) the services have, in fact, been provided (assuming all other expense accrual requirements have been satisfied). Section 461(h)(1) indicates that the all events test for an item cannot be treated as met until economic performance has occurred with respect to the item. Thereafter, § 461(h)(2) sets forth rules with respect to the timing of economic performance in different contexts. *See* Table 15.1.

TABLE 15.1 **Timing of Economic Performance Under the Accrual Method**

Nature of Taxpayer Liability	Timing of Economic Performance
Obligation for services provided to the taxpayer by another person	As the person provides the services
Obligation for property provided to the taxpayer by another person	As the person provides the property
Obligation for taxpayer's use of property	As the taxpayer uses the property
Taxpayer required to provide property or services	As the taxpayer provides the property or performs the services
Workers compensation and tort	As the payments to the relevant person are made by the taxpayer
Other	As determined under Treasury Regulations

3. Cash Receipts or Payments of Accrual Method Taxpayers

Per § 451(c)(1)(A), unless an accrual method taxpayer makes the appropriate election, the taxpayer's receipt of an advance payment triggers inclusion of the amount in gross income in the taxable year of receipt. Accordingly, amounts prepaid to an accrual method taxpayer for future services or other performance (including performance to occur during a future taxable year) may trigger immediate inclusion. Even so, you will recall from our brief discussion of loans that not every receipt of legal tender constitutes income; repayment obligations or other strings may well be attached. The Ninth Circuit Court of Appeals dealt with the treatment of a cash receipt by an accrual method taxpayer in the next case.

Case Preview

Westpac Pacific Food v. Commissioner

In *Westpac Pacific Food*, we find an accrual method taxpayer receiving cash as part of a bulk purchase arrangement with several wholesalers. Rather than receiving the bulk discount as it made purchases, however, the taxpayer received an up-front cash payment (i.e., an advance trade discount) and paid the "regular" price as it purchased merchandise in accord with the agreement. If the taxpayer failed to make sufficient purchases, it was obligated to return all or a portion of the up-front cash payment, depending on the extent to which it had complied with its purchasing obligation. Reviewing the decision of the Tax Court, the Ninth Circuit Court of Appeals addressed the question of whether the up-front cash payment constituted income of the taxpayer upon receipt. As you read the case, consider the following questions:

1. What conclusion did the Tax Court reach on this issue?
2. How, if at all, does the *Glenshaw Glass* decision support the Commissioner in this case?
3. Why does the court consider this case analogous to the *Indianapolis Power* case?
4. Would the court have reached a different conclusion if the taxpayer had used the cash receipts and disbursements method of accounting?

Westpac Pacific Food v. Commissioner
451 F.3d 970 (9th Cir. 2006)

KLEINFELD, Circuit Judge.

We must decide whether cash paid in advance by a wholesaler to a retailer, in exchange for a volume commitment, is "gross income" under 26 U.S.C. § 61. In the grocery trade, these are called "advance trade discounts."

It is hard to think of a way to make money by buying things. A child may think buying things is how one makes money: he sees his father give a clerk a single piece of paper money, and receive in exchange the goods purchased, several pieces of paper money, and a number of coins. And a person may jokingly say to a spouse "I made $100 today" after buying something on sale for $100 off. But everyone knows these are merely amusing remarks, not real ways to make money.

The facts outlined below sound more complicated than they are, so imagine a simple hypothetical. Harry Homeowner goes to the furniture store, spots just the right dining room chairs for $500 each, and says "I'll take four, if you give me a discount." Negotiating a 25% discount, he pays only $1,500 for the chairs. He has not made $500, he has spent $1,500. Now suppose Harry Homeowner is short on cash, and negotiates a deal where the furniture store gives him a 20% discount as a cash advance instead of the 25% off. This means the store gives him $400 "cash back" today, and he pays $2,000 for the four chairs when they are delivered shortly after the first of the year. Harry cannot go home and say "I made $400 today" unless he plans to skip out on his obligation to pay for the four chairs. Even though he receives the cash, he has not made money by buying the chairs. He has to sell the chairs for more than $1,600 if he wants to make money on them. The reason why the $400 "cash back" is not income is that, like a loan, the money is encumbered with a repayment obligation to the furniture store and the "cash back" must be repaid if Harry does not perform his obligation.

This case is that simple, except that it involves a little more math and a lot more money. The taxpayer promised to buy a lot of items and received cash in advance as its discount on its future, high-volume purchases. Using accrual accounting, the taxpayer treated the up-front cash discount as a liability when it was received, just like a loan. As goods were sold, the taxpayer applied the discount *pro rata* to the full purchase price it paid. The net effect was that Westpac reduced its cost of goods sold and increased its reported profit (and thus its taxable income). ***

The government concedes, and the Tax Court agreed, that Westpac's method was consistent with generally accepted accounting principles. *** Nevertheless, the Tax Court concluded that the cash discount received in advance was income, noting that tax principles do not serve the same purposes as accounting principles, such as reflecting to shareholders how their company is performing.

A company would indeed have a major problem if it accounted to its shareholders as the Tax Court would have it account to the government. Were a company to get very significant amounts of up-front cash discounts on its obligation to purchase goods in the future and tell stockholders and prospective stock purchasers that it had "made" this much "income," investors would be sorely disappointed to learn that all the money had to be paid back if their company did not sell all the goods it had promised to sell in the future. The company would be like Harry Homeowner claiming to have "made" $400 when he received his cash advance discount on the four chairs. Harry might have to spend the night on the couch, but the CEO could spend the night in jail.

FACTS

Three grocery store chains — Raley's, Save Mart, and Bel Air — organized the taxpayer, Westpac, as a partnership to purchase and warehouse inventory. Westpac is an accrual basis taxpayer.

Westpac's contracts

During 1990 and 1991, Westpac made four contracts to buy inventory and receive cash in advance: (1) lightbulbs from GTE Sylvania; (2) Hallmark cards from Ambassador; (3) bows, wrapping paper, and other products from American Greetings; and (4) spices from McCormick. Under each contract, Westpac promised to buy a minimum quantity of merchandise and received a volume discount in the form of cash up-front. If Westpac bought too few lightbulbs, spices, greeting cards, etc., then it was obligated to pay back the cash advance *pro rata*. Conversely, Westpac's obligation to repay the cash advance was extinguished if Westpac purchased the required volume. Westpac made other promises as well, such as exclusivity and shelf space, but the volume purchased determined whether it had to refund the cash advance and, if so, how much it had to refund.

GTE Sylvania Contract

In July of 1990, Westpac made a deal with the Sylvania Lighting division of GTE Products Corp. to (1) make GTE Sylvania its exclusive lightbulb supplier for Westpac and its member stores for four years; (2) "aggressively and regularly" advertise and promote GTE Sylvania's products; (3) dedicate on average at least 12 lineal feet of shelf space to GTE Sylvania's products in its member stores; and (4) purchase $17 million in lightbulbs during the term of the agreement. Given Westpac's volume purchase commitment, GTE Sylvania agreed to pay Westpac $1.1 million as an "unearned advance allowance." GTE Sylvania paid this to Westpac by check, and agreed to pay Westpac another $200,000 on the first, second, and third anniversaries of the agreement, provided that GTE Sylvania was satisfied with Westpac's warehouse distribution arrangement. The contract refers to the total $1.7 million in payments as the "Westpac Allowance" and contains the following clause:

Upon termination of this Agreement, Westpac will reimburse GTE Sylvania on a pro-rated basis for any portion of the Westpac Allowance advanced to Westpac but not earned due to the failure by Westpac to purchase at least $17.0 million in lamps.

During Westpac's 1991 tax year, GTE Sylvania paid the first $200,000 to Westpac.

Westpac could not resell enough lightbulbs to meet the minimum volume the contract called for, so it terminated the arrangement in October of 1994. Westpac's termination letter acknowledged its obligation to pay back a pro-rated portion of the Westpac Allowance, and it repaid $861,857 to GTE Sylvania in December.

[Discussion of the Ambassador, American Greetings, and McCormick contracts omitted.]

Westpac's Tax Reporting

In accord with standard accounting principles, Westpac accounted for the up-front cash as a liability at the time it received the cash. The cash advance got translated into taxable income through Westpac's inventory accounting. As Westpac purchased the goods for which it had the volume obligations, it subtracted *pro rata* portions of the advance cash discounts from what it paid. This had the effect of reducing the cost of goods sold (and increasing the taxable profits from sales) by the amount of the cash advances attributable to the goods sold.

The government took the position that Westpac and Save Mart under-reported over $5.5 million in gross income for 1990 and over $4.9 million for 1991 because they did not report the cash advances as gross income. Westpac filed a petition for readjustment and the government opposed it. Relying on *Commissioner of Internal Revenue v. Glenshaw Glass Co.,* the Tax Court held that the cash advance discounts were "income" under section 61 of the Internal Revenue Code. Westpac timely filed this appeal.

The sole issue before us is whether advance trade discounts constitute gross income when received. We hold that they do not and reverse the Tax Court.

ANALYSIS

There are no disputed findings of fact in this case, just the question of law: whether "advance trade discounts" subject to repayment if volume requirements are not met are income when received. We review the Tax Court's decision on questions of law *de novo.* ***

There appears to be no circuit court authority on point, but the Supreme Court authorities bracketing the question compel our answer: Cash advances in exchange for volume purchase commitments, subject to *pro rata* repayment if the volume commitments are not met, are not income when received.

The statutory definition of gross income is expansive. *Commissioner v. Glenshaw Glass Co.* held that punitive damages received by a successful litigant were "income" because they were "accessions to wealth, clearly realized, and over which the taxpayers have complete dominion." The government argues that the cash advances in this case fit that definition because Westpac had "complete dominion" over the money. It did not have to put the cash in a trust account and could spend the money as it chose. But that leaves out *sine qua non* of income: that it be an "accession to wealth." One may have "complete dominion" over money but it does not become income until it is an "accession to wealth." That is why borrowed money is not income, even though the borrower has "complete dominion" over the cash. "Because of this [repayment] obligation, the loan proceeds do not qualify as income to the taxpayer."

The Supreme Court decisions bracketing this case are *CIR v. Indianapolis Power & Light Co.* on one side, and *Automobile Club of Michigan v. CIR* and *Schlude v. CIR* on the other.

Indianapolis Power held that utility customers' security deposits are not income to the utility because of the obligation to repay the money when service ended. The decision analogizes the security deposits to loans because of the repayment obligation.

Automobile Club of Michigan holds that prepaid membership dues are income when received, despite the association's obligation to provide membership services — maps, tire repair and the like — during the subsequent year. The reason was that *pro rata* application of the dues to each month "bears no relation to the services" the club had to perform. Drivers do not call AAA once a month to repair a flat or send a map, and AAA is entitled to keep the membership dues regardless of whether the member ever requests any goods or services. *Schlude* held that cash paid to a dance studio for ballroom dancing lessons was income when received, not when the lessons were provided. The Court applied *Automobile Club of Michigan,* because the money was not refundable and the studio could keep it even if the student did not show up for dance lessons.

This case is like *Indianapolis Power,* not *Automobile Club of Michigan* or *Schlude.* The cash advance trade discounts are like the security deposits in that they are subject to repayment, and unlike the membership dues in that the recipient cannot keep the money regardless of what happens after receipt. Westpac could only retain the full, up front trade discount if it met the volume requirements. Like the security deposit, the cash advance is subject to repayment. The only difference is that the repayment amount in this case may not be the full amount advanced by the vendor, but that is because the repayment amount is reduced *pro rata* to the extent Westpac fails to fulfill its volume commitment.

Because the taxpayer here has to pay the money back if the volume commitments are not met, it is not an "accession to wealth" as required by *Glenshaw Glass.* Westpac either has to buy a specified volume of goods for more than it would otherwise pay or pay back the money, just like Harry Homeowner. Thus the cash advance discounts are, like a loan or customer security deposit, liabilities rather than income when received.

The Tax Court found that Westpac's accounting for the cash advances as affecting cost of goods sold complied with generally accepted accounting principles, but correctly held that accounting rules are not necessarily controlling for tax purposes. The regulations require that inventory accounting conform to best accounting practices *and* clearly reflect income. But that does not go far enough to transform the cash into "income" in the face of *Indianapolis Power.* We cannot agree with the government that Westpac's "unfettered use" of the money makes it income, because it was not an accession to wealth. Rather, it was merely an advance against an obligation, repayable if the obligation was not performed. ***

Westpac not only had a duty to repay the discounts, it actually did repay them when it did not meet the volume commitments. When Westpac did buy the required volume of goods, it paid list price rather than a discounted price, and realized the income for tax purposes.

It works out about the same as with Harry Homeowner: He has to sell the chairs for more than he paid in order to make money on them. Westpac had to sell the lightbulbs, ribbons, greeting cards, and such for more than they paid in order to make money on them. It remains exceedingly difficult to make money merely by buying things. Westpac did not get any richer when it received its volume discount in the form of cash up front than Harry Homeowner did when he got the $400 from the furniture store. There was no accession to wealth when Westpac got the cash, just an increase in cash assets offset by an equal liability for the advance trade discounts.

REVERSED.

Post-Case Follow-Up

Concluding that the taxpayer's business arrangement was analogous to the receipt of a loan or a security deposit and thus substantively similar to *Indianapolis Power*, the court held that the taxpayer had no includible income as a result of receiving the advance trade discount. Rejecting the Commissioner's appeal to *Glenshaw Glass*, the court confirmed that the taxpayer's potential repayment obligation meant that receipt of the up-front cash payment did not constitute an undeniable accession to wealth. Even accepting the court's logic, one can certainly appreciate the Commissioner's concern. The accrual method's occasional disregard of actual cash movement opens the door to potential abuse, and in the eyes of the Commissioner an advance trade discount looks like an acceleration of profit (in the form of millions of real dollars and real cents) with delayed inclusion operating as an aggressive distortion — rather than a clear reflection — of income. It's also true that rather than incorporating the use of an advance trade discount (with the specter of repayment), the wholesalers could simply have offered the bulk discount as companies made purchases. Doesn't that arrangement promise a simpler existence for all involved? Of course it does, but an aggressive wholesaler might prefer to take its competitive game to the next level by locking up future purchase commitments with the lure of up-front cash. A willing counterparty shouldn't face negative tax consequence if it truly is bargaining at arm's length in an effort to shore up its bottom line.

Westpac Pacific Food v. Commissioner: Real Life Applications

1. Toy Distributors, LLC ("TDL") is a wholesaler. It sells millions of dollars of toys to retailers over the course of a given year, and Fun Express, Inc. is one of its major customers. As the holiday season approaches, TDL begins to offer bulk purchase discounts in the form of post-purchase cash back. Assume that Fun Express, Inc. (an accrual method taxpayer) buys $800,000 of toys and two weeks later receives a bulk purchase discount of $80,000 by check from TDL. Must Fun Express, Inc. include the $80,000 received in its gross income?

2. *Same facts at Question #1*, except that TDL offers to pay the discount in cash prior to purchase. The parties understand that if the purchaser does not follow through 100 percent, the prepurchase discount must be repaid to TDL on a pro rata basis.

3. Empire Financial Bank ("Empire") hopes to survive an upcoming "stress" test by building up its base of depositors. Empire offers depositors $1,000 if they are willing to open a new account, deposit $25,000 in new funds (i.e., money not already on deposit at the bank), and maintain that amount as a minimum daily balance for at least 90 days. If Gary's Rib Shack (a sole proprietorship using the accrual method of accounting) takes advantage of this offer, when will the sole proprietor be required to include the $1,000 in income?

C. INSTALLMENT METHOD

Taxpayers making certain dispositions may take advantage of the so-called installment method of accounting with respect to gain on that transaction. Although some professors provide detailed and extensive coverage of the installment sale method, the approach taken here serves largely to communicate bare essentials, because you should already have a degree of familiarity with the core concepts. Section § 453(a) generally allows taxpayers to take advantage of the installment method with respect to what it refers to as installment sales. Section 453(b), in turn, defines an installment sale as "a disposition of property where at least 1 payment is to be received after the close of the taxable year in which the disposition occurs." Application of the installment method is not mandatory; taxpayers may elect out under § 453(d). Further, the method does not apply to all transactions (e.g., certain dealer dispositions and dispositions of taxpayer inventory). The availability of the method allows a clear reflection of income in some situations. Assume, for example, that a taxpayer purchased land several years ago for $300,000 and that the land currently has a fair market value of $1,000,000. If the taxpayer effects an installment sale of the land pursuant to which she is to receive five annual installments of $200,000, she has the option of recognizing her gain realized ($700,000) over the five-year period as payments are received (i.e., $140,000 per year). Section 453(c) essentially requires that a percentage of each payment received be included in gross income. That percentage is the quotient obtained by dividing the gross profit realized or to be realized ($700,000) by the total amount realized ($1,000,000). Thus, the percentage is 70 percent. If one multiplies the amount of each payment installment ($200,000) by the percentage (0.70), one will obtain the amount to be included each year over the five-year term (i.e., $140,000).

D. PRIORITIZATION: METHOD OF ACCOUNTING AND RULES OF SPECIFIC APPLICABILITY

It is worth noting, for the sake of avoiding confusion, that a taxpayer's method of accounting should be thought of as a complex of generally applicable rules regarding income inclusion and deduction. But more specific rules (many of which we have discussed previously) may take precedence. Thus, even if an expense appears to qualify for immediate deduction or immediate accrual, rules mandating capitalization will take precedence to the extent they apply. For example, a taxpayer using the accrual method of accounting may pay an independent contractor $4 million to construct a building to be used in its operations. Notwithstanding the fact that (i) all events have occurred establishing the fact of the liability, (ii) the amount of the liability can be ascertained with reasonable certainty, and (iii) economic performance has occurred, the taxpayer may not accrue the liability currently, because the amount paid to purchase a building constitutes a capital expenditure. Section 263(a) will govern. *See generally* Treas. Reg. § 1.461-1(a)(2)(iii) (referring to alternative timing rules that may be dictated by other provisions); *see also* Treas. Reg. § 1.461-1(a)(1) (discussing the taxable year of deduction for cash method taxpayers and referring to § 263 and the regulations thereunder for rules regarding capital expenditures).

Chapter Summary

- Taxpayers must compute their taxable income under the method of accounting they regularly use in computing their taxable income (e.g., the cash receipts and disbursements method of accounting or an accrual method of accounting).
- Taxpayers using the cash method generally include items in income upon actual receipt and deduct items upon actual payment. A taxpayer using the cash method must, nonetheless, immediately include in income amounts constructively received as well as amounts with respect to which he enjoys an economic benefit.
- Certain entities with gross receipts exceeding $5 million may not use the cash receipts and disbursements method of accounting. A broader rule generally requires that businesses with inventories use the accrual method.
- Taxpayers using the accrual method of accounting must include items in income when all events have occurred that fix their right to receive the income and the amount of such income can be determined with reasonable accuracy. For § 451 purposes, the all events test is met when (i) all events have occurred which fix the right to receive the income and (ii) the amount of the income can be determined with reasonable accuracy. Note that under § 451(b)(1), the all events test is deemed to have been met no later than when an item is taken into account as revenue in an applicable financial statement (or other financial statement specified by the Secretary of the Treasury).
- Taxpayers using the accrual method of accounting may take a deduction with respect to a liability when all events have occurred that establish the fact of liability, the amount thereof can be determined with reasonable accuracy, and economic performance has occurred with respect to the liability. Economic performance refers to the provision of services or property to the taxpayer, the provision of services or property by the taxpayer, and the use of property by the taxpayer. A mere cash disbursement will not, of necessity, dictate liability accrual.
- In some contexts, taxpayers disposing of property in an installment sale will be eligible to report gain over time as payments are made by the purchaser of the property.
- Specific rules governing the proper timing of inclusion or deduction of an item take precedence over general method of accounting rules.

Applying the Rules

1. Rail Transport, Inc. ("RTI") uses the calendar year as its taxable year and is an accrual method taxpayer. RTI provides rail delivery services to various customers throughout the United States and frequently delivers items at year-end for which it receives payment in the next taxable year. If RTI delivers 1,000 books on behalf of Academic Express LLC on December 31, 2019, but is paid (per standard fee schedule) in January 2020, must RTI accrue the income for 2019 or 2020? Why?

2. Assume that Fish Factory, Inc. ("Fish Factory") uses the calendar year as its taxable year and employs the cash receipts and disbursements method of accounting. Given the significance of superior cleanliness in its facilities, Fish Factory pays an independent contractor to clean its facilities on a nightly basis. If Fish Factory paid the independent contractor $12,000 for its services during 2019, may the company deduct the expense on its return for the 2019 taxable year?

3. *Same facts as Question #2*, except that Fish Factory decided to purchase the cleaning company outright for $500,000, an amount that included $15,000 in goodwill. May Fish Factory deduct the $500,000 purchase price on payment?

4. Assume that Nile Fashions, Inc. ("Nile") is an accrual method taxpayer using the calendar year as its taxable year. Nile has operated from the same location for several years, and it has become clear that the storefront needs a new paint job. Hoping to have the job done quickly, Nile paid an independent contractor $4,000 on December 30, 2019, to complete the job. Unwilling to brave particularly harsh elements (or work on holidays), the independent contractor did not start the job until January 7, 2020. May Nile accrue the expense in 2019?

5. In 1989, Alex purchased a tract of land for $300,000. Recently, he managed to sell it for $1.2 million with payments due in equal $100,000 installments over a 12-year period. Assuming application of the installment method, how much must Alex include in gross income with respect to each $100,000 payment?

Federal Income Taxation in Practice

1. One of your corporate clients recently received its property tax assessment. The company's general counsel feels sure that the assessment is excessive, and the Board of Directors has authorized him to take the necessary steps to contest it. The client's question, at this juncture, is whether the company can accrue any of the property tax liability in the current tax period. Conduct the research and follow up with the client by letter.

2. You are a partner in a law firm, and one of your growing clients is a sole proprietor who happens to have two businesses. The client would like to know whether he can use the cash receipts and disbursements method of accounting for one of his businesses while using an accrual method of accounting for his other business. See what you can find and prepare a brief letter to the client.

3. One of the senior partners you work for has a client contemplating a change in its method of accounting. The partner would like to know, in very basic terms, what steps the client must take to effect the change. Do the research and send the partner a brief memo.

Nonrecognition and Tax Impact Deferral

As we have seen in prior chapters, governing rules and doctrines often seek the clearest possible reflection of income by matching income inclusion to associated income-generation expenses. In this chapter, we focus on timing rules that also seek to achieve a clear reflection of income, but they do so by ensuring that income or loss itself is properly timed to the right taxable period. Section 1001(a) of the Code generally requires that we calculate gain or loss on the sale or exchange of property by measuring the difference between the amount realized on disposition and the adjusted basis of the property. Although § 1001(c) generally requires the immediate recognition of gains and losses realized, its introductory language bears critical significance. Immediate gain or loss recognition follows realization "*[e]xcept as otherwise provided in this subtitle,*" and as you will see in this course, and perhaps others, the Code contains a host of nonrecognition provisions. We turn our focus to a few of them in this chapter, but before doing so, we should highlight several overarching truths. First, the fact that a given Code provision halts recognition does not mean that *realization* does not occur; the realization events will often be starkly visible. The nonrecognition provision simply prevents immediate *recognition* of gain or loss. Second, the prevention of immediate recognition does not mean that any built-in gain or built-in loss in the property evaporates. Current nonrecognition merely results in the deferral of recognition. And finally, Congress uses somewhat convoluted basis rules to ensure that built-in gain or built-in loss is ultimately recognized after a nonrecognition event. We focus initially on like-kind exchanges of real property before turning to involuntary conversions and then, very briefly, to a simple incorporation transaction to give you a modest teaser to the complicated world of corporate taxation. Along the way, we discuss basis calculation rules, but only as needed and in measured doses.

Key Concepts

- Non-recognition of gain or loss realized
- Like-kind exchanges of real property
- Involuntary conversion
- Deferral of gain or loss
- Preservation of deferred gains or losses by use of asset basis rules

A. LIKE-KIND EXCHANGES OF REAL PROPERTY[1]

Although only some of you may be familiar with like-kind exchanges, the transactions are generally simple. A taxpayer owns real property, and he exchanges it for another taxpayer's real property. If you think about it, a taxpayer who holds one piece of land and exchanges it for another piece of land has undertaken a transaction that allows him to take ownership of an entirely new piece of property and endows him with a new set of rights and obligations (i.e., those associated with the new land as opposed to those associated with the old land). But, viewed from another perspective, the taxpayer started the deal with a tract of land and ended the deal with a tract of land. One could rationally conclude that his situation is fundamentally unchanged. Should the exchange give rise to the recognition of gain or loss? Notwithstanding the occurrence of a realization event, the Code justifies current nonrecognition with respect to such a transaction so long as the taxpayer simply exchanges one piece of real property for another that is of a like kind (e.g., transfers land solely in exchange for land) and satisfies other Code-based requirements. Transactions do, however, vary to some extent. The parties may need to employ limited amounts of cash or some combination of both like-kind and non-like-kind property. In the next few sections, we discuss several transactional variations of gradually increasing complexity and cover the rules governing the Code's treatment of specific taxpayers participating in them.

Key Statutory and Regulatory Provisions

- **Internal Revenue Code**
  - § 351(a)
  - § 358(a)(1) (except (A) and (B))
  - § 1001(a)
  - § 1001(b) (except (1) and (2))
  - § 1001(c)
  - § 1031(a)(1)–(3)
  - § 1031(b)–(d)
  - § 1031(h)
  - § 1033(a)(1)
  - § 1033(a)(2)(A) (1st 2 sentences)
  - § 1033(a)(2)(B) (skim)
  - § 1033(a)(2)(E)(ii)
  - § 1033(b)(1)–(2)
- **Treasury Regulations**
  - § 1.1031(a)-1(a)(2)
  - § 1.1031(a)-1(b) and (c)
  - § 1.1031(a)-2(a) and (b)(1)
  - § 1.1031(a)-2(c)
  - § 1.1031(k)-1(g)(4)(i) and (ii)

WARNING

The like-kind exchange rules apply only to exchanges of real property (excluding real property held primarily for sale (e.g., land held as a form of inventory)). *See generally* § 1031(a)(1)–(2). Keep in mind, however, that even if the like-kind exchange rules under § 1031 do not apply to a particular transaction, some exchanges of personal property will qualify for nonrecognition under other Code provisions (e.g., those governing exchanges of stock for stock as part of certain corporate transactions).

---

1. Although there will be occasional express reference to "real property," any textual reference to "property" in the like-kind exchange context should (unless otherwise indicated) be understood as a reference to real property.

1. Transactions Involving Taxpayer Receipt of Solely Like-Kind Real Property

The simplest like-kind exchanges involve nothing more than the like-kind properties, and the general nonrecognition rule applies. Section 1031(a)(1) provides as follows:

> No gain or loss shall be recognized on the exchange of real property held for productive use in a trade or business or for investment if such real property is exchanged solely for real property of like kind which is to be held for either productive use in a trade or business or for investment.

Note that this language incorporates several key elements. Section 1031(a)(1) will apply only if the taxpayer satisfies the following requirements:

- The taxpayer must have held the *relinquished* real property either for productive use in a trade or business *or* for investment;
- The taxpayer must exchange the relinquished real property solely for the replacement real property;
- The taxpayer must hold the *replacement* real property either for productive use in a trade or business *or* for investment; *and*
- The relinquished real property and the replacement real property must be of like kind.

Section 1031(a)(1) thus applies only with respect to a taxpayer's business or investment real property, only to an exchange of that real property solely for like-kind real property, and only to the extent the replacement real property will constitute business or investment property in the taxpayer's hands. Preserving built-in gains and built-in losses, the basis rule under § 1031(d) provides, in pertinent part, that "[i]f property was acquired on an exchange described in [§ 1031,] . . . then the basis shall be the same as that of the property exchanged . . . ." Let's see these rules in operation.

Example 1

Cayenne purchased Redacre for $400,000 and holds it as an investment. The property has a fair market value of $1,000,000. Grant owns Greenacre, which currently has a fair market value of $1,000,000. If Cayenne exchanges Redacre for Greenacre and proceeds to hold Greenacre either as an investment or for productive use in her trade or business, she will recognize no gain on the exchange. *See* § 1031(a)(1). Her basis in Greenacre will be $400,000 (i.e., the same as her basis in Redacre). *See* § 1031(d). Such a basis makes sense. Prior to the transaction, she held Redacre with a $600,000 built-in gain, yet she recognized no gain or loss in connection with the exchange. If she sells Greenacre for its fair market value (i.e., $1,000,000), her gain recognized will be $600,000.

Example 2

Cayenne purchased Redacre for $800,000 and holds it as an investment. The property has a fair market value of $500,000. Grant owns Greenacre, which currently has a fair market value of $500,000. If Cayenne exchanges Redacre for

Greenacre and proceeds to hold Greenacre either as an investment or for productive use in her trade or business, she will recognize no loss on the exchange. *See* § 1031(a)(1). Her basis in Greenacre will be $800,000 (i.e., the same as her basis in Redacre). *See* § 1031(d). Such a basis makes sense. Prior to the transaction, she held Redacre with a $300,000 built-in loss, yet she recognized no gain or loss in connection with the exchange. If she sells Greenacre for its fair market value (i.e., $500,000), her loss recognized will be $300,000.

Example 3

Cayenne purchased Redacre for $400,000 and holds it as an investment. The property has a fair market value of $1,000,000. Grant owns Greenacre, which currently has a fair market value of $1,000,000. If Cayenne exchanges Redacre for Greenacre and proceeds to build a personal residence on Greenacre, she will realize and recognize gain of $600,000 on the exchange under § 1001(a). Section 1031(a)(1) will not apply because Cayenne did not hold Greenacre as an investment or for productive use in her trade or business.

What about the exchange counterparty, Grant? Does it matter, in any fact scenario, in what capacity he held the property he relinquished and what he plans to do with the property he received in the exchanges? To speak in general terms, such factors may matter if the contract counterparty expects to take advantage of § 1031(a) or some other nonrecognition provision, but the prior or future actions of the contract counterparty cannot be allowed to govern the tax treatment of the taxpayer under focus. The taxpayer cannot control the activity of the contract counterparty and should not suffer (or enjoy) immediate recognition because of what the counterparty did previously with respect to property the counterparty relinquished or fails to do going forward with the property the counterparty received.

2. Transactions Involving Taxpayer Receipt of Like-Kind Real Property and Cash Boot

The general nonrecognition rule under § 1031(a)(1) applies only if the parties exchange *solely* properties of a like kind. Those seeking to delay the recognition of built-in gains generally favor this rule, and Congress, by allowing deferral, statutorily acknowledges that the taxpayer has, more or less, merely changed the form of his investment (or business asset) in a manner that does not merit immediate recognition. But what if a taxpayer receives both like-kind property and cash or some form of property that is not like kind to the relinquished property? Such additional consideration is referred to colloquially as **boot** or, more technically, as **nonqualifying consideration**. If a taxpayer participating in a like-kind exchange happens to receive both like-kind property and cash in exchange for property with built-in gain, some degree of gain recognition will follow. Rather than receiving purely like-kind property, the taxpayer has cashed out some portion (or possibly all) of the built-in gain, and it would be inappropriate to allow them to escape immediate taxation to the appropriate extent. Section 1031(b) provides, in pertinent part, as follows:

> If an exchange would be within the provisions of [1031(a)] . . . if it were not for the fact that the property received in exchange consists not only of property permitted by such provisions to be received without the recognition of gain, but also of other property or money, then the gain, if any, to the recipient shall be recognized, but in an amount not in excess of the sum of such money and the fair market value of such other property.

A simple example demonstrates the operation of this rule.

Example 4

Yuri purchased Yellowacre for $100,000 and holds it as an investment. The property has a fair market value of $800,000. Garth owns Greenacre, which currently has a fair market value of $600,000. Assume that Yuri exchanges Yellowacre for Greenacre and $200,000. If Yuri proceeds to hold Greenacre either as an investment or for productive use in his trade or business, he will recognize $200,000 of gain on the exchange. *See* § 1031(b).

As you address fact scenarios involving boot, it is extremely important that you keep in mind that the Code requires recognition with respect to *gain*. Resist the urge merely to require recognition with respect to *all* boot received. Let's alter the facts of the preceding example.

Example 5

Yuri purchased Yellowacre for $750,000 and holds it as an investment. The property has a fair market value of $800,000. Garth owns Greenacre, which currently has a fair market value of $600,000. Assume that Yuri exchanges Yellowacre for Greenacre and $200,000. If Yuri proceeds to hold Greenacre either as an investment or for productive use in his trade or business, he will recognize $50,000 of gain on the exchange. *See* § 1031(b). It's also true, under these facts, that Yuri would recognize $50,000 of gain on the transaction regardless of the capacity in which he held Greenacre.

Notwithstanding the fact that Yuri received $200,000, his built-in gain on Yellowacre was only $50,000. If Yuri received property and money with a total value of $800,000, there simply is no justification for taxing Yuri on more than $50,000, given his basis of $750,000. Tax the *gain* not the boot. If we alter the facts yet again to give Yuri a basis in Yellowacre of $800,000, then he would recognize no gain on receiving money and property worth $800,000 because he would have no gain to recognize. That's why the Code dictates that on the receipt of like-kind property and boot "the gain, *if any*, to the recipient shall be recognized" (emphasis added).

Calculating the basis of the replacement property when the like-kind exchange involves boot and gain recognition is slightly more convoluted than doing so with a pure like-kind exchange. Let's first consider the statutory rule. Section 1031(d) provides, in pertinent part, as follows:

> If property was acquired on an exchange described in [§ 1031], . . . then the basis shall be the same as that of the property exchanged, decreased in the amount of any money received by the taxpayer and increased in the amount of gain . . . to the taxpayer that was recognized on such exchange.

You may find the visual depiction of this rule in Exhibit 16.1 helpful.

With this basis calculation rule in mind, let's return to Example 4 and complete the picture of tax ramifications.

Example 4 (cont'd)

Yuri purchased Yellowacre for $100,000 and holds it as an investment. The property has a fair market value of $800,000. Garth owns Greenacre, which currently has a fair market value of $600,000. Assume that Yuri exchanges Yellowacre for Greenacre and $200,000. If Yuri proceeds to hold Greenacre either as an investment or for productive use in his trade or business, he will recognize $200,000 of gain on the exchange. *See* § 1031(b). His basis in Greenacre will be $100,000. That's because in calculating his final basis in Greenacre, we start with his basis in Yellowacre ($100,000), reduce that figure by the amount of money received ($200,000), and increase the resulting figure by the amount of gain recognized ($200,000) on the exchange. *See* § 1031(d). A basis of $100,000 in Greenacre makes sense. Prior to the transaction, Yuri held Yellowacre with built-in gain of $700,000, and he recognized $200,000 of it in connection with the exchange; $500,000 of gain was deferred. If Yuri sells Greenacre for its fair market value (i.e., $600,000), his gain recognized will be $500,000.

EXHIBIT 16.1   **Visual Depiction of § 1031(d) Basis Calculation Rule (*partial*)**

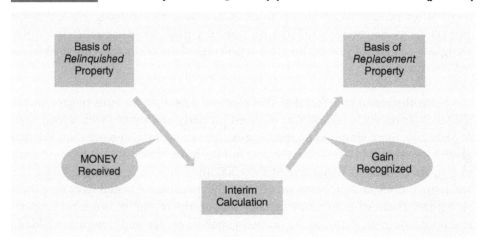

In most of the prior examples, the taxpayer held the relinquished property with built-in gain and received cash and like-kind property in connection with the exchange. As appropriate, gain recognition followed. If the taxpayer held such relinquished property subject to debt, an assumption of the debt by the contract counterparty would be treated as money received by the taxpayer. *See* § 1031(d) (last sentence).

Example 6

Yuri purchased Yellowacre for $500,000 and holds it as an investment; the property is encumbered by a mortgage of $150,000 and has a fair market value of $800,000. Garth owns Greenacre, which currently has a fair market value of $650,000. Assume that Yuri exchanges Yellowacre for (i) Greenacre and (ii) Garth's assumption of the $150,000 mortgage. If Yuri proceeds to hold Greenacre either as an investment or for productive use in his trade or business, he will recognize $150,000 of gain on the exchange. *See* § 1031(b). His basis in Greenacre will be $500,000 (i.e., his basis in Yellowacre ($500,000) reduced by the amount of money received ($150,000) and increased in the amount of gain recognized ($150,000) on the exchange). *See* § 1031(d). Mathematically, this basis makes sense. Prior to the transaction, Yuri held Yellowacre with built-in gain of $300,000, and he recognized $150,000 of it in connection with the exchange; $150,000 of gain was deferred. If Yuri sells Greenacre for its fair market value (i.e., $650,000), his gain recognized will be $150,000.

> **Note**
> ....
> Although the receipt of boot may trigger the recognition of built-in gain, the receipt of boot will *not* trigger the recognition of any built-in loss. *See* § 1031(c).

3. Transactions Involving Taxpayer Receipt of Like-Kind Real Property and Non-Cash Boot

Taxpayers participating in like-kind exchanges may receive boot in the form of cash or, perhaps, by having a contract counterparty assume a liability. Rather than tendering forth cash or assuming a liability, however, the contract counterparty may simply offer up boot in the form of personal property. Thus, the contract counterparty might tender, as consideration, both land and a Gutenberg Bible. The fact that the bible is not cash will not halt the recognition of the appropriate amount of built-in gain, if any. The boot will not be cash, but for gain recognition purposes, it must be treated like the non-like-kind property that it is. Consider the following example:

Example 7

Mira purchased Redacre for $2,000,000, and she holds it as an investment. The property currently has a fair market value of $7,000,000. Claude owns Blueacre (which currently has a fair market value of $5,500,000) and a Gutenberg Bible (which currently has a fair market value of $1,500,000). Assume that Mira exchanges Redacre for Blueacre and the Gutenberg Bible. If she proceeds to hold Blueacre as an investment or for productive use in her trade or business, she will recognize $1,500,000 of gain on the exchange. *See* § 1031(b).

The introduction of non-cash boot complicates basis calculations but only modestly. We will have to allocate the total basis for all replacement property to both the like-kind property and the non-like-kind property. Let's consider more of the basis calculation rule in § 1031(d).

> If property was acquired on an exchange described in [§ 1031], . . . then the basis shall be the same as that of the property exchanged, decreased in the amount of any money received by the taxpayer and increased in the amount of gain . . . to the taxpayer that was recognized on such exchange. If the property so acquired consisted in part of the type of property permitted by [§ 1031] to be received without the recognition of gain or loss, and in part of other property, the basis provided in this subsection shall be allocated between the properties (other than money) received, and for the purpose of the allocation there shall be assigned to such other property an amount equivalent to its fair market value at the date of the exchange.

Exhibit 16.2 depicts the operation of this rule as applied to *Example 7*.

Note two things. First, in compliance with the statute, we reduced the basis of Redacre by the amount of MONEY received. Although Example 7 involved the receipt of boot, it did not involve the receipt of money. Accordingly, we did not reduce the basis of Redacre to arrive at our interim calculation, but we did

EXHIBIT 16.2 **Visual Depiction of Basis Calculations for Example 7**

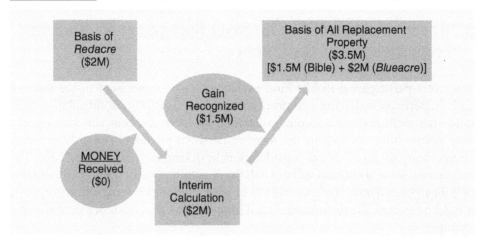

recognize gain. Second, a final basis of $2 million for Blueacre makes mathematical sense. Before the deal, Mira had a $5,000,000 built-in gain with respect to Redacre. She recognized $1,500,000 of gain in connection with the transaction; $3,500,000 was deferred. If Mira sells Blueacre (with a basis of $2,000,000) for its fair market value ($5,500,000), she will have gain recognized of $3,500,000.

4. Transactions Involving Taxpayer Transfer of Like-Kind Real Property and Non-Like-Kind Real or Personal Property

Up to this point, we have discussed like-kind exchanges that, at their most complex, involved the taxpayer receiving boot in the form of non-like-kind property. In fact, the taxpayer has always handed over solely like-kind property and has always received varying forms of property. Life does not always follow such a predictable pattern. Taxpayers participating in like-kind exchanges are just as likely to be handing over non-like-kind property as receiving it. If the non-like-kind property happens to be cash or property without built-in gain or loss, then no gain or loss will follow from handing that property over. It is key to remember to include the basis of *all* relinquished property as one starts the process of ascertaining the basis of the replacement property.

Example 8

Giovanni purchased Brownacre for $400,000, and he currently holds it as an investment. The property has a fair market value of $750,000. Tiara owns Whiteacre, which has a fair market value of $800,000. Assume that Giovanni exchanges $50,000 and Brownacre for Whiteacre and proceeds to hold Whiteacre as an investment. Giovanni will recognize no gain or loss on the transaction. His basis in Whiteacre will be his basis in the property exchanged ($400,000 + $50,000 = $450,000), decreased by the amount of money received ($0), and increased by the amount of gain recognized ($0). Thus, his basis in Whiteacre will be $450,000. Prior to the deal, Giovanni held Brownacre with a built-in gain of $350,000. He has recognized none of that gain. If he sells Whiteacre for $800,000, he will have gain recognized of $350,000.

With that general approach under your belt, consider the possibility that in addition to handing over *like-kind* real property with built-in gain or built-in loss, the taxpayer hands over *non-like-kind* real or personal property with built-in gain or built-in loss. If that happens, then the taxpayer *must* recognize the gain or loss *with respect to the real or personal property that is not like kind*. Section 1031 *only* applies to the exchange of the *like-kind* real property. The following example demonstrates application of the rules when the non-like-kind personal property has built-in gain.

Example 9

Giovanni purchased Brownacre for $400,000. He currently holds it as an investment, and its fair market value is $650,000. He also purchased a Greek vase for $100,000, and it now has a fair market value of $150,000. Tiara owns White-acre, which has a fair market value of $800,000. Assume that Giovanni exchanges both the Greek vase and Brownacre for Whiteacre and proceeds to hold Whiteacre as an investment. He will have gain recognized of $50,000 because of his dispo-sition of the Greek vase, but he will recognize none of the $250,000 gain realized with respect to the disposition of Brownacre. *See* § 1031(a). His basis in White-acre will be his basis in the property exchanged ($400,000 + $100,000 = $500,000), decreased by the amount of money received ($0), and increased by the amount of gain recognized ($50,000). Thus, his basis in Whiteacre will be $550,000. Prior to the deal, he held Brownacre with a built-in gain of $250,000. He has recognized none of *that* gain. If he sells Whiteacre for $800,000, he will have gain recognized of $250,000 (i.e., $800,000 – $550,000).

In *Example 9*, we saw that the $50,000 gain recognized factored into the basis calculations even though that gain arose from the disposition of non-like-kind property. That approach is entirely appropriate. We would also factor in the impact of loss recognition with respect to non-like-kind property. In pertinent part, sec-tion 1031(d) provides as follows:

> If property was acquired on an exchange described in [§ 1031], . . . then the basis shall be the same as that of the property exchanged, decreased in the amount of any money received by the taxpayer and increased in the amount of gain *or decreased in the amount of loss* to the taxpayer that was recognized on such exchange.

Section 1031(d) (emphasis added).

To see the impact of loss recognition from the disposition of non-like-kind property in connection with a like-kind exchange, consider the following example.

Example 10

Giovanni purchased Brownacre for $400,000. He currently holds it as an investment, and its fair market value is $650,000. He also purchased a Greek vase for $80,000, and it now has a fair market value of $50,000. Tiara owns White-acre, which has a fair market value of $700,000. Assume that Giovanni exchanges both the Greek vase and Brownacre for Whiteacre and proceeds to hold White-acre as an investment. He will have loss recognized of $30,000 because of his disposition of the Greek vase, but he will recognize none of the $250,000 gain realized with respect to the disposition of Brownacre. *See* § 1031(a). His basis in Whiteacre will be his basis in the property exchanged ($400,000 + $80,000 = $480,000), decreased by the amount of money received ($0), increased by the amount of gain recognized ($0), and decreased by the amount of loss recog-nized ($30,000) on the exchange. Thus, his basis in Whiteacre will be $450,000 (i.e., $480,000 – $0 + $0 – $30,000). Prior to the deal, he held Brownacre with a built-in gain of $250,000. He has recognized none of that gain. If he sells White-acre for its fair market value of $700,000, he will have gain recognized of $250,000 (i.e., $700,000 – $450,000).

5. Deferred Like-Kind Exchanges of Real Property

In the preceding sections of this chapter, we have discussed various like-kind exchange scenarios, and in each instance, the taxpayer under focus exchanged real property with a known and available counterparty. Often, however, the taxpayer has real property that would qualify for nonrecognition in a like-kind exchange and would like to participate in one, but no counterparty is at hand. The taxpayer has the option of pursuing a deferred like-kind exchange with the assistance of a qualified intermediary (whose job is to facilitate the transaction); for this purpose, the qualified intermediary is deemed not to be the taxpayer's agent. *See* Treas. Reg. § 1.1031(k)-1(g)(4)(i) and (ii). In general, the following steps occur in such a transaction:

1. The taxpayer transfers the relinquished real property to the qualified intermediary;
2. The taxpayer identifies replacement real property;
3. The qualified intermediary acquires the replacement real property; and
4. The qualified intermediary transfers the replacement real property to the taxpayer.

See generally § 1031(a)(3).

The deferred like-kind exchange avenue substantially broadens the opportunity to effect a like-kind exchange, but the taxpayer must act with dispatch and in full accord with the governing statutes and Treasury Regulations. In general, the taxpayer must identify the replacement property within 45 days of transferring the relinquished property to the qualified intermediary and must receive the replacement property within 180 days of such transfer. The receipt deadline will be earlier if the taxpayer's return for the year of the relinquishment is due in less than 180 days, but the return due date factors in extensions.

Sorting out the various tax ramifications associated with like-kind exchanges can appear daunting at first, but with focused study and practice, you will get the hang of it. Up to this point, we have intentionally focused on the mechanical operation of the rules. We now turn to substantive matters of significance and potential conflict in this context, including the meaning of "like kind."

B. THE "LIKE KIND" REQUIREMENT

Under prior law, taxpayers could defer taxation by participating in like-kind exchanges involving personal property as well as those involving real property, and it should come as no surprise that taxpayers often found themselves at odds with the IRS regarding whether specific items of property were like kind within the meaning of § 1031. Current law restricts application of § 1031's general rule to real property held for productive use in a trade or business or for investment. That change simplifies life to a considerable extent, but the like-kind requirement remains intact. Section 1031(h) makes it abundantly clear that real property located in the United States and real property located outside the United States are not property of like kind. What about domestic realty? The Treasury Regulations in this area reflect a healthy degree of accommodation. Treasury Regulations indicate that real property may be like kind regardless of whether the property is improved or unimproved because the absence or presence of improvements on the realty relates to its grade or quality but not its kind or class. *See* Treas. Reg. § 1.1031(a)-1(b); *see also* Treas. Reg. § 1.1031(a)-1(c) (indicating that a non-dealer can exchange city real estate for a farm or ranch). Notwithstanding the apparent flexibility taken with respect to classification of real property as like kind, thorny issues do arise from time to time.

Ruling Preview

Private Letter Ruling 9601046

The Treasury Regulations promulgated under § 1031 speak in fairly general terms when discussing real property. One gets the sense that exchanges of interests in real property (with or without improvements) readily qualify as like-kind exchanges. Even city land for farm land will do the trick. And yet, the universe of real property interests is quite diverse. Alongside fee simple absolute interests, we have leasehold interests, life estates, remainders, and easements. Do all such interests fall comfortably within the Internal Revenue Code's conception of "real property"? Add to that question the issue whether any given interest in real property can be used in effecting a deferred like-kind exchange. The Service provided a degree of guidance on these matters to a specific taxpayer in the following private letter ruling. Consider the following questions as you read the pronouncement.

Conservation Easements

Perpetual conservation easements help to preserve land in its natural, pristine state. Maintenance of the natural habitat benefits indigenous animal populations and, more generally, serves to protect ecological balance.

Credit: Randy Andy/Shutterstock.com.

1. What types of real property interests qualify as real property for like-kind exchange purposes?
2. What is a perpetual conservation easement?
3. Does a deferred like-kind exchange require that the parties exchange fee simple absolute interests?

Private Letter Ruling 9601046
1996 WL 4649

This letter is in response to your request for a private letter ruling dated September 5, 1995, submitted on behalf of the above referenced taxpayer. Specifically, you requested a ruling that the proposed perpetual conservation easement and a fee simple interest in the proposed replacement real property qualify as like-kind property under section 1031 of the Internal Revenue Code.

The taxpayer (and its predecessor) has owned, operated and leased real property in State Z (the "Property") for more than 10 years for productive use in the trade or business of cattle grazing and duck hunting. The United States of America, acting through the Department of Interior, Fish and Wildlife Service, wishes to acquire a perpetual conservation easement over the Property. The purpose of the proposed transfer will be to permit the Fish and Wildlife Service to maintain and use the lands and waters thereon for a seasonal habitat of migratory waterfowl, as authorized and set forth in the Migratory Bird Conservation Act of 1929 (16 U.S.C. § 17 et seq.), as amended.

The taxpayer has entered into an Option Agreement with the United States Department of Interior, Fish and Wildlife Service, for the acquisition by the United States of a perpetual conservation easement over the Property. Under the proposed conservation easement, the taxpayer will not be able to develop or alter the present character of the Property or interfere with its use as a waterfowl habitat without the express written approval of the Fish and Wildlife Service. Also, the Fish and Wildlife Service will be given certain water rights, including the right to use water from the taxpayer's wells and any other water rights appurtenant to the Property to the extent reasonably required to maintain a seasonal habitat for migrating waterfowl during a specified period of each year. The taxpayer will retain the right to all minerals underlying the Property and the right to hunt and operate a hunting club on the Property.

The transfer of the conservation easement is conditioned on the taxpayer acquiring in a multi-party exchange transaction, in accordance with section 1.1031(k)-1(g)(4)(i)-(iii) of the Income Tax Regulations, property of like kind which will qualify for nonrecognition of gain under section 1031 of the Code. The taxpayer desires to acquire either farm land, ranch land, or commercial real property as the replacement property. The taxpayer represents that it will hold the replacement real property for productive use in a trade or business or for investment.

Section A of the State Z Civil Code provides, in part, that a conservation easement is an interest in real property voluntarily created and freely transferable in whole or in part for the purposes stated in Section B of the State Z Civil Code. Section B of the State Z Civil Code provides, in part, that a conservation easement means any limitation in a deed in the form of an easement, restriction, covenant, or condition, the purpose of which is to retain land predominantly in its natural, scenic, historical, agricultural, forested, or open-space condition. Section C of the State Z Civil Code provides that a conservation easement shall be perpetual in duration.

Section 1031(a)(1) of the Code provides that no gain or loss shall be recognized on the exchange of property held for productive use in a trade or business or for investment if such property is exchanged solely for property of like kind which is to be held either for productive use in a trade or business or for investment.

Section 1.1031(a)-1(b) of the regulations provides, in part, that, as used in section 1031(a) of the Code, the words "like kind" have reference to the nature or character of the property and not to its grade or quality. One kind or class of property may not be exchanged for property of a different kind or class. The fact that any real estate involved is improved is not material, for that fact relates only to the grade or quality of the property and not to its kind or class. Unproductive real estate held by one other than a dealer for future use or future realization of the increment in value is held for investment and not primarily for sale. Section 1.1031(a)-1(c) provides, as an example, that no gain or loss is recognized if a taxpayer who is not a dealer in real estate exchanges city real estate for a ranch or farm, or exchanges a leasehold of a fee with 30 years or more to run for real estate, or exchanges improved real estate for unimproved real estate.

Rev. Rul. 55-749, 1955-2 C.B. 295, holds that where, under applicable state law, water rights are considered real property rights, the exchange of perpetual water rights for a fee interest in land constitutes a nontaxable exchange of property of like kind within the meaning of section 1031(a) of the Code.

Rev. Rul. 72–549, 1972–2 C.B. 472, holds that an easement and right-of-way that the taxpayer granted to an electric power company and the improved real properties acquired by the taxpayer are both continuing interests in real property and of the same nature and character, and as such qualify as like-kind property under section 1031 of the Code.

In the instant case, the proposed grant of a conservation easement in perpetuity, by virtue of state law, is an interest in real property. Based upon the above authorities and facts and representations that were submitted, the proposed conservation easement and the proposed replacement real property will qualify as like-kind property under section 1031 of the Code.

No opinion is expressed as to the tax treatment of these items (or transactions) under the provisions of any other section of the Code or regulations which may be applicable thereto, or the tax treatment of any conditions existing at the time of, or effects resulting from, the items (or transactions) described which are not specifically covered in the above ruling. Specifically, no opinion is expressed with respect to whether the proposed transaction meets the deferred like-kind exchange requirements of section 1.1031(k)-1 of the regulations.

A copy of this letter should be attached to the federal return for the year in which the transactions in question occurs.

This ruling is directed only to the taxpayer who requested it. Section 6110(j)(3) of the Code provides that it may not be used or cited as precedent.

Post-Ruling Follow-Up

The IRS concluded that the proposed conservation easement and the proposed replacement property were like kind within the meaning of § 1031. The Service refused to opine, however, on whether the proposed transaction would meet the requirements associated with a deferred like-kind exchange. Overall, the ruling confirms the general notion that "real property" in the like kind exchange context enjoys a broad interpretation and is clearly not confined to fee simple absolute interests.

Private Letter Ruling 9601046: Real Life Applications

1. Edward has held Blueacre as an investment for several years. The land is unimproved. Edward has been approached by Bouchet who has expressed interest in exchanging real estate he owns in fee simple absolute, Greenacre, for Edward's grant of a perpetual conservation easement with respect to Blueacre. If Edward grants a perpetual conservation easement with respect to Blueacre in exchange for Greenacre, will the exchange qualify for nonrecognition under § 1031, assuming Edward proceeds to hold Greenacre as an investment?

2. *Same facts as Question 1*, except that Greenacre is improved with a building.

Ruling Preview

Private Letter Ruling 201706009

The Treasury Regulations promulgated under § 1031 speak in fairly general terms when discussing real property. One gets the sense that exchanges of interests in real property (with or without improvements) readily qualify as like-kind exchanges. Even city land for farm land will do the trick. And yet, the universe of real property improvements is quite diverse. Indeed, it is diverse enough to give even taxpayers with sophisticated tax counsel reason to pause when contemplating the tax impact of a transaction with factual peculiarities well beyond the mere exchange of Blackacre solely for Blueacre. In PLR 201706009, the taxpayer felt compelled to seek the comfort and assurance of a private ruling from the IRS. As you read this pronouncement, see if you can answer the following questions:

1. Will state law classification of an interest as an interest in real property automatically result in the treatment of that interest as like kind to another real property interest in that state for purposes of § 1031?
2. May other taxpayers rely on this Private Letter Ruling ("PLR") as precedent?

Private Letter Ruling 201706009
2017 WL 537752

   This is in response to Taxpayer's request for a private letter ruling dated May 20, 2016, under § 1031 of the Internal Revenue Code. Specifically, the request concerns whether cellular towers that Taxpayer uses in its business and will relinquish are of like-kind under § 1031 to cable telecommunication signal distribution property Taxpayer intends to receive in exchange for the cellular towers.

FACTS

   Taxpayer is a communications services provider that offers communications infrastructure to its customers. Taxpayer currently owns fee simple or long-term leasehold interests in multiple wireless communication tower sites across the nation. Each tower site consists of fencing around the tower site, an antenna support structure for mounting antennas that are affixed to the land by a concrete foundation and attachment hardware (such as bolts and lashings), a nearby equipment hut with HVAC systems installed in the hut, and the land underlying the site itself ("Towers"). All of Taxpayer's Towers are permanently affixed to the land or would be extensively damaged if removed.

   Taxpayer is contemplating exchanging its Towers for fiber-optic and copper cables installed either above or below ground and various other associated properties, including telephone poles for carrying the cables, underground conduits, concrete pads, attachment hardware, pedestals, guy wires, and anchors ("Cable

Distribution Systems"). The Cable Distribution Systems are permanently affixed to the land or are intended never to be removed until the end of their respective useful lives.

LAW AND ANALYSIS

Section 1031 requires nonrecognition of gain or loss in an exchange of properties held for productive use in a trade or business or for investment if such properties are exchanged solely for like-kind properties held for productive use in a trade or business or for investment.

Section 1.1031(a)-1(b) of the Income Tax Regulations provides that the words "like kind" have reference to the nature or character of the property and not to its grade or quality. Under § 1031, one kind or class of property may not be exchanged for property of a different kind or class.

Several cases indicate that state law classifications of property are not the sole determiner of whether two sets of property are of like kind for § 1031 purposes. In *Fleming v. Commissioner*, 24 T.C. 818, 823-24 (1955), *aff'd sub nom. Commissioner v. P.G. Lake, Inc.*, 356 U.S. 260 (1958), *rev'g* 241 F.2d 78 (5th Cir. 1957), the court found that carved-out oil payments and a fee interest in real estate were not like-kind properties although the oil payment rights were an interest in real estate under applicable state law. In *Clemente Inc. v. Commissioner*, T.C. Memo. 1985-367, and *Oregon Lumber Co. v. Commissioner*, 20 T.C. 192 (1953), *acq.* 1953-2 C.B. 5, the courts considered more than state law classifications of property when determining whether properties were of like kind.

In addition, in *Morgan v. Commissioner*, 309 U.S. 78, 80-81 (1940), which concerned whether a state law classification of a power of appointment determined its character for federal tax purposes, the Supreme Court stated,

> State law creates legal interests and rights. The federal revenue acts designate what interests or rights, so created, shall be taxed . . . If it is found in a given case that an interest or right created by local law was the object to be taxed, the federal law must prevail no matter what name is given the interest or right by state law.

Therefore, consistent with *Fleming, Clemente, Inc., Oregon Lumber*, and *Morgan*, state law property classifications are not the sole basis for determining whether the Towers and the Cable Distribution Systems are like kind property for § 1031 purposes.

In this case, the Towers and the Cable Distribution Systems transmit or support the transmission of telecommunication signals across distances. Neither the Towers nor the Cable Distribution Systems are used for other activities. In addition, the Towers and the Cable Distribution Systems are, or are intended to be, permanently affixed to land. Under these facts, Taxpayer's Towers and the Cable Distribution Systems are like kind property for purposes of § 1031.

Taxpayer's real property improved with Towers *** is of like kind within the meaning of § 1031(a)(1) and § 1.1031(a)-1(b) to the real property improved with Cable Distribution Systems . . . . This ruling applies only to Towers and the Cable Distribution Systems being transferred and received by Taxpayer as relinquished or replacement property, respectively, in the exchange that are affixed or embedded in real property held in fee simple or similar interest or under a long-term lease, easement, right of way or similar long-term right of use arrangement, in each case having a duration of thirty years or more including optional renewal periods exercisable by the tenant or right of use holder.

Except as provided in the preceding paragraph, no opinion is expressed or implied concerning the tax consequences of any aspect of any transaction or item discussed or referenced in this letter under any provision of the Internal Revenue Code including § 1031. For example, this ruling pertains only to the Towers and the Cable Distribution Systems and does not pertain to any other properties exchanged by Taxpayer.

This ruling is directed only to Taxpayer. Section 6110(k)(3) of the Code provides that it may not be used or cited as precedent. Taxpayer must attach to any income tax return to which it is relevant a copy of this letter or, if it files its returns electronically, must include a statement providing the date and control number of this letter ruling. ***

Post-Ruling Follow-Up

In this ruling, the IRS concluded that the taxpayer's exchange of the Towers for the Cable Distribution Systems constituted a like-kind exchange. Each cluster of assets was affixed to land and performed the function of transmitting (or facilitating transmission of) signals over distances. The ruling nicely demonstrates how long-established statutory rules and regulations fit comfortably on assets not in existence or even contemplated at the time such rules or regulations were first drafted. The ruling also clarifies that state law determinations with respect to whether a given interest constitutes an interest in real property is but one factor in the federal-level determination of whether individual real property interests are like kind for § 1031 purposes. Unfortunately, the ruling says nothing (in generally applicable terms) with respect to additional factors a decision maker or advisor is to take into consideration beyond state-level determinations. We can only forge ahead knowing that the state-level determination will not, of necessity, carry the day.

Private Letter Ruling 201706009: Real Life Applications

1. Chelsea owns Greenacre in fee simple absolute as an investment. Kyle owns Blueacre in fee simple absolute. If Chelsea exchanges Greenacre solely for Blueacre and proceeds to hold Blueacre as an investment, will the exchange qualify for nonrecognition under § 1031?

2. Tien owns Greenacre in fee simple absolute as an investment. Madiha owns Redacre in fee simple absolute; Redacre is improved with a building. If Tien exchanges Greenacre solely for Redacre and its improvements (and proceeds to hold both as an investment), will the exchange qualify for nonrecognition under § 1031?

3. Mo has a fifty-year lease with respect to Blackacre and its improvement (a building) and holds both for productive use in his business. Ali owns Greenacre in fee simple absolute. Under state law, a lease with 30 or more years to run is the equivalent of a fee simple absolute interest; there are no federal statutes, regulations, cases, or IRS pronouncements contrary to this notion. If Mo exchanges his leasehold interest in Blackacre and its improvement for Greenacre and proceeds to hold Greenacre as an investment, will the exchange qualify for nonrecognition under § 1031?

C. INVOLUNTARY CONVERSIONS

Taxpayers participating in like-kind exchanges typically do so of their own volition and with full appreciation of the tax consequences that will result. Those seeking to avoid the recognition of gain can usually do so by ensuring that they receive solely property of like kind in exchange for the property they relinquish, thereby avoiding the receipt of cash or other nonqualifying consideration. But what if a taxpayer's property (regardless of its status as a business, investment, or personal-use asset) is lost in a fire or storm and results in the payment of a given dollar amount by an insurance company? Rather than having the ability to transfer qualifying property as part of a like-kind exchange, the taxpayer suffers the involuntary conversion of that property to cash and faces the specter of immediate taxation with respect to any built-in gain. Section 1033 makes several alternative outcomes possible.

In much the same way that like-kind exchanges vary, so do involuntary conversions. A taxpayer might lose property by fire or storm, but she might also suffer the loss of property as a result of condemnation, theft, seizure, or taking by eminent domain. Thereafter, the taxpayer may receive property, money, or some combination of property and money. And even if the taxpayer finds herself in receipt of money, she may pocket it or use some or all of it to replace the involuntarily converted property. The tax ramifications naturally depend on the facts of the transaction. As an initial matter, section 1033 generally contemplates two basic conversion scenarios. Property, "as a result of its destruction in whole or in part, theft, seizure, or requisition or condemnation or threat or imminence thereof," is compulsorily or involuntarily converted either (i) into property that is similar or related in service or use to the converted property or (ii) into money or into property that is not similar or related in service or use to the converted property. *See* § 1033(a).

1. Involuntary Conversion of Property Solely into Similar Property

Per the requirements of § 1033(a)(1), if property is involuntarily converted solely into property that is similar or related in service or use to the converted property, no

Hurricanes

Taxpayers suffering involuntary conversions as a result of storms often have hurricane-force winds and the associated storm surge to blame. These monstrous storms form near the equator over warm waters and can reach hundreds of miles in diameter. "They are called hurricanes in the Atlantic, Caribbean, and Eastern Pacific, apparently in reference to a god of the indigenous Caribbeans named 'Huracan.' In the Western Pacific, they are called typhoons, from the Cantonese word *tai fung*, meaning 'big wind.'" Juliane L. Fry et al., The Encyclopedia of Weather and Climate Change 166 (Univ. of California Press 2010).

Credit: Lavizzara / Shutterstock.com.

gain is recognized. Further, the taxpayer's basis in the new property will be the same as that of the converted property. *See* § 1033(b)(1). Consider the following example.

Example 11

Marley owns Brownacre, which he purchased for $500,000. The property now has a fair market value of $750,000. Assume that his local county takes the land by eminent domain for the construction of a bridge and conveys to him, at his request, Greenacre, which has a fair market value of $750,000. Per § 1033(a)(1), Marley will recognize no gain as a result of the conversion. His basis in Greenacre will be $500,000, the same as his basis in Brownacre. Recognition with respect to the original built-in gain of $250,000 is deferred.

2. Involuntary Conversion of Property into Similar Property and Cash

If a taxpayer holding property with built-in gain suffers the involuntary conversion of that property into similar property and cash, partial or full recognition of the gain will result, depending on the amount of built-in gain and the amount of cash received. The basis calculation rules are similar to those we saw when covering § 1031. We calculate the basis of the replacement property by starting with the basis of the converted property, decreasing that number by the amount of money received (and not used to purchase similar property), and increasing that number by the amount of gain (or decreasing that number by the amount of loss) recognized on the conversion. The following example demonstrates the operation of the relevant rules in this context.

Example 12

Marley owns Brownacre, which he purchased for $500,000. The property now has a fair market value of $750,000. Assume that his local county takes the land by eminent domain for the construction of a bridge and conveys to him, at his request, Greenacre (which has a fair market value of $700,000) and $50,000. Marley will recognize $50,000 of gain as a result of the conversion. His basis in Greenacre will be $500,000, that is, the same as his basis in Brownacre ($500,000), reduced by the amount of money received ($50,000), and increased by the amount of gain recognized ($50,000). Of the $250,000 gain realized, Marley recognized $50,000, and $200,000 was deferred. The remainder of the built-in gain is preserved by Marley taking a $500,000 basis in Greenacre.

3. Involuntary Conversion of Property into Money (With and Without Reinvestment)

If a taxpayer's property is involuntarily converted to money, he may choose to reinvest the proceeds (in whole or in part) in property that is similar or related in service or use to the converted property. Alternatively, he might simply choose to keep the money. In the latter context, he will realize and recognize all gain or loss realized on the conversion. In the former context, the treatment of the taxpayer will ultimately depend on the extent to which he reinvests the proceeds in property (within timing deadlines) that is similar or related in service or use to the converted property. Section 1033(a)(2)(A) provides, in pertinent part, as follows:

> If the taxpayer [within the established time limit], for the purpose of replacing the property so converted, purchases other property similar or related in service or use to the property so converted, or purchases stock in the acquisition of control of a corporation owning such other property, at the election of the taxpayer the gain shall be recognized only to the extent that the amount realized upon such conversion . . . exceeds the cost of such other property or such stock.

Assuming a taxpayer opts to purchase appropriate replacement property and manages to defer the recognition of gain (in whole or in part), his basis in the replacement property will be its cost, reduced by the amount of gain deferred. *See* § 1033(b)(2). The following example demonstrates the operation of the relevant rules in this context.

Example 13

Marley owns Brownacre, which he purchased for $500,000. The property now has a fair market value of $750,000. Assume that his local county takes the land by eminent domain for the construction of a bridge and provides just compensation in the amount of $750,000. If Marley uses most of the proceeds to purchase appropriate replacement property (Greenacre), which cost $700,000, he will recognize $50,000 of gain as a result of the conversion. His final basis in Greenacre will be $500,000. We arrive at that figure by starting with the cost of Greenacre ($700,000) and reducing that number by the amount of gain deferred ($200,000).

D. CERTAIN CORPORATE TRANSACTIONS

Students pursuing advanced study in the tax arena will likely take a full course in corporate taxation. We pause here for a remarkably brief glimpse into that arena to see nonrecognition at work in another context. Those of you who have taken Business Associations will likely recall that a sole proprietorship has one owner who has taken no steps to create an entity (e.g., a corporation, limited liability company, etc.) through which to operate the business. A major downside of being a sole proprietor, however, is the specter of personal liability. Taxpayers seeking to limit their personal liability often choose to form a corporation and then to transfer business assets to that corporation in exchange for shares of stock of the corporation. But there would appear to be a potential problem lurking on the horizon, at least in some circumstances. A taxpayer's business assets often have built-in gain (e.g., the assets have managed to maintain healthy fair market value, notwithstanding the fact that their bases have been adjusted downward). A transfer of those assets to a corporation (which is, after all, a wholly separate and distinct legal entity) in exchange for its stock *is* a realization event. Without some statutory intervention, recognition would follow as generally required by § 1001(c). Section 351 comes to the rescue and makes it possible, under the appropriate transactional circumstances, to incorporate without triggering built-in gains.

Section 351(a) provides that "[n]o gain or loss shall be recognized if property is transferred to a corporation by one or more persons solely in exchange for stock in such corporation and immediately after the exchange such person or persons are in control . . . of the corporation." In the case of a sole proprietor transferring property to a corporation in exchange for 100 percent of its stock, the sole proprietor will have the necessary control, and any built-in gain in the assets will not be recognized immediately. As it does in other contexts, Congress uses basis rules to

FYI

The fact that a sole proprietor takes steps to organize a corporation or, perhaps, a single-member limited liability company does not automatically result in the sole proprietor's business property becoming property of the new entity. After making the necessary filing to create the new entity, the former sole proprietor must transfer business assets to the new entity in order for it to become the legal owner of the assets.

Credit: Macrovector/Shutterstock.com.

preserve built-in gains and losses. Accordingly, the sole proprietor will take a basis in the stock received equal to the aggregate bases of the assets transferred. The following example demonstrates the operation of the relevant rules in this context.

Example 14

Earl has owned and operated the Burger Bench for several years as a sole proprietor. Although his basis in the business assets is $80,000, they have a fair market value of $300,000. Earl completes and files the appropriate documents and thereby organizes The Burger Bench, Inc. He transfers all of the business assets of his sole proprietorship to The Burger Bench, Inc. in exchange for 100 percent of its common stock. Although Earl's gain realized on the transaction is $220,000, his gain recognized is $0. *See* § 351(a). His basis in the stock received will be $80,000, his basis in the property transferred to the corporation. *See* § 358(a)(1).

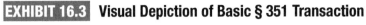

EXHIBIT 16.3 **Visual Depiction of Basic § 351 Transaction**

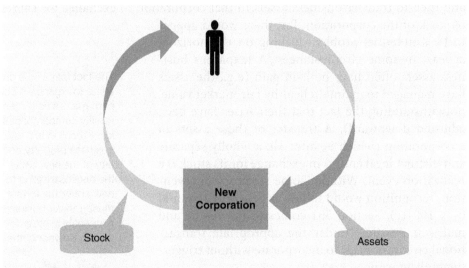

From a tax perspective, incorporation transactions can be fairly straightforward, but there are complicated variants. Your capable corporate tax professor will introduce you to them.

Chapter Summary

- Nonrecognition provisions merely defer the recognition of gain or loss. Basis rules operate to preserve deferred gains and losses.

- Like-kind exchanges of real property generally qualify for nonrecognition so long as the taxpayer relinquishes property held for productive use in a trade or business or for investment and holds the replacement property in either capacity. "Like kind" refers to the nature or character of property, not to its grade or quality. Note that domestic real property and foreign real property are not of a like kind.

- The receipt of boot in a like-kind exchange will trigger the recognition of gain, if any. The amount of gain recognized is limited to the lower of (i) the gain realized or (ii) the fair market value of the boot received. The receipt of boot will not trigger the recognition of any loss realized.

- The basis of replacement property is generally the same as the basis of the relinquished property reduced in the amount of money received and increased in the amount of any gain recognized on the exchange. Loss recognized on the transfer of non-like-kind property (whether real or personal) will impact basis calculations. The receipt of non-cash boot will require the allocation of aggregate replacement property basis.

- Section 1031 only applies to exchanges of like-kind real property, excluding real property that is held primarily for sale. If a taxpayer *transfers* non-like-kind real or personal property with built-in gain or built-in loss in connection with a like-kind exchange, such gain or loss will be recognized. The gain or loss recognized will factor into basis calculations with respect to property received on the exchange.

- Taxpayers may effect deferred like-kind exchanges by use of a qualified intermediary. For this purpose, the qualified intermediary is deemed not to be the taxpayer's agent.

- If a taxpayer's property is involuntarily converted into property that is similar or related in service or use, the taxpayer recognizes no gain as a result of the conversion. The taxpayer's basis in the new property will generally be the same as his basis in the converted property, decreased by the amount of money received (not expended on qualifying replacement property), and increased by the amount of gain recognized in connection with the conversion. The amount of any loss recognized will decrease basis in the replacement property.

- If a taxpayer's property is involuntarily converted to cash, gain (if any) will generally be recognized to the extent the taxpayer does not invest the conversion proceeds in property that is similar or related in service or use to the converted property. A taxpayer may also avoid some or all gain recognition by purchasing a control block of stock in a corporation owning the qualifying property. The taxpayer must purchase the replacement property or, as appropriate, the control block of stock within established time limits.

- A taxpayer will recognize no gain or loss on the transfer of property to a corporation solely in exchange for a control block of the corporation's stock. The taxpayer's basis in the stock will generally be the same as his basis in the property transferred.

Applying the Rules

1. Shane purchased Brownacre for $300,000, and he currently holds it as an investment. The property's fair market value is $900,000. Michael owns Redacre, which currently has a fair market value of $700,000. Assume that Shane exchanges Brownacre for Redacre and $200,000. Assume further that Shane proceeds to hold Redacre as an investment. What amount of gain, if any, will Share recognize on the exchange? What will be Shane's basis in Redacre?

2. *Same facts as Question #1*, except that Shane exchanges Brownacre for Redacre, $100,000 cash, and a car worth $100,000. What amount of gain, if any, will Shane recognize on the exchange? What will be Shane's basis in Redacre? What will be Shane's basis in the car?

3. Hannah purchased Blueacre for $500,000, and she currently holds it as an investment. The property's fair market value is $600,000. Hannah also purchased a gold-embellished African mask for $75,000, and its current fair market value is $100,000. Tess owns Greenacre, which has a fair market value of $700,000. If Hannah exchanges Blueacre and the African mask for Greenacre and proceeds to hold Greenacre as an investment, what amount of gain, if any, will Hannah recognize in connection with the transaction? What will be her basis in Greenacre?

4. Megan owns Whiteacre, which she purchased for $400,000. The property now has a fair market value of $900,000. Assume that her local county takes the land by eminent domain for the construction of a bridge and provides just compensation in the amount of $900,000. If Megan uses most of the proceeds to purchase appropriate replacement property that costs $825,000, how much gain, if any, will she recognize in connection with the conversion? What will be her basis in her replacement property?

5. Annie and Pearl decided to go into business together and to operate in the corporate form. Pearl plans to contribute $700,000 cash, and Annie plans to contribute a hair salon that she purchased for $450,000 but that now has a fair market value of $700,000. If Annie and Pearl contribute their respective properties to the newly organized corporation, La Coiffure Magnifique, Inc., in exchange for 50 percent of its stock (each), how much gain, if any, must Annie recognize in connection with this exchange? What will be Annie's basis in the stock she receives?

Federal Income Taxation in Practice

1. You are a junior associate in a large law firm. One of the firm's major clients is a TV broadcasting company. According to the assigning partner, the client is facing the loss of its right to operate in a specific bandwidth because the Federal Communications Commission seeks to take over that bandwidth and make it available for mobile device operations. The partner would like to know whether a sale of bandwidth rights under such duress (with application of the proceeds to other TV broadcasting operations) would be something covered by § 1033. See what you can find and follow up with the partner by memo.

2. A senior associate with whom you work recently had to hand off an assignment to you due to a family emergency. He claims that the question is simple, but he cannot focus on it at the moment. One of the firm's individual clients recently incorporated his sole proprietorship by transferring property (with built-in gain) to the corporation solely in exchange for stock. The client accepts the fact that his basis in his shares is equal to his basis in the transferred assets, but he would like to know (1) whether the corporation will face recognition as a result of receiving property in exchange for stock and (2) whether the corporation will have a basis in the assets equal to fair market value or some other amount. Conduct the research and follow up with the client by brief letter.

Assignment of Income and Income Splitting

During roughly the first four months of each calendar year, millions of individual taxpayers in the United States race to prepare and submit a timely tax return on or before April 15. The question of whether the income reported properly appears on *their* tax return is one most taxpayers never contemplate, and for the most part, there truly is no issue. Even taxpayers who are married filing jointly with respect to the income of one spouse have no concerns. What many of them may not know, however, is that married taxpayers did not always have the option of filing a joint federal income tax return. Under prior law, all taxpayers filed individual returns, and depending on how taxpayers arranged their financial affairs, proper taxpayer identification with respect to a given income item could easily become a thorny issue. Consider also the fact that proper taxpayer identification issues can arise in many contexts, such as when one taxpayer transfers income-producing property to another taxpayer by gift (e.g., a grandparent gives a favored grandchild stock in a company that regularly pays cash dividends) or when one taxpayer consciously attempts to shift income to another taxpayer as a means of lowering overall tax liability. We turn, in this chapter, to the rules, principles, and doctrines governing taxpayer identification for the purpose of appropriate income allocation.

A. TAX RATE PROGRESSIVITY AND THE NOTION OF ANTICIPATORY ASSIGNMENT OF INCOME

In prior chapters, we discussed the notion of tax rate progressivity. You will recall that as a taxpayer's taxable income rises, the rate of tax imposed gradually increases. *See generally* § 1. Take, for example, the rate schedule applicable to single taxpayers for calendar year 2018 depicted in Table 17.1.

Key Concepts

- Tax rate progressivity
- Assignment of income from services
- Assignment of income from property
- Transfer of income-producing property
- Marriage penalty and marriage bonus

TABLE 17.1 2018 Tax Rate Schedule for Single Taxpayers	
Taxable Income Range	**Applicable Rate of Tax**
$0–$9,525	10%
$9,526–$38,700	12%
$38,701–$82,500	22%
$82,501–$157,500	24%
$157,501–$200,000	32%
$200,001–$500,000	35%
Over $500,000	37%

Under this schedule, a taxpayer with taxable income of $350,000 would have a marginal tax rate of 35 percent, but that does not mean that all of her taxable income is taxed at that rate. Rather, she still gets the benefit of the lower rates. Thus, on her taxable income from $0 to $9,525, she will pay tax at a rate of 10 percent (i.e., $952.50), and on her taxable income from $9,526–$38,700, she will pay tax at a rate of 12 percent (i.e., $3,501), and so on. For each taxable year, taxpayers start over at the 10 percent rate, but alas, they get to start at 10 percent only once during that period. But what if, hypothetically, a taxpayer (Suzette) with a marginal rate of 37 percent could somehow manage to have the last $10,000 of her taxable income show up on the return of her live-in boyfriend, Guillermo, whose marginal tax rate is 12 percent? The money would stay in the same household, but rather than being taxed at 37 percent, that portion of taxable income would be taxed, at the most, at 12 percent. Given the opportunity, taxpayers would attempt to get as many starts from the bottom of the tax rate schedule as possible by assigning portions of their income to others within their economic unit. In fact, years ago, when all taxpayers (including those who were married) filed separate returns, it made a great deal of sense in a sole breadwinner context to have the husband report half of his income while his wife reported the other half. That way the household managed to get two starts at the bottom of the tax rate schedule. The difficulty, of course, was that the husband was the only individual actually earning income.

B. ASSIGNMENT OF INCOME FROM SERVICES

1. Allocation by Private Contract

Case Preview

Lucas v. Earl

Although married taxpayers currently have the option of filing a joint return, they (along with others) previously submitted individual tax returns. In the typical family of the 1920s, the husband was the sole breadwinner, and accordingly, only he had reason to file a federal income tax return. In *Lucas v. Earl*, the taxpayers (husband and wife) entered into a contract in 1901 regarding the income earned by Mr. Earl. Per the contract's terms, the income was deemed to be jointly held (with each reporting 50% of the total). Although the taxpayers were not attempting to "game the system" by having Ms. Earl report half of Mr. Earl's income (the Sixteenth Amendment had not been ratified), giving effect to the contract after such ratification would have resulted in the assignment of half of the husband's income to his wife, thereby allowing him to get two "starts at the bottom" of the rate structure with respect to his income (i.e., once on his return and another on his wife's). Not surprisingly, the Commissioner of Internal Revenue frowned on the result that would flow from respecting the couple's formal arrangement of their financial affairs in this manner. As you read through this landmark decision, consider the following questions:

1. Did the Court take issue with the basic validity of the contract?
2. How did the taxpayer attempt to justify his return position?
3. What factors did the Court consider key in reaching its decision?

Lucas v. Earl
281 U.S. 111 (1930)

Mr. Justice HOLMES delivered the opinion of the Court.

This case presents the question whether the respondent, Earl, could be taxed for the whole of the salary and attorney's fees earned by him in the years 1920 and 1921, or should be taxed for only a half of them in view of a contract with his wife which we shall mention. The Commissioner of Internal Revenue and the Board of Tax Appeals imposed a tax upon the whole, but their decision was reversed by the Circuit Court of Appeals. A writ of certiorari was granted by this court.

By the contract, made in 1901, Earl and his wife agreed "that any property either of us now has or may hereafter acquire * * * in any way, either by earnings (including salaries, fees, etc.), or any rights by contract or otherwise, during the existence of our marriage, or which we or either of us may receive by gift, bequest, devise, or inheritance, and all the proceeds, issues, and profits of any and all such property shall be treated and considered, and hereby is declared to be received, held, taken, and owned by us as joint tenants, and not otherwise, with the right of survivorship." The validity of the contract is not questioned, and we assume it to be unquestionable under the law of the State of California, in which the parties lived. Nevertheless we are of opinion that the Commissioner and Board of Tax Appeals were right.

Justice Oliver W. Holmes, Jr.

Oliver Wendell Holmes, Jr. joined the U.S. Supreme Court on the appointment of President Theodore Roosevelt. Although writing for the majority in *Lucas v. Earl*, Holmes is often referred to in legal and academic circles as the great dissenter.

Credit: Photo courtesy of the Library of Congress.

The Revenue Act of 1918 approved February 24, 1919, c. 18, §§ 210, 211, 212(a), 213(a), 40 Stat. 1057, 1062, 1064, 1065, imposes a tax upon the net income of every individual including "income derived from salaries, wages, or compensation for personal service * * * of whatever kind and in whatever form paid," § 213(a). The provisions of the Revenue Act of 1921, c. 136, 42 Stat. 227, 233, 237, 238, in sections bearing the same numbers are similar to those of the above. A very forcible argument is presented to the effect that the statute seeks to tax only income beneficially received, and that taking the question more technically the salary and fees became the joint property of Earl and his wife on the very first instant on which they were received. We well might hesitate upon the latter proposition, because however the matter might stand between husband and wife he was the only party to the contracts by which the salary and fees were earned, and it is somewhat hard to say that the last step in the performance of those contracts could be taken by anyone but himself alone. But this case is not to be decided by attenuated subtleties. It turns on the import and reasonable construction of the taxing act. There is no doubt that the statute could tax salaries to those who earned them and provide that the tax could not be escaped by anticipatory arrangements and contracts however skillfully devised to prevent the salary when paid from vesting even for a second in the man who earned it. That seems to us the import of the statute before us and we think that no distinction can be taken according to the motives leading to the arrangement by which the fruits are attributed to a different tree from that on which they grew.

Judgment reversed. ***

Post-Case Follow-Up

Notwithstanding the taxpayers' contractual division of income and other items, the Court in *Lucas v. Earl* held that the taxpayer must report all of the income he earned on his individual tax return. Today, of course, married taxpayers have the option of filing a joint return, so the precise issue presented in this decision does not arise. Even so, the principle for which it stands remains governing law. Taxpayers may not avoid including an item in gross income via anticipatory assignment.

Then again, a great deal turns on how one defines or views anticipatory assignment. Consider the general partnership context. To the extent no provision in the Partnership Agreement dictates otherwise, section 401(b) of the Revised Uniform Partnership Act ("RUPA") provides that "[e]ach partner is entitled to an equal share of the partnership profits . . . ." And yet, there is no RUPA provision requiring that each partner actually perform services on behalf of the partnership. Moreover, section 401 is merely the default rule. Partners generally have the freedom to allocate profits and losses amongst themselves however they see fit (at least in accordance with established tax principles); the Partnership Agreement governs, and the model statute largely sets forth an array of back-up rules. *See* RUPA § 103(a) ("To the extent the partnership agreement does not otherwise provide, this [Act] governs relations among the partners . . . .").

One could certainly argue that allocation of income by operation of external law differs fundamentally from a brazen attempt at allocation by a taxpayer. That notion has firm support, which we will turn to in the near term. But in this context, even the governing law expressly yields to taxpayer allocation of income. Viewed in that light, doesn't a partnership agreement allocating income on the basis of various factors (some of which may have nothing to do with the performance of specific services) bear uncomfortable resemblance to the kind of contractual arrangement we saw in *Lucas v. Earl*?

Lucas v. Earl: Real Life Applications

1. Stuart owns a three-bedroom home, which he rents to three college students each academic year. The monthly rent is $3,000. Assume that Stuart instructs the three students to pay the monthly rent to his aged Aunt Griselda for four months. If the students comply, who must include the $12,000 in gross income?

2. Recently, Parisia made a $1 million investment in a limited liability company ("LLC"). By doing so, she became a "member" of the LLC. As it turns out, this particular LLC is not run by its members. Instead, the LLC is run by its designated managers (i.e., it is a manager-managed LLC). Parisia is one of several passive investors. She does no work for the company and leaves day-to-day operations to the managers. The LLC's Operating Agreement, however, dictates that Parisia and the other passive investors received the vast majority of the income allocations and distributions. Does this arrangement represent an assignment of income from the managers to the members?

3. Stuart is a partner in a general partnership. In that capacity, Stuart is entitled to participate in the management of the general partnership, and he also has certain financial rights (i.e., the right to allocations of the partnership's profits and losses and the right to receive his portion of any distributions made). If Stuart sells his transferable partnership interest to a third person, that person will get Stuart's financial rights but have no management rights. Stuart recently transferred his transferable partnership interest to Esteban. During the taxable year, the partnership allocated and distributed $50,000 to Esteban. Must Stuart include this $50,000 in his gross income?

2. Allocation by Operation of Law

We previously mentioned the notion of income allocation by operation of law. Should it matter, one way or another, whether the taxpayers assign the income or whether such assignment flows from the operation of state law? As you might have predicted, the U.S. Supreme Court has weighed in on this issue.

Case Preview

Poe v. Seaborn

In *Lucas v. Earl*, the U.S. Supreme Court rejected the tax-payer's contractual assignment of income for federal income tax purposes. Not long after, the Court granted certiorari to hear *Poe v. Seaborn*, a case presenting a similar assignment of income issue but with a factual distinction. The taxpayer in *Poe v. Seaborn* resided in Washington State, a community property jurisdiction. Under Washington law, compensation for services rendered constituted community property from the instant it was earned, and from the tax-payer's perspective, that reality meant that he and his wife were each obligated to report half of his earnings on their individual tax returns. As you read the case, consider the following questions:

1. Given the supremacy of federal law, why was the law of Washington State of any significance?
2. Why was the Court's holding in *Lucas v. Earl* not dispositive?
3. How would you articulate the Commissioner's uniformity argument, and how does the Court address it?

Poe v. Seaborn
282 U.S. 101 (1930)

Mr. Justice [Owen] ROBERTS delivered the opinion of the Court.

Seaborn and his wife, citizens and residents of the State of Washington, made for the year 1927 separate income tax returns as permitted by the Revenue Act of 1926, c. 27, § 223 (USCA title 26, § 964).

During and prior to 1927 they accumulated property comprising real estate, stocks, bonds and other personal property. While the real estate stood in his name alone, it is undisputed that all of the property real and personal constituted community property and that neither owned any separate property or had any separate income.

The income comprised Seaborn's salary, interest on bank deposits and on bonds, dividends, and profits on sales of real and personal property. He and his wife each returned [i.e., reported on a tax return] one-half the total community income as gross income and each deducted one-half of the community expenses to arrive at the net income returned.

The Commissioner of Internal Revenue determined that all of the income should have been reported in the husband's return, and made an additional assessment against him. Seaborn paid under protest, claimed a refund, and on its rejection, brought this suit.

The District Court rendered judgment for the plaintiff; the Collector appealed, and the Circuit Court of Appeals certified to us the question whether the husband was bound to report for income tax the entire income, or whether the spouses were entitled each to return one-half thereof. This Court ordered the whole record to be sent up.

The case requires us to construe sections 210(a) and 211(a) of the Revenue Act of 1926 (44 Stat. 21, USCA tit. 26, §§ 951 note and 952 note), and apply them, as construed, to the interests of husband and wife in community property under the law of Washington. These sections lay a tax upon the net income of every individual. The Act goes no farther, and furnishes no other standard or definition of what constitutes an individual's income. The use of the word "of" denotes ownership. It would be a strained construction, which, in the absence of further definition by Congress, should impute a broader significance to the phrase.

The Commissioner concedes that the answer to the question involved in the cause must be found in the provisions of the law of the State, as to a wife's ownership of or interest in community property. What, then, is the law of Washington as to the ownership of community property and of community income including the earnings of the husband's and wife's labor?

The answer is found in the statutes of the State, and the decisions interpreting them.

These statutes provide that, save for property acquired by gift, bequest, devise or inheritance, all property however, acquired after marriage, by either husband or wife, or by both, is community property.

Justice Owen J. Roberts

Appointed to the U.S. Supreme Court by Herbert Hoover, Associate Justice Roberts served from 1930 to 1945. Previously, he had been appointed by President Calvin Coolidge to act as prosecutor in the Teapot Dome scandal.

Credit: Photo courtesy of Library of Congress.

On the death of either spouse his or her interest is subject to testamentary disposition, and failing that, it passes to the issue of the decedent and not to the surviving spouse. While the husband has the management and control of community personal property and like power of disposition thereof as of his separate personal property, this power is subject to restrictions which are inconsistent with denial of the wife's interest as co-owner. The wife may borrow for community purposes and bind the community property. Since the husband may not discharge his separate obligation out of community property, she may, suing alone, enjoin collection of his separate debt out of community property. She may prevent his making substantial gifts out of community property without her consent. The community property is not liable for the husband's torts not committed in carrying on the business of the community. ***

Without further extending this opinion it must suffice to say that it is clear the wife has, in Washington, a vested property right in the community property, equal with that of her husband; and in the income of the community, including salaries or wages of either husband or wife, or both. ***

Taxpayer arg

Commissioner's arg

The taxpayer contends that if the test of taxability under Sections 210 and 211 is ownership, it is clear that income of community property is owned by the community and that husband and wife have each a present vested one-half interest therein.

The Commissioner contends, however, that we are here concerned not with mere names, nor even with mere technical legal titles; that calling the wife's interest vested is nothing to the purpose, because the husband has such broad powers of control and alienation, that while the community lasts, he is essentially the owner of the whole community property, and ought so to be considered for the purposes of sections 210 and 211. He points out that as to personal property the husband may convey it, may make contracts affecting it, may do anything with it short of committing a fraud on his wife's rights. And though the wife must join in any sale of real estate, he asserts that the same is true, by virtue of statutes, in most States which do not have the community system. He asserts that control without accountability is indistinguishable from ownership, and that since the husband has this, quoad community property and income, the income is that "of" the husband under sections 210, 211 of the income tax law.

We think in view of the law of Washington above stated this contention is unsound. The community must act through an agent. This Court has said with respect to the community property system that "property acquired during marriage with community funds became an asset of the community and not the sole property of the one in whose name the property was bought, although by the law existing at the time the husband was given the management, control, and power of sale of such property. This right being vested in him, not because he was the exclusive owner, but because by law he was created the agent of the community." ***

The reasons for conferring such sweeping powers of management on the husband are not far to seek. Public policy demands that in all ordinary circumstances, litigation between wife and husband during the life of the community should be discouraged. Law-suits between them would tend to subvert the marital relation. The same policy dictates that third parties who deal with the husband respecting community property shall be assured that the wife shall not be permitted to nullify his transactions. The powers of partners, or of trustees of a spendthrift trust, furnish apt analogies.

The obligations of the husband as agent of the community are no less real because the policy of the State limits the wife's right to call him to account in a court. Power is not synonymous with right. Nor is obligation coterminous with legal remedy. The law's investiture of the husband with broad powers, by no means negatives the wife's present interest as a co-owner.

We are of opinion that under the law of Washington the entire property and income of the community can no more be said to be that of the husband, than it could rightly be termed that of the wife. ***

The Commissioner urges that we have, in principle, decided the instant question in favor of the Government. ***

In [*Lucas v. Earl*,] a husband and wife contracted that any property they had or might thereafter acquire in any way, either by earnings (including salaries, fees, etc.), or any rights by contract or otherwise, "shall be treated and considered, and hereby is declared to be received, held, taken, and owned by us as joint tenants. * * *" We held that assuming the validity of the contract under local law, it still remained true that the husband's professional fees, earned in years subsequent to the date of the contract, were his individual income, "derived from salaries, wages, or compensation for personal service," under section 210, 211, 212(a) and 213 of the Revenue Act of 1918 (40 Stat. 1062-1065). The very assignment in that case was bottomed on the fact that the earnings would be the husband's property, else there would have been nothing on which it could operate. That case presents quite a different question from this, because here, by law, the earnings are never the property of the husband, but that of the community.

Finally the argument is pressed upon us that the Commissioner's ruling will work uniformity of incidence and operation of the tax in the various states, while the view urged by the taxpayer will make the tax fall unevenly upon married people. *** [D]ifferences of state law, which may bring a person within or without the category designated by Congress as taxable, may not be read into the Revenue Act to spell out a lack of uniformity.

The District Court was right in holding that the husband and wife were entitled to file separate returns, each treating one-half of the community income as his or her respective incomes, and its judgment is affirmed. ***

Post-Case Follow-Up

Giving due regard to the community property law of Washington State, the Court concluded that one-half of the earned income of the husband was, indeed, income of the wife and reportable by her on her return. Distinguishing *Lucas v. Earl*, the court noted that in the prior case, the income was that of the husband, whereas in the case at hand the "earnings [were] never the property of the husband, but that of the community." Even while comprehending the Court's reasoning, it's hard to endorse the Court's unblinking, robotic deference to the dictates of state law. The differential treatment of married taxpayers residing in community property and non–community property jurisdictions explains, at least in part, Congress's ultimate embrace of joint filing by married taxpayers in all jurisdictions. In recent years, *Poe v. Seaborn*'s holding took on renewed significance as registered domestic partners living in community property jurisdictions sought to compel its application with respect to their tax affairs. As we discuss later in the chapter, achieving an equitable result was somewhat of an uphill battle, but with activity at the state level and in the federal courts, the dust appears to be settling.

Poe v. Seaborn: Real Life Applications

For purposes of these questions, please assume that all taxpayers must file an individual return (i.e., the notion of married filing jointly or married filing separately does not exist).

1. Quentin and Esther, husband and wife, live in a community property jurisdiction. Assume that during 2018 Quentin earned $75,000 and Esther earned $125,000. How much must each include in gross income on their federal income tax return?

2. Blake and Timothy live in a community property jurisdiction. Although they are not married, they live together and hold all property as joint tenants with the right of survivorship. Assume that during 2018, Blake earns $200,000 and that Timothy earns $35,000. How much must Blake include in gross income on his federal income tax return?

3. Scarlet and Hugh are registered domestic partners living in a community property jurisdiction. State law provides that registered domestic partners have all rights enjoyed by married persons and that they are generally subject to all community property laws. Such partners are not, however, allowed to treat earned income as community property. Assume that during 2018, Scarlet earns $100,000 and that Hugh earns $120,000. How much must Scarlet include in gross income on her federal income tax return?

3. Joint Filing, Marriage Penalties, and Marriage Bonuses

Today, married taxpayers must file their federal income tax returns either as married taxpayers filing jointly or as married taxpayers filing separately. While joint filing may well eliminate some of the issues presented under individual filing regimes, differences in tax rate structures may result in some married taxpayers suffering a marriage "penalty" or, as the case may well be, enjoying a marriage "bonus." Let's first consider the marriage bonus. Assume that a single taxpayer has taxable income of $250,000. In Table 17.2, we see that the taxpayer's marginal rate is 35 percent. If that same individual were married and filing jointly with a spouse lacking taxable income, he would have a marginal tax rate of only 24 percent under the tax rate schedule set forth in Table 17.3. The final liability difference constitutes a marriage bonus.

TABLE 17.2 **2018 Tax Rate Schedule for Single Taxpayers**

Taxable Income Range	Applicable Rate of Tax
$0–$9,525	10%
$9,526–$38,700	12%
$38,701–$82,500	22%
$82,501–$157,500	24%
$157,501–$200,000	32%
$200,001–$500,000	35%
Over $500,000	37%

TABLE 17.3 2018 Tax Rate Schedule for Married Taxpayers Filing Jointly and Surviving Spouses	
Taxable Income Range	**Applicable Rate of Tax**
$0–$19,050	10%
$19,051–$77,400	12%
$77,401–$165,000	22%
$165,001–$315,000	24%
$315,001–$400,000	32%
$400,001–$600,000	35%
Over $600,000	37%

The marriage penalty only affects some taxpayers, but it exists nonetheless. Assume that two individuals each have taxable income of $350,000. As individual taxpayers, each would have a marginal tax rate of 35 percent, but as married taxpayers filing jointly with taxable income of $700,000, they now have a marginal tax rate of 37 percent. The end result is a slightly higher rate of tax on (roughly) the last $100,000 of taxable income. Therein lies the marriage penalty.

C. ASSIGNMENT OF INCOME FROM PROPERTY

1. Transfer of Property That Produces Income

Lucas v. Earl and *Poe v. Seaborn* both dealt with assignments of income from services, the former by contract and the latter by operation of law. In this section, we turn to assignment of income issues that might arise in connection with certain transfers between taxpayers. How, if at all, should the tax ramifications differ when a taxpayer transfers income-producing property (e.g., dividend-paying stock) and when he transfers income from property while retaining ownership of the property itself (e.g., a limited stream of rents from a rental property)? Is it always easy to tell the difference between the two scenarios? The next two cases draw a line of demarcation. See if you think the dividing line is readily discernible.

Case Preview

Blair v. Commissioner

In *Blair v. Commissioner*, the taxpayer, the beneficiary of a testamentary trust, assigned the right to receive portions of the trust income to his children, although as originally established, the trust did not contemplate distributions to them. The Commissioner took the position that the father's act was a classic assignment of income. The taxpayer countered, arguing that he had effected the transfer of income-producing property and that the resulting income was that of his children. As you read the case, consider the following questions:

1. Was the assignment of income valid as a matter of state law?
2. Did the petitioner have an assignable interest in the corpus of the trust?
3. In the eyes of the Court, did the father effect an assignment of his income or a transfer of income-producing property?

Blair v. Commissioner
300 U.S. 5 (1937)

Mr. Chief Justice HUGHES delivered the opinion of the Court.

This case presents the question of the liability of a beneficiary of a testamentary trust for a tax upon the income which he had assigned to his children prior to the tax years and which the trustees had paid to them accordingly.

Chief Justice Charles E. Hughes, Sr.

Appointed as Chief Justice by President Herbert Hoover, Hughes served in that capacity from 1930 to 1945.

Credit: Photo courtesy of The Collection of the Supreme Court of the United States.

The trust was created by the will of William Blair, a resident of Illinois who died in 1899, and was of property located in that State. One-half of the net income was to be paid to the donor's widow during her life. His son, the petitioner Edward Tyler Blair, was to receive the other one-half and, after the death of the widow, the whole of the net income during his life. In 1923, after the widow's death, petitioner assigned to his daughter, Lucy Blair Linn, an interest amounting to $6,000 for the remainder of that calendar year, and to $9,000 in each calendar year thereafter, in the net income which the petitioner was then or might thereafter be entitled to receive during his life. At about the same time, he made like assignments of interests, amounting to $9,000 in each calendar year, in the net income of the trust to his daughter Edith Blair and to his son, Edward Seymour Blair, respectively. In later years, by similar instruments, he assigned to these children additional interests, and to his son William McCormick Blair other specified interests, in the net income. The trustees accepted the assignments and distributed the income directly to the assignees.

The question first arose with respect to the tax year 1923, and the Commissioner of Internal Revenue ruled that the income was taxable to the petitioner. The Board of Tax Appeals held the contrary. The Circuit Court of Appeals reversed the Board, holding that under the law of Illinois the trust was a spendthrift trust and the assignments were invalid. We denied certiorari. ***

[Subsequently the Superior Court of Cook County, Illinois held that that the trust was not a spendthrift trust and that the assignments were valid. Even though the Board of Tax Appeals agreed with the superior court's holding, the Circuit Court of Appeals reversed the Board. The Circuit Court of Appeal similarly disposed of the same issue with respect to subsequent tax years.]

[The Circuit Court] recognized the binding effect of the decision of the state court as to the validity of the assignments but decided that the income was still taxable to the petitioner upon the ground that his interest was not attached to the corpus of the estate and that the income was not subject to his disposition until he received it.

Because of an asserted conflict with the decision of the state court, and also with decisions of circuit courts of appeals, we granted certiorari. ***

The question remains whether, treating the assignments as valid, the assignor was still taxable upon the income under the federal income tax act. That is a federal question.

*** In [*Lucas v. Earl,*] the question was whether an attorney was taxable for the whole of his salary and fees earned by him in the tax years or only upon one-half by reason of an agreement with his wife by which his earnings were to be received and owned by them jointly. We were of the opinion that the case turned upon the construction of the taxing act. We said that "the statute could tax salaries to those who earned them and provide that the tax could not be escaped by anticipatory arrangements and contracts however skillfully devised to prevent the salary when paid from vesting even for a second in the man who earned it." That was deemed to be the meaning of the statute as to compensation for personal service and the one who earned the income was held to be subject to the tax. *** The tax here is not upon earnings which are taxed to the one who earns them. *** There is here no question of evasion or of giving effect to statutory provisions designed to forestall evasion; or of the taxpayer's retention of control.

In the instant case, the tax is upon income as to which, in the general application of the revenue acts, the tax liability attaches to ownership.

The Government points to the provisions of the revenue acts imposing upon the beneficiary of a trust the liability for the tax upon the income distributable to the beneficiary. But the term is merely descriptive of the one entitled to the beneficial interest. These provisions cannot be taken to preclude valid assignments of the beneficial interest, or to affect the duty of the trustee to distribute income to the owner of the beneficial interest, whether he was such initially or becomes such by valid assignment. The one who is to receive the income as the owner of the beneficial interest is to pay the tax. If under the law governing the trust the beneficial interest is assignable, and if it has been assigned without reservation, the assignee thus becomes the beneficiary and is entitled to rights and remedies accordingly. We find nothing in the revenue acts which denies him that status.

The decision of the Circuit Court of Appeals turned upon the effect to be ascribed to the assignments. The court held that the petitioner had no interest in the corpus of the estate and could not dispose of the income until he received it. Hence it was said that "the income was his" and his assignment was merely a direction to pay over to others what was due to himself. ***

The will creating the trust entitled the petitioner during his life to the net income of the property held in trust. He thus became the owner of an equitable interest in the corpus of the property. By virtue of that interest he was entitled to enforce the trust, to have a breach of trust enjoined and to obtain redress in case of breach. The interest was present property alienable like any other, in the absence of a valid restraint upon alienation. The beneficiary may thus transfer a part of his interest as well as the whole. ***

We conclude that the assignments were valid, that the assignees thereby became the owners of the specified beneficial interests in the income, and that as to these interests they and not the petitioner were taxable for the tax years in question. The judgment of the Circuit Court of Appeals is reversed and the cause is remanded with direction to affirm the decision of the Board of Tax Appeals.

It is so ordered.

Post-Case Follow-Up

Having concluded that the father held an equitable interest in the trust corpus (and thus the power of assignment), the Court held that the income paid by the trustee to the taxpayer's children was their income and not the income of the father. Distinguishing *Lucas v. Earl*, the Court noted that the case at hand did not involve income from the provision of services but income of the owner of property, and that the father's assignments made his children the owners of the beneficial interests. At first glance, the Court's conclusion that the person entitled to the income of a trust becomes the equitable owner of the trust corpus might appear to be a leap of logic over a chasm, but the Court's conclusion is well-rooted in trust law. Although the beneficiary of a *spendthrift* trust cannot reach the trust corpus and cannot voluntarily assign his beneficial interest (i.e., require the trustee to pay income to another), the beneficiary of a simple trust can, in fact, assign his interest in much the same way that he can transfer other personal property, assuming no articulated restraints on alienation exist. With the superior court's conclusion that the subject trust was not spendthrift in nature, the taxpayer could legitimately transfer ownership of his beneficial interest.

Blair v. Commissioner: Real Life Applications

1. In 1992, McGill inherited 500 shares of stock of Conglomerate, Inc. from his father. The stock has appreciated substantially in value since then. Assume that, in 2018, McGill transferred the stock to his cousin, Glen. Two months after the transfer, the corporation declared and paid a dividend of $5/share. Is McGill obligated to include the amount of the dividend in his gross income?

2. *Same facts at Question #1*, except that the company does not pay a dividend. Assume that Glen sells the stock and realizes a substantial gain. Must McGill include this gain on his federal income tax return?

3. A brilliant engineer, Khufu holds several patents, and each year, those taking advantage of his intellectual property pay him thousands of dollars for the privilege. Assume that Khufu transfers all rights associated with his patents to his daughter. In addition to the right to receive royalties, she also attained the right to enforce certain restrictions regarding use of the patents. Must Khufu include the royalty income generated in future years in his gross income for federal income tax purposes?

2. Transfer of Income from Retained Property

Case Preview

Helvering v. Horst

In *Blair v. Commissioner*, the taxpayer transferred income-producing property, and the Court concluded that the income was ultimately that of his transferee. One can easily imagine a similar result with respect to a transfer by gift of stock. To the extent the donee later receives dividends with respect to the stock, the income will be hers rather than that of her donor because the donor transferred outright ownership of the stock along with all the rights and privileges that flow from the ownership of corporate equity. But what if one holding stock simply directed that the dividends be paid over to a third person while the original stockholder maintained ownership of the stock? In *Helvering v. Horst*, we see a similar situation: A bondholder effects the payment of interest to his son while maintaining ownership of the bond itself. Should the maintenance of ownership by one party necessarily lead us to a result different from that reached in *Blair v. Commissioner*? Consider the following questions as you make your way through the case:

1. How did the bondholder effect payment of interest to his son?
2. How did the payment of interest to the son benefit the bondholder economically?
3. Does it matter that the interest coupons were detached prior to their maturity?
4. By what logic can a taxpayer using the cash method be taxed on cash he did not receive?

Helvering v. Horst
311 U.S. 112 (1940)

Mr. Justice STONE delivered the opinion of the Court.

The sole question for decision is whether the gift, during the donor's taxable year, of interest coupons detached from the bonds, delivered to the donee and later in the year paid at maturity, is the realization of income taxable to the donor.

Justice Harlan F. Stone

Having joined the U.S. Supreme Court as an Associate Justice in 1925, Harlan Fiske Stone became Chief Justice of the United States in 1941 on the nomination of President Franklin D. Roosevelt.

Credit: Photo courtesy of the Library of Congress.

In 1934 and 1935 respondent, the owner of negotiable bonds, detached from them negotiable interest coupons shortly before their due date and delivered them as a gift to his son who in the same year collected them at maturity. The Commissioner ruled that under the applicable § 22 of the Revenue Act of 1934, *** the interest payments were taxable, in the years when paid, to the respondent donor who reported his income on the cash receipts basis. The circuit court of appeals reversed the order of the Board of Tax Appeals sustaining the tax. We granted certiorari because of the importance of the question in the administration of the revenue laws and because of an asserted conflict in principle of the decision below with that of *Lucas v. Earl* and with that of decisions by other circuit courts of appeals.

The court below thought that as the consideration for the coupons had passed to the obligor, the donor had, by the gift, parted with all control over them and their payment, and for that reason the case was distinguishable from *Lucas v. Earl,* . . . where the assignment of compensation for services had preceded the rendition of the services, and where the income was held taxable to the donor.

The holder of a coupon bond is the owner of two independent and separable kinds of right. One is the right to demand and receive at maturity the principal amount of the bond representing capital investment. The other is the right to demand and receive interim payments of interest on the investment in the amounts and on the dates specified by the coupons. Together they are an obligation to pay principal and interest given in exchange for money or property which was presumably the consideration for the obligation of the bond. Here respondent, as owner of the bonds, had acquired the legal right to demand payment at maturity of the interest specified by the coupons and the power to command its payment to others which constituted an economic gain to him.

Admittedly not all economic gain of the taxpayer is taxable income. From the beginning the revenue laws have been interpreted as defining "realization" of income as the taxable event rather than the acquisition of the right to receive it. And "realization" is not deemed to occur until the income is paid. But the decisions and regulations have consistently recognized that receipt in cash or property is not the only characteristic of realization of income to a taxpayer on the cash receipts basis. Where the taxpayer does not receive payment of income in money or property realization may occur when the last step is taken by which he obtains the fruition of the economic gain which has already accrued to him.

In the ordinary case the taxpayer who acquires the right to receive income is taxed when he receives it, regardless of the time when his right to receive payment accrued. But the rule that income is not taxable until realized has never been taken to mean that the taxpayer, even on the cash receipts basis, who has fully enjoyed the benefit of the economic gain represented by his right to receive income, can escape taxation because he has not himself received payment of it from his obligor. The rule, founded on administrative convenience, is only one of postponement of the tax to the final event of enjoyment of the income, usually the receipt of it by the taxpayer, and not one of exemption from taxation where the enjoyment is consummated by some event other than the taxpayer's personal receipt of money or property. This may occur when he has made such use or disposition of his power to receive or control the income as to procure in its place other satisfactions which are of economic worth. The question here is, whether because one who in fact receives payment for services or interest payments is taxable only on his receipt of the payments, he can escape all tax by giving away his right to income in advance of payment. If the taxpayer procures payment directly to his creditors of the items of interest or earnings due him, *** or if he sets up a revocable trust with income payable to the objects of his bounty, *** he does not escape taxation because he did not actually receive the money.

Underlying the reasoning in these cases is the thought that income is "realized" by the assignor because he, who owns or controls the source of the income, also controls the disposition of that which he could have received himself and diverts the payment from himself to others as the means of procuring the satisfaction of his wants. The taxpayer has equally enjoyed the fruits of his labor or investment and obtained the satisfaction of his desires whether he collects and uses the income to procure those satisfactions, or whether he disposes of his right to collect it as the means of procuring them.

Although the donor here, by the transfer of the coupons, has precluded any possibility of his collecting them himself he has nevertheless, by his act, procured payment of the interest, as a valuable gift to a member of his family. Such a use of his economic gain, the right to receive income, to procure a satisfaction which can be obtained only by the expenditure of money or property, would seem to be the enjoyment of the income whether the satisfaction is the purchase of goods at the corner grocery, the payment of his debt there, or such non-material satisfactions as may result from the payment of a campaign or community chest contribution, or a gift to his favorite son. Even though he never receives the money he derives money's worth from the disposition of the coupons which he has used as money or money's worth in the procuring of a satisfaction which is procurable only by the expenditure of money or money's worth. The enjoyment of the economic benefit accruing to him by virtue of his acquisition of the coupons is realized as completely as it would have been if he had collected the interest in dollars and expended them for any of the purposes named.

In a real sense he has enjoyed compensation for money loaned or services rendered and not any the less so because it is his only reward for them. To say that one who has made a gift thus derived from interest or earnings paid to his donee has never enjoyed or realized the fruits of his investment or labor because he has assigned them instead of collecting them himself and then paying them over to the donee, is to affront common understanding and to deny the facts of common experience. Common understanding and experience are the touchstones for the interpretation of the revenue laws.

The power to dispose of income is the equivalent of ownership of it. The exercise of that power to procure the payment of income to another is the enjoyment and hence the realization of the income by him who exercises it. ***

Reversed.

[Separate opinion of Justice McReynolds omitted.]

Post-Case Follow-Up

In *Helvering v. Horst*, the court concluded that the taxpayer's transfer of detachable interest coupons to his son constituted an assignment of income. Although the circuit court of appeals viewed the transfer as an outright transfer of property that would yield income to the son and prevent receipt of the interest by the father, this Court concluded that realization of the income by the father did not require actual receipt by him. Such realization could occur, in the Court's view, if the father reaped the financial or economic benefit of having the funds paid over to a third person. Had the Court concluded otherwise, taxpayers would have enjoyed free reign to assign the income from their property to those with lower marginal tax rates. Those whose income derives almost exclusively from investments could disperse that income generously and thereby lower their effective tax rate. One could argue that taxpayers effectively assign income when they transfer property with built-in gain by gift. Rather than realization and recognition occurring in the hands of the donor, it occurs in the hands of the donee. Even with the recipient taking the donor's basis, nothing guarantees that on ultimate disposition the donee will be subject to the same marginal rate of tax on any resulting gain as the donor would have been. The catch, as it turns out, is that the donor must relinquish ownership. It's also true that neither Congress nor the courts would want to unnecessarily burden or complicate gratuitous transfers of property holding modest fair market value, and even if taxed at a lower rate, the built-in gain will likely get taxed to some extent (assuming the donee disposes of it in a taxable transaction prior to death).

Helvering v. Horst: Real Life Applications

1. Mahershala owns several rental properties, each of which generates over $2,000,000 per year in rents. Assume that Mahershala transfers one of his rental properties, The Peachtree Palace, to his daughter Khalia who proceeds to collect the rent from the tenants in that building. Must Khalia include the rents from that building in her gross income?

2. *Same facts as Question #1,* except that in addition to transferring the building to Khalia, Mahershala demands that Khalia execute a will naming him as sole beneficiary with respect to that building in the event of her death.

3. *Same facts as Question #1,* except that Mahershala does not transfer the property to Khalia. Instead, he directs the company charged with management of

the property to pay rents from that property (for one year) directly to one of Mahershala's creditors. Must Mahershala include such redirected rent payments in his gross income?

4. Five years ago, Whitney purchased a bearer bond. In addition to being entitled to periodic payments of interest prior to the bond's maturity date, any person bearing (or presenting) the bond on or after December 31, 2018, is entitled to receive a lump sum payment of $10,000 in readily available funds. If Whitney transfers this bond by gift to her brother, Pernell, must Whitney include in gross income the periodic payments of interest received by Pernell?

D. RECENT DEVELOPMENTS: TREATMENT OF INCOME OF REGISTERED DOMESTIC PARTNERS AND SAME-SEX MARRIED COUPLES FOR FEDERAL TAX PURPOSES

Earlier in this chapter, we discussed *Poe v. Seaborn*, the decision in which the U.S. Supreme Court concluded that a husband and a wife in a community property jurisdiction could report half of the income of the community on their individual tax returns. Today, married couples *must* file jointly or elect the "married filing separately" status. Recently, a question arose as to whether registered domestic partners living in a community property state qualified for the same tax treatment as that enjoyed by the spouses filing separate returns in *Poe v. Seaborn*. In Chief Counsel Advisory 200608038 (Feb. 24, 2006), the IRS concluded that *Poe v. Seaborn* only applied to married couples. Accordingly, registered domestic partners were required to report all income on their individual returns. The IRS reasoned that, notwithstanding recently enacted California law extending the rights and obligations of spouses to registered domestic partners, the law did not allow such couples to treat earned income as community property for state income tax purposes. A few years after the issuance of that pronouncement, California amended its law such that registered domestic partners could treat earned income as community property, and not long after, in deference to state law, the IRS extended application of *Poe v. Seaborn* to registered domestic partners. *See* Chief Counsel Advisory 201021050 (May 5, 2010). Even at this juncture, however, those in registered domestic partnerships and civil unions could not file joint federal income tax returns.

In 2013, the U.S. Supreme Court handed down its decision in *United States v. Windsor*, 570 U.S. 744 (2013), which held that Section 3 of the Defense of Marriage Act was unconstitutional because it violated the equal protection rights of citizens. The Service subsequently issued Revenue Ruling 2013-17, 2013-38 I.R.B. 201, clarifying that in the wake of the *Windsor* decision, same-sex taxpayers *married* under state law were eligible to file joint federal income tax returns (regardless of their state of domicile). This pronouncement was ultimately rendered obsolete by the issuance of consistent final Treasury Regulations in Treasury Decision 9785, I.R.B. 2016-38 (September 19, 2016), in the wake of *Obergefell v. Hodges*, 576 U.S. ____, 135 S. Ct. 2584 (2015) (authorizing same-sex marriage throughout the United States).

Chapter Summary

- Under prevailing tax rate schedules, taxpayers must pay progressively higher rates of tax as their taxable income rises.
- A taxpayer's marginal tax rate is generally the rate of tax imposed on the highest segment of his taxable income under the applicable rate schedule. The taxpayer does, however, benefit from the imposition of lower rates on other segments of taxable income.
- Taxpayers may not avoid taxation (or lower the rate of tax imposed) by the anticipatory assignment of their income.
- Allocations of income among taxpayers resulting from the operation of state law are not treated as prohibited assignments of income. Allocations of earned income typically occur with respect to certain taxpayers residing in community property jurisdictions.
- Depending on prevailing facts and circumstances, the progressive rate structure may result in marriage bonuses or marriage penalties for certain married taxpayers. All married couples must elect either the "married filing jointly" status or the "married filing separately" status. Registered domestic partners and those in civil unions may not file joint federal tax returns or elect the "married filing separately" status. If such couples reside in a community property jurisdiction that extends community property rights and obligations to such couples, they should be able to appeal to *Poe v. Seaborn* with respect to reporting the income of their community.
- A mere transfer of income from property will result in taxation of the donor with respect to the income.
- A transfer of income-producing property will result in taxation of the donee with respect to income from the property.

Applying the Rules

1. Several years ago, Heather purchased a famous painting, *Storm Clouds on the Horizon*. The art is currently on loan to a famous national museum. As compensation for allowing the exhibition of the work, the museum pays Heather a monthly fee. Assume that Heather transfers title to this art to Jackson and that the museum now pays the monthly fee to him. Must Heather include the amounts paid to Jackson in her gross income?

2. *Same facts as Question #1*, except that Heather does not transfer title to the painting. Instead, she retains title and directs to museum to make monthly payments due directly to Jackson. Must Heather include the amounts paid to Jackson in her gross income?

3. Pat works for Bakery, Inc. Her son, Alex, is in college and regularly asks her for money. Assume that Pat directs her employer to deposit 80 percent of her regular pay into her bank account and 20 percent into her son's bank account. Must Pat include the 20 percent paid to her son during the taxable year in her gross income?

4. Hank and Frank are registered domestic partners residing in a community property jurisdiction, and each earns considerable income. Under state law, the earned income of registered domestic partners is community property. With respect to earned income, what should Hank report as gross income on his federal income tax return?

Federal Income Taxation in Practice

1. Assume that you are a junior associate working in a large law firm. A tax partner has asked that you sit in on a conference call with the client later that afternoon. During the conference call, the partner indicates that he vaguely recollects a case concerning a former insurance agent who attempted to assign renewal commissions to various assignees. He has asked you to track the case down. See what you can find. If you find the case, send him a PDF file along with your summary of the facts and the holding.

2. You recently took a case on a contingent-fee basis. Although it looked as though the case was headed to trial, the parties ultimately settled the matter for a lump sum payment of money to the client. According to the settlement agreement, the counterparty is to pay 30 percent of the settlement amount directly to you and the remainder directly to the client. Your client is concerned that the 30 percent payment you are about to receive will be viewed by the taxing authorities as an anticipatory assignment of income from the client to you. Conduct the research on this issue and follow up with the client by letter.

3. One of your clients recently won the state lottery. At the outset, she opted to receive equal annual installments over a 20-year period. After receiving two payments, she decided to transfer her right to future payments to a third party specializing in such transactions. As consideration, she received a lump sum payment of approximately $7,000,000. The client would like to know whether the transfer of the right to the future lottery payments constitutes an anticipatory assignment of income requiring that she include amounts in income over time as the amounts are paid to the third party or whether she must currently include the lump sum payment in her gross income.

Transfers Incident to Marriage, Separation, and Divorce

In prior chapters, we discussed several of the Code's nonrecognition provisions, including those governing like-kind exchanges, involuntary conversions, and incorporations. Nonrecognition transactions or events frequently occur in a business setting, and deferral of gain or loss recognition may be conditioned on satisfaction of specific business, statutory, and common law standards. Students should not, however, surmise that nonrecognition transactions arise solely in the business context. As we will see in this chapter, certain transfers between spouses and former spouses face a nonrecognition mandate while others may have significant tax consequence. In a divorce or legal separation context, that reality has the potential to add tax volatility to the already combustible mixture of court-ordered property settlements, alimony, and child support. You will find that the statutory framework is fairly easy to navigate. Difficulty and conflict, if any, tend to arise when taxpayers take steps to exploit the governing rules to achieve tax results more closely aligned with their personal preferences. More often than not, they find their efforts blocked by contrary statutory edict.

A. PROPERTY TRANSFERS BETWEEN SPOUSES AND FORMER SPOUSES (EXCLUDING ALIMONY AND CHILD SUPPORT)

Although we will discuss the treatment of alimony and child support payments later in this chapter, our initial focus will be on transfers of other property between spouses and former spouses. Section 1041(a) of the Code generally provides that no gain or loss is recognized with respect to transfers of property between spouses. Although the

Key Concepts

- Impact of interspousal property transfers during marriage
- Impact of transfers *incident to the divorce*
- Treatment of *alimony* payment and receipt
- Treatment of child support payment and receipt
- Deemed characterization of amounts as alimony, child support, or property settlement

Key Statutory and Regulatory Provisions

▦ **Internal Revenue Code**
  ▦ § 1041(a)–(c)
▦ **Treasury Regulations**
  ▦ § 1.1041-1T

Alimony and Child Support

Later in this chapter, we will discuss specific rules governing the treatment of alimony and child support payments in greater depth. For the moment, note that for divorce and separation instruments executed after December 31, 2018, neither alimony nor child support is deductible by the payor. Also, in that context, neither amount is includible in the gross income of the recipient. For similar instruments executed on or before December 31, 2018 (and not amended thereafter to make current law applicable), alimony is deductible by the payor and includible in the gross income of the recipient. Child support, however, is neither deductible by the payor nor includible in the income of the recipient.

same rule applies to transfers between former spouses, the property transfers in that context must be incident to the divorce. Whether a taxpayer receives property from a spouse during marriage or from a former spouse incident to a divorce, he or she will be treated, for tax purposes, as receiving the property by gift. As a result, the taxpayer will take the property with a basis equal to the adjusted basis of the property in the hands of their transferring spouse (or former spouse). *See* § 1041(b). Note, specifically for this context, that even property with built-in loss will get this treatment. *See* Treas. Reg. § 1.1041-1T(d)(Q-11 and A-11).

It is often easy to think of § 1041 as applying largely and specifically to the division of property between divorcing spouses, but it is important to keep in mind that even if § 1041 is triggered in the divorce context, it applies with equal force to routine transfers or transactions between spouses, even when no divorce occurs or is even contemplated. *See* Treas. Reg. § 1.1041-1T(a). Thus, a taxpayer transferring stock with built-in gain to his spouse will recognize no gain on the transfer, and if such transfer occurs incident to a divorce, the same result follows. Section 1041(c) clarifies that a transfer occurs *incident to the divorce* in either of the following situations:

▦ The transfer occurs within one year after the date on which the marriage ceases; or
▦ The transfer is related to the cessation of the marriage.

As drafted, § 1041(c) articulates a statutory presumption for transfers occurring within one year of the cessation of the marriage (i.e., they are automatically deemed incident to a divorce), but it also incorporates a somewhat ambiguous degree of flexibility by including transfers related to the cessation of the marriage. Just how much does that standard encompass? Governing Treasury Regulations specify that to qualify as *related to the cessation of the marriage*, the property transfer must occur "pursuant to a divorce or separation instrument" and "not more than 6 years after the date on which the marriage ceases." *See* Treas. Reg. § 1.1041-1T(b)(Q-7 and A-7). The regulations go on to note the following:

> Any transfer not pursuant to a divorce or separation instrument and any transfer occurring more than 6 years after the cessation of the marriage is presumed to be not related to the cessation of the marriage. This presumption may be rebutted only by showing that the transfer was made to effect the division of property owned by the former spouse at the time of the cessation of the marriage.

Treas. Reg. § 1.1041-1T(b)(Q-7 and A-7). The next case gives us an opportunity to see the rules in this arena operate in a distinct factual setting.

Case Preview

Balding v. Commissioner

In the wake of certain changes in the community property law of California, the former spouse of Mr. Balding undertook to claim a community property share of his military pay. The parties reached a settlement requiring that Mr. Balding pay cash to his ex-wife over a three-year period in exchange for her relinquishing any claim to his military pay and foregoing any additional claims with respect to marital property. The Tax Court took up the question of whether the payments made to the taxpayer were includible in her gross income. As you read the case, consider the following questions:

1. Did the IRS take the position that the amounts paid by Mr. Balding constituted alimony?
2. What was the IRS's central argument?
3. Why did Congress enact § 1041, and why is legislative intent of any significance in this case?

Balding v. Commissioner
98 T.C. 368 (1992)

HALPERN, JUDGE:

Respondent determined deficiencies in petitioner's Federal income tax for the years 1986, 1987, and 1988, in the amounts of $3,605, $3,240, and $1,912, respectively. The sole issue we must decide is whether payments received by petitioner in settlement of her claim to a community property share of her ex-husband's military retirement pay are includable in gross income. ***

At the time of the filing of the petition in this case petitioner resided in Grover City, California.

Petitioner and Joe M. Balding (Balding) were married in 1962, less than 1 year after Balding entered the military. In December 1981, subsequent to Balding's retirement from the military, they were divorced. Among other things, the divorce court ordered a division of their community property and affirmed that Balding's military retirement pay was his sole and separate property. In 1984, because of changes in California's community property law, petitioner asked the divorce court to reopen its judgment of divorce and award her a community property share of Balding's military retirement pay. Before the divorce court could act, petitioner and Balding reached a settlement with regard to the retirement pay, which settlement was stipulated between them and entered as an order by the divorce court. Petitioner relinquished any claim to Balding's military retirement pay (and agreed not to bring any further claims with regard to marital property) in consideration of Balding's promise to pay to her $15,000, $14,000, and $13,000 in 1986, 1987, and 1988, respectively (hereinafter the settlement payments); petitioner also received Balding's promise not to make any future claims with regard to marital property. Petitioner did not include the settlement payments in her original returns for the years in question. After petitioner received a private letter ruling from respondent concluding that the settlement payments were includable, Priv. Ltr. Rul. 88-13-023 (Dec. 29, 1987), petitioner submitted unsigned Forms 1040X for 1986, 1987, and 1988, including in gross income for each year the settlement payment received in that year. We must determine whether any income is recognized to petitioner on account of receipt of such payments. We conclude that no income is recognized to her pursuant to the provisions of section 1041.

DISCUSSION

The settlement payments were received by petitioner on account of her divorce from Balding and in settlement of her claim to a community property interest in property that previously had been determined to be Balding's separate property. Respondent has not argued, nor would we agree, that the settlement payments constitute alimony or separate maintenance taxable to petitioner pursuant to sections 61(a)(8) and 71. Respondent has argued that petitioner's relinquishment of her community property interest in the retirement benefits in question constituted an anticipatory assignment of income such that the consideration she received therefor (i.e., the settlement payments) is immediately taxable to her. Outside of the marital context, we would have little trouble agreeing with respondent. Transfers of property, or releases of marital rights, incident to divorce, however, are subject to a special set of rules found in section 1041.

Section 1041 was enacted by section 421 of the Deficit Reduction Act of 1984 (DEFRA), Pub. L. 98-369, 98 Stat. 793-795. *** [It is] effective generally for transfers after July 18, 1984, in taxable years ending after such date. See DEFRA sec. 421(a), 98 Stat. 793.

Prior to the enactment of section 1041, the resolution of property rights incident to a divorce gave rise to differing tax results, depending on how each spouse's entitlements and obligations were viewed for State law purposes. The Supreme Court had ruled that a transfer of separately owned, appreciated property to a spouse (or former spouse) in exchange for the release of marital claims resulted in the recognition of gain to the transferor. *United States v. Davis*, 370 U.S. 65 (1962). However, in the case of an approximately equal division of community property on divorce, no gain was recognized on the theory that no sale or exchange had occurred but only a nontaxable partition. Respondent applied a like result to the partition of jointly held property. See Rev. Rul. 74-347, 1974-2 C.B. 26. The tax treatment of divisions of property between spouses involving other various types of ownership under the different State laws was often unclear and resulted in much litigation. Several States had amended their property law in an attempt to avoid the result in the *Davis* case.

Congress was dissatisfied with the aforesaid state of the law and desired to change the tax laws to make them as unintrusive as possible with respect to relations between spouses. Section 1041 was the result. In part, the Ways and Means Committee explained the new provision as follows:

The bill provides that the transfer of property to a spouse incident to a divorce will be treated, for income tax purposes, in the same manner as a gift. Gain (including recapture income) or loss will not be recognized to the transferor, and the transferee will receive the property at the transferor's basis (whether the property has appreciated or depreciated in value). A transfer will be treated as incident to a divorce if the transfer occurs within one year after the parties cease to be married or is related to the divorce. This nonrecognition rule applies whether the transfer is for the relinquishment of marital rights, for cash or other property, for the assumption of liabilities in excess of basis, or for other consideration and is intended to apply to any indebtedness which is discharged. Thus, uniform Federal income tax consequences will apply to these transfers notwithstanding that the property may be subject to differing state property laws. [*Id.*; fn. ref. omitted.]

Rule

The language of section 1041 specifies broad rules of exclusion for both the transferor spouse and the transferee spouse. If the language of the statute leaves any doubt, the relevant legislative history (quoted above) makes clear that, notwithstanding the nature of the consideration received (whether, for instance, the relinquishment of marital rights, cash, property, or "other consideration"), no gain or loss is to be recognized to the transferor spouse on account of any unrealized appreciation or depreciation in the property transferred. Likewise, the transferee spouse is to be viewed as having received the transferred property as if by nontaxable gift. ***

Here, petitioner released her claim to a community property share of her ex-husband's military retirement benefits in exchange for the settlement payments. Respondent has not argued, nor could we accept, that such receipt was not incident to the divorce. The state of the law in California with regard to community property was unsettled at the time petitioner and Balding entered into the settlement agreement. Nevertheless, whether we view petitioner's release as constituting (or equivalent to) a transfer of property, or simply a release of marital rights, the transaction whereby she received the settlement payments requires that we analyze her receipt in light of section 1041. The settlement payments having been received from her ex-husband, incident to her divorce (and in consideration of her release of any claim to his military retirement benefits), we must conclude that they constitute nontaxable gifts, pursuant to sections 1041 and 102. Respondent's determination of a deficiency, based on petitioner's failure to include such payments in gross income, cannot be sustained. To take account of a stipulation regarding the deductibility of attorney's fees,

Decision will be entered under Rule 155.

RE

Post-Case Follow-Up

While acknowledging that a different result would follow had unmarried taxpayers been involved, the court concluded that the taxpayer's relinquishment of her rights to her former husband's military pay in exchange for a series of payments merited application of § 1041 because the transfer was incident to the divorce. The holding highlights two practical realities.

First, changes in federal and California law made it possible to treat military retirement benefits as community property. Even so, a transfer incident to a divorce need not be a transfer solely with respect to marital property;

it can apply to a transfer of separate property. *See* Treas. Reg. § 1.1041-1T(d)(Q-10 and A-10). Second, the movement of money from one spouse to another years after entry of the original divorce decree presents an inherent risk, because such transfers are highly vulnerable to attempts to characterize them as transfers with negative tax consequences.

Balding v. Commissioner: Real Life Applications

1. Julia and her husband, Gordon, frequently argue about money. They have concluded that although they should continue to pay some obligations jointly, they should manage their other financial affairs separately. Very separately. For several years, Julia has been the sole owner of a log cabin nestled high in the mountains of Colorado. Gordon thinks that, if renovated, the cabin has rental revenue potential as a quiet get-a-way spot for individuals and couples. If Julia's basis in the cabin is $50,000, what tax results will follow if Gordon purchases it from her for $85,000?

2. *Same facts as Question #1*, except that Julia must transfer the log cabin to Gordon as part of a division of property pursuant to a divorce decree.

3. Assume that Locke and Serena divorced in 2018 and that as part of the property settlement he received several pieces of antique furniture. Eight years later, Serena approached Locke and inquired as to whether he would be willing to sell the antiques to her. He agreed. If Locke held the furniture with a $5,000 basis and sold it to Serena for $7,500, what was his gain recognized?

B. TREATMENT OF ALIMONY AND CHILD SUPPORT UNDER DIVORCE AND SEPARATION INSTRUMENTS EXECUTED AFTER DECEMBER 31, 2018

Per Code provisions existing prior to the enactment of the Tax Cuts and Jobs Act in 2017, taxpayers paying alimony could deduct such payments, and those receiving alimony were required to include the relevant payments in income. Child support payments, however, were neither deductible by the payor nor includible in the gross income of the recipients. With respect to divorce and separation instruments executed after December 31, 2018, the Tax Cuts and Jobs Act eliminated both the Code-based provision allowing the deduction of alimony payments and corresponding provisions requiring the inclusion of the alimony in the income of the recipient; the treatment of child support remained unchanged. Note that those with divorce or separation instruments executed on or before December 31, 2018, may amend them and apply current law, so long as the amendment expressly adopts applicable current law.

C. DELINEATING ALIMONY, CHILD SUPPORT, AND PROPERTY SETTLEMENTS FOR NON-AMENDED DIVORCE AND SEPARATION INSTRUMENTS EXECUTED ON OR BEFORE DECEMBER 31, 2018

In the wake of the Tax Cuts and Jobs Act, alimony paid pursuant to a divorce or separation instrument executed after December 31, 2018, is neither deductible by the payor nor includible in the gross income of the recipient. As of this writing, however, the vast and overwhelming majority of divorce or separation instruments were executed on or prior to that date and have not been amended for the express purpose of applying new tax law; divorced couples are often (though certainly not always) wise enough to let sleeping dogs lie. Given the substantial number of grandfathered agreements in effect, you will likely encounter taxpayers complying with the former statutory regime under which the characterization of an amount as child support, alimony, or property settlement remains critically important. Accordingly, given the potential relevance of various authorities, we turn to the body of law that developed as practitioners and others sought to delineate those categories.

1. In General

Although § 1041 generally governs the treatment of property transfers between spouses and former spouses, the Code contains specific and controlling rules with respect to the treatment of alimony and child support. In general, individuals making alimony or separate maintenance payments may deduct the amounts paid during the taxable year, and those receiving such payments must include them in gross income in the year of receipt. *See generally* §§ 215 and 71. Taxpayers may not, however, take a deduction with respect to child support payments, and the relevant recipients need

Credit: Pros and Cons used with the permission of King Features Syndicate and the Cartoonist Group. All rights reserved.

Key Statutory and Regulatory Provisions

- Internal Revenue Code (as of 12/21/17)
    - § 71(a)–(d)
    - § 215(a)–(b)
- Treasury Regulation (as of 12/21/17)
    - § 1.71-1T (skim)

not include such amounts in gross income. For the definition of *alimony or separate maintenance payment*, we turn to § 71. To qualify, the payment must conform to the following standard (bearing in mind that *spouse* also refers to former spouse):

- The payment must be in cash;
- Such payment must be received by (or on behalf of) a spouse under a divorce or separation instrument;
- The divorce or separation instrument may *not* designate the payment as one that is not includible in gross income under § 71 and not deductible under § 215;
- Individuals legally separated under a decree of divorce or separate maintenance may not be members of the same household at the time of the payment; and
- There can be no obligation to make the payment after the death of the payee spouse and no liability to make payment (in cash or property) as a substitute for such payment after the death of the payee spouse.

EXHIBIT 18.1   Record-Setting Divorce Settlements (as of November 2014)

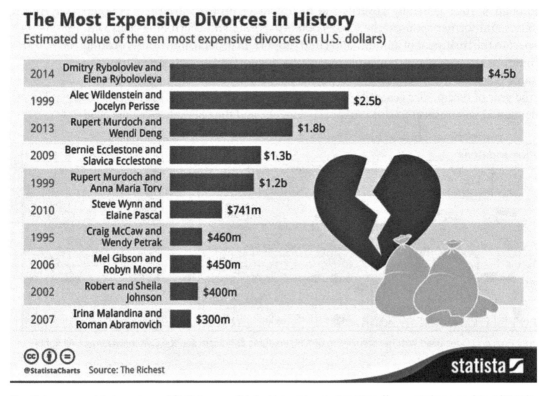

The Most Expensive Divorces in History
Estimated value of the ten most expensive divorces (in U.S. dollars)

Year	Couple	Value
2014	Dmitry Rybolovlev and Elena Rybolovleva	$4.5b
1999	Alec Wildenstein and Jocelyn Perisse	$2.5b
2013	Rupert Murdoch and Wendi Deng	$1.8b
2009	Bernie Ecclestone and Slavica Ecclestone	$1.3b
1999	Rupert Murdoch and Anna Maria Torv	$1.2b
2010	Steve Wynn and Elaine Pascal	$741m
1995	Craig McCaw and Wendy Petrak	$460m
2006	Mel Gibson and Robyn Moore	$450m
2002	Robert and Sheila Johnson	$400m
2007	Irina Malandina and Roman Abramovich	$300m

@StatistaCharts   Source: The Richest

statista

Credit: Image provided courtesy of Statista.com. Original image located at https://www.statista.com/chart/2949/the-most-expensive-divorces-in-history (last visited August 8, 2017).

From time to time, as we will soon see, courts must often determine whether a given amount falls within or outside the boundaries of the defined terms. Demonstrating little, if any, sympathy for inadvertent variance or legal foot-fault, courts typically demand strict compliance with statutory mandates. As a result, what the parties (or even some courts) often think can qualify as alimony turns out, on further examination, to be a recognition-prohibited property settlement (governed by § 1041) or a nondeductible, nonincludible child support payment (governed by § 71(c)).

2. Alimony v. Property Settlement

In the immediate aftermath of a divorce, the likelihood is strong that substantial amounts of property and money will change hands between former spouses. As Exhibit 18.1 makes abundantly clear, the dollar amounts can be staggering. Notable divorce settlements involving U.S. celebrities include those depicted in Exhibit 18.2.

From the perspective of the former spouse charged with paying alimony and surrendering property, both the availability of the deduction with respect to alimony payments and the prohibition of recognizing gain or loss in connection with a property settlement often weigh heavily in favor of characterizing a given transfer as alimony. In fact, such an individual has every incentive to attempt to morph what truly is a property settlement into some form of alimony payment. Taxpayers attempting to forcibly extract such a deduction from a property settlement by

EXHIBIT 18.2 **Select Celebrity Divorce Settlement Estimates**

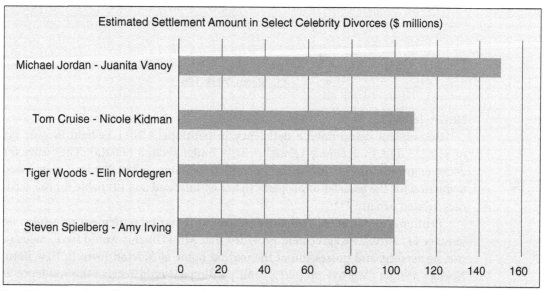

Credit: Data from https://www.statista.com/statistics/532368/the-most-expensive-divorces-among-celebrities-by-estimated-settlement/ (last visited August 8, 2017).

making substantial up-front payments of "alimony" will find their effort stymied by § 71(f). Under that provision, the abusive front-loading of alimony payments will result in corrective inclusion (of the excess) by the original payor and corresponding corrective deduction (of such excess) by the original payee. *See* § 71(f)(1). But even if the taxpayers are not attempting to game the system, they may find themselves unwittingly outside the protective definitional ambit of § 71(b) if they fail to give consistent and sufficient regard to its strictures.

Case Preview

Mehriary v. Commissioner

In the immediate aftermath of her divorce, Christina Mehriary found herself the recipient of a personal residence and, at the same time, the party obligated to pay alimony of $4,000 per month to her former spouse. A short while after entry of the original divorce decree, Ms. Mehriary attempted to satisfy a portion of her alimony obligation by transferring the personal residence she had received back to her former spouse. Worsening matters further, she proceeded to take a loss deduction with respect to the transfer, notwithstanding the prohibitions of § 1041. As you watch this case unfold, consider the following questions:

1. Why did the court conclude that the conveyance of the property back to Mr. Williams was a transaction covered by § 1041?
2. How did the court react to the petitioner's argument that the transfer of the property was tantamount to a payment of alimony?
3. Why did the court conclude that the imposition of an accuracy-related penalty was justified?

Mehriary v. Commissioner
T.C. Memo. 2015-126

NEGA, Judge:

Respondent determined a deficiency in petitioner's 2011 Federal income tax of $19,225 and an accuracy-related penalty under section 6662(a). The issues for decision are whether petitioner is (1) entitled to claim an $80,000 loss or itemized deduction for the transfer of property to her ex-husband and (2) liable for the accuracy-related penalty. ***

Petitioner and Bradley Williams entered into a marital settlement agreement on January 11, 2010. The agreement provided that Mr. Williams would have exclusive use, ownership, and possession of the marital home at Morton Road in New Bern, North Carolina (Morton property), and petitioner would receive the residence at Sweet Briar Road in New Bern, North Carolina (Sweet Briar property). Mr. Williams transferred his interest in the Sweet Briar property to petitioner via a quitclaim deed dated February 18, 2010.

The agreement further provided that petitioner would pay Mr. Williams $4,000 per month for 60 months, commencing February 1, 2010, as nonmodifiable lump-sum alimony. All payments were to be made to Wells Fargo Bank to pay the mortgage on the Morton property. In the event that the mortgage was paid in full before full payment of the lump-sum alimony, petitioner would continue to pay the remaining lump-sum alimony directly to Mr. Williams. Finally, the agreement advised the parties to seek the opinion and advice of a tax professional as to the tax ramifications of the agreement. On February 19, 2010, the Circuit Court for Escambia County, Florida (hereinafter circuit court), entered a final judgment of dissolution of marriage.

Sometime thereafter, petitioner submitted to Mr. Williams a modification to the marital agreement which stated that petitioner would convey (through a quitclaim deed) the Sweet Briar property back to Mr. Williams in lieu of $80,000 of the alimony obligation. Mr. Williams agreed to and signed the modification.

Petitioner quitclaimed the Sweet Briar property to Mr. Williams on February 16, 2011. On September 28, 2011, petitioner sent a letter to the circuit court requesting that the court modify the divorce decree to reflect the transfer of the Sweet Briar property to Mr. Williams in lieu of $80,000 of her alimony obligation.

On Schedule A, Itemized Deductions, of her 2011 tax return, petitioner claimed an $80,000 loss deduction for the transfer of the Sweet Briar property to Mr. Williams. At trial petitioner stated that she claimed the loss deduction because her insurance company characterized the Sweet Briar property as investment property.

OPINION

The Commissioner's determinations set forth in a notice of deficiency are generally presumed correct, and the taxpayer bears the burden of proving them erroneous. ***

Section 1041(a) provides that no gain or loss is recognized on the transfer of property from one spouse to another or to a former spouse, but only if the transfer is incident to divorce. A transfer of property is incident to divorce if the transfer occurs within one year after the date on which the marriage ceases, or is related to the cessation of the marriage. A transfer of property is related to the cessation of the marriage if the transfer is pursuant to a divorce or separation instrument, as defined in section 71(b)(2), and the transfer does not occur more than six years after the date on which the marriage ceases. A divorce or separation instrument includes a "written instrument incident to such a decree."

Petitioner transferred the Sweet Briar property to Mr. Williams in lieu of $80,000 of her alimony obligation. The final judgment of divorce was entered on February 19, 2010, and the Sweet Briar property was transferred on February 16, 2011. This transfer is considered a transfer of property incident to divorce because the transfer occurred within one year after the date on which the marriage ceased. Furthermore, the written modification to the marital agreement signed by petitioner and Mr. Williams was a divorce or separation instrument. Because the transfer of the Sweet Briar property was pursuant to petitioner's and Mr. Williams' modification agreement and occurred within one year of petitioner's divorce from Mr. Williams, the transfer was related to the cessation of their marriage. As such, the transfer was incident to their divorce in all respects. Therefore, under section 1041(a) petitioner may not recognize an $80,000 loss upon the transfer of the Sweet Briar property to Mr. Williams.

Wife's 2nd Arg: Is it deductible as alimony?

Alternatively, petitioner argues that the transfer of the Sweet Briar property to Mr. Williams is a deductible alimony payment.

Alimony (or separate maintenance) payments are deductible from income by the payor and includable in the income of the payee. The payments must meet certain requirements to be deductible, however. One requirement is that payments be made in cash or a cash equivalent. A check or money order that is payable on demand is a cash equivalent. Transfers of services or property do not qualify as alimony payments.

H: No, because it was transfer of property, not cash payment

Petitioner's argument that the transfer of $80,000 (the fair market value of the Sweet Briar property) was deductible as an alimony payment fails because it was not a payment in cash. Instead the transfer was a transfer of property and therefore does not constitute an alimony payment. Although petitioner and Mr. Williams agreed that petitioner's transfer of the Sweet Briar property would replace $80,000 of petitioner's alimony obligation, the intent of the parties does not determine the deductibility of a payment as alimony under section 71. Instead the test for whether a payment is deductible as alimony is a straightforward, objective test that rests entirely on the fulfillment of explicit requirements set forth in section 71, including that the payment be made in cash or a cash equivalent. Accordingly, we sustain respondent's determination.

Section 6662(a) and (b)(1) and (2) imposes a 20% accuracy-related penalty on any portion of an underpayment of Federal income tax attributable to, among other things, a taxpayer's negligence or disregard of rules or regulations, or a substantial understatement of income tax. An understatement of income tax is substantial if it exceeds the greater of 10% of the tax required to be shown on the return or $5,000.

***

I: Penalty

H: She must pay penalty

RE

Petitioner set forth no specific facts to show that she acted with reasonable cause and in good faith. Petitioner was advised to seek the opinion of a tax professional when she signed her marital settlement agreement, but she did not offer any testimony or other evidence to show that she relied on professional tax advice. Petitioner merely testified that she relied on her insurance company's characterization of the Sweet Briar property as investment property. The insurance company did not provide tax advice, and the record does not reflect that it ever represented itself as a competent professional. Accordingly, petitioner is liable for the accuracy-related penalty under section 6662(a) for the 2011 taxable year.

To reflect the foregoing,

Decision will be entered for respondent.

Post-Case Follow-Up

Unwilling to relax the definitional boundaries in § 1041, the court concluded that the taxpayer's transfer of the residential property to Mr. Williams was incident to the divorce not only because it occurred within one year of the divorce but also because it was clearly related to the cessation of the marriage. Rejecting the taxpayer's argument that the transfer of the residence was a form of alimony, the court emphasized the statutory requirement that alimony payments take the form of cash. One can hardly fault the court for applying the letter of the law as written. At the same time, the situation itself tends to call more for the elevation of substance over form than a wooden and unblinking demand for the required form. Surely a naked attempt by an alimony obligor to substitute property for cash over the objection of the intended recipient should meet with judicial opprobrium. But, real estate is unique. It is somewhat odd that when an alimony recipient freely agrees to accept real property in lieu of cash, the statute recasts the transaction in a manner at odds with the intent of the parties.

Mehriary v. Commissioner: Real Life Applications

1. After 18 difficult years of marriage, Boyd and Leslie divorced. Under the divorce decree, Leslie was entitled to receive the dining room table and matching chairs, but Boyd was entitled to receive the china hutch. Boyd was also obligated to pay Leslie $3,000 per month in alimony. Assume that six months after entry of the final divorce decree and in response to Leslie's pleas, Boyd agreed to pay her $1,000 and to transfer the china hutch in lieu of paying her $3,000 for one month of alimony. How will this transaction be treated for federal income tax purposes?

2. Although Helen and Natalie felt sure that marriage was the step they needed to take to calm their stormy relationship, they soon found themselves filing for divorce, citing irreconcilable differences. Under the divorce decree, Natalie was obligated to pay Helen alimony of $4,000 per month. Knowing that Helen firmly believe that no investment in the world was better than Apple, Inc. stock, Natalie offered to transfer 100 shares of Apple, Inc. stock to Helen in satisfaction of the first three months of her alimony obligation. Helen enthusiastically accepted. Natalie's basis in the stock was $1,000, and as of the date of the transfer, the stock had a fair market value of $12,000. How will the transfer of the stock be treated for federal income tax purposes?

3. *Same facts as Question #2*, except that just prior to the intended transfer date, the value of Apple, Inc. stock rose dramatically, and Natalie decided to retain her stock. She paid Helen $4,000 per month in accord with the divorce decree. How will the payment be treated?

3. Alimony v. Child Support

Section 71(a) generally requires that those receiving alimony or separate maintenance payments include those amounts in gross income. This inclusion mandate does not apply, however, with respect to any fixed portion of the payment that, under the terms of the divorce or separation instrument, is for the support of the payor spouse's children. *See* § 71(f). Although § 215 allows a deduction for the payment of alimony, no corresponding provision covers the payment of child support, and in much the same way that taxpayers may attempt to secure a deduction for property settlements by denominating them "alimony," they may attempt to disguise a child support payment as alimony. The ruse is often exposed, however, by terms of the divorce or separation instrument calling for a reduction of amounts paid on the happening of specific child-related events (e.g., graduation from high school, attaining a certain age, etc.). Under § 71(c)(2), a reduction in "alimony" timed to coincide with certain child-related events (e.g., marriage, death, leaving school, etc.) will be treated as child support, as will reductions that can be readily associated with such events (e.g., a sudden and inexplicable reduction on a given date in a specific calendar year). This result will follow even if the relevant instruments separately state a child support obligation. Notwithstanding the clarity and simplicity of these rules, taxpayers and their legal advisors routinely manage to run afoul of them, with decidedly negative tax consequences.

Case Preview

Johnson v. Commissioner

In *Johnson v. Commissioner*, the taxpayer and his spouse divorced after 15 years of marriage. Although Mr. Johnson was obligated to make what was referred to as "spousal maintenance" payments, that obligation was subject to termination on the occurrence of specific events, including one related to their youngest child. In light of the Code's directives, the case's outcome is not surprising, but it does serve well as a cautionary tale for aspiring attorneys, especially those brave souls contemplating careers in family law. At the end of the day, Mr. Johnson could have found himself on the hook for more than mere child support. Consider the following questions as you read the case:

1. Did the spousal support payments suffer reduction or elimination on the occurrence of specific events?
2. What role did the taxpayer's accountant play, and why was that of significance to the court?

Johnson v. Commissioner
T.C. Memo. 2014-67

BUCH, Judge:

Allen Johnson divorced in 2006. Pursuant to a divorce decree Mr. Johnson made "spousal maintenance" payments to his ex-wife and claimed an alimony deduction on his 2008 Federal income tax return. The spousal maintenance payments were subject to a child-related contingency. Specifically, Mr. Johnson's payment obligation terminates when his youngest child graduates from high school. Respondent disallowed Mr. Johnson's alimony deduction, determined a deficiency of $15,532, and imposed an accuracy-related penalty under section 6662(a). Under section 71(c)(2), the amount of any payment that is subject to a child-related contingency is child support and not alimony. Because the spousal maintenance payments terminate based on a child-related contingency, we hold that Mr. Johnson is not entitled to deduct the payments to his ex-wife as alimony. Mr. Johnson is not liable for the section 6662(a) penalty, however, because he acted reasonably and in good faith.

[handwritten margin notes: Rule; H: He cannot deduct, but no Penalty]

FINDINGS OF FACT

At the time the petition was filed, Mr. Johnson resided in Minnesota.

Mr. Johnson married in 1989. After more than 15 years of marriage, he divorced in 2006. At the time of the divorce Mr. Johnson and his ex-wife had three minor children.

A divorce decree entered on September 19, 2006, required Mr. Johnson to pay spousal maintenance of $6,068 per month. In addition to the spousal maintenance payments, the divorce decree also required Mr. Johnson to pay 40% of his gross bonus to his ex-wife. Both the periodic spousal maintenance payments and the additional payment terminate upon the occurrence of any one of the following events:

[handwritten margin note: Decree]

(a) the graduation from high school of the youngest child;
(b) the remarriage of Mr. Johnson's ex-wife; or
(c) the death of either Mr. Johnson or his ex-wife.

The divorce decree states that the spousal maintenance should be deductible to Mr. Johnson under section 215 and includible in his ex-wife's gross income under section 71.

The divorce decree further obligated Mr. Johnson to pay $500 per month, adjusted for cost of living, for the support of his minor children until any one of a series of events occurs (including graduation from high school).

In July 2008 the Family Court of the State of Minnesota issued an order modifying the spousal maintenance amount from $6,068 per month to $4,000 per month and the child support amount from $500 to $200 per month. The termination clause of the spousal maintenance remained the same. On his 2008 Form 1040, U.S. Individual Income Tax Return, Mr. Johnson deducted the total of $54,788 in spousal maintenance payments as alimony. A certified public accountant (C.P.A.) prepared the original return based on the divorce decree, which Mr. Johnson provided.

[handwritten margin note: His tax return]

In a notice of deficiency dated October 19, 2011, respondent disallowed the alimony deduction and determined a deficiency of $15,532 in Mr. Johnson's 2008 Federal income tax and an accuracy-related penalty under section 6662(a) of $3,106. Mr. Johnson filed a petition disputing the adjustment and the accuracy-related penalty.

[handwritten margin note: Deficiency/ Penalty]

On February 17, 2012, after the petition was filed, Mr. Johnson's C.P.A. amended the 2008 tax return and reported an alimony deduction of $70,848. The amendment increased the reported alimony to include the portion of Mr. Johnson's bonus that he paid to his ex-wife pursuant to the decree, which Mr. Johnson did not claim on his original return. Mr. Johnson amended his petition to include the additional amount paid with respect to his bonus.

Mr. Johnson's ex-wife reported all of the spousal support payments received from Mr. Johnson as taxable income on her return.

OPINION

The issues for decision are: (1) whether Mr. Johnson is entitled to an alimony deduction for spousal maintenance payments made during 2008, and (2) whether he is liable for a section 6662(a) accuracy-related penalty.

The Commissioner's determinations in a notice of deficiency are generally presumed to be correct and taxpayers bear the burden of proving otherwise. Income tax deductions are a "matter of legislative grace," and the burden of proving entitlement to any claimed deduction rests on the taxpayer. Here, the facts are not in dispute, and all of the questions to be resolved are questions of law.

The issue in this case concerns the characterization of the spousal maintenance payments that Mr. Johnson made in 2008: whether they are alimony or child support. The tax consequences as to both the payor and the recipient turn on the characterization.

Section 215(a) allows a deduction to the payor for an amount equal to the alimony paid during the taxable year to the extent it is includible in the recipient spouse's gross income under section 71(a). Whether a payment constitutes alimony is determined by reference to section 71(b)(1), which defines "alimony" as any cash payment if: (1) the payment is received by a spouse under a divorce or separation instrument; (2) the divorce or separation instrument does not state that the payment is neither includible in gross income nor allowable as a deduction; (3) the payor and payee spouses are not members of the same household when the payment is made; and (4) the payment obligation terminates at the death of the payee spouse and there is no liability to make either a cash or a property payment as a substitute for the payment after the death of the payee spouse.

Section 71(c)(2), however, provides that the amount of any payment that is subject to "contingencies involving child" must be considered payment made for the support of the child. The Code specifically lists "[child] leaving school" as an example of such a contingency.

We have previously decided that even if there are separately allocated child support payments, other monthly payments made pursuant to a decree will still qualify as child support if the decree contains an explicit contingency related to a child. In _Hammond v. Commissioner,_ the taxpayer made monthly payments pursuant to a divorce decree that stated that the payments would terminate on the taxpayer's child's 18th birthday or at the time of remarriage of the taxpayer's ex-wife. In addition to these monthly payments, the taxpayer was obligated to make separately allocated, fixed payments for child support. The taxpayer in _Hammond_ argued that because there was separately allocated child support, the monthly payments at issue were alimony. We found no authority in support of the taxpayer's proposition and held that the amount of any payment that "will be reduced on the happening of a contingency relating to a child" is child support and not alimony regardless of the existence of a separate child support payment.

In this case, the divorce decree clearly states that the support payments will terminate upon the graduation of the youngest child. With this kind of contingency, the statute compels us to characterize the payments as child support. The fact that the divorce decree specifies that the payments are to be deducted by Mr. Johnson is not controlling. The Court does not rely on the intent of the parties when defining alimony for Federal income tax purposes but applies the explicit requirements laid out in section 71. Therefore, Mr. Johnson's argument that the graduation of the youngest child from high school was intended as a mere reference point for the termination of spousal support holds no value.

Accordingly, we hold that Mr. Johnson is not entitled to an alimony deduction regarding the support payments made to his ex-wife.

We must also decide whether Mr. Johnson is liable for an accuracy-related penalty under section 6662(a). ***

I: Penalty?
H: No.

We are satisfied on this record, however, that Mr. Johnson reasonably relied on the professional advice of his return preparer. Mr. Johnson hired a C.P.A. to prepare his 2008 tax return and provided his C.P.A. with a copy of the divorce decree, which was necessary for the completion of the tax return. The record does not indicate that the C.P.A. was incompetent or inexperienced. It was reasonable for Mr. Johnson to rely on his C.P.A., and he was not required to second-guess his C.P.A.'s advice.

RE

Accordingly, Mr. Johnson is not liable for the section 6662(a) accuracy-related penalty. *** On the basis of our examination of the record before us and the parties' arguments at trial, we find that Mr. Johnson is not entitled to an alimony deduction for the spousal maintenance payments.

However, Mr. Johnson is not liable for an accuracy-related penalty because he was able to show that he acted reasonably and in good faith.

To reflect the foregoing,

Decision will be entered for respondent as to the deficiency and for petitioner as to the accuracy-related penalty under section 6662(a).

Post-Case Follow-Up

Given the clear mandate of § 71(c)(2) regarding child-related contingencies, the Tax Court promptly disposed of the taxpayer's alimony deduction claim in *Johnson*. Notwithstanding the decree's inclusion of standard alimony contingencies concerning remarriage of the recipient or the death of either former spouse, the child-related contingency fundamentally altered the nature of the payment. Indeed, in light of the fact that payments would cease altogether (rather than merely being reduced) when the youngest child graduated from high school, the case for child support characterization is compelling. Moreover, but for the taxpayer's reliance on his CPA, the court might have imposed an accuracy-related penalty. The attempt to get a deduction by wrapping child support payments in the see-through cloak of alimony was simply bad tax planning on someone's part. Perhaps a better approach (at least for modest dollar amounts) would have been to have Mr. Johnson agree to pay child support in exchange for his former spouse's execution of IRS Form 8332 (releasing her claim to exemption for the children). That way, she would include only actual alimony in income, she would exclude child support received, and her former husband would get a tax break by claiming the children as dependents (possibly reaping the benefit of certain refundable tax credits). Of course, all of the foregoing assumes that the former spouses have not declared absolute and total war on each other.

Johnson v. Commissioner: Real Life Applications

1. After only five turbulent years of marriage and the controversy-as-to-paternity birth of their daughter (Brittany), Ryan and Cassidy finally decided to call it quits. The divorce decree (executed on August 8, 2013) required that Ryan pay Cassidy $1,000 per month in child support (until Brittany reaches 18 years of age) and $2,000 per month in spousal maintenance, but this amount was to be reduced to $500 per month on December 1, 2022. Although the decree does not mention it, Brittany will turn 18 on November 15, 2022. How will Ryan's payments be treated for federal income tax purposes?

2. *Same facts as Question #1*, except that all payments are to terminate on December 1, 2022.

3. Jae and Betty were married for 20 years. Acknowledging that they had drifted apart years ago, they decided to occupy separate bedrooms and to take separate vacations before finally accepting the reality that a friendly divorce was in order. Under the terms of the divorce decree (executed on December 10, 2010), Jae was obligated to pay Betty $2,000 per month as alimony, but this obligation would terminate in the event of Betty's remarriage, Betty's cohabitation, or the death of either Jae or Betty. How will Jae's payments be treated for federal income tax purposes?

Chapter Summary

- No gain or loss is recognized if property is transferred from one spouse to another spouse. The spouse receiving the property will take it with a basis equal to the adjusted basis of the property in the hands of the transferring spouse. The property transfer need not be done in contemplation of separation or divorce, and no such event need ultimately occur.

- No gain or loss is recognized if property is transferred from an individual to his former spouse so long as the transfer is incident to the divorce. The former spouse receiving the property will take it with a basis equal to the adjusted basis of the transferring former spouse.

- A transfer is incident to a divorce if (1) it occurs within one year after the date on which the marriage ceases or (2) is related to the cessation of the marriage.

- A transfer of property is related to the cessation of the marriage if it occurs pursuant to a divorce or separation instrument and occurs within six years of the date of the cessation of the marriage. Otherwise, a rebuttable assumption exists that the transfer was not related to the cessation of the marriage.

- Those paying alimony pursuant to a divorce or separation instrument executed on or before December 31, 2018, are entitled to a deduction equal to the amount of alimony includible in the gross income of the recipient, assuming the instrument has not been amended to make current law applicable. An amount will constitute alimony only if it meets the definitional requirements set forth in § 71 (in effect as of the date of the execution of the instrument).

■ Those paying alimony pursuant to divorce or separation instrument executed after December 31, 2018, are not entitled to a deduction, and the recipient need not include the payment in income.

■ Those paying child support may not take a deduction with respect to the payment, and those receiving child support need not include the amount received in gross income.

■ Amounts denominated alimony but subject to a child-related contingency will be treated as child support.

Applying the Rules

1. Ali and Kendall divorced on January 20, 2018. Under the terms of the divorce decree Kendall was obligated to convey the vacation residence to Ali, but she was unable to do so until February 28, 2020. Assume that Kendall's basis in the vacation home was $180,000 and that as of the date of its transfer to Ali, the fair market value was $300,000. How will Kendall and Ali be treated in connection with this property transfer?

2. Mallory and Sean have been married for almost 15 years. They have always resided in California, a community property state. At the time of their marriage, Mallory held several assets, and accordingly, after marriage, these items constituted her separate property. Assume that Mallory's downtown condominium is her separate property and that her basis in it is $400,000. If Mallory sells her condominium to Sean for $550,000, how will the transaction be treated for federal income tax purposes?

3. Pursuant to a divorce decree executed on December 7, 2017, Alex is obligated to pay Mark spousal support of $2,000 per month and child support of $3,000 per month with respect to their 16-year old daughter, Hera. Assume that the spousal support payments are to remain at $2,000 per month until Hera turns 18. At that point, both the spousal support and child support payments are to terminate. How will the payments made by Alex be treated for federal income tax purposes?

4. Roberto and Evita recently divorced, and pursuant to the terms of the divorce decree (executed on July 4, 2016), Roberto is obligated to pay Evita alimony of $2,000 per month. Since divorcing, Roberto has acquired several real estate properties, most of which he sells immediately. On occasion, however, he will retain a property and rent it out to various tenants. Assume that Roberto and Evita agree that Evita will live rent-free in one of Roberto's homes for one year as a means of collecting her alimony from him for that year. If the two secure an amendment to their divorce decree (reflecting the agreement) and proceed according to plan, how will the arrangement be treated for federal income tax purposes?

5. After three years of marriage and six months of couple's therapy, Carlos and Pristina divorced. Under the terms of the divorce decree (executed on June 19, 2018), Pristina was required to transfer her interest in the marital home to Carlos, and Carlos was required to pay Pristina both alimony of $2,500 per month and child support of $1,500 per month. If Carlos and Pristina comply with the divorce decree, how will they be treated for federal income tax purposes?

Federal Income Taxation in Practice

1. Assume that you are a mid-level associate in the tax group of a major national law firm. One of the assigning partners has heard good things about you over the years and would like you to handle a question presented by one of the firm's wealthy individual clients, Flavio Gonzales. As you understand the facts, Flavio is the sole shareholder of The Pasta Factory, Inc. ("TPF"). Flavio's wife, Tyra, would like to purchase property from TPF, but Flavio is concerned that such a sale would generate income at the corporate level because the property Tyra has an interest in has built-in gain. The partner has asked you whether Flavio's status as the sole shareholder of TPF and Tyra's husband will result in the application of § 1041 to a sale from TPF to Tyra. Conduct the research and follow up with the partner by brief memorandum. Remember that this assigning partner is not a tax partner.

2. Four years ago, Frieda and Pierce divorced. Under the terms of the divorce decree (executed on February 12, 2014), Frieda must pay Pierce alimony of $2,500 per month. The difficulty, unfortunately, is that Pierce has never been good with managing his money. In fact, during their marriage, Pierce's financial ineptitude and irresponsibility gave rise to many heated arguments. Frieda and Pierce have asked for your legal opinion with respect to the following contemplated course of action. If Pierce and Frieda agree in writing that Frieda is to pay $2,500 directly to the bank holding a mortgage on Pierce's home until the mortgage is paid off and thereafter directly to Pierce, how will the various payments be treated for federal income tax purposes? If Pierce refuses to agree to such an arrangement, may Frieda pursue an alternative strategy? Conduct the research and follow up with them by letter.

3. Your client, Gaston, has been married for several years, but he is now in the process of getting a divorce. The couple will execute the relevant divorce papers on November 22, 2017, and Gaston accepts the fact that he will have to pay alimony. In fact, to the extent that money will have to flow from him to his soon-to-be-former spouse, he would much prefer that the amount be characterized as alimony because, as he understands the law, alimony payments are generally deductible for federal income tax purposes. He shows you the following tentative schedule of payments.

Year	Amount to Be Paid
1	$42,000
2	$32,000
3	$12,000
4	$12,000
5	$12,000

You believe that there may be an issue because the initial payments are notably higher than subsequent payments. Consult § 71 (as in effect as of the date of the execution of the instrument), and follow up with the client by brief letter.

19

Capital Gains and Losses

Throughout our coverage of the tax law to this point, we have discussed a number of statutory and regulatory provisions, including those governing income inclusion, exclusions, deductions, proper timing, and taxpayer identification. Our ultimate goal has been to understand how these rules impact and ultimately determine a given taxpayer's taxable income during a specific taxable year. All along, our underlying assumption has been that taxpayer income has a degree of sameness. Jill may earn a salary, and Ali may earn hourly wages, but the basic nature of what they have earned (money) is the same. Similarly, deductions and exclusions may relate to specific items, but as a class, deductions are deductions and exclusions are exclusions. Notwithstanding these realities, federal income tax law does not subject all forms of income (or loss) to the same treatment. The tax law assigns various forms of income and loss a specific "character," and under the established classification scheme, items are either "ordinary" or "capital" in nature. Much of what we have discussed up to this point concerned both "ordinary" income and deductions or "ordinary" losses offsetting ordinary income. Even if we previously encountered items of gain or loss that were technically "capital" in character, we did not highlight that fact. In this chapter, we focus decidedly on income character and discuss the rules governing the treatment of capital gains and capital losses. Although specific rules govern the treatment of the capital gains and losses of corporate taxpayers, we limit our coverage in this context to the rules governing *noncorporate* taxpayers.

A. OVERVIEW

If an individual receives a salary, hourly wages, or fees for services rendered, the income is "ordinary" in character. Assuming calculations ultimately result in taxable income, the individuals can determine their final tax liability by application of

Key Concepts

- The character of income or loss as "ordinary" or "capital"
- Treatment of capital gains and losses (long term and short term)
- Treatment of § 1231 gains and losses and depreciation recapture
- Definition of capital asset
- The "sale or exchange" requirement and the meaning of "property" under § 1221

the appropriate progressive rate schedule. If, however, that same individual purchases stock in a large corporation (as a personal investment) and later sells it for an amount exceeding his basis, the income will constitute "capital gain" and may qualify for preferential tax treatment. Under the appropriate circumstances, the capital gain will not be taxed according to the progressive rate structure applicable to ordinary income (under which rates can be as high as 37 percent) but, instead, will generally enjoy preferential treatment and likely be taxed at a rate of up to 20 percent. Clearly, characterization of income as ordinary or capital in nature has considerable impact, and in this chapter we will study the classification and taxation scheme Congress has put in place. One preliminary question merits attention: Why does Congress grant preferential tax treatment to certain forms of capital gain income?

Originally, capital gains did not enjoy preferential tax treatment, and even today, only specific capital gains enjoy such preferential treatment. As to why Congress ultimately embraced the notion of taxing specific capital gains at more favorable rates, commentators often reason that such treatment stimulates taxpayer investment activity, enhances the mobility of capital, and minimizes the tax impact of recognizing all gains (which may have accumulated over several years) in a single taxable year. Taxpayers with income available for investment have the option of retaining that income and allowing it to generate interest (which typically constitutes ordinary income). Taxing capital gains at preferential rates provides an incentive for such a taxpayer to remove those funds from savings and make them available to capital-hungry businesses and the larger investment community. If the taxpayer later decides to pursue an alternative investment, preferential capital gains rates facilitate the movement of money from one investment to another (i.e., sale of one investment for cash (i.e., liquidation) followed by prompt reinvestment of the proceeds). Thus, investors are not "locked in" to an investment for fear of negative tax impact on disposition of the asset at a profit. And to the extent the taxpayer held his original investment and accumulated gains over several years, he is not penalized for "bunching" all of his capital gains in a single taxable year. Put differently, the existence of preferential rates means that a liquidation event will not subject the taxpayer to more burdensome taxation merely because she chose to realize her gains in a lump sum rather than taking them in smaller increments over time. Whatever the actual or purported benefits of the preferential treatment of capital gains, the ordinary/capital dichotomy has, unfortunately, given rise to serious issues and problems.

Under ideal circumstances, operation of the federal tax system results in both horizontal and vertical taxpayer equity, and to a considerable extent, the progressive rate structure applicable to ordinary income helps to achieve those twin goals. But the existence of preferential rates for certain capital gains represents a frontal assault on both horizontal and vertical equity. A taxpayer who earns $50,000 of ordinary taxable income in a given year is not taxed the same way as a taxpayer who earns $50,000 of long-term capital gain in a given year (offending horizontal equity). Moreover, even if one taxpayer has $25,000 of long-term capital gain in a given year, his rate of tax may be no lower than that of a taxpayer with $50,000 in long-term capital gain in a given year (offending vertical equity). And the inequities heighten as the dollar amounts increase. Under current law, individual taxpayers with taxable income ("ordinary" in character) above $500,000 face a marginal tax rate of 37 percent, whereas individuals with *millions* of dollars in realized long-term capital gains would likely pay tax on such gains at rates at or below 20 percent. It should come as no surprise, then, that Warren Buffet, a multibillionaire known for his investment acumen, famously quipped that his average tax rate is lower than that of his secretary. In addition to the foregoing issues, a vexing and somewhat chronic problem flows from the differential treatment of "ordinary" and "capital" amounts; taxpayers have regularly attempted to manipulate the character of their income items and their losses to suit their tax goals. Congress has established ground rules to sort out the items it seeks to reward with preferential treatment, but courts must often intervene to effect congressional intent and keep taxpayers in check.

B. BASIC TREATMENT OF CAPITAL GAINS AND LOSSES

The rules governing the treatment of capital gains and losses reflect the pursuit of several congressional goals. But even as Congress seeks to reward long-term investment while facilitating the mobility of capital, there remains not only the need to police taxpayers (who might attempt to manipulate income or loss character) but also the desire to limit the revenue impact of allowing taxpayers to recognize certain losses, even if such losses are unambiguously capital in nature. Later in this chapter we will study the precise mechanical rules operating in this area to sort out the gains Congress seeks to favor and the losses it seeks to keep within sensible confines. You will better understand the broader scheme, however, if we start with a somewhat oversimplified sneak preview of the governing rules. As for terminology (e.g., "short term," "long term," "capital asset," etc.), you need not be concerned. We will flesh out some terms as we go along and explore others in greater depth later in the chapter. For the moment, let's focus on the nuts and bolts.

Capital gains and capital losses arise when a taxpayer sells, exchanges, or otherwise disposes of a capital asset. If the taxpayer is fortunate, the taxpayer will realize a capital gain, and if he is not so fortunate, he will realize a capital loss, all of which simply depends on his amount realized relative to his basis in the capital asset. The further characterization of the capital gain or loss as short term or long term generally turns on the amount of time the taxpayer held the capital asset prior to its sale, exchange, or other disposition (i.e., the taxpayer's **holding period**). For assets held one year or less by the taxpayer, the capital gain or loss will be short term, and for assets held for more than one year, the capital gain or loss will be long term. With those basic rules in mind, take note of the following fundamental concepts:

■ Congress reserves preferential tax treatment only for long-term capital gains; short-term capital gains are taxed at the rates applicable to ordinary income.

■ Capital losses can be used to offset capital gains and a *limited* amount of ordinary income. Beyond those offsets, such losses must be carried forward to future taxable years as capital losses.

Special Note Re Holding Period and "Tacking"

Section 1223 contains a number of special rules regarding a taxpayer's holding period. Note, in particular, that certain inherited property is deemed to have been held for more than one year, even if disposed of within one year of receipt. *See* § 1223(9). Also, taxpayers acquiring property and taking a carryover basis with respect to it (e.g., a gift) may add to *their* holding period (in that asset) the holding period of their predecessor(s) in title. *See* § 1223(2). This addition is referred to as "tacking." Similarly, a taxpayer takes a holding period in property received in an exchange equal to his holding period in the property relinquished, *if* the relinquished property was a capital asset (or § 1231 property) and he holds the new property with a substituted basis. *See* § 1223(1).

The following examples should prove helpful in terms of familiarizing you with some of the essential rules. In each instance, we do make a few baseline assumptions (which need not concern you at the moment) in addition to assuming that the transaction mentioned is the taxpayer's *sole* capital asset transaction during the relevant taxable year.

Example 1

On February 15, 2018, Zhao purchased 1,000 shares of stock for $10,000. A few weeks later, on March 30, 2018, he sold those shares for $15,000. In 2018, Zhao had a *short-term capital gain* of $5,000. That gain will be included in his gross income and taxed at the rates applicable to ordinary income.

Example 2

On January 4, 2018, Chase purchased 1,000 shares of stock for $10,000. A few years later, on July 1, 2020, he sold those shares for $25,000. In 2020, Chase had a *long-term capital gain* of $15,000. That gain will be included in his gross income, *but it will qualify for taxation at preferential rates.*

Example 3

On July 10, 2018, Ariana purchased 1,000 shares of stock for $10,000. Days later, the company announced that its second quarter earnings had not met the expectations of investment analysts. For the company and its investors, this was bad news. The value of Ariana's stock plummeted immediately, and she sold it on

August 12, 2018, for $8,000. In 2018, Ariana had a *short-term capital loss* of $2,000. Ariana may deduct this loss and thereby offset her ordinary income. Note that if the loss had been $4,000, she would have been able to offset only $3,000 of ordinary income, but she would have had to carry over the remaining $1,000 (as a *short-term capital loss*) to 2019.

Example 4

On July 10, 2018, Chetna purchased 1,000 shares of stock for $10,000. On October 15, 2021, the company announced that its third quarter earnings had not met the expectations of investment analysts. The value of Chetna's stock plummeted immediately, and she sold it on October 18, 2021, for $7,000. In 2021, Ariana had a *long-term capital loss* of $3,000. Chetna may use this loss deduction to offset her ordinary income. Note that if the loss had been $5,000, she would have been able to offset $3,000 of ordinary income, but she would have had to carry over the remaining $2,000 (as a *long-term capital loss*) to 2022.

The picture emerging should be sharpening in focus. Short-term capital gains get taxed at ordinary income rates, but long-term capital gains qualify for preferential tax treatment. Capital losses have the ability to offset limited amounts of ordinary income, but beyond that offset, they must be carried forward as capital losses. In deeply oversimplified terms, that's the lay of the land. We can explore the precise mechanical rules governing the treatment of capital gains and losses with a baseline understanding of the broader scheme.

C. MECHANICAL RULES FOR CALCULATING CAPITAL GAINS, CAPITAL LOSSES, AND NET CAPITAL AMOUNTS

Understanding the mechanical rules governing the calculation of capital gains and losses requires digesting a series of definitions set forth in § 1222, and you should pause for a moment to study them very carefully. You will note that several definitions apply only if and to the extent that a given gain or loss is taken into account in computing gross income or taxable income. This language is critically important because not every capital gain or loss can or should be taken into account in computing gross or taxable income. Individuals, for example, may take losses into account under § 165(a) in computing their taxable income only if and to the extent such losses qualify under § 165(c), and you'll recall that § 165(c)(3) losses may be taken into account only to a limited extent as a result of the rules set forth

Wash Sales

In some circumstances, a taxpayer disposing of stock at a loss will be unable to deduct the loss. If, for example, a taxpayer disposes of 100 shares of stock at a loss but immediately purchases 100 shares of the same company's stock, she is essentially in the same financial posture and cannot deduct a loss. She cannot circumvent the rule by purchasing 100 additional shares just before disposing of the first 100 shares at a loss. Section 1091(a) generally provides that a taxpayer disposing of stock at a loss will not be able to take that loss into account if she purchases substantially identical stock within 30 days before or after the sale that resulted in the realization of a loss.

in § 165(h) and the various Treasury Regulations promulgated under § 165. Note also that under § 165(f), losses from the sale or exchange of capital assets may be taken into account only as allowed under §§ 1211 and 1212. Bearing these boundaries in mind, let's move on to the mechanical calculation rules.

In the preceding section, we focused on the treatment of isolated capital asset transactions that produced short-term or long-term capital gain or loss. In reality, of course, a taxpayer might have a single capital asset transaction in a given taxable year, but it is equally if not more likely that a taxpayer will have capital asset transactions resulting in a mixture of short-term capital gains, long-term capital losses, short-term capital losses, and long-term capital gains. Rather than focusing rigidly on each and every transaction, Congress expects taxpayers to report net or final results. Its approach is to use defined terms. For example, under § 1222(5), *net short-term capital gain* is defined as "the excess of short-term capital gains for the taxable year over the short-term capital losses for the taxable year." Thus, if a taxpayer has a short-term capital gain of $10 and a short-term capital loss of $4 during the same taxable year, Congress expects the taxpayer merely to report a *net* short-term capital *gain* of $6. Other defined terms operate in a similar manner. Necessarily, at the outset, Congress provides basic definitions for short-term capital gain, short-term capital loss, long-term capital gain, and long-term capital loss. From there, it defines other terms, many of which require netting. First, short-term capital gains and losses are netted against each other. In the end, a net short-term capital gain or a net short-term capital loss may result. In Exhibit 19.1, we get a net short-term capital gain.

EXHIBIT 19.1 **Netting of Short-Term Capital Gains and Losses**

Short-Term Capital Gains	Short-Term Capital Losses
$10,000	$8,000
$15,000	$7,000
Total Gains: $25,000	Total Losses: $15,000
Net Short-Term Capital Gain = $10,000	

Next, long-term capital gains and losses are netted against each other. In the end, a net long-term capital gain or a net long-term capital loss may result.

EXHIBIT 19.2 **Netting of Long-Term Capital Gains and Losses**

Long-Term Capital Gains	Long-Term Capital Losses
$10,000	$18,000
$15,000	$17,000
Total Gains: $25,000	Total Losses: $35,000
Net Long-Term Capital Loss = $10,000	

Finally, ascertaining the dollar amount corresponding to certain defined terms requires computations involving both short-term and long-term capital transaction amounts. For example, we accept the general notion that long-term capital gains get preferential tax treatment, but now, we have to cultivate a more precise understanding of the governing rules. If we look at the preferential rate provision in § 1(h)(1), it actually refers to net capital gain. Accordingly, Congress is not merely preferring a taxpayer's long-term capital gains or even their net long-term capital gains, but something quite specific, "net capital gain." Technically, preferential rates apply to a taxpayer only with respect to their *net capital gain*, which is defined under § 1222(11) as "the excess of the net long-term capital gain for the taxable year over the net short-term capital loss for such year." The following exhibits (both Exhibits 19.3 and 19.4) demonstrate how such an amount can ultimately result from a mix of capital asset transactions.

> ## Treatment of Qualified Dividend Income
>
> Under the appropriate circumstances, certain dividends are taxed at preferential rates. Section 1(h)(11) generally provides that net capital gain includes qualified dividend income. If a taxpayer does not hold the associated stock for a sufficient time period relative to the stock's **ex-dividend date** (i.e., the first day on which purchasers of the stock will *not* receive the subject dividend), the dividends will not constitute qualified dividend income. *See generally* §§ 1(h)(11)(A).

EXHIBIT 19.3 **Determining Net Capital Gain**

Short-Term Capital Transactions		Long-Term Capital Transactions	
Short-Term Capital Gains:	$10,000	Long-Term Capital Gains:	$28,000
Short-Term Capital Losses:	$15,000	Long-Term Capital Losses:	$12,000
Net Short-Term Capital Loss:	$5,000	Net Long-Term Capital Gain:	$16,000
	Net Capital Gain = $11,000		

In Exhibit 19.4, we arrive at a net capital gain of $16,000 even when we get a net short-term capital *gain*. How? Under that scenario, a *net* short-term capital loss amount simply does not exist, so we assign it a value of $0. Accordingly, the net capital gain is $16,000, because that is the excess of the net long-term capital gain ($16,000) over the net short-term capital loss ($0). The net capital gain of $16,000 will be taxed at preferential rates, and the net *short*-term capital gain of $7,000 will be taxed at ordinary income tax rates.

EXHIBIT 19.4 **Determining Net Capital Gain**

Short-Term Capital Transactions		Long-Term Capital Transactions	
Short-Term Capital Gains:	$15,000	Long-Term Capital Gains:	$28,000
Short-Term Capital Losses:	$8,000	Long-Term Capital Losses:	$12,000
Net Short-Term Capital Gain:	$7,000	Net Long-Term Capital Gain:	$16,000
	Net Capital Gain = $16,000		

D. TREATMENT OF CAPITAL GAINS

As was noted previously, not all gains from capital asset transactions enjoy preferential tax treatment. Short-term capital gains are taxed at ordinary income tax rates, and long-term capital gains generally qualify for taxation at preferential rates. More precisely, preferential tax rates apply only to a taxpayer's net capital gain, and even then, under § 1(h)(1), different net capital gains may be taxed at different preferential rates (i.e., 0 percent, 10 percent, 15 percent, 20 percent, 25 percent, and 28 percent). The larger netting process can produce final net gains in several different contexts. In Exhibits 19.5, 19.6, and 19.7, we consider three different scenarios and the treatment of the resulting gains.

EXHIBIT 19.5 Determining Capital Gain Net Income

Short-Term Capital Transactions		Long-Term Capital Transactions	
Short-Term Gains:	$800	Long-Term Gains:	$500
Short-Term Losses:	$200	Long-Term Losses:	$800
Net Short-Term Capital Gain:	$600	Net Long-Term Capital Loss:	$300

Capital Gain Net Income = $300

Tax Treatment: In this situation, net short-term gain exceeds net long-term loss. Thus, net gain dominates. In definitional terms, we cannot say that we have net short-term capital gain of $300, because of that defined amount we actually have $600. For this situation, Congress defines the amount by which total capital gains ($1,300) exceed total capital losses ($1,000) as *capital gain net income.* See § 1222(9). No portion of this amount qualifies for preferential tax rates. Instead, ordinary income tax rates apply to the entire amount.

EXHIBIT 19.6 Determining Net Capital Gain

Short-Term Capital Transactions		Long-Term Capital Transactions	
Short-Term Gains:	$400	Long-Term Gains:	$900
Short-Term Losses:	$500	Long-Term Losses:	$600
Net Short-Term Capital Loss:	$100	Net Long-Term Capital Gain:	$300

Net Capital Gain = $200

Tax Treatment: In this situation, net long-term capital gain exceeds net short-term capital loss. By statutory definition under § 1222(11), we have net capital gain, *and this amount qualifies for preferential treatment under § 1(h).* One could also say that we have capital gain net income of $200 (i.e., $1,300 − $1,100). In this scenario, all capital gain net income is simultaneously net capital gain, but preferential tax treatment follows only because we have net capital gain.

EXHIBIT 19.7 **Determining Capital Gain Net Income and Net Capital Gain**

Short-Term Capital Transactions		Long-Term Capital Transactions	
Short-Term Gains:	$400	Long-Term Gains:	$900
Short-Term Losses:	$200	Long-Term Losses:	$600
Net Short-Term Capital Gain:	$200	Net Long-Term Capital Gain:	$300

Capital Gain Net Income = $500; Net Capital Gain = $300

Tax Treatment: In this situation, we have capital gain net income of $500 (i.e., $1,300 – $800), but of this total amount, we have net capital gain of $300 because net long-term gains ($300) exceed net short-term losses ($0). Accordingly, the $300 of net capital gain qualifies for preferential tax treatment, while the remaining $200 of capital gain net income does not; it is taxed at ordinary income rates.

E. TREATMENT OF CAPITAL LOSSES

Compared to the treatment of capital gains, the treatment of capital losses is slightly more complicated. We know, at this juncture, that capital losses can offset capital gains, but we also know that to the extent taxpayers have total capital losses exceeding total capital gains, they can use a limited amount of such losses to offset ordinary income. Any losses remaining after the latter offset must be carried over as capital losses to a subsequent taxable year. Sections 1211 and 1212 are the governing provisions. Section 1211(b) generally provides that with respect to capital losses, noncorporate taxpayers may use them to offset capital gains and, assuming capital losses exceed capital gains, to offset a limited amount of ordinary income. But remember that Congress needs to ensure the collection of healthy amounts of revenue, so Congress does not allow taxpayers to offset all ordinary income from a taxable year with capital losses they realized. An annual ordinary-income-offset limit applies, and it is the *lower* of either (1) the actual amount by which total capital losses exceed total capital gains, or (2) $3,000. The operation of this rule is demonstrated by Exhibits 19.8 and 19.9.

EXHIBIT 19.8 **Treatment of Capital Losses (Situation #1)**

Ordinary Income	Short-Term Capital Transactions		Long-Term Capital Transactions	
$85,000	Short-Term Gains:	$4,000	Long-Term Gains:	$9,000
	Short-Term Losses:	$9,000	Long-Term Losses:	$6,000
	Net Short-Term Capital Loss:	$5,000	Net Long-Term Capital Gain:	$3,000

Excess of Total Capital Losses over Total Capital Gains = $2,000

Tax Treatment: Total capital losses ($15,000) exceed total capital gains ($13,000) by $2,000. The taxpayer may use this $2,000 capital loss excess as a deduction offsetting ordinary income, reducing it to $83,000.

EXHIBIT 19.9   Treatment of Capital Losses (Situation #2)

Ordinary Income	Short-Term Capital Transactions		Long-Term Capital Transactions	
$85,000	Short-Term Gains:	$ 4,000	Long-Term Gains:	$9,000
	Short-Term Losses:	$10,000	Long-Term Losses:	$7,000
	Net Short-Term Capital Loss:	$ 6,000	Net Long-Term Capital Gain:	$2,000

Excess of Total Capital Losses over Total Capital Gains = $4,000

Tax Treatment: Total capital losses ($17,000) exceed total capital gains ($13,000) by $4,000. The taxpayer may use $3,000 of the capital losses excess as a deduction offsetting ordinary income, reducing it to $82,000. Section 1212 will govern the precise character of the $1,000 of capital loss excess not used in the current tax year and carried over to the next taxable year.

The rules set forth in § 1212 govern not only the amount of capital loss carryover but also its precise character (i.e., short-term capital loss or long-term capital loss). Logically enough, the basic rule under § 1212(b)(1) operates on the assumption that capital losses exceed the amount allowed under § 1211. Technically, then, this excess is defined as a *net capital loss* under § 1222(10) (i.e., "the excess of the losses from sales or exchanges of capital assets over the sum allowed under § 1211").

Determining the precise character of the capital loss carryover is simple, but there is a twist. The carryover will be short term (in the next tax year) to the extent that in the current year net short-term capital loss exceeds net long-term capital gain. *See* § 1212(b)(1)(A). The carryover will be long term (in the next tax year) to the extent that in the current year net long-term capital loss exceeds net short-term capital gain. *See* § 1212(b)(1)(B). But, here's the twist. In performing the calculations under § 1212(b)(1)(A) or (B) to determine the precise character of the capital loss carryover, *one must treat the ordinary income offset amount (i.e., the § 1211(b) amount) as a short-term capital gain for the current year.* One could be forced to use "adjusted taxable income" if that amount is lower, but for the sake of simplicity we will ignore that possibility and focus on the ordinary income offset amount. Exhibits 19.10 and 19.11 demonstrate the operation of these rules. We start with familiar standard calculations.

EXHIBIT 19.10   Standard Capital Transaction Calculations

Short-Term Capital Transactions		Long-Term Capital Transactions	
Short-Term Capital Gains:	$ 8,000	Long-Term Capital Gains:	$7,000
Short-Term Capital Losses:	$15,000	Long-Term Capital Losses:	$6,000
Net Short-Term Capital Loss:	$7,000	Net Long-Term Capital Gain:	$1,000

Excess of Total Capital Losses over Total Capital Gains = $6,000

Tax Treatment: Total capital losses ($21,000) exceed total capital gains ($15,000) by $6,000. The taxpayer may use $3,000 of the capital loss excess as a deduction offsetting ordinary income. Section 1212 will govern the precise character of the remaining $3,000 capital loss to be carried over. *See* Exhibit 19.11.

And now, *solely* for the purpose of determining the precise character of the capital loss carryover, we recompute, treating the ordinary income offset as a new short-term capital gain.

EXHIBIT 19.11   Capital Transaction Calculations <u>with Deemed Short-Term Gain</u>

Short-Term Capital Transactions	Long-Term Capital Transactions	
S.T.C.G.: $8,000 + <u>$3,000</u> = $11,000	L.T.C.G.:	$7,000
S.T.C.L.: $15,000	L.T.C.L.:	$6,000
Net Short-Term Capital Loss: $4,000	Net Long-Term Capital Gain: $1,000	

Excess of Net Short-Term Capital Loss over Net Long-Term Capital Gain = $3,000

Tax Treatment: Per § 1212(b)(1)(A), the $3,000 excess of the net short-term capital loss over net long-term capital gain will constitute a short-term capital loss in the subsequent taxable year.

With the essentials in hand, consider an additional possibility as reflected in Exhibits 19.12 and 19.13.

EXHIBIT 19.12   Standard Capital Transaction Calculations

Short-Term Capital Transactions	Long-Term Capital Transactions	
S.T.C.G.:	$8,000	L.T.C.G.:	$ 3,000
S.T.C.L.:	$10,000	L.T.C.L.:	$10,000
Net Short-Term Capital Loss: $2,000	Net Long-Term Capital Loss: $7,000	

Excess of Total Capital Losses over Total Capital Gains = $9,000

Tax Treatment: Total capital losses ($20,000) exceed total capital gains ($11,000) by $9,000. The taxpayer may use $3,000 of the capital loss excess as a deduction offsetting ordinary income. Section 1212 will govern the precise character of the $6,000 capital loss to be carried over. *See* Exhibit 19.14.

EXHIBIT 19.13   Capital Transaction Calculations <u>with Deemed Short-Term Gain</u>

Short-Term Capital Transactions	Long-Term Capital Transactions	
S.T.C.G.: $8,000 + <u>$3,000</u> = $11,000	L.T.C.G.:	$3,000
S.T.C.L.: $10,000	L.T.C.L.:	$10,000
Net Short-Term Capital Gain: $1,000	Net Long-Term Capital Loss: $7,000	

Excess of Net Long-Term Capital Loss over Net Short-Term Capital Gain = $6,000

Tax Treatment: Per § 1212(b)(1)(B), the $6,000 excess of the net long-term capital loss over net short-term capital gain will constitute a long-term capital loss in the subsequent taxable year.

Is it possible to have a carryover of both a short-term capital loss and a long-term capital loss? Yes. *See* Exhibits 19.14 and 19.15.

EXHIBIT 19.14 **Standard Capital Transaction Calculations**

Short-Term Capital Transactions		Long-Term Capital Transactions	
S.T.C.G.:	$8,000	L.T.C.G.:	$3,000
S.T.C.L.:	$17,000	L.T.C.L.:	$10,000
Net Short-Term Capital Loss: $9,000		Net Long-Term Capital Loss: $7,000	

Excess of Total Capital Losses over Total Capital Gains = $16,000

Tax Treatment. Total capital losses ($27,000) exceed total capital gains ($11,000) by $16,000. The taxpayer may use $3,000 of the capital loss excess as a deduction offsetting ordinary income. Section 1212 will govern the precise character of the $13,000 capital loss to be carried over. *See* Exhibit 19.15.

EXHIBIT 19.15 **Capital Transaction Calculations with Deemed Short-Term Gain**

Short-Term Capital Transactions		Long-Term Capital Transactions	
S.T.C.G.: $8,000 + $3,000 = $11,000		L.T.C.G.:	$3,000
S.T.C.L.:	$17,000	L.T.C.L.:	$10,000
Net Short-Term Capital Loss: $6,000		Net Long-Term Capital Loss: $7,000	

Excess of Net Short-Term Capital Loss over Net Long-Term Capital Gain ($0) = $6,000
Excess of Net Long-Term Capital Loss over Net Short-Term Capital Gain ($0) = $7,000

Tax Treatment. Per § 1212(b)(1)(A), the excess of the net short-term capital loss ($6,000) over net short-term capital gain ($0) will constitute a short-term capital loss in the subsequent taxable year. Per § 1212(b)(1)(B), the excess of the net long-term capital loss ($7,000) over the net short-term capital gain ($0) will be a long-term capital loss in the subsequent taxable year.

Section 1231(b) Property

"Property used in the trade or business" is defined under § 1231(b) and includes the following (assuming, in both instances, that the property is neither inventory nor property held primarily for sale to customers in the ordinary course of business and avoids other statutory categories):

- Property used in in the trade or business that is depreciable under § 167 and has been *held for more than one year*; and
- Real property used in the trade or business that has been *held for more than one year.*

F. SPECIAL RULES REGARDING GAIN OR LOSS CHARACTER

1. Section 1231 Gain and Loss

In general, the rules defining capital gains and losses reside in §1222, and as we have just seen, related rules in the Code govern the basic treatment and use of those items (e.g., §§ 1, 61, 1211, and 1212). We turn to and explore § 1231 and other pertinent provisions at this juncture because they can have an impact on the character and amount of specific gains and losses recognized with respect to certain taxpayer property in a particular taxable year.

Although § 1231 affects certain capital assets held in connection with a trade or business or a transaction entered into for profit, the provision also affects property used in the taxpayer's trade or business that would fall outside § 1221's definition of "capital asset." Accordingly, under normal circumstances, a sale or exchange with respect to the latter category of property would generate either ordinary losses or ordinary gains as the case may be. As you might suspect, the specter of recognizing ordinary gain on the disposition of business property might have an associated lock-in effect, even though the economy as a whole might benefit from the enhanced mobility of such business assets. Section 1231 creates a taxpayer-friendly statutory regime that

> **"Compulsory or Involuntary Conversion"**
>
> Section 1231(a)(3)(A)(ii) refers to compulsory or involuntary conversions resulting from destruction (in whole or in part), theft, seizure, or an exercise of the power of requisition or condemnation or the threat or imminence thereof).

carefully but effectively greases the wheels of commerce in this context by altering the default *character* of the gain or loss recognized on the occurrence of specific events with respect to certain business assets.

In general, items affected by § 1231 fall into the following two basic categories:

- "Property used in the trade or business" that (by definition under § 1231(b)) has been held for more than one year; and
- Capital assets (held for more than one year) that are held in connection with a trade or business or in connection with a transaction entered into for profit.

Section 1231 steps in to govern the character of gain or loss recognized when the following transactions or events occur with respect to § 1231 property:

- The sale or exchange of property used in the trade or business;
- The compulsory or involuntary conversion (into property or money) of property used in the trade or business; and
- The compulsory or involuntary conversion (into property or money) of any capital asset held for more than one year and held in connection with a trade or business or a transaction entered into for profit.

See generally § 1231(a)(3).

When these events occur, they are likely to produce a mix of § 1231 gains and § 1231 losses. The final character of those gains or losses turns on whether recognized § 1231 gains or recognized § 1231 losses predominate in a given taxable year. If a taxpayer's § 1231 gains exceed § 1231 losses for a given taxable year, then all of such gains and losses are to be characterized as long-term capital gains or long-term capital losses. *See* § 1231(a)(1). But if the taxpayer's § 1231 losses exceed § 1231 gains for a given taxable year, then such gains or losses are *not* to be treated as gains or losses from the sale of capital assets. *See* § 1231(a)(2). To simplify, gain dominance will result in long-term *capital* gains, but loss dominance will result in *ordinary* losses. Thus, section 1231 has the power to transform what would have been an ordinary gain into a tax-favored long-term capital gain while at the same time transforming what would have been a tax-restricted capital loss into an ordinary loss.

The operation of the general rules in § 1231(a)(1) and (2) are subject to the special rules set forth in § 1231(a)(4). Section 1231(a)(4)(A) clarifies that in determining whether § 1231 gains or losses predominate, the taxpayer is to include § 1231 gains only if and to the extent they are taken into account in computing gross income and to include § 1231 losses only if and to the extent they are taken into account in computing taxable income, except that § 1211 (which restricts loss allowances) is deemed inapplicable. Section 1231(a)(4)(B) requires that losses resulting from the destruction (total or partial), theft, seizure, requisition, or condemnation of § 1231 property be treated as a loss from a compulsory or involuntary conversion. The rule in § 1231(a)(4)(C) bears special significance because it works to remove certain items from § 1231(a) altogether (i.e., they are not taken into account in assessing § 1231 gain or loss predominance). Although the involuntary conversion of erstwhile § 1231 property due to fire, storm, shipwreck, or other casualty or from theft would ordinarily be taken into account under § 1231(a), such conversion events are not to be taken into account under that provision *IF* during the taxable year the recognized losses from such conversions exceed the recognized gains from such conversions. Thus, the character of the gains and losses resulting from such conversions will not be affected by § 1231(a) under those specific facts.

2. Recapture of Net Ordinary Losses Under § 1231(c)

If you think a world of long-term capital gains and ordinary losses for all time sounds a bit too good to be true in every instance, you're right. After all, if a taxpayer has a multiyear string of *ordinary* losses as a result of § 1231's operation, should he be able to treat his next-arriving § 1231 gain as *capital* in nature? Or should he be forced to somehow make up for all those ordinary losses by treating what might have been a § 1231 long-term capital gain as ordinary, at least until things balance out in a sense? Congress says "yes" to the latter. When this happens, the taxpayer is said to "recapture" the ordinary losses. Fortunately, the taxpayer need not search back for net § 1231 losses in perpetuity. Under the Code, the taxpayer must search back through the five preceding taxable years for nonrecaptured net § 1231 losses before proceeding to treat a net § 1231 gain as capital in nature. *See* § 1231(c). Let's consider a simple example.

Example 5

In 2017, Shira's § 1231 losses of $4,000 exceeded her § 1231 gains of $3,000. As a result, such gains and losses were not treated as capital, and Shira had a net § 1231 loss of $1,000, which was ordinary in character. In 2018, Shira's § 1231 gains of $5,000 exceeded her § 1231 losses of $2,000. Because she had $1,000 of nonrecaptured net § 1231 loss (from 2017), she must treat $1,000 of her net § 1231 gain from 2018 as ordinary income, and she may treat the remaining $2,000 as long-term capital gain.

3. Section 1245 and Depreciation Recapture; *Arrowsmith* Doctrine

Section 1245 operates, to some extent, in a manner similar to § 1231 in terms of altering character, but its focus is on prior depreciation deductions taken by the taxpayer. Section 1231 creates the possibility that the sale or exchange of certain depreciable property can result in the recognition of capital gain. Bear in mind, however, that a taxpayer's prior depreciation deductions with respect to a tangible wasting asset have been taken against the taxpayer's ordinary income over time. Even if § 1231 makes it possible for gain realized with respect to depreciable business property to be characterized as long-term capital gain, section 1245 halts § 1231 long enough to recapture (as ordinary income) an amount equal to prior depreciation taken with respect to the asset. *See generally* § 1245. Consider the following example, while assuming that no § 1231 losses occurred in the current or prior taxable years.

Example 6

Carlos owns and operates a grocery store. Several years ago, he purchased an industrial-sized freezer for $500,000 for the business. The freezer is a tangible, wasting asset subject to depreciation, and Carlos now has an adjusted basis in the freezer of $375,000. If Carlos sells the freezer for $510,000, he will realize a gain of $135,000. Although § 1231 would ordinarily dictate that this amount be characterized as long-term capital gain, § 1245 takes precedence. *See* § 1245(d). Of the total gain realized, the taxpayer must treat $125,000 as ordinary income. Per § 1231, he may treat the remaining $10,000 as long-term capital gain.

Although Example 6 demonstrates § 1245's operation under specific facts, the statutory provisions necessarily anticipate various situations in which recapture of prior allowances (e.g., depreciation or amortization) as ordinary income might be necessary. Exhibit 19.16 depicts the general rule visually.

EXHIBIT 19.16   **Visual Depiction of General Rule in § 1245(a)**

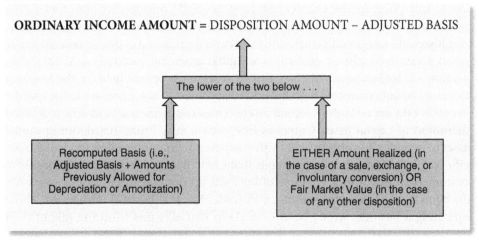

ORDINARY INCOME AMOUNT = DISPOSITION AMOUNT – ADJUSTED BASIS

The lower of the two below . . .

Recomputed Basis (i.e., Adjusted Basis + Amounts Previously Allowed for Depreciation or Amortization)

EITHER Amount Realized (in the case of a sale, exchange, or involuntary conversion) OR Fair Market Value (in the case of any other disposition)

In Example 6, we see that the recomputed basis was $500,000 ($375,000 + $125,000). Carlos's amount realized (and the fair market value of the asset) was $510,000. Thus, the Disposition Amount was $500,000, and the amount of depreciation recaptured as ordinary income was $125,000 (i.e., $500,000 – $375,000). Section 1231 operated to characterize the remaining $10,000 of gain as long-term capital gain.

> **Note**
>
> Section 1245 may operate, in many instances, to require the recapture of prior depreciation or amortization as ordinary income, but the provision does not apply in every situation. Section 1245(a) does not apply to dispositions by gift, nor does it generally apply to transfers at death. For additional exceptions and limitations, see § 1245(b).

Alongside statutory provisions aimed at what one might loosely term character mismatches, we also find corresponding judicial doctrines. The so-called *Arrowsmith* doctrine comes to us from *Arrowsmith v. Commissioner*, 344 U.S. 6 (1952). In that decision, shareholders received final liquidating distributions from a corporation. As a result, they were treated as though that had simply sold their stock, and capital gain treatment followed. In a subsequent taxable year, however, the shareholders were required to pay a judgment rendered against the former corporation. Although the taxpayers treated the subsequent payment as an ordinary loss, the Court ultimately held that the current loss was to be coordinated with the prior capital gain. Accordingly, the taxpayers were unable to take an ordinary loss with respect to the payment, being required, instead, to treat it as a capital loss.

G. DEFINITION OF "CAPITAL ASSET"

Up to this point in the chapter, we have devoted considerable attention to the mechanical calculation rules applicable to short-term and long-term capital gains and losses. As was noted earlier, however, capital gains and capital losses only arise when a taxpayer sells or exchanges a capital asset. *See generally* § 1222(1)–(4). Section 1221(a) generally defines *capital asset* as "property held by the taxpayer (whether or not connected with his trade or business)," but it goes on to list specific items that do *not* constitute capital assets. Thus, rather than articulating a detailed definition of capital asset, Congress first casts a very broad net defining capital asset to include all property held by the taxpayer before proceeding to identify specific items as noncapital. For example, items held by taxpayers primarily for sale to customers in the ordinary course of business do not constitute capital assets nor do items held as inventory or stock in trade. *See* § 1221(a)(1). Otherwise, those operating a business would be able to claim that all gains from the sale of their merchandise was capital in nature. Congress also defines "capital asset" to exclude other items used or acquired in a taxpayer's trade or business (e.g., depreciable property, real property, supplies regularly used or consumed, and accounts or notes receivable arising from providing services or selling inventory or other merchandise). *See* § 1221(a)(2) and (8). In many instances, determining whether a taxpayer holds property as inventory or merchandise for sale to customers presents no difficulty, but from time to time issues can arise in this context, and as we know from prior discussion, the character of gain or loss may have considerable ramifications with respect to its treatment under the mechanical rules.

Case Preview

David Taylor Enterprises, Inc. v. Commissioner

Prior to his sudden death, David Taylor, Sr. ("Taylor") was the sole shareholder of David Taylor Enterprises, Inc. The company operated several automobile dealerships and generally sold new, used, and classic cars. In the immediate aftermath of Taylor's death, the company sold a large number of classic cars, and although one might readily conclude that such a sale was simply a sale of inventory in the ordinary course of the company's business (rather than the sale of capital assets), Taylor's long-time love of classic cars gave rise to an issue as to whether the classic cars held by the dealership constituted true inventory or simply property held by the dealership, albeit not primarily for sale to customers. Consider the following questions as you make your way through the case:

1. Did the taxpayer hold the classic cars and the other vehicles in the same facility? Did that factor influence the characterization analysis?
2. What factors did the court use in making its determinations?
3. Why did the taxpayer dispose of a large volume of classic cars in a short time period? Does that factor influence the court's characterization analysis?

David Taylor Enterprises, Inc. v. Commissioner
T.C. Memo. 2005-127

KROUPA, J.

Respondent determined deficiencies of $431,114 for 1999 and $113,390 for 2000 in petitioner's Federal income taxes. The issue to be decided is whether losses realized on the sale of classic cars during the years at issue are capital or ordinary losses under section 1221(a). Resolution of this issue depends on whether the classic cars were held primarily for sale to customers in the ordinary course of business or were held instead for investment purposes. We hold that petitioner held the classic cars for sale to customers.

FINDINGS OF FACT

The parties have stipulated some facts. The stipulation of facts and accompanying exhibits are incorporated by this reference and are so found.

David Taylor Enterprises

Petitioner is an affiliated group of corporations that files consolidated income tax returns. The common parent of the affiliated group is David Taylor Enterprises, Inc. (DTE). Until his death, David Taylor, Sr. (Mr. Taylor) owned all the shares of DTE. DTE's principal place of business was Houston, Texas, at the time it filed the petition.

David Taylor Cadillac

Cars were Mr. Taylor's love and passion, and he was involved in the car business throughout his life. When he was a child, Mr. Taylor's father was an Oldsmobile–Cadillac dealer in Port Arthur, Texas. From 1975 until his untimely death in 1997, Mr. Taylor was a car dealer and engaged in the trade or business of selling cars. ***

In 1974, Mr. Taylor sold a Buick Dealership in Beaumont, Texas, and a year later acquired the right from General Motors to open a Cadillac dealership in Houston, Texas, known as David Taylor Cadillac (the dealership). The dealership was one of the largest Cadillac dealers in the world, and was, at the time of trial, a subsidiary of petitioner. The dealership is the main focus of our case.

The dealership owned new, used, and classic cars. The new and used cars were located in Houston, Texas, while the classic cars were located in Galveston, Texas.

Classic Cars

The dealership began to acquire classic cars in 1979. Initially, the dealership purchased a 1931 Cadillac Roadster for $40,000. The dealership then purchased two classic cars in the mid–1980s, a 1934 Ford Roadster and a 1932 Ford Victoria, that came as kits and required assemblage. After the initial purchases, the dealership acquired additional classic cars, either by purchase, exchange of one classic car for another, or as trade-ins from new car customers to reduce the purchase price of a new Cadillac or Buick. The dealership's purpose in acquiring the classic cars was to enhance their value by restoring them and selling them at a premium price.

The dealership viewed potential buyers of the classic cars as a select group of mostly wealthy classic car enthusiasts, and designed a strategy to reach them. The dealership's strategy involved building the dealership's reputation as a source of high quality classic cars by entering the cars in auctions, auto shows, classic car competitions, and displaying them at promotional events for the dealership or third parties. For instance, the classic cars were displayed at events frequented by wealthy individuals, like the Alley Theatre and the annual Lakewood Yacht Club Wooden Keels and Classic Wheels event. The classic cars were also prominently advertised in brochures, booklets, newspapers, and magazine articles, and a placard describing each car was also placed on each vehicle.

Potential buyers of the classic cars were directed to Mr. Taylor or a broker the dealership hired after Mr. Taylor died. Until his death, Mr. Taylor personally negotiated the sales of the classic cars.

To command a premium price for the classic cars, a priority for the dealership and Mr. Taylor, the classic cars had to be restored to classic condition, maintained, and driveable at any time by potential customers. Restoring the cars involved a long process of fundamentally rebuilding the car to near perfection. After the cars were fully restored, the dealership carefully maintained them by setting the cars on jack stands so the tires maintained air pressure, starting the engines every 6 weeks, and changing the oil every 6 months.

In addition, the dealership kept the classic cars indoors to protect them from inclement weather. Initially, the classic cars were kept at the dealership or in Mr. Taylor's garage, and later were moved to a building the dealership bought that was located across the street from its main showroom. The cars were eventually moved to three adjacent buildings in Galveston, Texas (the Galveston property) that the dealership purchased to provide the classic cars with a climate-controlled environment and to expose them to the public.

The dealership intended to recoup its costs of restoring the classic cars by selling them at a profit. In 1990, the dealership sold a Packard convertible for $330,000, earning a profit of $143,340. The dealership made three more sales that year, and three in the succeeding year. The dealership thereafter strategically began acquiring more classic cars and increasing its participation in promotional events to generate interest, win competitions, and service the wealthy clientele the dealership hoped would follow. This plan was abruptly derailed in 1997 when Mr. Taylor died, within a month of being diagnosed with lung cancer.

Mr. Taylor's shares in the dealership represented most of the value of his estate. To raise money for the estate tax, Mr. Taylor's estate requested a liquidation of the DTE shares [Author Note: His estate asked that the corporation, the taxpayer here, purchase Mr. Taylor's shares.] [The taxpayer agreed to do so] and resolved to sell the classic cars to raise the necessary capital. The dealership hired a broker and sold approximately 69 classic cars during 1999 and 2000, the years at issue.

The dealership accounted for the new, used, and classic cars consistently. Every car was treated as inventory and assigned an individual stock number. Costs associated with the purchase and restoration of the classic cars were posted to the car's stock number, which allowed a running total of the dealership's cost basis in each car. The dealership did not deduct any costs as they were incurred, nor did the dealership depreciate any of the cars. No part of the dealership's cost basis in any classic car was recognized except when the car was sold or disposed of. The dealership included the sales price of the car, whether new, used, or classic, in the dealership's gross receipts and included all accumulated costs of each specific car in the costs of goods sold.

Whenever a car was sold, whether new, used, or classic, the dealership reported the gain or loss on the sale at ordinary income rates. For all years prior to the years at issue, the dealership reported sales on 11 classic cars at ordinary income rates. During the years at issue, the dealership reported sales on 69 cars, also at ordinary income rates.

Petitioner timely filed its Forms 1120, U.S. Corporation Income Tax Return, for 1999 and 2000, reporting the losses at issue. Upon examination of those returns,

[handwritten margin note: Commissioner's way]

[handwritten margin note: Taxpayer's]

respondent issued a Notice of Deficiency to petitioner on February 25, 2003, determining that the classic cars were held for investment purposes and should be accorded capital loss treatment, not ordinary loss.

Petitioner filed a petition contesting respondent's determination and argued that the classic cars were held for sale and should be accorded ordinary income treatment. We must therefore determine whether the losses from the sales of the classic cars are ordinary or capital losses.

OPINION

We are asked to decide whether the dealership held the classic cars for investment or for sale. If the dealership held the classic cars as capital assets for investment, then we must sustain respondent's determination. Conversely, if the dealership held the classic cars for sale to customers, then we must find for petitioner. We begin with who has the burden of proof.

A. Burden of Proof

[handwritten margin note: Burden of proof]

The Commissioner's determination in the notice of deficiency is generally presumed to be correct, and the taxpayer bears the burden of proving otherwise. If a taxpayer introduces credible evidence with respect to a factual issue relevant to ascertaining the taxpayer's tax liability, however, the burden shifts to the Commissioner with respect to that issue, assuming the taxpayer meets certain other requirements. Sec. 7491(a)(1). The burden of proof does not shift unless the taxpayer has complied with the substantiation requirements, maintained required records, and cooperated with the Commissioner's reasonable requests for witnesses, information, and meetings. Sec. 7491(a)(2)(A) and (B). The taxpayer has the burden of establishing that each requirement of section 7491(a)(2) has been met. Respondent concedes that petitioner has met the cooperation and substantiation requirements, but argues that petitioner has not met the credible evidence requirement. We disagree.

Credible evidence means the quality of evidence the Court would find sufficient upon which to base a decision on the issue if no contrary evidence were submitted.

[handwritten margin note: Court rules taxpayer offered enough evidence to shift burden to Commissioner]

Petitioner introduced evidence with respect to the factual issue in the case, through witness testimony and business records of the dealership, sufficient, in the absence of contrary evidence, to prove by a preponderance of the evidence that the classic cars were inventory held primarily for sale to customers in the ordinary course of business. Specifically, petitioner produced evidence that it advertised the classic cars for sale, sold a substantial number of classic cars, and consistently reported the sales at ordinary income rates and consistently treated the classic cars as inventory on its corporate books. We find this evidence credible as to the factual issue in dispute and thus sufficient to shift the burden to respondent under section 7491 to prove the classic cars were held as an investment and subject to capital treatment.

Williford Factors

Our Court generally uses a number of factors to determine whether property is held for investment or held for sale. See *Williford v. Commissioner,* T.C. Memo.

1992–450. In *Williford,* we examined whether a taxpayer's art collection was held primarily for sale to customers in the ordinary course of business. The taxpayer in *Williford* was a part-time art dealer and bought some paintings for resale and others for investment. The taxpayer kept separate his private art collection and the paintings for resale. The taxpayer classified the paintings in his private collection as capital assets and reported capital gains on the sale of these paintings. The Commissioner objected to the capital treatment, arguing that the taxpayer was an art dealer and derived the sales proceeds in the ordinary course of business. The Tax Court agreed with the taxpayer and held that the paintings were capital assets held for investment.

The Court used eight factors to analyze whether the art collection was held primarily for sale to customers in the ordinary course of the taxpayer's trade or business. The eight factors are: (1) Frequency and regularity of sales; (2) the substantiality of sales; (3) the duration the property was held; (4) the nature of the taxpayer's business and the extent to which the taxpayer segregated the collection from his or her business inventory; (5) the purpose for acquiring and holding the property before sale; (6) the extent of the taxpayer's sales efforts by advertising or otherwise; (7) the time and effort the taxpayer dedicated to the sales; and (8) how the sales proceeds were used. We apply these factors to determine whether the dealership held the classic cars for investment or for sale.

1. *Frequency and Regularity of Sales*

The frequency and regularity of sales are among the most important factors in determining whether an asset is held for investment or as inventory. The inference, generally, is that frequent sales serve as an indicium that the assets are being held for sale, while infrequent sales serve as an indicium that the assets are being held for investment.

Whether the number of sales was sufficiently frequent must be viewed in the context of the particular industry at issue. Respondent and petitioner have provided us with no caselaw concerning the sale of classic cars, or cars in general, but rather have highlighted cases concerning sales of real estate and artwork. Each case turned on the unique facts at issue, and we can discern no standard from the caselaw to apply here. We therefore view the frequency of sales factor in the context of our own facts and apply no standardized test to determine whether the sales were sufficiently frequent.

Petitioner sold 80 cars over approximately 12 years. The parties focus on different time periods to support their arguments. Petitioner focuses upon the higher number of sales in the years at issue to argue that the cars were held for sale as inventory. In contrast, respondent focuses upon the smaller number of sales between 1989 and 1998 to argue that the cars were held for investment purposes. The holding purpose inquiry begins at the time the property is acquired and spans the entire course of ownership.

We first note that sales increased in the years at issue for understandable reasons. Mr. Taylor died unexpectedly at age 60, and petitioner's board agreed to redeem the shares of DTE *** that Mr. Taylor owned before his death. The increase in sales does not negate a finding that the cars were previously held for sale. Petitioner explains that the dealership sold fewer classic cars in the earlier years because it was in the nascent phase of building inventory, restoring the cars, establishing a reputation, and publicizing the classic cars to potential clientele, but that the cars were nonetheless held for sale at all times. We found testimony for the dealership compelling, and find the total number of sales, 80 sales over 12 years, and 69 sales over the 2 years at issue, sufficiently frequent to support a finding that the classic cars were held for sale. This factor favors petitioner.

2. *Substantiality of Sales*

Courts generally view frequent sales generating substantial income as tending to show that property was held for sale rather than for investment. Where substantial profits result from capital appreciation, however, and not from the taxpayer's efforts, infrequent sales generating large profits tend to show that the property was held for investment.

While the cars in this case appreciated in value, most of the gains from the sales were due to the dealership's efforts in restoring and refurbishing the cars. Further, the dealership consistently sold the classic cars before the years at issue for a profit, with the exception of two sales. The dealership reported all sales at ordinary income rates, as it did for sales of new and used cars. This factor favors petitioner.

3. *Duration of Ownership*

Longer holding periods suggest an asset is held for investment. The Court in *Williford* found that holding periods of 19 years and 13 years served as indicia that the paintings were held for investment. The classic cars in this case were held 7 to 10 years. Of the classic cars sold prior to the years at issue, seven were held less than 2 years, one was held less than 4 years, and one was held less than 10 years. None of the classic cars were held for as long as the periods set forth in *Williford*.

Moreover, in *Williford*, the paintings did not require work akin to the extensive time and effort the dealership devoted to refurbishing and restoring the classic cars. The attendant length of ownership is therefore longer in the case of value-added classic cars. In comparison, the dealership's new and used cars were held shorter periods for readily apparent reasons. Respondent's argument comparing the shorter periods for the new and used cars vis-à-vis the classic cars, therefore, is not dispositive.

The value of the new and used cars, as petitioner explained, depreciated quickly, demanding quicker turnover. In contrast, the classic cars appreciated in value over time and, consequently, did not necessitate the same rapid turnover period. We find, therefore, that the holding period for the classic cars is consistent with finding the dealership held the classic cars for sale. This factor favors petitioner.

4. *Segregation of Classic Cars From New and Used Cars*

Property held for sale and property held for investment must be separately identified. This factor suggests property segregated from other property may indicate some assets are held for investment while others are held for sale.

In *Williford,* the Court found that the paintings held as inventory were kept in a location separate from those held for investment. While the classic cars were physically segregated from the new and used cars, we find the physical segregation of the cars of no moment. A dealership could have numerous physical locations. The fact remains that the classic cars were on display to the public at all times in contrast to the paintings the taxpayer held in his home that were not on display to the public. Moreover, the classic cars were held separately in buildings on the Galveston property because they required protection from the elements, unlike the new and used cars. ***

Overall, we do not find the segregation of the dealership's classic cars relevant to our determination whether they were for investment or for sale. We therefore find this factor neutral.

5. *Purpose of Acquisition*

This factor relates to whether the taxpayer intended to hold the property for sale or to hold the property for investment. *Williford v. Commissioner, supra.* Respondent argues that the dealership's application for "exhibition" license plates indicates that the dealership did not hold the classic cars for sale. Instead, respondent argues that the exhibition plates essentially meant the classic cars were not for sale. As petitioner countered, the exhibition plates did not restrict the cars from being sold but merely were a means of informing the public that the classic cars were at least 25 years old.

Respondent also argues that the dealership acquired the classic cars to hold them for investment because Mr. Taylor was "passionate" about cars in general and classic cars in particular. Testimony established that every classic car the dealership owned was acquired so it could be sold for a profit. We do not find it relevant whether Mr. Taylor was passionate about classic cars.

The dealership's accounting treatment of the classic cars was no different from the new or used cars. Each car, whether new, used, or classic, was assigned a stock inventory number. Any costs associated with the car were added to the basis of that car, and no depreciation or current deduction was claimed. The dealership reported each car sale, whether new, used, or classic, as a sale of inventory at ordinary income rates. That the dealership reported sales at ordinary income rates in the 10 years prior to the years at issue and consistently held the classic cars out to third parties as inventory bolsters its argument that its purpose was to hold the cars for sale.

Further, we cannot accept respondent's assertion that the primary holding purpose of the classic cars was merely to exhibit them as "museum pieces." We question whether the dealership would expend effort to acquire, rebuild, and maintain the classic cars if the purpose were merely to display them, stationary, at a museum. On the contrary, each car was rebuilt to near perfection, and the dealership maintained standards so that each car could be driveable at any time and therefore command the highest price. The dealership started the car engines every 6 weeks and changed the oil every 6 months to maintain them in driving condition. Designating the Galveston property as a museum made business sense as a means to gain exposure for the classic cars specifically and the dealership in general, and to cover overhead.

We found the testimony that the classic cars were acquired as inventory to be honest, forthright, and credible. This factor favors petitioner.

6. *Sales and Advertising Effort*

Sales and advertising efforts indicate the assets are held for sale, not investment. Respondent argues that the dealership did not advertise the classic cars for sale and compares the advertising strategies the dealership used to market the new and used cars with the less overt methods the dealership used to market the classic cars. Again, we find this analogy artificial. The holding period was shorter for new and used cars, and the advertising methods consequently more immediate. The dealership could be selective in its sales so long as its activity was consistent, overall, with its treatment of the classic cars as inventory for sale.

Petitioner argues that the dealership used various advertising methods to market the classic cars for sale. These included entering the cars in auctions and auto shows, displaying the cars at numerous events frequented by wealthy individuals, hosting events at the Galveston property for wealthy car enthusiasts, designing and printing brochures featuring the cars, arranging for newspaper and magazine articles about the cars, displaying the cars at the dealership and promotional events, and publishing a large booklet on the cars. Personnel of the dealership testified that they referred serious inquiries regarding the classic cars to Mr. Taylor, or to a broker retained by the dealership after Mr. Taylor died. There was also testimony that Mr. Taylor was frequently on the Galveston property negotiating with interested buyers.

We find that the dealership always held the classic cars as inventory for sale. The dealership was merely more flexible regarding the classic car's price during the years at issue because of the immediate need for capital. In addition, we find that the dealership made efforts to advertise and sell the classic cars in years before those at issue. Mr. Taylor personally negotiated these sales, and he would often accompany potential customers on test drives of the cars. If a potential customer ever expressed an interest in a classic car, testimony established that personnel would direct the potential customer to Mr. Taylor or the broker appointed to sell the classic cars after Mr. Taylor's death.

Even though, as respondent contends, the dealership did not market the classic cars as it marketed the new and used cars, we find the record replete with evidence that the dealership held the classic cars as inventory for sale. Mr. Taylor frequently stated that every classic car was for sale. In fact, the dealership's general manager testified that Mr. Taylor said everything was for sale for the right price. Testimony also indicates that Mr. Taylor rejected a suggestion to form a foundation to own the classic cars. Mr. Taylor rejected the suggestion when he learned that the profits from selling the classic cars would go to the foundation rather than the dealership. Mr. Taylor wanted the profits to flow to the dealership. This factor favors petitioner.

7. *Time Devoted to Sales Activity*

That a taxpayer devotes little time or effort to the selling of assets may suggest that the assets are held for investment purposes. A taxpayer does not hold property for sale if the taxpayer did not initiate sales, advertise, have a sales office, or spend a great deal of time on the transactions.

We find that the dealership here devoted substantial time to the sales activity. *[substantial time spent]* This includes the time spent coordinating advertising and promotional events, and the time Mr. Taylor spent at classic car shows and auctions negotiating with potential customers, as well as the time the broker spent negotiating sales following Mr. Taylor's death. This factor favors petitioner.

C. Conclusion

The ultimate inquiry in this case is whether the classic cars were held primarily for sale. We find that they were. We find compelling the dealership's continuous and consistent treatment of the classic cars as held for sale. We also find testimony concerning the dealership's sales efforts credible and persuasive. From the date the dealership first acquired a classic car, the dealership has been in the business of selling cars. The dealership's classic cars were consistently treated for book purposes and tax purposes as held for sale. We surmise respondent now objects because of the ordinary losses generated by the sales in the years at issue. Respondent was apparently content to collect tax at ordinary income rates on gains from sales of the dealership's classic cars in prior years.

We have found that all of the pertinent factors favor petitioner or were neutral. The factors, however, are not dispositive, and each case must rest upon its own facts. The focus here is upon the statute, which excludes from capital asset treatment property held by the taxpayer primarily for sale to customers in the ordinary course of his or her trade or business.

Respondent had the burden to prove by a preponderance of the evidence that the classic cars were not held for sale. He did not meet that burden. We conclude that the dealership's classic cars were held for sale and hence qualify for an exception from capital asset status under section 1221(a)(1). Accordingly, we do not sustain respondent's determination.

Decision will be entered for petitioner.

Post-Case Follow-Up

Applying the *Williford* factors, the Tax Court concluded in this case that the taxpayer did not hold the classic cars as capital assets because they were held primarily for sale to customers. As basic inventory, the vehicles fell squarely within the capital asset exclusion of § 1221(a)(1). Having made its way carefully through each *Williford* factor, the court managed to introduce a modest ambiguity by noting that the *Williford* factors were not dispositive and that future decisions would turn on the unique facts and circumstances at hand. Even so, it is difficult to frown because a court opts to reserve a degree of flexibility with respect to future decisions.

The noncapital versus capital distinctions can be particularly difficult to make in some instances, and taxpayer-specific factors can prove crucial. Consider the case of traditional investments. A taxpayer may purchase and hold stock as a capital asset because he thinks the value of the stock will rise in the future. Similarly, he might think that oranges will be very scarce (and thus very expensive) in the future, and he might contract with a counterparty the right to buy oranges in the future at a price set today (i.e., he will hold a "futures" contract). If he is correct, and the price of oranges skyrockets, he can forego taking delivery of the oranges and simply sell the now-valuable contract at a profit to someone desperately in need of oranges (or willing to speculate further on the price of oranges). In that context, the futures contract is simply another form of capital asset, and its sale produces capital gain.

But what if that taxpayer was in the business of selling oranges (or orange juice) and needed some contractual insurance against a sudden spike in the cost of oranges? Is that futures contract still a speculation-fueled capital asset? Or is the nexus between the contract and the buyer's core businesses so tight that the contract should be viewed as a much-needed, insurance-type business asset (the sale of which would produce ordinary income or loss)? In *Corn Products Refining Co. v. Commissioner*, 350 U.S. 46 (1955), the taxpayer purchased corn futures contracts and, depending on market conditions and its needs, either sold the contract or took delivery of the corn. Rejecting the taxpayer's argument that its sale of futures contracts produced capital gains and losses, the Court reasoned that in light of the taxpayer's business purpose in purchasing the contracts (to protect itself from price spikes), the futures contracts should be classified as business assets and not capital assets in the nature of investments. Accordingly, sale of the contracts resulted in ordinary gains or losses. The taxpayer in *Arkansas Best Corp. v. Commissioner*, 485 U.S. 212 (1988), attempted to argue that its stock purchases were made for "business" reasons and not as investments in the hope that it could rely on *Corn Products* to treat gains and losses from disposition of the stock as ordinary gains and losses. Dismissing the effort, the Court concluded that the taxpayer's articulated motive in purchasing an asset is irrelevant in terms of its basic and default classification as capital in nature. The Court did, however, emphasize that the business link matters with respect to whether a given asset falls within a statutory exception (e.g., inventory). The Court went on to distinguish *Corn Products* as involving a taxpayer using futures contracts as a hedge to protect itself against the need for raw materials destined to become part of its inventory. Congress's addition of §§ 1221(a)(7) and (8) to the Code brought a degree of clarity to this area by directly addressing the classification of hedging transactions and supplies used or consumed in the ordinary course of a trade or business.

David Taylor Enterprises, Inc. v. Commissioner: Real Life Applications

1. Since her early college years, Cleo has been a raving fan of Impressionist-era art. She currently owns and operates an art gallery. Although many visit the gallery merely to view the art, the gallery's literature makes it abundantly clear that each item on display is for sale at a price deemed mutually agreeable by the gallery and the purchaser. Cleo recently purchased a work by Vincent van Gogh and placed it on display in her dining room. From time to time over the years, a

dinner guest would attempt to purchase the work from her, but she respectfully declined; that is until she received a blowout offer that she could not refuse. Will Cleo's gain from the sale of her work by Van Gogh constitute ordinary income or capital gain?

2. Dr. Marilyn Grandy completed her Ph.D. in the history of art several years ago. For her dissertation, she chose to focus on the works of Hieronymus Bosch. Dr. Grandy now owns and operates an art gallery. Although the gallery's literature states that all works on display are for sale, Dr. Grandy rarely (but occasionally) approves the sale of any of the gallery's Bosch works. Does Dr. Grandy hold her Bosch works as capital assets?

3. A long-time history buff, Belvedere owns and operates a store featuring memorabilia from the Civil War and World War II. Items range from war-bond related literature to private letters, photos, uniforms, and instruments used in field surgery hospitals. Does Belvedere hold these items as capital assets?

H. THE "SALE OR EXCHANGE" REQUIREMENT

In addition to relating solely to a taxpayer's capital assets, the definitions set forth in § 1222 regarding capital gains and losses apply only when there has been a sale or exchange of a given capital asset. Under ordinary circumstances, once it is established that the taxpayer holds property as a capital asset, only occasionally does an issue arise as to whether a sale or exchange has occurred with respect to it. But things can get murky (and right quickly at that). The Code does not define "sale" or "exchange," and yet property changes hands in many contexts.

Case Preview

Kenan v. Commissioner

In the classic sale transaction, one party provides property to a counterparty for cash. An exchange typically differs only in the fact that the parties exchange non-cash properties or, perhaps, services. But just how narrowly or broadly should one construe "sale or exchange"? If one party is obligated to another and simply decides to satisfy that obligation by transferring property with built-in gain (foregoing an outright sale), does the transaction fall within or outside the relevant sphere? In the next case, the court takes up the issue whether such a transfer qualifies as a sale or exchange and thereby triggers recognition of the built-in gain. Consider the following questions as you read the case:

1. Why did the trustees feel that any taxation in connection with the transfer was inappropriate?

2. Will the built-in gain be subject to double-taxation?
3. What did the court conclude with respect to the Commissioner's character argument?

Kenan v. Commissioner
114 F.2d 217 (2d Cir. 1940)

AUGUSTUS N. HAND, Circuit Judge.

The testatrix, Mrs. Bingham, died on July 27, 1917, leaving a will under which she placed her residuary estate in trust and provided in item "Seventh" that her trustees should pay a certain amount annually to her niece, Louise Clisby Wise, until the latter reached the age of forty, "at which time or as soon thereafter as compatible with the interests of my estate they shall pay to her the sum of Five Million ($5,000,000.00) Dollars." The will provided in item "Eleventh" that the trustees, in the case of certain payments including that of the $5,000,000 under item "Seventh," should have the right "to substitute for the payment in money, payment in marketable securities of a value equal to the sum to be paid, the selection of the securities to be substituted in any instance, and the valuation of such securities to be done by the Trustees and their selection and valuation to be final."

Louise Clisby Wise became forty years of age on July 28, 1935. The trustees decided to pay her the $5,000,000 partly in cash and partly in securities. The greater part of the securities had been owned by the testator and transferred as part of her estate to the trustees; others had been purchased by the trustees. All had appreciated in value during the period for which they were held by the trustees, and the Commissioner determined that the distribution of the securities to the niece resulted in capital gains which were taxable to the trustees under the rates specified in Section 117 of the Revenue Act of 1934, which limits the percentage of gain to be treated as taxable income on the "sale or exchange" of capital assets. On this basis, the Commissioner determined a deficiency of $367,687.12 in the income tax for the year 1935.

The Board overruled the objections of the trustees to the imposition of any tax and denied a motion of the Commissioner to amend his answer in order to claim the full amount of the appreciation in value as ordinary income rather than a percentage of it as a capital gain, and confirmed the original deficiency determination. The taxpayers contend that the decision of the Board was erroneous because they realized neither gain from the sale or exchange of capital assets nor income of any character by delivering the securities to the legatee pursuant to the permissive terms of the will. The Commissioner contends that gain was realized by the delivery of the securities but that such gain was ordinary income not derived from a sale or exchange and therefore taxable in its entirety. The trustees have filed a petition to review the order of the Board determining the deficiency of $365,687.12 and the Commissioner has filed a cross-petition claiming a deficiency of $1,238,841.99, based on his contention that the gain was not governed by Section 117, and therefore not limited by the percentages therein specified.

The amount of gain is to be determined under Section 111 of the Revenue Act of 1934, which provides:

"(a) Computations of gain or loss. The gain from the sale or other disposition of property shall be the excess of the amount realized therefrom over the adjusted basis * * * .

"(b) Amount realized. The amount realized from the sale or other disposition of property shall be the sum of any money received plus the fair market value of the property (other than money) received."

Section 113, 26 U.S.C.A. Int. Rev. Code, 113, is claimed by the taxpayers to be relevant and provides:

"(a) The basis of property shall be the cost of such property; except that —

"(5) Property transmitted at death. If the property was acquired by bequest, devise, or inheritance, or by the decedent's estate from the decedent, the basis shall be the fair market value of such property at the time of such acquisition."

THE TAXPAYER'S APPEAL.

In support of their petition the taxpayers contend that the delivery of the securities of the trust estate to the legatee was a donative disposition of property pursuant to the terms of the will, and that no gain was thereby realized. They argue that when they determined that the legacy should be one of securities, it became for all purposes a bequest of property, just as if the cash alternative had not been provided, and not taxable for the reason that no gain is realized on the transfer by a testamentary trustee of specific securities or other property bequeathed by will to a legatee.

We do not think that the situation here is the same as that of legacy of specific property. The legatee was never in the position occupied by the recipient of specific securities under a will. She had a claim against the estate for $5,000,000, payable either in cash or securities of that value, but had no title or right to the securities, legal or equitable, until they were delivered to her by the trustees after the exercise of their option. She took none of the chances of a legatee of specific securities or of a share of a residue that the securities might appreciate or decline in value between the time of the death of the testator and the transfer to her by the trustees, but instead had at all times a claim for an unvarying amount in money or its equivalent.

If there had merely been a bequest to the legatee of $5,000,000 and she had agreed with the trustees to take securities of that value, the transaction would have been a "sale or other disposition" of the securities under *Suisman v. Eaton*, 15 F.Supp. 113, *affirmed*, 2 Cir., 83 F.2d 1019, *certiorari denied* 299 U.S. 573, 57 S. Ct. 37, 81 L. Ed. 422. There, a will creating a trust provided that each of the testator's children was to receive $50,000 on attaining the age of twenty-five. The trustee transferred stock of the value of $50,000 to one of the children, Minerva, in satisfaction of her legacy. Judge Hincks said in the district court that the "property which the trust estate received from the 'sale or other disposition' of said stocks was the discharge of the corpus from Minerva's equitable right to receive $50,000 therefrom; the amount realized, i.e., the 'fair market value of the property (other than money) received,' * * * was $50,000; and the excess of the amount realized over the basis was properly computed by the Commissioner, legally assessed as part of the taxable income of the trust estate, and the tax thereon was legally collected."

In the present case, the legatee had a claim which was a charge against the trust estate for $5,000,000 in cash or securities and the trustees had the power to determine whether the claim should be satisfied in one form or the other. The claim, though enforceable only in the alternative, was, like the claim in *Suisman v. Eaton, supra,* a charge against the entire trust estate. If it were satisfied by a cash payment securities might have to be sold on which (if those actually delivered in specie were selected) a taxable gain would necessarily have been realized. Instead of making such a sale the trustees delivered the securities and exchanged them pro tanto for the general claim of the legatee, which was thereby satisfied.

It is said that this transaction was not such a "sale or other disposition" as is intended by Section 111(a) or was dealt with in *Suisman v. Eaton,* because it was effectuated only by the will of the trustees and not, as in *Suisman v. Eaton,* through a mutual agreement between trustee and legatee. The Board made no such distinction, and we are not inclined to limit thus the meaning of the words "other disposition" used in Section 111(a), or of "exchange" used in Section 117. The word "exchange" does not necessarily have the connotation of a bilateral agreement which may be said to attach to the word "sale." Thus, should a person set up a trust and reserve to himself the power to substitute for the securities placed in trust other securities of equal value, there would seem no doubt that the exercise of this reserved power would be an "exchange" within the common meaning of the word, even though the settlor consulted no will other than his own, although, of course, we do not here advert to the problems of taxability in such a situation.

The Board alluded to the fact that both here and in *Suisman v. Eaton* the bequest was fixed at a definite amount in money, that in both cases there was no bequest of specific securities (nor of a share in the residue which might vary in value), that the rights of the legatee, like those in the *Suisman* case, were a charge upon the corpus of the trust, and that the trustees had to part either with $5,000,000 in cash or with securities worth that amount at the time of the transfer. It added that the increase in value of the securities was realized by the trust and benefited it to the full extent, since, except for the increase, it would have had to part with other property ***. Under circumstances like those here, where the legatee did not take securities designated by the will or an interest in the corpus which might be more or less at the time of the transfer than at the time of decedent's death, it seems to us that the trustees realized a gain by using these securities to settle a claim worth $5,000,000, just as the trustee in *Suisman v. Eaton* realized one.

It seems reasonably clear that the property was not "transmitted at death" or "acquired by bequest * * * from the decedent." Section 113(a)(5). It follows that the fears of the taxpayers that double taxation of this appreciation will result because the legatee will take the basis of the decedent under *Brewster v. Gage,* 280 U.S. 327, 50 S. Ct. 115, 74 L. Ed. 457, are groundless. It is true that under Section 113(a)(5) the basis for property "acquired by bequest, devise, or inheritance" is "the fair market value of such property at the time of such acquisition" and that under *Brewster v. Gage, supra,* the date of acquisition has been defined as the date of death of the testator. But the holding of the present case is necessarily a determination that the property here acquired is acquired in an exchange and not "by bequest, devise or inheritance," since Sections 117 and 113(a)(5) seem to be mutually exclusive. The legatee's basis would seem to be the value of the claim surrendered in exchange for the securities; and the Board of Tax Appeals has so held.

THE COMMISSIONER'S APPEAL.

We have already held that a taxable gain was realized by the delivery of the securities. It follows from the reasons that support that conclusion that the appreciation was a capital gain, taxable at the rates specified in Section 117. Therefore, neither under Section 111(a) nor under Section 22(a) *** can the gain realized be taxed as ordinary income.

***

If the trustees had sold the securities, they would be taxed at capital gain rates. Both the trustees and the Commissioner, in their arguments as respondent and cross-respondents, draw the analogy between the transaction here and a sale, and no injustice is done to either by taxing the gain at the rates which would apply had a sale actually been made and the proceeds delivered to the legatee. It seems to us extraordinary that the exercise by the trustees of the option to deliver to the legatee securities, rather than cash, should be thought to result in an increased deficiency of enormous proportions.

Orders affirmed.

Post-Case Follow-Up

Dismissing the taxpayer's objections, the court concluded that the distribution of appreciated property by the trustees to the legatee in accordance with the terms of Mrs. Bingham's will did, in fact, constitute an exchange of property. Accordingly, the trustees were obligated to recognize the built-in gain with respect to the stock transferred. The Commissioner attempted to have the gain taxed as ordinary income, but the court reasoned that the taxpayers should be treated just as they would have been treated had they simply sold the relevant stock for cash (generating capital gain) and distributed the funds received to the legatee. The court's logic in *Kenan* is not difficult to follow. In fact, the decision can be thought of as the mere tip of an iceberg. Over the years, IRS pronouncements and cases have confirmed that a wide range of transactions constitute sales or exchanges (or are to be treated as such), even though one might not think of them in that light as an initial matter. Some, such as transferring property to satisfy a debt, involve transactions comparable (if not identical) to those in *Kenan*. Others differ significantly (e.g., certain voluntary and involuntary dispositions (e.g., foreclosures), abandonments, and some distributions made by a corporation to its shareholders with respect to its stock).

Kenan v. Commissioner: Real Life Applications

1. Justin owns and operates The Victoria & Albert Grille, an upscale restaurant. Over the years, the business has done very well, and Justin has long-standing

relationships with various vendors, including Sam's Seafood Emporium ("SSE"). Recently, due to an economic downturn, Justin's restaurant began to encounter financial difficulty, so much so that a few of the restaurant's accounts payable are now past due. Determined to preserve his ongoing business relationship with SSE, Justin transferred several shares of Orange, Inc. stock to SSE in satisfaction of the past-due account payable. Will Justin's transfer of the stock constitute a sale or exchange with respect to that stock?

2. *Same facts at Question #1,* except that Justin asks Dwayne to pay the past-due account at SSE, promising to transfer the Orange, Inc. stock to Dwayne if he does so. Assuming all goes according to plan, will there be a sale or exchange with respect to the Orange, Inc. stock?

In *Kenan*, Ms. Wise received both cash and stock in her capacity as legatee, and the only real issue was whether distribution of the stock to her constituted a sale or exchange with respect to the trustees. The existence of differing consideration components is not inherently problematic, but issues can certainly arise when sophisticated transactions are at hand and a capital asset sale or exchange is merely part of a larger, multi-faceted transactional mix. Without abundant clarity and a true meeting of all the minds involved, the taxpayer may find himself at odds with the IRS over whether consideration received at or after closing of the deal was for the capital asset or for something else altogether.

Case Preview

Brinkley v. Commissioner

Brian Brinkly made it abundantly clear at all times that he was willing to part with his stock in Zave Networks, Inc. ("Zave") as part of Google, Inc.'s acquisition of the company. Although he was of the opinion that he would be selling his stock for approximately $3 million, other parties to the transaction placed a much lower valuation on his stock. In the end, Brinkley received roughly $3 million as part of the deal, but under the terms of the documents he and others ultimately executed, a substantial portion of the consideration did not appear to be in exchange for his stock. Determined and strongly motivated to cast the transaction as one generating long-term capital gain and not ordinary income, Brinkley took issue with the notion that he had received consideration as compensation of any sort. As you read the case, consider the following questions:

1. Is the question of whether Brinkley received long-term capital gain or ordinary income ultimately a function of the terms of the documents executed by the parties?
2. What weight, if any, did the court assign to the fact that Brinkley had a separate employment agreement with Google, Inc. for future services as an employee?

3. What "service" did Brinkley perform in connection with the acquisition transaction?
4. If you were representing Brinkley, how would you have attempted to achieve the results your client desired? What are the risks of proceeding in that manner?

Brinkley v. Commissioner
808 F.3d 657 (5th Cir. 2015)

EDWARD C. PRADO, Circuit Judge:

Respondent-Appellee the Commissioner of Internal Revenue issued Petitioner-Appellant Brian Brinkley a notice of deficiency for the 2011 tax year. The Commissioner charged that Brinkley had mischaracterized $1.8 million of the $3.1 million he received as a result of the merger between his company (Zave Networks, Inc.) and Google, Inc., as long-term capital gain rather than ordinary income. The Commissioner therefore found a federal income tax deficiency of $369,071 and assessed an accuracy-related penalty of $48,036.15. Brinkley petitioned the U.S. Tax Court to challenge both the deficiency and the penalty. Following a bench trial, the tax court sustained the Commissioner's determinations in a written order. We affirm the tax court's decision.

I. FACTUAL AND PROCEDURAL BACKGROUND

A. Factual Background

Brinkley was a founding member of Zave Networks, Inc. ("Zave"), a company offering digital coupon services under the name "Zavers." Brinkley began his career with Zave in 2006 as an independent contractor, but in 2010 he became a salaried employee as Zave's Chief Technology Officer. Commencing in 2006, in addition to Brinkley's monetary compensation, Zave issued Brinkley restricted stock grants.

Brinkley initially owned roughly 9.8% of Zave's stock. However, as investors contributed additional capital to the company, Brinkley's equity interest was diluted. Brinkley threatened to leave Zave if his interest fell below 3%, so in 2009, Zave's President Thad Langford agreed to issue Brinkley additional restricted stock grants to maintain his stake.

In 2011, Google, Inc., ("Google") began negotiations to acquire Zave as a wholly owned subsidiary. Brinkley took no part in the negotiations. In September 2011, Google acquired all of Zave's stock pursuant to a merger agreement. At closing, Brinkley held 1,340,000 shares of Zave common stock, 200,000 of which were unvested; Brinkley estimated that his equity interest in Zave at this time was between one and three percent. Although Brinkley was only a minority shareholder of Zave, he maintained that Zave needed his stock and his consent to effectuate the merger because he was one of the "key holders" of Zave's intellectual property (IP) and Google wanted both that IP and a commitment by Brinkley to work for the company.

Before the merger terms were finalized, Brinkley met with Ronald and Lance LeMay, two of Zave's directors, to discuss Brinkley's payout. The LeMays advised

Brinkley that Zave would be sold to Google for $93 million and that Brinkley's Zave stock was worth approximately $800,000. Brinkley contested this valuation, asserting that because he owned 3% of Zave, his stock was worth "about $3 million or at least 3 percent of the company."

[Brinkley and Zave continued their discussions and correspondence. Brinkley insisted that he was due approximately $3 million, and that all of it was to be consideration for the sale of his stock. Although the parties ultimately executed "Letter Agreement II," the final terms of the letter (in conjunction with the merger agreement and other executed transaction documents) effectively cast the bulk of what Brinkley was to receive as deferred compensation rather than as payment in exchange for his stock.]

Following the merger closing in September 2011, Brinkley was entitled to total compensation of $3,027,515, and he received a paycheck from Zave that listed $1,879,779 as "stock compensation pay" subject to federal income tax withholding. Brinkley's W-2 form *** similarly characterized this sum as "stock compensation pay" and included it in Brinkley's taxable income. Recognizing that such tax treatment denoted that Zave had characterized the $1.8 million as ordinary income, rather than as part of the $3 million he believed Zave had agreed to pay for his stock, Brinkley [sought corrective action. He eventually filed an income tax return asserting that the so-called stock compensation pay was, in fact, consideration paid for the sale of his stock and that accordingly, its character was long-term capital gain and not ordinary income.]

B. Procedural Background

On January 9, 2013, the Commissioner issued Brinkley a notice of deficiency for 2011, asserting an income tax deficiency of $369,071 and assessing an accuracy-related penalty of $48,036 under I.R.C. § 6662(a). As the ground for the deficiency, the Commissioner found that the $1.8 million that Brinkley received from Zave and characterized as capital gain was in fact ordinary income.

Brinkley petitioned the tax court to challenge the Commissioner's determinations. Following a bench trial ***, the tax court upheld the Commissioner's findings. *** Brinkley timely appealed.

III. DISCUSSION

Brinkley brings three challenges to the tax court's decision. First, he contends that under I.R.C. §§ 6201(d) and 7491(a), the burden of proof regarding his tax liability should have shifted back to the Commissioner. Second, he claims clear error in the tax court's finding that the $3.1 million he received in the merger represents more than just the proceeds of his stock sale, and in its subsidiary finding that the $1.8 million he claimed in capital gain was in fact ordinary income. Third, he asserts clear error in the tax court's finding that he was not entitled to the "reasonable cause and good faith" defense against an accuracy-related penalty under I.R.C. § 6664.

A. The Allocation of the Burden of Proof

[The court proceeded to conclude that any error in the allocation of the burden of proof was harmless.]

B. The Character of the Consideration

1. Standard of Review

This Court applies the same standard of review to tax court decisions and district court decisions: Findings of fact are reviewed for clear error and issues of law are reviewed de novo. ***

The tax court's conclusion regarding the character of Brinkley's consideration has both factual and legal components—the finding that Brinkley's merger income was the product of more than just the sale of his stock is a factual determination, and the holding that the $1.8 million in contested income qualifies as ordinary income rather than capital gain is a conclusion of law.

2. Governing Law

Gain from the sale of a capital asset, such as stock, may receive the preferential tax treatment of long-term capital gain if certain conditions are satisfied. *See* I.R.C. §§ 1(h), 1221(a), 1222(3). As the Supreme Court has noted, "not every gain growing out of a transaction concerning capital assets is allowed the benefits of the capital gains tax provision"—"[t]hose are limited by definition to gains from 'the sale or exchange' of capital assets." *Dobson v. Comm'r*, 321 U.S. 231, 231–32. "[W]hether or not a sale or exchange has taken place for income tax purposes must be ascertained from all relevant facts and circumstances," and "the form of an agreement is not of itself determinative of the question of whether payments to the taxpayer should be treated as ordinary income or capital gains." *Estate of Nordquist v. Comm'r*, 481 F.2d 1058, 1061 (8th Cir. 1973). Rather, "[a] transaction's tax consequences depend on its substance, not its form." *Chemtech*, 766 F.3d at 460 (quoting *Southgate*, 659 F.3d at 478–79). Ordinary-income treatment is afforded to compensation for services rendered, *e.g., Roscoe v. Commissioner*, 215 F.2d 478, 480–81 (5th Cir. 1954), and to consideration for the execution of a contract such as a covenant not to compete, *e.g., Sonnleitner v. Commissioner*, 598 F.2d 464, 466 (5th Cir. 1979).

When there is evidence that part of the consideration for a sale of stock amounts to compensation for ordinary-income-producing activities, the portion of the consideration exceeding that attributable to the exchange of the capital assets themselves may be taxable as ordinary income rather than capital gain. *See Roscoe*, 215 F.2d at 480–81. ***

3. Analysis

Here, the tax court held that the preponderance of the evidence supported the Commissioner's finding that Brinkley's $3.1 million merger payout could not be ascribed exclusively to the sale of Brinkley's interest in Zave and that the $1.8 million difference between Brinkley's claimed capital gain and the actual value of his stock was taxable as ordinary income.

Brinkley contends that the tax court's finding was clearly erroneous. Brinkley argues he negotiated a price for the sale of his stock well above its value as calculated by Zave—$3.1 million versus $787,671 for the same block of 1,340,000 shares—and that the correspondence culminating in letter agreement II reflected the parties' mutual assent to this arrangement. Brinkley cites his agreement with Zave, under which he was assured that his equity interest would not dip below 3% of the company, and his negotiating power as a key employee and the holder of certain IP, as proof that Zave had an incentive to pay him far more than the value of his shares in order to secure his consent to the merger. He also points to the text of the various letter agreements as evidence that he and Zave arrived at the sum of $3.1 million without reference to past or future services, and he contends that none of this amount could be for deferred compensation because he has never held any deferred-compensation plan. Further, Brinkley asserts the compensation could not be for future services because the separate employment agreement he signed with Google already generously compensated him for his future services by providing him an annual salary of $231,000, an annual discretionary bonus of 25% of his peer-group salary, and a $2.5 million stay bonus.

Brinkley's arguments are unpersuasive for several reasons. First and foremost, the plain text of letter agreement II supports the Commissioner's position. It sets forth two conditions on Brinkley's receipt of the merger consideration: (1) the exchange of Brinkley's Zave shares and (2) the execution of a Key Employee Offer Letter and Proprietary Information and Inventions Assignment Agreement with Google. Brinkley argues that the entire $3.1 million in consideration must have been for the first condition alone, as this amount had been set in letter agreements I and I(a) — which contained no reference to the second condition — and he was set to receive generous compensation from Google for his future employment. *** [N]either letter agreement I nor I(a) were ultimately executed by the parties and are thus of limited relevance. Both parties ultimately executed letter agreement II, which unambiguously lists both conditions and includes a merger clause that supersedes all prior agreements.

As for Brinkley's argument concerning his future compensation as a Google employee, it is not inconsistent with letter agreement II for Zave to assign value to Brinkley's willingness to execute the employment and assignment agreements, separate and apart from Google's valuation of Brinkley's future services. *** At root, Brinkley's position seems to hinge on the premise that once the parties fixed the sum of $3.1 million for his 3% stake in the company, they could not later adjust the portions of that sum allocable to stock, past or future compensation, and commitments to execute work-related agreements. But this is precisely what letter agreement II does.

Further, Brinkley signed the shareholder-consent form, which affirmed that he had read the merger agreement and bound him to accept its terms. The schedules to the merger agreement identified Brinkley as a recipient of deferred compensation and characterized letter agreement II as a deferred-compensation plan. Brinkley responds that letter agreement II does not appear to be a deferred-compensation plan, and he points out that he was not asked to sign the consent form required of other deferred-compensation recipients. This may be true, but it misses the mark. Even if Brinkley's payout was not part of a formal deferred-compensation plan, this does not mean that the payout could not be properly characterized as deferred compensation. The primary definition of the term "deferred compensation" actually just describes a method of payment: "Payment for work performed, to be paid in the future or when some future event occurs." Black's Law Dictionary 343 (10th ed.2014). Brinkley's signing of the employment and assignment agreements, per the requirement of letter agreement II, was the service he performed that entitled him to the additional $1.8 million payment that Zave would later distribute to him. *** Zave's treatment of this payment as deferred compensation subject to ordinary-income tax withholding is consistent with the definition of deferred compensation and with the terms of letter agreement II.

Finally, the facts in this case are broadly similar to *Roscoe. See* 215 F.2d at 479–81. As in *Roscoe,* there is substantial evidence that the consideration paid to Brinkley, although nominally for the exchange of his stock, was partly compensation for services rendered. Although the taxpayers in *Roscoe* were compensated for past services rendered, and Brinkley was more likely compensated for future service to be rendered — namely, his execution of the employment and assignment agreements — Brinkley's future service was an ordinary-income producing activity and was not entitled to long-term capital gains treatment, *see, e.g., Sonnleitner,* 598 F.2d at 466. Also similar to the taxpayers in *Roscoe,* Brinkley argues that his stock was more valuable than other shares because he was a critical employee and because Zave viewed his consent as necessary to the merger. Nevertheless, Brinkley fails to offer "convincing testimony" that his shares were in fact more valuable than other shares and that Zave was not simply compensating him for future services as the plain language of letter agreement II indicates. Following *Roscoe,* therefore, we find no clear error in the tax court's conclusion that the outstanding $1.8 million in compensation qualifies as ordinary income rather than capital gain. ***

[The court proceeded to discuss and allow the imposition of an accuracy-related penalty.]

For the foregoing reasons, we AFFIRM the tax court's decision.

Post-Case Follow-Up

Though not bound by the form of the transaction structured by the parties, the court in *Brinkley* concluded that the $1.8 million received by the taxpayer was ordinary income for services rendered (i.e., executing agreements) and not consideration for the sale of his stock. Based solely on the facts at hand, it's remarkably easy to dissent. To the extent that any compensation paid to Brinkley was deductible by Zave, the company would have had a strong interest in characterizing the bulk of what was paid to Brinkley as compensation rather than as consideration for his stock. Even so, the court casually hangs its hat on Brinkley's execution of specific agreements as the future "service" entitling him to substantial consideration while dismissing the significance of his separate employment agreement with Google which included a salary and a hefty $2.5 million stay bonus. The court cites *Estate of Nordquist* to emphasize that the form adopted by the parties is not determinative as to whether a sale or exchange of a capital asset has occurred, but in *Brinkley,* the court seems curiously determined to surrender to the four corners of form.

Brinkley v. Commissioner: Real Life Applications

1. Maxwell owns 52 percent of the issued and outstanding shares of Pacific Products, Inc. ("PPI"). Acquiring Conglomerate, Inc. ("ACI") has taken an interest in purchasing all of the stock of PPI on or about December 15, 2018. Maxwell is interested in selling his stock, but he thinks the price ACI is offering is too low. Maxwell contacts ACI's representatives and explains to them that if they are willing to give him a control premium for his bloc of shares (i.e., pay him more per share than is paid to the holders of the other 48 percent of shares), he will proceed with the sale. If ACI agrees to Maxwell's terms and proceeds with the purchase, how will Maxwell be treated for federal income tax purposes?

2. For the past 15 years, Salazar has been a loyal employee of Vanguard Security International, Inc. ("VSI"). He also owns 2 percent of the company's issued and outstanding shares. Although he and a number of other shareholders are unhappy about the fact, VSI will soon be merged with and into Gladiator Shield Corporation ("GSC"), and Salazar's position will be eliminated. Salazar's contract requires that he be paid severance, but he and VSI are at odds over the exact amount due. Salazar offers to just "let it go" if the consideration to be paid for his stock is increased by $200,000. If GSC ultimately purchases Salazar's stock for the enhanced consideration amount, how will the transaction be treated for federal income tax purposes?

3. ***Same facts at Question #2***, except that Salazar owns 30 percent of the company and is not eligible for severance. Salazar knows that certain VSI employees will be getting approximately $500,000 of severance on the closing of the acquisition, and he has been told by his attorneys that governing state law requires supermajority shareholder approval (i.e., 75 percent) of these transactions for them to qualify as valid acquisitions under state law. If Salazar brings this fact to the attention of the negotiators and manages to get a $500,000 increase in consideration for his shares, how will the transaction be treated if GSC accedes to his demands?

I. DEFINING "PROPERTY" IN THE CAPITAL ASSET CONTEXT

With the exception of specific items, section § 1221(a) defines capital asset as "property held by the taxpayer (whether or not connected with his trade or business)." Congress may have resorted to § 1221's definitional strategy to control the deduction of losses and to ensure that individuals could not claim capital gain treatment for the sale of inventory or other items used in their trades or business; however, the flip-side risk is that taxpayers will capitalize on the definition's prophylactic ambit to claim that any sale or exchange of property they happen to hold constitutes capital gain as opposed to ordinary income. Not surprisingly, regulatory provisions and judicial doctrines intervene to impose necessary restraints.

Case Preview 	## *Womack v. Commissioner*

Much to his apparent glee, Roland Womack won a portion of a handsome $8,000,000 Florida Lottery prize. Winners in Womack's position were initially allowed to receive their winnings only in annual installments over a period of years, but a change in Florida law allowed him to assign his rights to future installments to a third party. Viewing his right to future installments as "property" satisfying the definition of a capital asset, he took the position that the assignment proceeds he received constituted capital gain. Not surprisingly, the Commissioner disagreed. As you read the 11th Circuit's opinion in *Womack*, consider the following questions:

1. Does the court embrace a literal reading of the definition of "capital asset" under § 1221?
2. What is the "substitute for ordinary income" doctrine?
3. In the opinion of the court, does the taxpayer's right to receive future installment payments constitute "property" within the meaning of § 1221(a)?

Womack v. Commissioner
510 F.3d 1295 (11th Cir. 2007)

MARTIN, District Judge:

   This is an appeal by Florida State Lottery winners from the United States Tax Court's decision that proceeds from the sale of the rights to future installment payments from lottery winnings ("Lottery Rights") are taxable as ordinary income, rather than at the lower tax rate applied to the sale of a long-term capital asset. The Tax Court specifically held that Lottery Rights are not capital assets as defined in 26 U.S.C. § 1221 ("Section 1221"), under the judicially established substitute for ordinary income doctrine. We affirm.

I. BACKGROUND

Roland Womack won a portion of an $8,000,000 Florida State Lottery ("Florida Lotto") prize on January 20, 1996. At the time, the prize was payable only in twenty annual installments of $150,000. Mr. Womack received four such annual installments from 1996 to 1999, and he reported those payments as ordinary income on the federal tax returns he filed jointly with his wife, Marie Womack.

   In 1999, Florida amended its law to permit lottery winners to assign Lottery Rights. Mr. Womack subsequently sold the right to receive the remaining sixteen payments to Singer Asset Finance Company ("Singer") in exchange for a sum of $1,328,000. The total face value of the remaining payments was $2,400,000. The Womacks reported the amount received from Singer on their 2000 joint federal income tax return as proceeds from the sale of a long-term capital asset.

F: Second Winner

Maria Spiridakos is also a Florida Lotto winner. She won a $6,240,000 prize on January 6, 1990, payable in 20 annual installments of $312,000. She received ten annual payments and, from 1990 to 1999, she and her husband, Anastasios Spiridakos, reported those payments as ordinary income on their jointly filed federal income tax returns. Ms. Spiridakos sold the right to receive her remaining payments to Singer for $2,125,000, which the Spiridakoses reported on their 2000 joint federal income tax return as proceeds from the sale of a long-term capital asset.

The IRS issued notices of deficiency to the Womacks and the Spiridakoses (collectively, "Taxpayers") for failure to pay tax on the lump sum payment as ordinary income. Taxpayers each filed a petition with the Tax Court seeking a redetermination. The Tax Court consolidated the petitions and denied both on November 7, 2006. Taxpayers now appeal.

II. STANDARD OF REVIEW

We have jurisdiction in this case pursuant to 26 U.S.C. § 7482, which specifies that we review Tax Court decisions "in the same manner and to the same extent as decisions of the district courts in civil actions tried without a jury." 26 U.S.C. § 7482(a)(1). We review the Tax Court's interpretations of the Internal Revenue Code *de novo*.

III. DISCUSSION

General

The question before us is whether Lottery Rights are "capital assets" as defined by Section 1221 of the Internal Revenue Code, 26 U.S.C. § 1221. Income representing proceeds from the sale or exchange of a capital asset that a taxpayer holds for over a year is considered a "capital gain," 26 U.S.C. § 1222(3), and is taxed at a favorable rate. Other income, or "ordinary income," is taxed at a higher rate. Section 1221 defines a capital asset as any property the taxpayer holds, but excludes certain items from the definition. Taxpayers held their Lottery Rights for more than one year before selling them, so Taxpayers may report the lump sum payment they received in consideration as a capital gain if Lottery Rights are considered a capital asset. [Author's Note: The court, in each instance, is referring to long-term capital gains as defined by § 1222(3).]

Taxpayer's met time (for (over one year))

The Tax Court and the four U.S. Circuit Courts to consider the question have concluded that Lottery Rights are not a capital asset within the definition set forth in Section 1221. *E.g., Prebola v. Comm'r*, 482 F.3d 610 (2d Cir. 2007); *Watkins v. Comm'r*, 447 F.3d 1269 (10th Cir. 2006); *Lattera v. Comm'r*, 437 F.3d 399 (3d Cir. 2006), *cert. denied*, 549 U.S. 1212, 127 S. Ct. 1328, 167 L.Ed.2d 86 (2007); *United States v. Maginnis*, 356 F.3d 1179 (9th Cir. 2004); *Davis v. Comm'r*, 119 T.C. 1, 2002 WL 1446631 (2002). These decisions are based on the so-called substitute for ordinary income doctrine, which provides that when a party receives a lump sum payment as "essentially a substitute for what would otherwise be received at a future time as ordinary income" that lump sum payment is taxable as ordinary income as well. *Comm'r v. P.G. Lake, Inc.*, 356 U.S. 260, 265, 78 S. Ct. 691, 694, 2 L. Ed. 2d 743 (1958). We agree that the substitute for ordinary income doctrine applies to Lottery Rights, and therefore that proceeds from the sale of Lottery Rights are taxable as ordinary income.

Rule for being ordinary income

A. The Substitute for Ordinary Income Doctrine

The statutory definition of capital asset "has ... never been read as broadly as the statutory language might seem to permit, because such a reading would encompass some things Congress did not intend to be taxed as capital gains." *Maginnis,* 356 F.3d at 1181. Congress intended ordinary income to be the default tax rate, with capital gains treatment an exception applicable only in appropriate cases. In fact, "the term 'capital asset' is to be construed narrowly in accordance with the purpose of Congress to afford capital-gains treatment only in situations typically involving the realization of appreciation in value accrued over a substantial period of time." *Comm'r v. Gillette Motor Transp., Inc.,* 364 U.S. 130, 134, 80 S. Ct. 1497, 1500, 4 L. Ed. 2d 1617 (1960). This interpretation prevents taxpayers from circumventing ordinary income tax rates by selling rights to future ordinary income payments in exchange for a lump sum.

The doctrine is attributed to four seminal Supreme Court cases: *Hort v. Commissioner, Commissioner v. P.G. Lake, Inc., Commissioner v. Gillette Motor Transport, Inc.,* and *United States v. Midland-Ross Corp.* The taxpayer in *Hort,* a building owner, received a lump sum in exchange for cancelling a lease on the property. The sum was taxable as ordinary income because it was "essentially a substitute" for the rental payments, themselves obviously ordinary income. In *Lake,* the taxpayer, a corporation, assigned a portion of oil and sulphur payment rights to its president in consideration for the cancellation of a debt the corporation owed to the president. The Supreme Court considered the profit to be in essence a substitution for the oil and sulphur payments that the corporation would have otherwise received in the future, and held it taxable as ordinary income for that reason. *Id.* at 265, 78 S. Ct. at 694. ***

The overall effect of these cases has been to narrow what a mechanical application of Section 1221 would otherwise cause to be treated as a capital asset.

With that background, four Circuits have reviewed the precise legal question we face here under materially identical circumstances. Each Circuit has concluded that Lottery Rights are substitutes for ordinary income . . . . ***

We agree with our sister circuits that Lottery Rights are a clear case of a substitute for ordinary income. A lottery winner who has *not* sold the right to his winnings to a third party must report the winnings as ordinary income whether the state pays him in a lump sum or in installments. Thus, when a lottery winner sells the right to his winnings, he replaces future ordinary income. In defining "capital asset," Congress did not intend for taxpayers to circumvent ordinary income tax treatment by packaging ordinary income payments and selling them to a third party.

There are important differences between Lottery Rights and the typical capital asset. The sale of a capital asset captures the increased value of the underlying asset. Perhaps the most common example occurs when a taxpayer purchases shares of stock, owns the shares for longer than a year, and then sells them at a higher price. The taxpayer makes an underlying investment in a capital asset when he purchases the stock. When he sells the shares at a higher price, the gain represents an increase in the value of the original investment. As the Ninth Circuit noted in *Maginnis,* 356 F.3d at 1183, Lottery Rights lack these characteristics emblematic of capital assets — Lottery Rights involve no underlying investment of capital.

Furthermore, any "gain" from their sale reflects no change in the value of the asset. It is simply the amount Taxpayers would have received eventually, discounted to present value.

Furthermore, when a lottery winner sells Lottery Rights, he transfers a right to income that is already earned, not a right to earn income in the future. ***

A capital asset has the potential to earn income in the future based on the owner's actions in using it. Lottery winners, by contrast, are "entitled to the income merely by virtue of owning the property." Thus, income from a lottery payment is earned income despite the fact that it does not accrue until the scheduled annual payment date. Proceeds from the sale of Lottery Rights are a clear substitute for ordinary income and are taxable as ordinary income.

***

B. "Property" Under Section 1221

As Taxpayers note, *Arkansas Best* makes clear that if a given asset is not listed within Section 1221's exclusions, it is a capital asset unless it is not considered "property." The pertinent Treasury Department regulation also provides that "[t]he term capital assets includes all classes of property not specifically excluded by section 1221." 26 C.F.R. § 1.1221-1(a). The parties do not dispute that Lottery Rights are not within the statutory exclusions. Therefore, in deciding that the substitute for ordinary income doctrine applies, we necessarily find that Lottery Rights do not constitute "property" as that term is used in Section 1221.

Taxpayers also note that Lottery Rights are property in the ordinary sense of the term and for purposes of other state and federal laws. We recognize that Lottery Rights are property for most other purposes, but "property" under Section 1221 is a narrower concept. As the Supreme Court has stated, "it is evident that not everything which can be called property in the ordinary sense and which is outside the statutory exclusions qualifies as a capital asset." *Gillette,* 364 U.S. at 134, 80 S. Ct. at 1500. ***

This interpretation, which courts repeatedly adopt, gives effect to congressional intent. In defining "capital asset," *** "Property" in the most general sense means anything owned, which would also include income and any rights or claims to it. Even if other statutes use "property" in this broad sense, to exclude substitutes for income in determining what constitutes a capital asset is consistent with the word "property." No other interpretation of "property" would harmonize with the statute's purpose, as the very nature of the term "capital asset" excludes what is in essence ordinary income. *** Lottery Rights, as we explained above, are substitutes for ordinary income. ***

IV. CONCLUSION

For the foregoing reasons, we hold that proceeds from the sale of Lottery Rights should be taxed as ordinary income under the substitute for ordinary income doctrine. The Tax Court's decision is AFFIRMED.

Post-Case Follow-Up

With a straightforward application of the substitute for ordinary income doctrine, the court quickly concluded that the proceeds received by Womack (and similarly situated taxpayers) on the sale of his rights to future lottery payments constituted ordinary income. The decision certainly accords with congressional intent with respect to the taxation of ordinary income and capital gains, but does the court go too far in crafting a special meaning of "property" for purposes of § 1221(a)? Rather than straining so vigorously to tear the taxpayer's right to future payments away from the definition of property, the court could have acknowledged that the taxpayer's rights constitute "property" in the legal sense while simply clarifying that well-established judicial doctrine dictates the exclusion of this form of taxpayer property from the otherwise applicable definition of capital asset. The approach taken jumbles and confuses the meaning of "property" and thereby manages to expose both the taxpayer and the IRS to judicial whim.

Womack v. Commissioner: Real Life Applications

1. In the aftermath of a serious accident in which he suffered physical injury, Cory prevailed in a lawsuit and was awarded compensatory damages of $500,000 and punitive damages of $1.5 million. According to the award, Cory was to receive the punitive damages in equal installments over a fifteen-year period. If Cory sells the right to receive his future punitive damage payments to a third party for an immediate lump-sum payment of $1 million, will the amount constitute capital gain?
2. *Same facts as Question #1*, except that Cory was entitled to receive his compensatory damages over time and sold that right to a third party for a lump sum payment.
3. Dee recently decided to change jobs. In a matter of weeks, she got lucky and found a new position in a nearby state. Her new company needed her to start in three weeks. Dee approached her landlord to find out whether he would be willing to waive her lease's early termination fee. He declined but told her that if she let him keep her used car (worth approximately $5,000), the two could "call it even." If Dee complies, will the landlord realize income that is capital or ordinary in character?

Chapter Summary

- For federal income tax purposes, items of income or loss have a specific character. Items are either "ordinary" or "capital" in nature.

- Capital gains and losses will be either short term or long term, depending on the taxpayer's holding period with respect to the asset. The sale or exchange of an asset with a holding period of more than one year will result in long-term capital gain or loss. Otherwise, such amounts will be short term in character.

- Section § 1222 contains definitions of short-term capital gain, short-term capital loss, long-term capital gain, and long-term capital loss. Other defined terms (e.g. net short-term capital gain) require the netting of short-term and long-term amounts or, quite possibly, calculations involving simultaneous reference to both long-term and short-term amounts (e.g., net capital gain).

- Amounts will constitute short-term or long-term capital gain only if and to the extent such items are taken into account in computing gross income. Amounts will constitute short-term or long-term capital loss only if and to the extent such items are taken into account in computing taxable income.

- Congress reserves preferential tax treatment for a taxpayer's net capital gain. Net capital gain is the excess of a taxpayer's net long-term gains over his net short-term losses during a taxable year. Note that it may be necessary to assign a $0 value to net short-term capital losses if no such losses exist for a given taxable year. Under § 1(h), different tax rates may apply to a taxpayer's net capital gains.

- If a taxpayer's total capital losses exceed his total capital gains for a taxable year, he may generally offset his ordinary income by the lesser of (1) the actual excess amount or (2) $3,000. Any remaining losses must be carried over as a capital loss to subsequent taxable years. Calculations under § 1212 determine the precise character of the capital loss carried over.

- A taxpayer's § 1231 gains will generally be taxed as long-term capital gain, and a taxpayer's § 1231 losses will generally be treated as ordinary losses. If a taxpayer has nonrecaptured § 1231 losses from the preceding five taxable years, current § 1231 gains will be taxed as ordinary income to the extent of such nonrecaptured § 1231 losses.

- On the disposition of specific assets, § 1245 may require the recapture of previously taken depreciation or amortization. Recapture refers to the treatment of realized gain as ordinary income.

- Under the *Arrowsmith* doctrine, a taxpayer may be required to coordinate related transactions separated by taxable years to avoid a mismatch of character (e.g., taking an ordinary loss after recognizing a capital gain in a related transaction).

- The term capital asset includes all property held by the taxpayer with the exception of various items listed in § 1221. Not every asset generally considered property will constitute property for purposes of § 1221 (e.g., property which serves as a substitute for ordinary income).

- The various forms of capital gain and loss are defined terms. Both short-term and long-term capital gains (or losses) arise only with respect to the sale or exchange of a capital asset. Unrealized amounts do not qualify, nor do amounts received for noncapital property or for services rendered, even if such amounts are received in a larger transaction involving capital assets.

Applying the Rules

For purposes of the following questions, please assume that all gains from capital asset transactions are taken into account in full in computing gross income and that all capital loss transactions are taken into account in full in computing taxable income.

1. On July 16, 2018, Amy purchased 1,000 shares of stock of Corporation X for $10,000. The stock gradually rose in value, and on August 22, 2019, she sold it for $12,000. Assuming Amy had no other capital asset transactions during 2018 and 2019, how will this transaction be treated for federal income tax purposes?

2. *Same facts as Question #1*, except that Amy purchased the stock for $12,000 and sold it for $10,000. What if she had only been able to sell it for $8,000?

3. On January 17, 2018, Sun purchased 100 shares of Vanderbilt, Inc. for $800,000. Approximately four weeks later, she sold the stock for $850,000. Assuming Sun had no other capital asset transactions during 2018, how will this transaction be treated for federal income tax purposes?

4. Assume that a taxpayer has the following capital asset transactions during a single taxable year. How will the taxpayer be treated with respect to these transactions for federal income tax purposes?

Short-Term Capital Transactions		Long-Term Capital Transactions	
Short-Term Gains:	$20,000	Long-Term Gains:	$90,000
Short-Term Losses:	$28,000	Long-Term Losses:	$60,000

5. Assume that a taxpayer has the following capital asset transactions during a single taxable year. How will the taxpayer be treated with respect to these transactions for federal income tax purposes?

Short-Term Capital Transactions		Long-Term Capital Transactions	
Short-Term Gains:	$8,000	Long-Term Gains:	$7,000
Short-Term Losses:	$3,000	Long-Term Losses:	$16,000

6. On January 3, 2019, Rakesh purchased 5,000 shares of Pure Nutrition, Inc. ("PNI") for $250,000. On February 6, 2019, PNI announced that shareholders of record on February 28, 2019, would be entitled to receive a dividend of $1/share (to be paid on March 8, 2019). Such shareholders would also be entitled to vote at the company's upcoming annual meeting (scheduled for April 16, 2019).

On March 6, 2019, Rakesh sold his PNI shares to Soledad for $300,000. Under the terms of the purchase agreement they both executed, Soledad agreed to pay Rakesh $300,000 for the stock, but the document also indicated that Rakesh's signature would automatically assign to Soledad the right to receive the dividend to be paid on March 8, 2019. How will Rakesh be treated with respect to this transaction for federal income tax purposes?

7. *Same facts as Question #6*, except that Rakesh simply sold Soledad his right to receive the dividend to be paid on March 8, 2019. Will that transaction result in his recognition of capital gain with respect to a capital asset (i.e., his right to receive a dividend)?

Federal Income Taxation in Practice

1. One of the junior partners you work with has a basic question he would like you to research. He understands that preferential tax rates apply to net capital gain, and that even if a taxpayer has a net capital gain, it might be taxed at a 15 percent, 20 percent, 25 percent, or 28 percent rate, depending on many factors, including the nature of the underlying capital asset. One of the firm's individual clients owns a very expensive work of art, although she is not, herself, in the trade or business of selling art. The partner would like to know whether this work of art is a "collectible" for purposes of § 1(h). Conduct the research and follow up with him by preparing and submitting a short memorandum.

2. You are a summer associate in a large law firm. One of the senior associates is working on a project for one of the firm's clients and needs some basic legislative history on § 1221(a)(7). He has asked that you find out when this provision was added to the Code and why. See what you can find and follow up with him by e-mail.

3. You are a member of Congress, and you serve on the House Ways and Means Committee. The committee will be considering a number of items in the future, including the tax rates to be applied to long-term capital gains and qualified dividends. Review the material in Exhibit 19.17 from the Congressional Budget Office and prepare a one-page memorandum summarizing your thoughts and arguments.

EXHIBIT 19.17   **Excerpt from Congressional Budget Office, Options for Reducing the Deficit: 2017–2026 (Option 3: Tax Rates on Long-Term Capital Gains and Qualified Dividends)**

132   OPTIONS FOR REDUCING THE DEFICIT: 2017 TO 2026   DECEMBER 2016

Revenues—Option 3

Raise the Tax Rates on Long-Term Capital Gains and Qualified Dividends by 2 Percentage Points

											Total	
Billions of Dollars	2017	2018	2019	2020	2021	2022	2023	2024	2025	2026	2017–2021	2017–2026
Change in Revenues	6.7	-2.8	6.0	6.1	6.4	6.5	6.7	6.9	7.1	7.5	22.4	57.1

Source: Staff of the Joint Committee on Taxation.

This option would take effect in January 2017.

When individuals sell an asset for more than the price at which they obtained it, they generally realize a capital gain that is subject to taxation. Most taxable capital gains are realized from the sale of corporate stocks, other financial assets, real estate, and unincorporated businesses. Since the adoption of the individual income tax in 1913, long-term gains (those realized on assets held for more than a year) have usually been taxed at lower rates than other sources of income, such as wages and interest. Since 2003, qualified dividends, which include most dividends, have been taxed at the same rates as long-term capital gains. Generally, qualified dividends are paid by domestic corporations or certain foreign corporations (including, for example, foreign corporations whose stock is traded in one of the major securities markets in the United States).

The current tax rates on long-term capital gains and qualified dividends depend on several features of the tax code:

■ The statutory tax rates on long-term capital gains and qualified dividends depend on the statutory tax rates that would apply if they were considered to be ordinary income—that is, all income subject to the individual income tax from sources other than long-term capital gains and qualified dividends. A taxpayer does not pay any taxes on long-term capital gains and qualified dividends that otherwise would be taxed at a rate of 10 percent or 15 percent if those earnings were treated as ordinary income. Long-term capital gains and qualified dividends become taxable when they would be taxed at a rate that ranged from 25 percent through 35 percent if they were treated as ordinary income; those gains and dividends are taxed, instead, at a rate of 15 percent. All other long-term capital gains and qualified dividends are subject to a tax rate of 20 percent—nearly 20 percentage points lower than the rate that would apply if they were considered ordinary income.

■ Certain long-term capital gains and qualified dividends are included in net investment income, which is subject to the Net Investment Income Tax (NIIT) of 3.8 percent. Taxpayers are subject to the NIIT if their modified adjusted gross income is greater than $200,000 for unmarried filers and $250,000 for married couples filing joint tax returns. (Adjusted gross income, or AGI, includes income from all sources not specifically excluded by the tax code, minus certain deductions. Modified AGI includes foreign income that is normally excluded from AGI.) The additional tax is applied to the smaller of two amounts: net investment income or the amount by which modified AGI exceeds the thresholds. Therefore, for taxpayers subject to the NIIT, the marginal tax rate (that is, the percentage of an additional dollar of income that is paid in taxes) on long-term capital gains and qualified dividends effectively increases from 20 percent to 23.8 percent.

■ Other provisions of the tax code—such as those that limit or phase out other tax preferences—may further increase the tax rate on long-term capital gains and dividends. For example, for each dollar by which taxpayers' AGI exceeds certain high thresholds, the total value of certain itemized deductions is reduced by 3 cents. As a result, the amount of income that is taxable will increase: For example, for taxpayers in the 39.6 percent tax bracket for ordinary income, taxable income will effectively rise by $1.03 for each additional dollar of long-term capital gains. That increase in taxable income will cause their marginal tax rate to rise by more than 1 percentage point (0.396 times 3 percent).

With all of those provisions taken into account, the tax rate on long-term capital gains and dividends is nearly 25 percent for most people in the top income tax bracket. Although that bracket applies to less than 1 percent of all

EXHIBIT 19.17 **Excerpt from Congressional Budget Office, Options for Reducing the Deficit: 2017–2026 (Option 3: Tax Rates on Long-Term Capital Gains and Qualified Dividends) (*cont'd*)**

taxpayers, the income of those taxpayers accounts for roughly two-thirds of income from dividends and realized long-term capital gains.

This option would raise the statutory tax rates on long-term capital gains and dividends by 2 percentage points. Those rates would then be 2 percent for taxpayers in the 10 percent and 15 percent brackets for ordinary income, 17 percent for taxpayers in the brackets ranging from 25 percent through 35 percent, and 22 percent for taxpayers in the top bracket. The option would not change other provisions of the tax code that also affect taxes on capital gains and dividends. The staff of the Joint Committee on Taxation estimates that this option would raise federal revenues by $57 billion over the 2017–2026 period.

One advantage of raising tax rates on long-term capital gains and dividends, rather than raising tax rates on ordinary income, is that it would reduce the incentive for taxpayers to try to mischaracterize labor compensation and profits as capital gains. Such strategizing occurs under current law even though the tax code and regulations governing taxes contain numerous provisions that attempt to limit it. Reducing the incentive to mischaracterize compensation and profits as capital gains would reduce the resources devoted to circumventing the rules.

Another rationale for raising revenue through this option is that it would be progressive with respect to people's wealth and income. Most capital gains are received by people with significant wealth and income, although some are received by retirees who have greater wealth but less income than some younger people who are still working. Overall, raising tax rates on long-term capital gains would impose, on average, a larger burden on people with significant financial resources than on people with fewer resources.

A disadvantage of the option is that raising tax rates on long-term capital gains and dividends would influence investment decisions by increasing the tax burden on investment income. By lowering the after-tax return on investments, the increased tax rates would reduce the incentive to invest in businesses. Another disadvantage is that the option would exacerbate an existing bias that favors debt-financed investment by businesses over equity-financed investment. That bias is greatest for investors in firms that pay the corporate income tax because corporate profits are taxed once under the corporate income tax and a second time when those profits are paid out as dividends or reinvested and taxed later as capital gains on the sale of corporate stock. In contrast, profits of unincorporated businesses, rents, and interest are taxed only once. That difference distorts investment decisions by discouraging investment funded through new issues of corporate stock and encouraging, instead, either borrowing to fund corporate investments or the formation and expansion of noncorporate businesses. The bias against equity funding of corporate investments would not expand if the option exempted dividends and capital gains on corporate stock—limiting the tax increase to capital gains on those assets that are not taxed under both the corporate and the individual income taxes. That modification, however, would also reduce the revenue gains from the option.

Another argument against implementing the option is related to the fact that taxation of capital gains encourages people to defer the sale of their capital assets, sometimes even leading them to never sell some of the assets during their lifetime. In the former case, the taxation of capital gains is postponed; in the latter case, it is avoided altogether because if an individual sells an inherited asset, the capital gain is the difference between the sale price and the fair-market value as of the date of the previous owner's death. By raising tax rates on long-term capital gains and dividends, this option could further encourage people to hold on to their investments only for tax reasons, which could reduce economic efficiency by preventing some of those assets from being put to more productive uses.

RELATED OPTIONS: Revenues, Options 1, 2, 9, 12, 41

RELATED CBO PUBLICATIONS: *The Distribution of Asset Holdings and Capital Gains* (August 2016), www.cbo.gov/publication/51831; *The Distribution of Household Income and Federal Taxes, 2013* (June 2016), www.cbo.gov/publication/51361; *Taxing Capital Income: Effective Marginal Tax Rates Under 2014 Law and Selected Policy Options* (December 2014), www.cbo.gov/publication/49817; *The Distribution of Major Tax Expenditures in the Individual Income Tax System* (May 2013), www.cbo.gov/publication/43768; Tim Dowd, Robert McClelland, and Athiphat Muthitacharoen, *New Evidence on the Tax Elasticity of Capital Gains*, Working Paper 2012-09 (June 2012), www.cbo.gov/publication/43334

Tax Avoidance and Tax Shelters

Decades ago, Judge Learned Hand famously noted that anyone "may so arrange his affairs that his taxes shall be as low as possible; he is not bound to choose that pattern which will best pay the Treasury . . . ." *Helvering v. Gregory*, 69 F.2d 809, at 810 (2d Cir. 1934). Soon thereafter, Justice Sutherland of the U.S. Supreme Court echoed that notion, writing as follows, "The legal right of a taxpayer to decrease the amount of what otherwise would be his taxes, or altogether avoid them, by means which the law permits, cannot be doubted. The question for determination is whether what was done, apart from the tax motive, was the thing which the statute intended." *Gregory v. Helvering*, 293 U.S. 465, at 469 (1935) (citations omitted). Without question, Justice Sutherland's sentiment has continuing vitality, but the unfortunate and long-standing truth is that certain taxpayers habitually focus more on their right to minimize (or, ideally, eliminate) their tax liabilities and less on achieving that goal within means permitted by governing federal law. Rather than respecting established boundaries, they are ever on the search to find (or, if need be, create) a "loophole." Many attempt to exploit the rules to secure unwarranted deductions. Others seek to manipulate the character of their income or losses, and yet others aim simply to defer the recognition of gains long enough to reap time-value-of-money benefits with respect to the funds they manage to deflect from public coffers for a season. They seek to *appear* to do that "which the statute intended" while doing anything but. To be sure, Congress, the IRS, and the courts have responded, but the difficulty they encounter is attempting to derail abuses while, at the same time, ensuring that legitimate activity suffers no negative tax impact. And, as if that task was not difficult enough, there is the chronic problem of migration. As

Key Concepts

- Passive activity and passive activity losses
- Material participation
- At-risk limitations
- Economic substance doctrine

soon as the damage is halted in one corner, taxpayers move their strategies to a new arena of opportunity, hoping to chew away as much as they can before the legislative, administrative, or judicial exterminators arrive there. Even with considerable resources at their disposal, Congress, the IRS, and the courts often have difficulty keeping up with creative and well-seasoned tax strategists who routinely petition taxpayers for an audience in order to hawk their wares. In this chapter, we turn to specific provisions that serve, in at least some instances, to arrest taxpayer abuse of various Code-based allowances.

A. IN GENERAL

In Chapter 1, we discussed the role that taxes played in sparking the American Revolution. While some colonists may have been so loyal to Great Britain that they willingly paid taxes without representation in Parliament, others were adamant in their opposition, going so far as to toss taxable tea into the waters of Boston Harbor and to bestow coats of tar and feathers upon would-be tax collectors. In more modern times, taxpayers do not resort to such drastic measures, but more passive aggression is not uncommon. Even if taxpayers generally realize the futility of resisting the collection of taxes, they have certainly been known to make facile attempts to shelter their income from the burden of taxation and thereby reduce what they would otherwise owe (e.g., claiming pets and phantom children as dependents or taking deductions for nonexistent charitable contributions). But those moves are the easily detected efforts of ham-handed, small-time amateurs. Corporate and sophisticated individual taxpayers (who routinely operate in the multi-million-dollar financial stratosphere) have concocted (or embraced) a host of "strategies" and "solutions" in an effort to minimize their tax liabilities. More often than not, the attempt involves abuse of Code provisions making allowances for depreciation or interest payments. Administrative or judicial intervention is usually the first line of defense, but abusive activity may ultimately prompt Congress to act. To get a more concrete sense of how tax shelters have operated in the past and how Congress intervened, we turn to rules governing passive activity losses, at-risk limitations, and the economic substance doctrine.

B. PASSIVE ACTIVITY LOSSES

The passive activity loss rules set forth in § 469 arose largely in response to taxpayer abuse of the Code's depreciation provisions. Putting money into a real estate investment while delegating management and other real work to agents was a fairly common "passive" taxpayer activity. The classic scheme involved several individuals acting in concert first to borrow money and then to use the loan proceeds to invest in real estate (e.g., a large apartment building). If successful, the venture would generate rental income, and the bulk of that income would be offset by available deductions (e.g., interest on the loan, building maintenance, employee salaries, etc.). The taxpayers' chief motivation in executing the transaction, however, was to reap the benefit of the depreciation deductions flowing from ownership of the building. Such deductions offset the income from their other income-generating activities and effectively "sheltered" that income from taxation. At the same time, the basis of the building was regularly adjusted downward. Even if the taxpayers recognized gain on subsequent sale of the building at a profit and were forced to recapture prior depreciation as ordinary income, the prior depreciation deductions reduced their tax burdens in earlier years. As a result, the taxpayers managed to enjoy, temporarily at least, the time-value-of-money benefits of the funds they would otherwise have surrendered as taxes in prior years. Today, this gambit no longer works.

As an initial matter, a taxpayer participating in such a transaction may no longer deduct the interest paid with respect to the loan. Section 163(h)(2)(B) may appear to facilitate the deduction of investment interest by excluding it from the definition of *personal interest*, but § 163(d)(3)(B)(ii) clarifies that *investment interest* does not include "any interest which is taken into account under § 469 in computing income or loss from a passive activity of the taxpayer." That definition leads us to the primary provision impeding the classic real estate tax shelter, § 469.

Final Disposition of Passive Activity in Fully Taxable Transaction

A taxpayer may be barred from taking a deduction with respect to a passive activity loss for several taxable years, but he will be able to take such losses into account if he disposes of his entire interest in the passive activity in a fully taxable transaction. *See generally* §§ 469(b) and (g)(1).

Limited Relief for Certain Active Participants

Section 469 contains specific rules under which all rental activity is deemed passive unless the taxpayer can satisfy the standards set forth in § 469(c)(7). A relief provision exists, however, under which a portion of a taxpayer's passive activity losses are deductible. Such losses must be attributable to rental real estate activity in which the taxpayer actively participated. *See* § 469(i)(1). A $25,000 cap applies, and even this amount may be completely phased out as the taxpayer's adjusted gross income rises.

Although § 469 sweeps somewhat broadly, we limit our focus here to its impact on individuals with losses flowing from specific activities. Under § 469(a)(1), an individual taxpayer is barred from deducting any passive activity losses incurred during the taxable year, and per § 469(d)(1), *passive activity loss* refers to the amount (if any) by which aggregate losses from all passive activities for the taxable year exceed aggregate income from all passive activities for such taxable year. Thus, losses and income from passive activities may operate to offset each other, but the statute specifically targets the *excess* of losses over income. This approach makes sense because Congress seeks to prevent the use of such excess losses to offset the taxpayer's *other* income. Of course, this specific rule only operates with respect to the taxpayer's passive activities. Section 469(c) defines *passive activity* as any activity (1) that involves the conduct of a trade or business and (2) in which the taxpayer does not materially participate. Material participation requires taxpayer involvement in operations on a regular, continuous, and substantial basis. *See* § 469(h)(1). Intent on preventing the use of specific real estate investments as tax shelters (while aiming to protect legitimate business activity), Congress felt the need to devote focused statutory attention to rental activities.

Although § 469(c) generally defines passive activity as the conduct of a trade or business in which the taxpayer does not materially participate, § 469(c)(2) declares that with limited exception, any rental activity will constitute a passive activity, and under § 469(c)(4), such characterization will persist regardless of whether the taxpayer materially participates in the activity. The narrow and limited exception (set forth in § 469(c)(7)) is intended to protect those who truly are in the real property trade or business, and by that, Congress means only those able to satisfy both of the following requirements:

- More than one-half of the personal services performed in trades or businesses by the taxpayer during such taxable year are performed in real property trades or businesses in which the taxpayer materially participates; and
- Such taxpayer performs more than 750 hours of services during the taxable year in real property trades or businesses in which the taxpayer materially participates.

See § 469(c)(7)(B)(i) and (ii). The rigorous application of this rule is softened only by a relief provision of limited applicability. *See* § 469(i).

Today, much of the controversy and litigation under § 469 involves taxpayers who feel entitled to the relief provided by § 469(c)(7) because, so they assert, they are genuinely and legitimately involved in the real property trade or business. As the next case well demonstrates, arguing that one is involved in the relevant trade or business and being able to establish that fact to a court's satisfaction are two different things.

Case Preview

Almquist v. Commissioner

Having worked in the rental real estate business for several years, Talbot Almquist had considerable industry experience as an employee. Even so, his work in the industry did not qualify him automatically as someone involved in the real property trade or business with respect to rental real estate he and his wife owned and operated in their individual, nonemployee capacities. Section 469(c)(7)(D)(ii) provides that services as an employee do not count in terms of satisfying the § 469(c)(7)(B) requirements unless the employee is a 5 percent owner of the employer. Thus, the Almquists had to satisfy the personal service requirements based on their activities outside their formal employment. As you read through the decision, consider the following questions:

1. Did Mr. Almquist's work at Oakwood help him qualify as one participating in the real property trade or business?
2. Was the taxpayer required to keep detailed daily records of his real property business activities to satisfy the statutory requirements?
3. If the taxpayer could prove that he performed more than 750 hours of services in real property trades or businesses, would he have satisfied the statutory requirements?

Almquist v. Commissioner
T.C. Memo. 2014-40

WHERRY, Judge:

This case is before the Court on a petition for redetermination of a deficiency in income tax respondent determined for petitioners' 2008 tax year. Petitioners timely filed a joint Federal income tax return for the 2008 tax year ***. Respondent issued a notice of deficiency on April 13, 2011, for the 2008 tax year disallowing a deduction for petitioners' losses from their rental real estate activity as passive and determining an accuracy-related penalty under section 6662(a).

After concessions by the parties, the only issues for decision are (1) whether petitioners' real estate loss of $154,835 reported on Schedule E, Supplemental Income and Loss, for the tax year 2008 is subject to the passive loss limitation under section 469 and (2) whether petitioners are liable for the section 6662(a) accuracy-related penalty.

FINDINGS OF FACT

Some of the facts have been stipulated and are so found. The stipulations of the parties with accompanying exhibits are incorporated herein by reference. At the time the petition was filed, petitioners resided in Encino, California. ***

Talbot Matthew Almquist worked as an executive at Oakwood Worldwide (Oakwood) a.k.a. R & B Realty Group for over 15 years including the 2008 tax calendar year. While working for Oakwood Mr. Almquist managed 15 rental buildings and oversaw 300 employees. Since 2001 Mr. Almquist and Rula Almquist have owned and managed from one to three rental properties of their own. ***

In 2008 Mr. Almquist worked as the vice president of operations for Oakwood and received a salary of $180,748. In 2008 Mr. Almquist estimated that he spent no more than 20 hours a week working for Oakwood and that over the course of the year he worked between 885 and 980 hours. Petitioners did not provide any paperwork from Oakwood or other documents supporting Mr. Almquist's claim that he worked no more than 885 to 980 hours in 2008 for Oakwood. Mr. Almquist continued to work for Oakwood until 2010 when his job was terminated and he was provided with a severance check for $180,799.

In 2008 Mrs. Almquist worked as an operations manager for Archstone Communities, LLC (Archstone). Mrs. Almquist oversaw Archstone's properties, buildings, and apartments. ***

In 2008 petitioners owned two rental real estate properties. One of their rental properties is in Indio, California (Indio property). Petitioners' home in Oakwood, California, is approximately 130 miles from Indio, California. The Indio property is an approximately 2,700-square-foot residence purchased new in 2006. Petitioners rented the Indio property out to Beverly Humphrey in 2007 and renewed the lease from January 9 through April 9, 2008, for $3,000 a month. Mr. Almquist maintained the Indio property, which, although purchased new, did not come with the amenities needed to rent it as a furnished apartment. Accordingly, he spent considerable time preparing it for potential renters. Some of the preparation activities included replacing the air conditioner condenser, landscaping the yard, posting ads, and making sure the property had sufficient furnishings.

The other rental property is in Naples, Florida (Naples property). The Naples property was constructed in 1993 and is approximately 1,500 square feet in size. On May 29, 2007, petitioners hired Naples Realty Services, Inc. (Realty), to find possible renters for the Naples property. In 2008 petitioners did not visit the Naples property. Petitioners rented out the Naples property to one renter starting January 28, 2008, for one year. Realty collected the $1,500 per month rent from the renter, withheld its 10% fee, and then forwarded the remaining rent to petitioners.

Both of petitioners' properties were furnished and were intended to be rented out as fully furnished units. Generally, renting furnished residential property requires more upkeep and time than renting unfurnished residential property because the furnished property should be equipped with reasonable appliances, furnishings, and necessities for the renters.

Renters and potential renters faxed correspondence to an electronic fax number; then the correspondence was automatically forwarded to Mrs. Almquist's email address. Mr. Almquist had access to Mrs. Almquist's email, and he worked on the rental property business using her email. ***

Petitioners provided one calendar and two different logs describing the hours worked on the rental properties. At the start of respondent's examination of petitioners' 2008 tax return petitioners created the calendar from very brief cryptic notes in Mr. Almquist's personal spiral notebook daily records. He did this about a year after the fact, long after the asserted work was completed. The calendar's short notes about the days Mr. Almquist worked on the rental properties occasionally included the hours worked as respondent's revenue agent requested that this information be included when petitioners prepared the calendar. Mr. Almquist contends that the calendar was created on the advice of petitioners' certified public accountant and was, as noted, purportedly based on Mr. Almquist's daily record handwritten notes. Petitioners did not provide the purported supporting handwritten notes to the Court.

More than a year after the work was completed petitioners also created the first log purportedly based on the calendar, documents, and emails. The first log listed the hours Mr. Almquist spent working on the properties and a brief description of the type of work he performed. That log indicated that Mr. Almquist worked 486 hours on the Indio property and 188 hours on the Naples property. The first log also indicated that Mr. Almquist spent another 101 hours looking for investment properties and attending open houses. Other than the calendar prepared after the audit started, petitioners did not provide any of the purported supporting documents or emails to the Court. Mr. Almquist explained: "[W]e've moved twice since then, so I can't find the original spiral, but, you know, it was transferred to this, which then was transferred to the final document."

After a meeting with a revenue agent, petitioners created a second log listing additional time allocated to the activity. Mr. Almquist contends that the second log lists more hours because it included additional activities, such as craigslist ads and emails he did not previously include, as well as additional hours for his drive to the Indio property. Petitioners contend the 280-mile round trip takes on average as much as six to seven hours because of Los Angeles traffic and gas stops. This second greatly expanded log containing many more entries indicated that Mr. Almquist worked 759 hours on the Indio property and 84 hours on the Naples property. Among the changes from the first log to the second log was a modification for November 2008 where the first log reported that Mr. Almquist spent 25 hours on the Indio property, but the second log reported that Mr. Almquist spent a little over 135 hours on the Indio property. Petitioners did not provide the Court with any of the purported new supporting documents or other emails for the later log.

OPINION

As a general rule, the Commissioner's determination in the notice of deficiency is presumed correct, and the taxpayer bears the burden of proving by a preponderance of the evidence that the determination is improper. ***

Deductions are a matter of legislative grace, and taxpayers bear the burden of proving that they are entitled to any claimed deductions. Taxpayers are required to identify each deduction, maintain adequate records, substantiate each deduction, and show that they have met all requirements.

I. Real Estate Activity

A taxpayer is generally allowed deductions for certain business and profit-seeking investment expenses. Section 469 disallows a taxpayer's deductions attributable to a passive activity loss for the taxable year. Section 469(d)(1) defines "passive activity loss" as "the amount (if any) by which — (A) the aggregate losses from all passive activities for the taxable year, exceed (B) the aggregate income from all passive activities for such year." Passive activity is defined as any activity "which involves the conduct of any trade or business, and * * * in which the taxpayer does not materially participate." § 469(c)(1)(A) and (B). The Code specifically provides that the term "passive activity" also includes any rental activity. Sec. 469(c)(2). The Code then provides an exception from that rule for rental real estate activity of a taxpayer who is engaged in a real property trade or business. *See* § 469(c)(7).

Consequently, the first issue is whether Mr. Almquist was actively engaged in a real property trade or business (real estate professional) as provided in section 469(c)(7). A taxpayer qualifies as a real estate professional if

(i) more than one-half of the personal services performed in trades or businesses by the taxpayer during such taxable year are performed in real property trades or businesses in which the taxpayer materially participates, and

(ii) such taxpayer performs more than 750 hours of services during the taxable year in real property trades or businesses in which the taxpayer materially participates.

Sec. 469(c)(7)(B)(i) and (ii).

Unless the taxpayer timely elects otherwise, the taxpayer must satisfy the requirement of material participation as applied separately to each rental real estate interest. Sec. 469(c)(7)(A).

In determining whether a taxpayer performs more than 750 hours of service in a real property trade or business, any time spent as an employee performing real estate activities is ignored, except if the employee is also a 5% owner as defined in section 416(i)(1)(B). See sec. 469(c)(7)(D)(ii). Mr. Almquist does not contend that he was a 5% owner of Oakwood; therefore, any time spent managing property as Oakwood's employee is not included in determining whether Mr. Almquist is a real estate professional.

Petitioners do not contend that Mrs. Almquist qualifies as a real estate professional. In the case of a joint return, a spouse must separately satisfy the requirements of section 469(c)(7) to qualify as a real estate professional. *See* § 469(c)(7)(B). Petitioners do not allege, nor does the record support, that Mrs. Almquist spent any time on the rental properties that should be included in determining whether there was material participation. Therefore, any time Mrs. Almquist spent working on the rental properties is not included in determining whether Mr. Almquist qualifies as a real estate professional.

All of a taxpayer's real property trade or business activity is taken into account in determining whether the 750-hour requirement is satisfied. A real property trade or business is defined in section 469(c)(7)(C) as "any real property development, redevelopment, construction, reconstruction, acquisition, conversion, rental, operation, management, leasing, or brokerage trade or business." This list does not include any research or other preparatory activities.

The regulations provide that "the extent of an individual's participation in an activity may be established by any reasonable means." Sec. 1.469-5T(f)(4), Temporary Income Tax Regs., 53 Fed.Reg. 5727 (Feb. 25, 1988).

Contemporaneous daily time reports, logs, or similar documents are not required if the extent of such participation may be established by other reasonable means. Reasonable means * * * may include but are not limited to the identification of services performed over a period of time and the approximate number of hours spent performing such services during such period, based on appointment books, calendars, or narrative summaries. *Id.*

Although "reasonable means" may be interpreted broadly, "a postevent 'ballpark guesstimate'" will not suffice. *Moss v. Commissioner*, 135 T.C. 365, 369, 2010 WL 3633505 (2010) (citing *Bailey v. Commissioner*, T.C. Memo.2001–296, and *Goshorn v. Commissioner*, T.C. Memo.1993–578).

Petitioners introduced a calendar containing cryptic brief notes about the work completed on the two rental properties. The calendar occasionally stated some of the hours Mr. Almquist purportedly worked. Petitioners purportedly created the first log using the calendar, supporting documents, and emails. However, other than the calendar, petitioners did not supply the Court with any of the purported supporting documents or emails.

Even if this Court were to accept petitioner's calendar and first log as accurate, Mr. Almquist would still not qualify as a real estate professional because the first log shows that Mr. Almquist spent only 486 hours on the Indio property, 188 hours on the Naples property, and 101 hours on investment property. Combined, these would account for 775 hours worked on real estate property, which would only be enough for the 750 hour requirement. Petitioners have not shown that Mr. Almquist spent more than one-half of his trade or business personal service time in a real property trade or business in which he materially participates as required by section 469(c)(7)(B)(i).

Mr. Almquist estimated that he spent somewhere between 885 and 980 hours working at Oakwood. If this Court were to accept Mr. Almquist's assertion and generously place him at the low end of his estimate of 885 hours worked at Oakwood, Mr. Almquist would still not qualify as a real estate professional.

Petitioners contend that this Court should look past the fact that petitioners did not provide any supporting documentation of the hours Mr. Almquist worked, should ignore petitioners' calendar and first log, and should look only to the second log in determining whether Mr. Almquist is a real estate professional. We again emphasize that the Court was not provided any of the purported supporting documentation or email and was provided only petitioners' self-serving testimony.

We are not required to accept such self-serving testimony, and we are not willing to rely on that testimony to establish petitioners' position. Without any supporting documentation, the second log, created by petitioners over a year after the work was completed, is nothing more than "a postevent 'ballpark guesstimate.'"

Therefore, Mr. Almquist does not meet the minimum requirements for a qualified real estate professional. Accordingly, petitioners' rental real estate activity shall be treated as passive and the claimed deduction relating to the passive activity losses is disallowed for the 2008 tax year.

[The court also confirmed the propriety of imposing an accuracy-related penalty.]

The Court has considered all of petitioners' contentions, argument, requests, and statements. To the extent not discussed herein, we conclude that they are meritless, moot, or irrelevant. To reflect the foregoing,

Decision will be entered under Rule 155.

Post-Case Follow-Up

Noting the taxpayer's abject failure to document and substantiate the extent of their services in a real property trade or business, the court concluded in *Almquist* that the taxpayer failed to satisfy the requirements of § 469(c)(7)(B)(i) and(ii). Accordingly, the taxpayers were unable to deduct the passive activity losses they incurred during the taxable year. Oddly enough, the court spends a considerable amount of time berating the taxpayer for failing to substantiate the extent of his real estate activities before pointing out that even if the sloppy recordkeeping had been accepted, the taxpayer still would not have satisfied the statute's other requirement (i.e., that more than one-half of the personal services performed in trades or businesses by the taxpayer were performed in real property trades or businesses in which the taxpayer materially participated). Note, in particular, that detailed daily records are not required. As the court notes, Temporary Treasury Regulations allow proof of the extent of a taxpayer's participation in the activity "by any reasonable means." Treas. Reg. § 1.469-5T(f)(4).

Almquist v. Commissioner: Real Life Applications

1. Seven years ago, Casey became a 10 percent owner of the Sterling Properties LLC ("Sterling"). Since its inception, Sterling has owned several apartment buildings in downtown Chicago, and Casey serves as the property manager for two adjacent buildings. In 2019, she spent approximately 2,000 hours managing the properties, and although she had income from other sources, she conducted no other trades or businesses. Do Casey's activities constitute a passive activity within the meaning of § 469(c)?

2. Assume that Brandi is a property manager for Shanghai Properties International, Inc. ("Shanghai"). In 2019, she worked approximately 2,000 hours for Shanghai and spent approximately 500 hours performing various services with respect to three rental properties she owned. Will Brandi's rental activity constitute a passive activity for her 2019 taxable year?

3. Five years ago, Myla retired after 30 years of teaching at a local public school. In 2020, Myla spent approximately 180 hours as a school crossing guard and 900 managing her four rental properties. Will Myla's rental property activities constitute a passive activity within the meaning of § 469(c)?

C. AT-RISK LIMITATION

Those of you who have gambled at casinos have a good sense of how at least a few of the games work. If you hand over a $100 bill in exchange for gambling chips and then place them on the blackjack table to play a hand against the casino (i.e., the "house"), you might get lucky or, as fate might have it, you might find the swift hands of the house's dealer swiping your hard-earned chips away as you reel in defeat. It all depends on the cards you're dealt relative to those dealt to and played by the house. In any event, you fully understand that no matter what, the most you can lose on that specific play of the cards is $100, because that is the amount you gambled or put "at risk" of loss. Similarly, if you purchase 1,000 shares of stock for $100,000, the stock may appreciate in value, but assuming the stock falls in

> **Key Statutory Provisions**
>
> ▦ **Internal Revenue Code**
> ▦ **§ 465(a)(1)–(2)**
> ▦ **§ 465(b)(1)–(2), (4)–(6)**
> ▦ **§ 465(c)(1) & (3)(A)**

value to $0, the most you can lose in that scenario (excluding any transaction costs) is $100,000. Nothing more, nothing less. Prior to the enactment of § 465, taxpayers attempted to abuse various Code provisions by taking loss deductions in excess of their at-risk amounts. Often, the ruse was to treat borrowed amounts (for which they were not personally liable) as at-risk amounts in the hope of triggering an interest or other deduction that could give rise to losses that, in turn, could be used to shelter income from other sources. The at-risk rules under § 465 serve to ensure that to the extent a taxpayer attempts to take a loss deduction with respect to a given transaction, they can claim as a loss no more than the amount they truly have "at risk."

In the examples presented thus far, ascertaining the taxpayer's at-risk amount was easy enough. But things can get far more complicated, and as you might suspect, complexity can serve to cloak the tax dodge. If a taxpayer invests $100,000 of her own money in a business venture and borrows an additional $5 million to invest in the same venture, what amount does she have at risk? Is it $100,000 or $5,100,000? The answer, of course, turns on the terms of the loan. If she is personally liable with respect to the loan proceeds, then her amount at risk is $5,100,000; otherwise, she has only $100,000 at risk. As one might guess, loans take many forms. The creditor may lend money or extend credit without demanding that the debtor put up security (i.e. collateral) to ensure repayment. Under such circumstances, the creditor is described as **unsecured**. In other situations, the creditor is willing to lend money or extend credit, but it may demand that the debtor make some form of property serve as security or collateral for repayment of the debt (e.g., the car itself for a car loan or the residence itself for a mortgage). Logically enough, such a creditor is described as being **secured**. If the debtor defaults on the loan and the secured creditor is forced to proceed against or take possession of the asset and sell it to get the funds to cover its debt, that remedy may be the end of it. But what if the sale of the collateral does not produce enough money to cover the outstanding debt (i.e., a deficiency exists)? If the loan is **recourse**, the creditor can proceed against the debtor and his other assets to collect the deficiency, but if the loan is **nonrecourse**, the creditor has exercised its *only* remedy, proceeding against the asset serving as security and selling it in the hope of recovering any outstanding loan balance. Returning to our prior fact scenario, we can assume that most financial institutions willing to lend $5 million will expect some form of direct personal liability or some form of marketable collateral as security. If our investor assumed personal liability on the debt, her amount at risk was $5,100,000. But if the loan was secured only by collateral, then her amount at risk turned on whether the loan was recourse or nonrecourse. With these notions in mind, let's turn the rules set forth in § 465.

The Right to Repossess

Although secured creditors generally have the right to repossess collateral if the debtor defaults with respect to the relevant obligation, such a creditor may not breach the peace in exercising that right. If a breach of the peace is threatened during a given repossession attempt and the secured creditor temporarily abandons the effort, the secured creditor (or, more likely, its stealthy agents) may try again. And again . . .

Credit: Roman S., Photographer/ Shutterstock.com.

Qualified Nonrecourse Financing

Section 465(b)(6) makes special provision for qualified nonrecourse financing in the sense that such financing can be considered amounts at risk for those obtaining the financing under the appropriate circumstances. The rule applies only with respect to the activity of holding real property and only if such property serves as security for the qualified nonrecourse financing. Qualified nonrecourse financing generally refers to amounts borrowed with respect to the holding of real property on a nonrecourse basis from the government or from a financial institution engaged in the business of lending money. *See generally* § 465(b)(6).

The general rule under § 465(a)(1) clarifies that, for tax purposes, losses incurred by an individual with respect to specific taxpayer activities are limited to the aggregate amount the taxpayer has at risk. Under § 465(c)(1) and (3), the scope of covered activities is broad enough to include any activity "engaged in by the taxpayer in carrying on a trade or business or for the production of income," and the definition of at-risk amount is set forth in § 465(b)(1). In general, an individual's at-risk amount includes (1) money contributed to the activity, (2) the adjusted basis of property contributed to the activity, and (3) amounts borrowed with respect to the activity (within the meaning of § 465(b)(2)). A taxpayer is considered at risk with respect to amounts borrowed for use in the activity only if the taxpayer is personally liable for repayment of the debt or has pledged property as security for repayment of the debt (excluding property used in the activity). *See* § 465(b)(1) and (2). Note that the latter amount only refers to the net fair market value of the taxpayer's interest in the property. *See* § 465(b)(2)(B).

Given the importance of personal taxpayer liability with respect to amounts to be treated as at risk, the parties to a given transaction have an incentive to cast it as a recourse liability, even if on close examination it would be readily apparent that the taxpayer is not, in fact, personally liable for the debt. Section 465(b)(4) anticipates the potential for deceptive transactional form and dictates that "a taxpayer shall not be considered at risk with respect to amounts protected against loss through nonrecourse financing, guarantees, stop loss agreements, or other similar arrangements." We see this rule in operation in Revenue Ruling 83-133.

Ruling Preview

Revenue Ruling 83-133

In this Revenue Ruling, the IRS creates a hypothetical taxpayer, *A*, and has the taxpayer participate in a transaction in which he contributes a specific dollar amount to an activity and signs a recourse note with respect to the activity bearing a face amount equal to three times that amount. Although the taxpayer claimed to be at risk with respect to both his cash investment and his recourse borrowing, the precise terms and conditions of the deal indicated otherwise. As you read the ruling, consider the following questions:

1. In what way did the taxpayer's recourse note differ from a traditional recourse note?

2. What was the taxpayer's apparent motive for entering into the various transactions discussed?
3. To what extent, if any, was the taxpayer actually at risk?

Rev. Rul. 83-133
1983-2 C.B. 15

ISSUE

For purposes of computing the investment tax credit and determining the allowable loss from an activity, is an investor at risk with respect to the amount of a note, under the circumstances described below?

FACTS

In July 1981 *P*, a promoter, offered to sell to investors electronic moving message boards that display news, information and advertising. The equipment is 5 year recovery property within the meaning of section 168(c) of the Internal Revenue Code. *P* recommended that investors hire *X*, a service corporation, to supply all the necessary support systems. *P* represented that investors will be able to claim an investment tax credit based upon the total purchase price of the equipment and will be "at risk" within the meaning of section 465(b) for that amount.

A, an individual, purchased a set of four message boards from *P* for 40*x* dollars. *A* made a cash down payment of 10*x* dollars and executed a recourse note to *P* for the balance. The note provides that principal plus interest at the rate of 9 percent per annum is payable in equal monthly installments over a 10-year period. The note also provides that failure to pay any or all of a payment when it is due will not cause a default on the note. The amount not paid when due will be added to the remaining balance of principal.

A hired *X* to install, maintain and service the boards, program the news, information and entertainment features, sell advertising time, develop and schedule the advertising messages, and provide bookkeeping, accounting and other administrative services to *A* in exchange for 50 percent of the gross operating revenue generated. The service agreement provides that *A* must retain *X* for 36 months. If *A* decides to withdraw from the project at any time after the 36-month period has passed, *X* agrees to assume ownership of *A*'s equipment and all financial responsibility on *A*'s note to *P*.

A offered the message boards for lease but received no income from the activity during 1981. *A* made no payments on the note during 1981. On *A*'s 1981 federal income tax return, *A* used 40*x* dollars for the purpose of computing the investment tax credit, for determining basis and depreciation, and for purposes of limiting *A*'s loss from the activity to *A*'s amount of risk.

LAW AND ANALYSIS

[The Service first discusses provisions related to the investment tax credit, including § 38.]

Section 465(a)(1) of the Code provides that, in the case of an individual engaged in an activity to which section 465 applies, any loss from the activity for the taxable year shall be allowed only to the extent of the aggregate amount with respect to which the taxpayer is at risk for the activity at the close of the taxable year.

Section 465(b)(1) of the Code provides that, for purposes of section 465, the amounts with respect to which a taxpayer shall be considered at risk for an activity shall include the amount of money and the adjusted basis of other property contributed by the taxpayer to the activity, and certain amounts borrowed with respect to the activity.

Section 465(b)(2) of the Code provides that, for purposes of section 465, a taxpayer shall be considered at risk with respect to amounts borrowed for use in an activity to the extent that the taxpayer is personally liable for the repayment of the amounts, or has pledged property, other than property used in the activity, as security for the borrowed amount (to the extent of the net fair market value of the taxpayer's interest in the property).

Section 465(b)(4) of the Code provides that a taxpayer shall not be considered at risk with respect to amounts protected against loss through nonrecourse financing, guarantees, stop loss agreements or other similar arrangements.

The message boards qualify as "section 38 property." Therefore A can claim an investment tax credit based on the amount A is at risk with respect to the property at the close of the taxable year. According to the terms of the note, A will not be in default for failing to make payments on the note when due, but such amounts will be added to the remaining balance of principal. Further, A is able to be relieved of financial responsibility on the note at any time after 36 months by transferring the property to X.

Although A is personally liable on the note to P, the terms of the note and the arrangement with X, in effect, indemnify A against any loss from the activity. The arrangement with X, in conjunction with the terms of the note, constitutes a protection against loss arrangement under section 465(b)(4). Therefore, for purposes of section 465(b) of the Code, the investor is not at risk with respect to the amount of the note.

HOLDING

At the time of purchase A is not at risk for the amount of the note. A's at risk amount is 10x dollars, the amount of cash paid for the message boards.

For purposes of this revenue ruling, it has been assumed that A is the owner of the property and had entered into the transaction to make a profit and that the value of the set of four message boards is 40x dollars. The analysis and scope of this revenue ruling is, therefore, limited to determining the amount A is at risk within the meaning of section 465 of the Code. This ruling does not address the question concerning who actually owns the property nor does it address the question as to what is the correct fair market value of the property.

Post-Ruling Follow-Up   In this Revenue Ruling, the Service confirms that even if a promissory note is recourse in form, its substance will prove determinative. Because *A* invested no more than 10*x* dollars and was protected against both default and liability on the associated promissory note, *A* was at risk for no more than 10*x* dollars. The facts presented by the Service are somewhat simple, and detecting the taxpayer's true at-risk amount is not difficult. To the extent sophisticated and well-advised taxpayers are involved, however, detecting risk-relieving countermeasures may prove far more difficult, especially with enhanced complexity and ongoing innovation in the financial instruments arena.

Revenue Ruling 83-133: Real Life Applications

1. Randy recently decided to go into the solar panel business. He invested $25,000 from his personal savings and managed to get a $75,000 loan from the First Federal Savings & Loan Bank ("FFSLB"). Under the terms of the loan, Randy was expected to make monthly payments of interest and principal, but the governing agreement clarified that the loan itself is unsecured and "without recourse" as to Randy. By what amount is Randy at risk with respect to his solar panel business activity?

2. Several months ago, Fatima decided to go into the antique furniture business. At the outset, she invested $50,000 from her personal savings account. She also borrowed $50,000 from The Empire State Bank of Manhattan ("Empire"). Although the loan documents reflect that Empire is unsecured, they also make it clear that Fatima has assumed personal liability for repayment of the debt along with interest at rates that are adjustable (within established limits) from time to time. By what amount is Fatima at risk with respect to her business?

3. ***Same facts as Question #2***, except that Empire has a guarantee from Fatima's grandfather for repayment of the debt and has agreed (in writing) to seek nothing beyond what it can collect under the guarantee from her grandfather.

Given the unpredictability of the business cycle, taxpayers may experience regular success, steady losses, or (more likely) some combination of profitable years and not-so-profitable years. As a result, taxpayers who invest wisely and reap profits may never run into their at-risk limitations. If fortune does not prevail, taxpayers may find that their losses in a given period are allowed to some extent (because the loss is less than their at-risk amount) or disallowed in whole or in part as a result of the at-risk limits. Section 465 contains two important rules you should be aware of. The first appears under § 465(a)(2) and provides that a loss disallowed in a particular taxable year as a result of the at-risk limitation is to be treated as a deduction allocable to the activity in the first succeeding taxable year. Thus, if a taxpayer started the taxable year with an at-risk amount of $25,000 and suffered a loss of $30,000 during the taxable year, she will be barred from deducting any amount in excess of $25,000. Accordingly, she will have a $5,000 deduction allocable to the activity in the first succeeding taxable year. The second rule appears in § 465(b)(5) and generally provides for the reduction of the taxpayer's future at-risk amount to the extent that a loss is actually allowed in a given taxable year. Thus, if a taxpayer started the taxable year with $50,000 at risk and is allowed a loss deduction of $20,000 in that taxable year, his amount at risk in the succeeding taxable year is $30,000 (assuming all else remains the same).

D. ECONOMIC SUBSTANCE

Earlier in this chapter, it was noted that the first line of defense against taxpayer abuse of Code-based allowances often takes the form of judicial or administrative intervention. The so-called economic substance doctrine reflects a tag-team assault: objection to the taxpayer's efforts by the IRS followed by recognition of the doctrine by the courts. Today, the economic substance doctrine has achieved codification, but before turning to the language of the Internal Revenue Code, let's develop of sense of the taxpayer behavior this doctrine serves to attack.

> **Key Statutory Provisions**
>
> ■ Internal Revenue Code
> ■ § 7701(o)(1) and (5)
> ■ § 7701(o)(2)–(4) (skim)

In Chapter 6, we discussed life insurance contracts. You'll recall that the traditional life insurance arrangement works for both the insured and the insurance company because the individual pays premiums over time, and the insurance company invests those premiums such that they generate returns in the form of interest, dividends, capital gains, and the like. These returns generally remain with the company. If insurance company experts have relied properly on mortality and morbidity statistics in pricing the insurance and have invested the premiums they received wisely, the insurance company should have funds sufficient to pay a full death benefit promptly when called on to do so. To state the situation in more technical terms, the policyholder pays premiums to the insurance company, and as time passes, the value (or the so-called cash surrender value) of the life insurance contract builds. Ideally, the value of the contract at the time of the death of the covered individual will be sufficient to pay out a full death benefit. As long as the insured has an insurable interest in the covered individual at the outset (e.g., a spouse covering a spouse or a corporate employer covering a key employee), the basic scheme should operate smoothly, barring sudden mortality spikes or financial ineptitude at the insurance company level.

Although many life insurance contracts operate in the traditional manner just discussed, some insurance contracts have a special feature that allows the policyholder to borrow money from the insurance company in an amount determined by reference to the cash surrender value of the policy. Interest is due on the loan, and (at least prior to effective Congressional intervention under § 264) taxpayers entitled to an interest deduction with respect to such loans aggressively sought to exploit a lucrative tax-sheltering opportunity. If such a taxpayer borrowed modestly and repaid responsibly, the arrangement still worked as life insurance. The policy loan operated like a true loan, and the interest payment truly provided payment for the use of money. But if such a taxpayer sought to exploit the deductibility of the policy loan interest, it had every incentive to take out contracts of insurance on thousands of employees largely to turn right around and systematically drain the cash surrender values of the contracts via policy "loans." With the coverage of tens of thousands of employees, a sizeable policy loan interest deduction would result. At the end of the day, the policyholder may have had little if anything in the way of a death benefit, but it didn't care, and in all likelihood, the arrangement was terminated long before substantial deaths actually occurred. It was never about covering the life of the individual. Rather, the goal was to take advantage of the interest deduction from the policy loan and thereby shelter the business's income from taxation. Notwithstanding the general propriety of tax minimization as a motive, the actual transactions undertaken must amount to more than a mere façade. But in this instance, the whole transaction was a sham. Put in more diplomatic terms, the arrangement never had the hallmark of true insurance. It was insurance in form only; it lacked any real economic substance as insurance. Accordingly, the "loan" was never truly a loan on a policy of insurance, and the "interest" was never truly interest. With Congress gradually addressing the issue and attempting to keep pace with taxpayer machinations and abuses, the Service had every right to intercede in the meantime, wielding the economic substance doctrine to prevent the deduction of the so-called "policy loan interest." Let's now consider Congress's codification of the judicially created economic substance doctrine.

Section 7701(o)(5)(A) notes that "[t]he term 'economic substance doctrine' means the common law doctrine under which tax benefits . . . with respect to a transaction are not allowable if the transaction does not have economic substance or lacks a business purpose." We then find that under § 7701(o)(1), if the economic substance doctrine is relevant to a transaction, it will be treated as having true economic substance only if the following requirements are satisfied:

- The transaction changes in a meaningful way (apart from federal income tax effects) the taxpayer's economic position; and
- The taxpayer has a substantial purpose (apart from federal income tax effects) for entering into such transaction.

Notwithstanding the importance of the economic substance doctrine being "relevant," the Code simply states that the "determination of whether the economic substance doctrine is relevant to a transaction shall be made in the same manner as if this subsection had never been enacted." Section 7701(o)(5)(C). This language leaves it up to the IRS and the courts, once again, to determine whether economic substance is an issue worth raising with respect to a given taxpayer transaction or, as the case may be, series of transactions. *See* § 7701(o)(5)(D). Although the next case arose long before the codification of the economic substance doctrine, it does give us an opportunity to see the kind of transaction in which the doctrine is considered relevant and how courts have employed it to reign in and address questionable taxpayer transactions.

Knetsch v. United States

Knetsch is a landmark decision in the tax arena. You will note that it involves the deduction of interest by a taxpayer, but you should keep in mind that the rules governing the deductibility of personal interest in the current version of the Code were not in effect at the time this case arose. Even though the taxpayer's transaction differs in some respects from the abusive life insurance scheme discussed previously, you need not get bogged down in technical transactional details. Simply bear in mind that the scam still involves the attempt to take advantage of the deductibility of interest. Consider the following questions as you make your way through the case.

1. The court mentions *Gregory v. Helvering*. Why is that decision relevant in this case?
2. What impact should this decision have on other arrangements involving loans taken against cash value? Can it be said that they all lack economic substance?
3. How would you articulate the taxpayer's § 264 argument, and how does the court address it?

Knetsch v. United States
364 U.S. 361 (1960)

Justice William J. Brennan, Jr.

An appointee of President Eisenhower, Justice Brennan served on the U.S. Supreme Court from 1956 to 1990. *See* Owen M. Fiss, *William Joseph Brennan, Jr.*, 2 THE WORLD BOOK ENCYCLOPEDIA 593 (World Book 2013).

Credit: Photo courtesy of the Library of Congress.

Mr. Justice BRENNAN delivered the opinion of the Court.

This case presents the question of whether deductions from gross income claimed on petitioners' 1953 and 1954 joint federal income tax returns, of $143,465 in 1953 and of $147,105 in 1954, for payments made by petitioner, Karl F. Knetsch, to Sam Houston Life Insurance Company, constituted "interest paid . . . on indebtedness" within the meaning of § 23(b) of the Internal Revenue Code of 1939 and § 163(a) of the Internal Revenue Code of 1954. The Commissioner of Internal Revenue disallowed the deductions and determined a deficiency for each year. The petitioners paid the deficiencies and brought this action for refund in the District Court for the Southern District of California. The District Court rendered judgment for the United States, and the Court of Appeals for the Ninth Circuit affirmed. Because of a suggested conflict with the decision of the Court of Appeals for the Fifth Circuit in *United States v. Bond*, 258 F.2d 577, we granted certiorari.

On December 11, 1953, the insurance company sold Knetsch ten 30-year maturity deferred annuity savings bonds, each in the face amount of $400,000 and bearing interest at 2 1/2% compounded annually. The purchase price was $4,004,000. Knetsch gave the Company his check for $4,000, and signed $4,000,000 of nonrecourse annuity loan notes for the balance. The notes bore 3 1/2% interest and were secured by the annuity bonds. The interest was payable in advance, and Knetsch on the same day prepaid the first year's interest, which was $140,000. Under the Table of Cash and Loan Values made part of the bonds, their cash or loan value at December 11, 1954, the end of the first contract year, was to be $4,100,000. The contract terms, however, permitted Knetsch to borrow any excess of this value above his indebtedness without waiting until December 11, 1954. Knetsch took advantage of this provision only five days after the purchase. On December 16, 1953, he received from the company $99,000 of the $100,000 excess over his $4,000,000 indebtedness, for which he gave his notes bearing 3 1/2% interest. This interest was also payable in advance and on the same day he prepaid the first year's interest of $3,465. In their joint return for 1953, the petitioners deducted the sum of the two interest payments, that is $143,465, as "interest paid * * * within the taxable year on indebtedness," under § 23(b) of the 1939 Code.

The second contract year began on December 11, 1954, when interest in advance of $143,465 was payable by Knetsch on his aggregate indebtedness of $4,099,000. Knetsch paid this amount on December 27, 1954. Three days later, on December 30, he received from the company cash in the amount of $104,000, the difference less $1,000 between his then $4,099,000 indebtedness and the cash or loan value of the bonds of $4,204,000 on December 11, 1955. He gave the company appropriate notes and prepaid the interest thereon of $3,640. In their joint return for the taxable year 1954 the petitioners deducted the sum of the two interest payments, that is $147,105, as "interest paid * * * within the taxable year on indebtedness," under § 163(a) of the 1954 Code.

The tax years 1955 and 1956 are not involved in this proceeding, but a recital of the events of those years is necessary to complete the story of the transaction. On December 11, 1955, the start of the third contract year, Knetsch became obligated to pay $147,105 as prepaid interest on an indebtedness which now totaled $4,203,000. He paid this interest on December 28, 1955. On the same date he received $104,000 from the company. This was $1,000 less than the difference between his indebtedness and the cash or loan value of the bonds of $4,308,000 at December 11, 1956. Again he gave the company notes upon which he prepaid interest of $3,640. Petitioners claimed a deduction on their 1955 joint return for the aggregate of the payments, or $150,745.

Knetsch did not go on with the transaction for the fourth contract year beginning December 11, 1956, but terminated it on December 27, 1956. His indebtedness at that time totaled $4,307,000. The cash or loan value of the bonds was the $4,308,000 value at December 11, 1956, which had been the basis of the "loan" of December 28, 1955. He surrendered the bonds and his indebtedness was canceled. He received the difference of $1,000 in cash.

The contract called for a monthly annuity of $90,171 at maturity (when Knetsch would be 90 years of age) or for such smaller amount as would be produced by the cash or loan value after deduction of the then existing indebtedness. It was stipulated that if Knetsch had held the bonds to maturity and continued annually to borrow the net cash value less $1,000, the sum available for the annuity at maturity would be $1,000 ($8,388,000 cash or loan value less $8,387,000 of indebtedness), enough to provide an annuity of only $43 per month.

The trial judge made findings that "(t)here was no commercial economic substance to the * * * transaction," that the parties did not intend that Knetsch "become indebted to Sam Houston," that "(n)o indebtedness of (Knetsch) was created by any of the * * * transactions," and that "(n)o economic gain could be achieved from the purchase of these bonds without regard to the tax consequences * * *." His conclusion of law, based on this Court's decision in *Deputy v. du Pont*, 308 U.S. 488, 60 S. Ct. 363, 84 L. Ed. 416, was that "(w)hile in form the payments to Sam Houston were compensation for the use or forbearance of money, they were not in substance. As a payment of interest, the transaction was a sham."

We first examine the transaction between Knetsch and the insurance company to determine whether it created an "indebtedness" within the meaning of § 23(b) of the 1939 Code and § 163(a) of the 1954 Code, or whether, as the trial court found, it was a sham. We put aside a finding by the District Court that Knetsch's "only motive in purchasing these 10 bonds was to attempt to secure an interest deduction." As was said in *Gregory v. Helvering*, 293 U.S. 465, 469, 55 S. Ct. 266, 267, 79 L. Ed. 596: "The legal right of a taxpayer to decrease the amount of what otherwise would be his taxes, or altogether avoid them, by means which the law permits, cannot be doubted. * * * But the question for determination is whether what was done, apart from the tax motive, was the thing which the statute intended."

When we examine "what was done" here, we see that Knetsch paid the insurance company $294,570 during the two taxable years involved and received $203,000 back in the form of "loans." What did Knetsch get for the out-of-pocket difference of $91,570? In form he had an annuity contract with a so-called guaranteed cash value at maturity of $8,388,000, which would produce monthly annuity payments of $90,171, or substantial life insurance proceeds in the event of his death before maturity. This, as we have seen, was a fiction, because each year Knetsch's annual borrowings kept the net cash value, on which any annuity or insurance payments would depend, at the relative pittance of $1,000. Plainly, therefore, Knetsch's transaction with the insurance company did "not appreciably affect his beneficial interest except to reduce his tax * * *." For it is patent that there was nothing of substance to be realized by Knetsch from this transaction beyond a tax deduction. What he was ostensibly "lent" back was in reality only the rebate of a substantial part of the so-called "interest" payments. The $91,570 difference retained by the company was its fee for providing the facade of "loans" whereby the petitioners sought to reduce their 1953 and 1954 taxes in the total sum of $233,297.68. There may well be single premium annuity arrangements with nontax substance which create an "indebtedness" for the purposes of § 23(b) of the 1939 Code and § 163(a) of the 1954 Code. But this one is a sham.

The petitioners contend, however, that the Congress in enacting § 264 of the 1954 Code, 26 U.S.C.A. § 264, authorized the deductions. They point out that § 264(a) (2) denies a deduction for amounts paid on indebtedness incurred to purchase [or] carry a single-premium annuity contract, but only as to contracts purchased after March 1, 1954. The petitioners thus would attribute to Congress a purpose to allow the deduction of pre-1954 payments under transactions of the kind carried on by Knetsch with the insurance company without regard to whether the transactions created a true obligation to pay interest. Unless that meaning plainly appears we will not attribute it to Congress. "To hold otherwise would be to exalt artifice above reality and to deprive the statutory provision in question of all serious purpose." *Gregory v. Helvering, supra*, 293 U.S. at page 470, 55 S. Ct. at page 268. We, therefore, look to the statute and materials relevant to its construction for evidence that Congress meant in § 264(a)(2) to authorize the deduction of payments made under sham transactions entered into before 1954. We look in vain.

[The court proceeds to discuss the evolution of § 264 and its treatment of interest on indebtedness incurred to purchase or carry certain instruments producing fully-tax-exempt income (e.g., death benefits from a life insurance contract) or partially-tax-exempt income (e.g., annuity contract benefits). The court rejects the notion that by addressing specific transactions, Congress directly or indirectly sanctioned the deductibility of interest on sham transactions.]

***These are signs that Congress' long-standing concern with the problem of interest allocable to partially exempt income, and not any concern with sham transactions, explains the provision.

Moreover, the provision itself negates any suggestion that sham transactions were the congressional concern, for the deduction denied is of certain interest payments on actual "indebtedness." And we see nothing in the Senate Finance and House Ways and Means Committee Reports on § 264, ***, to suggest that Congress in exempting pre-1954 annuities intended to protect sham transactions. ***

The judgment of the Court of Appeals is affirmed.

Affirmed.

[Dissenting opinion of Mr. Justice Douglas omitted.]

Post-Case Follow-Up

Concluding that Knetsch's annuity contract transactions were shams, the Court had little difficulty siding with the United States and denying the taxpayer's interest deductions. Although the taxpayer hoped to draw support from the fact that Congress had devoted specific attention to the deductibility of interest on indebtedness incurred to purchase or carry certain contracts and had, apparently, left that taxpayer's transactions unscathed, the Court dismissed the effort. Congress's actions, noted the Court, were directed at interest on *actual* indebtedness. Years later, taxpayers appealed to the same *Knetsch*-type arguments in the hope of obtaining a deduction for interest paid with respect to policy loans on corporate-owned life insurance ("COLI"), and not surprisingly, the arguments suffered the same *Knetsch*-type fate. *See, e.g., AEP v. United States*, 326 F.3d 737 (6th Cir. 2003); *In re CM Holdings*, 301 F.3d 96 (3d Cir. 2002).

Congressional attention notwithstanding, the taxpayer must still ensure that their statutorily compliant transactions reflect true economic substance. Insurance must be true insurance, the loan must be a true loan, and the interest must be true interest. Doing the statutory dance of form without the statutory music of substance will not go over well with the judges. Even so, the taxpayers do have a point. If Congress, fully cognizant of abusive taxpayer tendencies, crafts a rule of prohibition but establishes a carve-out, how can a court justify denying a taxpayer an interest deduction when Congress appears to have given its full attention to the matter and drawn its own sharp line in the sand? Given that Congress prohibits, under certain circumstances, an interest deduction "pursuant to a plan . . . which contemplates the systematic direct or indirect borrowing of part or all of the increases in the cash value of such contracts" under § 264(a)(3), how can a court object when a taxpayer takes pains to comply with one of *four* of Congress's articulated exceptions to application of its general rule (e.g., §264(d)(1))? If the taxpayer can comply with the statutory rules and still manage to squeeze five quarters from a dollar, should Congress be left to fix the problem? Or has Congress, in its wisdom, left the economic substance doctrine in place and provided a basic statutory standard while delegating "relevance" of the doctrine to the IRS and judiciary. Such an approach may well serve as Congress's own insurance against taxpayer efforts that, even if remarkably creative, seek to exploit legislative blunders or to abuse Congress's benevolence and legislative grace.

Knetsch v. United States: Real Life Applications

1. American Energy, Inc. ("AEI") recently purchased life insurance policies on each of its 70,000 employees. Under the terms of each policy, AEI is entitled to take out policy loans against the cash value of each policy, and AEI does so for several years. Examination of the arrangement reveals that if AEI continues its pattern of taking policy loans, the death benefit resulting with respect to each policy will be $100. Further, the overall arrangement would actually result in a loss to AEI but for the fact that AEI appears to be entitled to deduct the interest paid on the policy loans. Factoring in such a deduction, the arrangement results in millions of dollars in tax savings to AEI. Does this arrangement have economic substance?

2. *Same facts as Question #1*, except that AEI only purchased policies on the lives of its key, upper-management-level employees. Further, due to contractual limitations, the company rarely takes policy loans, and in any event, each policy will produce a net death benefit of $1 million. The chance that the arrangement could result in a loss to AEI is, at best, 5 percent. Does this transaction have economic substance?

3. Billy and Betty Doster recently purchased a brand-new principal residence. They made a down payment of $2,000 and financed the remainder with an interest-only mortgage of $998,000. Under the terms of the loan, the Dosters will pay only the interest component of their mortgage for the first five years. As a result, they will make no progress with respect to paying off the underlying

mortgage loan, but they do plan to take annual deductions with respect to the qualified residence interest they pay. After the first five years, they have many options. They may commence payment of principal and interest, or they may simply sell the residence, assuming the fair market value of the home is sufficient to pay off the outstanding loan balance. If the home's value is insufficient to cover the debt (i.e., they are "underwater"), then a sale of the home will result in a deficiency, exposing them to the bank's aggressive collection efforts. Does this mortgage transaction have economic substance?

Chapter Summary

- Although losses from passive activites may offset income from passive activities, taxpayers generally may not deduct any excess of such losses over such gains incurred during the taxable year. A taxpayer may be able to carry forward disallowed loss excesses as passive activity deductions in the next taxable year.
- A passive activity is a trade or business or income-producing activity in which the taxpayer does not materially participate. Material participation, by definition, requires involvement that is regular, continuous, and substantial.
- In general, all real estate rental activity constitutes a passive activity, but such characterization does not apply with respect to taxpayers who, by satisfying a statutory standard, qualify as conducting a real property trade or business.
- Taxpayers may deduct losses from an activity, but only to the extent of the taxpayer's aggregate amount at risk with respect to the activity. Amounts at risk include money contributed to the activity, the adjusted basis of property contributed to the activity, and amounts borrowed for use in the activity (under specific circumstances). If losses are allowed in a given taxable year, the taxpayer's at-risk amount is reduced accordingly in the next taxable year. Disallowed losses are treated as activity-related deductions in the first succeeding taxable year.
- Activity-linked borrowed amounts include only those amounts for which the taxpayer is personally liable or has pledged nonactivity property as security (to the extent of the net fair market value of the taxpayer's interest in the property). At risk amounts do not include those against which the taxpayer is protected against loss via nonrecourse financing, guarantees, and other similar arrangements.
- The economic substance doctrine requires the disallowance of tax benefits with respect to any transaction lacking economic substance or a business purpose. A transaction has economic substance only if the transaction (i) changes in a meaningful way (apart from federal income tax effects) the taxpayer's economic position, and (ii) the taxpayer has a substantial purpose (apart from federal income tax effects) for entering into such transaction.

Applying the Rules

1. Eddie owns several homes in the metropolitan Cincinnati area, and he rents each of them to various tenants. He does not actively participate in the rental activity, and under the prevailing facts, his real estate activities constitute passive activities within the meaning of § 469. Eddie uses the calendar year as his taxable year, and during 2019 his rental activities produced losses of $20,000 and income of $32,000. To what extent, if any, will § 469 operate to disallow Eddie's losses?

2. In an effort to capitalize on the fragility of various features of smartphones and other popular electronic devices, Hamilton recently decided to go into the business of designing and selling durable mobile device protectors. In January of 2019, he invested $50,000 of his personal savings, and he borrowed an additional $200,000 from the First National Bank of Bermuda ("FNBB") for use in the business. Under the terms of the loan agreement with FNBB, Hamilton was not personally liable on the debt, but he did provide collateral as security for repayment. None of the encumbered property (which had a net fair market value of $200,000) was used in the business. By what amount is Hamilton at risk with respect to this business venture?

3. *Same facts as Question #2.* Assume that Hamilton ended the year 2020 with an at-risk amount of $300,000 and that during that year the business produced a loss of $40,000. What impact will this loss have on Hamilton's at-risk amount in subsequent taxable years?

4. Jennifer owns several homes, and she regularly rents them out to tenants. Assume that Jennifer uses the calendar year as her taxable year and that she actively participates in the rental activity, although she is not in the real property trade or business within the meaning of § 469. During 2020, Jennifer had losses from her rental activities of $50,000 and income of $30,000. If Jennifer's adjusted gross income was $80,000 in 2020 (excluding any passive activity items), to what extent, if any, will § 469 impact the deductibility of any passive activity loss?

Federal Income Taxation in Practice

1. Assume that you are a new associate in a large law firm. The partner with whom you work has been asked to provide an opinion with respect to what appears to be a tax shelter. She would like you to find, read, and summarize *AEP v. United States*, 326 F.3d 737 (6th Cir. 2003), for her. Find the case, and follow up with her by brief e-mail.

2. The same partner has come back to you with an additional research assignment. She would like you to find out when § 7702(o) was added to the Code and whether any legislative history exists regarding the provision.

The Alternative Minimum Tax

Up to this point in our coverage of federal income taxation, we have focused on a very wide array of rules, some concerning deductions, others addressing exclusions, and yet others guiding taxpayers with respect to timing of recognition events or, perhaps, the character of gain or loss. Our common goal, throughout, has been to understand how these rules operate because, at root, taxpayers must apply them in order to determine their taxable income. Common and widespread knowledge of the operating rules facilitates effective tax planning, but such a reality also presents opportunities. Even if, as Judge Learned Hand noted, taxpayers do nothing wrong in minimizing their tax obligations within the bounds of the law, some taxpayers may employ existing rules to effectively eliminate or drastically reduce their tax liabilities, notwithstanding the fact that they managed to derive substantial amounts of gross income during the taxable year. To prevent this outcome, Congress imposes the alternative minimum tax ("AMT") and thereby ensures that those taxpayers (who might otherwise pay too little or nothing in taxes) shoulder what Congress considers an acceptable tax burden. The AMT rules are complex, and the scope of coverage here will be limited. Even in maintaining that limited focus, we stay well within relatively familiar territory (and steer clear of baroque detail of limited pedagogical value) to enhance your ability to grasp the core concepts.

A. OVERVIEW

In applying the complex of rules we have covered thus far, we have focused (from a broad and holistic perspective) on ascertaining a taxpayer's taxable income for the purpose of calculating their "normal"

Key Concepts

- *Alternative minimum tax*, regular tax, and *tentative minimum tax*
- *Alternative minimum taxable income*
- Exemption amounts and phase-out thresholds
- *Taxable excess* and calculation of the *tentative minimum tax*
- Inflation adjustment of relevant dollar amounts

or regular tax. Ascertaining whether a taxpayer owes an alternative minimum tax requires a series of calculations using a modestly altered version of the same rules with which you are now familiar. Remember that in this context, application of the rules in their natural state threatens to result in too little or no tax liability, so something has to change to give us a different result. Our new goal, then, becomes determining the individual's alternative minimum tax. With that figure in hand, we can ultimately ensure that the individual is paying an acceptable amount of tax overall.

Calculating an individual's AMT requires that we take several steps. We will explore the individual steps in greater detail in the remainder of this chapter, but here at the outset, you should develop some appreciation of the larger process.

■ Step #1 requires that we calculate the taxpayer's alternative minimum taxable income ("AMTI"). That process essentially requires that we calculate the taxpayer's taxable income using modestly altered rules. As applied, these rules deprive taxpayers of certain deductions and allowances while at the same time forcing an increase in gross income by stripping them of certain tax benefits they would ordinarily enjoy.

■ Step #2 requires that we reduce the AMTI just calculated by an exemption amount which varies depending on the taxpayer's filing status. Recall that in arriving at AMTI, the rules deprived taxpayers of several items. The exemption amount serves to protect a low-income taxpayer from undue harshness in this environment, but as the individual's AMTI rises, he no longer qualifies in any meaningful sense as low-income. Accordingly, his exemption amount may be decreased or phased out entirely. By definition, the amount by which the taxpayer's AMTI exceeds his exemption amount is referred to as his *taxable excess*.

■ Step #3 requires that we apply specific tax rates to the taxable excess. Up to a point, the applicable rate is 26 percent, but it then shifts to 28 percent. Application of the relevant rates to the taxable excess will give us the taxpayer's *tentative minimum tax*.

■ Finally, Step #4 requires that we compare the tentative minimum tax that we have calculated with the taxpayer's regular tax liability. If the tentative minimum tax is higher than the regular tax, the taxpayer is effectively responsible for the full tentative minimum tax amount. Stated in precise technical terms, if the taxpayer's tentative minimum tax exceeds his regular tax, he must pay both the amount of the excess and his regular tax. The shorthand reference to this "excess" is the *alternative minimum tax*. Thus, if a taxpayer's regular tax is $5,000, and his tentative minimum tax is $7,500, he must pay both his regular tax of $5,000 and his alternative minimum tax of $2,500. *See, e.g.*, Exhibit 21.1. Of course, if the taxpayer's regular tax is higher than his tentative minimum tax, he is responsible for paying his regular tax, and there simply is no AMT with respect to that taxpayer for that taxable year. *See, e.g.*, Exhibit 21.2.

EXHIBIT 21.1 Tentative Minimum Tax Exceeds Regular Tax: Both Regular Tax and AMT Due

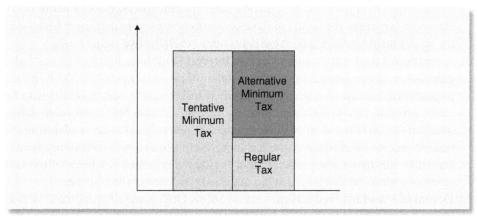

EXHIBIT 21.2 Regular Tax Exceeds Tentative Minimum Tax: Regular Tax Due with No AMT Imposed

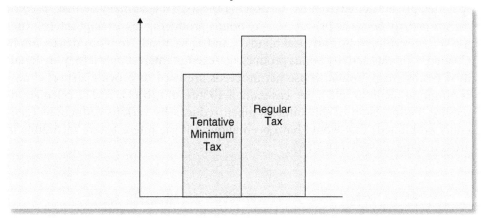

B. CALCULATING ALTERNATIVE MINIMUM TAXABLE INCOME

As noted earlier, calculating taxpayers' AMTI requires, in essence, calculating their traditional or regular "taxable income" with modestly altered rules. Section 55(b)(2) directs that we take this approach by defining *alternative minimum taxable income* as "the taxable income of the taxpayer for the taxable year determined with the adjustments provided in section 56 and section 58 and increased by the amount of the items of tax preference described in section 57." Although we will not explore all of the adjustments and tax preference items set forth in those provisions, we will take a passing glance at several just to give you a sense of how the AMTI calculus differs from what we have seen previously. Some of the adjustments called for in § 56 include the following:

▧ **Denial of Certain Itemized Deductions.** Section 56(b)(1)(A)(ii) disallows any deduction for the payment of real or personal property taxes as well as any deduction for the payment of state and local income taxes (i.e., the so-called **SALT deduction**). For some taxpayers, the denial of these deductions is a severe detriment because in the aggregate (or *individually*) these items often reach the five-figure range.

▧ **Alteration of the Deduction for Certain Interest Paid.** Although § 163(h) excludes qualified residence interest from the definition of personal interest, § 56(b)(1)(C)(i) dictates that instead of referring to qualified residence interest, § 163(h) is to be applied by referring to "qualified housing interest." Section 56(e) goes on to define *qualified housing interest* as qualified residence interest "paid or accrued during the taxable year on indebtedness which is incurred in acquiring, constructing, or substantially improving any property" that is either a principal residence of the taxpayer or a qualified dwelling that is a qualified residence of the taxpayer.

▧ **Denial of Standard Deduction.** Section 56(b)(1)(E) generally prohibits the taking of a standard deduction under § 63(c).

In addition to incorporating the adjustments under §§ 56 and 58, AMTI calculations also require that a taxpayer's regular taxable income be increased by items of tax preference set forth in § 57. One such item of tax preference is the interest on specified private activity bonds. Section 57(a)(5)(C)(i) essentially defines *specified private activity bonds* as private activity bonds producing tax-exempt interest (per § 103 (concerning state and local bonds)), and as we recall from our discussion in Chapter 6, private activity bonds produce tax-exempt interest only if they are "qualified bonds" (e.g., bonds whose net proceeds are used to provide airports, mass commuting facilities, etc.). *See generally* § 103(a) and (b)(1). AMTI calculations require the inclusion of this interest, albeit reduced by various deductions (generally prohibited) that would have been allowed if the interest were includible in gross income. *See* § 57(a)(5)(A).

C. ASCERTAINING THE ALTERNATIVE MINIMUM TAX

As you can see, because of the various adjustments and increases required, a taxpayer's AMTI stands a good chance of exceeding a taxpayer's "regular" taxable income. But as was noted earlier, one does not apply applicable rates to AMTI. Instead, those rates apply only to the so-called taxable excess (i.e., AMTI reduced by an exemption amount). Exemption amounts vary, depending on the taxpayer's filing status. For taxable years beginning after December 31, 2017, and before January 1, 2026, married taxpayers filing a joint return (and surviving spouses) have an exemption amount of $109,400, and unmarried taxpayers have an exemption amount of $70,300. *See generally* § 55(d)(1)(A)-(B) and (d)(4)(A)(i). These exemption amounts are subject to reduction (or elimination), and phase-outs begin as AMTI exceeds $1,000,000 in the case of married taxpayers filing jointly (and surviving spouses) and $500,000 in the case of unmarried individuals. *See generally* § 55(d)(2) and (d)(4)(A)(ii).

The taxpayer's AMTI reduced by the exemption amount yields the taxable excess, and this amount is used to calculate the taxpayer's tentative minimum tax.

Under § 55(b)(1)(A), a taxpayer's *tentative minimum tax* is generally defined as the following sum:

(i)   26% of the taxable excess (up to $175,000); plus
(ii) 28% of the taxable excess (with respect to amounts above $175,000).

This definition is fine-tuned by other provisions to take into account proper credits (e.g., the alternative minimum tax foreign tax credit) and preferential rates for net capital gain. *See* § 55(b)(3). Having calculated both the taxpayer's regular tax under standard rules and their tentative minimum tax under the special rules discussed, one can readily ascertain whether the taxpayer must pay only their regular tax or both their regular tax and an alternative minimum tax. *See* Exhibits 21.1 and 21.2. Section 55(a) provides, in technical terms, "[i]n the case of a taxpayer other than a corporation, there is hereby imposed (in addition to any other tax imposed by this subtitle) a tax equal to the excess (if any) of the tentative minimum tax for the taxable year over the regular tax for the taxable year."

Special Note: Cost of Living Adjustments

A number of the items of relevance in AMT calculations require reference to specific dollar amounts. Under § 55(d)(3), these amounts must be periodically adjusted for inflation.

D. EXPLORING THE ISSUES

As one might well imagine, many taxpayers disapprove of the AMT with its deduction-stripping and allowance-limiting edicts. Even so, many taxpayers would likely take offense at the notion that some taxpayers could escape taxation (or come close to doing so) by taking advantage of a raft of deductions. Given that AMTI calculations often operate to deprive taxpayers of itemized deductions, it obviously has primary impact on those whose itemized deductions are so substantial that they exceed the corresponding standard deduction amount. But does that mean that the AMT is largely a headache of the wealthy? Should it be?

Case Preview

Kamara v. Commissioner

In *Kamara v. Commissioner*, the taxpayer found himself facing an AMT obligation. Reasoning that the AMT was largely intended to impose minimal tax obligations on the wealthy, the taxpayer reasoned that any effort to impose the AMT on him was simply inappropriate. The court thought otherwise. As you read the case consider the following questions:

1. What items would the taxpayer be deprived of in AMTI calculations?
2. Does the AMT apply only if the taxpayer has items of tax preference?

Kamara v. Commissioner
T.C. Summary Op. 2007–103

NIMS, Judge.

***

Respondent determined a deficiency in petitioner's 2003 Federal income tax in the amount of $4,176. The issue for decision is whether petitioner is liable for the alternative minimum tax (AMT) for the 2003 taxable year.

BACKGROUND

*** At the time the petition was filed, petitioner resided in New York, New York.

Petitioner timely filed a 2003 Form 1040, U.S. Individual Income Tax Return, for the year ended December 31, 2003. *** On the return petitioner indicated his status as head of household and claimed his parents as dependents. In 2003, petitioner worked as a licensed practical nurse for St. Mary's Center, Inc., and De Sales Assisted Living. He reported $121,309 [as] wages on his return.

Petitioner [claimed the following as itemized deductions on his Form 1040 Schedule A]: $6,450 of medical and dental expenses, $10,298 of State and local income taxes, $4,203 of other taxes, $7,680 of gifts to charity, $13,762 of unreimbursed employee business expenses, $250 of tax preparation fees, and $1,250 of attorney and accounting fees.

Petitioner calculated his total income tax liability to be $14,976. Petitioner failed to include any AMT or attach Form 6251, Alternative Minimum Tax—Individuals. After subtracting $13,137 for Federal income tax withheld and $2,225 for excess Social Security tax withheld, petitioner requested a refund in the amount of $386.

On July 12, 2005, respondent issued to petitioner a notice of deficiency for his 2003 Federal income tax. Respondent determined a deficiency of $4,176, which was attributable to the AMT. Petitioner filed a petition seeking redetermination of the deficiency.

Petitioner has conceded that respondent's arithmetic in computing petitioner's AMT is correct. Petitioner has also conceded that respondent computed the alternative minimum tax in accordance with the Internal Revenue Code. Petitioner nevertheless contends that respondent inappropriately applied the AMT to his circumstances.

DISCUSSION

Section 55 imposes an AMT in addition to all other taxes imposed by [S]ubtitle A. A taxpayer's AMT liability is the amount by which the taxpayer's tentative tax exceeds his or her regular tax. Sec. 55(a). For noncorporate taxpayers, the tentative tax is calculated by using the taxpayer's alternative minimum taxable income [reduced by any available exemption amount]. Sec. 55(b)(1)(A). As relevant to the case before us, alternative minimum taxable income is a recomputation of taxable income without the benefit of certain itemized deductions and personal exemptions. See secs. 55(b)(2), 56(b). Pursuant to this statutory scheme, respondent calculated petitioner's AMT liability to be $4,176.

As previously mentioned, petitioner does not challenge respondent's calculation of his AMT liability and agrees that the calculation was in accordance with the Internal Revenue Code. Petitioner's objection is simply that respondent erred in applying the AMT to petitioner. He asserts that Congress did not intend for the AMT to apply to taxpayers like him, who are in the nonwealthy working class. He believes he should not be subject to the AMT since he works two jobs, night shifts, weekends, and overtime to support his family. Petitioner also points out that he did not claim any tax preferences that are targets of the AMT. (Items of tax preference are described in section 57 and include depletion, intangible drilling costs, tax-exempt interest, certain accelerated depreciation or amortization, and exclusion for gains on sale of certain small business stock.)

Petitioner provides no authority to support his position. His arguments are based on criticisms of the AMT in newspaper articles and his misreading of Internal Revenue Service Publication 17, Your Federal Income Tax. These are not authoritative sources of Federal tax law.

Furthermore, petitioner's arguments have been previously rejected by this Court. As set forth in the statute, the AMT does apply to lower-income taxpayers, not just the wealthy. Although tax preferences play a part in the computation of the AMT, a taxpayer may still be liable for the AMT even if he claimed no tax preferences.

We are not unsympathetic to petitioner's concerns about the AMT's reach. This Court has stated:

> The unfortunate consequences of the AMT in various circumstances have been litigated since shortly after the adoption of the AMT. In many different contexts, literal application of the AMT has led to a perceived hardship, but challenges based on equity have been uniformly rejected. [Citations omitted.]

*** Accordingly, we sustain respondent's deficiency determination.

To reflect the foregoing,

Decision will be entered for respondent.

Post-Case Follow-Up

The taxpayer's plight in *Kamara v. Commissioner* is typical. As the court concluded, the AMT applies to taxpayers across the board, regardless of whether they might think of themselves as wealthy and even if their regular taxable income reflects no items of tax preference. For years, taxpayers complained that they were unfairly impacted by the AMT, and truth be told, the tax was gradually affecting those Congress simply did not intend to reach. Congress repeatedly amended a number of the provisions in § 55(d) (concerning exemption amounts) to ensure that certain taxpayers remain unaffected by the AMT before finally providing for inflation adjustments in § 55(d)(3). *See generally* American Taxpayer Relief Act of 2012, P.L. 112–240, at § 104(b)(1). The Tax Cuts and Jobs Act enhanced exemption amounts and substantially increased the AMTI dollar amounts at which exemption phaseouts begin (e.g., $1M for a married couple filing jointly).

Kamara v. Commissioner: Real Life Application

1. Elena and Harris are married taxpayers who file a joint return. A local IRS agent has concluded that the taxpayers must pay an alternative minimum tax (in addition to their regular tax). The taxpayers challenge the asserted AMT obligation on the grounds that they received no tax-exempt bond interest and had no other items of tax preference. They also note that they are of decidedly modest financial means. Will these arguments likely prevail?

Chapter Summary

- The imposition of an alternative minimum tax is Congress's way of ensuring that taxpayers pay an acceptable minimum amount of tax.
- Calculating a taxpayer's alternative minimum taxable income requires recalculation of their taxable income with the adjustments set forth in §§ 56 and 58 and the increases dictated by § 57. In general, the modifications deprive taxpayers of various deductions and eliminate items of tax preference they would otherwise enjoy.
- Applicable tax rates are not applied to the taxpayer's alternative minimum taxable income. Instead, such rates apply to the individual's taxable excess, an amount determined by subtracting an exemption amount from the taxpayer's AMTI. Exemption amounts vary, depending on filing status, and are subject to phase-out. Exemption and phase-out amounts are adjusted over time for inflation.
- Application of specific tax rates to an individual's taxable excess yields his tentative minimum tax. If the tentative minimum tax exceeds the taxpayer's regular tax, the taxpayer must pay the excess (i.e., an alternative minimum tax) in addition to his regular tax. If the taxpayer's regular tax exceeds his tentative minimum tax, he must pay the regular tax.
- Although wealthy taxpayers with substantial itemized deductions are more likely impacted by the imposition of an alternative minimum tax, all taxpayers are subject to the alternative minimum tax.

Applying the Rules

1. For his 2019 taxable year, Alan's regular tax is $15,000. His tentative minimum tax, however, is $18,500. What amount, if any, is Alan's alternative minimum tax?

2. *Same facts as Question #1*, except that Alan's regular tax is $18,700. What amount, if any, is Alan's alternative minimum tax?

3. Assume that for the 2018 taxable year, Jane and Travis (married individuals filing jointly) had alternative minimum taxable income of $148,000 and an

exemption amount of $109,400. Assume further that the applicable dollar amount set forth in § 55(b)(1)(A) is $175,000. What will be their tentative minimum tax?

4. Assume that for his 2020 taxable year, Terrell (an unmarried individual) had alternative minimum taxable income of $117,000 and an exemption amount of $70,300. Assume further that the applicable dollar amounts set forth in § 55(b)(1)(A) is $175,000. If Terrell's regular tax is $11,000, what amount, if any, will be his alternative minimum tax?

Federal Income Taxation in Practice

1. You are working on a litigation project for a senior associate in your firm. You would like to know not only when § 55 was added to the Code but also if any legislative history is available. See what you can find and add a brief memo to your personal files for future reference.

2. One of your colleagues is concerned that she may have to pay an alternative minimum tax based on what she sees in a relatively current version of the Internal Revenue Code. You know that a number of the dollar amounts of relevance in the AMT context are adjusted for inflation. See if you can locate any pronouncements providing current inflation-adjusted dollar amounts for use in calculating alternative minimum taxes.

Federal Withholding, Estimated Tax Payments, and Worker Classification

For some taxpayers, the arrival of tax season brings with it considerable stress. Their annual ritual requires the cutting of yet another check payable to the United States Treasury, and if payment-in-full on the designated date is not possible, they face the specter of the imposition of penalties and interest. Fortunately, for a substantial percentage of taxpayers in the United States, the arrival of tax season occasions no dread beyond that associated with the need to gather a healthy amount of paperwork and seek out a return preparer (or gear up for a lengthy session with tax preparation software). If a refund is on the way, financial anticipation heightens. Recently, in fact, the rapid refund industry has managed to thrive because individuals often stand to receive thousands of dollars as a result of either employer overwithholding or the taxpayer's ability to take advantage of refundable tax credits; for the truly fortunate, excess withholding and refundable tax credits combine to produce a very real opportunity to splurge. In general, the system works for both the United States and the taxpayer.

Employees expect that various taxes will be withheld from their regular pay, and employers are generally obligated both to withhold such taxes and to pay them to the federal government at regular intervals. Even in this context, however, issues may arise. Employers have withholding obligations but only with respect to "wages" paid to employees, and not every dollar paid by an employer to an employee constitutes wages. For that matter, not all money paid by a business or employer is paid to one who is technically an "employee,"

Key Concepts

- The meaning of *wages* for income tax and employment tax purposes
- FICA taxes and the FICA Wage Base
- Estimated tax payments
- Worker classification as employee or independent contractor
- The impact of penalties and interest with respect to underpayments

and in those contexts, withholding is (as a general matter) neither expected nor allowed. Although one can often classify a worker as an employee with little difficulty, some relationships involve considerable classification uncertainty and thereby introduce a degree of ambiguity with respect to the question of withholding obligations. Adding to this complexity is the fact that some individuals are self-employed, yet even they must tender forth revenue to the sovereign on a timely basis. We turn, in this chapter, to the complex of rules governing the withholding and payment of taxes and the proper classification of workers.

A. FEDERAL WITHHOLDING ON "WAGES"

1. In General

Background and Current Statutory Framework

Section 1 of the Code imposes a tax on an individual's taxable income, but the provision itself does not address the subject of the involuntary withholding of taxes with respect to wages. Even so, today, employees generally accept both the normality and regularity of the withholding of taxes from their compensation. In prior years, however, the involuntary withholding of taxes from an individual's pay was not the norm because the income tax itself applied only to a very small percentage of the population (i.e., the very wealthy). *See* JOEL SLEMROD AND JON BAKIJA, TAXING OURSELVES 19 (The MIT Press 2008). With the involvement of the United States in World War II, the need for substantial amounts of revenue suddenly arose, and it became necessary to collect income taxes from a larger segment of the population. To facilitate rapid collection, Congress mandated the withholding of taxes on wages in the early 1940s. *See id.* at 20–21. Such a system also had the benefit of substantially reducing (if not eliminating) the risk that new taxpayers would find themselves obligated to pay taxes but lacking the financial wherewithal to do so.

Under current law, we find the wage withholding obligation in § 3402, which generally provides that "every employer making payment of wages shall deduct and withhold upon such wages a tax determined in accordance with tables or computational procedures prescribed by the Secretary [of the Treasury]." Section 3403, in turn, clarifies that the employer is liable for payment of the tax deducted and withheld. Although § 3402 makes reference to *wages*, we find the term itself defined in § 3401 as "all remuneration . . . for services performed by an employee for his employer . . . ." The provision does, however, exclude several items from

Key Statutory Provisions

■ **Internal Revenue Code**
  ■ § 164(f)
  ■ § 1401(a)–(b)(1)
  ■ § 1411(a)(1) (skim)
  ■ § 3101(a)–(b)
  ■ § 3102(a) (first sentence)
  ■ § 3111(a)–(b)
  ■ § 3121(a) (initial language)
  ■ § 3401(a) (initial language)
  ■ § 3402(a) (first sentence)
  ■ § 3403
  ■ § 3509 (skim)
  ■ § 6601 (skim)
  ■ § 6621 (skim)
  ■ § 6651 (skim)
  ■ § 6654 (skim)
  ■ § 6662 (skim)
  ■ § 6663 (skim)
  ■ § 6664 (skim)

the definition of wages, including amounts likely to qualify for exclusion at the employee level (e.g., a cash advance to cover anticipated business travel expenses (the value of which, we recall, is excludable by the employee under § 132 as a working condition fringe benefit)). *See, e.g.,* § 3401(a)(19).

Exploring the Meaning of "Wages" in the Withholding Context

Under fairly standard circumstances, an employee reporting for work and doing the job unquestionably earns wages because he or she is, quite literally, being compensated for the performance of services. But just how narrowly or broadly can the term wages be construed? If a potential employee demands a signing bonus, will the amount paid constitute wages even though the person has yet to perform any services? And what about the payment of severance? Presumably, the employee received adequate compensation for services performed during the employment relationship. Can amounts paid in connection with the termination of services be viewed, under any rational interpretation of the Code, as having been paid *for* the performance of services? Courts and administrative agencies have addressed these questions over the years.

Case Preview

Central Illinois Public Service Co. v. United States

Several chapters ago, we discussed *de minimis fringe benefits*. Section 132(d) generally defines such items as "property or service the value of which is (after taking into account the frequency with which similar fringes are provided by the employer to the employer's employees) so small as to make accounting for it unreasonable or administratively impracticable." Accordingly, an employee taking home leftover hamburgers at the end of his shift at a fast food restaurant or enjoying a slice of pizza during a monthly meeting need not include the value of the item in gross income. Likewise, an employee who receives free meals from her employer on the business premises (and for her employer's convenience) may exclude the value of her meals from gross income per § 119. But what if an employer provides a daily cash allowance for lunch to employees whose jobs require that they perform services away from business headquarters? The fact that the allowance is daily and takes the form of cash for meals off the employer's business premises dooms any real hope of taxpayer exclusion, but given that the amount pays for food and, arguably, not for services per se, can one accurately characterize the amount as "wages" under § 3401? The U.S. Supreme Court took up this issue in *Central Illinois*. As you read the case, consider the following questions:

1. Were all employees entitled to a lunch allowance?
2. If the allowance is income to the employees and paid to them by their employer, do the amounts necessarily received constitute "wages"?
3. Why is proper characterization by the employer critically important?

Central Illinois Public Service Co. v. United States
435 U.S. 21 (1978)

Mr. Justice BLACKMUN delivered the opinion of the Court.

This case presents the issue whether an employer, who in 1963 reimbursed lunch expenses of employees who were on company travel but not away overnight, must withhold federal income tax on those reimbursements. Stated another way, the issue is whether the lunch reimbursements qualify as "wages" under § 3401(a) of the Internal Revenue Code of 1954.

I

The facts are not in any real dispute. Petitioner Central Illinois Public Service Company (Company) is a regulated public utility engaged, in downstate Illinois, in the generation, transmission, distribution, and sale of electric energy, and in the distribution and sale of natural gas. Its principal office is in Springfield. It serves a geographic area of some size. In order adequately to serve the area, the Company, in accord with long-established policy, reimburses its employees for reasonable, legitimate expenses of transportation, meals, and lodging they incur in travel on the Company's business. Some of these trips are overnight; on others, the employees return before the end of the business day.

Justice Harry A. Blackmun

Appointed by President Nixon, Associate Justice Harry A. Blackmun joined the U.S. Supreme Court in 1970 and served until 1994.

Credit: Photo courtesy of the U.S. Library of Congress.

In 1963, the tax year in issue, the Company had approximately 1,900 employees. It reimbursed its union employees and the operating employees of its western division (its only nonunionized division) for noon lunches consumed, while on authorized travel, in an amount not to exceed $1.40 per lunch. *** Other salaried employees were reimbursed for actual reasonable luncheon expenses up to a specified maximum amount.

An employee on an authorized trip prepared his expense account on a company form. This was turned in to his supervisor for approval. The $1.40 rate sometimes was in excess of the actual lunch cost, but at other times it was insufficient to cover that cost. An employee who took lunch from home with him on a company trip was entitled to reimbursement. If, because of the locality of his work assignment on a particular day, the employee went home for lunch, he was not entitled to reimbursement. Many employees were engaged in open-air labor. Even in 1963 the $1.40 rate was "modest."

The employee on travel status rendered no service to the Company during his lunch. He was off duty and on his own time. He was subject to call, however, as were all employees at any time as emergencies required. The lunch payment was unrelated to the employee's specific job title, the nature of his work, or his rate of pay. "[T]his lunch payment arrangement was beneficial and convenient for the company and served its business interest. It saved the company employee time otherwise spent in travelling back and forth as well as the usual travel expenses."

During 1963 the Company paid its employees a total of $139,936.12 in reimbursement for noon lunches consumed while away from normal duty stations on nonovernight trips. It did not withhold federal income tax for its employees with respect to the components of this sum. The Company in 1963, however, did withhold and pay federal income withholding taxes totaling $1,966,489.87 with respect to other employee payments.

Upon audit in 1971, the Internal Revenue Service took the position that the lunch reimbursements in 1963 qualified as wages subject to withholding. A deficiency of $25,188.50 in withholding taxes was assessed. The Company promptly paid this deficiency together with $11,427.22 interest thereon, a total of $36,615.72. It then immediately filed its claim for refund of the total amount so paid and, with no action forthcoming on the claim for six months, instituted this suit in the United States District Court for the Southern District of Illinois to recover the amount so paid.

The District Court ruled in the Company's favor, holding that the reimbursements in question were not wages subject to withholding. The United States Court of Appeals for the Seventh Circuit reversed. Because that decision appeared to be in conflict with the views and decision of the Fourth Circuit in *Royster Co. v. United States*, 479 F.2d 387 (1973), we granted certiorari.

II

In *Commissioner of Internal Revenue v. Kowalski*, 434 U.S. 77 (1977), decided earlier this Term, the Court held that New Jersey's cash reimbursements to its highway patrol officers for meals consumed while on patrol duty constituted income to the officers, within the broad definition of gross income under § 61(a) of the 1954 Code, 26 U.S.C. § 61(a), and, further, that those cash payments were not excludable under § 119 of the Code relating to meals or lodging furnished for the convenience of the employer.

Kowalski, however, concerned the federal income tax and the issue of what was income. Its pertinency for the present withholding tax litigation is necessarily confined to the income tax aspects of the lunch reimbursements to the Company's employees.

The income tax issue is not before us in this case. We are confronted here, instead, with the question whether the lunch reimbursements, even though now they may be held to constitute taxable income to the employees who are reimbursed, are or are not "wages" subject to withholding, within the meaning and requirements of §§ 3401-3403 of the Code. ***

The income tax is imposed on taxable income. Generally, this is gross income minus allowable deductions. Section 61(a) defines as gross income "all income from whatever source derived" including, under § 61(a)(1), "[c]ompensation for services." The withholding tax, in some contrast, is confined to wages, § 3402(a), and § 3401(a) defines as "wages," "all remuneration (other than fees paid to a public official) for services performed by an employee for his employer, including the cash value of all remuneration paid in any medium other than cash." The two concepts — income and wages — obviously are not necessarily the same. Wages usually are income, but many items qualify as income and yet clearly are not wages. Interest, rent, and dividends are ready examples. And the very definition of "wages" in § 3401(a) itself goes on specifically to exclude certain types of remuneration for an employee's services to his employer (*e.g.*, combat pay, agricultural labor, certain domestic service). Our task, therefore, is to determine the character of the lunch reimbursements in the light of the definition of "wages" in § 3401(a), and the Company's consequent obligation to withhold under § 3402(a).

***

The Government, straightforwardly and simplistically, argues that the definition of "wages" in § 3401(a) corresponds to the first category of gross income set forth in § 61(a)(1), and that the two statutes "although not entirely congruent [in their] relationship," have "equivalent scope." It is claimed that the meal allowance was compensatory, for it was paid for the performance of assigned service at the place the employer determined. Thus, it is said, there was a direct causal connection between the receipt of the allowance and the performance of services. The allowance, then, was part of a total package of remuneration designed to attract and hold the employee to the Company. The Government further argues that this is in accord with the Court's pronouncements as to what is compensation for purposes of the tax statutes. It states that § 3401(a) broadly defines "wages," and it cites *Old Colony Trust Co. v. Commissioner of Internal Revenue*, 279 U.S. 716 (1929), where the Court held employees taxable for the amount of their income taxes paid by their employers. *** [I]t urges that what is important is that the payments at issue were a result of the employment relationship and were a part of the total of the personal benefits that arose out of that relationship.

V

We do not agree with this rather facile conclusion advanced by the Government. The case, of course, would flow in the Government's favor if the mere fact that the reimbursements were made in the context of the employer-employee relationship were to govern the withholding tax result. That they were so paid is obvious. But it is one thing to say that the reimbursements constitute income to the employees for income tax purposes, and it is quite another thing to say that it follows therefrom that the reimbursements in 1963 were subject to withholding. There is a gap between the premise and the conclusion and it is a wide one. Considerations that support subjectability to the income tax are not necessarily the same as the considerations that support withholding. To require the employee to carry the risk of his own tax liability is not the same as to require the employer to carry the risk of the tax liability of its employee. Required withholding, therefore, is rightly much narrower than subjectability to income taxation.

As we have noted above, withholding, under § 3402, is required only upon wages, and § 3401(a) defines wages as "all remuneration . . . for services performed by an employee for his employer." ***

Decided cases have made the distinction between wages and income and have refused to equate the two in withholding or similar controversies.***

An expansive and sweeping definition of wages, such as was indulged in by the Court of Appeals and is urged by the Government here, is not consistent with the existing withholding system. As noted above, Congress chose simplicity, ease of administration, and confinement to wages as the standard in 1942. This was a standard that was intentionally narrow and precise. It has not been changed by Congress since 1942, although, of course, as is often the case, administrative and other pressures seek to soften and stretch the definition. Because the employer is in a secondary position as to liability for any tax of the employee, it is a matter of obvious concern that, absent further specific congressional action, the employer's obligation to withhold be precise and not speculative.

***

This is not to say, of course, that the Congress may not subject lunch reimbursements to withholding if in its wisdom it chooses to do so by expanding the definition of wages for withholding. It has not done so as yet. And we cannot justify the Government's attempt to do so by judicial determination.

The judgment of the Court of Appeals is reversed.

It is so ordered.

[Concurring opinions omitted.]

Post-Case Follow-Up

Readily acknowledging that the lunch allowances constituted gross income to the affected employees, the Court concluded that such amounts did not constitute wages. As a result, the employer had no withholding obligation with respect to the amounts provided. The Court emphasized the fact that not all payments made in connection with the employer-employee relationship constitute wages and went on to softly chastise the administrative attempt to "soften and stretch the definition." As a practical matter, one can certainly appreciate the Commissioner's logic. Far better to put the employer, a taxpayer with financial wherewithal, on the hook than to audit and chase down employees who may have failed to include all gross income on their returns.

The IRS's recent pronouncements reflect consistent and aggressive effort to advance a broad and expansive definition of wages, even under circumstances reflecting a less than firm link between the amounts paid and the performance of services. In Revenue Ruling 2004-109, for example, the Service found it necessary to revoke prior inconsistent rulings to conclude that amounts paid to an employee as a signing bonus (for his first baseball contract with a future employer) constituted wages subject to withholding. Similarly, the IRS had to wrestle with its own prior pronouncements in concluding that employment contract cancellation payments constituted wages in Revenue Ruling 2004-110. At least one court has prevented expansion of the definitional ambit of wages to encompass damages paid for illegal refusal to hire. *See, e.g., Newhouse v. McCormick & Co, Inc.*, 157 F.3d 582 (8th Cir. 1998). But the IRS's posture has managed to gain considerable traction in several other contexts. Erroneously or not, it now appears that almost any amount paid by an employer to an employee in connection with the employment relationship will constitute wages, even if the payment constitutes severance or compensation for egregious employer misconduct. *See, e.g., United States v. Quality Stores, Inc.*, 572 U.S. _____ (2014) (concluding that the term "wages" includes severance payments).

Central Illinois Public Service Co. v. United States: Real Life Applications

1. In May of 2018, the owner of The Mini Mart hired Seymour to work as a cashier. Seymour had expected to earn the prevailing minimum wage, but his employer decided to pay him a full $1.00/hour more than minimum wage. Seymour did an excellent job, and in December of that year, his employer decided to award him a $1,000 bonus. Will Seymour's bonus constitute wages for federal income tax purposes?

2. Applicable law requires that all employees paid on an hourly basis be paid 1.5 times their standard hourly rate for any time worked during a given week in excess of 40 hours. Joette's employer was recently found to be in violation of the governing law and required to pay her back pay to compensate her properly for overtime. Will the amounts paid to Joette under these circumstances constitute wages for federal income tax purposes?

3. In connection with a recent sexual harassment suit, Paula and her former employer reached a settlement. Under the terms of the agreement, the former employer was obligated to pay Paula $100,000, and Paula was obligated not to disclose the amount of the settlement or any of the facts and circumstances surrounding the incident. Will the amount paid to Paula constitute wages for federal income tax purposes?

---

2. Employment Taxes

In General

Although § 1 imposes a tax on the taxable income of individuals, the uncomfortable reality is that several other Code provisions operate to impose additional taxes in certain contexts. Employers, employees, and the self-employed must contend, for example, with employment taxes imposed under the Federal Insurance Contributions Act ("FICA"). These taxes include the following:

▪ A tax with respect to Old Age, Survivors, and Disability Insurance ("OASDI"); these amounts generally cover the cost of Social Security and Disability Benefits.

■ A tax with respect to Hospital Insurance ("HI"); these amounts generally cover the cost of Medicare.

Old Age, Survivors, and Disability Insurance

As we just noted, OASDI is only one of the taxes imposed under the Federal Insurance Contributions Act. Nonetheless, one will frequently see reference to what is technically OASDI as FICA, and for ease of reference, we will temporarily adopt that convention. Many workers see FICA on their pay stubs for the first time when they are young and earning modest hourly wages. Initially, the employee may find the acronym perplexing and question his employer's ability to reduce further his already meager compensation. Understanding that these amounts are linked to his grandmother's Social Security benefits and his uncle's disability benefits may do little to soften the financial sting.

> ### Tax "Incidence"
>
> Just because Congress imposes a tax on a specific taxpayer, nothing truly guarantees that the targeted taxpayer will ultimately shoulder the burden of the tax. If the targeted taxpayer manages to pass the burden of the tax on to another taxpayer, we say that the incidence of the tax actually falls on the other taxpayer. Thus, although Congress imposes certain employment taxes on employers and employees, the likelihood is quite strong that the incidence of the employer's portion of the tax ultimately falls on the employee in the form of slightly lower wages.

One critically important thing to keep in mind is that FICA is imposed at both the employer and the employee level. Section 3101 imposes the tax at a rate of 6.2 percent on the wages received by an individual with respect to employment (with both wages and employment defined in § 3121). Similarly, § 3111(a) imposes on every *employer* an excise tax, with respect to having individuals in his employ, equal to 6.2 percent of the wages paid by the employer with respect to employment (with both wages and employment defined in § 3121). In addition to submitting the employer's share of FICA, the employer must deduct the employee's share of FICA from the employee's wages and pay that amount to the federal government. *See* § 3102(a) and (b).

Another important aspect of FICA should be remembered. Although a casual reading of §§3101 and 3111 might cause one to assume that FICA taxes apply to all wages paid with respect to employment, an annual cap or limit, the so-called FICA Wage Base (also known as the Contribution and Benefits Base) applies. This means that FICA is imposed on employee wages but only up to a specific dollar amount of wages per taxable year. Once the taxpayer and his employer have paid the FICA tax on this dollar amount in a taxable year, no further FICA tax is due; the employee will note that the FICA line item on his pay stub literally drops to $0 until the new tax year begins. The nasty truth about the FICA Wage base, however, is that the number is frequently adjusted from year to year, and the number almost always rises; by law, the amount cannot decrease. If you believe that the annual "adjustment to the FICA Wage Base" serves as a euphemism for "tax hike," you're not alone. It is true that FICA Wage Base adjustments are linked to national average wages and to cost-of-living adjustments for those receiving Social Security and related benefits, but even so, the adjustment eats away at more and more of an employee's regular pay as the years go by. Just recently, the FICA Wage Base was less than $100,000, and for several years, the number did not rise. As Exhibit 22.1 indicates, the FICA Wage Base now marches onward and upward with real vigor. Technically, Congress achieves taxation only on FICA Wage Base amounts by restricting the definition of wages. Bearing in mind that the employment taxes only apply to wages (as defined under § 3121), note that § 3121 provides a general definition of wages but also clarifies that certain amounts do not constitute wages. With respect to the provisions imposing the employee's share of FICA (§ 3101(a)) and the employer's share of FICA (§ 3111(a)), the term wages does *not* include remuneration paid in excess of the applicable FICA Wage Base. Accordingly, because such amounts are not wages, the FICA tax does not apply. For 2018, after the employer and the employee have paid the FICA tax on $128,400, no FICA tax is due on amounts paid above and beyond that.

Medicare

In addition to the tax imposed with respect to OASDI, Congress also imposes a tax with respect to Hospital Insurance to fund Medicare and related programs. Note, here at the outset, that although a FICA Wage Base applies in the OASDI context, in the HI context no cap exists. In fact, you will find that as wages rise, more HI tax must be paid.

Section 3101(b)(1) provides for a tax on the employee's share of HI. More precisely, the Code imposes "on the income of every individual a tax equal to 1.45 percent of wages (as defined in section 3121(a)) received by him with respect to employment (as defined in section 3121(b))." In addition, for wage amounts exceeding certain thresholds (which vary depending on one's filing status), section 3101(b)

EXHIBIT 22.1   **FICA Wage Base: Selected Years 1990–2018**

Year	FICA Wage Base
1990	$51,300
2000	$76,200
2007	$97,500
2008	$102,000
2009	$106,800
2010	$106,800
2011	$106,800
2012	$110,100
2013	$113,700
2014	$117,000
2015	$118,500
2016	$118,500
2017	$127,200
2018	$128,400

See https://www.ssa.gov/oact/cola/cbb.html (last visited March 14, 2018).

(2) imposes an *additional* tax of 0.90 percent. Employers must withhold and pay over the employee's share of HI tax. *See* § 3102(a) and (b). Although § 3111(b) generally imposes a 1.45 percent tax on employers (i.e., the employer's share of HI), no employer is subject to the additional 0.90 percent that may be imposed on some employees.

Employment Taxes and the Self-Employed

Thus far in this chapter, we have discussed the tax imposed with respect to OASDI and HI, and we have noted that, in general, these taxes have an employee's

> ## The Other Medicare Tax
>
> The taxes imposed under §§ 3101(b) and 3111(b) apply to wages with respect to employment. Some taxpayers may find that they are subject to the Unearned Income Medicare Contribution, a 3.8 percent tax imposed under § 1411. In some instances, this tax will apply to those with substantial amounts of investment income.

share and an employer's share. What happens with respect to the self-employed? If the same individual is both the employer and the employee, does she simply get to choose one role for the purpose of paying employment taxes? No, but the news is not all bad. A self-employed individual must pay both the employer's share *and* the employee's share of the FICA taxes owed. With respect to OASDI, section 1401(a) provides that "there shall be imposed for each taxable year, on the self-employment income of every individual, a tax equal to 12.4 percent of the amount of the self-employment income for such taxable year." With respect to HI, section 1401(b) provides for a tax of "2.9 percent of the amount of the self-employment income for such taxable year" as well as the additional 0.9 percent tax on self-employment income above a certain threshold. Those of you who aspire to becoming law firm partners should know that once you have attained that goal, you will be self-employed and thereafter have the pleasure of paying both the employer's share and the employee's share of FICA taxes. The good news is that all self-employed individuals may generally deduct, per § 164(f), half of the employment taxes paid, except any additional HI tax imposed under § 1401(b)(2).

Exploring the Meaning of "Wages" in the Employment Tax Context

Earlier in this chapter, we discussed the withholding of taxes with respect to wages, and you will recall that in discussing basic withholding, we referred to § 3401 for a definition of *wages* (i.e., "all remuneration . . . for services performed by an employee for his employer"). In the employment tax context, however, note that the term *wages* is defined in § 3121(a) as "all remuneration for employment," and § 3121(b), in turn, generally defines employment as "any service, of whatever nature, performed . . . by an employee for the person employing him . . . ." The definitions in § 3401 and § 3121 are strikingly similar, but we already know (because of the FICA Wage Base) that an amount may constitute wages for withholding purposes but not wages for OASDI purposes. For example, if an individual has already paid all OASDI taxes due with respect to § 3121(a) wages because they cleared the FICA Wage Base, then *for purposes of § 3121(a)*, additional amounts received from their employer do not, by definition, constitute wages subject to the OASDI tax.

Yet, these same additional amounts paid by the employer will be subject to general income tax withholding because they fall within the basic definition of wages under § 3401. Section 3401 does *not* cut off "wages" at the FICA Wage Base. Even if this definitional dichotomy makes sense when discussing OASDI tax obligations, what about other situations? Is it possible that a given amount received from an employer will constitute wages under § 3401 but not § 3121? If the IRS has its way, the definition of wages will sweep broadly in every context, but taxpayers can be counted on to resist an expansionist reading of the statute.

Case Preview

University of Pittsburgh v. United States

The *University of Pittsburgh* decision involved payments made to certain tenured faculty members. Rather than compensating the faculty members to deliver lectures, keep office hours, or perform other professorial tasks, these payments compensated them for relinquishing tenure, thereby fundamentally altering their relationship with the university. These so-called tenure buy-outs gave rise to an intriguing tax issue. Even if one concedes that the affected faculty members must include the payments in gross income, should the payments be subject to employment taxes? Do the payments, in any sense, constitute payments for services performed within the meaning of § 3121? Consider the following questions as you read the case:

1. What factors determined whether an employee could participate in the program?
2. If a former employer pays an amount to a former employee, can the amount constitute wages for employment tax purposes?
3. Why does the court consider the method by which tenure is earned significant?

University of Pittsburgh v. United States
507 F.3d 165 (3d Cir. 2007)

FUENTES, Circuit Judge.

The issue in this case is whether early retirement payments made by the University of Pittsburgh (the University) to its tenured faculty are taxable as "wages" under the Federal Insurance Contribution Act (FICA), 26 U.S.C. § 3121-28. From 1996 to 2001, the University paid over $2 million in FICA taxes on these payments. In 2001, however, it sought a refund from the Internal Revenue Service (IRS), on the ground that the early retirement payments were not "wages," but instead were "buy outs" not subject to FICA taxes. The IRS denied the refund, and the University filed this action in the District Court for the Western District of Pennsylvania. The District Court granted the University's motion for summary judgment, concluding that the payments were not wages, and denied the government's cross-motion for summary judgment. This appeal followed.

Because we agree with the government that the retirement payments are within the Act's definition of wages we will vacate the District Court's grant of summary judgment, and remand for entry of judgment in favor of the government.

I. BACKGROUND

The following facts are not disputed. Between 1982 and 1999, the University offered five successive Early Retirement Plans (the Plans) to tenured faculty members and administrators, as well as non-tenured librarians whose contracts provided an "expectation of continued employment." Payments under all five Plans were made monthly, and were based on an employee's salary at the time of retirement, as well as length of service to the University. *** To participate, employees were required to execute an irrevocable Contract for Participation. Employees who held tenure were required to relinquish their tenure rights.

Pursuant to University policy, "tenure" constitutes recognition by the University that a person so identified is qualified by achievements and contributions to knowledge as to be ranked among the most worthy of the members of the faculty engaged in scholarly endeavors: research, teaching, professional training, or creative intellectual activities of other kinds.

A non-tenured faculty member can serve without tenure for a maximum of seven years (with some exceptions not relevant here). After seven years, a faculty member can be terminated for failing to meet the requirements for tenure, or be granted tenure at the discretion of the Chancellor and the Chief Executive of the University.

According to the University, tenure fosters an environment of free inquiry because, once conferred, it affords faculty "rights and immunities," including immunity from termination except for cause or financial exigency. The University also may not terminate a tenured faculty member without a hearing that comports with standards of procedural due process under the Fourteenth Amendment.

As noted above, the University paid over $2 million in FICA taxes on payments under the Plans between 1996 and 2001. On November 19, 2001, the University filed claims with the IRS for refunds totaling $2,196,942, the total amount of the University's FICA tax payments since 1996, including employee-paid portions. Employees who participated in the Plans consented to have the University seek a refund on their behalf.

On October 30, 2002, the IRS denied the refund request, and on October 21, 2004, the University filed this suit in the District Court. The parties filed cross-motions for summary judgment, which the Court referred to Magistrate Judge Robert Mitchell. The Magistrate Judge recommended granting the University's motion with respect to Plan payments to tenured employees, but recommended granting the government's cross-motion with respect to Plan payments to non-tenured librarians.

On November 22, 2005, the District Court adopted the Magistrate Judge's Report and Recommendation, granting each party's motion for summary judgment in part, and denying each in part. The Court entered judgment in favor of the University in the amount of $2,088,358, plus statutory interest. Only the government appealed.

II. LEGAL FRAMEWORK

A. *"Wages" Under FICA*

The purpose of FICA taxes, as distinct from income taxes, is to "fund a national system of social insurance that supports important and extensive social security and medicare health programs." *Temple Univ. v. United States*, 769 F.2d 126, 130 (3d Cir.1985). FICA taxes include a tax to fund old-age, survivors, and disability insurance, and a tax to fund hospital insurance. In *Temple* we cited the Senate's comments explaining the underlying purpose of FICA:

> "The social security program aims to replace the income of beneficiaries when that income is reduced on account of retirement and disability. Thus, the amount of 'wages' is the measure used both to define income which should be replaced and to compute FICA tax liability. Since the security system has objectives which are significantly different from the objective underlying the income tax withholding rules, the committee believes that amounts exempt from income tax withholding should not be exempt from FICA unless Congress provides an explicit FICA tax exclusion."

769 F.2d at 130 (quoting S.Rep. No. 23, 98th Cong., 1st Sess. 41, reprinted in 1983 U.S.C.C.A.N. 143, 183).

Under the Internal Revenue Code, employers and employees are liable for payment of FICA taxes on all "wages" that are received by an employee "with respect to employment." Section 3121(a) defines "wages" subject to FICA taxes as "all remuneration for employment, including the cash value of all remuneration (including benefits) paid in any medium other than cash." Section 3121(b) defines "employment" as "any service, of whatever nature, performed . . . by an employee for the person employing him."

The Supreme Court has interpreted the term "employment" — a component of the definition of wages — broadly: "The very words any service . . . performed . . . for his employer, with the purpose of the Social Security Act in mind import breadth of coverage." *See Social Sec. Bd. v. Nierotko*, 327 U.S. 358, 365 (1946) (internal quotation marks omitted) (emphasis added). *Nierotko* concluded, specifically, that "service" in the phrase "any service performed" means not only work actually performed, but also "the entire employer-employee relationship for which compensation is paid to the employee by the employer." *Id.* at 365–66. Applying this interpretation, *Nierotko* held that "back pay" awarded under the National Labor Relations Act to a wrongfully discharged employee had to be taxed as wages under the Social Security Act. *See id.* at 364.

Treasury regulations further provide that "[t]he name by which . . . remuneration for employment is designated is immaterial." 26 C.F.R. § 31.3121(a) –1(c). Thus, for example, "salaries, fees, bonuses, and commissions on sales or on insurance premiums, are wages if paid as compensation for employment." *Id.* Likewise, "the basis upon which the remuneration is paid is immaterial in determining whether the remuneration constitutes wages." *Id.* at § 31.3121(a) –1(d). For example, "it may be paid on the basis of piecework, or a percentage of profits; and it may be paid hourly, daily, weekly, monthly, or annually." *Id.* Unless remuneration for employment is specifically excepted, it "constitutes wages even though at the time paid the relationship of employer and employee no longer exists between the person in whose employ the services were performed and the individual who performed them." *Id.* at § 31.3121(a)–1(i).

B. Relevant IRS Revenue Rulings

Both parties rely on IRS revenue rulings interpreting the Code and regulations to support their characterization of the Plan payments. We have explained that "although revenue rulings are entitled to great deference, . . . courts may disregard them if they conflict with the statute they purport to interpret or its legislative history, or if they are otherwise unreasonable." *Reese Bros., Inc. v. United States*, 447 F.3d 229, 237–38 (3d Cir.2006); *see also United States v. Mead Corp.*, 533 U.S. 218, 228 (2001) ("The weight [accorded to an administrative] judgment in a particular case will depend upon the thoroughness evident in its consideration, the validity of its reasoning, its consistency with earlier and later pronouncements, and all those factors which give it power to persuade, if lacking power to control.") (internal quotation marks omitted). Neither party challenges the validity of the applicable revenue rulings, but they dispute which among them is most analogous to this case. [The court proceeds to discuss various Revenue Rulings. Given the shift in the IRS's perspective on these issues over time, some rulings favor the IRS while others favor the taxpayer.]

***

C. The Circuit Split

This case presents an issue of first impression in our Court. Two other Courts of Appeals have addressed these precise questions, however, and have reached contrary conclusions. The University relies on *North Dakota State Univ. v. United States*, 255 F.3d 599 (8th Cir.2001), which held that early retirement payments to faculty who were required to relinquish their tenure rights, *were not* wages under FICA. The government relies on *Appoloni v. United States*, 450 F.3d 185 (6th Cir.2006) which held that early retirement payments made to public school teachers, who relinquished their statutory tenure rights, *were* wages under FICA.

In *North Dakota State*, the Eighth Circuit determined that a university's early retirement payments were made "in exchange for the relinquishment of [the faculty's] contractual and constitutionally protected tenure rights rather than as remuneration for services to [the University]." 255 F.3d at 607. After examining the relevant revenue rulings, the court reasoned:

> Under the terms of [North Dakota State's] Early Retirement Program, the tenured faculty received a negotiated amount of money in exchange for . . . their tenure rights. They did not receive what they were entitled to under their contracts, which was continued employment absent fiscal constraints or adequate cause for termination. Rather, they gave up those rights, making this case more analogous to Revenue Ruling 58-301 than to Revenue Ruling 74-252.

Id. at 607.

The District Court adopted this reasoning. ***

Subsequent to the District Court's decision, the Sixth Circuit declined to follow *North Dakota State. See Appoloni,* 450 F.3d 185. *Appoloni* summarized its reasoning as follows:

> [W]e find [it of] great significance that the tenure rights at issue were earned through service to the employer. This is for two reasons. First, we see no reason to differentiate tenure rights from any other right an employee earns through service to any employer. . . . [C]ourts have found the relinquishment of seniority rights, rights to bring suit, and other types of rights in exchange for a severance payment constitute FICA wages. Secondly, because these rights were earned through service rather than contracted for at the time of employment, this suggests Rev. Rul. 75-44 is more on point than Rev. Rul. 58-301.
>
> We also want to again emphasize the importance of the school district's principal purpose in offering these severance payments. The school district's purpose here was not to "buy" tenure rights. It was to induce those at the highest pay scales to voluntarily retire early. Relinquishment of tenure rights was incidental to the acceptance of the severance payment. A school district could not offer an early retirement payment and permit the teacher to keep his/her tenure and remain employed.

450 F.3d at 195-96 (footnote and citations omitted).

III. ANALYSIS

The weight of authority holds that compensation paid to an employee for services to her employer constitutes wages under FICA regardless of whether it is prospective (for lost earning potential), or retrospective (as a reward for past service). For the following reasons, we conclude that the relinquishment of tenure rights — although a condition precedent to the payments — does not alter the Plan payments' character as compensation for services, and therefore as wages.

First, the eligibility requirements for payments under the Plans are linked to past services at the University, not relinquishment of tenure. As *Appoloni* explained, "[i]n determining whether a payment constitutes wages, courts have looked to eligibility requirements, specifically longevity, as an important factor." 450 F.3d at 191. In this case, there is no dispute that eligibility for the Plans, for *both* tenured and non-tenured Plan participants, was based on the employee's age and years of service. These requirements link the Plan payments to past services for the employer, not the specific rights being relinquished, and weigh heavily in favor of treating the payments as wages.

Second, the Plans themselves make clear that the payments were viewed as compensation for service to the University. For example, the face of the 1998–2002 Plan reveals that an important motivation for the Plans was to keep the University's compensation package competitive with peer universities. Also, the 1983 Plan states that, in addition to making room for new faculty, the University offered the Plan because it "deem[ed] it desirable and appropriate to provide maximum flexibility and opportunities for its faculty members to retire voluntarily prior to the mandatory retirement age." Subsequent plans state a similar desire to reward valued faculty members.

To the extent the payments are a reward for service — as the Plans themselves indicate — they qualify as wages: "Payments for hard work and faithful service arise directly from the employee-employer relationship and are payments which recognize the value or character of the services performed for the employer." *Associated*

Electric, 226 F.3d at 1327 (finding manager's testimony that early out payments were "the right thing to do [because] [t]hese people had worked hard, and were good people," indicated payments were reward for past service and therefore wages) (second alteration in original).

Third, even if the University made the payments *in part* to secure relinquishment of tenure rights, their main purpose was to provide for employees' early retirement. In this way, they were indistinguishable from severance payments, which are generally taxed as wages. In this regard, we agree with the Sixth Circuit's statement in *Appoloni* that it

> fail[ed] to see how this is different from other severance packages just because a "tenure" right was exchanged. In almost all severance packages an employee gives up something, and we have a hard time distinguishing this case from similar cases where an employee, pursuant to a severance package, gives up rights in exchange. Courts have consistently held that severance payments for the relinquishment of rights in the course of an employment relationship are FICA wages. In fact, we are at a loss to find a case, other than the Eighth Circuit's decision, to hold otherwise.

450 F.3d at 193. This reasoning is consistent with numerous cases treating payment for the relinquishment of rights gained over the course of employment — including severance packages requiring waiver of all rights to sue — as wages.

The University seeks to distinguish these accrued-seniority and severance cases on the ground that the employees had "at will" employment contracts, whereas here, "tenure is obligatory for the University, optional with the faculty member." This distinction misses the point. Regardless of whether an employee voluntarily ended the employment relationship, or whether the employee had a due process right to maintain his employment, the rights relinquished were gained through the employee's past services to the employer.

***

Fourth, and relatedly, we reject the University's suggestion that because tenure is wholly discretionary and affords new rights to the recipient, it is necessarily the start of a new employment relationship ***. The University's policy on "Appointment and Tenure" shows that the award is contingent on past performance and is more like a promotion than an entirely new contract ***.

The fact that tenure is awarded on a very limited, discretionary basis does not change the fact that it is awarded based on service to the University. In this regard, we agree with *Appoloni* that courts

> must not look simply at what is being relinquished at the point a severance payment is offered, but rather, *how the right relinquished was earned.* Thus, we cannot understate the importance of the fact that a teacher earns tenure by successfully completing a probationary period. In other words, a teacher does not obtain tenure at the onset of employment; it is a right that is earned like any other job benefit. Admittedly, the grant of this right is guaranteed and protected by statute. But we fail to see how the fact that this right is protected by statute takes away from the point that it still *must be earned through services to the employer.*

450 F.3d at 192-93 (citations omitted) (emphasis added).

In sum, because tenure is a form of compensation for past services to the University, payments offered as a substitute for tenure are compensation and therefore taxable as wages. *See* 26 U.S.C. § 3121(a) ("[W]ages" includes "all remuneration for employment, including the cash value of all remuneration (including benefits) paid in any medium other than cash."); *Appoloni,* 450 F.3d at 195 ("Tenure rights were previously paid in kind — job security — and now are being paid in cash."); CSX, 52 Fed. Cl. at 221 ("Pursuant to [§ 3121(a)] . . . the value of the benefits and protections that each employee held in his or her position — rights to vacation pay, sick pay, layoff pay, and seniority — constituted part of the employee's total compensation package and, hence, constituted wages. Therefore, when these job-related benefits are relinquished in favor of a lump-sum payment, the transaction simply amounts to a redemption, paid in cash, of wage amounts previously paid in kind. . . . [W]hat were wages at the start remain wages at the end.").

IV. CONCLUSION

The record in this case shows that payments under the Plans were primarily in consideration for employees' past service to the University. Relinquishment of tenure rights, while a condition precedent to the payments, was not the primary consideration that employees offered. The payments therefore qualify as wages subject to FICA taxation. Accordingly, we will vacate the District Court's entry of summary judgment in favor the University, and remand to the District Court for entry of summary judgment in favor of the government.

[Dissenting opinion omitted.]

Post-Case Follow-Up

Noting that an employee earns tenure by providing services to the university, the court in *University of Pittsburgh* concludes that tenure buyout payments constitute wages for employment tax purposes. Emphasizing that courts have long treated severance payments as wages subject to employment taxes, the court found the apparent parallel compelling. But do the severance and buy-out decisions go too far? To be sure, an employee need not be "on the clock" to be earning wages. Few would contend that vacation pay or sick leave pay falls outside the bounds of wages for income tax or employment tax purposes just because vacations and illness do not involve the sweat of the employee's brow. Indeed, entitlement to such amounts generally forms part of a comprehensive employee compensation package. Perhaps one could say the same with respect to severance rights, but severance is undeniably an amount paid with respect to the termination of services. Does the employee earn a full salary and, simultaneously and surreptitiously, accrue the right to severance? Some courts comfortably dispense with the analytical niceties and simply conclude that severance is sufficiently linked to the employer/employee relationship to constitute wages for all federal tax purposes. Even if one willingly embraces such a broad conception of wages, can one truly justify characterizing amounts paid to an employee in the wake of egregious employer misconduct "wages with respect to employment" and therefore fully subject to all federal employment taxes? Even if Congress meant to reach far, could it possibly have meant to reach that far in its quest for revenue? Arguably, an extraordinarily broad interpretation of wages stretches the concept to the point of analytical rupture and effectively rewrites the statute to read "all amounts paid from an employer (or former employer) to an employee (or former employee)" rather than "wages with respect to employment." For additional commentary on this issue, see Bobby L. Dexter, *Tenure Buyouts: Employment Death Taxes and the Curious Obesity of "Wages,"* 70 U. Pitt. L. Rev. 343 (2009) (Lead Article); *see also* Bobby L. Dexter, *The Hate Exclusion: Moral Tax Equity for Damages Received for Race, Sex, or Sexual Orientation Discrimination,* 13 Pitt. Tax Rev. 197 (2016).

University of Pittsburgh v. United States: Real Life Applications

To the extent relevant in the following questions, please assume that no payment made with respect to an individual includes amounts that would be in excess of the relevant FICA Wage Base with respect to that employee.

1. Fulton currently teaches at a local law school. Although Fulton is not on tenure-track, he and the law school entered into a five-year employment contract in 2017. For reasons unknown to Fulton, the law school terminated his contract early and paid him a lump sum of $25,000. Will this amount constitute wages subject to federal employment taxes?

2. Sheila and her former employer recently settled a race discrimination lawsuit. Under the terms of the settlement agreement, her former employer must pay her $150,000. Will this amount constitute wages subject to federal employment taxes?

3. In an effort to recruit the best law students, Stiles & Currier LLP pays new associates a $10,000 signing bonus. If Austin accepts the firm's offer of employment and receives a signing bonus, will the amount constitute wages subject to federal employment taxes?

3. Worker Classification: Employee Versus Independent Contractor

Overview

For tax purposes, workers are generally classified as either employees or independent contractors. Proper classification is paramount because the withholding rules we have discussed thus far apply only in contexts involving an employer and an employee. Thus, if a business employs a full-time administrative assistant as an

Backup Withholding

In some contexts, a payor may be required to withhold taxes from amounts due to a payee. Such withholding ensures the collection of some amount of revenue in contexts in which ultimate collection from the payee may be jeopardized (e.g., the payee refuses to provide information (such as a Social Security Number or Taxpayer Identification Number) that would facilitate accurate and timely information reporting by the payor).

employee, it must withhold both employment taxes and income taxes from the employee's wages. But if that same business pays an independent contractor, for example, to repair several computers or to inspect a fire sprinkler system, it is neither obligated nor authorized to withhold such taxes from the amounts due for the services rendered. In many instances, one can promptly and accurately classify a worker. On occasion, however, determining whether a worker is an employee or an independent contractor can prove exceedingly difficult, especially if a business has a long-standing relationship with a service provider and their interactions are regular and continuous. Misclassification of an employee as an independent contractor leads to retroactive and decidedly unpleasant tax corrections. By default, the errant employer is responsible for both general income and employment taxes that should have been withheld and paid over, and the problem is exacerbated if (as is often the case) the misclassification involved several employees and withholding failures extending over several years. Workers also face unpleasant consequences from misclassification. Those who realize that they have paid a portion of self-employment taxes in error will have ample reason to complain, especially if they find themselves on the wrong side of a statute of limitations. Accordingly, all parties involved need clear and abundant worker classification guidance.

According to IRS Publication 15-A, *Employer's Supplemental Tax Guide*, workers fall into one of the following classifications:

- Independent contractor;
- Common-law employee;
- Statutory employee; or
- Statutory nonemployee.

Notwithstanding the presence of four distinct classification categories, two reflect statutory classification mandate. In practice, lawyers more frequently encounter classification issues involving independent contractors and common-law employees. Accordingly, we will focus exclusively on the standards that facilitate resolution in that context.

For decades, the task of classifying a worker required undertaking a 20-factor analysis of a given business relationship to ascertain whether the purported employer had the requisite level of control over the purported employee. To the extent actual control (or merely the right to control) existed, employee classification followed. Revenue Ruling 87-41 (quoted below) set forth the relevant factors and, at the same time, discussed their potential bearing on ultimate classification. The factors are as follows:

1. INSTRUCTIONS. A worker who is required to comply with other persons' instructions about when, where, and how he or she is to work is ordinar-

ily an employee. This control factor is present if the person or persons for whom the services are performed have the RIGHT to require compliance with instructions.

2. TRAINING. Training a worker by requiring an experienced employee to work with the worker, by corresponding with the worker, by requiring the worker to attend meetings, or by using other methods, indicates that the person or persons for whom the services are performed want the services performed in a particular method or manner.

3. INTEGRATION. Integration of the worker's services into the business operations generally shows that the worker is subject to direction and control. When the success or continuation of a business depends to an appreciable degree upon the performance of certain services, the workers who perform those services must necessarily be subject to a certain amount of control by the owner of the business.

4. SERVICES RENDERED PERSONALLY. If the Services must be rendered personally, presumably the person or persons for whom the services are performed are interested in the methods used to accomplish the work as well as in the results.

5. HIRING, SUPERVISING, AND PAYING ASSISTANTS. If the person or persons for whom the services are performed hire, supervise, and pay assistants, that factor generally shows control over the workers on the job. However, if one worker hires, supervises, and pays the other assistants pursuant to a contract under which the worker agrees to provide materials and labor and under which the worker is responsible only for the attainment of a result, this factor indicates an independent contractor status.

6. CONTINUING RELATIONSHIP. A continuing relationship between the worker and the person or persons for whom the services are performed indicates that an employer-employee relationship exists. A continuing relationship may exist where work is performed at frequently recurring although irregular intervals.

7. SET HOURS OF WORK. The establishment of set hours of work by the person or persons for whom the services are performed is a factor indicating control.

8. FULL TIME REQUIRED. If the worker must devote substantially full time to the business of the person or persons for whom the services are performed, such person or persons have control over the amount of time the worker spends working and impliedly restrict the worker from doing other gainful work. An independent contractor on the other hand, is free to work when and for whom he or she chooses.

9. DOING WORK ON EMPLOYER'S PREMISES. If the work is performed on the premises of the person or persons for whom the services are performed, that factor suggests control over the worker, especially if the work could be done elsewhere. Work done off the premises of the person or persons receiving the services, such as at the office of the worker, indicates some freedom from control. However, this fact by itself does not mean that the worker is not an employee. The importance of this factor depends on the nature of

the service involved and the extent to which an employer generally would require that employees perform such services on the employer's premises. Control over the place of work is indicated when the person or persons for whom the services are performed have the right to compel the worker to travel a designated route, to canvass a territory within a certain time, or to work at specific places as required.

10. ORDER OR SEQUENCE SET. If a worker must perform services in the order or sequence set by the person or persons for whom the services are performed, that factor shows that the worker is not free to follow the worker's own pattern of work but must follow the established routines and schedules of the person or persons for whom the services are performed. Often, because of the nature of an occupation, the person or persons for whom the services are performed do not set the order of the services or set the order infrequently. It is sufficient to show control, however, if such person or persons retain the right to do so.

11. ORAL OR WRITTEN REPORTS. A requirement that the worker submit regular or written reports to the person or persons for whom the services are performed indicates a degree of control.

12. PAYMENT BY HOUR, WEEK, MONTH. Payment by the hour, week, or month generally points to an employer-employee relationship, provided that this method of payment is not just a convenient way of paying a lump sum agreed upon as the cost of a job. Payment made by the job or on a straight commission generally indicates that the worker is an independent contractor.

13. PAYMENT OF BUSINESS AND/OR TRAVELING EXPENSES. If the person or persons for whom the services are performed ordinarily pay the worker's business and/or traveling expenses, the worker is ordinarily an employee. An employer, to be able to control expenses, generally retains the right to regulate and direct the worker's business activity.

14. FURNISHING OF TOOLS AND MATERIALS. The fact that the person or persons for whom the services are performed furnish significant tools, materials, and other equipment tends to show the existence of an employer-employee relationship.

15. SIGNIFICANT INVESTMENT. If the worker invests in facilities that are used by the worker in performing services and are not typically maintained by employees (such as the maintenance of an office rented at fair value from an unrelated party), that factor tends to indicate that the worker is an independent contractor. On the other hand, lack of investment in facilities indicates dependence on the person or persons for whom the services are performed for such facilities and, accordingly, the existence of an employer-employee relationship. Special scrutiny is required with respect to certain types of facilities, such as home offices.

16. REALIZATION OF PROFIT OR LOSS. A worker who can realize a profit or suffer a loss as a result of the worker's services (in addition to the profit or loss ordinarily realized by employees) is generally an independent contrac-

tor, but the worker who cannot is an employee. For example, if the worker is subject to a real risk of economic loss due to significant investments or a bona fide liability for expenses, such as salary payments to unrelated employees, that factor indicates that the worker is an independent contractor. The risk that a worker will not receive payment for his or her services, however, is common to both independent contractors and employees and thus does not constitute a sufficient economic risk to support treatment as an independent contractor.

17. WORKING FOR MORE THAN ONE FIRM AT A TIME. If a worker performs more than de minimis services for a multiple of unrelated persons or firms at the same time, that factor generally indicates that the worker is an independent contractor. However, a worker who performs services for more than one person may be an employee of each of the persons, especially where such persons are part of the same service arrangement.

18. MAKING SERVICE AVAILABLE TO GENERAL PUBLIC. The fact that a worker makes his or her services available to the general public on a regular and consistent basis indicates an independent contractor relationship.

19. RIGHT TO DISCHARGE. The right to discharge a worker is a factor indicating that the worker is an employee and the person possessing the right is an employer. An employer exercises control through the threat of dismissal, which causes the worker to obey the employer's instructions. An independent contractor, on the other hand, cannot be fired so long as the independent contractor produces a result that meets the contract specifications.

20. RIGHT TO TERMINATE. If the worker has the right to end his or her relationship with the person for whom the services are performed at any time he or she wishes without incurring liability, that factor indicates an employer-employee relationship.

Rev. Rul. 87-41, 1987-1 C.B. 296 (citations omitted).

These factors continue to be important, although the more modern approach (as set forth in IRS Publication 15-A) restructures the analysis without fundamentally changing it. Currently, classification requires an assessment of the working relationship by reference to the following three factor categories: (1) behavioral control, (2) financial control, and (3) established relationship type. Determining whether behavioral control is present requires consideration of (i) the extent to which instructions are given to the worker (e.g., when and where to do work, what tools or equipment to use, where to purchase supplies, and what order or sequence to follow), and (ii) the extent to which training is provided to the worker (e.g., training a waiter to how to serve prepared meals and how to clear dinnerware). The financial control assessment requires consideration of several factors, including whether the worker has unreimbursed business expenses, has invested in his own tools or equipment, can make his services available to others, and can reap a profit or suffer a loss. The substantive nature or type of relationship the parties have established is generally indicated by contractual descriptions of the relationship, the absence or presence of traditional employee benefits (e.g., vacation pay and sick pay), the intended relationship term, and the extent to which the worker is integrated into the business.

Section 530 Relief

As was noted earlier, misclassification of an employee as an independent contractor can result in substantial tax liabilities for the employer, and those who misclassify in the hope of avoiding employment taxes and various withholding obligations stand to suffer at the hands of the revenue collectors. Congress realized years ago, however, that for some taxpayers, misclassification of a specific worker or class of workers amounts to honest mistake, and so long as the employer has been consistent in its treatment and has otherwise followed the proper tax rules regarding such workers, relief from otherwise applicable employment tax levies was in order. For those who qualify, § 530 of the Revenue Act of 1978 (as amended) provides the needed relief. Note that § 530 does not appear in the Internal Revenue Code; it governs in this context but merely exists as part of the larger body of federal law.

IRS Publication 1976, *Do You Qualify for Relief under Section 530?*, summarizes the relevant requirements. Errant employers must have (1) had a reasonable basis for not treating the worker as an employee, (2) maintained substantive consistency, and (3) maintained reporting consistency. Affected employers can establish that they had a reasonable basis for treating a given worker as a nonemployee by proving proper reliance on any of the following:

- Judicial authority concerning federal taxes;
- A private ruling issued to the taxpayer;
- Post-1996 audits of the taxpayer (including worker classification assessments) in which the same or similar workers were not reclassified as employees;
- Treatment of similar workers in a significant segment of the taxpayer's industry; or
- Reasonable reliance on the advice of business lawyers or accountants familiar with the taxpayer's business.

A business satisfies the substantive consistency requirement by establishing that it (and any predecessor business) treated the relevant workers (and any similar workers) as independent contractors. Finally, a business satisfies the reporting consistency requirement by establishing that it has filed all required federal tax returns (including information returns) consistent with the treatment of the worker as an independent contractor. An **information return** (the filing of which may be required in certain contexts) allows one providing payment to a third party to notify or inform the IRS that the payment has been made to a specific payee (generally identified by a Social Security Number or some other Taxpayer Identification Number); the payment recipient also gets a copy. As depicted in Exhibit 22.2, IRS Form 1099-MISC is typical of information returns more generally.

EXHIBIT 22.2   **2017 IRS Form 1099-MISC**

☐ VOID ☐ CORRECTED		
PAYER'S name, street address, city or town, state or province, country, ZIP or foreign postal code, and telephone no.	**1 Rents** $ **2 Royalties** $	**OMB No. 1545-0115** **2017** Form **1099-MISC**
		Miscellaneous Income
	3 Other income $	**4 Federal income tax withheld** $
PAYER'S federal identification number | RECIPIENT'S identification number	**5 Fishing boat proceeds** $	**6 Medical and health care payments** $
RECIPIENT'S name	**7 Nonemployee compensation** $	**8 Substitute payments in lieu of dividends or interest** $
Street address (including apt. no.)	**9 Payer made direct sales of $5,000 or more of consumer products to a buyer (recipient) for resale ▶** ☐	**10 Crop insurance proceeds** $
City or town, state or province, country, and ZIP or foreign postal code	**11**	**12**
Account number (see instructions) | FATCA filing requirement ☐	**13 Excess golden parachute payments** $	**14 Gross proceeds paid to an attorney** $
15a Section 409A deferrals $ | **15b Section 409A income** $	**16 State tax withheld** $	**17 State/Payer's state no.** | **18 State income** $

Copy 1
For State Tax Department

Form **1099-MISC**   www.irs.gov/form1099misc   Department of the Treasury - Internal Revenue Service

Other Forms of Relief and Accommodation

Although many taxpayers will find employment tax relief under § 530, others will find that they cannot satisfy its requirements. Congress provides a degree of relief (in appropriate circumstances) under § 3509 of the Code. Barring circumstances involving intentional disregard of the rules, an employer failing to withhold and deduct withholding taxes and employee social security taxes will generally escape 100 percent liability. With respect to withholding taxes, the employer will generally be liable for 1.5 percent of wages paid to the employee, and with respect to social security taxes (which should have been deducted and withheld with respect to the employee's share), the employer will be liable for 20 percent of the amount; the employer remains liable for 100 percent of the employer's share of the social security taxes. Employers who failed to treat the relevant workers as employees and further failed to comply with information reporting requirements must shoulder a heightened burden (i.e., 3 percent of wages and 40 percent of the employee's share of social security taxes). *See generally* § 3509(a)–(c). Note that § 3509 does not apply to the improper classification of statutory employees or in situations in which the employer deducted and withheld with respect to withholding taxes but failed to do so with respect to social security taxes. *See* § 3509(d)(2)–(3). Note further that § 3509 does not operate to relieve the payee of tax liabilities or empower the employer to recover amounts paid under § 3509 from the employee. *See* § 3509(d)(1).

Employers currently treating certain workers as nonemployees and who seek, on a voluntary basis, to treat such workers as employees in the future may be able to take advantage of the Voluntary Classification Settlement Program. *See IRS Publication 15, (Circular E), Employer's Tax Guide.*

Exploring the Issues

Depending on prevailing facts and circumstances, proper worker classification can be a task that is easy, difficult, or somewhere in between; it is a calculus of multiple variables. Although relief provisions and programs are often available, the costs of misclassification can be uncomfortably high for some taxpayers. Adding to the complexity is the fact that a given business may contain a mix of employees and independent contractors and exist in somewhat of a state of flux. Individuals may consciously and overtly intend transition from independent contractor status to employee status and vice versa, but the labels used by the parties do not, of necessity, govern. Practical realities do.

Case Preview

Keller v. United States

The taxpayer in *Keller* operated an auto body shop, and while some of the workers maintained a regular daily presence as vital and integral parts of the business, others appeared more on an as-needed basis, albeit with some apparent regularity. The Tax Court took up the issue of classifying various workers. As you make your way through the case, consider the following questions:

1. Did AAB withhold any amounts with respect to any of its workers?
2. Did the absence of written employment contracts have any bearing on the court's analysis?
3. Must an employer exercise actual control over a worker, or is the right to control sufficient?
4. Why did the taxpayer not qualify for § 530 relief?

Keller v. United States

T.C. Memo. 2012-62

WHERRY, Judge:

This case is before the Court on a petition for review of a notice of determination of worker classification for petitioner's 1998 tax year which also determined that petitioner was liable for a $97,421.38 deficiency and $26,365 in penalties and additions to tax. The issues for decision are:

(1) whether the workers listed in the notice of determination should be legally classified as petitioner's employees for Federal employment tax purposes;

(2) whether petitioner is entitled to relief under the Revenue Act of 1978, Pub. L. No. 95–600, sec. 530, 92 Stat. at 2885, as amended (section 530), which in certain circumstances deems an individual not to be an employee;

(3) whether petitioner is liable for the employment taxes in the notice of determination;

(4) whether petitioner is liable for a section 6651(a)(1) addition to tax for failing to file Forms 941, Employer's Quarterly Federal Tax Return, and a Form 940, Employer's Annual Federal Unemployment Tax Return;

(5) whether petitioner is liable for a section 6656 penalty for failing to make timely deposits of employment taxes.

FINDINGS OF FACT

***

Petitioner was a 50% partner in Action Auto Body (AAB), which operated a paint and auto body shop. Petitioner's uncle, David Keller, was the other 50% partner. Petitioner managed the daily operations of the business. AAB had a contract with Mercury Insurance to make estimates for repairs and then would often repair those vehicles. AAB also took in business outside of Mercury.

On September 3, 2009, respondent sent petitioner a notice of determination of worker classification for the 1998 tax year, determining that [various individuals were to be legally classified as his employees]:

[Tabular data omitted.]

For three years before opening AAB, petitioner and Tony Red worked together repairing cars as independent contractors. Mr. Red was a mechanic and also restored cars. Kevin Walker, Javier Mendoza, and Walter Black worked as auto body repair technicians for AAB. Alex Martinez worked as a detailer for AAB. Tom Thompson and Kurt Hirsch worked as auto body painters for AAB. Each of these seven auto body workers had his own space on AAB's premises to perform his work but did not pay any rent. Petitioner paid all of AAB's auto workers weekly by check; the amount varied depending on commissions and the type of work they performed.

Eric Mark started out by cleaning the shop and assisting other workers at AAB and moved up to writing estimates for repairs. Mr. Mark received on-the-job training from petitioner and the other technicians at AAB. Petitioner also paid Mr. Mark weekly by check.

Lorna Dinger and Nicole Gonzalez performed secretarial duties for AAB such as serving as a receptionist, answering the phones, and filing. Petitioner paid them weekly by check.

Petitioner did not withhold any payroll tax from the amounts paid to any of the workers at AAB and did not issue Forms W-2, Wage and Tax Statement, or Forms 1099-MISC, Miscellaneous Income. AAB did not issue any employee manuals, and no employment contracts were ever signed between the workers of AAB and AAB.

OPINION

I. Burden of Proof

As a general rule, the Commissioner's determination of a taxpayer's liability is presumed correct, and the taxpayer bears the burden of proving that the determination is improper. However, pursuant to section 7491(a), the burden of proof on factual issues that affect the taxpayer's tax liability may be shifted to the Commissioner where the "taxpayer introduces credible evidence with respect to * * * such issue." The burden will shift only if the taxpayer has, inter alia, complied with substantiation requirements pursuant to the Code and "cooperated with reasonable requests by the Secretary for witnesses, information, documents, meetings, and interviews." Sec. 7491(a)(2)(B). Petitioner failed to cooperate, and the burden of proof remains on him.

II. The Workers' Legal Classification

Whether an individual is an independent contractor or an employee is a question of fact. Common law rules are applied to determine whether an individual is an employee or an independent contractor. Secs. 3121(d)(2), 3306(i).

In determining whether a worker is a common law employee or an independent contractor, the Court, inter alia, generally considers: "(1) The degree of control exercised by the principal; (2) which party invests in work facilities used by the individual; (3) the opportunity of the individual for profit or loss; (4) whether the principal can discharge the individual; (5) whether the work is part of the principal's regular business; (6) the permanency of the relationship; and (7) the relationship the parties believed they were creating." This list of factors is not exclusive, and other factors may also be considered such as the provision of employee benefits. All of the facts and circumstances of each case are considered, and no single factor is dispositive.

A. Degree of Control

The right of the principal to exercise control over the agent, whether or not the principal in fact does so, is the "crucial test" for the employer-employee relationship. "The employment relationship exists when the principal retains the *right* to direct the manner in which the work is done, and to control the methods used in doing the work, and to control the details and means by which the desired result is accomplished." In order to show the requisite degree of control, "the alleged employer need not 'stand over the employee and direct every move that he makes.'"

Petitioner argues that he could not control the persons working for AAB and that they set their own hours and chose their own work. Petitioner credibly testified that "each outside service provider provided an individual direct service, from pinstriping to windows to glass to bumper repair to bumpers" and that the individuals worked at their own pace with their own methods to create a finished, deliverable product.

Petitioner did not control the workers engaged in the actual body work of AAB. As the person for whom the services were performed, in order for the workers to be employees petitioner needed to have "the right [whether or not exercised] to control and direct the individual who performs the services, not only as to the result to be accomplished by the work but also as to the details and means by which that result is accomplished. That is, an employee is subject to the will and control of the employer not only as to what shall be done but how it shall be done. * * *"

See *Simpson v. Commissioner,* 64 T.C. at 984 (quoting section 31.3121(d)–1(c)(2), Employment Tax Regs.). This was simply not the case for those persons engaged in auto work at AAB.

However, as to Mr. Mark and the two workers who performed secretarial duties, the record is extremely sparse on petitioner's ability to control. It seems to show that petitioner had the right to control their work, and petitioner did not prove that he did not control their work. Accordingly, this factor weighs heavily in favor of independent contractor status for the auto workers and employee status for Ms. Dinger, Ms. Gonzalez, and Mr. Mark.

B. *Investment in Facilities*

The fact that a worker provides his or her own tools or owns a vehicle that is used for work is indicative of independent contractor status. Additionally, maintenance of a home office is consistent with, but not determinative of, independent contractor status.

Petitioner argues that each of the persons working at AAB owned his own tools. Unfortunately, the stipulation of facts, *** explicitly states that each of the listed workers did not own his own tools. At trial petitioner did not present any evidence contrary to the stipulation of facts besides his and Ms. Dinger's testimony. Ms. Dinger stated that the workers owned their own hand tools but explained that AAB owned and maintained heavy equipment such as sprayers, a framing machine, and lift equipment. This Court finds it especially unconvincing that the two workers who performed secretarial tasks provided their own equipment. There is no evidence whether any of the workers maintained a home office. The Court concludes that this factor weighs in favor of an employer-employee relationship for all of AAB's workers.

C. *Opportunity for Profit or Loss*

Compensation on a commission basis is entirely consistent with an employer-employee relationship. However, compensation in the form of commissions can also be indicative of independent contractor status. See *Simpson v. Commissioner,* 64 T.C. at 988. In *Simpson* the Court found, inter alia, that because the worker's opportunity for "profit or loss in any given year was solely dependent upon his own efforts and skill" he was an independent contractor. *Id.* Petitioner paid the auto body workers weekly with the amount depending on the commissions and the type of work they performed. Although the auto workers were paid on the basis of their own efforts and skill, they were not entirely dependent on themselves because petitioner was responsible for finding most of the work. Nevertheless, the auto body workers also obtained some of their own work independently from AAB. There is no evidence in the record as to how the compensation of Mr. Mark and the workers performing secretarial duties was determined. Accordingly, this factor is neutral for the auto workers and weighs in favor of employee status for Ms. Dinger, Ms. Gonzalez, and Mr. Mark.

D. *Right To Discharge*

Employers typically have the power to terminate employees at will. At trial petitioner explained that as to the persons working at AAB "could they be discharged by me? Absolutely. If I didn't like their service or we were done for whatever reason." Accordingly, the Court concludes that this factor weighs in favor of an employer-employee relationship.

E. *Integral Part of Business*

Before the workers listed in the notice of determination began working at AAB, petitioner performed all of the services himself. However, once the business expanded, petitioner needed the flexibility of independent workers to handle the varying types of jobs and numbers of cars. Because petitioner paid the auto workers commissions based on the work they did, he could support different amounts of business. As the business expanded the workers became an important part of AAB. We note that when workers are an essential part of the taxpayer's normal operations the Court has found this factor to weigh in favor of an employer-employee relationship. *See Day v. Commissioner,* T.C. Memo. 2000–375. However this case is distinguishable from *Day* because petitioner's main job was to estimate repairs for Mercury Insurance, and he would then refer vehicles to the workers for repairs.

    The Court concludes that this factor is neutral. The business could have survived without the workers; the workers had previously survived and in the future could and did survive without AAB. Petitioner was capable of performing the services on his own and could have cut back the number of vehicles he took in to accommodate his loss of workers. Alternatively he could have referred or subcontracted the repair work out to other independent contractors. Therefore this factor indicates neither independent contractor nor employee status.

F. *Permanency of the Relationship*

A transitory work relationship may weigh in favor of independent contractor status. The principal's right to discharge the worker, and the worker's right to quit, at any time, is a factor. The workers at AAB were all allowed to leave or quit at will, and some did. They could also have been discharged at will. At least six body workers left, and respondent treated them as independent contractors. Because both independent contractors and employees can be terminated at will, we accord this factor less weight. Accordingly, this factor weighs slightly in favor of independent contractor status.

G. *Relationship the Parties Thought They Created*

Petitioner certainly thought that he was creating independent contractor relationships with workers at AAB. For three years before opening AAB, petitioner and Mr. Red had worked together repairing cars as independent contractors. The former workers who testified seemed aware that petitioner believed that they were independent contractors while working for him, and they agreed. Thus, the Court concludes that both petitioner and the AAB workers listed in the notice of determination intended to create independent contractor relationships.

H. Provision of Employee Benefits

Petitioner did not offer the workers listed in the notice of determination any employee benefits. Benefits are typically provided to employees rather than independent contractors. When AAB closed or a worker left, none of the workers claimed unemployment benefits under California law. Accordingly, this factor tends to weigh in favor of independent contractor status.

I. Conclusion

After weighing the above factors, the Court concludes that the auto body repair workers listed in the notice of determination were independent contractors and Ms. Dinger, Ms. Gonzalez, and Mr. Mark were employees.

III. Section 530 Relief

Respondent also determined that petitioner is not entitled to relief from employee classification of its workers under section 530.

Section 530(a)(1) provides that an individual will be deemed not to be an employee of a taxpayer for purposes of applying employment taxes to that taxpayer, if the taxpayer satisfies three requirements: (1) the taxpayer must not have treated the individual as an employee for any period; (2) the taxpayer must have consistently treated the individual as not being an employee on all tax returns for periods after December 31, 1978; (3) the taxpayer must have had a reasonable basis for not treating the individual as an employee.

Respondent concedes that petitioner meets the first requirement because he did not treat any of the workers as employees for any period. Respondent, however, contends that petitioner failed to meet the second requirement because he never filed Forms 1099-MISC for any of the workers in question as required by sections 6041(a) and 6041A(a). We note that "For tax periods after December 31, 1978, relief under § 530 is available only if * * * [the taxpayer] filed required tax or information returns. § 530(a)(1)." *Gen. Inv. Corp. v. United States,* 823 F.2d 337, 341 (9th Cir. 1987). To qualify for relief under section 530(a)(1), a taxpayer must satisfy all three requirements; and because we have found that petitioner fails to meet the second requirement, he does not qualify for relief under section 530.

IV. Employment Taxes

Because this Court found that three persons, Ms. Dinger, Ms. Gonzalez, and Mr. Mark, listed in the notice of determination were his employees and he did not present any evidence that the amounts of employment tax listed in the notice of determination were incorrect, petitioner is liable for the employment taxes related to those three employees.

V. Section 6651 Addition To Tax and Section 6656 Penalty

Under section 6656(a), if a taxpayer fails to make a required deposit on the date prescribed for that deposit, a penalty equal to the applicable percentage of the amount of the underpayment, determined pursuant to section 6656(b), shall be imposed. Section 6656(a) also provides that the penalty shall not be imposed if "it is shown that such failure is due to reasonable cause and not due to willful neglect." Likewise section 6651(a)(1) imposes an addition to tax for failure to timely file the tax return. This addition to tax is also not to be imposed if the failure to pay was due to reasonable cause and not willful neglect.

Although we did find that certain of petitioner's workers were independent contractors and others were employees, we do not find that he had reasonable cause for failing to make the required deposits and timely pay tax for the three employees. As discussed *supra* petitioner did not issue a Form W-2 or a Form 1099-MISC to any of his workers, and it would be inconsistent for us to find that petitioner did not have reasonable cause for treating his employees as independent contractors but had reasonable cause for failing to make the required deposits and timely pay tax. Petitioner also did not provide any evidence of or explanation as to reasonable cause at trial. Petitioner is liable for the section 6656(a) penalty and the section 6651(a)(1) addition to tax for the three workers that this Court has found to be employees.

The Court has considered all of the parties' contentions, arguments, requests, and statements. To the extent not discussed herein, we conclude that they are meritless, moot, or irrelevant.

To reflect the foregoing,

Decision will be entered under Rule 155.

Post-Case Follow-Up

After weighing the relevant factors, the court in *Keller* concluded that the auto body workers were independent contractors with respect to AAB and that those workers performing secretarial functions and writing estimates were employees of AAB. Because AAB failed to file appropriate information returns with respect to any of its workers, it could not qualify for employment tax relief under Section 530 of the Revenue Act of 1978. AAB's failure in this regard (with respect to its employees) also subjected it to penalties and additions to tax. The decision itself does little if anything to alter the legal landscape. More so than anything, the decision clarifies that to the extent a worker is retained to accomplish a specific task but is not subject to control with respect to how the task is to be accomplished, he operates as an independent contractor. Time will tell whether the governing worker classification standards update well. Today, technology makes it possible for many individuals to work from home. Some may be expected to accomplish a specific task with little supervision or direction, but no one questions whether an employer-employee relationship exists. How much does such a situation differ from one in which a worker who is generally treated as an independent contractor is charged with accomplishing the same or a substantially similar task under identical terms?

Perhaps technological evolution will ultimately result in searching analysis with respect to the right to control a worker, regardless of whether the right is regularly or rarely exercised.

Keller v. United States: Real Life Applications

1. Apollo Express, Inc. ("Apollo") operates a moving service. Its drivers may not provide services for any other companies. Further, each driver must comply with several rules in connection with performing their work (e.g., driving below a set speed limit, refraining from the use of controlled substances at all times, limiting driving to a set number of hours per day, refraining from the use of all electronic devices while the truck engine is running, submitting to annual physical exams, etc.). Based on the facts presented, is it likely that Apollo's drivers are employees or independent contractors?

2. Perdue owns and operates a farm on which he grows various crops. Each year in October, he hires several workers to pick the pecans that have been shaken from the trees on which they grew. Perdue pays the workers based on the weight of the pecans they have picked during the course of the day, but in general, he does not supervise the workers as they go about the task of picking the pecans. Are the workers likely to be classified as Perdue's employees?

3. Package Express, Inc. ("PE") operates a package delivery service. Given that business picks up considerably during the holiday season, PE brings in several workers during the month of December. Although the workers and PE fully understand that they have been brought on for no more than four weeks, the workers must comply with PE's general operating procedures in whatever capacity they happen to be working (e.g., loading packages, unloading packages, performing secretarial tasks, or delivering packages). Is it likely that these seasonal workers will be classified as PE's employees?

B. ESTIMATED TAX PAYMENTS

Thus far in this chapter, we have devoted considerable attention not only to an employer's obligation to deduct and withhold various amounts from wages paid to employees but also to that employer's obligation to pay those amounts over to the federal government on a timely basis. The employer does not deduct and withhold the relevant amounts and pay them over to the federal government in a single lump sum at the end of a taxable year. Instead, the employer must regularly deposit the withheld amounts, typically on a monthly or semiweekly basis. The *Keller* decision, while focused largely on worker classification issues, also introduced us to potential penalties the employer might face both for failing to pay over proper amounts (which should have been withheld with respect to employees) and for failing to file the appropriate information returns with respect to amounts paid to employees. Those who are self-employed stand in the shoes of both the employer and the employees, and they too operate in this environment but with a few key differences.

Self-employed individuals must make payments with respect to their tax liabilities, but they do so by using tax liability estimates and submitting payments on what is essentially a quarterly basis. To employ an oversimplification, assume that Carmella earns $10,000 in January, February, and March of 2018. If she expects to continue earning at that rate, she can expect to earn a total of $120,000 in 2018. At the same time, based on her business expenses and other tax-relevant facts (e.g., her ability to take a standard deduction, etc.), she can estimate that her total tax liability for the year will be $28,000. Carmella will be obligated to make four quarterly payments of $7,000 to the federal government. For a given tax year, the due dates will generally be April 15, June 15, September 15, and January 15 of the following taxable year. If Carmella fails to pay a quarterly installment, pays the installment late, or pays too little with respect to any installment, she may be required to pay penalties and interest. *See generally* § 6654. Precise calculation of the required installment amount under various scenarios (and within a range of options) is beyond the intended scope of this casebook. Of primary importance, at this juncture, is that you grasp the notion that self-employed individuals must make adequate and timely quarterly estimated tax payments or suffer the consequences of failing to do so in accord with established statutory dictates.

C. SPECIFIC TAX PENALTIES AND THE IMPOSITION OF INTEREST ON TAX OBLIGATIONS

In reviewing tax cases in this course and others, you will regularly encounter fact scenarios in which the IRS seeks not only to collect an asserted deficiency from a taxpayer but also seeks to have the relevant decision maker impose penalties. Commonly, the IRS pursues the imposition of an accuracy-related penalty (e.g., for negligence, substantial understatements of income tax, or disregard of the rules or regulations), but as you might suspect, the IRS can appeal to a rich universe of potential penalties for taxpayer misconduct conduct or oversight, including the following:

- Penalty for Failure to File Tax Return or Pay Tax. *See* § 6651.
- Penalty for Failure of Individual to Pay Estimated Income Tax. *See* § 6654.
- Accuracy-Related Penalty. *See* § 6662.
- Fraud Penalty. *See* § 6663.

Notwithstanding the existence of various penalties, they are not generally imposed as a matter of strict taxpayer liability. Even in the penalty arena, Congress displays some degree of legislative grace. The failure to file penalty, for example, will apply "unless it is shown that such failure is due to reasonable cause and not due to willful neglect." *See* § 6651(a)(1). Similarly, with respect to the accuracy-related penalty and the fraud penalty, we see a special rule in § 6664, which generally provides that "[n]o penalty shall be imposed under section 6662 or 6663 with respect to any portion of an underpayment if it is shown that there was a reasonable cause for such portion and that the taxpayer acted in good faith with respect to such portion." Section 6664(c)(1).

In addition to imposing penalties with respect to taxpayer underpayments, the Code also provides for the collection of interest. *See* § 6601(a). Section 6621(a)(2) provides for standard underpayment interest rates, but enhanced interest rates (i.e., so-called hot interest) may apply to large corporate underpayments, which are generally defined as those exceeding $100,000. As was mentioned much earlier in the casebook, taxpayers facing asserted deficiencies have the ability to stop the tolling of interest by paying the assessment. Thereafter, they may pursue recovery of the amount paid by filing a refund suit against the United States in the appropriate venue; successful taxpayers may pursue interest on the overpayment at the overpayment rate set forth in § 6621(a). *See* 28 U.S.C. § 2411.

Food for Thought: The Accuracy-Related and Civil Fraud Penalties

For underpayments arising from negligence, disregard of rules/regulations, substantial understatement of income, and certain other taxpayer conduct, § 6662 imposes a penalty equal to 20 percent of the applicable underpayment. For civil tax fraud, however, the penalty rises to 75 percent, per mandate of § 6663. Interestingly enough, reasonable cause relief under § 6664(c) applies to both accuracy-related and civil tax fraud penalties to the extent that that taxpayer can establish reasonable cause for the underpayment and action rooted in good faith. Barring egregious reliance on a third party, do reasonable cause and good faith provide a viable path to civil tax fraud relief?

Chapter Summary

- Employers are generally obligated to deduct, withhold, and pay over federal income taxes with respect to wages paid to their employees. For this purpose, the term wages is defined in § 3401. Not all amounts paid from an employer to an employee constitute wages.
- Under the Federal Insurance Contributions Act, employers are generally obligated to deduct, withhold, and pay over federal employment taxes with respect to wages paid to their employees. For this purpose, the term wages is defined in § 3121. Employment taxes are imposed both on the employer and the employee. The tax imposed with respect to OASDI applies each taxable year only on compensation up to the so-called FICA Wage Base. The tax imposed with respect to HI has no cap, and those with wages above a certain amount must pay additional HI taxes. The FICA Wage Basis is subject to annual adjustment, but the number cannot decrease.

- The self-employed must pay both the employer's and the employee's share of FICA. Further, such individuals must estimate their total tax liability for a given taxable year and make quarterly estimated tax payments. Self-employed individuals may be entitled to a deduction with respect to a portion of the employment taxes paid.

- An amount may constitute wages for income tax purposes but not for employment tax purposes.

- Workers are classified as independent contractors, common-law employees, statutory employees, and statutory nonemployees. Wage-based withholding obligations apply only in contexts involving employers and employees.

- In general, a worker is an employee if he or she is subject to the control of an employer with respect to the precise means by which the work is to be done. Decision makers take various factors into consideration in classifying a worker as an employee or an independent contractor. To the extent that an employer failed to classify a worker as an employee, the employer may qualify for the relief provided by § 530 of the Revenue Act of 1978 (as amended).

- Section 3509 of the Code may provide relief to some employers failing to properly classify employees as such.

- For various forms of taxpayer conduct, the IRS may impose penalties and collect interest with respect to underpayments.

Applying the Rules

1. The Sterling Company LLC ("TSC") operates apartment complexes throughout the metropolitan Atlanta area. The region has abundant sunshine and rain such that the trees in TSC's communities need regular trimming. Assume that on April 30 and September 30, TSC paid $5,000 to The Chainsaw Gang (a local business) for tree trimming services. Was TSC obligated to withhold any taxes with respect to these payments?

2. For several years, Parcel Service of America, Inc. ("PSA") has treated all of its long-haul truck drivers as independent contractors. Recently, it was determined that these drivers should have been classified as employees. According to PSA, almost every business in the industry treats long-haul drivers as independent contractors. Further, PSA has always treated such workers (and any worker operating in a similar capacity) as an independent contractor, and PSA has filed all returns (including Form 1099-MISC) in a manner consistent with the treatment of the workers as independent contractors. Will PSA be required to pay employment taxes with respect to these workers as though they were employees all along?

3. Assume that in 2018, the FICA Wage Base is $130,000, and that as of August 31, 2018, Susan has been paid $140,000 in wages subject to employment taxes. What employment taxes, if any, should be withheld from Susan's pay for the remainder of the year?

4. Garilli is a cash-basis, self-employed individual who uses the calendar year as his taxable year. As of March 31, he estimates that his final tax liability for the full year will be $40,000. What amount must he pay in estimated taxes on April 15 of that year?

Federal Income Taxation in Practice

1. One of your fellow law partners has received a question from one of her clients, a large corporation. Apparently, the client has treated a number of its traveling salespeople as independent contractors, although it appears that they may be employees. Some reference has been made to statutory employees, and your fellow partner has asked that you give her a better sense of what a statutory employee is and how that differs, if at all, from a common-law employee. Conduct the research and follow up with the partner by brief memorandum.

2. The same partner from Question #1 has come to you again with another worker classification question. She has heard of something called the VCSP, and her understanding is that it is some form of voluntary worker classification program. She'd like to know more about it and what it basically entails for the affected business. Conduct the research and follow up with her by brief e-mail.

3. You and several of your friends landed jobs at major international law firms and have been working diligently for several months. During a Happy Hour celebration in February of the current year, someone noted that everyone's take home pay is supposed to increase at some point during the year because of something called the FICA Wage Base. Everyone knows that you're a tax associate, so they turn to you and ask when they can expect their paycheck to increase. You don't know everyone's salary, so the best you can do is tell them that no more OASDI will be taken once the amount withheld reaches a specific number. What will that number be?

Tax Controversy and Litigation: A Brief Overview

Each year, millions of taxpayers in the United States submit timely federal income tax returns, and given that audits are more the exception than the rule, issues rarely arise. But as the preceding chapters have made abundantly clear, tax laws can be notoriously complex, and interpretive differences can quickly evolve into litigation-worthy disagreement. To the extent that the IRS and a taxpayer are at odds, many paths can lead to resolution, some ending in a place of complete accord, others requiring passage through contentious litigation, and yet others directing parties to a mutually satisfactory destination just short of the courthouse steps, albeit not without a few uncomfortable bumps and detours along the way. Fortunately for all involved, well-established rules govern the process. In fact, entire courses are devoted to procedural and other rules applicable in the tax controversy context, and we will come nowhere close to addressing all relevant statutory provisions or potential resolution scenarios. The aim at this juncture is to offer a very basic introduction to the tax controversy and litigation landscape. Knowledge of the core fundamentals set forth here will facilitate your smooth transition to a clinical or early practice setting.[1]

A. THE NOTION OF ASSESSMENT

Many of you will recall language from various tax opinions indicating that the Commissioner of Internal Revenue generally enjoys a presumption of correctness with respect to determinations of a taxpayer's liability. This notion has common sense appeal, but there's far more to it than meets the eye at first glance. In general, before a taxpayer can be held officially responsible for payment of a tax, the tax must be properly "assessed," and the assessment requirement allows taxpayers

---

[1]Portions of this Appendix 1 reflect a synthesis of material from BLOOMBERG BNA, 2015 FEDERAL TAX GUIDE (Tax Management 2014).

to assert and enjoy various procedural protections. Section 6201 both authorizes and requires assessments, and § 6203 dictates that the IRS formally assess taxes by recording the liability in its records.

1. "Self-Assessment" by Taxpayer

Taxpayers filing returns are, essentially, authorizing an assessment that they themselves have determined, but as a technical matter, the final and true assessment from a tax return is made by the IRS. On receipt of a return reflecting "total tax," the IRS can summarily assess the amount shown. *See* Exhibit A1.1.

Although assessment gives the IRS the authority to collect any unpaid amounts through lien and levy procedures, taxpayers may be able to take advantage of various relief-type arrangements to the extent they are subject to tax assessments and lack the ability to pay immediately or in full. Offers in Compromise and Installment Agreements are common arrangements.

Offers in Compromise

Section 7122 allows the IRS to agree to accept less than 100 percent of a taxpayer's assessed liability under certain circumstances by entering into an **offer in compromise**. As a matter of policy, the IRS tends to compromise the liability when full collection of the liability is unlikely and the taxpayer's offer reflects likely collectability. The tax must be assessed, and there must be (i) doubt as to liability, (ii) doubt as to collectability, or (iii) facts indicating that a compromise with respect to the liability will promote effective administration of the tax laws (i.e., avoid undue economic hardship or prevent the undermining of public confidence that administration of the tax laws is fair and equitable). Ordinarily, the taxpayer will complete and execute IRS Form 656 (depicted in Exhibit A1.2).

EXHIBIT A1.1   **Excerpt from IRS Form 1040**

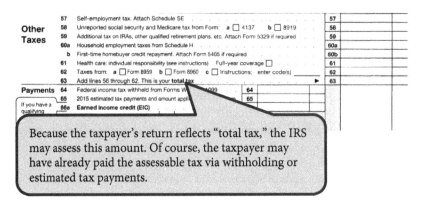

EXHIBIT A1.2   **IRS Form 656 (Page 1)**

Form **656**
(Rev. February 2016)

Department of the Treasury — Internal Revenue Service
Offer in Compromise

▶ **To: Commissioner of Internal Revenue Service**

In the following agreement, the pronoun "we" may be assumed in place of "I" when there are joint liabilities and both parties are signing this agreement.

I submit this offer to compromise the tax liabilities plus any interest, penalties, additions to tax, and additional amounts required by law for the tax type and period(s) marked in Section 1 or Section 2 below.

Did you use the Pre-Qualifier tool located on our website at http://irs.treasury.gov/oic_pre_qualifier/ **prior to filling out this form?**
  ☐ Yes   ☐ No

Note: The use of the Pre-Qualifier tool is not mandatory before sending in your offer. However, it is recommended.

Include the $186 application fee and initial payment (*personal check, cashier's check, or money order*) with your Form 656. You must also include the completed Form 433-A (OIC) and/or 433-B (OIC) and supporting documentation. You should fill out either Section 1 or Section 2, but not both, depending on the tax debt you are offering to compromise.

Section 1	**Individual Information (Form 1040 filers)**

If you are a 1040 filer, an individual with personal liability for Excise tax, individual responsible for Trust Fund Recovery Penalty, self-employed individual, individual personally responsible for partnership liabilities, and/or an individual who operates as a single member LLC or a disregarded entity taxed as an sole proprietorship you should fill out Section 1. You must also include all required documentation including the Form 433-A (OIC), the $186 application fee, and initial payment.

Your First Name, Middle Initial, Last Name	Social Security Number (SSN)	**IRS Received Date**
	- -	
If a Joint Offer, Spouse's First Name, Middle Initial, Last Name	Social Security Number (SSN)	
	- -	
Your Physical Home Address (*Street, City, State, ZIP Code*)		
Mailing Address (*if different from above or Post Office Box number*)		
Employer Identification Number		
-		

Individual Tax Periods
If Your Offer is for Individual Tax Debt Only

☐ 1040 Income Tax-Year(s) _____

☐ Trust Fund Recovery Penalty as a responsible person of (*enter business name*) _____

  for failure to pay withholding and Federal Insurance Contributions Act taxes (Social Security taxes), for period(s) ending _____

☐ 941 Employer's Quarterly Federal Tax Return - Quarterly period(s) _____

☐ 940 Employer's Annual Federal Unemployment (FUTA) Tax Return - Year(s) _____

☐ Other Federal Tax(es) [specify type(s) and period(s)] _____

Note: If you need more space, use attachment and title it "Attachment to Form 656 dated _____." Make sure to sign and date the attachment.

Catalog Number 16728N   www.irs.gov   Form **656** (Rev. 2-2016)

EXHIBIT A1.2 **IRS Form 656 (Page 2)**

Low-Income Certification *(Individuals and Sole Proprietors Only)*

Do you qualify for Low-Income Certification? You qualify if your gross monthly household income is less than or equal to the amount shown in the chart below based on your family size and where you live. If you qualify, you are not required to submit any payments during the consideration of your offer. Businesses other than sole proprietors or disregarded single member LLCs taxed as a sole proprietor do not qualify for the low income waiver.

☐ Check this box if your household's gross monthly income is equal to or less than the monthly income shown in the table below.

Size of family unit	48 contiguous states and D.C.	Hawaii	Alaska
1	$2,475	$2,848	$3,092
2	$3,338	$3,840	$4,171
3	$4,200	$4,831	$5,250
4	$5,063	$5,823	$6,329
5	$5,925	$6,815	$7,408
6	$6,788	$7,806	$8,488
7	$7,652	$8,798	$9,567
8	$8,538	$9,794	$10,650
For each additional person, add	$867	$996	$1,083

Section 2 **Business Information (Form 1120, 1065, etc., filers)**

If your business is a Corporation, Partnership, LLC, or LLP and you want to compromise those tax debts, you must complete this section. You must also include all required documentation including the Form 433-B (OIC), and a separate $186 application fee, and initial payment.

Business Name

Business Address *(Street, City, State, ZIP Code)*

Employer Identification Number (EIN)	Name and Title of Primary Contact	Telephone Number
-		( ) -

Business Tax Periods

If Your Offer is for Business Tax Debt Only

☐ 1120 Income Tax-Year(s)

☐ 941 Employer's Quarterly Federal Tax Return - Quarterly period(s)

☐ 940 Employer's Annual Federal Unemployment (FUTA) Tax Return - Year(s)

☐ Other Federal Tax(es) [specify type(s) and period(s)]

Note: If you need more space, use attachment and title it "Attachment to Form 656 dated _____." Make sure to sign and date the attachment.

Section 3 **Reason for Offer**

☐ **Doubt as to Collectibility** - I have insufficient assets and income to pay the full amount.

☐ **Exceptional Circumstances (Effective Tax Administration)** - I owe this amount and have sufficient assets to pay the full amount, but due to my exceptional circumstances, requiring full payment would cause an economic hardship or would be unfair and inequitable. I am submitting a written narrative explaining my circumstances.

Explanation of Circumstances *(Add additional pages, if needed)* – The IRS understands that there are unplanned events or special circumstances, such as serious illness, where paying the full amount or the minimum offer amount might impair your ability to provide for yourself and your family. If this is the case and you can provide documentation to prove your situation, then your offer may be accepted despite your financial profile. Describe your situation below and attach appropriate documents to this offer application.

Catalog Number 16728N　　　　　www.irs.gov　　　　　Form **656** (Rev. 2-2016)

EXHIBIT A1.2   **IRS Form 656 (Page 3)**

Section 4	Payment Terms

▼ Check one of the payment options below to indicate how long it will take you to pay your offer in full. You must offer more than $0. The offer amount should be in whole dollars only. ▼

Lump Sum Cash

☐ Check here if you will pay your offer in 5 or fewer payments within 5 or fewer months from the date of acceptance:

Enclose a check for 20% of the offer amount (waived if you are an individual or sole proprietor and met the requirements for Low Income Certification) and fill in the amount(s) of your future payment(s).

Total Offer Amount	-	20% Initial Payment	=	Remaining Balance
$	-	$	=	$

You may pay the remaining balance in one payment after acceptance of the offer or up to five payments, but cannot exceed 5 months.

Amount of payment	$	payable within	1	Month after acceptance
Amount of payment	$	payable within	2	Months after acceptance
Amount of payment	$	payable within	3	Months after acceptance
Amount of payment	$	payable within	4	Months after acceptance
Amount of payment	$	payable within	5	Months after acceptance

Periodic Payment

☐ Check here if you will pay your offer in full in 6 to 24 months.

Enter the amount of your offer $ _____

Note: The total amount must equal all of the proposed payments including the first and last payments.

Enclose a check for the first month's payment.

$ _____ is included with this offer then $ _____ will be sent in on the _____ day of each month thereafter

for a total of _____ months with a final payment of $ _____ to be paid on the _____ day of the _____ month.

Note: The total months may not exceed a total of 24 months, including the first payment. Your first payment is considered to be month 1; therefore, the remainder of the payments must be made within 23 months for a total of 24.

You must continue to make these monthly payments while the IRS is considering the offer *(waived if you met the requirements for Low Income Certification)*. Failure to make regular monthly payments will cause your offer to be returned with no appeal rights.

IRS Use Only

☐ Attached is an addendum dated (insert date) _____ setting forth the amended offer amount and payment terms.

Section 5	Designation of Payment and Deposit

Designation of Payment

If you want your payment to be applied to a specific tax year and a specific tax debt, such as a Trust Fund Recovery Penalty, please tell us the tax

year/quarter _____ . If you do not designate a preference, we will apply any money you send to the government's best interest. If you wish to designate any payments not included with this offer, you must designate a preference for each payment at the time the payment is made. However, you cannot designate the $186 application fee or any payment after the IRS accepts the offer.

Deposit

If you are paying **more than** the initial payment when you submit your offer and want any part of that payment treated as a deposit, check the box below and insert the amount. Deposits will be returned to you if the offer is rejected, returned, or withdrawn, unless you provide a request in writing that you want your payment(s) to be applied to your tax debt.

☐ My payment of $ _____ includes the $186 application fee and $ _____ for my first month's payment. I am requesting the

additional amount of $ _____ be held as a deposit.

CAUTION: Do NOT designate the amounts sent in with your offer to cover the initial payment and application fee as "deposits." Doing so will result in the return of your offer with no right to appeal.

EXHIBIT A1.2   **IRS Form 656 (Page 4)**

Section 6   Source of Funds, Making Your Payment, Filing Requirements, and Tax Payment Requirements

Source of Funds

Tell us where you will obtain the funds to pay your offer. You may consider borrowing from friends and/or family, taking out a loan, or selling assets.

_____

_____

_____

Making Your Payment

Include separate checks for the payment and application fee.

Make checks payable to the "United States Treasury" and attach to the front of your Form 656, Offer in Compromise. All payments must be in U.S. dollars. **Do not send cash.** Send a separate application fee with each offer; do not combine it with any other tax payments, as this may delay processing of your offer. Your offer will be returned to you if the application fee and the required payment are not included, or if your check is returned for insufficient funds.

Filing Requirements

☐ I have filed all required tax returns.

☐ I was not required to file a tax return for the following years: _____

Tax Payment Requirements *(check all that apply)*

☐ I have made all required estimated tax payments for the current tax year.

☐ I am not required to make any estimated tax payments for the current tax year.

☐ I have made all required federal tax deposits for the current quarter.

☐ I am not required to make any federal tax deposits for the current quarter.

Section 7   Offer Terms

By submitting this offer, I have read, understand and agree to the following terms and conditions:

Terms, Conditions, and Legal Agreement	a) I request that the IRS accept the offer amount listed in this offer application as payment of my outstanding tax debt (including interest, penalties, and any additional amounts required by law) as of the date listed on this form. I authorize the IRS to amend Section 1 and/or Section 2 if I failed to list any of my assessed tax debt or tax debt assessed before acceptance of my offer. I also authorize the IRS to amend Section 1 and/or Section 2 by removing any tax years on which there is currently no outstanding liability. I understand that my offer will be accepted, by law, unless IRS notifies me otherwise, in writing, within 24 months of the date my offer was received by IRS. I also understand that if any tax debt that is included in the offer is in dispute in any judicial proceeding it/ they will not be included in determining the expiration of the 24-month period.
IRS will keep my payments, fees, and some refunds.	b) I voluntarily submit the payments made on this offer and understand that they will not be returned even if I withdraw the offer or the IRS rejects or returns the offer. Unless I designate how to apply each required payment in Section 5, the IRS will apply my payment in the best interest of the government, choosing which tax years and tax debts to pay off. The IRS will also keep my application fee unless the offer is not accepted for processing.
	c) The IRS will keep any refund, including interest, that I might be due for tax periods extending through the calendar year in which the IRS accepts my offer. I cannot designate that the refund be applied to estimated tax payments for the following year or the accepted offer amount. If I receive a refund after I submit this offer for any tax period extending through the calendar year in which the IRS accepts my offer, I will return the refund within 30 days of notification. The refund offset does not apply to offers accepted under the provisions of Effective Tax Administration based on public policy/equity considerations.
	d) I understand that the amount I am offering may not include part or all of an expected or current tax refund, money already paid, funds attached by any collection action, or anticipated benefits from a capital or net operating loss.
	e) The IRS will keep any monies it has collected prior to this offer. Under section § 6331(a) the IRS may levy up to the time that the IRS official signs and acknowledges my offer as pending, which is accepted for processing and the IRS may keep any proceeds arising from such a levy. No levy will be issued on individual shared responsibility payments. However, if the IRS served a continuous levy on wages, salary, or certain federal payments under sections 6331(e) or (h), then the IRS could choose to either retain or release the levy.
	f) The IRS will keep any payments that I make related to this offer. I agree that any funds submitted with this offer will be treated as a payment unless I checked the box to treat any amount more than the required initial payment as a deposit. Only amounts that exceed the mandatory payments can be treated as a deposit. I also agree that any funds submitted with periodic payments made after the submission of this offer and prior to the acceptance, rejection, or return of this offer will be treated as payments, unless I identify the amount more than the required payment as a deposit on the check submitted with the corresponding periodic payment. A deposit will be returned if the offer is rejected, returned, or withdrawn. I understand that the IRS will not pay interest on any deposit.
	g) If my offer is accepted and my final payment is more than the agreed amount by $50 or less, the IRS will not return the difference, but will apply the entire overpayment to my tax debt. If my final payment is more than the agreed amount by $50 or more, the IRS will return the overpayment to me.

EXHIBIT A1.2   **IRS Form 656 (Page 5)**

Page 5 of 6

Section 7 *(Continued)*	**Offer Terms**

Pending status of an offer and right to appeal

h) Once an authorized IRS official signs this form, my offer is considered pending as of that signature date and it remains pending until the IRS accepts, rejects, returns, or I withdraw my offer. An offer is also considered pending for 30 days after any rejection of my offer by the IRS, and during the time that any rejection of my offer is being considered by the Appeals Office. An offer will be considered withdrawn when the IRS receives my written notification of withdrawal by personal delivery or certified mail or when I inform the IRS of my withdrawal by other means and the IRS acknowledges in writing my intent to withdraw the offer.

i) I waive the right to an Appeals hearing if I do not request a hearing in writing within 30 days of the date the IRS notifies me of the decision to reject the offer.

I must comply with my future tax obligations and understand I remain liable for the full amount of my tax debt until all terms and conditions of this offer have been met.

j) I will comply with all provisions of the internal revenue laws, including requirements to timely file tax returns and timely pay taxes for the five year period beginning with the date of acceptance of this offer and ending through the fifth year, including any extensions to file and pay. I also agree to promptly pay any liabilities assessed after acceptance of this offer for tax years ending prior to acceptance of this offer that were not otherwise identified in Section 1 or Section 2 of this agreement. If this is an offer being submitted for joint tax debt, and one of us does not comply with future obligations, only the non-compliant taxpayer will be in default of this agreement. An accepted offer will not be defaulted solely due to the assessment of an individual shared responsibility payment.

k) I agree that I will remain liable for the full amount of the tax liability, accrued penalties and interest, until I have met all of the terms and conditions of this offer. Penalty and interest will continue to accrue until all payment terms of the offer have been met. If I file for bankruptcy before the terms and conditions of the offer are met, I agree that the IRS may file a claim for the full amount of the tax liability, accrued penalties and interest, and that any claim the IRS files in the bankruptcy proceeding will be a tax claim.

l) Once the IRS accepts my offer in writing, I have no right to challenge the tax debt(s) in court or by filing a refund claim or refund suit for any liability or period listed in Section 1 or Section 2, even if I default the terms of the accepted offer.

I understand what will happen if I fail to meet the terms of my offer (e.g., default).

m) If I fail to meet any of the terms of this offer, the IRS may levy or sue me to collect any amount ranging from one or more missed payments to the original amount of the tax debt (less payments made) plus penalties and interest that have accrued from the time the underlying tax liability arose. The IRS will continue to add interest, as required by Section § 6601 of the Internal Revenue Code, on the amount the IRS determines is due after default Shared responsibility payments are excluded from levy.

I agree to waive time limits provided by law.

n) To have my offer considered, I agree to the extension of the time limit provided by law to assess my tax debt (statutory period of assessment). I agree that the date by which the IRS must assess my tax debt will now be the date by which my debt must currently be assessed plus the period of time my offer is pending plus one additional year if the IRS rejects, returns, or terminates my offer or I withdraw it. (Paragraph (h) of this section defines pending and withdrawal.) I understand that I have the right not to waive the statutory period of assessment or to limit the waiver to a certain length or certain periods or issues. I understand, however, that the IRS may not consider my offer if I refuse to waive the statutory period of assessment or if I provide only a limited waiver. I also understand that the statutory period for collecting my tax debt will be suspended during the time my offer is pending with the IRS, for 30 days after any rejection of my offer by the IRS, and during the time that any rejection of my offer is being considered by the Appeals Office.

I understand the IRS may file a Notice of Federal Tax Lien on my property.

o) The IRS may file a Notice of Federal Tax Lien during consideration of the offer. The IRS may file a Notice of Federal Tax Lien to protect the Government's interest on offers that will be paid over time. This tax lien will be released 30 days after the payment terms have been satisfied and the payment has been verified. If the offer is accepted, the tax lien will be released within 30 days of when the payment terms have been satisfied and the payment has been verified. The time it takes to transfer funds to the IRS from commercial institutions varies based on the form of payment. The IRS will not file a Notice of Federal Tax Lien on any individual shared responsibility debt.

Correction Agreement

p) I authorize IRS, to correct any typographical or clerical errors or make minor modifications to my/our Form 656 that I signed in connection to this offer.

I authorize the IRS to contact relevant third parties in order to process my offer.

q) By authorizing the IRS to contact third parties, I understand that I will not be notified of which third parties the IRS contacts as part of the offer application process, including tax periods that have not been assessed, as stated in §7602 (c) of the Internal Revenue Code. In addition, I authorize the IRS to request a consumer report on me from a credit bureau.

I am submitting an offer as an individual for a joint liability.

r) I understand if the liability sought to be compromised is the joint and individual liability of myself and my co-obligor(s) and I am submitting this offer to compromise my individual liability only, then if this offer is accepted, it does not release or discharge my co-obligor(s) from liability. The United States still reserves all rights of collection against the co-obligor(s).

Shared Responsibility Payment (SRP)

s) If your offer includes any shared responsibility payment (SRP) amount that you owe for not having minimum essential health coverage for you and, if applicable, your dependents per Internal Revenue Code Section 5000A - Individual shared responsibility payment, it is not subject to penalties, except applicable bad check penalty, or to lien and levy enforcement actions. However, interest will continue to accrue until you pay the total SRP balance due. We may apply your federal tax refunds to the SRP amount that you owe until it is paid in full.

Catalog Number 16728N	www.irs.gov	Form **656** (Rev. 2-2016)

EXHIBIT A1.2   **IRS Form 656 (Page 6)**

Page 6 of 6

Section 8	**Signatures**	

Under penalties of perjury, I declare that I have examined this offer, including accompanying schedules and statements, and to the best of my knowledge and belief, it is true, correct and complete.

▶ Signature of Taxpayer/Corporation Name	Phone Number	Date *(mm/dd/yyyy)*
▶ Signature of Spouse/Authorized Corporate Officer	Phone Number	Date *(mm/dd/yyyy)*

Section 9	**Paid Preparer Use Only**	
Signature of Preparer	Phone Number	Date *(mm/dd/yyyy)*
Name of Paid Preparer	Preparer's CAF no. or PTIN	

Firm's Name (or yours if self-employed), Address, and ZIP Code

If you would like to have someone represent you during the offer investigation, include a valid, signed Form 2848 or 8821 with this application or a copy of a previously filed form. You should also include the current tax year.

IRS Use Only. I accept the waiver of the statutory period of limitations on assessment for the Internal Revenue Service, as described in Section 7(k).		
Signature of Authorized Internal Revenue Service Official	Title	Date *(mm/dd/yyyy)*

Privacy Act Statement

We ask for the information on this form to carry out the internal revenue laws of the United States. Our authority to request this information is section § 7801 of the Internal Revenue Code.

Our purpose for requesting the information is to determine if it is in the best interests of the IRS to accept an offer. You are not required to make an offer; however, if you choose to do so, you must provide all of the taxpayer information requested. Failure to provide all of the information may prevent us from processing your request.

If you are a paid preparer and you prepared the Form 656 for the taxpayer submitting an offer, we request that you complete and sign Section 9 on Form 656, and provide identifying information. Providing this information is voluntary. This information will be used to administer and enforce the internal revenue laws of the United States and may be used to regulate practice before the Internal Revenue Service for those persons subject to Treasury Department Circular No. 230, Regulations Governing the Practice of Attorneys, Certified Public Accountants, Enrolled Agents, Enrolled Actuaries, and Appraisers before the Internal Revenue Service. Information on this form may be disclosed to the Department of Justice for civil and criminal litigation.

We may also disclose this information to cities, states and the District of Columbia for use in administering their tax laws and to combat terrorism. Providing false or fraudulent information on this form may subject you to criminal prosecution and penalties.

Installment Agreements

Installment agreements generally allow the taxpayer to pay an established deficiency in installments. The taxpayer requests the arrangement by completing IRS Form 9465 (depicted in Exhibit A1.3).

EXHIBIT A1.3   IRS Form 9465 (Page 1)

Form **9465**	**Installment Agreement Request**	
(Rev. February 2017) Department of the Treasury Internal Revenue Service	► Information about Form 9465 and its separate instructions is at *www.irs.gov/form9465*. ► If you are filing this form with your tax return, attach it to the front of the return. ► See separate instructions.	OMB No. 1545-0074

Tip: If you owe $50,000 or less, you may be able to establish an installment agreement online, even if you have not yet received a bill for your taxes. Go to IRS.gov to apply to pay online. **Caution:** *Don't file this form if you can pay your balance in full within 120 days. Instead, call 1-800-829-1040. Don't file if your business is still operating and owes employment or unemployment taxes. Instead, call the telephone number on your most recent notice. If you are in bankruptcy or we have accepted your offer-in-compromise, see* **Bankruptcy or offer-in-compromise,** *in the instructions.*

Part I

This request is for Form(s) (for example, Form 1040 or Form 941) ►_____   and for tax year(s) (for example, 2012 and 2013) ►_____

1a Your first name and initial	Last name	Your social security number
If a joint return, spouse's first name and initial	Last name	Spouse's social security number

Current address (number and street). If you have a P.O. box and no home delivery, enter your box number.		Apt. number

City, town or post office, state, and ZIP code. If a foreign address, also complete the spaces below (see instructions)

Foreign country name	Foreign province/state/county	Foreign postal code

1b   If this address is new since you filed your last tax return, check here   . . . . ► ☐

2   Name of your business (must be no longer operating)   Employer identification number (EIN)

3 Your home phone number Best time for us to call	**4** Your work phone number Ext. Best time for us to call
5 Name of your bank or other financial institution: Address City, state, and ZIP code	**6** Your employer's name: Address City, state, and ZIP code

7   Enter the total amount you owe as shown on your tax return(s) (or notice(s)) **7**

8   Enter the amount of any payment you are making with your tax return(s) (or notice(s)). See instructions   **8**

9   Subtract line 8 from line 7 and enter the result **9**

10   Enter the amount you can pay each month. Make your payments as large as possible to limit interest and penalty charges. **The charges will continue until you pay in full. If no payment amount is listed on line 10, a payment will be determined for you by dividing the balance due by 72 months** . .   **10**

11   Divide the amount on line 9 by 72 and enter the result **11**

• If the amount on line 10 is less than the amount on line 11 and you are unable to increase your payment to the amount on line 11, complete and attach Form 433-F, Collection Information Statement.

• If the amount on line 10 is equal to or greater than the amount on line 11 but the amount you owe is greater than $25,000 but not more than $50,000, you must complete either line 13 or 14, if you do not wish to complete Form 433-F.

• If the amount on line 9 is greater than $50,000, complete and attach Form 433-F, Collection Information Statement.

12   Enter the date you want to make your payment each month. **Do not** enter a date later than the 28th ►_____

13   If you want to make your payments by direct debit from your checking account, see the instructions and fill in lines 13a and 13b. This is the most convenient way to make your payments and it will ensure that they are made on time.

►   **a**   Routing number   ☐☐☐☐☐☐☐☐☐

►   **b**   Account number   ☐☐☐☐☐☐☐☐☐☐☐☐☐☐☐☐☐

I authorize the U.S. Treasury and its designated Financial Agent to initiate a monthly ACH debit (electronic withdrawal) entry to the financial institution account indicated for payments of my Federal taxes owed, and the financial institution to debit the entry to this account. This authorization is to remain in full force and effect until I notify the U.S. Treasury Financial Agent to terminate the authorization. To revoke payment, I must contact the U.S. Treasury Financial Agent at **1-800-829-1040** no later than 14 business days prior to the payment (settlement) date. I also authorize the financial institutions involved in the processing of the electronic payments of taxes to receive confidential information necessary to answer inquiries and resolve issues related to the payments.

14   If you want to make your payments by payroll deduction, check this box and attach a completed Form 2159, Payroll Deduction Agreement   . . . . ► ☐

Your signature	Date	Spouse's signature. If a joint return, **both** must sign.	Date

For Privacy Act and Paperwork Reduction Act Notice, see instructions.   Cat. No. 14842Y   Form **9465** (Rev. 2-2017)

EXHIBIT A1.3 **IRS Form 9465 (Page 2)**

Form 9465 (Rev. 2-2017) Page **2**

Part II **Additional information.** Complete this part only if you have defaulted on an installment agreement within the past 12 months and the amount you owe is greater than $25,000 but not more $50,000 and the amount on line 10 is equal to or greater than the amount on line 11. If you owe more than $50,000, complete and attach Form 433-F, Collection Information Statement.

15 In which county is your primary residence? _____

16a Marital status:
☐ Single. Skip question 16b and go to question 17.
☐ Married. Go to question 16b.
 b Do you share household expenses with your spouse?
☐ Yes.
☐ No.

17 How many dependents will you be able to claim on this year's tax return?. . . . . | **17** |_____

18 How many people in your household are 65 or older? . . . . | **18** |_____

19 How often are you paid?
☐ Once a week.
☐ Once every two weeks.
☐ Once a month.
☐ Twice a month.

20 What is your net income per pay period (take home pay)? . . . . | **20** |$ |_____

21 How often is your spouse paid?
☐ Once a week.
☐ Once every two weeks.
☐ Once a month.
☐ Twice a month.

22 What is your spouse's net income per pay period (take home pay)? . . . . | **22** |$ |_____

23 How many vehicles do you own? . . . . | **23** |_____

24 How many car payments do you have each month? . . . . | **24** |_____

25a Do you have health insurance?
☐ Yes. Go to question 25b.
☐ No. Skip question 25b and go to question 26a.
 b Are your premiums deducted from your paycheck?
☐ Yes. Skip question 25c and go to question 26a.
☐ No. Go to question 25c.
 c How much are your monthly premiums? . . . . | **25c** |$ |_____

26a Do you make court-ordered payments?
☐ Yes. Go to question 26b.
☐ No. Go to question 27.
 b Are your court-ordered payments deducted from your paycheck?
☐ Yes. Go to question 27.
☐ No. Go to question 26c.
 c How much are your court-ordered payments each month? . . . . | **26c** |$ |_____

27 Not including any court-ordered payments for child and dependent support, how much do you pay for child or dependent care each month? . . . . | **27** |$ |_____

Form **9465** (Rev. 2-2017)

2. Assessment by the IRS

Most taxpayers accurately determine the amount of tax they owe with respect to a given taxable year, especially if they do so with the assistance of a seasoned tax return preparer or tax preparation software. But putting aside those prone to mathematical error, income oversight, or simple substantive misstep (e.g., excluding punitive damages paid in connection with personal physical injury), some taxpayers give in to their dark side. Even with substantial mathematical aptitude and full cognizance of the governing rules, some taxpayers remain willing to cheat aggressively and play the audit lottery. Fortune often smiles on their machinations, although the IRS does occasionally make an example of those guilty of egregious abuses or those who have the misfortune of being very famous and tax-delinquent at the same time.

Unfortunately, the IRS still fails to detect a healthy degree of noncompliance. As a result, a so-called **tax gap** will develop, or more precisely, a **gross tax gap**, the difference between aggregate taxes owed by all taxpayers and the amounts paid voluntarily and on time. Late payments and IRS enforcement efforts ultimately reduce this amount, but even in the wake of these events, a **net tax gap** remains (i.e., the difference between (i) the gross tax gap and (ii) the amounts ultimately paid voluntarily or collected by enforcement); the latest tax gap information is available on the IRS website (www.irs.gov). Looking to tax year 2006, the IRS estimated a gross tax gap of $450 billion and a net tax gap of $385 billion, reflecting $65 billion in late payments and enforcement-derived revenues. *See* James M. Bickley, *Tax Gap, Tax Compliance, and Proposed Legislation in the 112th Congress* (Congressional Research Service 2012), *available at* https://www.fas.org/sgp/crs/misc/R42739.pdf. With revenue shortfalls measured in the hundreds of billions of dollars (not to mention skyrocketing federal budget deficits), the IRS needs and must regularly wield its ample assessment powers in various contexts. Commonly, we see the IRS exercising its assessment powers after detecting a taxpayer **deficiency**, which one can think of in simple terms as the difference between the amount of tax actually due from a taxpayer over the amount shown on his tax return (assuming a return was actually filed). The IRS does not, however, have the luxury of sleeping on its assessment powers in perpetuity. Because a **statute of limitations on assessment** (i.e., a maximum amount of time during which the IRS may assess taxes with respect to a taxable year) applies, timing is quite critical. In general, the IRS must assess any additional taxes within three years after the taxpayer files a return. Accordingly, both before and during any tax controversy, all parties involved must give timing their full and rapt attention. Limited exceptions to the three-year rule include the following:

- Understatements of income by more than 25 percent of the gross income shown on the return extends the statute of limitations on assessment to six years.
- No statute of limitations applies on assessment with respect to the filing of a fraudulent return.
- No statute of limitations applies on assessment with respect to a taxable year in which the taxpayer did not file a return.

Note that in some instances (e.g., the filing of a fraudulent return), the IRS has the option of assessing taxes due at any time or commencing collection efforts without previously assessing taxes. Note further that even if the clock is ticking with respect to a statute of limitations on assessment, the clock may be halted by statute in some contexts or the taxpayer may extend or waive (indefinitely) the assessment period. If the IRS requests a waiver and the taxpayer refuses to grant it, the IRS may dispense with polite requests and resort to more aggressive tactics to ensure that, in any event, the IRS will be able to make a timely assessment and collect the tax.

B. CONTROVERSY AND LITIGATION

1. In General

Notwithstanding that a very small percentage of filed returns undergo audit, the risk of formal examination remains quite real. Individuals, businesses entities, estates, and so on are all subject to audit, but our immediate focus here will be on the audit of individual taxpayers. Audits tend to fall into one of three categories. **Correspondence audits** occur between the taxpayer and the IRS wholly by way of correspondence (e.g., mail, telephone conversations, etc.). **Office audits**, which generally require the taxpayer to appear and present requested documentation and discuss specific issues with IRS personnel, typically occur at IRS offices in the general vicinity of the taxpayer's residence. **Field audits** typically occur at a taxpayer's place of business, giving IRS personnel direct access to potentially voluminous documents, books, records, and other items. On completion of the relevant audit, the IRS may recommend no changes, effectively accepting the taxpayer's return as filed. The IRS may, however, propose adjustments that would increase the amount of tax owed. Keep in mind, however, that barring exceptional circumstances, the IRS does *not* have the power to summarily assess taxes not shown as due on a filed return. Accordingly, the IRS must establish its right to assess additional taxes or somehow persuade the taxpayer to waive the restrictions imposed on the IRS with respect to assessment and collection of deficiencies. Taxpayers agree to the waiver by completing and executing IRS Form 870.

EXHIBIT A1.4 **IRS Form 870 (Page 1)**

Form **870** (Rev. March 1992)	Department of the Treasury—Internal Revenue Service **Waiver of Restrictions on Assessment and Collection of Deficiency in Tax and Acceptance of Overassessment**	Date received by Internal Revenue Service

Names and address of taxpayers *(Number, street, city or town, State, ZIP code)* — Social security or employer identification number

Increase (Decrease) in Tax and Penalties

Tax year ended	Tax	Penalties		

(For instructions, see back of form)

Consent to Assessment and Collection

I consent to the immediate assessment and collection of any deficiencies *(increase in tax and penalties)* and accept any overassessment *(decrease in tax and penalties)* shown above, plus any interest provided by law. I understand that by signing this waiver, I will not be able to contest these years in the United States Tax Court, unless additional deficiencies are determined for these years.

YOUR SIGNATURE HERE ➤		Date
SPOUSE'S SIGNATURE ➤		Date
TAXPAYER'S REPRESENTATIVE HERE ➤		Date

CORPORATE NAME ➤		
CORPORATE OFFICER(S) SIGN HERE ➤	Title	Date
	Title	Date

Catalog Number 16894U   Form **870** (Rev. 3-1992)

Getting the taxpayer to waive assessment and collection restrictions may be a simple matter of reasoned explanation of the IRS's position. When the IRS proposes adjustments after an audit, it issues a report to the taxpayer setting forth its position with respect to why it considers the adjustments appropriate (i.e., the so-called **revenue agent's report** or **R.A.R.**). The taxpayer's response will be either **agreed** (accepting all proposed adjustments), **partially agreed** (accepting some but not all proposed adjustments), or **unagreed** (disputing all proposed adjustments). Ideally, the taxpayer and the IRS can work things out at this stage of the process and proceed to formalize the understanding.

Closing Agreements

The IRS and the taxpayer may come to an agreement with respect to the amount ultimately due (or to be refunded) and sign a **closing agreement**. Disputes can be resolved for any dollar amount and need not be based strictly on the law. Although both parties likely contemplate the "hazards of litigation," the IRS often has a keen interest in avoiding the issuance of a published decision that could serve as unfavorable precedent. Section 7121(a) provides that "[t]he Secretary is authorized to enter into an agreement in writing with any person relating to the liability of such person (or of the person or estate for whom he acts) in respect of any internal revenue tax for any taxable period." Section 7121(b) essentially confirms the finality of such agreements in the absence of fraud, malfeasance, or misrepresentation of a material fact. *Cf.* Exhibit A1.5, IRS Form 866.

EXHIBIT A1.5   **IRS Form 866 (Page 1 *excerpt*)**

Form **866**
(Rev. July 1981)

Department of the Treasury - Internal Revenue Service

Agreement as to Final Determination of Tax Liability

(Complete three copies of this form)

Under Section 7121 of the Internal Revenue Code, _____
(Taxpayer's name. address, and identifying number)

and the Commissioner of Internal Revenue agree that the liability of the above taxpayer for the taxable periods and kinds of tax listed in this agreement is as follows: (The applicability or inapplicability of interest or penalties, including additions to tax or additional amounts authorized by Subchapter A of Chapter 68 of the Code, is not determined except as provided in this agreement.)

Taxable Period	Kind of Tax or Penalty	Chapter Number and Subchapter Letter of Internal Revenue Code	Total Tax Liability for Period

This agreement is final and conclusive except:

   (1)   the liability it relates to may be reopened in the event of fraud, malfeasance, or misrepresentation of material fact and

   (2)   it is subject to the Internal Revenue Code sections that expressly provide that effect be given to their provisions notwithstanding any other law or rule of law except Code section 7122.

   By signing this agreement, the above parties certify they have read and agreed to its terms.

Your signature _____   Date signed _____

Spouse's signature *(If a joint return was filed)* _____   Date signed _____

_____

Signature of taxpayer's representative _____   Date signed _____

Taxpayer (other *than individual*) _____

   By _____   Date signed _____

   Title _____

Commissioner of Internal Revenue

   By _____   Date signed _____

   Title _____

Part 1 – Original	Cat. No. 16889B	(See back)	Form **866** (Rev. 7-81)

EXHIBIT A1.5   **IRS Form 866 (Page 2 *excerpt*)**

I have examined the return(s) and recommend approval of the proposed agreement.

_____
(Receiving Officer)   (Date)

_____
(Title)

I have reviewed the return(s) and recommend approval of the proposed agreement.

_____
(District/Appeals Reviewing Officer)   (Date)

_____
(Title)

---

2. Resolving Disputed Issues

Taxpayers who find themselves at odds with the IRS have a number of important decisions to make; no one path leads to ultimate dispute resolution. Some taxpayers will strenuously attempt to work things out administratively while consciously avoiding litigation, whereas others will dismiss administrative negotiation altogether, fixing their sights rigidly on litigation from the very start. Some, of course, fall somewhere in between, open to multiple attempts at administrative resolution but fully willing to litigate. Whatever the course of events, a few commonalities emerge in terms of procedural requirements, temporal landmarks, standard correspondence, and the like. You will have a better understanding of the various paths to resolution with a few key terms and concepts under your belt, some of which we have already covered (i.e., the notion of assessment, the variety of audit types, and the role of taxpayer waiver). Additional items that you should add to your working vocabulary include the following:

- **No-change letter.** If the IRS determines that the original tax return was correct, it will issue this letter. Fortunate taxpayer advocates will see a lot of these!
- **Information document request** ("IDR"). During an audit, the IRS employs the IDR to request documents informally.
- **Administrative summons.** The IRS employs the administrative summons to formally request the production of documents or testimony in an audit; this summons can be enforced in federal district court.
- **Thirty-day letter.** If a taxpayer has been unable to achieve satisfactory resolution of disputed issues by discussion or conference with IRS audit personnel, the IRS will likely provide him with a thirty-day letter. This letter essentially informs the taxpayer that he can take the matter to the next level by filing a protest (or other required correspondence) with the IRS Office of Appeals. The taxpayer must act within thirty days and follow established guidelines and procedures.

■ **Protest.** For proposed tax increases exceeding $25,000, taxpayers must file this document when pursuing administrative resolution with the IRS Office of Appeals. Taxpayers must provide specific information, including facts and law supporting their position. Taxpayers facing proposed tax increases of $25,000 or less may forego the submission of a formal written protest and make a small case request using IRS Form 12203, *Request for Appeals Review. See* Exhibit A1.6.

■ **IRS Office of Appeals.** This is an independent organization within the IRS. Its stated goal is to resolve disputes and thereby allow the IRS and the taxpayer to avoid litigation.

■ **Ninety-day letter** or **statutory notice of deficiency.** This letter (required by statute) informs taxpayers that they have ninety days to file a petition in Tax Court for redetermination of the IRS's asserted deficiency. *See* § 6213(a). Accordingly, practitioners commonly refer to the ninety-day letter as the "ticket to Tax Court." Note that in general, until the letter is mailed (and for 90 days thereafter), the IRS may not assess any deficiencies, levy, or pursue collection via judicial process with respect to the deficiency at issue. Further, if the taxpayer timely files a petition in Tax Court, those prohibitions continue until the decision of the Tax Court becomes final. *See id.* If the taxpayer fails to file the petition during the ninety-day period, the IRS may assess the tax immediately thereafter. Although a taxpayer's ninety-day period generally includes Saturdays, Sundays, and all legal holidays, his ninety-day period may not *end* on a Saturday, Sunday, or a day that is a legal holiday in the District of Columbia. *See id.*

■ **Tax Court.** This court has specialized tax expertise. If a taxpayer seeks to litigate disputed issues and has received a ninety-day letter, he has ninety days to file a petition for redetermination with this court. Prior payment of the deficiency is not required, and the suit filed will be against the Commissioner of Internal Revenue. Either the taxpayer or the Commissioner may appeal the decision of the Tax Court to the relevant Circuit Court of Appeals and from there to the United States Supreme Court.

■ **District Court.** This trial-level federal court is available to certain taxpayers. If a taxpayer has paid an asserted IRS deficiency and failed to secure a demanded refund (either by express IRS denial or after the expiration of six months), they may pursue refund litigation against the United States in the appropriate federal district court (i.e., the court with jurisdiction over the geographic area in which the taxpayer resided at the time of the filing of the petition). Proceeding in this forum allows the case to be tried by a jury. Either the taxpayer or the United States may appeal the decision of this court to the relevant Circuit Court of Appeals and from there to the United States Supreme Court.

■ **Court of Federal Claims.** This trial-level federal court is available to certain taxpayers. If a taxpayer has paid an asserted IRS deficiency and failed to secure a demanded refund (either by express IRS denial or after the expiration of six months), they may pursue refund litigation against the United States in this court. In this forum, only a bench trial is available. Either the taxpayer or the United States may appeal the decision of this court to the Court of Appeals for the Federal Circuit and from there to the United States Supreme Court.

EXHIBIT A1.6 **IRS Form 12203 (Page 1)**

Form **12203** (February 2016)	Department of the Treasury - Internal Revenue Service **Request for Appeals Review**

Complete the information in the spaces below, including your signature and the date.

Taxpayer name(s)	Taxpayer Identification Number(s)
Mailing address	Tax form number
City	Tax period(s) ended

State	ZIP Code	
Your telephone number(s)		Best time to call

Identify the item(s) *(for example: filing status, exemptions, interest or dividends)* you disagree with in the proposed change or assessment report you received with the enclosed letter. Tell us why you disagree. You can add more pages if this is not enough space.

Disagreed item	Reason why you disagree

Disagreed item	Reason why you disagree

Disagreed item	Reason why you disagree

Disagreed item	Reason why you disagree

Name of Taxpayer	Signature	Date
Name of Taxpayer	Signature	Date

Name and signature of authorized representative **(If a representative is signing this form, please attach a copy of your completed Form 2848, Power of Attorney and Declaration of Representative.)**

Name	Signature	Date
Your telephone number	Best time to call	

Catalog Number 27136N   www.irs.gov   Form **12203** (Rev. 2-2016)

3. Typical Scenarios

Although taxpayers can resolve disputed issues with the IRS in more than one way, controversies do follow a fairly predictable pattern. The following examples should give you a sense of how cases generally evolve. Unless the facts indicate otherwise, you should assume that the parties are unable to reach agreement and must proceed to the next stage.

Example 1

In connection with an audit of Taxpayer's 2015 tax return, an IRS agent proposed an adjustment increasing the amount owed. Taxpayer attempted to work it out in conference with the agent and her supervisor, but to no avail. As a result, Taxpayer declined to sign a waiver with respect to assessment, and the IRS sent him a thirty-day letter. Taxpayer filed a protest with the IRS Office of Appeals, but even after going over the issue in appeals, the parties could not reach agreement. Taxpayer decided to litigate the issue against the Commissioner. As required by statute, the IRS sent the taxpayer a ninety-day letter, and Taxpayer proceeded to file a timely petition with the Tax Court.

Example 2

In connection with an audit of Taxpayer's 2015 tax return, an IRS agent proposed an adjustment increasing the amount owed. Taxpayer attempted to work it out in conference with the agent and her supervisor, but to no avail. As a result, Taxpayer declined to sign a waiver with respect to assessment, and the IRS sent him a thirty-day letter. Taxpayer filed a protest with the IRS Office of Appeals, but even after going over the issue in appeals, the parties could not reach agreement. Taxpayer decided to pay the proposed assessment and sue the United States for a refund of the amount paid. Accordingly, at this juncture, Taxpayer signed the waiver with respect to assessment and paid the proposed assessment. He immediately requested a refund from the IRS. The IRS expressly declined to issue a refund. Taxpayer then proceeded to sue the United States for a refund in [District Court or the Court of Federal Claims].

Example 3

In connection with a correspondence audit of Taxpayer's 2015 tax return, an IRS agent requested documentation with respect to two itemized deductions taken by Taxpayer. After Taxpayer provided the relevant documents, the IRS issued a No Change Letter.

Example 4

In connection with an audit of Taxpayer's 2015 tax return, an IRS agent proposed an adjustment increasing the amount owed. Taxpayer attempted to work it out in conference with the agent and her supervisor, but to no avail. Taxpayer decided to litigate the issue in federal court. Accordingly, Taxpayer signed a waiver with respect to assessment, paid the proposed assessment, and immediately requested a refund of the amount paid. The IRS did nothing for six months after the request. Taxpayer then proceeded to sue the United States for a refund in [District Court or the Court of Federal Claims].

Example 5

In connection with an audit of Taxpayer's 2015 tax return, an IRS agent identified several issues and proposed several adjustments increasing the amount of taxes owed. After substantial discussion and analysis, Taxpayer and the IRS found common ground and entered into a closing agreement with respect to Taxpayer's final tax liability.

Example 6

In connection with an audit of Taxpayer's 2015 tax return, an IRS agent proposed an adjustment increasing the amount of taxes owed. Taxpayer attempted to work it out in conference with the agent and her supervisor, but to no avail. Accordingly, Taxpayer refused to sign a waiver with respect to assessment. The IRS sent the taxpayer a thirty-day letter to which Taxpayer did not respond. After expiration of the thirty-day period, the IRS sent Taxpayer a ninety-day letter. Soon thereafter, Taxpayer filed a timely petition in Tax Court.

> **Special Note**
> ....
> In this example, Taxpayer opted to forego the Office of Appeals and proceeded directly to Tax Court. If Taxpayer takes this route, he may take the case to Appeals after filing his petition, so long as IRS counsel consents and the process does not run afoul of Tax Court deadlines.

Example 7

In connection with an audit of Taxpayer's 2015 tax return, an IRS agent proposed an adjustment increasing the amount of taxes owed. Taxpayer attempted to work it out in conference with the agent and her supervisor, but to no avail. Given that the expiration of the statute of limitations on assessment was rapidly approaching, the IRS asked that Taxpayer agree to an extension of the assessment time period. Taxpayer refused. The IRS then proceeded to issue a ninety-day letter. Note that Form 872 extends the assessment period for a limited time. *See* Exhibit A1.7. Indefinite extensions require Form 872-A. *See* Exhibit A1.8.

EXHIBIT A1.7   **IRS Form 872 (Page 1)**

Form **872** (Rev. July 2014)	Department of the Treasury-Internal Revenue Service **Consent to Extend the Time to Assess Tax**	In reply refer to: TIN

_____

_____
(Name(s))

taxpayer(s) of   _____

_____
(Address)

and the Commissioner of Internal Revenue consent and agree to the following:

(1) The amount of any Federal _____ Income _____ tax due on any return(s) made by or
(Kind of tax)

for the above taxpayer(s) for the period(s) ended

_____

may be assessed at any time on or before _____ . If a provision
(Expiration date)

of the Internal Revenue Code suspends the running of the period of limitations to assess such tax, then, when, under the Internal Revenue Code, the running of the period resumes, the extended period to assess will include the number of days remaining in the extended period immediately before the suspension began.

(2) The taxpayer(s) may file a claim for credit or refund and the Service may credit or refund the tax within 6 months after this agreement ends, except with respect to the items in paragraph (4).

(3) Paragraph (4) applies only to any taxpayer who holds an interest, **either directly or indirectly,** in any partnership subject to subchapter C of chapter 63 of the Internal Revenue Code.

(4) Without otherwise limiting the applicability of this agreement, this agreement also extends the period of limitations for assessing any tax (including penalties, additions to tax and interest) attributable to any partnership items (see section 6231 (a)(3)), affected items (see section 6231(a)(5)), computational adjustments (see section 6231(a)(6)), and partnership items converted to nonpartnership items (see section 6231(b)). Additionally, this agreement extends the period of limitations for assessing any tax (including penalties, additions to tax, and interest) relating to any amounts carried over from the taxable year specified in paragraph (1) to any other taxable year(s). This agreement extends the period for filing a petition for adjustment under section 6228(b) but only if a timely request for administrative adjustment is filed under section 6227. For partnership items which have converted to nonpartnership items, this agreement extends the period for filing a suit for refund or credit under section 6532, but only if a timely claim for refund is filed for such items.

(5) This Form contains the entire terms of the Consent to Extend the Time to Assess Tax. There are no representations, promises, or agreements between the parties except those found or referenced on this Form.

With respect to the returns for the period(s) listed in paragraph (1) above, if the three-year period for assessing tax, under Internal Revenue Code section 6501(a), ended prior to the date of this consent, then this consent serves to extend the time to assess tax under any other provision of section 6501 for which the period of time to assess tax has not ended as of the date of this consent.

This consent does not serve to shorten the statutory period of time to assess tax for any return.

Your Rights as a Taxpayer

You have the right to refuse to extend the period of limitations or limit this extension to a mutually agreed-upon issue(s) or mutually agreed-upon period of time. *Publication 1035, Extending the Tax Assessment Period,* provides a more detailed explanation of your rights and the consequences of the choices you may make. If you have not already received a Publication 1035, the publication can be obtained, free of charge, from the IRS official who requested that you sign this consent or from the IRS' web site at www.irs.gov or by calling toll free at 1-800-TAX-FORM (1-800-829-3676). Signing this consent will not deprive you of any appeal rights to which you would otherwise be entitled.

(Space for signature is on the back of this form and signature instructions are attached)

EXHIBIT A1.7   **IRS Form 872 (Page 2)**

TIN	Period Ending		Expiration Date

SIGNING THIS CONSENT WILL NOT DEPRIVE THE TAXPAYER(S) OF ANY APPEAL RIGHTS TO WHICH THEY WOULD OTHERWISE BE ENTITLED.

YOUR SIGNATURE HERE ➤ _____   *(Date signed)*

_____
(Type or Print Name)

I am aware that I have the right to refuse to sign this consent or to limit the extension to mutually agreed-upon issues and/or period of time as set forth in I.R.C. § 6501(c)(4)(B).

SPOUSE'S SIGNATURE ➤ _____   *(Date signed)*

_____
(Type or Print Name)

I am aware that I have the right to refuse to sign this consent or to limit the extension to mutually agreed-upon issues and/or period of time as set forth in I.R.C. § 6501(c)(4)(B).

TAXPAYER'S REPRESENTATIVE SIGN HERE ➤ _____   *(Date signed)*
(Only needed if signing on behalf of the taxpayer.)
_____
(Type or Print Name)

I am aware that I have the right to refuse to sign this consent or to limit the extension to mutually agreed-upon issues and/or period of time as set forth in I.R.C. § 6501(c)(4)(B). In addition, the taxpayer(s) has been made aware of these rights.

If this document is signed by a taxpayer's representative, the Form 2848, Power of Attorney and Declaration of Representative, or other power of attorney document must state that the acts authorized by the power of attorney include representation for the purposes of Subchapter C of Chapter 63 of the Internal Revenue Code in order to cover items in paragraph (4).

CORPORATE NAME ➤ _____

CORPORATE OFFICER(S) SIGN HERE ➤ _____   *(Title)*   *(Date signed)*

_____
(Type or Print Name)

➤ _____   *(Title)*   *(Date signed)*

_____
(Type or Print Name)

I (we) am aware that I (we) have the right to refuse to sign this consent or to limit the extension to mutually agreed-upon issues and/or period of time as set forth in I.R.C. § 6501 (c)(4)(B).

INTERNAL REVENUE SERVICE SIGNATURE AND TITLE

_____   _____
(IRS Official's Name - see instructions)   *(IRS Official's Title - see instructions)*

_____   _____
(IRS Official's Signature - see instructions)   *(Date signed)*

EXHIBIT A1.8   **IRS Form 872-A (Page 1)**

Form **872-A** (Rev. February 2005)	Department of the Treasury-Internal Revenue Service **Special Consent to Extend the Time to Assess Tax**	In reply refer to Taxpayer Identification Number

(Name(s))

Taxpayer(s) of _____

(Number, street, city or town, state, zip code)

and the Commissioner of Internal Revenue consent and agree as follows:

(1) The amount of any Federal_____ tax due on any return(s) made by or for the

(Kind of tax)

above taxpayer(s) for the period(s) ended _____
may be assessed on or before the 90th (ninetieth) day after: (a) the date on which a Form 872-T, *Notice of Termination of Special Consent to Extend the Time to Assess Tax,* is received by the division operating unit of the Internal Revenue Service having jurisdiction over the taxable period(s) at the address provided in paragraph (4) below or the address designated by the division operating unit in a Form 872-U, *Change of IRS Address to Submit Notice of Termination of Special Consent to Extend the Time to Assess Tax,* which address will supersede the address provided in paragraph (4) below; or (b) the Internal Revenue Service mails Form 872-T to the last known address of the taxpayer(s); or (c) the Internal Revenue Service mails a notice of deficiency for such period(s); except that if a notice of deficiency is sent to the taxpayer(s), the time for assessing the tax for the period(s) stated in the notice of deficiency will end 60 days after the period during which the making of an assessment is prohibited. A final adverse determination subject to declaratory judgment under sections 7428, 7476, or 7477 of the Internal Revenue Code will not terminate this agreement.

(2) This agreement ends on the earlier of expiration date determined in paragraph (1) above or the assessment date of an increase in the above tax or the overassessment date of a decrease in the above tax that reflects the final determination of tax and the final administrative appeals consideration. An assessment or overassessment for one period covered by this agreement will not end this agreement for any other period it covers. Some assessments do not reflect a final determination and appeals consideration and therefore will not terminate the agreement before the expiration date. Examples are assessments of: (a) tax under a partial agreement; (b) tax in jeopardy; (c) tax to correct mathematical or clerical errors; (d) tax reported on amended returns; and (e) advance payments. In addition, unassessed payments, such as amounts treated by the Service as cash bonds and advance payments not assessed by the Service, will not terminate this agreement before the expiration date determined in (1) above. This agreement ends on the date determined in (1) above regardless of any assessment for any period includable in a report to the Joint Committee on Taxation submitted under section 6405 of the Internal Revenue Code.

(3) This agreement will not reduce the period of time otherwise provided by law for making such assessment.

(4) This agreement may be terminated by either the taxpayer or the Internal Revenue Service with the use of Form 872-T which is available from the division operating unit of the Internal Revenue Service considering the taxpayer's case. For a termination initiated by the taxpayer to be valid, the executed Form 872-T must be delivered to one of the following addresses or the address designated by the division operating unit considering the taxpayer's case in a Form 872-U, which address will supersede the address below:

If **MAILING** Form 872-T, send to: If **HAND CARRYING** Form 872-T, deliver to:

(5) The taxpayer(s) may file a claim for credit or refund and the Service may credit or refund the tax within 6 (six) months after this agreement ends.

(Signature instructions and space for signature are on the back of this form)   www.irs.gov   Catalog Number 20760B Form **872-A** (Rev. 2-2005)

EXHIBIT A1.8 **IRS Form 872-A (Page 2)**

Your Rights as a Taxpayer

You have the right to refuse to extend the period of limitations or limit this extension to a mutually agreed-upon issue(s) or mutually agreed-upon period of time. Publication 1035, *Extending the Tax Assessment Period,* provides a more detailed explanation of your rights and the consequences of the choices you may make. If you have not already received a Publication 1035, you can obtain one, free of charge, from the IRS official who requested that you sign this consent or from the IRS' web site at www.irs.gov or by calling toll free at **1-800-829-3676**. Signing this consent will not deprive you of any appeal rights to which you would otherwise be entitled.

Your signature here	Date signed
I am aware that I have the right to refuse to sign this consent or to limit the extension to mutually agreed-upon issues and/or period of time as set forth in I.R.C. §6501(c)(4)(B).	

Spouse's signature	Date signed
I am aware that I have the right to refuse to sign this consent or to limit the extension to mutually agreed-upon issues and/or period of time as set forth in I.R.C. §6501(c)(4)(B).	

Taxpayer's Representative signature	Date signed
I am aware that I have the right to refuse to sign this consent or to limit the extension to mutually agreed-upon issues and/or period of time as set forth in I.R.C. §6501(c)(4)(B). In addition, the taxpayer(s) has been made aware of these rights.	

(You must also attach written authorization as stated in the instructions below.)

Corporate Officer's signature
I (we) am aware that I (we) have the right to refuse to sign this consent or to limit the extension to mutually agreed-upon issues and/or period of time as set forth in I.R.C. §6501(c)(4)(B).

Authorized Official signature and title *(see instructions)*	Date signed
Authorized Official signature and title *(see instructions)*	Date signed

INTERNAL REVENUE SERVICE SIGNATURE AND TITLE

Division Executive name *(see instructions)*	Division Executive title *(see instructions)*

BY	
Authorized Official signature and title *(see instructions)*	Date signed

Instructions

If this consent is for income tax, self-employment tax, or FICA tax on tips and is made for any year(s) for which a joint return was filed, both husband and wife must sign the original and copy of this form unless one, acting under a power of attorney, signs as agent for the other. The signatures must match the names as they appear on the front of this form.

If this consent is for gift tax and the donor and the donor's spouse elected to have gifts to third persons considered as made one-half by each, both husband and wife must sign the original and copy of this form unless one, acting under a power of attorney, signs as agent for the other. The signatures must match the names as they appear on the front of this form.

If this consent is for Chapter 41, 42, or 43 taxes involving a partnership, only one authorized partner need sign.

If this consent is for Chapter 42 taxes, a separate Form 872-A should be completed for each potential disqualified person or entity that may have been involved in a taxable transaction during the related tax year. See Revenue Ruling 75-391, 1975-2 C.B. 446.

If you are an attorney or agent of the taxpayer(s), you may sign this consent provided the action is specifically authorized by a power of attorney. If the power of attorney was not previously filed, you must include it with this form.

If you are acting as a fiduciary *(such as executor, administrator, trustee, etc.)* and you sign this consent, attach Form 56, *Notice Concerning Fiduciary Relationship,* unless it was previously filed.

If the taxpayer is a corporation, sign this consent with the corporate name followed by the signature and title of the officer(s) authorized to sign.

Instructions for Internal Revenue Service Employees

Complete the Division Executive's name and title depending upon your division:

- Small Business and Self-Employed Division = Area Director; Director, Specialty Programs; Director, Compliance Campus Operations, etc.
- Wage and Investment Division = Area Director; Director, Field Compliance Services.
- Large and Mid-Size Business Division = Director, Field Operations for your industry.
- Tax Exempt and Government Entities Division = Director, Exempt Organizations; Director, Employee Plans; Director, Federal, State and Local Governments; Director, Indian Tribal Governments; Director, Tax Exempt Bonds.
- Appeals = Chief, Appeals.

The appropriate authorized official within your division must sign and date the signature and title line.

Taxpayers attempting to resolve disputes with the IRS may approach the matter from different angles and achieve resolution (favorable or not) by different means. At least one possibility not yet presented is complete taxpayer apathy. What happens when the IRS audits a taxpayer and proposes an adjustment increasing the amount owed only to face the taxpayer's appalled silence? As you might suspect, the IRS will first send a thirty-day letter. If the taxpayer fails to respond, the IRS proceeds to send a ninety-day letter. Assuming the taxpayer fails to file a petition in Tax Court within ninety days, the IRS will then assess the additional taxes due and proceed with collection. Of course, taxpayers rarely do absolutely nothing, and tax controversies ultimately lead to mutually agreeable (or at least final) resolutions. A taxpayer, having put up the good fight in court, might simply pay the amount of an asserted deficiency in full (or, in chronic defiance, test the IRS's collection apparatus). From time to time, of course, the taxpayer emerges battle-scarred but triumphant.

C. ETHICS IN TAX PRACTICE: CIRCULAR 230

Attorneys representing taxpayers before the IRS are generally duly admitted members of a state bar. Such admission does not, however, guarantee that an attorney will always have the privilege of representing clients before the IRS. Treasury Department Circular 230 sets forth the regulations governing practice before the IRS, and it merits close attention. Attorneys have an obligation to be zealous advocates for their clients, and in many instances, lawyers may be able to get away with taking various liberties. Zealous advocacy does, however, have its limits, and Circular 230 makes that reality abundantly clear. Those who seek the continuous privilege of practicing before the IRS are expected to conduct themselves in accordance with the Circular's mandates, and the price of noncompliance can be quite high. In this Appendix, we present, as an introductory educational reference, specific sections of the Circular most likely to be of relevance to attorneys representing tax clients before the IRS. The Circular will likely change over time. For the most current rules, please refer to the IRS website.

Exhibit A1.9

Selected Sections from Treasury Department Circular 230

Students should devote special attention to 31 U.S.C. § 330 and to the following provisions in this circular:

§ 10.2

§ 10.3(a)

§ 10.20–10.24

§ 10.31–33

§ 10.34(a)(1)(ii)

§ 10.34(a)(2)

§ 10.34(b)–(e)

§ 10.35–10.37

§ 10.5 (except subsection (b))

§ 10.51(a) (skim)

§ 10.52

§ 10.53 (skim)

**Treasury Department
Circular No. 230
(Rev. 6-2014)**

Catalog Number 16586R
www.irs.gov

**Regulations Governing Practice before
the Internal Revenue Service**

Department
of the
Treasury

**Internal
Revenue
Service**

**Title 31 Code of Federal Regulations,
Subtitle A, Part 10,
published (June 12, 2014)**

31 U.S.C. §330. Practice before the Department

(a) Subject to section 500 of title 5, the Secretary of the Treasury may —
  (1) regulate the practice of representatives of persons before the Department of the Treasury; and
  (2) before admitting a representative to practice, require that the representative demonstrate —
   (A) good character;
   (B) good reputation;
   (C) necessary qualifications to enable the representative to provide to persons valuable service; and
   (D) competency to advise and assist persons in presenting their cases.

(b) After notice and opportunity for a proceeding, the Secretary may suspend or disbar from practice before the Department, or censure, a representative who —
  (1) is incompetent;
  (2) is disreputable;
  (3) violates regulations prescribed under this section; or
  (4) with intent to defraud, willfully and knowingly misleads or threatens the person being represented or a prospective person to be represented.

The Secretary may impose a monetary penalty on any representative described in the preceding sentence. If the representative was acting on behalf of an employer or any firm or other entity in connection with the conduct giving rise to such penalty, the Secretary may impose a monetary penalty on such employer, firm, or entity if it knew, or reasonably should have known, of such conduct. Such penalty shall not exceed the gross income derived (or to be derived) from the conduct giving rise to the penalty and may be in addition to, or in lieu of, any suspension, disbarment, or censure of the representative.

(c) After notice and opportunity for a hearing to any appraiser, the Secretary may —
  (1) provide that appraisals by such appraiser shall not have any probative effect in any administrative proceeding before the Department of the Treasury or the Internal Revenue Service, and
  (2) bar such appraiser from presenting evidence or testimony in any such proceeding.

(d) Nothing in this section or in any other provision of law shall be construed to limit the authority of the Secretary of the Treasury to impose standards applicable to the rendering of written advice with respect to any entity, transaction plan or arrangement, or other plan or arrangement, which is of a type which the Secretary determines as having a potential for tax avoidance or evasion.

(Pub. L. 97–258, Sept. 13, 1982, 96 Stat. 884; Pub. L. 98–369, div. A, title I, §156(a), July 18, 1984, 98 Stat. 695; Pub. L. 99–514, §2, Oct. 22, 1986, 100 Stat. 2095; Pub. L. 108–357, title VIII, §822(a)(1), (b), Oct. 22, 2004, 118 Stat. 1586, 1587; Pub. L. 109–280, title XII, §1219(d), Aug. 17, 2006, 120 Stat. 1085.)

[Pages 3 to 5 omitted.]

§ 10.2 Definitions.

(a) As used in this part, except where the text provides otherwise —

(1) *Attorney* means any person who is a member in good standing of the bar of the highest court of any state, territory, or possession of the United States, including a Commonwealth, or the District of Columbia.

(2) *Certified public accountant* means any person who is duly qualified to practice as a certified public accountant in any state, territory, or possession of the United States, including a Commonwealth, or the District of Columbia.

(3) *Commissioner* refers to the Commissioner of Internal Revenue.

(4) *Practice before the Internal Revenue Service* comprehends all matters connected with a presentation to the Internal Revenue Service or any of its officers or employees relating to a taxpayer's rights, privileges, or liabilities under laws or regulations administered by the Internal Revenue Service. Such presentations include, but are not limited to, preparing documents; filing documents; corresponding and communicating with the Internal Revenue Service; rendering written advice with respect to any entity, transaction, plan or arrangement, or other plan or arrangement having a potential for tax avoidance or evasion; and representing a client at conferences, hearings, and meetings.

(5) *Practitioner* means any individual described in paragraphs (a), (b), (c), (d), (e), or (f) of §10.3.

(6) A *tax return* includes an amended tax return and a claim for refund.

(7) *Service* means the Internal Revenue Service.

(8) *Tax return preparer* means any individual within the meaning of section 7701(a)(36) and 26 CFR 301.7701-15.

(b) *Effective/applicability date.* This section is applicable on August 2, 2011.

§ 10.3 Who may practice.

(a) *Attorneys.* Any attorney who is not currently under suspension or disbarment from practice before the Internal Revenue Service may practice before the Internal Revenue Service by filing with the Internal Revenue Service a written declaration that the attorney is currently qualified as an attorney and is authorized to represent the party or parties. Notwithstanding the preceding sentence, attorneys who are not currently under suspension or disbarment from practice before the Internal Revenue Service are not required to file a written declaration with the IRS before rendering written advice covered under §10.37, but their rendering of this advice is practice before the Internal Revenue Service.

(b) *Certified public accountants.* Any certified public accountant who is not currently under suspension or disbarment from practice before the Internal Revenue Service may practice before the Internal Revenue Service by filing with the Internal Revenue Service a written declaration that the certified public accountant is currently qualified as a certified public accountant and is authorized to represent the party or parties. Notwithstanding the preceding sentence, certified public accountants who are not currently under suspension or disbarment from practice before the Internal Revenue Service are not required to file a written declaration with the IRS before rendering written advice covered under §10.37, but their rendering of this advice is practice before the Internal Revenue Service.

(c) *Enrolled agents.* Any individual enrolled as an agent pursuant to this part who is not currently under suspension or disbarment from practice before the Internal Revenue Service may practice before the Internal Revenue Service.

(d) *Enrolled actuaries.*

(1) Any individual who is enrolled as an actuary by the Joint Board for the Enrollment of Actuaries pursuant to 29 U.S.C. 1242 who is not currently under suspension or disbarment from practice before the Internal Revenue Service may practice before the Internal Revenue Service by filing with the Internal Revenue Service a written declaration stating that he or she is currently qualified as an enrolled actuary and is authorized to represent the party or parties on whose behalf he or she acts.

(2) Practice as an enrolled actuary is limited

[Pages 7 to 18 omitted.]

Subpart B — Duties and Restrictions Relating to Practice Before the Internal Revenue Service

§ 10.20 Information to be furnished.

(a) *To the Internal Revenue Service.*

(1) A practitioner must, on a proper and lawful request by a duly authorized officer or employee of the Internal Revenue Service, promptly submit records or information in any matter before the Internal Revenue Service unless the practitioner believes in good faith and on reasonable grounds that the records or information are privileged.

(2) Where the requested records or information are not in the possession of, or subject to the control of, the practitioner or the practitioner's client, the practitioner must promptly notify the requesting Internal Revenue Service officer or employee and the practitioner must provide any information that the practitioner has regarding the identity of any person who the practitioner believes may have possession or control of the requested records or information. The practitioner must make reasonable inquiry of his or her client regarding the identity of any person who may have possession or control of the requested records or information, but the practitioner is not required to make inquiry of any other person or independently verify any information provided by the practitioner's client regarding the identity of such persons.

(3) When a proper and lawful request is made by a duly authorized officer or employee of the Internal Revenue Service, concerning an inquiry into an alleged violation of the regulations in this part, a practitioner must provide any information the practitioner has concerning the alleged violation and testify regarding this information in any proceeding instituted under this part, unless the practitioner believes in good faith and on reasonable grounds that the information is privileged.

(b) *Interference with a proper and lawful request for records or information.* A practitioner may not interfere, or attempt to interfere, with any proper and lawful effort by the Internal Revenue Service, its officers or employees, to obtain any record or information unless the practitioner believes in good faith and on reasonable grounds that the record or information is privileged.

(c) *Effective/applicability date.* This section is applicable beginning August 2, 2011.

§ 10.21 Knowledge of client's omission.

A practitioner who, having been retained by a client with respect to a matter administered by the Internal Revenue Service, knows that the client has not complied with the revenue laws of the United States or has made an error in or omission from any return, document, affidavit, or other paper which the client submitted or executed under the revenue laws of the United States, must advise the client promptly of the fact of such noncompliance, error, or omission. The practitioner must advise the client of the consequences as provided under the Code and regulations of such noncompliance, error, or omission.

§ 10.22 Diligence as to accuracy.

(a) *In general.* A practitioner must exercise due diligence —

(1) In preparing or assisting in the preparation of, approving, and filing tax returns, documents, affidavits, and other papers relating to Internal Revenue Service matters;

(2) In determining the correctness of oral or written representations made by the practitioner to the Department of the Treasury; and

(3) In determining the correctness of oral or written representations made by the practitioner to clients with reference to any matter administered by the Internal Revenue Service.

(b) *Reliance on others.* Except as modified by §§10.34 and 10.37, a practitioner will be presumed to have exercised due diligence for purposes of this section if the practitioner relies on the work product of another person and the practitioner used reasonable care in engaging, supervising, training, and evaluating the person, taking proper account of the nature of the relationship between the practitioner and the person.

(c) *Effective/applicability date.* Paragraph (a) of this section is applicable on September 26, 2007. Paragraph (b) of this section is applicable beginning June 12, 2014.

§ 10.23 Prompt disposition of pending matters.

A practitioner may not unreasonably delay the prompt disposition of any matter before the Internal Revenue Service.

§ 10.24 Assistance from or to disbarred or suspended persons and former Internal Revenue Service employees.

A practitioner may not, knowingly and directly or indirectly:

(a) Accept assistance from or assist any person who is under disbarment or suspension from practice before the Internal Revenue Service if the assistance relates to a matter or matters constituting practice before the Internal Revenue Service.

(b) Accept assistance from any former government employee where the provisions of § 10.25 or any Federal law would be violated.

§ 10.25 Practice by former government employees, their partners and their associates.

(a) *Definitions.* For purposes of this section —

(1) *Assist* means to act in such a way as to advise, furnish information to, or otherwise aid another person, directly, or indirectly.

(2) *Government employee* is an officer or employee of the United States or any agency of the United States, including a special Government employee as defined in *18 U.S.C. 202(a)*, or of the District of Columbia, or of any State, or a member of Congress or of any State legislature.

(3) *Member of a firm* is a sole practitioner or an employee or associate thereof, or a partner, stockholder, associate, affiliate or employee of a partnership, joint venture, corporation, professional association or other affiliation of two or more practitioners who represent nongovernmental parties.

(4) *Particular matter involving specific parties* is defined at 5 CFR 2637.201(c), or superseding post-employment regulations issued by the U.S. Office of Government Ethics.

(5) *Rule* includes Treasury regulations, whether issued or under preparation for issuance as notices of proposed rulemaking or as Treasury decisions, revenue rulings, and revenue procedures published in the Internal Revenue Bulletin (see *26 CFR 601.601(d)(2)(ii)(b)*).

(b) *General rules —*

(1) No former Government employee may, subsequent to Government employment, represent anyone in any matter administered by the Internal Revenue Service if the representation would violate *18 U.S.C. 207* or any other laws of the United States.

(2) No former Government employee who personally and substantially participated in a particular matter involving specific parties may, subsequent to Government employment, represent or knowingly assist, in that particular matter, any person who is or was a specific party to that particular matter.

(3) A former Government employee who within a period of one year prior to the termination of Government employment had official responsibility for a particular matter involving specific parties may not, within two years after Government employment is ended, represent in that particular matter any person who is or was a specific party to that particular matter.

(4) No former Government employee may, within one year after Government employment is ended, communicate with or appear before, with the intent to influence, any employee of the Treasury Department in connection with the publication, withdrawal, amendment, modification, or interpretation of a rule the development of which the former Government employee participated in, or for which, within a period of one year prior to the termination of Government employment, the former government employee had official responsibility. This paragraph (b)(4) does not, however, preclude any former employee from appearing on one's own behalf or from representing a taxpayer before the Internal Revenue Service in connection with a particular matter involving specific

[Pages 21 to 23 omitted.]

communication was mailed or otherwise distributed. The copy must be retained by the practitioner for a period of at least 36 months from the date of the last transmission or use.

(d) *Improper associations.* A practitioner may not, in matters related to the Internal Revenue Service, assist, or accept assistance from, any person or entity who, to the knowledge of the practitioner, obtains clients or otherwise practices in a manner forbidden under this section.

(e) *Effective/applicability date.* This section is applicable beginning August 2, 2011.

(Approved by the Office of Management and Budget under Control No. 1545-1726)

§ 10.31 Negotiation of taxpayer checks.

(a) A practitioner may not endorse or otherwise negotiate any check (including directing or accepting payment by any means, electronic or otherwise, into an account owned or controlled by the practitioner or any firm or other entity with whom the practitioner is associated) issued to a client by the government in respect of a Federal tax liability.

(b) *Effective/applicability date.* This section is applicable beginning June 12, 2014.

§ 10.32 Practice of law.

Nothing in the regulations in this part may be construed as authorizing persons not members of the bar to practice law.

§ 10.33 Best practices for tax advisors.

(a) *Best practices.* Tax advisors should provide clients with the highest quality representation concerning Federal tax issues by adhering to best practices in providing advice and in preparing or assisting in the preparation of a submission to the Internal Revenue Service. In addition to compliance with the standards of practice provided elsewhere in this part, best practices include the following:

(1) Communicating clearly with the client

regarding the terms of the engagement. For example, the advisor should determine the client's expected purpose for and use of the advice and should have a clear understanding with the client regarding the form and scope of the advice or assistance to be rendered.

(2) Establishing the facts, determining which facts are relevant, evaluating the reasonableness of any assumptions or representations, relating the applicable law (including potentially applicable judicial doctrines) to the relevant facts, and arriving at a conclusion supported by the law and the facts.

(3) Advising the client regarding the import of the conclusions reached, including, for example, whether a taxpayer may avoid accuracy-related penalties under the Internal Revenue Code if a taxpayer acts in reliance on the advice.

(4) Acting fairly and with integrity in practice before the Internal Revenue Service.

(b) *Procedures to ensure best practices for tax advisors.* Tax advisors with responsibility for overseeing a firm's practice of providing advice concerning Federal tax issues or of preparing or assisting in the preparation of submissions to the Internal Revenue Service should take reasonable steps to ensure that the firm's procedures for all members, associates, and employees are consistent with the best practices set forth in paragraph (a) of this section.

(c) *Applicability date.* This section is effective after June 20, 2005.

§ 10.34 Standards with respect to tax returns and documents, affidavits and other papers.

(a) *Tax returns.*

(1) A practitioner may not willfully, recklessly, or through gross incompetence —

(i) Sign a tax return or claim for refund that the practitioner knows or reasonably should know contains a position that —

(A) Lacks a reasonable basis;

(B) Is an unreasonable position as described in section 6694(a)(2) of the Internal Revenue Code (Code) (including the related regulations and other published guidance); or

(C) Is a willful attempt by the practitioner to understate the liability for tax or a reckless or intentional disregard of rules or regulations by the practitioner as described in section 6694(b)(2) of the Code (including the related regulations and other published guidance).

(ii) Advise a client to take a position on a tax return or claim for refund, or prepare a portion of a tax return or claim for refund containing a position, that —

(A) Lacks a reasonable basis;

(B) Is an unreasonable position as described in section 6694(a)(2) of the Code (including the related regulations and other published guidance); or

(C) Is a willful attempt by the practitioner to understate the liability for tax or a reckless or intentional disregard of rules or regulations by the practitioner as described in section 6694(b)(2) of the Code (including the related regulations and other published guidance).

(2) A pattern of conduct is a factor that will be taken into account in determining whether a practitioner acted willfully, recklessly, or through gross incompetence.

(b) *Documents, affidavits and other papers* —

(1) A practitioner may not advise a client to take a position on a document, affidavit or other paper submitted to the Internal Revenue Service unless the position is not frivolous.

(2) A practitioner may not advise a client to submit a document, affidavit or other paper to the Internal Revenue Service —

(i) The purpose of which is to delay or impede the administration of the Federal tax laws;

(ii) That is frivolous; or

(iii) That contains or omits information in a manner that demonstrates an intentional disregard of a rule or regulation unless the practitioner also advises the client to submit a document that evidences a good faith challenge to the rule or regulation.

(c) *Advising clients on potential penalties* —

(1) A practitioner must inform a client of any penalties that are reasonably likely to apply to the client with respect to —

(i) A position taken on a tax return if —

(A) The practitioner advised the client with respect to the position; or

(B) The practitioner prepared or signed the tax return; and

(ii) Any document, affidavit or other paper submitted to the Internal Revenue Service.

(2) The practitioner also must inform the client of any opportunity to avoid any such penalties by disclosure, if relevant, and of the requirements for adequate disclosure.

(3) This paragraph (c) applies even if the practitioner is not subject to a penalty under the Internal Revenue Code with respect to the position or with respect to the document, affidavit or other paper submitted.

(d) *Relying on information furnished by clients.* A practitioner advising a client to take a position on a tax return, document, affidavit or other paper submitted to the Internal Revenue Service, or preparing or signing a tax return as a preparer, generally may rely in good faith without verification upon information furnished by the client. The practitioner may not, however, ignore the implications of information furnished to, or actually known by, the practitioner, and must make reasonable inquiries if the information as furnished appears to be incorrect, inconsistent with an important fact or another factual assumption, or incomplete.

(e) *Effective/applicability date.* Paragraph (a) of this section is applicable for returns or claims for refund filed, or advice provided, beginning August 2, 2011. Paragraphs (b) through (d) of this section are applicable to tax returns, documents, affidavits, and other papers filed on or after September 26, 2007.

§ 10.35 Competence.

(a) A practitioner must possess the necessary competence to engage in practice before the Internal Revenue Service. Competent practice requires the appropriate level of knowledge, skill, thoroughness, and preparation necessary for the matter for which the practitioner is engaged. A practitioner may become competent for the matter for which the practitioner has been engaged through various methods, such as consulting with experts in the relevant area or studying the relevant law.

(b) *Effective/applicability date.* This section is applicable beginning June 12, 2014.

§ 10.36 Procedures to ensure compliance.

(a) Any individual subject to the provisions of this part who has (or individuals who have or share) principal authority and responsibility for overseeing a firm's practice governed by this part, including the provision of advice concerning Federal tax matters and preparation of tax returns, claims for refund, or other documents for submission to the Internal Revenue Service, must take reasonable steps to ensure that the firm has adequate procedures in effect for all members, associates, and employees for purposes of complying with subparts A, B, and C of this part, as applicable. In the absence of a person or persons identified by the firm as having the principal authority and responsibility described in this paragraph, the Internal Revenue Service may identify one or more individuals subject to the provisions of this part responsible for compliance with the requirements of this section.

(b) Any such individual who has (or such individuals who have or share) principal authority as described in paragraph (a) of this section will be subject to discipline for failing to comply with the requirements of this section if—

(1) The individual through willfulness, recklessness, or gross incompetence does not take reasonable steps to ensure that the firm has adequate procedures to comply with this part, as applicable, and one or more individuals who are members of, associated with, or employed by, the firm are, or have, engaged in a pattern or practice, in connection with their practice with the firm, of failing to comply with this part, as applicable;

(2) The individual through willfulness, recklessness, or gross incompetence does not take reasonable steps to ensure that firm procedures in effect are properly followed, and one or more individuals who are members of, associated with, or employed by, the firm are, or have, engaged in a

pattern or practice, in connection with their practice with the firm, of failing to comply with this part, as applicable; or

(3) The individual knows or should know that one or more individuals who are members of, associated with, or employed by, the firm are, or have, engaged in a pattern or practice, in connection with their practice with the firm, that does not comply with this part, as applicable, and the individual, through willfulness, recklessness, or gross incompetence fails to take prompt action to correct the noncompliance.

(c) *Effective/applicability date.* This section is applicable beginning June 12, 2014.

§ 10.37 Requirements for written advice.

(a) *Requirements.*

(1) A practitioner may give written advice (including by means of electronic communication) concerning one or more Federal tax matters subject to the requirements in paragraph (a)(2) of this section. Government submissions on matters of general policy are not considered written advice on a Federal tax matter for purposes of this section. Continuing education presentations provided to an audience solely for the purpose of enhancing practitioners' professional knowledge on Federal tax matters are not considered written advice on a Federal tax matter for purposes of this section. The preceding sentence does not apply to presentations marketing or promoting transactions.

(2) The practitioner must—

(i) Base the written advice on reasonable factual and legal assumptions (including assumptions as to future events);

(ii) Reasonably consider all relevant facts and circumstances that the practitioner knows or reasonably should know;

(iii) Use reasonable efforts to identify and ascertain the facts relevant to written advice on each Federal tax matter;

(iv) Not rely upon representations, statements, findings, or agreements (including projections, financial forecasts, or appraisals) of the taxpayer or any other person if reliance on them would be unreasonable;

(v) Relate applicable law and authorities to facts; and

(vi) Not, in evaluating a Federal tax matter, take into account the possibility that a tax return will not be audited or that a matter will not be raised on audit.

(3) Reliance on representations, statements, findings, or agreements is unreasonable if the practitioner knows or reasonably should know that one or more representations or assumptions on which any representation is based are incorrect, incomplete, or inconsistent.

(b) *Reliance on advice of others.* A practitioner may only rely on the advice of another person if the advice was reasonable and the reliance is in good faith considering all the facts and circumstances. Reliance is not reasonable when—

(1) The practitioner knows or reasonably should know that the opinion of the other person should not be relied on;

(2) The practitioner knows or reasonably should know that the other person is not competent or lacks the necessary qualifications to provide the advice; or

(3) The practitioner knows or reasonably should know that the other person has a conflict of interest in violation of the rules described in this part.

(c) *Standard of review.*

(1) In evaluating whether a practitioner giving written advice concerning one or more Federal tax matters complied with the requirements of this section, the Commissioner, or delegate, will apply a reasonable practitioner standard, considering all facts and circumstances, including, but not limited to, the scope of the engagement and the type and specificity of the advice sought by the client.

(2) In the case of an opinion the practitioner knows or has reason to know will be used or referred to by a person other than the practitioner (or a person who is a member of, associated with, or employed by the practitioner's firm) in promoting, marketing, or recommending to one or more taxpayers a partnership or other entity, investment plan or arrangement a significant purpose of which is the avoidance or evasion of any tax imposed by the Internal Revenue Code, the Commissioner, or delegate, will apply a reasonable practitioner standard, considering all

facts and circumstances, with emphasis given to the additional risk caused by the practitioner's lack of knowledge of the taxpayer's particular circumstances, when determining whether a practitioner has failed to comply with this section.

(d) *Federal tax matter.* A Federal tax matter, as used in this section, is any matter concerning the application or interpretation of---

(1) A revenue provision as defined in section 6110(i)(1)(B) of the Internal Revenue Code;

(2) Any provision of law impacting a person's obligations under the internal revenue laws and regulations, including but not limited to the person's liability to pay tax or obligation to file returns; or

(3) Any other law or regulation administered by the Internal Revenue Service.

(e) *Effective/applicability date.* This section is applicable to written advice rendered after June 12, 2014.

§ 10.38 Establishment of advisory committees.

(a) *Advisory committees.* To promote and maintain the public's confidence in tax advisors, the Internal Revenue Service is authorized to establish one or more advisory committees composed of at least six individuals authorized to practice before the Internal Revenue Service. Membership of an advisory committee must be balanced among those who practice as attorneys, accountants, enrolled agents, enrolled actuaries, enrolled retirement plan agents, and registered tax return preparers. Under procedures prescribed by the Internal Revenue Service, an advisory committee may review and make general recommendations regarding the practices, procedures, and policies of the offices described in §10.1.

(b) *Effective date.* This section is applicable beginning August 2, 2011.

Treasury Department Circular No. 230

§ 10.38 — Page 27

Subpart C — Sanctions for Violation of the Regulations

§ 10.50 Sanctions.

(a) *Authority to censure, suspend, or disbar.* The Secretary of the Treasury, or delegate, after notice and an opportunity for a proceeding, may censure, suspend, or disbar any practitioner from practice before the Internal Revenue Service if the practitioner is shown to be incompetent or disreputable (within the meaning of §10.51), fails to comply with any regulation in this part (under the prohibited conduct standards of §10.52), or with intent to defraud, willfully and knowingly misleads or threatens a client or prospective client. Censure is a public reprimand.

(b) *Authority to disqualify.* The Secretary of the Treasury, or delegate, after due notice and opportunity for hearing, may disqualify any appraiser for a violation of these rules as applicable to appraisers.

(1) If any appraiser is disqualified pursuant to this subpart C, the appraiser is barred from presenting evidence or testimony in any administrative proceeding before the Department of Treasury or the Internal Revenue Service, unless and until authorized to do so by the Internal Revenue Service pursuant to §10.81, regardless of whether the evidence or testimony would pertain to an appraisal made prior to or after the effective date of disqualification.

(2) Any appraisal made by a disqualified appraiser after the effective date of disqualification will not have any probative effect in any administrative proceeding before the Department of the Treasury or the Internal Revenue Service. An appraisal otherwise barred from admission into evidence pursuant to this section may be admitted into evidence solely for the purpose of determining the taxpayer's reliance in good faith on such appraisal.

(c) *Authority to impose monetary penalty —*

(1) *In general.*

(i) The Secretary of the Treasury, or delegate, after notice and an opportunity for a proceeding, may impose a monetary penalty on any practitioner who engages in conduct subject to sanction under paragraph (a) of this section.

(ii) If the practitioner described in paragraph (c)(1)(i) of this section was acting on behalf of an employer or any firm or other entity in connection with the conduct giving rise to the penalty, the Secretary of the Treasury, or delegate, may impose a monetary penalty on the employer, firm, or entity if it knew, or reasonably should have known of such conduct.

(2) *Amount of penalty.* The amount of the penalty shall not exceed the gross income derived (or to be derived) from the conduct giving rise to the penalty.

(3) *Coordination with other sanctions.* Subject to paragraph (c)(2) of this section —

(i) Any monetary penalty imposed on a practitioner under this paragraph (c) may be in addition to or in lieu of any suspension, disbarment or censure and may be in addition to a penalty imposed on an employer, firm or other entity under paragraph (c)(1)(ii) of this section.

(ii) Any monetary penalty imposed on an employer, firm or other entity may be in addition to or in lieu of penalties imposed under paragraph (c)(1)(i) of this section.

(d) *Authority to accept a practitioner's consent to sanction.* The Internal Revenue Service may accept a practitioner's offer of consent to be sanctioned under §10.50 in lieu of instituting or continuing a proceeding under §10.60(a).

(e) *Sanctions to be imposed.* The sanctions imposed by this section shall take into account all relevant facts and circumstances.

(f) *Effective/applicability date.* This section is applicable to conduct occurring on or after August 2, 2011, except that paragraphs (a), (b)(2), and (e) apply to conduct occurring on or after September 26, 2007, and paragraph (c) applies to prohibited conduct that occurs after October 22, 2004.

§ 10.51 Incompetence and disreputable conduct.

(a) *Incompetence and disreputable conduct.* Incompetence and disreputable conduct for which a practitioner may be sanctioned under §10.50 includes, but is not limited to —

(1) Conviction of any criminal offense under the Federal tax laws.

(2) Conviction of any criminal offense involving dishonesty or breach of trust.

(3) Conviction of any felony under Federal or State law for which the conduct involved renders the practitioner unfit to practice before the Internal Revenue Service.

(4) Giving false or misleading information, or participating in any way in the giving of false or misleading information to the Department of the Treasury or any officer or employee thereof, or to any tribunal authorized to pass upon Federal tax matters, in connection with any matter pending or likely to be pending before them, knowing the information to be false or misleading. Facts or other matters contained in testimony, Federal tax returns, financial statements, applications for enrollment, affidavits, declarations, and any other document or statement, written or oral, are included in the term "information."

(5) Solicitation of employment as prohibited under §10.30, the use of false or misleading representations with intent to deceive a client or prospective client in order to procure employment, or intimating that the practitioner is able improperly to obtain special consideration or action from the Internal Revenue Service or any officer or employee thereof.

(6) Willfully failing to make a Federal tax return in violation of the Federal tax laws, or willfully evading, attempting to evade, or participating in any way in evading or attempting to evade any assessment or payment of any Federal tax.

(7) Willfully assisting, counseling, encouraging a client or prospective client in violating, or suggesting to a client or prospective client to violate, any Federal tax law, or knowingly counseling or suggesting to a client or prospective client an illegal plan to evade Federal taxes or payment thereof.

(8) Misappropriation of, or failure properly or promptly to remit, funds received from a client for the purpose of payment of taxes or other obligations due the United States.

(9) Directly or indirectly attempting to influence, or offering or agreeing to attempt to influence, the official action of any officer or employee of the Internal Revenue Service by the use of threats, false accusations, duress or coercion, by the offer of any special inducement or promise of an advantage or by the bestowing of any gift, favor or thing of value.

(10) Disbarment or suspension from practice as an attorney, certified public accountant, public accountant, or actuary by any duly constituted authority of any State, territory, or possession of the United States, including a Commonwealth, or the District of Columbia, any Federal court of record or any Federal agency, body or board.

(11) Knowingly aiding and abetting another person to practice before the Internal Revenue Service during a period of suspension, disbarment or ineligibility of such other person.

(12) Contemptuous conduct in connection with practice before the Internal Revenue Service, including the use of abusive language, making false accusations or statements, knowing them to be false, or circulating or publishing malicious or libelous matter.

(13) Giving a false opinion, knowingly, recklessly, or through gross incompetence, including an opinion which is intentionally or recklessly misleading, or engaging in a pattern of providing incompetent opinions on questions arising under the Federal tax laws. False opinions described in this paragraph (a)(13) include those which reflect or result from a knowing misstatement of fact or law, from an assertion of a position known to be unwarranted under existing law, from counseling or assisting in conduct known to be illegal or fraudulent, from concealing matters required by law to be revealed, or from consciously disregarding information indicating that material facts expressed in the opinion or offering material are false or misleading. For purposes of this paragraph (a)(13), reckless conduct is a highly unreasonable omission or misrepresentation involving an extreme departure from the standards of ordinary care that a practitioner should observe under the circumstances. A pattern of conduct is a factor that will be taken into account in determining whether a practitioner acted knowingly, recklessly, or through gross incompetence. Gross incompetence

includes conduct that reflects gross indifference, preparation which is grossly inadequate under the circumstances, and a consistent failure to perform obligations to the client.

(14) Willfully failing to sign a tax return prepared by the practitioner when the practitioner's signature is required by Federal tax laws unless the failure is due to reasonable cause and not due to willful neglect.

(15) Willfully disclosing or otherwise using a tax return or tax return information in a manner not authorized by the Internal Revenue Code, contrary to the order of a court of competent jurisdiction, or contrary to the order of an administrative law judge in a proceeding instituted under §10.60.

(16) Willfully failing to file on magnetic or other electronic media a tax return prepared by the practitioner when the practitioner is required to do so by the Federal tax laws unless the failure is due to reasonable cause and not due to willful neglect.

(17) Willfully preparing all or substantially all of, or signing, a tax return or claim for refund when the practitioner does not possess a current or otherwise valid preparer tax identification number or other prescribed identifying number.

(18) Willfully representing a taxpayer before an officer or employee of the Internal Revenue Service unless the practitioner is authorized to do so pursuant to this part.

(b) *Effective/applicability date.* This section is applicable beginning August 2, 2011.

§ 10.52 Violations subject to sanction.

(a) A practitioner may be sanctioned under §10.50 if the practitioner —

(1) Willfully violates any of the regulations (other than §10.33) contained in this part; or

(2) Recklessly or through gross incompetence (within the meaning of §10.51(a)(13)) violates §§ 10.34, 10.35, 10.36 or 10.37.

(b) *Effective/applicability date.* This section is applicable to conduct occurring on or after September 26, 2007.

§ 10.53 Receipt of information concerning practitioner.

(a) *Officer or employee of the Internal Revenue Service.* If an officer or employee of the Internal Revenue Service has reason to believe a practitioner has violated any provision of this part, the officer or employee will promptly make a written report of the suspected violation. The report will explain the facts and reasons upon which the officer's or employee's belief rests and must be submitted to the office(s) of the Internal Revenue Service responsible for administering or enforcing this part.

(b) *Other persons.* Any person other than an officer or employee of the Internal Revenue Service having information of a violation of any provision of this part may make an oral or written report of the alleged violation to the office(s) of the Internal Revenue Service responsible for administering or enforcing this part or any officer or employee of the Internal Revenue Service. If the report is made to an officer or employee of the Internal Revenue Service, the officer or employee will make a written report of the suspected violation and submit the report to the office(s) of the Internal Revenue Service responsible for administering or enforcing this part.

(c) *Destruction of report.* No report made under paragraph (a) or (b) of this section shall be maintained unless retention of the report is permissible under the applicable records control schedule as approved by the National Archives and Records Administration and designated in the Internal Revenue Manual. Reports must be destroyed as soon as permissible under the applicable records control schedule.

(d) *Effect on proceedings under subpart D.* The destruction of any report will not bar any proceeding under subpart D of this part, but will preclude the use of a copy of the report in a proceeding under subpart D of this part.

(e) *Effective/applicability date.* This section is applicable beginning August 2, 2011.

[Pages 31 to 44 omitted.]

Federal Income Taxation Research

The largely electronic nature of today's legal research environment places considerable resources instantly and constantly at our disposal. Although having a vast information network available to us might appear desirable as an initial matter, such a resource-rich environment poses the risk of nourishing a false sense of security and implanting unrealistic expectations in those with ready access to it. Surely, the Internet produces highly useful information in a host of contexts, and its various features have markedly enhanced communications, entertainment, commerce, and several other spheres of human activity. But notwithstanding the fact that the Internet can serve as an extraordinary (indeed, critically necessary) tool as one goes about the practice of law, the Internet *cannot* practice law for an attorney nor, for that matter, can it conduct effective legal research at the attorney's behest. Computers, search engines, and legal databases produce mere output. The utility and quality of the output derived from these resources correlates positively with the substantive and technical expertise of the individual providing the necessary research prompts. With a solid knowledge base and proper training, an attorney can conduct professional-level research with intelligence rather than casting a net and later sifting hopefully through a pile of instant, electronic results.

Getting useful research results is just the first step in the larger process of client service. Attorneys must be able to make informed judgments with respect to the relevance of the sources found and proceed to take those sources, digest them, and turn them into a professional work product reflecting thorough analysis and clear, audience-sensitive explanation. Substantively, tax law can prove quite difficult to digest at first, but with practice and experience, an aspiring tax professional will gradually develop the necessary aptitude. Fortunately, those charged with conducting research in the federal tax arena have a distinct advantage. No matter how vast, the tax universe is, at the least, generally organized by Code section, and that reality makes for a structured, well-streamlined research environment. In this appendix, we start with basic substantive knowledge sources. From there, we turn to standard tax research methodology and direct our focus to the research process as it relates to specific source materials of relevance to tax professionals.

A. KNOWING THE LAW AND ESTABLISHING A STANDARD METHODOLOGY

1. Substantive Knowledge

Effective tax research necessarily starts with acquisition of the substantive fundamentals. Although students may establish a healthy knowledge base by taking several tax courses at the J.D. level, taking the further step of obtaining an LLM in Taxation not only ensures a degree of substantive breadth and depth but also enhances an aspiring attorney's ability to secure gainful employment; many law and accounting firms have come to value the LLM credential and routinely expect their entry-level tax professionals to have it. After graduation, tax professionals must also keep abreast of current developments, with heightened attention devoted to those events of relevance to the attorney's client base. Knowledge of recent and ongoing developments will inform and improve the attorney's research efforts in the near term and may even prove beneficial weeks, months, or years later. Frequently, tax professionals stay current by subscribing to and reviewing various electronic update resources (typically received each business day by e-mail). Examples include the Daily Tax Report published by Bloomberg BNA and the Daily Federal Tax News published by Commerce Clearing House ("CCH"). *See, e.g.,* Exhibits A2.1 and A2.2.

EXHIBIT A2.1   Sample Daily Tax Report Update (Reprinted with permission from *Daily Tax Report*, Number 101 (May 26, 2017). Copyright 2017 by The Bureau of National Affairs, Inc. (800-372-1033), http://www.bna.com.)

Bloomberg BNA

Daily Tax Report

May 26, 2017 - Number 101

Federal Tax & Accounting

Accounting
Software's Subscription Model Could Ease Revenue Rule Compliance
Subscription-based software providers such as Adobe Systems Inc. and Workday Inc. stand to benefit from new revenue recognition rules, while companies with less certain revenue streams could be hurt.

Accounting
U.S. Accounting Rulemakers Urged to Mull GOP Tax Reform Impacts
U.S. accounting rulemakers should start to informally engage with companies about the implications of potential U.S. tax law changes.

Capital Gains
How to Handle the $85 Million Gain From That Basquiat Windfall
As the auction hammer fell at Sotheby's in New York last week, a painting by Jean-Michel Basquiat fetched a record $110.5 million. Now another hammer will come down: the tax man's.

Tax Decisions & Rulings

Estate Taxes
Conservative Group Takes IRS to Court on Estate Tax Rules
The IRS is facing a legal demand to say why it thinks its controversial estate tax valuation rules don't have an economic impact that requires analysis under the Regulatory Flexibility Act.

Tax Compliance
Whistle-Blower Agreed to Award Amount, Can't Ask for More
A whistle-blower who accepted a $2.1 million IRS award that had been reduced by the Budget Control Act of 2011 can't retroactively challenge the agency for the full award amount.

Tax Court
Tax Court Shorts
The U.S. Tax Court ruled May 25 that the IRS could levy a taxpayer who conveyed property to his daughter for negligible consideration but claimed financial hardship.

Chiarelli v. Commissioner

Whistleblower 4496-15W v. Commissioner

EXHIBIT A2.2   **Sample CCH Tracker News (selected portions)**

⊕CCH Tracker News

Add or modify your Trackers

Jump To:
Federal Tax Legislation Watch | Daily Federal Tax News

Federal Tax Legislation Watch

House Approves Aviation Bill Exempting Certain Expense Payments from Federal Excise Tax (Jul. 14, 2016)

> Jessica Jeane, Wolters Kluwer The House Ways and Means Committee on July 13 approved, by voice vote, a bipartisan, bicameral bill that would exempt amounts paid for aircraft management services from federal excise taxes imposed on transportation by air. HR 3608 would resolve potential ambiguities in the ticket tax by codifying the current IRS practice regarding the treatment of aircraft management services, Chairman Kevin Brady, R-Tex., said during opening statements. The bill now heads to the...

Senate Approves Bill to Exempt Olympic Medals and Awards from Taxation (Jul. 14, 2016)

> Jessica Jeane, Wolters Kluwer The Senate approved the United States Appreciation for Olympians and Paralympians Bill (Sen 2650) by unanimous consent on July 12. The measure now heads to the House for consideration. If enacted, the value of any medals awarded in, or any prize money received from the U.S. Olympic Committee on account of, competition in the Olympic or Paralympic Games would be exempt from income taxation, beginning with the 2016 Olympic Games in Brazil. The bipartisan bill,...

Daily Federal Tax News   Back to top

House Approves Aviation Bill Exempting Certain Expense Payments from Federal Excise Tax (Jul. 14, 2016)

> Jessica Jeane, Wolters Kluwer The House Ways and Means Committee on July 13 approved, by voice vote, a bipartisan, bicameral bill that would exempt amounts paid for aircraft management services from federal excise taxes imposed on transportation by air. HR 3608 would resolve potential ambiguities in the ticket tax by codifying the current IRS practice

1

Source: CCH; used with the permission of Wolters Kluwer.

2. Research Methodology

The approach taken in conducting federal income tax research depends, to a great extent, on the assignment parameters. In general, however, one starts by consulting governing Code provisions and Treasury Regulations before proceeding to cases,

IRS pronouncements, legislative history, and various secondary resources. Ultimately, each attorney must find a standard research methodology with which he or she is comfortable and can employ consistently and that generally assures thorough examination of the issue at hand.

B. STATUTES

1. Basic Statutory Text

The Internal Revenue Code is the logical starting point for most basic tax research assignments. In planning for transactions or events likely to occur in the future, the current version of the Code should suffice. Most tax attorneys will have physical copies of the text in bound volumes on their desks, although the Code is, of course, available in several electronic databases. The vast majority of tax statutes are found in Title 26 of the United States Code. Accordingly, finding the current version of a specific provision is simply a matter of entering its citation in a search window in a legal research database. Entering "26 U.S.C. 104" will produce the result set forth in Exhibit A2.3.

In addition to being useful for planning purposes, the current version of the Code will likely suffice with respect to research questions flowing from relatively recent events. Such is the case because of the low likelihood that governing provisions will

EXHIBIT A2.3 Westlaw Research Result for "26 U.S.C. 104"

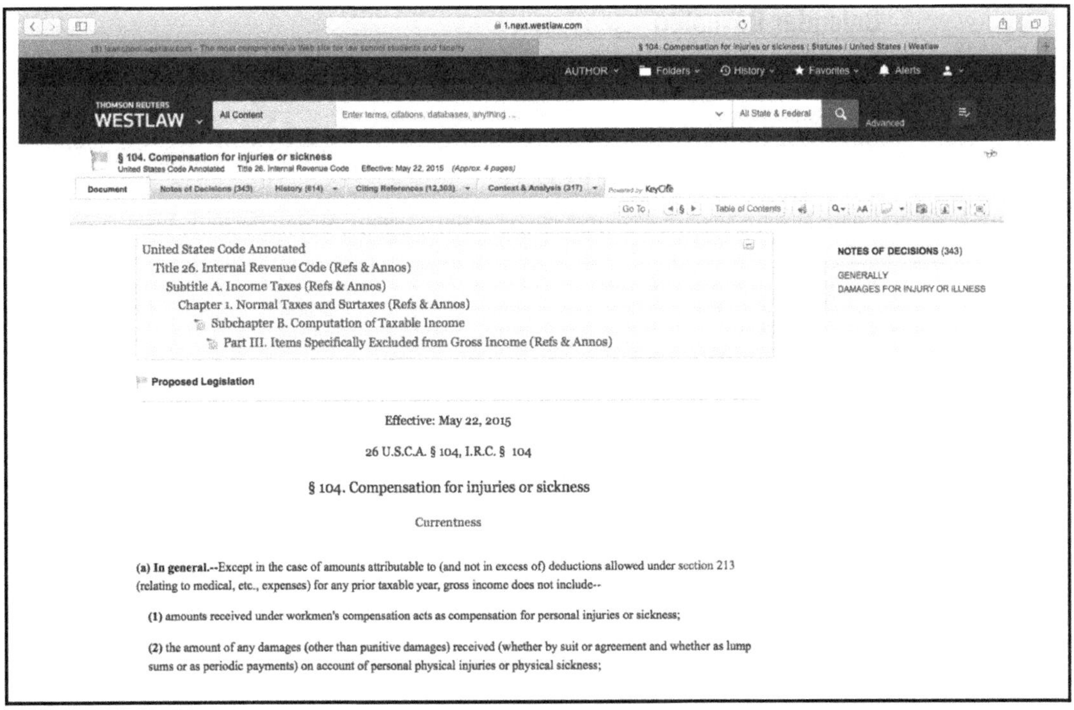
THOMSON REUTERS WESTLAW

§ 104. Compensation for injuries or sickness

United States Code Annotated Title 26. Internal Revenue Code Effective: May 22, 2015 (Approx. 4 pages)

NOTES OF DECISIONS (343)

GENERALLY

DAMAGES FOR INJURY OR ILLNESS

United States Code Annotated

Title 26. Internal Revenue Code (Refs & Annos)

Subtitle A. Income Taxes (Refs & Annos)

Chapter 1. Normal Taxes and Surtaxes (Refs & Annos)

Subchapter B. Computation of Taxable Income

Part III. Items Specifically Excluded from Gross Income (Refs & Annos)

Proposed Legislation

Effective: May 22, 2015

26 U.S.C.A. § 104, I.R.C. § 104

§ 104. Compensation for injuries or sickness

Currentness

(a) In general.--Except in the case of amounts attributable to (and not in excess of) deductions allowed under section 213 (relating to medical, etc., expenses) for any prior taxable year, gross income does not include--

(1) amounts received under workmen's compensation acts as compensation for personal injuries or sickness;

(2) the amount of any damages (other than punitive damages) received (whether by suit or agreement and whether as lump sums or as periodic payments) on account of personal physical injuries or physical sickness;

Source: Westlaw; used with the permission of Thomson Reuters.

have undergone substantial (if any) amendment in the short term. As time passes, however, the likelihood of amendment is a reality that cannot be ignored. If an attorney is conducting research with respect to prior transactions or events or, perhaps, in connection with tax controversy or litigation, *the attorney must apply the version of the Internal Revenue Code in existence at the relevant time.* If a previously filed tax return is at issue, the relevant time is generally in the temporal vicinity of the return's filing date. The relevant statutory language may or may not be identical to the current statutory language, but the rule applies; taxpayers of yesteryear cannot be expected to have complied with a statute not in existence at the time of their transactions (i.e., the current version). In prior years, law libraries would maintain decades of prior versions of the Internal Revenue Code, and for some years, it may still be necessary to seek out the physical text of the statute. For relatively recent years, researchers need not rely so heavily on the law librarian's Code-keeping diligence. The researcher cannot obtain the prior version of the statute by merely entering the section's standard citation; as we now know, the database will return the current version of the provision. To access the prior version of a given provision, one must start by accessing the Internal Revenue Code database. From the Westlaw home page, one can open the tab for "Practice Areas" and then follow the links for "Tax," "Statutes and Court Rules," and "Internal Revenue Code." Having arrived at that page, one would then click the box for "Effective Date," enter the relevant date, and click "Go" to access the proper version of the Code. Exhibit A2.4 depicts the Internal Revenue Code database page with the date selection calendar revealed.

EXHIBIT A2.4   **Westlaw's Internal Revenue Code Database Page with Date Selection Calendar Revealed**

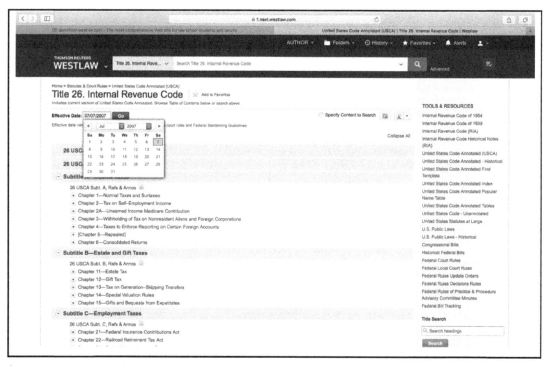

Source: Westlaw; used with the permission of Thomson Reuters.

Note that after a researcher clicks "Go," the proper Code version will be present, but locating a specific provision will *not* be a function of entering a citation in the search window; that action will still take you to the current statute. Instead, one must locate the date-specific provision by expanding line items in the Code outline (of the prior version) that is now set forth on the opening page. Exhibit A2.5 depicts expansion of relevant Code outline items; from this screen, a researcher would be able to click on the appropriate link and view § 104 as it existed on January 1, 2001.

Non-Code Provisions

Bear in mind that although the vast majority of tax laws have been codified as part of the Internal Revenue Code, a few tax provisions exist in the larger body of federal statutes that have not been made part of the Internal Revenue Code. In Chapter 22, we noted the existence of one such non-Code tax provision, Section 530 of the Revenue Act of 1978 (as amended).

EXHIBIT A2.5 **Westlaw Page Depicting Outline of Internal Revenue Code as of January 1, 2001** *(with selected expansions under Subtitle A, Chapter 1)*

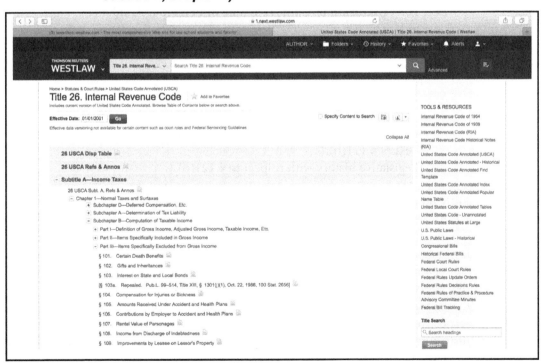

Source: Westlaw; used with the permission of Thomson Reuters.

2. Legislative History

In addition to locating and applying statutory provisions, a researcher may find it necessary to explore the legislative history of a given section or subsection. Such will often be the case if the language of the statute is ambiguous and other resources do not provide meaningful guidance. Many commercially available versions of the Code anticipate this research need. They will include not only the text of the statute but also annotations with respect to the legislative history of various sections and subsections. Placement of the annotations varies. Some sources provide the entire text of a specific Code section, and all legislative history annotations for that section appear only at the end of the statutory text. The following generically exemplifies this approach:

Sec. 121 - Exclusion of Gain from Sale of Principal Residence

[Full Text of § 121.]
***
[Legislative history annotations with respect to § 121.]

In other instances, the presentation of the core statutory text is more fragmented because individual subsections are presented and followed immediately by relevant legislative history annotations; the presentation of additional statutory text continues only after the legislative history of the preceding subsection has been presented. The following generically exemplifies this approach:

Sec. 121 - Exclusion of Gain from Sale of Principal Residence

[Sec. 121(a)]

[Text of § 121(a).]

[Sec. 121(b)]

[Text of § 121(b).]
[Legislative history with respect to § 121(b).]

Both presentation approaches have some benefits. The first approach facilitates rapid comprehension of the entire provision because it allows a reader to review it without the interruption of legislative history annotations. The second approach facilitates focused research. Attorneys conducting research with respect to a given subsection can often see (with little additional effort) references to the legislation that added the specific subsection to the Code and how amendments have changed that subsection over time. In an electronic database, one has many options with respect to finding legislative history. On Westlaw, one could conduct legislative history research by accessing the "Legislative History" database or by locating a

EXHIBIT A2.6   **Research Result for "26 U.S.C. 104" with "History" Menu Revealed**

Source: Westlaw; used with the permission of Thomson Reuters.

specific statutory provision and following the "History" tab. As you can see from Exhibit A2.6, one can take the latter approach when locating legislative history with respect to a specific Code section.

As you can see, however, following the Legislative History Materials link only brings one a step closer to the sought-after research results. Ideally, a researcher will have narrowed his focus to a specific legislative development and can proceed to do further research with a Public Law number in hand. Legislative history annotations in the researcher's Internal Revenue Code will likely reference specific legislative developments and provide both a Public Law number and the name of the relevant legislation. In addition to the legislative history resources discussed above, tax researchers should also be familiar with what tax attorneys refer to as the "Bluebook." Unrelated to the text used in connection with legal citation, the tax Bluebook (generally pale blue in color when in physical form) is published by the Staff of the Joint Committee on Taxation and typically provides a general explanation of tax legislation enacted during a specific time period. Ideally, the researcher will find full discussion of Present Law (i.e., pre-amendment law), Reasons for Change, Explanation of Provision, and Effective Date. *See, e.g.*, Exhibit A2.7. Note that many Bluebooks are available on the Joint Committee on Taxation website, in HeinOnline, and in commercial databases (including Westlaw).

EXHIBIT A2.7 Bluebook Excerpt Concerning Legislation Excluding Certain Items
from the Gross Income of Participants in Olympic and
Paralympic Games (Page 1)

GENERAL EXPLANATION OF
TAX LEGISLATION ENACTED IN 2016

_____

PREPARED BY THE STAFF

OF THE

JOINT COMMITTEE ON TAXATION

February 2017

JCX-4-17

EXHIBIT A2.7   **Bluebook Excerpt Concerning Legislation Excluding Certain Items from the Gross Income of Participants in Olympic and Paralympic Games (Page 2)**

PART FOUR: UNITED STATES APPRECIATION FOR
OLYMPIANS AND PARALYMPIANS ACT OF 2016
(PUBLIC LAW 114-239)[30]

A. Exclusion from Gross Income for the Value of Medals Awarded at Olympic
or Paralympic Games and for Certain Prizes or Awards Paid
by the U.S. Olympic Committee to Competitors
(sec. 2 of the Act and sec. 74 of the Code)

<u>Present Law</u>

U.S. citizens and residents are subject to U.S. taxation on their worldwide income, from whatever source derived,[31] absent a specific statutory exception. Prizes and awards are specifically included in income.[32] If prizes or awards are provided in the form of goods or services, the fair market value of the goods or services provided is the amount to be included in income.[33]

There are three exceptions to the general rule of inclusion of prizes and awards: First, qualified scholarships described in section 117; second, certain employee achievement awards; and third, awards for religious, charitable, scientific, educational, artistic, literary or civic achievement, provided that the recipient takes no action to be considered for the award, requests that the monetary award be transferred to a designated governmental unit or tax-exempt organization to which deductible charitable contributions are permitted, and is not required to render future substantial services as a condition of the award.[34] Examples of awards that may qualify for the third exception if the monies associated with the award are timely donated include the Nobel and Pulitzer prizes. In contrast, prizes or awards in recognition of athletic achievement are generally ineligible for the exception.[35]

The United States Olympic Committee ("USOC") is a corporation created by statute to serve as a coordinating body for United States participation in international competitive amateur

---

[30] H.R. 5946. The Senate passed S. 2650, a bill similar to H.R. 5946, on July 12, 2016. The House Committee on Ways and Means reported H.R. 5946 on September 20, 2016 (H.R. Rep. No. 114-762). The House passed the bill on September 22, 2016. The Senate passed the bill without amendment on September 29, 2016. The President signed the bill on October 7, 2016.

[31] Sec. 61.

[32] Sec. 74.

[33] Treas. Reg. sec. 1.74-1(a)(2).

[34] Treas. Reg. sec. 1.74-1(b).

[35] *Wills v. Commissioner*, 48 T.C. 308 (1967), aff'd 411 F.2d 537 (9th Cir. 1969), in which the Court held that the value of the S. Rae Hickock Belt, awarded to baseball player Maury Wills as outstanding professional athlete of the year, was includible in income as a prize or award given for athletic achievement, and ineligible for the exception available for awards based on educational, civil, literary, scientific or artistic achievement.

13

sports, in order to provide "the most competent amateur representation possible in each event" in the Olympic, Paralympic and Pan-American Games.[36] As part of its activities, the USOC awards each U.S. Olympic athlete prize money for each medal won, in the amounts of $25,000 for each gold medal, $15,000 for each silver medal, and $10,000 for each bronze medal. U.S. Paralympic athletes receive $5,000, $3,500 and $2,500 respectively for each gold, silver and bronze medal awarded.[37] All U.S. Olympians and U.S. Paralympians are required to be U.S. citizens.[38] As a result, these performance awards from the USOC are includible as prizes and awards, regardless of whether the athletes derive the income for activities performed inside, or outside, the United States.[39] Both the prize money awarded to U.S. athletes by the USOC, as well as the fair market value of gold, silver, and bronze medals, are includible in gross income.

Reasons for Change

The Congress believes that the athletes who represent the United States on the global stage at the Olympic and Paralympic games perform a valuable patriotic service. The athletes do so only after years of personal sacrifice to attain the level of excellence required to compete at the Olympic and Paralympic games. The Congress also believes that during their years of

---

[36] See generally, 36 U.S.C. secs. 220501 through 220512. The organization does not generally receive Federal funding, although specific programs for veterans of U.S. military service receive Federal assistance. Instead, the organization raises funds from donors as well as revenue from licensing of use of the US Olympic team name and insignia, as well as granting of broadcast rights in the United States. The purposes of the organization are enumerated in section 220503, and include promotion of physical fitness and sports participation generally, financial assistance to athletes or sport federations, development of training facilities and technical support to amateur athletic programs that support sports that are included in the Olympics, Paralympics and Pan-Am games. The USOC provides a quadrennial report to Congress on its operations. The most recent report, covering the period 2009 through 2012, was issued June 1, 2013, and is available at http://www.teamusa.org/Footer/Legal/Governance-Documents.

[37] Based on recent metal prices, the approximate value of the medals awarded at the Rio games are $565 for the gold, $305 for the silver and $5 for the bronze. See, Reid Carlson, "The Monetary Worth of the 2016 Rio Olympic Medals," SwimSwam, available at https://swimswam.com/monetary-worth-rio-medals.

[38] The international governing bodies of the Olympic and Paralympic games permit certain exceptions for athletes from countries that do not have national organizations eligible to enter teams in the games. See, Rule 41 and related by-laws, *The International Olympic Committee Charter*, available at http://www.teamusa.org/About-the-USOC/Inside-the-USOC/Olympic-Movement/Structure, and Chapter 3.1, *The International Paralympic Committee Handbook*, available at https://www.paralympic.org/sites/default/files/document/160523070735592_Rio%2BQG_23_May_2016.pdf. Peter Spiro, "Citizenship and the Olympics," 5 *Insights*, (Spring 2016), published by American Bar Association, http://www.americanbar.org/publications/insights_on_law_andsociety/16/spring-2016/citizenship-and-the-olympics.

[39] A credit may be allowed for any foreign income tax imposed on awards for games held outside the United States. Many Olympic host countries (including the United States) exempt nonresident athletes from income tax on awards. As in the United States, these exemptions may be part of a host country's tax law, and some contracts between the International Olympic Committee and Olympic host cities confirm the exemption. Under a typical contract, the host city and the host city's Organizing Committee promise either that the host country will not tax performance awards or, if the host country does tax performance awards, that the host city or Organizing Committee will reimburse athletes for the amount of the tax. For example, Rio de Janeiro entered into a Host City Contract containing this clause. A draft contract corresponding to the 2022 Olympics in China also contains this clause.

EXHIBIT A2.7   **Bluebook Excerpt Concerning Legislation Excluding Certain Items from the Gross Income of Participants in Olympic and Paralympic Games (Page 4)**

training and preparation, many athletes representing the United States in the games earn little or no money from participation in their chosen sports, and often defer pursuit of careers outside sports. Monetary prizes awarded by the USOC to medalists on the United States teams are intended to reward such sacrifices and to provide incentives to other athletes who seek to represent the United States on a global stage. The Congress believes that providing this exclusion for the receipt of an Olympic or Paralympic medal and other prizes awarded by the USOC generally should be without tax consequences.

Explanation of Provision

The provision creates a new exception to the general rule requiring inclusion of prizes and awards in gross income. Under the terms of the exception, neither the value of the medals awarded to U.S. Olympic or Paralympic athletes nor the cash prizes given by the USOC are includible in income for Federal tax purposes. This exclusion does not apply to taxpayers whose adjusted gross income (determined without regard to the value of such medals or rewards) is in excess of $1,000,000 (or half such amount in the case of a married taxpayer filing a separate return).

Effective Date

The provision applies to prizes and awards received after December 31, 2015.

C. TREASURY REGULATIONS

Although those conducting tax research may be able to resolve all necessary issues by consulting the Code, it is often the case that researchers must go much further. Consulting Treasury Regulations (discussed previously in Chapter 1) makes sense as the next logical step in the process. Attorneys will likely have a full, multivolume set of Treasury Regulations on their desks or bookshelves, but as with the Internal Revenue Code, the resource is available and searchable electronically. One can access the Treasury Regulations databases by opening the "Practice Areas" tab from the Westlaw home page, following the "Tax" link, following the link for "Regulations," and then selecting "Treasury Regulations." A researcher should be able to locate proposed regulations by opting for the "Proposed and Adopted Regulations" link as opposed to the "Regulations" link. Temporary Regulations are available in both the "Regulations" and the "Proposed and Adopted Regulations" databases because Temporary Regulations take immediate effect but are issued in proposed form at the same time for purposes of notice and comment before they are finalized. Note that as was the case with Code provisions, for prior transactions and events, a researcher must locate and apply Treasury Regulations as they existed at the relevant time. Note further that attorneys in private practice will likely be alerted to the promulgation of proposed, temporary, and finalized regulations by reviewing a daily tax resource.

D. CASES

Tax cases appear at all levels of the federal judiciary and can prove particularly useful in the research context. Practitioners can search as narrowly or as broadly as they choose by following the appropriate links to restrict database content. After opening the "Practice Areas" tab on the Westlaw home page and following the "Tax" link, one will have the ability to go further by following the "Cases" link. Having followed that link, the researcher can search all tax cases or only those in a given set of federal courts by following the appropriate link. *See, e.g.,* Exhibit A2.8.

EXHIBIT A2.8 **Westlaw Tax Cases Database Page**

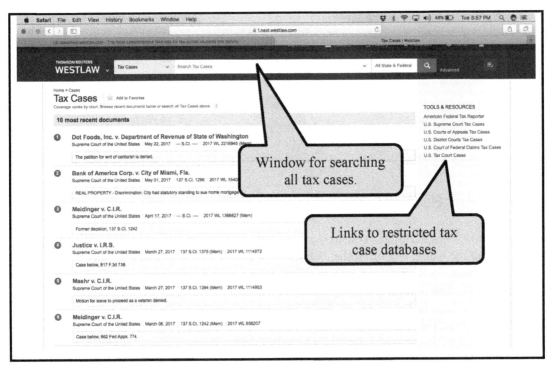

Source: Westlaw; used with the permission of Thomson Reuters.

Those opting to search with restricted scope (e.g., only the decisions of a specific District Court or a specific Circuit Court of Appeals) can follow the "Federal Materials" tab (from the Westlaw home page) and the "Federal Cases" link before selecting the appropriate court's database. *See, e.g.,* Exhibit A2.9.

EXHIBIT A2.9　**Westlaw Federal Cases Database Page**

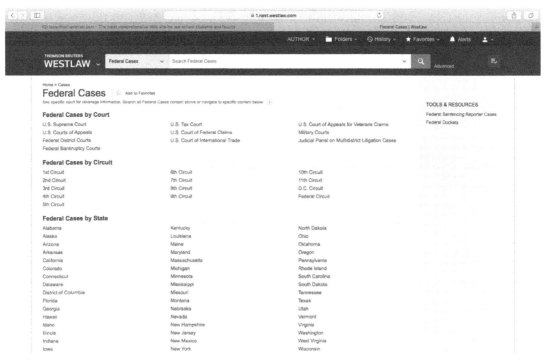

Source: Westlaw; used with the permission of Thomson Reuters.

For some taxpayers, the ability to search the decisions of a specific court is quite important. Although taxpayers unable to pay a proposed assessment prior to litigation must proceed in Tax Court, those with the financial wherewithal to pay the proposed assessment up front have maximum flexibility because pre-litigation payment will grant them the option of proceeding in either a U.S. District Court or the U.S. Court of Federal Claims. If such a taxpayer decides to go to Tax Court, they may do so, provided that they forego payment of the proposed assessment prior to filing their petition in Tax Court. In any event, taxpayers with maximum flexibility can get a sneak preview of sorts (i.e., shopping each forum) by seeing how specific courts have decided the issue at hand in the past. If an attorney in private practice is fortunate, she might find binding precedent that disposes of the IRS's proposed tax enhancements and forces full concession at the protest phase. Such silver bullets are rare, indeed, but they do exist.

E.　SPECIFIC IRS PRONOUNCEMENTS

In Chapter 1, we discussed various IRS pronouncements (e.g., Revenue Rulings, Revenue Procedures, Private Letter Rulings, etc.). Attorneys in private practice will likely first become aware of the publication and release of these documents by reviewing a daily tax resource. Previously released pronouncements are available in various electronic databases, and one will generally be able to search broadly or narrowly. On Westlaw, after opening the Practice Areas tab and following the links for "Tax" and "Administrative Decisions & Guidance," one can enter search terms for a broad search or follow links to restrict the search to a specific pronouncement type. *See, e.g.,* Exhibit A2.10.

EXHIBIT A2.10   **Westlaw Database for Tax Administrative Decisions & Guidance**

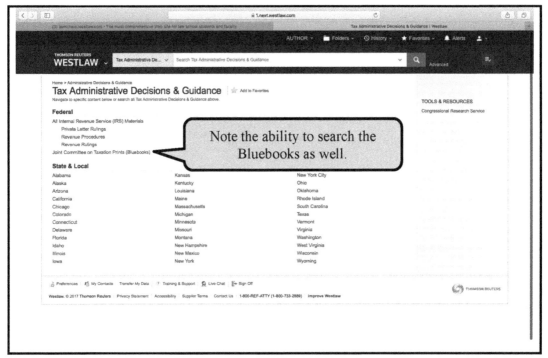

Source: Westlaw; used with the permission of Thomson Reuters.

F. ADDITIONAL SECONDARY SOURCES

Tax attorneys have a number of research resources at their disposal, including several outside traditional and well-known legal research databases. CLE materials, scholarly articles, treatises, and the like may offer the clear and direct explanation a practitioner or government attorney needs. One high-quality resource of long-standing value to tax practitioners is the Bloomberg BNA Tax Management Portfolio series. Drafted by leading experts, the portfolios present a detailed and comprehensive analysis of various areas of tax law. A number of law libraries subscribe to the series and will devote a section of the library to the portfolio texts. The portfolios are also available by online subscription, and for those operating in a sophisticated and demanding legal environment, access to the series can substantially enhance research efficiency and quality. Exhibits A2.11 and A2.12 (respectively) depict the beginning of the list of income tax portfolios and an excerpt of

EXHIBIT A2.11 Page 1 of List of Bloomberg BNA Tax Portfolios (U.S. Income Tax) (screen shot shown taken as of 05/31/2017) (Reprinted with permission from Bloomberg BNA Tax and Accounting Center, "List of U.S. Income Portfolios, Classification Guide, Numerical Finding List." Copyright 2017 by The Bureau of National Affairs, Inc. (800-372-1033), http://www.bna.com.)

EXHIBIT A2.12 Excerpt from Detailed Analysis in Bloomberg BNA Tax Portfolio (U.S. Income Tax) on Annuities, Life Insurance, and Long-Term Care Insurance Products (screen shot shown taken as of 08/20/2017) (Reprinted with permission from Annuities, Life Insurance, and Long-Term Care Insurance Products, Tax Management Portfolio No. 546-1st, Chapter 2, Section D ("Exclusion Ratio"), Bloomberg BNA Tax and Accounting Center. Copyright 2017 by The Bureau of National Affairs, Inc. (800-372-1033), http://www.bna.com.)

the detailed analysis from the portfolio on annuities, life insurance, and long-term care insurance products.

Tax professionals have also long relied on the rich universe of tax resources presented by Commerce Clearing House ("CCH"), a Wolters Kluwer business. Tax attorneys, in particular, regularly consult CCH's Standard Federal Tax Reporter, which is organized by Code section and contains statutory and regulatory language as well as legislative history, explanations, and useful annotations. The Standard Federal Tax Reporter is available electronically in the CCH IntelliConnect database. *See, e.g.*, Exhibit A2.13 (depicting a page from the coverage of § 163).

EXHIBIT A2.13 **Page from Standard Federal Tax Reporter (2017) Coverage of § 163 (within CCH IntelliConnect database)**

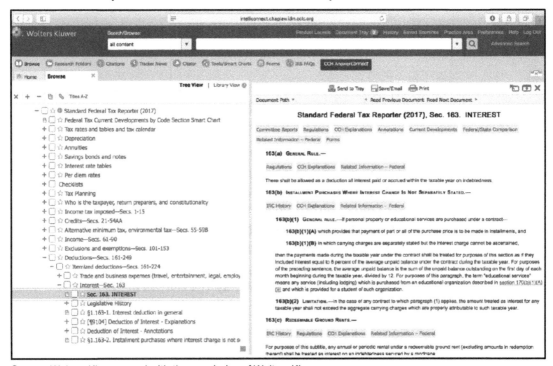

Source: Wolters Kluwer; used with the permission of Wolters Kluwer.

G. MAINTAINING AN EXPERIENCE PROFILE AND KEEPING GOOD FILES

Throughout the course of an attorney's career, he or she will likely address a wide range of issues and undertake responsibility for a host transactional and litigation matters. After years of practice, it is easy to be left with the sense that one has touched a thousand things but only long enough to complete the matter at hand before moving on to the next. A backward glance can leave one wondering what ground has been covered from a substantive history perspective. For any number of reasons, then, it's important that an attorney maintain and regularly update an experience profile. Think of this document as a resume supplement that can provide a potential employer or client a more concrete sense of *exactly* what an attorney has done over the years as he or she practiced law. The profiles of junior attorneys will likely reflect substantial research work (e.g., "Researched whether the stock of a specific foreign corporation would be treated as 'voting stock' for federal income tax purposes"), but over the years, more substantial tasks and accomplishments will appear (e.g., "Drafted protest on worker classification issue and thereby achieved a 100% IRS concession" and "Conducted research for and drafted private letter ruling request which ultimately resulted in client's desired outcome with respect to corporate reorganization"). *Note that even as you prepare the experience profile, you must speak in generic terms to avoid breaching client confidentiality.*

Even with research completed and deals closed, the attorney's work is not yet done. Truly efficient practice requires the keeping of good records and files. Issues tend to resurface, and both you and your colleagues may find yourselves in earnest need of old memos or transaction documents. Today, most attorneys rely on some form of electronic storage either locally or in the ever-ubiquitous "cloud," but even if one opts for electronic work product preservation, remember that relying on the storage of one electronic copy in one location is never a good idea. Systems crash, and files get corrupted. Wholly aside from such unfortunate incidents, attorneys cannot ignore the modern-day realities of persistent hacking and aggressive cyberattacks. One method of insuring against the vagaries of electronic storage is to embrace the old-fashioned habit of printing and filing documents. Preserve your best work both within and outside the electronic medium. More broadly, place yourself amongst the wisest and most successful attorneys by establishing and maintaining your own best professional practices.

APPENDIX 3

Additional Budget Options for Reducing the Deficit

EXHIBIT A3.1   **Excerpt from Congressional Budget Office, Options for Reducing the Deficit: 2017–2026 (Option 39: Value-Added Tax)**

Revenues—Option 39

Impose a 5 Percent Value-Added Tax

Billions of Dollars	2017	2018	2019	2020	2021	2022	2023	2024	2025	2026	Total 2017–2021	Total 2017–2026
Change in Revenues												
Broad base	0	180	270	280	290	300	320	330	340	350	1,030	2,670
Narrow base	0	110	180	190	190	200	210	220	230	240	670	1,770

Source: Staff of the Joint Committee on Taxation.

This option would take effect in January 2018.

A value-added tax (VAT) is a type of consumption tax that is levied on the incremental increase in value of a good or service. The tax is collected at each stage of the production process and passed on until the full tax is paid by the final consumer. Although the United States does not have a broad, consumption-based tax, federal excise taxes are imposed on the purchase of several goods (gasoline, alcohol, and cigarettes, for example). In addition, most states impose sales taxes, which, unlike a VAT, are levied on the total value of goods and services purchased.

More than 140 countries—including all members of the Organisation for Economic Co-operation and Development (OECD), except for the United States—have adopted VATs. The tax bases and rate structures of VATs differ greatly among countries. Most European countries have implemented VATs that have a narrow tax base, with certain categories of goods and services—such as food, education, and health care—excluded from the tax base. In Australia and New Zealand, the VAT has a much broader tax base, with exclusions generally limited only to those goods and services for which it is difficult to determine a value. In 2016, the average national VAT rate for OECD countries was 19.2 percent, ranging from 5 percent in Canada to 27 percent in Hungary. All OECD countries that impose a VAT also collect revenues from taxes on individual and corporate income.

This option includes two different approaches that would impose a 5 percent VAT. Each of the approaches would become effective on January 1, 2018—a year later than most of the revenue options presented in this volume—to provide the Internal Revenue Service time to set up and administer the tax.

■ The first approach would apply the VAT to a broad base that would include most goods and services.

Certain goods and services would be excluded from the base, because their value is difficult to measure. Those include financial services without explicit fees, existing housing services, primary and secondary education, and other services provided by government agencies and nonprofit organizations for little or no fee. (Existing housing services encompass the monetary rents paid by tenants and rents imputed to owners who reside in their own homes. Although existing housing services would be excluded under this alternative, the broad base would include all future consumption of housing services by taxing the purchase of new residential housing.) In addition, government-reimbursed expenditures for health care—primarily costs paid by Medicare and Medicaid—would also be excluded from the tax base under this approach. With those exclusions taken into account, the tax base would encompass approximately 65 percent of household consumption in 2018. This approach would increase revenues by $2.7 trillion over the 2018–2026 period, the staff of the Joint Committee on Taxation (JCT) estimates. (Because a VAT, like excise taxes, reduces the tax base of income and payroll taxes, implementing such a tax would lead to reductions in revenues from those sources. The estimates shown here reflect those reductions.)

■ Under the second approach, the VAT would apply to a narrower base. In addition to those items excluded under the broad base, the narrow base would exclude certain goods and services that are considered necessary for subsistence or that provide broad social benefits. Specifically, purchases of new residential housing, food purchased for home consumption, health care, and postsecondary education would be excluded from the tax base. With those exclusions taken into account,

EXHIBIT A3.1 **Excerpt from Congressional Budget Office, Options for Reducing the Deficit: 2017–2026 (Option 39: Value-Added Tax)** (*cont'd*)

the tax base would include about 46 percent of household consumption in 2018. This approach would increase revenues by $1.8 trillion over the 2018–2026 period, according to JCT's estimates.

Both approaches would employ the "credit-invoice method," which is the most common method used by other countries to administer a VAT. That method would tax the total value of a business's sales of a particular product or service, and the business would claim a credit for the taxes paid on the purchased inputs—such as materials and equipment—it used to make the product or provide the service. With a credit-invoice method, goods and services could be either "zero-rated" or "exempt" from the VAT; in both cases, the VAT would not apply to purchased items. If the purchased item was zero-rated, however, the seller would be able to claim a credit for the VAT that had been paid on the production inputs. In contrast, if the purchased item was exempted, the seller would not be able to claim a credit for the VAT paid on the production inputs.

Under both variants, primary and secondary education and other noncommercial services provided by government or nonprofit organizations for little or no fee would be zero-rated, and financial services and existing housing services would be exempt from the VAT. In addition, under the option with the narrow base, food purchased for home consumption, new housing services, health care, and postsecondary education would be zero-rated.

One argument in favor of the option is that it would raise revenues without discouraging saving and investment by taxpayers. In any given period, income can be either consumed or saved. Through exclusions, deductions, and credits, the individual tax system provides incentives that encourage saving, but those types of preferences do not apply to all methods of saving and increase the complexity of the tax system. In contrast to a tax levied on income, a VAT applies only to the amount of income consumed and therefore would not discourage private saving and investment in the economy.

A drawback of the option is that it would require the federal government to establish a new system to monitor compliance and collect the tax. As with any new tax, a VAT would impose additional administrative costs on the federal government and additional compliance costs on businesses. A study conducted by the Government Accountability Office in 2008 showed that all of the

countries evaluated in the study—Australia, Canada, France, New Zealand, and the United Kingdom—devoted significant resources to addressing and enforcing compliance.[1] Because such compliance costs are typically more burdensome for smaller businesses, many countries exempt some small businesses from the VAT.

Another argument against implementing a VAT is that, as specified under both alternatives in this option, it would probably be regressive—that is, it would be more burdensome for individuals and families with fewer economic resources than it would be for individuals and families with more economic resources. The regressivity of a VAT, however, depends significantly on how its effects are measured. Furthermore, there are ways to design a VAT—or implement complementary policies—that could ameliorate distributional concerns.

If the burden of a VAT was measured as a share of annual income, the tax would be regressive, primarily because lower-income families generally consume a greater share of their income than higher-income families do. If, however, the burden of a VAT was measured over a much longer period, the tax would appear to be less regressive than if the burden was measured in a single year. For example, the burden of a VAT relative to a measure of lifetime income—which would account for both life-cycle income patterns and temporary fluctuations in annual income—would be less regressive than the burden of a VAT relative to a measure of annual income that does not account for those patterns and anomalies. Furthermore, in the initial year, the distributional effects of a VAT would depend on its impact on consumer prices. Adopting a VAT would probably cause an initial jump in the consumer price index, which would be based on prices that would reflect the new consumption tax. That initial price increase would be equivalent to a onetime implicit tax on existing wealth because of the immediate reduction in purchasing power. To the extent that wealth and annual income are positively correlated, the distributional effects of a VAT in the initial year—if measured relative to annual income—would be less regressive than in subsequent years because of the onetime increase in price levels.

---

1. See Government Accountability Office, *Value-Added Taxes: Lessons Learned From Other Countries on Compliance Risks, Administrative Costs, Compliance Burden, and Transition*, GAO-08-566 (April 2008), www.gao.gov/products/GAO-08-566.

EXHIBIT A3.1 **Excerpt from Congressional Budget Office, Options for Reducing the Deficit: 2017–2026 (Option 39: Value-Added Tax) (*cont'd*)**

One way to make a VAT less regressive would be to exclude from the tax base certain basic goods and services—just as the narrow-base alternative of this option does. Applying a VAT to that narrower tax base would be less regressive because low-income individuals and families spend a relatively larger share of their budgets on those basic goods and services than higher-income individuals and families do. (Alternatively, lower rates could be applied to such items.) Those preferences, however, generally would make the VAT more complex and would reduce revenues from the new tax. In addition, a VAT with a narrow base would distort economic decisions to a greater degree than would a VAT with a broader base. An alternative approach to offset the regressive impact of a VAT would be to increase or create additional exemptions or refundable credits under the federal income tax for low-income individuals and families. That approach, however, would add to the complexity of the individual income tax and reduce individual income tax revenues, offsetting some of the revenue gains from a VAT.

There are alternative forms of a broad-based consumption that would potentially be easier to implement or be less regressive. A national retail sales tax, for example, would initially be easier to implement than a VAT. However, it would require the federal government to coordinate tax collection and administration with state and local governments. In addition, there are more incentives to underreport national retail sales taxes because they are collected only when the final user of the product makes a purchase, whereas a VAT is collected throughout the entire production chain. A cash-flow tax would be an alternative to a VAT that would be less regressive. A cash-flow tax applies to the difference between a business's cash receipts and cash payments, which would be equivalent to a consumption tax on income sources other than wages and salaries. Because consumption from wages and salaries would not be included in the tax base, a cash-flow tax would generally have a narrower base than a VAT and would be substantially less regressive than a VAT—and potentially progressive depending on how it was measured. Implementing a cash-flow tax would probably require modifications to the current corporate income tax system but would more easily incorporate the value of financial services in the tax base than a VAT.

RELATED CBO PUBLICATIONS: *Comparing Income and Consumption Tax Bases* (July 1997), www.cbo.gov/publication/10599; *The Economic Effects of Comprehensive Tax Reform* (July 1997), www.cbo.gov/publication/10355; testimony of Robert D. Reischauer, Director, before the Senate Committee on Energy and Natural Resources, *Effects of Energy Taxes and Value-Added Taxes (VAT)* (February 24, 1993), www.cbo.gov/publication/20834; *Distributional Effects of Substituting a Flat-Rate Income Tax and a Value-Added Tax for Current Federal Income, Payroll, and Excise Taxes* (April 1992), www.cbo.gov/publication/20766; *Effects of Adopting a Value-Added Tax* (February 1992), www.cbo.gov/publication/20769

EXHIBIT A3.2 **Excerpt from Congressional Budget Office, Options for Reducing the Deficit: 2017–2026 (Option 40: Fee on Large Financial Institutions)**

Revenues—Option 40

Impose a Fee on Large Financial Institutions

Billions of Dollars	2017	2018	2019	2020	2021	2022	2023	2024	2025	2026	Total	
											2017–2021	2017–2026
Change in Revenues	5.2	10.4	10.4	10.4	10.4	10.3	10.4	10.4	10.3	10.3	46.7	98.3

Sources: Staff of the Joint Committee on Taxation; Congressional Budget Office.

This option would take effect in January 2017.

During the financial crisis that occurred between 2007 and 2009, the federal government provided substantial assistance to major financial institutions, effectively protecting many uninsured creditors from losses. Although most of that assistance was ultimately recovered, it could have resulted in great cost to taxpayers. That assistance reinforced investors' perceptions that large financial firms are "too big to fail"—in other words, so important to the financial system and the broader economy that the firms' creditors are likely to be protected by the government in the event of large losses.

In the wake of that crisis, legislators and regulators adopted a number of measures designed to prevent the failure of large, systemically important financial institutions and to resolve any future failures without putting taxpayers at risk. One of those measures provided the Federal Deposit Insurance Corporation (FDIC) with orderly liquidation authority. That authority is intended to allow the FDIC to quickly and efficiently settle the obligations of such institutions, which can include companies that control one or more banks (also known as bank holding companies) or firms that predominantly engage in lending, insurance, securities trading, or other financial activities. In the event that a large financial institution fails, the FDIC will be appointed to liquidate the company's assets in an orderly manner and thus maintain critical operations of the failed institution in an effort to avoid consequences throughout the financial system.

Despite the new safeguards, if one or more large financial institutions were to fail, particularly during a period of broader economic distress, the FDIC might need to borrow funds from the Treasury to implement its orderly liquidation authority. The law mandates that those funds be repaid either through recoveries from the failed firm or through a future assessment on the surviving firms. As a result, individuals and businesses dealing with those firms could be affected by the costs of the assistance provided

to the financial system. For example, if a number of large firms failed and substantial cash infusions were needed to resolve those failures, the assessment required to repay the Treasury would have to be set at a very high amount. Under some circumstances, the surviving firms might not be able to pay that assessment without making significant changes to their operations or activities. Those changes could result in higher costs to borrowers and reduced access to credit at a time when the economy might be under significant stress.

Under this option, an annual fee would be imposed beginning in 2017 on financial institutions subject to the orderly liquidation authority—that is, bank holding companies (including foreign banks operating in the United States) with $50 billion or more in total assets and nonbank financial companies designated by the Financial Stability Oversight Council for enhanced supervision by the Board of Governors of the Federal Reserve. The annual fee would be 0.15 percent of firms' covered liabilities, defined primarily as total liabilities less deposits insured by the FDIC. Covered liabilities also include certain types of noncore capital and exclude certain reserves required for insurance policies. The sums collected would be deposited in an interest-bearing fund that would be available for the FDIC's use when exercising its orderly liquidation authority. The outlays necessary to carry out the FDIC's orderly liquidation authority are estimated to be the same under this option as under current law. If implemented on January 1, 2017, such a fee would generate revenues totaling $103 billion from 2017 through 2026, the staff of the Joint Committee on Taxation estimates. (Such a fee would reduce the tax base of income and payroll taxes, leading to reductions in income and payroll tax revenues. The estimates shown here reflect those reductions.)

In its current-law baseline projections for the 2017–2026 period, the Congressional Budget Office accounted for

EXHIBIT A3.2   **Excerpt from Congressional Budget Office, Options for Reducing the Deficit: 2017–2026 (Option 40: Fee on Large Financial Institutions) (*cont'd*)**

the probability that the orderly liquidation authority would have to be used and that an assessment would have to be levied on surviving firms to cover some of the government's costs. Net proceeds from such assessments are projected to total roughly $5 billion over the next decade. Under the option, CBO expects that the receipts from the fee would provide a significant source of funds for the FDIC to carry out its orderly liquidation authority and thus reduce the likelihood that an assessment would be needed during the coming decade. Therefore, to determine the net effect on revenues, CBO subtracted $5 billion in projected assessments under current law from the amount the new fee is projected to generate ($103 billion), yielding net additional revenues of $98 billion from 2017 through 2026.

At 0.15 percent, the fee would probably not be so high as to cause financial institutions to significantly change their financial structure or activities. The fee could nevertheless affect institutions' tendency to take various business risks, but the net direction of that effect is uncertain; in some ways, it would encourage greater risk-taking, and in other ways, less risk-taking. One approach might be to vary the amount of the fee so that it reflected the risk posed by each institution, but it might be difficult to assess that risk precisely.

The main advantage of this option is that it would help defray the economic costs of providing a financial safety net by generating revenues when the economy is not in a financial crisis, rather than in the immediate aftermath of one. Another advantage of the option is that it would provide an incentive for banks to keep assets below the $50 billion threshold, diminishing the risk of spillover effects to the broader economy from a future failure of a particularly large institution (although at the expense of potential economies of scale). Alternatively, if larger financial institutions reduced their dependence on liabilities subject to the fee and increased their reliance on equity, their vulnerability to future losses would be reduced. The fee also would improve the relative competitive position of small and medium-sized banks by charging the largest institutions for the greater government protection they receive.

The option would also have two main disadvantages. Unless the fee was risk-based, stronger financial institutions that posed less systemic risk—and consequently paid lower interest rates on their debt as a result of their lower risk of default—would face a proportionally greater increase in funding costs than would weaker financial institutions. In addition, the fee could reduce the profitability of larger institutions, which might create an incentive for them to take greater risks in pursuit of higher returns to offset their higher costs.

RELATED OPTION: Revenues, Option 41

RELATED CBO PUBLICATIONS: *The Budgetary Impact and Subsidy Costs of the Federal Reserve's Actions During the Financial Crisis* (May 2010), www.cbo.gov/publication/21491; letter to the Honorable Charles E. Grassley providing information on the President's proposal for a financial crisis responsibility fee (March 4, 2010), www.cbo.gov/publication/21020

EXHIBIT A3.3 **Excerpt from Congressional Budget Office, Options for Reducing the Deficit: 2017–2026 (Option 41: Tax on Financial Transactions)**

Revenues—Option 41

Impose a Tax on Financial Transactions

Billions of Dollars	2017	2018	2019	2020	2021	2022	2023	2024	2025	2026	Total 2017–2021	Total 2017–2026
Change in Revenues	-53.6	13.3	62.9	85.0	92.6	95.9	98.7	101.3	104.1	106.9	200.3	707.3

Source: Staff of the Joint Committee on Taxation.

This option would take effect in January 2018.

The United States is home to large financial markets, with hundreds of billions of dollars in stocks and bonds—collectively referred to as securities—traded on a typical business day. The total dollar value, or market capitalization, of U.S. stocks was roughly $23 trillion in March 2016, and about $265 billion in shares is traded on a typical day. The value of outstanding bond market debt was about $40 trillion at the end of 2015, and average trading volume in debt, concentrated mostly in Treasury securities, amounts to over $700 billion on a typical day. In addition, large volumes of derivatives—contracts that derive their value from another security or commodity and include options, forwards, futures, and swaps—are traded on U.S. financial markets every business day. None of those transactions are taxed in the United States, although most taxpayers who sell securities for more than they paid for them owe tax on their gains.

This option would impose a tax on the purchase of most securities and on transactions involving derivatives. For purchases of stocks, bonds, and other debt obligations, the tax generally would be 0.10 percent of the value of the security. For purchases of derivatives contracts, the tax would be 0.10 percent of all payments actually made under the terms of the contract, including the price paid when the contract was written, any periodic payments, and any amount to be paid when the contract expires. Trading costs for institutional investors tend to be very low—in many cases less than 0.10 percent of the value of the securities traded—so this option would generate a notable increase in trading costs for those investors.

The tax would not apply to the initial issuance of stock or debt securities, transactions in debt obligations with fixed maturities of no more than 100 days, or currency transactions (although transactions involving currency derivatives would be taxed). The tax would be imposed on transactions that occurred within the United States and on transactions that took place outside of the country, as

long as any party to an offshore transaction was a U.S. taxpayer (whether a corporation, partnership, citizen, or resident). The tax would apply to transactions occurring after December 31, 2017. This option would be effective a year later than nearly all of the other revenue options analyzed in this report to provide the government and firms sufficient time to develop and implement the new reporting systems that would be necessary to accurately collect the tax.

The tax would increase revenues by $707 billion from 2017 through 2026, according to estimates by the staff of the Joint Committee on Taxation (JCT). The option would result in a revenue loss in 2017 because the transaction tax would lower the value of financial assets and thus lower capital gains. JCT assumes that, until 2020, when all reporting systems are expected to be in place, financial transactions will be underreported. Revenues would be lower if implementation of the option was phased in because of delays in developing the new reporting systems. (Because a financial transaction tax would reduce the tax base of income and payroll taxes, it would lead to reductions in revenues from those sources. The estimates shown here reflect those reductions.) The additional revenues generated by the option would depend significantly on the extent to which transactions subject to the tax fell in response to the policy.

One argument in favor of a tax on financial transactions is that it would significantly reduce the amount of short-term speculation and computer-assisted high-frequency trading that currently takes place and direct the resources dedicated to those activities to more productive uses. Speculation can destabilize markets and lead to disruptive events, such as the October 1987 stock market crash and the more recent "flash crash" that occurred when the stock market temporarily plunged on May 6, 2010. Although neither of those events had significant effects

EXHIBIT A3.3   **Excerpt from Congressional Budget Office, Options for Reducing the Deficit: 2017–2026 (Option 41: Tax on Financial Transactions) (*cont'd*)**

on the general economy, the potential exists for negative spillovers from future events.

A disadvantage of the option is that the tax would discourage all short-term trading, not just speculation—including some transactions by well-informed traders and transactions that stabilize markets. Empirical evidence suggests that, on balance, a transaction tax could make asset prices less stable: In particular, a number of studies have concluded that higher transaction costs lead to more, rather than less, volatility in prices. (However, much of that evidence is from studies conducted before the rise of high-frequency trading programs, which now account for a significant share of trading in the stock market.)

The tax could also have a number of negative effects on the economy stemming from its effects on asset prices and the frequency of trading. Traders and investors would seek to recoup the cost of trading by raising the return they require on financial assets, thereby lowering the value of those assets. However, because the tax would be small relative to the returns that investors with long-term horizons could earn, the effect on asset prices would be partly mitigated when traders and investors reduced the frequency of their trading, which would have a trade-off in terms of lowering liquidity and reducing the amount of information reflected in prices. Consequently, investment could decline (leaving aside the positive effects of higher tax revenues lowering federal borrowing and thus increasing the funds available for investment) because of the following: the increase in the cost of issuing debt and equity securities that would be subject to the tax and the potential negative effects on derivatives trading that could make it more difficult to efficiently distribute risk in the economy. The cost to the Treasury of issuing federal debt would increase (again, leaving aside the effects of deficit reduction) because of the increase in trading costs and the reduction in liquidity. Household wealth would decline with the reduction in asset prices, which would lower consumption.

In addition, traders would have an incentive to reduce the tax they must pay either by developing alternative instruments not subject to the tax or by moving their trading out of the country (although offshore trades by U.S. taxpayers would be taxed). Such effects would be mitigated if other countries enacted financial transaction taxes; currently, many members of the European Union are considering implementing such a tax.

RELATED OPTIONS: Revenues, Options 3, 40

RELATED CBO PUBLICATION: Letter to the Honorable Orrin G. Hatch responding to questions about the effects of a tax on financial transactions that would be imposed by the Wall Street Trading and Speculators Tax Act, H.R. 3313 or S. 1787 (December 12, 2011), www.cbo.gov/publication/42690

EXHIBIT A3.4 **Excerpt from Congressional Budget Office, Options for Reducing the Deficit: 2017–2026 (Option 42: Tax on Emissions of Greenhouse Gases)**

Revenues—Option 42

Impose a Tax on Emissions of Greenhouse Gases

											Total	
Billions of Dollars	**2017**	**2018**	**2019**	**2020**	**2021**	**2022**	**2023**	**2024**	**2025**	**2026**	**2017–2021**	**2017–2026**
Change in Revenues	57.4	90.3	93.6	96.5	98.6	101.3	104.6	108.1	111.5	115.2	436.5	977.2

Sources: Staff of the Joint Committee on Taxation; Congressional Budget Office.

This option would take effect in January 2017.

Many estimates suggest that the effect of climate change on the nation's economic output, and hence on federal tax revenues, will probably be small over the next 30 years and larger, but still modest, in later years.[1] Nonetheless, significant uncertainty surrounds those estimates. The accumulation of greenhouse gases (GHG) in the atmosphere—particularly carbon dioxide (CO_2), which is released when fossil fuels (such as coal, oil, and natural gas) are burned, and as a result of deforestation—could generate damaging and costly changes in the climate around the world. Although the consequences of those changes are highly uncertain and would probably vary widely across the United States and the rest of the world, many scientists think there is at least some risk that large changes in global temperatures will trigger catastrophic damage. Among the less uncertain effects of climate change on humans, some would be positive, such as fewer deaths from cold weather and improvements in agricultural productivity in certain areas; however, others would be negative, such as the loss of property from storm surges as sea levels rise and declines in the availability of fresh water in areas dependent on snowmelt. Many scientists agree that reducing global emissions of greenhouse gases would decrease the extent of climate change and the expected costs and risks associated with it. The federal government regulates some of those emissions but does not directly tax them.

This option would place a tax of $25 per metric ton on most emissions of greenhouse gases in the United States—specifically, on most energy-related emissions of CO_2 (for example, from electricity generation, manufacturing, and transportation) and some other GHG emissions from large manufacturing facilities. Emissions would be measured in CO_2 equivalents (CO_2e), which

reflect the amount of carbon dioxide estimated to cause an equivalent amount of warming. The tax would increase at an annual real (inflation-adjusted) rate of 2 percent. During the first decade the tax was in effect, the Congressional Budget Office estimates, cumulative emissions from sources subject to the tax would fall by roughly 9 percent.

According to estimates by the staff of the Joint Committee on Taxation and CBO, federal revenues would increase by $977 billion between 2017 and 2026. (The tax would increase businesses' costs, which would reduce the tax bases for income and payroll taxes. The estimates shown here reflect the resulting reduction in revenues from those sources.)

The size of the tax used for these estimates was chosen for illustrative purposes, and policymakers who wanted to pursue this approach might prefer a smaller tax or a larger one. The appropriate size of a tax on GHG emissions, if one was adopted, would depend on the value of limiting emissions and their associated costs, the way in which the additional revenues were used, the effect on emissions overseas, and the additional benefits and costs that resulted from the tax.

One argument in support of the option is that it would reduce emissions of greenhouse gases at the lowest possible cost per ton of emissions because each ton would be subject to the same tax. That uniform treatment would increase the cost of producing and consuming goods and services in proportion to the amount of greenhouse gases emitted as a result of that production and consumption. Those higher production costs, and corresponding increases in prices for final goods and services, would create incentives for firms, households, governments, and other entities throughout the U.S. economy to undertake reductions of greenhouse gases that cost up to $25 per metric ton of CO_2e to achieve. This approach would

1. Congressional Budget Office, *Potential Impacts of Climate Change in the United States* (May 2009), www.cbo.gov/publication/41180.

CBO

EXHIBIT A3.4   **Excerpt from Congressional Budget Office, Options for Reducing the Deficit: 2017–2026 (Option 42: Tax on Emissions of Greenhouse Gases) (*cont'd*)**

minimize the cost of achieving a given level of emissions because the tax would motivate reductions that cost less than $25 per ton to achieve, but not those that would cost more than $25 per ton. An alternative approach to reducing GHG emissions that is currently being pursued by the federal government is to issue regulations based on various provisions of the Clean Air Act (CAA). However, standards issued under the CAA (for example, specifying an emissions rate for a given plant or an energy-efficiency standard for a given product) would offer less flexibility than a tax and, therefore, would achieve any given amount of emission reductions at a higher cost to the economy than a uniform tax that was applied to all sectors of the economy.

Another argument in favor of a GHG tax is that such a program could generate "co-benefits." Co-benefits would occur when measures taken to reduce GHG emissions—such as generating electricity from natural gas rather than from coal—also reduced other pollutants not explicitly limited by the cap, thereby reducing the harmful effects estimated to be associated with those emissions. However, measures taken to decrease CO_2 emissions could also result in additional costs depending on how the emissions were reduced. For example, increased use of nuclear power could exacerbate potential problems created by the lack of adequate long-term storage capacity for nuclear waste.

An argument against a tax on GHG emissions is that curtailing U.S. emissions would burden the economy by raising the cost of producing emission-intensive goods and services while yielding benefits for U.S. residents of an uncertain magnitude. For example, most of the benefits of limiting emissions and any associated reductions in climate change might occur outside of the United States, particularly in developing countries that are at greater risk from changes in weather patterns and an increase in sea

levels. Another argument against this option is that reductions in domestic emissions could be partially offset by increases in emissions overseas if carbon-intensive industries relocated to countries that did not impose restrictions on emissions or if U.S. reductions in energy consumption led to decreases in fuel prices outside of the United States. More generally, averting the risk of future damage caused by emissions would depend on collective global efforts to cut emissions. Most analysts agree that if other countries with high levels of emissions do not cut those pollutants substantially, reductions in emissions in this country would produce only small changes in the climate (although such reductions would still diminish the probability of catastrophic damage).

An alternative approach for reducing emissions of greenhouse gases would be to establish a cap-and-trade program that set caps on such emissions in the United States. Under such a program, allowances that conveyed the right to emit 1 metric ton of CO_2e apiece would be sold at open auction, and the cap would probably be lowered over time. If the caps were set to achieve the same cut in emissions that was anticipated from the tax, then the program would be expected to raise roughly the same amount of revenues between 2017 and 2026 as the tax analyzed here. Both a tax on GHG emissions and a cap-and-trade program for those emissions would represent market-based approaches to cutting emissions and would achieve any desired amount of emission reduction at a lower cost than the regulatory approach described above. In contrast with a tax, a cap-and-trade program would provide certainty about the quantity of emissions from sources that are subject to the cap (because it would directly limit those emissions), but it would not provide certainty about the costs that firms and households would face for the greenhouse gases that they continued to emit.

RELATED CBO PUBLICATIONS: *Effects of a Carbon Tax on the Economy and the Environment* (May 2013), www.cbo.gov/publication/44223; *How Policies to Reduce Greenhouse Gas Emissions Could Affect Employment* (May 2010), www.cbo.gov/publication/41257; *The Costs of Reducing Greenhouse-Gas Emissions* (November 2009), www.cbo.gov/publication/20933; Testimony of Douglas W. Elmendorf, Director, before the Senate Committee on Energy and Natural Resources, *The Economic Effects of Legislation to Reduce Greenhouse-Gas Emissions* (October 14, 2009), www.cbo.gov/publication/41254; *Potential Impacts of Climate Change in the United States* (May 2009), www.cbo.gov/publication/41180

Glossary

Accelerated cost recovery A cost recovery method in which initial cost recovery amounts in initial taxable years are higher relative to those taken in subsequent taxable years.

Accelerated depreciation *See* Accelerated cost recovery.

Accrual method of accounting A method of accounting under which taxpayers generally include amounts in income when the right to income has been established/earned and deduct expenses when the obligations have been incurred.

Accumulation phase The time during which premiums paid with respect to an annuity, life insurance, or similar contract generate investment returns (prior to the commencement of payments under the contract).

Action on Decision IRS pronouncements made in response to tax litigation developments (i.e., the judicial disposition of an issue that the IRS will not appeal in the instant case).

Adjusted basis In general, the cost basis of an asset after adjustment to take into account specific asset-related events.

Administrative Summons A formal request from the IRS (during an audit) for the production of documents or for testimony (and which is subject to judicial enforcement).

Agreed A taxpayer's response to a Revenue Agent's Report in which the taxpayer accepts all proposed adjustments.

Amount realized In general, the sum or money received plus the fair market value of property (other than money received) on the sale or other disposition of property. *See generally* § 1001(b).

Annual Percentage Rate (APR) In the mortgage loan context, an interest rate that factors in all costs and fees associated with the loan transaction.

Annuitant The individual designated to receive payments under an annuity contract.

ARM Adjustable rate mortgage.

Bartering transaction A transaction in which one party provides property or services and receives, in exchange, property or services.

Basis In general, the cost of property. *See generally* § 1012.

Boot A general reference to property received by a taxpayer that does not qualify for non-recognition upon its receipt by the taxpayer.

Built-in gain   The amount by which the fair market value of a taxpayer's property exceeds its basis or its "adjusted basis."

Capital expenditure   An item the cost of which has been capitalized.

Capitalize   To record the cost of an asset in a taxpayer's financial books and records and forego immediate deduction with respect to it for federal income tax purposes.

Carryback   Use of a net operating loss from one taxable year to offset taxable income from a prior taxable year (relative to the loss year).

Carryover   Use of a net operating loss from one taxable year to offset taxable income of a future taxable year (relative to the loss year).

Cash disbursements and receipts method of accounting   A method of accounting under which taxpayers generally report income when received and deduct items upon actual payment.

Closing agreement   An agreement between the taxpayer and the IRS concerning the amount ultimately due (or to be refunded) with respect to a given taxable year.

Closing Disclosure   In the mortgage loan context, a document setting forth the final loan details and associated transaction facts.

Closing escrow   In the mortgage loan context, the event marking the completion of all tasks necessary to effect the legal transfer of the home from the seller to the buyer.

Commissioner of Internal Revenue (Commissioner)   Leader of the Internal Revenue Service.

Conference Committee   A joint congressional committee comprised of members from both chambers who work together to iron out differences in legislation as originally passed by the House and the Senate.

Conference Committee Report   A report generated by the Conference Committee that discusses specific tax legislation.

Constructive receipt   Receipt of income in effect, even if the income has not been reduced to the taxpayer's actual possession due to failure to complete some ministerial act.

Correspondence audits   Taxpayer audits occurring between the taxpayer and the IRS wholly by way of correspondence (e.g., mail, telephone conversations, etc.).

Cost recovery   *See* Depreciation deductions.

Deferred compensation   Compensation provided for during a specific period of employee service but made available to (or accessed by) the employee at a later date.

Deficiency   In general, the difference between the amount of tax actually due from a taxpayer over the amount shown on his tax return (assuming a return was actually filed).

Department of the Treasury   A department within the executive branch of the federal government charged with formulating tax policy and administering the tax laws.

Depreciation deductions   Amounts allowed as deductions to account for exhaustion, wear, and tear with respect to a business asset.

Dividend   A distribution by a corporation of money or property to its shareholders (with respect to its stock) of current or accumulated earnings and profits.

Earnest money   In the mortgage loan context, a portion of the purchase price provided by the buyer to take the property off the market for the purpose of ultimately purchasing the property.

Economic benefit theory   Theory mandating the inclusion of amounts in income to the extent that such amounts have been (1) paid over to a third party on the taxpayer's behalf or (2) set aside for the taxpayer irrevocably and in such a manner that the amounts are no longer within the reach of the payor's creditors.

Equity interest   An ownership interest in an entity.

Escrow agent   In the mortgage loan context, a trusted third party who facilitates execution of the transaction by performing various services (including the receipt, holding, and disbursement of money).

Ex-dividend date   The first day on which purchasers of the stock will *not* receive the subject dividend.

Facial applicability   Laws that, based on a straightforward reading of their plain language, appear to apply.

Federal budget year   The federal government's fiscal year, which starts on October 1 and ends on September 30 of the following calendar year.

FICO score   A number generated by the Fair Isaac Corporation using information in an individual's credit report and based on a host of factors, including an individual's history of managing personal debt.

Field audits   In general, audits that occur at a taxpayer's place of business.

Filing status   An individual taxpayer's familial status for federal income tax purposes (e.g., "single," "head of household," or "married filing jointly").

Flat tax   An alternative approach to income taxation in which tax would be imposed at a single rate on gross income or, perhaps, gross income above a certain exemption amount.

Fully depreciated   A term describing an asset the cost of which has been recovered in full through depreciation deductions.

Gain realized   In general, the excess of amount realized over basis (or adjusted basis) on the sale or other disposition of property. *See generally* § 1001(a).

Gain recognized   The amount of gain realized by a taxpayer that is included on the taxpayer's federal income tax return.

Goodwill   A general reference to a business's good name or reputation.

Grandfathered   This term refers to a status in which the taxpayer may continue to apply the old rules to some extent. Note that Congress may allow grandfathering, albeit with a host of carefully tailored limitations and restrictions.

Gross tax gap   The difference between aggregate taxes owed by all taxpayers and the amounts paid voluntarily and on time.

Holding period   In general, a reference to the time a taxpayer has held an asset prior to its sale, exchange, or other disposition.

Horizontal equity   The notion that a tax system achieves fairness if taxpayers who are similarly situated in an economic sense shoulder the same tax burden.

House Ways and Means Committee   A standing committee in the House of Representatives that is responsible for addressing tax-related measures.

House Ways and Means Committee Report   A report generated by the House Ways and Means Committee which discusses specific tax legislation.

Information Document Request   An informal mechanism employed by the IRS to request documents during an audit.

Information return   In general, a document filed by a third party that notifies or informs the IRS that payment has been made to a specific payee (generally identified by a Social Security Number or some other Taxpayer Identification Number).

In-kind compensation   Compensation in a form other than cash.

Insolvent   The condition of having liabilities in excess of assets.

Installment agreement   An agreement under which a taxpayer is generally allowed to pay an established deficiency in installments.

Intangible asset   An asset that lacks a tangible or physical manifestation.

Interest rate   In the mortgage loan context, the rate of interest to be paid over time on outstanding loan principal.

Internal Revenue Code   A codification of substantially all-governing federal tax laws (e.g., the Internal Revenue Code of 1986 (as amended)).

Internal Revenue Code of 1986 (as amended) (the "Code")   The current version of the Internal Revenue Code.

Internal Revenue Service (IRS)   The federal agency charged with the administration and enforcement of the federal tax laws.

Interstitial law-making   A form of judicial law making in which courts fill in gaps left by current statutes and regulations.

IRS Office of Appeals   An independent organization within the IRS that seeks to resolve disputes without resort to litigation.

Lien   An encumbrance upon property that will allow a secured party to proceed against the property if a specific obligation is not paid according to agreed-upon terms.

Loan Estimate   In the mortgage loan context, a document providing basic details about the proposed loan.

Lock-in effect   The phenomenon in which one holding property with built-in gain continues to hold it, largely to avoid being taxed on the gain that would be realized on the property's sale or other disposition.

Marginal tax rate   The rate of tax applicable to the highest segment of a taxpayer's taxable income.

Matching   For federal income tax purposes, the timing of deductions with respect to an asset or activity such that they appear on the same taxable year return as income generated from the use of the asset or the conduct of the business activity.

Mortgagee   A lender that secures repayment by requiring that the mortgagee provide property as collateral.

Mortgagor   A borrower whose property will serve as security for repayment of the obligation to the mortgagee.

Net tax gap   The difference between (1) the gross tax gap and (2) the amounts ultimately paid voluntarily or collected by enforcement.

Ninety-Day Letter   *See* Statutory Notice of Deficiency.

No Change Letter   A post-audit letter indicating the IRS's conclusion that the original tax return was correct.

Non-qualifying consideration   *See* Boot.

Non-recourse   An obligation with respect to which the creditor does not have the right to proceed against the debtor and his assets (other than assets securing the obligation) to collect an unpaid debt.

Offer in compromise   A mechanism by which the IRS is able to accept less than 100% of a taxpayer's assessed liability under certain circumstances.

Office audits   Taxpayer audits that generally require the taxpayer to appear and present requested documentation and discuss specific issues with IRS personnel, typically at IRS offices in the general vicinity of the taxpayer's residence or business location.

Office of Appeals   An office within the IRS that aims to settle tax controversies without litigation.

Office of Chief Counsel   A division within the IRS providing guidance and advice regarding federal tax laws.

Opening escrow   In the mortgage loan context, the payment of earnest money (typically to an Escrow Agent) and the removal of the home from the housing purchase market.

Partially Agreed   A taxpayer's response to a Revenue Agent's Report in which the taxpayer accepts some but not all proposed adjustments.

Payout phase   The time period during which payments are made in accordance with the terms of an annuity, life insurance, or similar contract (generally after an accumulation phase).

Points (or "discount points")   In the mortgage loan context, amounts representing prepaid interest that buyers ordinarily pay to lower the mortgage loan's interest rate.

Private Letter Ruling   A pronouncement issued by the IRS to a specific taxpayer with respect to an issue the taxpayer currently faces or an actual transaction the taxpayer contemplates.

Progressivity   The imposition of progressively higher rates of taxation as a taxpayer's taxable income rises.

Proposed Treasury Regulations Regulations promulgated by the Treasury Department that generally serve to provide non-binding but needed taxpayer guidance; only after a public comment period and further administrative procedure are they issued as final Treasury Regulations.

Protest A document (including specific facts and applicable law) that must be filed by taxpayers as part of pursuing administrative resolution with the IRS Office of Appeals if the taxpayer faces a proposed adjustment exceeding $25,000.

Realization event An event in which potential or hypothetical tax impact becomes real.

Recourse An obligation with respect to which the creditor has the right to proceed against the debtor and his assets to collect an unpaid debt.

Revenue Agent's Report (RAR) A post-audit report provided to the taxpayer setting forth the IRS's position with respect to why it considers proposed adjustments appropriate.

Revenue Procedures IRS pronouncements that provide guidance or specific instructions with respect to the proper procedure to be followed under varying circumstances.

Revenue Ruling A pronouncement of the IRS articulating its official position with respect to its treatment of a given transaction or item.

Scutage A tax paid in lieu of military service.

Secretary of the Treasury Leader of the Department of the Treasury.

Secured An obligation for which security (i.e., collateral) has been provided to protect against the possibility of non-payment.

Senate Finance Committee A standing committee in the U.S. Senate that is responsible for addressing tax-related measures.

Senate Finance Committee Report A report generated by the Senate Finance Committee that discusses specific tax legislation.

Servicer In the mortgage loan context, the institution charged with managing various aspects of the loan after closing (e.g., sending invoices and receiving monthly payments).

Stamp Act One of the first acts passed by Great Britain's Parliament to extract taxes from the American colonies. The act required that various documents carry a revenue stamp.

Statute of limitations on assessment A maximum amount of time during which the IRS may assess taxes with respect to a taxable year.

Statutory Notice of Deficiency A letter from the IRS (required by statute) that informs taxpayers that they have ninety days to file a petition in Tax Court for redetermination of the IRS's asserted deficiency.

Stock dividend In general, the distribution of shares of a corporation to existing shareholders.

Stock option The right or option to purchase a company's stock at a specific price.

Straight line depreciation A cost recovery method in which cost recovery amounts are equal during the cost recovery period.

Sub-prime mortgage A mortgage loan generally made available to those with poor credit histories.

Sunset In the tax context, the expiration of a temporary provision.

Tax Court The federal court that specializes in tax matters and whose judges have tax expertise (formerly the Board of Tax Appeals).

Tax credit An allowance that effects a direct reduction in a taxpayer's tax liability (and may or may not result in a refund).

Tax Incidence The individual or person that ultimately bears the financial burden of a given tax, even if the tax is not imposed directly upon them.

Technical Advice Memoranda IRS pronouncements issued to fellow IRS personnel as guidance in connection with the examination of a specific taxpayer.

Temporary Regulations Regulations promulgated by the Treasury Department to provide needed rules of immediate applicability (although such regulations are also typically issued in proposed form to elicit feedback and commentary before such regulations are finalized).

Thirty-Day Letter A letter informing a taxpayer that unresolved audit-related issues may be taken to the IRS Office of Appeals, provided that the taxpayer does so within thirty days and follows established guidelines and procedures.

Townshend Acts Revenue-generation measures passed by Great Britain's Parliament imposing taxes on various mundane items such as glass, tea, and paper to extract revenue from the American colonies.

Treasury Regulations Official Treasury Department interpretations of Internal Revenue Code provisions. Treasury Regulations may be promulgated in proposed and/or temporary form before becoming final.

Unagreed A taxpayer's response to a Revenue Agent's Report in which the taxpayer disputes all proposed adjustments.

Underwater In the mortgage context, a situation in which the fair market value of a mortgagor's home is less than the amount of the outstanding mortgage debt.

Underwriter In the mortgage loan context, those who ultimately decide, based on all relevant facts and circumstances, whether a mortgage loan application is to be approved or denied.

Unrealized gain *See* Built-in gain.

Unsecured An obligation for which no security (i.e., collateral) has been provided to protect against the possibility of non-payment.

Useful life A general reference to the defined period during which it is anticipated that an asset will be of use to the business (and thus the period during which cost recovery deductions will be allowed).

Vertical equity The notion that a tax system achieves fairness if taxpayers with greater ability to pay (as measured by higher levels of taxable income) are required to pay more taxes *and* at progressively higher rates.

Table of Cases

Table of Internal Revenue Code Sections

Table of Miscellaneous IRS Pronouncements

Table of Revenue Rulings

Table of Treasury Regulations

Index